Learn cocos2D 2

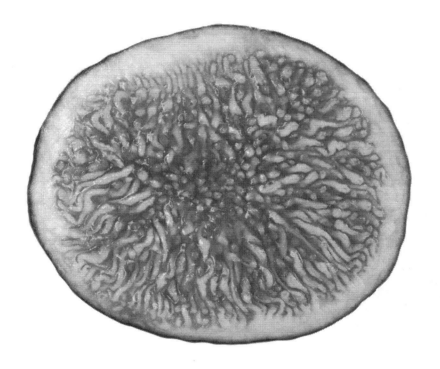

Steffen Itterheim
Andreas Löw

Apress®

Learn cocos2D 2

Copyright © 2012 by Steffen Itterheim and Andreas Löw

ISBN-13 (pbk): 978-1-4302-4416-5

ISBN-13 (electronic): 978-1-4302-4417-2

President and Publisher: Paul Manning
Lead Editor: Steve Anglin
Development Editor: Tom Welsh
Technical Reviewers: Boon Chew & Tony Hillerson
Editorial Board: Steve Anglin, Mark Beckner, Ewan Buckingham, Gary Cornell, Morgan Ertel, Jonathan Gennick, Jonathan Hassell, Robert Hutchinson, Michelle Lowman, James Markham, Matthew Moodie, Jeff Olson, Jeffrey Pepper, Douglas Pundick, Ben Renow-Clarke, Dominic Shakeshaft, Gwenan Spearing, Matt Wade, Tom Welsh
Coordinating Editor: Brigid Duffy
Copy Editors: Corbin Collins
Compositor: SPi Global
Indexer: SPi Global
Artist: SPi Global
Cover Designer: Anna Ishchenko

Distributed to the book trade worldwide by Springer Science+Business Media, LLC., 233 Spring Street, 6th Floor, New York, NY 10013. Phone 1-800-SPRINGER, fax (201) 348-4505, e-mail orders-ny@springer-sbm.com, or visit www.springeronline.com.

For information on translations, please e-mail rights@apress.com, or visit www.apress.com.

Apress and friends of ED books may be purchased in bulk for academic, corporate, or promotional use. eBook versions and licenses are also available for most titles. For more information, reference our Special Bulk Sales–eBook Licensing web page at www.apress.com/info/bulksales.

The source code for this book is available to readers at www.apress.com and www.learn-cocos2d.com/store/book-learn-cocos2d.

To Gabi, the one and only space ant.
Sometimes alien, often antsy, always loved.

—Steffen

To Saskia & Renate for making it possible to
spend my time with things I love most.

—Andreas

Contents at a Glance

Contents

About the Authors

Steffen Itterheim has been a game development enthusiast since the early 1990s. His work in the Doom and Duke Nukem 3D communities landed him his first freelance job as a beta tester for 3D Realms. He has been a professional game developer for more than a decade, having worked most of his career as a game play and tools programmer for Electronic Arts Phenomic. His first contact with cocos2d was in 2009, when he cofounded an aspiring iOS games start-up company called Fun Armada. He loves to teach and enable other game developers so that they can work smarter, not harder. Occasionally you'll find him strolling around in the lush vineyards near his domicile at daytime, and the desert of Nevada at night, collecting bottle caps.

Andreas Löw has been a computer feak since he the age of 10 when he got is first Commodore C16. Teaching himself how to write games, he released his first computer game, Gamma Zone, for Commodore Amiga in 1994, written in pure assembly language. After his diploma in electrical engineering, he worked for Harman International, in the department responsible for developing navigation and infotainment systems with speech recognition for the automotive industy. He invented his own programming language and development tools, which are in use by every car with speech recognition technology around the world.

With the iPhone, he found his way back to his roots and began developing a game called TurtleTrigger. He realized there is a huge demand for good tools in the cocos2d community. With his knowledge in both game and tool development, his products TexturePacker and PhysicsEditor quickly became essential development tools for any cocos2d user.

About the Technical Reviewers

Boon Chew is the managing director for Nanaimo Studio, a game studio based in Seattle and Shanghai that specializes in web and mobile games. He has extensive experience with game development and interactive media, having previously worked for companies such as Vivendi Universal, Amazon, Microsoft, and various game studios and advertising agencies. His passion is in building things and working with great people. You can reach Boon at boon@nanaimostudio.com.

Tony Hillerson is a mobile developer and cofounder at Tack Mobile. He graduated from Ambassador University with a bachelor's degree in Management Information Systems. On any given day, he may be working with Objective-C, Java, Ruby, CoffeeScript, JavaScript, HTML, or shell scripts. Tony has spoken at RailsConf, AnDevCon, and 360|Flex. He is the creator of the popular O'Reilly Android screencasts.

In his free time, Tony enjoys playing the bass and Warr Guitar, and making electronic music. Tony lives outside Denver, Colorado, with his wife, Lori, and sons, Titus and Lincoln.

Acknowledgments

This is the part of the book that makes me a little anxious. I don't want to forget anyone who has been instrumental and helpful in creating this book, yet I know I can't mention each and every one of you. If you're not mentioned here, that doesn't mean I'm not thankful for your contribution! Give me a pen, and I'll scribble your name right here in your copy of the book, and I'll sincerely apologize for not having mentioned you here in the first place.

My first thanks go to you, dear reader. Without you, this book wouldn't make any sense. Without knowing that you might read and enjoy this book, and hopefully learn from it, I probably wouldn't even have considered writing it in the first place. I've received valuable insights and requests from my blog readers and other people I've met or mailed during the course of this book. Thank you, all!

My first thanks go to Jack Nutting, who put the idea of writing a book about cocos2d in my head in the first place. I'm grateful that he did not sugarcoat how much work goes into writing a book so that I wasn't unprepared.

Clay Andres I have to thank for being such a kind person, whose input on my chapter proposals were invaluable and to the point. He helped me form the idea of what the book was to become, and he's generally a delightful person to talk to. Clay, I hope that storm did not flood your house.

Many thanks to Kelly Moritz, Corbin Collins and Brigid Duffy, the coordinating editors. When chaos ensued, they were the ones to put everything back in order and made it happen.

Lots and lots of feedback and suggestions I received from Brian MacDonald and Chris Nelson, the development editors for the book, and Boon Chew, the technical reviewer. They made me go to even greater lengths. Brian helped me understand many of the intricacies of writing a book, while Boon pointed out a lot of technical inaccuracies and additional explanations needed. Many thanks to both of you. Chris was a tremendous help for the second edition; he pointed out a lot of the small but crucial improvements. He shall forever be known as CCCC: Code Continuation Character Chris.

Many thanks go to the copy editor, Kim Wimpsett. Without you, the book's text would be rife with syntax errors and compiler warnings, to put it in programmer's terms.

I also wish to thank Bernie Watkins, who managed the Alpha Book feedback and my contracts. Thanks also to Chris Guillebeau for being an outstanding inspirational blogger and role model.

Of course, my friends and family all took some part in writing this book, through both feedback and plain-and-simple patience with putting up with my writing spree. Thank you!

Preface

In May 2009 I made first contact. For the first time in my life, I was subjected to the Mac OS platform and started learning Xcode, Objective-C, and cocos2d. Even for experienced developers like me and my colleagues, it was a struggle. It was then that I realized cocos2d was good, but it lacked documentation, tutorials, and how-to articles—especially when compared with the other technologies I was learning at the time.

Fast-forward a year to May 2010. I had completed four cocos2d projects. My Objective-C and cocos2d had become fluent. It pained me to see how other developers were still struggling with the same basic issues and were falling victim to the same misconceptions that I did about a year earlier. The cocos2d documentation was still severely lacking.

I saw that other cocos2d developers were having great success attracting readers to their blogs by writing tutorials and sharing what they know about cocos2d. To date, most of the cocos2d documentation is actively being created in a decentralized fashion by other developers. I saw a need for a web site to channel all of the information that's spread over so many different web sites.

I created the `www.learn-cocos2d.com` web site to share what I knew about cocos2d and game development, to write tutorials and FAQs, and to redirect readers interested in cocos2d to all the important sources of information. In turn, I would be selling cocos2d-related products, hoping it might one day bring me close to the ultimate goal of becoming financially independent. I knew I could make the web site a win for everyone.

Then, within 24 hours of taking the web site live, Jack Nutting asked me if I had considered writing a cocos2d book. The rest is history, and the result is the book you're reading right now.

I took everything I had in mind for the web site and put it in the book. But that alone would have amounted to maybe a quarter of the book, at most. I hope the five months in 2010 I spent writing the book full-time paid off by being able to provide an unprecedented level of detail on how cocos2d works and how to work with cocos2d.

I learned a lot in the process, and even more so during the many months updating the chapters to the second and then the third edition. I wish nothing more than for you to learn a great deal about cocos2d and game development from this book.

What I learned from writing about cocos2d is that I can provide a solution for cocos2d that removes most of the initial hurdles for cocos2d developers. The result of that is Kobold2D, which you'll find an introduction to in Chapter 16 and of course on www.kobold2d.com. What sets it apart from cocos2d is that it has an installer, all the documentation, bundles the important libraries, has ARC enabled, over a dozen example projects and additional features on top of that. Obviously one of my goals for the third edition was to make it 100% compatible with Kobold2D 2.0.

Steffen Itterheim

Introduction

Have you ever imagined yourself writing a computer game and being able to make money selling it? With Apple's iTunes App Store and the accompanying mobile iPhone, iPod touch, and iPad devices, doing that is now easier than ever. Of course, that doesn't mean it's easy—there's still a lot to learn about game development and programming games. But you are reading this book, so I believe you've already made up your mind to take this journey. And you've chosen one of the most interesting game engines to work with: cocos2d for iOS.

Developers using cocos2d come from a huge variety of backgrounds. Some, like me, have been professional game developers for years, or even decades. Others are just starting to learn programming for iOS devices or are freshly venturing into the exciting field of game development. Whatever your background might be, I'm sure you'll get something out of this book.

Two things unite all cocos2d developers: we love games, and we love creating and programming them. This book pays homage to that, yet doesn't forget about the tools that help ease the development process. Most of all, you'll be making games that matter along the way, and you'll see how this knowledge is applied in real game development.

You see, I get bored by books that spend all their pages teaching me how to make yet another dull Asteroids clone using some specific game-programming API (application programming interface. What's more important, I think, are game-programming concepts and tools—the things you take with you even as APIs or your personal programming preferences change. I've amassed hundreds of programming and game development books over 20 years. The books I value the most to this day are those that went beyond the technology and taught me why certain things are designed and programmed the way they are. This book will focus not just on working game code but also on why it works and which trade-offs to consider.

I would like you to learn how to write games that matter—games that are popular on the App Store and relevant to players. I'll walk you through the ideas and technical concepts behind these games in this book and, of course, how cocos2d and Objective-C make these games tick. You'll find that the source code that comes with the book is enriched with a lot of comments, which should help you navigate and understand all the nooks and crannies of the code.

Learning from someone else's source code with a guide to help focus on what's important is what works best for me whenever I'm learning something new—and I like to think it will work great

1

for you too. And because you can base your own games on the book's source code, I'm looking forward to playing your games in the near future! Don't forget to let me know about them!

You can share your projects and ask questions on Cocos2D Central (www.cocos2d-central.com), and you can reach me at steffen@learn-cocos2d.com. You should definitely visit the book's companion web site at www.learn-cocos2d.com. Since the first edition of this book, I began improving cocos2d with the Kobold2D project, which you can also use while reading this book. You can learn more about Kobold2D by visiting www.kobold2d.com.

What's New in the Third Edition?

This third edition is a complete overhaul to bring the book up to date with the latest developments, including but not limited to iOS 6 and Xcode 4.4.

For one, cocos2d 2.0 is fresh out of the box. All the source code and descriptions have been adapted to the latest incarnation of cocos2d and OpenGL ES 2.0. Although you cannot deploy cocos2d 2.0 apps on 1st- and 2nd-generation devices, in March 2012 these devices only made up about 16% of all iOS devices sold thus far. There's no doubt that by the time you're reading this book this number will have gone down to around 10% and be still falling as the newer devices continue to sell at an ever increasing rate.

I've also received plenty of questions from many readers all wanting to know the same thing: can the book be used with Kobold2D as well? Previously I had to say "Yes, but there are a few things that are slightly different." The third edition changes my answer to a resounding "Yes, by all means!" Whenever there's anything that works differently in Kobold2D, I mention that. I also highlight all the things that you don't need to do anymore if you were using Kobold2D, because that's what Kobold2D is all about: making cocos2d easier to use.

In case you passed on the second edition, here's a quick recap of what was new in the second edition and was further adapted for this edition. First Andreas Löw joined as a co-author for the book, providing valuable help to improve the book with instructions for his Texture Packer and Physics Editor tools. Together we overhauled a lot of the graphics and significantly improved several chapters with additional code and new features. And two new chapters were added: one about integrating cocos2d in a UIKit app and the other an introduction to the (then newly released) Kobold2D.

All About ARC

Then there's ARC. Woof? What? ARC? Yes, automatic reference counting (ARC) is Apple's new and proven technology to simplify memory management for Objective-C applications. In essence it does away with reference counting, meaning you no longer have to concern yourself with remembering how many times you or other code has retained an object, requiring you to release it the exact same number of times. Autoreleasing objects further complicated that matter. If you didn't get retain, release, and autorelease 100% matched up correctly every time for every object, you were either leaking memory or the app would be prone to crashing.

It's also good to know that ARC is not garbage collection. It works fully deterministic, which means if you run the same program through the exact same process every time, it will behave exactly the same. ARC is also not a runtime component—it's the compiler inserting retain, release, and autorelease statements automatically for you whenever they are needed. There is a set of simple rules followed by ARC that every Objective-C programmer previously had to follow to avoid memory leaks and crashes. You can imagine that if a human being does that job, a lot more errors sneak in, whereas ARC is not only able to perform this job without fail, it also optimizes your code along the way. For example, in manual reference counting you had the ability to retain objects multiple times. ARC, however, realizes when additional retains are unnecessary and omits them.

Now, the compiler has taken over the tedious job of retaining and releasing objects in memory, and all the source code throughout the book has been converted to use ARC. This means fewer code lines to write, and fewer potentially lethal drugs … err, bugs.

The two biggest concerns from Objective-C programmers towards ARC are loss of control and learning a new programming paradigm. Both are terrible arguments against using ARC. I offer an analogy: think of ARC being like automatic transmission in a car, and manual reference as shifting gears manually. If you leave the world of the clutch and gear stick, are you really giving up control? Yes, but it's not control that you really need. Do you need to learn something new? No, you only need to unlearn a few things and you actually have to do less.

With manual transmission, you can easily miss a gear even after years of driving, possibly damaging the engine. That is equivalent to over-releasing or over-retaining an object. You may also kill the engine with the clutch every now and then. That's the equivalent of crashing your app due to a dangling (over-released) pointer. And with an automatic transmission, the engine always changes gears at the optimal rate, typically reducing the fuel consumption rate to a comparable manually shifted car (and a typical driver). Wasting gas is the equivalent of leaking memory.

To sum it up: ARC does not take control away from you. You can still control everything that is important to your app. Code that requires more memory management control than is available to you under ARC does not exist. The issue of loss of control is purely psychological and possibly based on misconceptions about how ARC works. Which brings me to the learning aspect: yes, there are a few things you can and should learn about ARC. But this is so little compared to what a programmer learns every day, and it's far easier than picking up (let alone mastering) manual reference counting if you're new to Objective-C. You only need to read Apple's relatively short Transitioning to ARC Release Notes summary: `http://developer.apple.com/library/ios/#releasenotes/ObjectiveC/RN-TransitioningToARC/Introduction/Introduction.html`. You may also want to read my blog post covering everything you need to know about automatic reference counting: `www.learn-cocos2d.com/2011/11/everything-know-about-arc`.

Why Use cocos2d for iOS?

When game developers look for a game engine, they first evaluate their options. I think cocos2d is a great choice for a lot of developers, for many reasons.

It's Free

First, it is free. It doesn't cost you a dime to work with it. You are allowed to create both free and commercial iPhone, iPod, and iPad apps. You can also create Mac OS X apps with it. You don't have to pay any royalties. Seriously, no strings attached.

It's Open Source

The next good reason to use cocos2d is that it's open source. This means there's no black box preventing you from learning from the game engine code or making changes to it where necessary. That makes cocos2d both extensible and flexible.

It's Objective, See?

Cocos2d is written in Objective-C, Apple's native programming language for writing iOS apps. It's the same language used by the iOS SDK, which makes it easy to understand Apple's documentation and implement iOS SDK functionality.

A lot of other useful APIs, such as Facebook Connect and OpenFeint, are also written in Objective-C, which makes it easy to integrate those APIs, too.

Note   I advise learning Objective-C, even if you prefer some other language. I have a strong C++ and C# background, and the Objective-C syntax looked very odd at first glance. I wasn't happy at the prospect of learning a new programming language that was said to be old and outdated. Not surprisingly, I struggled for a while to get the hang of writing code in a programming language that required me to let go of old habits and expectations.

Don't let the thought of programming with Objective-C distract you, though. It does require some getting used to, but it pays off soon enough, if only for the sheer amount of documentation available. I promise you won't look back!

It's 2D

Of course, cocos2d carries the 2D in its name for a reason. It focuses on helping you create 2D games. It's a specialization few other iOS game engines currently offer.

It doesn't prevent you from loading and displaying 3D objects. In fact, an entire add-on product aptly named cocos3d has been created as an open source project to add 3D rendering support to cocos2d. Unfortunately, cocos3d is not compatible with cocos2d 2.0 at this point since cocos3d is still using OpenGL ES 1.1.

I have to say that the iOS devices are an ideal platform for great 2D games. The majority of new games released on the iTunes App Store are still 2D-only games even today, and even a lot of 3D games are essentially 2D games, gameplay-wise. 2D games are generally easier to develop, and the algorithms in 2D games are easier to understand and implement, making them ideal for beginners. In almost all cases, 2D games are less demanding on hardware, allowing you to create more vibrant and more detailed graphics.

It's Got Physics

You can also choose from two physics engines that are already integrated with cocos2d. On the one hand there's Chipmunk, and on the other there's Box2D. Both physics engines superficially differ only in the language they're written in: Chipmunk is written in C, and Box2D is written in C++. The feature set is almost the same in the two products. If you're looking for differences, you'll find some, but it requires a good understanding of how physics engines work to base your choice on the differences. In general, you should simply choose the physics engine you think is easier to understand and better documented. For most developers, that tends to be Box2D. On the other hand Chipmunk has a commercial Pro version which, among other things, gives you a native Objective-C interface to its API.

It's Less Technical

What game developers enjoy most about cocos2d is how it hides the low-level OpenGL ES code. Most of the graphics are drawn using simple sprite classes that are created from image files. A sprite is a texture that can have scaling, rotation, and color applied to it by simply changing the appropriate Objective-C properties of the CCSprite class. You don't have to be concerned about how this is implemented using OpenGL ES code, which is a good thing.

At the same time, cocos2d gives you the flexibility to add your own OpenGL ES code, including vertex and fragment shaders, at any time for any game object that needs it. Shaders are a way to program the graphics hardware and are beyond the scope of this book. If you're thinking about adding some Cocoa Touch user interface elements, you'll appreciate knowing that these can be miXEd in as well.

And cocos2d doesn't just shield you from the OpenGL ES intricacies; it also provides high-level abstraction of commonly performed tasks, some of which would otherwise require extensive knowledge of the iOS SDK. But if you do need more low-level access or want to make use of iOS SDK features, cocos2d won't hold you back.

It's Still Programming

In general, you could say that cocos2d makes programming iOS games simpler while still requiring truly excellent programming skills first and foremost. Other iOS game engines such as Unity, Unreal, iTorque 2D, and Shiva focus their efforts on providing tool sets and workflows to reduce the amount of programming knowledge required. In return, you give away some technical freedom—and cash, too. With cocos2d, you have to put in a little extra effort, but you're as close to the core of game programming as possible without having to actually deal with the core.

It's Got a Great Community

The cocos2d community always has someone who will answer a question quickly, and developers are generally open to sharing knowledge and information. You can get in touch with the community on the official forum (www.cocos2d-iphone.org/forum) or on my own forum Cocos2D Central (http://cocos2d-central.com). Cocos2D Central is the best place to reach me personally.

New tutorials and sample source code are released on almost, and most of it's for free. And scattered over the Internet you'll find plenty of other resources to learn from and get inspired by.

Tip   To stay up to date with what's happening in the cocos2d community, I recommend following cocos2d on Twitter: http://twitter.com/cocos2d.

While you're at it, you might want to follow me and Kobold2D as well: http://twitter.com/gaminghorror

http://twitter.com/kobold2d

Next, enter **cocos2d** in Twitter's search box and then click the "Save this search" link. That way, you can regularly check for new posts about cocos2d with a single click. More often than not, you'll come across useful cocos2d-related information that would otherwise have passed you by. And you'll definitely get to know your fellow developers who are also working with cocos2d.

Once your game is complete and released on the App Store, you can even promote it on the cocos2d web site. At the very least, you'll get the attention of fellow developers and ideally valuable feedback.

Why Use Kobold2D over cocos2d-iphone?

First of all, it's a lot easier to get started with cocos2d-iphone development if you use Kobold2D from the start. You only need to run the Kobold2D installer to get everything you need: the source code, additional useful source code libraries, the template projects, the documentation, the tools, and more. You can start a new project right away.

You get 15 template projects instead of just 3, and all of them are ARC enabled. You'll recognize that most of the template projects are variations of the projects you'll create throughout the book. So you'll feel right at home.

The most commonly used source code libraries are also integrated and ready to use. This includes the cocos2d-iphone-extensions project, the Lua scripting language, ObjectAL, iSimulate, SneakyInput, and more.

Kobold2D has additional convenience features that cocos2d-iphone doesn't have. There's helper code for Game Center, Ad Banners, Gesture Recognizers, PiXEl-Perfect Collision Detection, and simplified user input handling. KKInput gives you an easy-to-use, platform-independent wrapper to use Gesture Recognizers, the Gyroscope, Keyboard, and Mouse.

Additionally, most Kobold2D projects have targets for both iOS and Mac OS X. So if you plan on releasing your game to both App Stores, Kobold2D makes this dual-platform development a lot smoother and offers other enhancements under the hood, such as optimized Build Settings for each platform.

Then there's KoboldScript. It's a modern, powerful, yet simple Lua interface backed by Kobold2D to develop iOS and Mac OS X apps with. At the time of this writing it's still a work in progress, so please visit www.koboldscript.com for the latest news and updates.

Finally, I use Kobold2D each and every day for my own work. I continue to tweak and improve it, and I make sure it stays up-to-date with the latest developments, be they new iOS devices, new Xcode versions, or simply new releases of cocos2d and the other libraries provided by Kobold2D. You'll get a timely update and you'll be able to upgrade your projects safely to a newer Kobold2D version with just one mouse click.

Other cocos2d Game Engines

You may have noticed that versions of cocos2d exist for a great variety of platforms, including Windows, JavaScript, and Android. There's even a C++ version of cocos2d dubbed cocos2d-x that supports multiple mobile platforms all in one, including iOS and Android.

These cocos2d ports all share the same name and design philosophy but are written in different languages by different authors and are generally quite different from cocos2d for iOS. For example, the Android cocos2d port is written in Java, which is the native language when developing for Android devices.

If you're interested in porting your games to other platforms, you should know that the various cocos2d game engines differ by a lot. Porting your cocos2d-iphone game to Android, for example, isn't an easy task. First there's the language barrier—all your Objective-C code must be rewritten in Java. When that's done, you still need to make a lot of modifications to cope with numerous changes in the cocos2d API or possibly unsupported features of the port or the target platform. Finally, every port can have its own kind of bugs, and every platform has its own technical limitations and challenges.

Overall, porting iOS games written with cocos2d to other platforms that also have a cocos2d game engine entails almost the same effort as rewriting the game for the target platform using some other game engine. This means there's no switch you can flip and it'll work. The similarity of the cocos2d engines across various platforms is in name and philosophy only. If cross-platform development is your goal, you should take a look at cocos2d-x, which has most of the features of cocos2d-iphone, is backed financially by China Unicom, and continues to be updated and improved at an incredible pace.

In any case, I think you should still know about the most popular cocos2d game engines. Table 1–1 lists the cocos2d game engines that are frequently updated and are stable enough for production use. I didn't include in this list cocos2d ports that are significantly out of date and haven't been updated for months, if not years. That includes the defunct cocos2d for Windows project, whose only release dates back to May 2010, and the long obsolete ShinyCocos, a Ruby Wrapper based on cocos2d-iphone v0.8.2.

Table 1–1. Most Popular cocos2d Game Engine Ports

Name	Language	Platforms	Web Site
cocos2d-iphone	Objective-C	iOS, Mac OS X	www.cocos2d-iphone.org
Kobold2D	Objective-C, Lua	iOS, Mac OS X	www.kobold2d.com
cocos2d-x	C++, Lua	iOS, Android, Samsung Bada, BlackBerry Tablet OS, Windows, Linux	www.cocos2d-x.org
cocos2d-x for XNA	C#	Windows Phone 7	http://github.com/cocos2d/cocos2d-x-for-xna/
cocos2d-javascript	JavaScript	Web browsers	www.cocos2d-javascript.org
cocos2d-android-1	Java	Android	http://code.google.com/p/cocos2d-android-1
cocos2d	Python	Mac OS, Windows, Linux	www.cocos2d.org

This Book Is for You

I'd like to imagine you picked this book because its title caught your interest. I suppose you want to make 2D games for iPhone, iPod touch, and iPad, and the game engine of your choice is cocos2d for iOS. Or maybe you don't care so much about the game engine but you do want to make 2D games for iOS devices in general. Maybe you're looking for some in-depth discussion on cocos2d, if you've been using it for a while already. Whatever your reasons for choosing this book, I'm sure you'll get a lot out it.

Prerequisites

As with every programming book, some prerequisites are nice to have and some are almost mandatory.

Programming Experience

The only thing that's mandatory for this book is some degree of programming experience, so let's get that out of the way first. You should have an understanding of programming concepts such as loops, functions, classes, and so forth. If you have written a computer program before, preferably using an object-oriented programming language, you should be fine.

Still with me? Good.

Objective-C

So, you do have programming experience, but maybe you've never written anything in that obscure language called Objective-C.

You don't need to know Objective-C for this book, but it definitely helps to know the language's basics. If you're already familiar with at least one other object-oriented programming language, such as C++, C#, or Java, you may be able to pick it up as you go. But to be honest, I found it hard to do that myself even after roughly 15 years of programming experience with C++, C#, and various scripting languages. There are always those small, bothersome questions about tiny things that you just don't get right away, and they tend to steal your attention away. In that case, it's handy to have a resource you can refer to whenever there's something you need to understand about Objective-C.

Objective-C may seem scary with its square brackets, and you may have picked up some horror stories about its memory management and how there's no garbage collection on iOS devices. Worry not.

First, Objective-C is just a different set of clothes. It looks unfamiliar, but the underlying programming concepts such as loops, classes, inheritance, and function calls still work in the same way as in other programming languages. The terminology might be different; for example, what Objective-C developers call *sending messages* is in essence the same as *calling a method*. As for memory management, with ARC you practically don't have to concern yourself with memory management anymore. The very few exceptions are explained in the book, and for the most part they're only telling the compiler that what you're doing is intentional, and not an error, by adding a fancy-sounding keyword.

I learned from one invaluable Objective-C book, and I recommend it wholeheartedly as a companion book in case you want to learn more about Objective-C and Xcode: *Learn Objective-C on the Mac* by Mark Dalrymple and Scott Knaster, published by Apress.

There is also Apple's "Introduction to the Objective-C Programming Language," which proved valuable as an online reference. It's available here: `http://developer.apple.com/mac/library/DOCUMENTATION/Cocoa/Conceptual/ObjectiveC/Introduction/introObjectiveC.html`.

What You Will Learn

I provide you with a fair share of my game-development experiences to show how interactive games are made. I believe that learning to program is not at all about memorizing API methods, yet a lot of game-development books I've read over the past two decades follow that "reference handbook" approach. But that's what the API documentation is for. When I started programming some 20 years ago, I thought I'd never learn to program just by looking at a huge stack of compiler reference handbooks and manuals. Back at that time, compiler manuals were still printed, thick and heavy, and obviously didn't come with fully searchable online versions. The World Wide Web was still in its infancy. All that information was stacked some 15 inches high on my desk, and it seemed very daunting to try to learn any of it, let alone all of it.

Today, I can't recall most methods and APIs from memory, and I keep forgetting about those I used to know. I look them up time and time again. After 20 years of programming, I do know what's really important to learn: the concepts, what works well and what doesn't, where to look for info when I need to learn, and why it's important to learn and follow best practices. Good programming concepts and best practices stick around for a long time, and they help with programming in any language. Learning concepts is done best by understanding the rationale behind the choices that were made in designing, structuring, and writing the source code. That's what I focus on the most.

What Beginning iOS Game Developers Will Learn

I also ease you into the most important aspects of cocos2d and Kobold2D. I focus on the kind of classes, methods, and concepts you should be able to recall from memory just because they are so fundamental to programming with cocos2d.

You'll also learn about the essential tools supporting or being supported by cocos2d. Without these tools, you'd be only half the cocos2d programmer you can be. You'll use tools like TexturePacker and ParticleDesignerto create games that are increasingly complex and challenging to develop. Because of the scope of this book, these games aren't complete and polished games, nor can I discuss every line of code. Instead I annotate the code with many helpful comments so that it's easy to follow and understand.

I leave it up to you to improve on these skeleton game projects, and I'm excited to see your results. I think giving you multiple starting points to base your own work on works better than walking you through the typical Asteroids games over the course of the whole book.

I chose the game projects for this book based on popularity on the App Store and relevance for game developers, who often inquire about how to solve the specific problems that these games present. For example, the line-drawing game genre is a huge favorite among cocos2d game developers, yet line-drawing games require you to overcome deceivingly complex challenges.

I've also seen a fair bit of other developers' cocos2d code and followed the discussions on code design, structure, and style. I base my code samples on a framework that relies on composition over inheritance and explain why this is preferable. One other frequent question that has to do with code design is how different objects should communicate with each other. There are interesting pros and cons for each approach to code design and structure, and I want to convey these concepts because they help you write more stable code with fewer bugs and better performance.

What iOS App Developers Will Learn

So, you're an iOS app developer, and you've worked with the iOS SDK before? Perfect. Then you'll be most interested in how making games work in a world without Interface Builder. In fact, you'll be using other tools. They may not be as shiny as Apple's tools, but they're useful nonetheless.

The programming considerations will change, too. You don't normally send and receive a lot of events in game programming, and you let a larger number of objects decide what to do with an event. For performance reasons and to reduce user input latency, game engine systems often work more closely connected with each other. A lot of work is done in loops and update methods, which are called at every frame or at specific points in time. Whereas a user interface-driven application spends most of its time waiting for a user's input, a game keeps pushing a lot of data and piXEls behind the scenes, even when the player is not doing anything. So there's a lot more going on, and game code tends to be more streamlined and efficient because of concerns for performance.

What Cocos2d Developers Will Learn

You're already familiar with cocos2d? You may be wondering whether you can learn anything new from this book. I say you will. Maybe you want to skip the first chapters, but you'll definitely get hooked by the games' sample source code supplied with the book. You'll learn how I structure my code and the rationale behind it. You'll probably find inspiration reading about the various games and how I implemented them. You'll also benefit from a good number of tips and you'll learn how Kobold2D helps you develop games faster.

Most importantly, this book isn't written by some geek you've never heard of and never will hear from again, with no e-mail address or web site to post your follow-up questions. Instead, it's written by a geek you may not have heard of but who will definitely be around. I'm actively engaged with the cocos2d community at the book's companion blog `www.learn-cocos2d.com`, where I'll continue to improve this book as well as improving how we write App Store games with Kobold2D and KoboldScript.

What's in This Book

Here's a brief overview of the chapters in this book. The second edition added two entirely new chapters: Chapter 15 discusses integration of UIKit views with cocos2d, and Chapter 16 introduces Kobold2D, my own take on a cocos2d development environment with additional convenience features. The third edition sees all chapters updated to Cocos2D v2.0 and made compatible with Kobold2D v2.0, and all source code is using ARC.

Chapter 2, "Getting Started"

I cover setting up cocos2d for development, installing project templates, and creating the first "Hello World" project. You'll learn about cocos2d basics, such as scenes and nodes.

Chapter 3, "Essentials"

I explain the essential cocos2d classes that you'll need most often, such as sprites, transitions, and actions. And you'll learn how to use them, of course.

Chapter 4, "Your First Game"

Enemies drop from the top, and you have to avoid them by tilting your device. This will be our first simple game using accelerometer controls.

Chapter 5, "Game Building Blocks"

Now prepare yourself for a bigger game, one that requires a better code structure. You'll learn how scenes and nodes are layered and the various ways that game objects can exchange information.

Chapter 6, "Sprites In-Depth"

You'll learn what a texture atlas is and why you'll be using it for the next game and how to create a texture atlas with the TexturePacker tool.

Chapter 7, "Scrolling with Joy"

With the texture atlas ready, you'll learn how to implement a parallax scrolling shooter game, controlled by touch input.

Chapter 8, "Shoot 'em Up"

Without enemies, our shooter wouldn't have much to shoot at, right? I show you how to add game-play code to spawn, move, hit, and animate the enemy hordes.

Chapter 9, "Particle Effects"

By using the ParticleDesigner tool, you'll add some particle effects to the side-scrolling game.

Chapter 10, "Working with Tilemaps"

Infinitely jumping upward, you'll apply what you've learned from the side-scrolling game in portrait mode to create another popular iOS game genre.

Chapter 11, "Isometric Tilemaps"

Because cocos2d supports the TMX file format, you'll take a look at how to create tile-based games using the Tiled editor.

Chapter 12, "Physics Engines"

This is a primer on using the Chipmunk and Box2D physics engines—and the crazy things you can do with them.

Chapter 13, "Pinball Game"

In this chapter you'll create a basic pinball table using the Box2D physics engine. The collision shapes are created with the help of the PhysicsEditor tool.

Chapter 14, "Game Center"

Learn how to turn the isometric tilemap game from Chapter 11 into a multiplayer game for two, complete with leaderboards and achievements.

Chapter 15, "Cocos2d and UIKit Views"

This chapter goes into depth on how to mix and match cocos2d with regular Cocoa Touch, particularly UIKit views. You'll learn how to add UIKit views to a cocos2d game but also the reverse: how to integrate cocos2d in an existing UIKit app.

Chapter 16, "Kobold2D Introduction"

Kobold2D is my take on improving the cocos2d game engine by making it easier to work with while adding features such as ARC compatibility and Lua scripting to it. In this chapter you'll learn how to set up new Kobold2D projects and what's special about Kobold2D.

Chapter 17, "Conclusion"

This is where the book ends and your journey continues. You'll get lots of inspiration on where to go from here and food for thought.

Where to Get the Book's Source Code

One of the most frequently asked questions following the release of the first edition of this book was about where to get the book's source code. I've added this little section to answer this question.

You can get the book's source code on the book's page at `www.apress.com`. The source code is available on the Source Code/Downloads tab.

Alternatively, you can download the source code from the Downloads section on Learn Cocos2D: `www.learn-cocos2d.com/store/book-learn-cocos2d`.

Of course, you can always type the code directly from the book if you prefer. But it may come in handy to have the code ready, in case you need to compare what you typed with what the code is supposed to look like. I also continue to upgrade the downloadable source code on Learn Cocos2D to fix issues with newer Xcode or iOS versions.

Most importantly the source code download contains the exact versions of cocos2d and Kobold2D used by the source code in this book. Because both projects continue to be improved, there's a possibility that the latest download from the web site may not be 100% compatible with the book's descriptions and source code. Therefore I recommend you install and use the versions distributed with the source code while you're reading the book.

Questions and Feedback

I do hope I get the right mixture of easing you into cocos2d and iOS game development while challenging you with advanced game-programming concepts.

If at any time I fail and leave you wondering, please feel free to ask your questions on Cocos2D Central (`www.cocos2d-central.com`). I'll also continue to post frequently about cocos2d news and developments on the Learn Cocos2D companion web site for this book at `www.learn-cocos2d.com`. Your feedback is always welcome!

Chapter **2**

Getting Started

I'll get you up to speed on developing cocos2d games as quickly as possible. By the end of this chapter, you'll be able to create new cocos2d projects based on the supplied Xcode project templates. I'll also introduce you to the important bits of knowledge you need to keep in mind during game development.

And because it's been a big source of confusion, I'll explain how to enable automatic reference counting (ARC) in a cocos2d project. At the end of this chapter, you'll have a first cocos2d project based on one of the cocos2d project templates up and running.

What You Need to Get Started

In this section, I'll quickly walk you through the requirements and necessary steps to get started. Getting registered as an iOS developer and creating the necessary provisioning profiles are both excellently documented by Apple, so I won't re-create that detailed information here.

System Requirements

Here are the minimum hardware and software requirements for developing iOS applications:

- Intel-based Mac computer
- Mac OS X 10.6 (Snow Leopard) or newer, Mac OS X 10.7 (Lion) or newer for iOS 5.1 features.
- Any iOS device

For development, any Intel-based Mac computer suffices. Even the Mac mini and MacBook Air are perfectly fine for developing iOS applications and games. Having at least 2GB of RAM installed will make using your computer smoother, especially because game development tools often require much more memory than most other software. You'll be handling a lot of images, audio files, and program code, and you'll probably be running all these tools in parallel.

Note that Apple typically only supports the current and previous Mac OS X versions for iOS and Mac OS X development. Right now these are Mac OS X 10.7 Lion and Mac OS X 10.8 Mountain Lion, with development on Mac OS X 10.6 Snow Leopard still an option albeit not with the latest features. Be prepared to update your Mac to a newer Mac OS X version frequently, typically once every 12 to 24 months. Note that there's always the option to install Mac OS X separately to an external hard drive if for some reason you don't want to or can't update your Mac's operating system.

If you're running an older Mac computer please consult the Max OS X Technical Specifications web site (`www.apple.com/macosx/specs.html`) to learn whether your Mac meets the system requirements and how to purchase and upgrade to the latest Mac OS X version.

Register as an iOS Developer

If you haven't already done so, you might want to register yourself as an iOS developer with Apple. Access to the iOS Developer Program costs $99 per year. If you plan to submit Mac OS X apps to the Mac App Store, you'll also have to register as a Mac OS X developer, for an additional $99 per year.

You can register as an iOS developer at `http://developer.apple.com/programs/ios`.

To register as a Mac OS X developer, go to `http://developer.apple.com/programs/mac`.

Strictly speaking you do not need to register as a developer right away. You can also download Xcode for free and take your first steps with the iOS Simulator.

But as a registered developer you get additional benefits. For example, you have access to the iOS Developer Portal where you can set up your development devices and provisioning profiles to deploy your app to one or more iOS devices. You also get access to iTunes Connect where you can manage your contracts, manage and submit your apps, and review financial reports.

In addition, you'll be offered beta versions, sometimes also called preview versions, of Apple software. You should generally refrain from using Apple beta software however. I know it's cool to have access to it and tempting to use the latest software as part of an exclusive club. But trust me on this: you'll easily run into compatibility issues that no one can help you with because the Apple beta software can not be publicly discussed. I strictly refrain from using Apple beta versions because even minor incompatibilities can be huge productivity killers.

Tip   If you do want to try out Apple beta software, be sure to install it separately so that you can switch back to the official version at any time. This is specifically important if you plan to install a beta Mac OS X version, because it's very possible that either cocos2d or any of the other tools and libraries you're using has severe compatibility issues with the beta OS. Don't allow the beta OS to permanently replace your current OS, or you'll be stuck and alone with any issues you may encounter. Install Mac OS beta versions on a separate (external) hard drive instead and use the System Preferences Startup Disk tool to switch between startup disks.

Certificates and Provisioning Profiles

Eventually you'll want to deploy the games you're building onto your iOS device. To do so, you must create an iOS development certificate, register your iOS device, and enable it for development. You complete this setup with Xcode's Organizer, where you can download and install your development and distribution provisioning profiles.

All these steps are well explained on the iOS Provisioning Portal. Apple has done an excellent job of documenting them on the How To tabs of each section of the Provisioning Portal. Registered iOS developers can access the iOS Provisioning Portal at `http://developer.apple.com/ios/manage/overview/index.action`.

Download and Install Xcode and the iOS SDK

You can download the latest Xcode version, which includes the iOS SDK, from the Xcode web site: `https://developer.apple.com/xcode`. The 1.5GB download may take a while to download and install, so you may want to start downloading it right away.

After you've installed Xcode, you're set with everything you need to develop iOS applications. If you've never worked with Xcode before, I suggest you familiarize yourself with it by reading the Xcode 4 User Guide:
`https://developer.apple.com/library/ios/documentation/ToolsLanguages/Conceptual/Xcode4UserGuide/index.html`

Specifically, you should know the names of the four main areas of the Xcode window as shown in Figure 2-1: the Navigation (left), Editor (center), Utility (right), and Debug (bottom) areas. With the exception of the Editor area, you can hide and unhide any of these areas from view via the Xcode View menu.

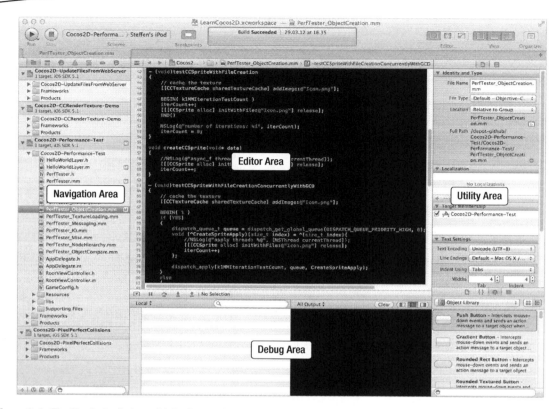

Figure 2-1. *The Xcode 4 window with its four main areas: Navigation, Editor, Utility, and Debug*

Download cocos2d or Kobold2D

The next step is to download either cocos2d-iphone or Kobold2D. If you download the book's source code (see Chapter 1) you'll find the exact cocos2d and Kobold2D versions that the book's source code was written for. The latest versions available from the Web may not be 100% compatible with the book because they're continually improved. Unless you feel comfortable deviating from the book's source code on occasion, you should stick to the cocos2d and Kobold2D versions provided with the book.

You can download the book's source code, including the corresponding cocos2d and Kobold2D versions, from the Downloads section on the Learn Cocos2D book's store page: www.learn-cocos2d.com/store/book-learn-cocos2d.

Download the latest cocos2d versions from www.cocos2d-iphone.org/download. The latest Kobold2D installer package is available from www.kobold2d.com/display/KKSITE/Kobold2D+Download.

Install Kobold2D

Kobold2D users only need to run the installer package. Doing so also installs the Kobold2D Template Projects and the Xcode documentation for cocos2d-iphone, Box2D, Chipmunk, and other libraries.

After installation has succeeded, you'll find the Kobold2D files in your home directory under ~/Kobold2D. You can safely move the ~/Kobold2D folder anywhere else on your hard disk if you want, but I recommend leaving it as is for now.

Each new version of Kobold2D is installed to a subfolder of ~/Kobold2D, typically named Kobold2D-2.0.0 or similar, depending on the version number. That's where your Kobold2D projects for this particular Kobold2D version are located, as well as the Kobold2D Project Starter and Project Upgrader tools.

> **Note** To uninstall Kobold2D simply delete the Kobold2D folder. Remember, your projects also reside in that folder, so make a backup of your projects before deleting it. You may also want to delete the Kobold2D documentation for Xcode by deleting the files beginning with com.kobold2d in the folder ~/Library/Developer/Shared/Documentation/DocSets.

Create a Kobold2D Project

Kobold2D projects are created with the Kobold2D Project Starter.app, which you'll find in each versioned Kobold2D subfolder—for example, in ~/Kobold2D/Kobold2D-2.0.0. Runing this app will show a dialog like the one in Figure 2-2.

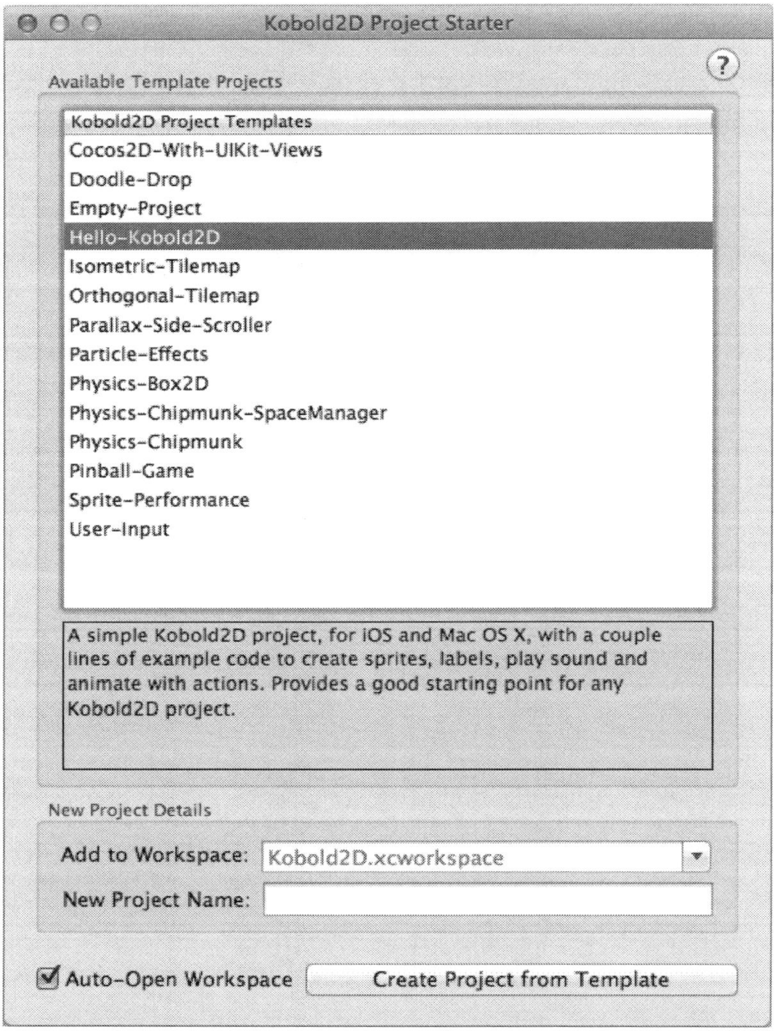

Figure 2-2. The Kobold2D Project Starter tool

You can choose a Template Project to use for your project. The Hello-Kobold2D and the Empty-Project templates are ideal if you want to start from scratch, as are the Physics templates. All other templates are more or less complete games or illustrate some aspect of Kobold2D or cocos2d. All the template projects have ARC enabled.

By default, new projects are added to the Kobold2D.xcworkspace, but you can override this by entering a workspace name. It helps to have closely related projects in the same workspace.

Enter a name for your project and click Create Project from Template. With Auto-Open Workspace checked, Xcode will automatically open the workspace with your newly created project. You can get started right away, and your project has ARC enabled automatically.

Note   Kobold2D makes creating and sharing project templates very easy. You can change an existing project's name, provide a description file, and start sharing the template with other users. This process is documented at www.kobold2d.com/x/TgUO. To create a new Kobold2D project, you'll be using the Kobold2D Project Starter app exclusively. You can't create new Kobold2D projects from within Xcode, but in return you get a lot more projects to choose from and you can make your own project templates easily.

Click the Run button and you should see the iPhone Simulator starting up, as in Figure 2-3.

Figure 2-3. The Hello Kobold2D project

> **Caution**   Due to a bug in Xcode, you should not open more than one Kobold2D workspace of the
> same Kobold2D version at the same time. Xcode will only load the Kobold2D-Libraries project for one
> workspace, leaving any other Kobold2D workspace temporarily dysfunctional, typically resulting in a
> nondescript "failed with exit code 1" type of error. To resolve this, close all open Xcode windows and then
> re-open just the workspace you want to work with. Builds will also fail if you open the Kobold2D project's
> `.xcodeproj` file instead of the `.xcworkspace` because the Kobold2D-Libraries project reference will
> be missing. The Kobold2D FAQ explains all these closely related issues and how to identify them and
> provides solutions: `www.kobold2d.com/x/IQkO`.

Install cocos2d and its Xcode Project Templates

> **Tip**   If you've already installed Kobold2D and are planning to use it, you can skip ahead to the section
> "Anatomy of cocos2d and Kobold2D Applications." If not, keep in mind that for cocos2d you'll have to
> enable ARC in each cocos2d project separately following the instructions given in the upcoming section
> "How to enable ARC in a cocos2d Project." Alternatively, download the book's source code and use the
> supplied ARC-enabled cocos2d template projects. In any case, you can safely install both cocos2d and
> Kobold2D, and there will be no conflicts between them.

To use cocos2d, you need to extract the downloaded file by double-clicking it. This should
create a folder named `cocos2d-iphone-2.0` or similar, depending on the exact version number
and other suffiXEs. You can move or rename this folder as you please.

To install the cocos2d Xcode templates, open the Terminal app (in the Utilities folder under
Applications in Finder—or just search for `Terminal.app` in Spotlight to locate it). The cocos2d
Xcode project templates installation procedure is driven by a shell script that you'll have to run
from the command-line program Terminal.

First, change to the directory where cocos2d is installed. For example, if you downloaded and
extracted cocos2d in the Downloads folder, you will have a folder named cocos2d-iphone-2.0 or
similar. If the path to cocos2d-iphone varies on your system, be sure to use the correct path. In
this example, you would have to enter the following:

```
./Downloads/cocos2d-iphone-2.0/install-templates.sh -f
```

Press Return to run the template installation script. If everything goes fine, you should see a
number of lines printed in the Terminal window. Most of them will start with "…copying." If that's
the case, the templates should now be installed.

Note that the leading dot before the path is essential—without it, you'll most likely get a "No
such file or directory" error.

The templates are copied to the user's Developer directory, which is `~/Library/Developer/Xcode/`
`Templates`. This is the directory to browse to in Finder if you ever want to delete the cocos2d
Xcode templates. The `-f` switch forces the script to replace any existing cocos2d template files
so that you don't get any errors if you've previously installed the cocos2d Xcode templates.

Remember that you will have to run this script each time you download a new cocos2d version to upgrade the Xcode project templates to the latest version.

> **Note**   To uninstall cocos2d, simply delete the cocos2d-iphone-2.0 folder and any cocos2d projects you no longer need. To remove the cocos2d Xcode templates, delete the two folders beginning with `cocos2d` in `~/Library/Developer/Xcode/Templates` and `~/Library/Developer/Xcode/Templates/ File Templates`.

How to Create a cocos2d Project

After installing the cocos2d project templates, open Xcode and select File ➤ New Project. Clicking the cocos2d v2.x entry on the left-hand side should display the three cocos2d icons shown in Figure 2-4. If that's not what you're seeing, go back to the previous section and verify that installing the cocos2d Xcode project templates succeeded without errors.

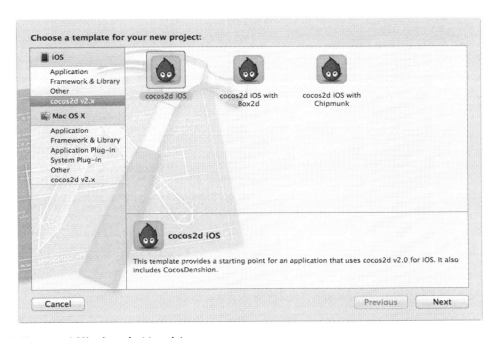

Figure 2-4. The cocos2d Xcode project templates

> **Note**   I discuss the Box2D and Chipmunk application templates in Chapter 13. Feel free to try them if you want to have some fun with physics right now.

Choose the cocos2d iOS template, click Next, name it, and save it anywhere on your computer.

Tip   It's good practice not to use space characters in Xcode project names. Xcode doesn't mind, but some tools you use might. It's a matter of defensively avoiding any potential hiccups. Even today, occasional problems occur related to spaces and special characters in filenames. I always restrict myself to naming anything code-related—whether projects, source files, or resources—to letters, digits, and the dash and underscore characters. Note that the app's name, as it appears on iTunes or on the device, defaults to the project's name. You can change this in the `Info.plist` file by entering the app's real name in the Bundle Display Name entry.

Xcode will create the cocos2d project based on the selected template. An Xcode project window like the one in Figure 2-5 will open.

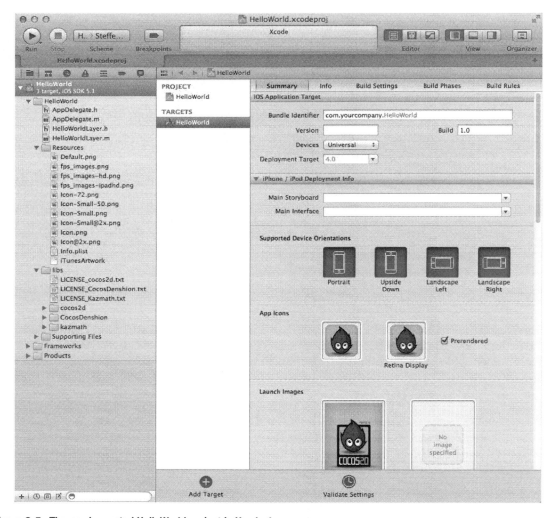

Figure 2-5. The newly created HelloWorld project in Xcode 4

When you click Run, the project will build and then run in the iOS Simulator. The result should look like Figure 2-6.

Figure 2-6. *The template project works and displays a "Hello World" label running in the iPhone Simulator*

How to Enable ARC in a cocos2d Project

Although all Kobold2D projects have ARC enabled automatically, cocos2d projects don't. Moreover, it's not as simple as flipping a switch. To enable ARC in a newly created cocos2d project, you need to perform the steps outlined In this section (Kobold2D users can skip this entire section).

Build the cocos2d code as a Static Library

Cocos2d may be compatible with ARC, but the cocos2d source code is not compliant with ARC. That means you have to build the cocos2d source code with ARC disabled if you want to use it in a project that has ARC enabled. By far the best way to do that is to build the cocos2d code as a static library, allowing the code to be built without ARC. Then you can safely link the cocos2d static library with your application's target, which has ARC enabled.

First, locate and delete the libs group in the Navigation area. When the confirmation dialog in Figure 2-7 pops up, click Remove References. Don't trash the files because you'll be needing them later.

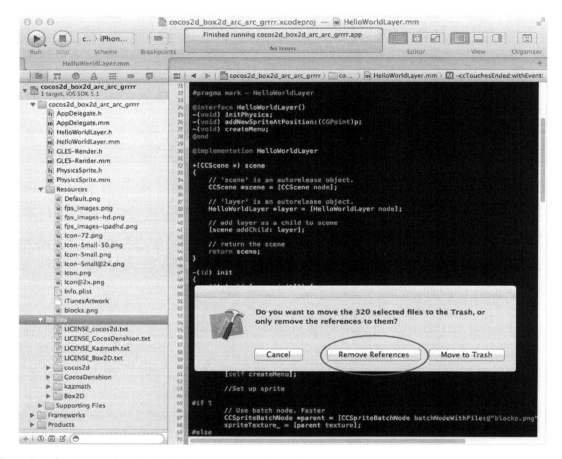

Figure 2-7. Remove but do not trash the libs group from the project

Select the Project itself in the Navigation area, as seen in Figure 2-8. The project is always the first entry and has a blue document icon. Then click the Add Target button at the bottom.

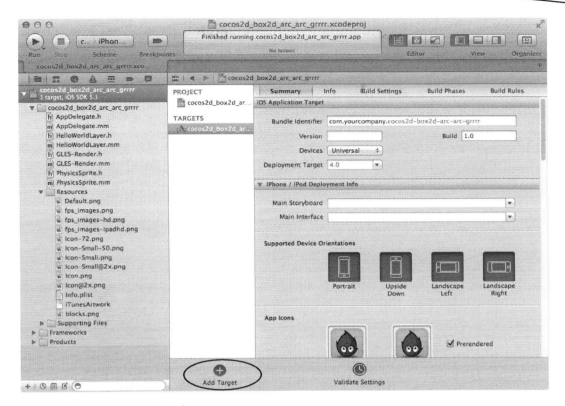

Figure 2-8. *Add a new target to the project*

In the Add Target template dialog shown in Figure 2-9, navigate to the Framework & Library group and select Cocoa Touch Static Library. Then click Next.

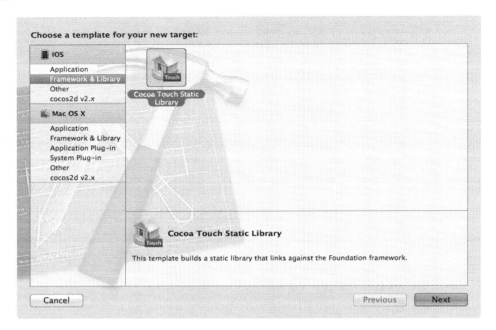

Figure 2-9. Select the Cocoa Touch Static Library template

Name the static library appropriately—for example, cocos2d-library would be a good name. Be sure to deselect both Include Unit Tests and Use Automatic Reference Counting. The settings should match those in Figure 2-10. Then click Finish to add the static library target to your project.

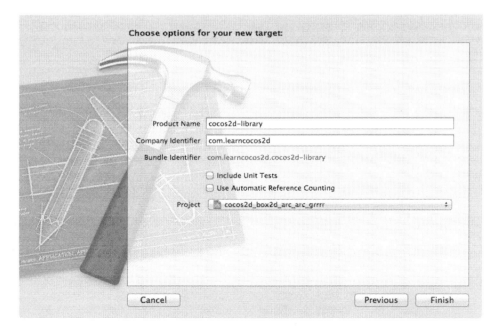

Figure 2-10. Name the static library and deselect both check boXEs

After creating the cocos2d-library target, select it, and the Build Settings pane is shown. You need to browse the Build Settings to make two changes in the Search Paths section. The easiest way to find those is by entering *search* in the search filter textbox in the upper right-hand corner of the Build Settings pane (see Figure 2-11). Set the Always Search User Paths setting to Yes and set the User Header Search Paths to the somewhat cryptic ./** string.

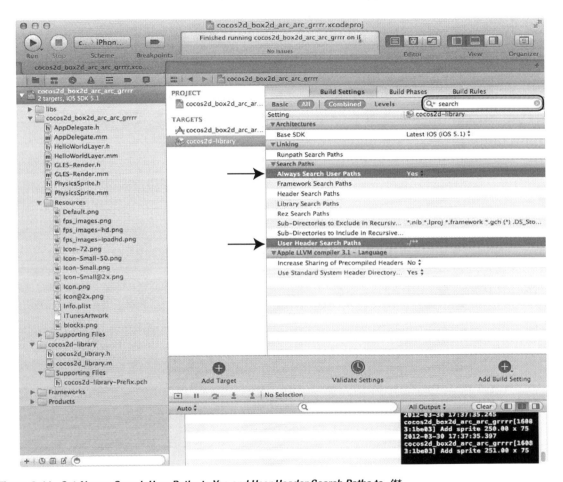

Figure 2-11. *Set Always Search User Paths to Yes and User Header Search Paths to ./***

Note   You can edit the User Header Search Paths setting in two ways: by clicking it twice with a delay between the clicks—this allows you to enter the text directly—or by double-clicking the field, which brings up an additional dialog with a nondescript check box in it. In that case, either enter just a dot and click the check box or enter the full string ./** but don't check the check box. Otherwise you might end up with the string ./**/** which will cause compiler errors. Be sure to verify that the string is correct after the edit dialog closes.

Now select the other target of the project. That's the one that was already there when you created the project. Select the Build Phases tab and expand the Link Binary With Libraries list, as shown in Figure 2-12.

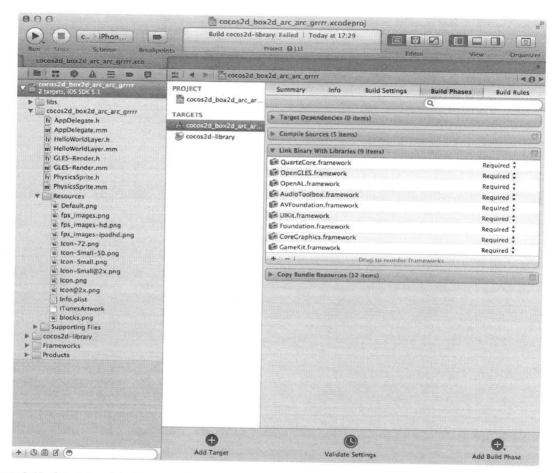

Figure 2-12. Select the original target and expand the Link Binary With Libraries list

Click the small + button below the list to bring up the selection dialog shown in Figure 2-13. From that, select the `libcocos2d-library.a` entry and click Add.

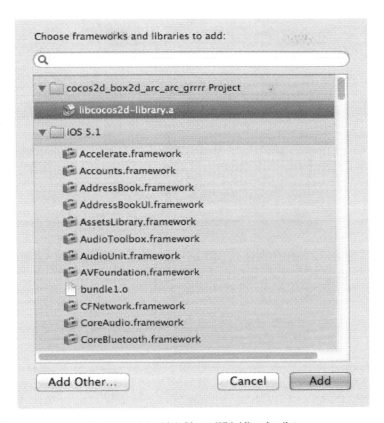

Figure 2-13. *Select the original target and expand the Link Binary With Libraries list*

The last step is to re-add the cocos2d files to the static library target. Click File ➤ Add Files to "name-of-project" to bring up the file dialog shown in Figure 2-14. Navigate to your project's folder and then locate and select the libs folder. Make sure the "Copy items into destination group's folder (if needed)" check box is not checked and that the "Create groups for any added folders" radio button is selected. Finally verify that the cocos2d-library target is the only target whose check box is checked before clicking the Add button. If in doubt, compare your settings with Figure 2-14.

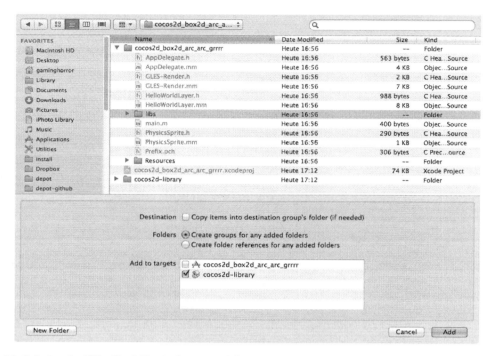

Figure 2-14. *Select and add the libs folder to the cocos2d-library target*

Now build and run the project to verify that everything is working. The cocos2d code and any other library source code provided by cocos2d is now built as a static library and linked with the application target.

Tip   The cocos2d-library project has created additional files that are not needed in your project. Locate the `cocos2d-library.h` and `cocos2d-library.m` files in the navigation area and delete the files. It's just an empty stub class that Xcode always creates when adding a static library target.

Refactor the Project's Source Code to ARC

With the cocos2d source code building as a static library that has ARC disabled, the next step is to enable ARC for your project's source code. Fortunately, Xcode provides a convenience function to convert existing code to ARC.

From the Xcode menu choose Edit ➤ Refactor ➤ Convert to Objective-C ARC.... This brings up the dialog shown in Figure 2-15, where you can select the targets to convert. Select only your app's target and not the cocos2d-library target. Then click Check.

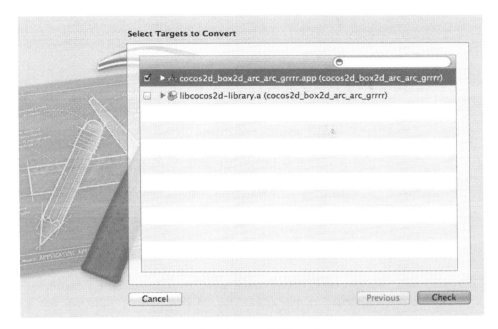

Figure 2-15. Convert only your project's target and not the cocos2d-library target

Xcode first tries to build your code with ARC enabled to determine the changes it will have to make. This only takes a few seconds. When complete, an introduction dialog explains what comes next. Read the text and click Next. The dialog shown in Figure 2-16 allows you to review the changes it is about to make. You can safely accept them all by clicking Save.

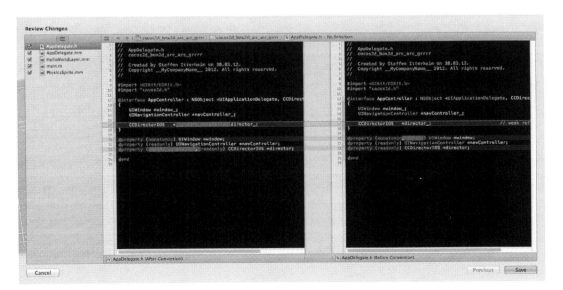

Figure 2-16. Review how Xcode is changing the code to make it comply with ARC

Afterwards, Xcode has also enabled the Objective-C Automatic Reference Counting build setting for the converted target. The code should build and run with ARC enabled, so go ahead and try it out now.

The Anatomy of cocos2d and Kobold2D Applications

So you now know how to create ARC-enabled cocos2d and Kobold2D projects. Perfect. Say no more, say no more.

But now you want to know how it works, right? Well, I didn't expect you'd let me off the hook so easily. And something tells me that however deep I go into the details over the course of the book, you'll want to know more. That's the spirit!

Let's check what's in the respective "Hello World" projects and see how it all works together so you get a rough overview of how things are connected. Feel free to play around with this "Hello World" project. If anything breaks, you can just start over by creating a new project based on one of the project templates.

Figure 2-17 shows the Project Navigator area for both a Kobold2D and a cocos2d project. You'll notice they're mostly identical as far as the source code is concerned. Because Kobold2D utilizes an Xcode workspace, you'll also find an additional project named Kobold2D-Libraries. That's where you can access all the library source code. In a cocos2d project these files are located in the libs group.

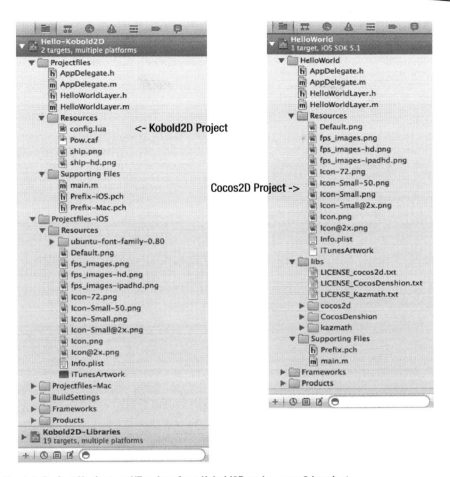

Figure 2-17. Xcode's Project Navigator eXEmplary for a Kobold2D and a cocos2d project

Caution   Xcode's Project Navigator pane looks a lot like folders and files in Finder. But the folders with yellow icons are actually called *groups*, and they're like virtual folders. Groups allow you to arrange files logically without affecting their actual folder location. You can move files between groups and rename groups but the files will remain at the same location in Finder. Likewise, if you move a file in Finder or rename a folder with files in it, Xcode doesn't automatically update the files in the project and instead displays the files in red, indicating that it was unable to locate the files.

Both cocos2d and Kobold2D projects essentially reference two different types of files: source code files and resource files (for example, images and property lists). I get to the resource files over the course of the book, so let's concentrate on the most important ones.

The Default.png file is the image displayed when iOS is loading your app, and Icon.png is, of course, the app's icon. Several variations of these files may be used, depending on the device. For example, Retina devices will load the image files with the @2x suffix. For a full list of image sizes and formats of app icons, launch images, and others, refer to Apple's Custom Icon and Image Creation Guidelines: http://developer.apple.com/library/ios/#documentation/userexperience/conceptual/mobilehig/IconsImages/IconsImages.html.

Cocos2d uses the fps_images.png files to display the framerate; you should not remove or modify them.

Inside the Info.plist file you'll find a number of settings for your application. You only need to make changes here when you get close to publishing your app. You can also change the most important Info.plist settings, such as supported device orientations, more conveniently if you select your project's target (see Figure 2-5).

The Supporting Files Group

If you're familiar with programming in C or similar languages, you may recognize main.m in the Supporting Files group as the starting point of the application. The only other file in this group is the precompiled header file Prefix.pch, respectively Prefix-iOS.pch and Prefix-Mac.pch in Kobold2D projects.

The main Function

Everything that happens between the main function and the AppDelegate class is part of the behind-the-scenes magic of the iOS SDK, over which you have no control. because you'll practically never need to change main.m, you can safely ignore its contents. Still, it never hurts to peek inside.

The main function creates an @autoreleasepool and then calls UIApplicationMain to start the application using AppController as the class that implements the UIApplicationDelegate protocol. You can find the implementation of the AppController class in the files named AppDelegate. This is what the main function looks like in an ARC-enabled cocos2d application:

```
int main(int argc, char *argv[])
{
    @autoreleasepool
    {
        int retVal = UIApplicationMain(argc, argv, nil, @"AppController");
        return retVal;
    }
}
```

The only interesting point to take away from this is that every iOS application uses an @autoreleasepool, which ARC needs to manage memory.

In Kobold2D apps, the main function only calls KKMain which performs the preceding and ends up using the AppDelegate class as well. But KKMain also initializes Lua, loads the config.lua file, and calls the appropriate startup function depending on the operating system (iOS or Mac OS).

```
int main(int argc, char *argv[])
{
    // Forward main to a default implementation provided by Kobold2D™.
    return KKMain(argc, argv, NULL);
}
```

The Prefix Header Files

In case you're wondering what the Prefix.pch header files are for, they're special header files used to speed up compilation. The PCH abbreviation stands for Pre-Compiled Header. You're supposed to add the header files of frameworks that rarely or never change to the prefix header. This causes the framework's code to be compiled in advance and made available to all your classes. Unfortunately, it also has the disadvantage that, if a header added to the prefix header changes, all your code will have to be recompiled—which is why you should only add header files that rarely or never change.

For example, the cocos2d.h header file is a good candidate to add to the prefix header of a cocos2d project, as shown in Listing 2-1. To create a noticeable increase in compilation time, your project would need to be reasonably complex, however, so don't get your stopwatch out just yet. But it's good practice to add cocos2d.h as a prefix header right away, if only to never have to write #import "cocos2d.h" in any of your source files again.

Listing 2-1. Adding the cocos2d.h Header File to the Prefix Header

```
#ifdef __OBJC__
    #import <Foundation/Foundation.h>
    #import <UIKit/UIKit.h>
    #import "cocos2d.h"
#endif
```

> **Note** The Prefix header files in a Kobold2D project already have the cocos2d.h added to it, as well as a number of other reasonable header files.

The AppDelegate Class

Every iOS application has one AppDelegate class that implements the UIApplicationDelegate protocol. In our HelloWorld project, it's simply called AppDelegate.

The AppDelegate is a global concept found in every iOS application. It tracks state changes of the application by receiving messages from the iOS at certain points in time. For example, it allows you to determine when the user gets an incoming phone call or when the application is low on memory. Cocos2d is typically initialized in the applicationDidFinishLaunching method.

The AppDelegate class in a Kobold2D project is a subclass of the KKAppDelegate class provided by Kobold2D. Like the AppController class, it subclasses NSObject and implements the UIApplicationDelegate protocol. KKAppDelegate does a lot of the work behind the scenes, leaving you to deal with only three callback functions that you may want to use or not. For example, the initializationComplete method is called by Kobold2D just before the first scene is run. This is where you should add any code that needs to run before the first scene is initialized. All the other settings you'd normally modify the source code of the AppDelegate class for can be altered more conveniently in the config.lua file in Kobold2D projects.

To learn more about the AppDelegate's various methods, what they do, and when these messages are sent by the iOS SDK, you can look it up in Apple's reference documentation on the UIApplicationDelegate protocol at http://developer.apple.com/iphone/library/documentation/uikit/reference/UIApplicationDelegate_Protocol.

> **Note**   I'm talking about application startup, so I might as well talk about application shutdown. You may eventually notice an oddity with the AppDelegate's dealloc method. It never gets called! Any breakpoint set in the AppDelegate's dealloc method will never be hit!
>
> This is normal behavior. When iOS terminates an application, it simply wipes the memory clean to speed up the shutdown process. That's why any code inside the dealloc method of the AppDelegate class is never run. As it's very bad practice to call dealloc manually, this and calling [super dealloc] is forbidden under ARC because ARC itself takes care of that for you. If you ever need to run code in your AppDelegate just before the application terminates, do it inside the applicationWillTerminate method.

In a pure cocos2d project the most commonly changed lines of code in the AppDelegate class are:

```
[director_ setDisplayStats:YES];
[director_ setAnimationInterval:1.0/60];
```

In a Kobold2D application, you can modify these and other settings in the config.lua file. Look for these two lines:

```
DisplayFPS = YES,
MaxFrameRate = 60,
```

Display Stats

The setDisplayStats method enables the numbers you see in the lower left-hand corner of the screen. See Figure 2-3 for an example. The numbers are stacked in three lines. From top to bottom, the first line indicates the number of draw calls. You want to keep this number as low as possible because a draw call is an expensive operation (more on this later). The second line is the time it took to update the frame. It tells you how much headroom you have before the framerate starts dropping. And the bottom-most number is the current framerate.

> **Caution**   Except for the number of draw calls, you have to entirely disregard the frame time and framerate numbers when running your app on the iOS Simulator. The Simulator performance has simply no significance, as it may be faster or slower by factors than an actual iOS device. It's like trying to measure the performance of a sports car while driving it through a cornfield. It sort of works, it may even be fun, but you still don't know what its street performance will be. Yet that's the only thing that matters.

If you need to tweak the responsiveness of the FPS display, you can do so by modifying the CC_DIRECTOR_STATS_INTERVAL line in ccConfig.h. By default it's set to 0.1, which means the framerate display will be updated ten times per second. If you increase the value, the frames per second (FPS) display will average out over a longer period of time. However, you won't be able to see any sudden, short drops in framerate, which can still be noticeable.

Animation Interval

The animation interval determines how often cocos2d updates the screen. Effectively, this affects the maximum framerate your game can achieve. The animation interval is not given in frames per second, though. It's the inverse because it determines how frequently cocos2d should update the screen. That's why the parameter is 1 divided by 60, because that results in 0.0167 seconds. If your app takes longer than this to update the game logic and render the screen, the framerate will drop below 60 FPS. It's your responsibility to keep the game running at a high framerate. Don't worry, I explain techniques to improve performance throughout the book.

In some cases, locking the framerate to 30 frames per second may be preferable. Doing so may be helpful in very complex games where you know you can't achieve 60 FPS consistently, and the framerate fluctuates anywhere between 30 and 60 FPS. In such a case, it's often better to lock the framerate to the lowest common denominator, because a lower but steady framerate is perceived as smoother by players than a framerate that tends to fluctuate abruptly, even when the actual average framerate may be higher. Human perception is a tricky thing.

> **Note**   You can't render more than 60 FPS on iOS devices. The device's display is locked to update at 60 frames per second (Hz), and forcing cocos2d to render more frames than 60 per second is, at best, not doing anything. At worst, it can actually slow down your framerate. Stick with the `animationInterval` of 1.0/60 if you want to run cocos2d at the fastest possible rate.

HelloWorldLayer

The `HelloWorldLayer` class is where cocos2d code does its magic to display the "Hello World" label. Before I get into that, you should understand that cocos2d uses a hierarchy of `CCNode` objects to determine what's displayed where.

The base class of all nodes is the `CCNode` class, which contains a position but has no visual representation. It's the parent class for all other node classes, including the two most fundamental ones: `CCScene` and `CCLayer`.

`CCScene` is an abstract concept and does nothing more than allow proper placement of objects in the scene according to their piXEl coordinates. A `CCScene` node is thus always used as the parent object for every cocos2d scene hierarchy. You can only have one running scene at any time.

The `CCLayer` class does very little by itself other than allow touch and accelerometer input. You'll normally use it as the first class added to the `CCScene`, simply because most games use at least simple touch input. Strictly speaking `CCLayer` is not needed to layer objects—you can achieve the same effect with `CCNode` or any other class derived from `CCNode`.

If you open the `HelloWorldLayer.h` header file, you'll see that the `HelloWorldLayer` class is derived from `CCLayer`. So where does the `CCScene` class come into play?

Because `CCScene` is merely an abstract concept, the default way of setting up a scene in cocos2d has always been to use a static initializer `+(id) scene` in your class. This method creates a regular `CCScene` object and then adds an instance of the `HelloWorldLayer` class to the scene. In almost all cases, that's the only place where a CCScene is created and used. The following is a generic example of the +(id) scene method:

```
+(id) scene
{
    CCScene *scene = [CCScene node];
    id layer = [HelloWorldLayer node];
    [scene addChild:layer];

    return scene;
}
```

First, a CCScene object is created using the class method +(id) node of the CCScene class. Next, the HelloWorldLayer class is created using the same +(id) node method and then added to the scene. The scene is then returned to the caller.

In a Kobold2D project,you may notice that the +(id) scene method is absent. You can use the config.lua setting FirstSceneClassName to instruct Kobold2D to run this particular class as the first scene:

```
FirstSceneClassName = "HelloWorldLayer",
```

If this particular class doesn't derive from CCScene, Kobold2D will create the CCScene object automatically behind the scenes.

Moving on to the -(id) init method of the HelloWorldLayer class, that's where the code starts to deviate between cocos2d, Kobold2D, and each individual project template. There are some commonalities though. Listing 2-2 represents a minimal init code for a "Hello World" app. The actual code in the project differs, but you'll definitely see a CCLabelTTF being added in the project you created earlier.

Notice something that might seem odd: self is assigned the return value from the init message sent to the super object in the call to self = [super init]. If you come from a C++ background, you'll shudder in pain looking at this. Don't get too upset; it's all right. It simply means that in Objective-C you have to manually call the superclass's init method. There's no automatic call to the parent class. And you do have to assign self the return value of the [super init] message because it might return nil.

Listing 2-2. The init Method Creates and Adds a "Hello World" Label

```
-(id) init
{
    if ((self = [super init]))
    {
        // create and initialize a label
        CCLabelTTF* label = [CCLabelTTF labelWithString:@"Hello World"
                                fontName:@"Marker Felt"
                                fontSize:64];

        // get the window (screen) size from CCDirector
        CGSize size = [[CCDirector sharedDirector] winSize];

        // position the label at the center of the screen
        label.position = CGPointMake(size.width / 2, size.height / 2);
```

```
        // add the label as a child to this Layer
        [self addChild:label];
    }
    return self;
}
```

The CCLabelTTF class draws text on the screen using a TrueType font.

If you're deeply concerned by the way Objective-C programmers write the call to [super init], here's an alternative that might ease your mind, even though it's not as common among cocos2d developers. It's fundamentally the same, and Apple also uses this style:

```
-(id) init
{
    self = [super init];
    if (self != nil)
    {
        // do init stuff here ...
    }
    return self;
}
```

Now let me explain how the label is added to the scene. If you look again at the init method in Listing 2-2, you'll see that a CCLabelTTF object is created using one of init's static initializer methods. It'll return a new instance of the CCLabelTTF class. To not have its memory freed after control leaves the init method, you have to add the label to self as a child using the [self addChild:label] message. In essence, holding a reference to an object keeps the object alive. In this case, cocos2d takes control over the object's memory until you remove it from the scene or switch scenes.

In between creating and adding the label, the label is assigned a position at the center of the screen. Note that whether you assign the position before or after the call to addChild doesn't matter.

Memory Management with ARC

If you've never done any Objective-C programming before, good for you! You'll come to take for granted memory management that works as you would expect. As long as you keep a reference to an object, it will be kept alive. You don't need to worry about allocating or freeing memory at all.

If you have programmed with Objective-C before, you may have to overcome the uneasy feeling of "just letting go." ARC is not magic, but it can be trusted to do the right thing 100% of the time. You might want to read Apple's Transitioning to ARC Release Notes here: http://developer.apple.com/library/ios/#releasenotes/ObjectiveC/RN-TransitioningToARC/Introduction/Introduction.html.

To give you an example, these two lines of code are identical in ARC:

```
CCSprite* sprite = [CCSprite spriteWithFile:@"file.png"];
CCSprite* sprite = [[CCSprite alloc] initWithFile:@"file.png"];
```

Before ARC, you actually had to differentiate between allocating an autorelease object (first line) or a regularly initialized object (second line). With ARC, you should prefer the first version if available because it's more readable and is faster under ARC. But either way is fine, and both create an object whose memory is freed when the `sprite` variable goes out of scope. It's as simple as that.

The only thing that doesn't change with ARC is that you have to send the `alloc` message to a class to create an instance of that class. This also allocates and initializes the object's memory.

Changing the World

What good is a template project like HelloWorld if I don't have you tinker with it at least a little? I'll have you change the world by touching it! How's that for a start?

First you'll make two changes to the `init` method to enable touch input and to use a tag value to retrieve the label at a later point. The changes are highlighted in Listing 2-3.

Listing 2-3. Enabling Touch and Gaining Access to the Label Object

```
-(id) init
{
    if ((self = [super init]))
    {
        // create and initialize a label
        CCLabelTTF* label = [CCLabelTTF labelWithString:@"Hello World"
                            fontName:@"Marker Felt"
                            fontSize:64];

        // get the window (screen) size from CCDirector
        CGSize size = [[CCDirector sharedDirector] winSize];

        // position the label at the center of the screen
        label.position = CGPointMake(size.width / 2, size.height / 2);

        // add the label as a child to this Layer
        [self addChild: label];

        // our label needs a tag so we can find it later on
        // you can pick any arbitrary number
        label.tag = 13;

        // must be enabled if you want to receive touch events!
        self.isTouchEnabled = YES;
    }
    return self;
}
```

The `label` object gets 13 assigned to its tag property. Now why did you do that? I know, I told you to, but I must have had a reason, right? In the previous section, I explained that that's how you can later access a child object of your class—you can refer to it by its tag. The tag number is completely arbitrary, other than that it must be a positive number and every object should have its own tag number, so there aren't two with the same number, or you couldn't tell which you'd be retrieving.

> **Tip**   Instead of using magic numbers like 13 as tag values, you should get in the habit of defining
> constants to use with tags. You'll have a hard time remembering what tag number 13 stands for,
> compared to writing a meaningful variable name like kTagForLabel. I get to this in Chapter 5.

In addition, self.isTouchEnabled is set to YES. This property of the CCLayer class tells it that you
want to receive touch messages. Only then will the method ccTouchesBegan be called:

```
-(void) ccTouchesBegan:(NSSet*)touches withEvent:(UIEvent*)event
{
    CCLabelTTF* label = (CCLabelTTF*)[self getChildByTag:13];
    label.scale = CCRANDOM_0_1();
}
```

By using [self getChildByTag:13], you can access the CCLabelTTF object by its tag property,
which you assigned in the init method. You can then use the label as usual. In this case, we use
cocos2d's handy CCRANDOM_0_1() macro to change the label's scale property to a value between
0 and 1. This will change the label's size every time you touch the screen.

Because getChildByTag will always return the label, you can safely cast it to a(CCLabelTTF*)
object. However, be aware that doing so will crash your game if the retrieved object isn't derived
from the CCLabelTTF class for some reason. This could easily happen if you accidentally give
another object the same tag number 13. For that reason, it's good practice to use a defensive
programming style and verify that what you're working with is exactly what you expect.
Defensive programming uses assertions to verify that assumptions made are true. For this, you
should use the NSAssert method:

```
-(void) ccTouchesBegan:(NSSet*)touches withEvent:(UIEvent*)event;
{
    CCNode* node = [self getChildByTag:13];

    // defensive programming: verify the returned node is a CCLabelTTF
    NSAssert([node isKindOfClass:[CCLabelTTF class]], ↵
        @"node is not a CCLabelTTF!");

    CCLabelTTF* label = (CCLabelTTF*)node;
    label.scale = CCRANDOM_0_1();
}
```

In this case, you expect the node returned by getChildByTag to be an object derived from
CCLabelTTF, but you can never be sure, which is why adding an NSAssert to verify the fact is
helpful in finding errors before they lead to a crash.

Note that this adds two more lines of code, but in terms of performance things remain the
same. The call to NSAssert is completely removed in Release builds, and the cast CCLabelTTF*
label = (CCLabelTTF*)node; is what you've done already, just on the same line. Essentially,
both versions perform exactly the same, but in the second case you get the benefit of being
notified when you didn't get the expected CCLabelTTF object, instead of crashing with an
EXC_BAD_ACCESS error.

What Else You Should Know

Because this is the "Getting Started" chapter, I think it's important to take the opportunity to introduce you to some vital but often overlooked aspects of iOS game development. I want you to be aware of the subtle differences among various iOS devices. In particular, available memory is often incorrectly considered because you can use only a fraction of each device's memory safely.

I also want you to know that the iOS Simulator is a great tool for testing your game, but it can't be used to assess performance, memory usage, and other features. The Simulator experience can differ greatly from running your game on an actual iOS device. Don't fall into the trap of making assessments based on your game's behavior in the iOS Simulator. Only the device counts.

The iOS Devices

When you develop for iOS devices, you need to take into account their differences. Most independent and hobby game developers can't afford to purchase each slightly different iOS device—of which there are eight at the time of this writing, with roughly two more to be released each year. At the very least, you need to understand that there are important differences.

You might want to refer to Apple's spec sheets to familiarize yourself with the iOS device technical specifications. The following links list the iPhone, iPod touch, and iPad device specifications, respectively:

- http://support.apple.com/specs/#iphone
- http://support.apple.com/specs/#ipodtouch
- http://support.apple.com/specs/#ipad

Table 2-1 summarizes the most important hardware differences that concern game developers. The iPhone and iPod touch models are listed by generation, with the corresponding iPhone model suffix in brackets. Where there are two numbers for Processor speed or memory, the first number is that of the iPhone model and the second number is that of the iPod touch model.

Table 2-1. *iOS Hardware Differences*

Device	Processor	Graphics	Resolution	Memory (RAM)
First generation	412 MHz	PowerVR MBX	480×320	128MB
Second generation (3G)	412/533 MHz	PowerVR MBX	480×320	128MB
Third generation (3GS)	600 MHz	PowerVR SGX535	480×320	256MB
Fourth generation (4)	800 MHz	PowerVR SGX535	960×640	512/256MB
iPhone 4S	2x 800 MHz	PowerVR SGX535 Dual	960×640	512MB
iPad first generation	1 GHz	PowerVR SGX535	1024×768	256MB
iPad second generation	2x 1 GHz	PowerVR SGX543 Dual	1024×768	512MB
iPad third generation	2x 1 GHz	PowerVR SGX543 Quad	2048×1536	1GB

As you can see, with every new generation, iOS devices usually have a faster CPU, a more powerful graphics chip, and increased memory and screen resolution. This trend will continue, with newer devices getting more and more powerful.

With cocos2d 2.0 you can't target the first- and second-generation devices, which make up an increasingly smaller fraction of the iOS market. That means you're looking at a minimum of 256MB of memory on the oldest devices you can support. However, there's still a wide range between 256MB and 1024MB of memory, respectively a 600 MHz CPU and a Dual-Core CPU with 2x 1 GHz on the third-generation iPad.

Usually when game developers look at hardware features, they tend to focus on the CPU speed and graphics chip to assess what's technically possible. However, being mobile devices, the iOS devices (until the most recent iPhone 4) are limited mostly by the amount of available memory. This is also quite frequently underestimated by new developers. For example, a 1000x1000 tilemap can easily consume several hundred megabytes of memory, not counting the texture memory. And a 2048x2048 texture with 32-bit color depth already consumes 16MB of memory, so you can't have too many of them in memory at the same time.

> **Note**   Don't confuse RAM with the flash storage memory where MP3s, videos, apps, and photos are stored, of which even the smallest iOS device has 8GB. Flash storage memory is equivalent to the hard drive on your desktop computer. RAM is the memory your application uses to store code, data, and textures while it's running. When I talk about memory, I mean RAM.

About Memory Usage

Current iOS devices have between 256MB and 1GB of RAM installed. However, that's not the amount of memory available to apps. iOS uses a big chunk of memory all the time, and this is compounded by iOS multitasking introduced with iOS 4.

Over time, iOS developers have been able to close in on the theoretical maximum amount of RAM an app can use before it's forcibly closed by the OS. Table 2–2 shows what you can expect to work with.

Table 2–2. Installed Memory Is Not Available Memory

Installed Memory	Available Memory	Memory Warning Threshold
128MB	Around 30MB	Around 20MB
256MB	Around 90MB	Around 70MB
512MB	Around 300MB	Around 250MB (estimated)

Ideally, you want to keep your memory usage below the number in the Memory Warning Threshold column at all times. Around that point your app might start receiving Memory Warning notifications. You can ignore Memory Warning Level 1 notifications, but if the app continues to use more memory, you may get a Memory Warning Level 2 message, at which point the OS basically threatens to close your app if you don't free some memory right now. It's like your mom threatening not to buy your new computer if you don't clean up your room right now! Please oblige.

Cocos2d and Kobold2D automatically free memory by calling the purgeCachedData method whenever the AppDelegate class receives an applicationDidReceive MemoryWarning message.

If you're developing on a device with 512MB or more memory, keep in mind that a great number of iOS devices are models with only 256MB. It's a good idea to have an actual device around from the oldest generation of devices that you aim to support. You might want to buy a cheap, used, third-generation device to test your game primarily with that device in order to catch memory warnings and performance issues early in development. That's when they are still easy and cheap to fix, especially if they require a change in the game's design. In general, it's advisable to use the device for development that's the weakest one available to you in terms of hardware capabilities.

You can measure the memory usage of your app using the Instruments application, explained in Apple's Instruments User Guide:
https://developer.apple.com/library/ios/#documentation/DeveloperTools/Conceptual/
InstrumentsUserGuide/Introduction/Introduction.html.

The iOS Simulator

Apple's iOS SDK allows you to run and test iPhone and iPad applications on your Mac with the iOS Simulator. The primary purpose of the iOS Simulator is to let you more rapidly test your application, because deployment to an iOS device takes longer and longer as your game gets bigger and bigger. Games in particular use a lot of images and other assets that need to be transferred, slowing down deployment.

However, there are several caveats to using the iOS Simulator. The following sections reveal what the iOS Simulator does not allow you to do. For all these reasons, I recommend that you test your game early and often on a device. At least after every major change or near the end of the day, you should run a test on your iOS device to verify that the game behaves exactly as intended.

Can't Assess Performance

The performance of your game running in the iOS Simulator depends entirely on your computer's CPU. The graphics-rendering process doesn't even use the hardware acceleration capabilities of your Mac's graphics chip. That's why the framerate of your game running in the simulator has no meaning at all. You can't even be sure that comparing the framerate before and after a change will reveal the same results on the device. Always do your performance testing on the device using the Release build configuration.

Can't Assess Memory Usage

The iOS Simulator can use all the memory available on your computer, so there's a lot more memory available on the Simulator than on the device. This means you won't get Memory Warning notifications, and your game will run fine on the iOS Simulator, but you may be in for a shock (a crash) when you try the game for the first time on an iOS device.

You can, however, assess how much memory is currently used by your game using the iOS Simulator and Instruments. You can also send a fake memory warning message to your app from the iOS Simulator menu via Hardware ➤ Simulate Memory Warning.

Can't Use All iOS Device Features

Some features, such as device orientation, can be simulated using menu items or keyboard shortcuts, but this comes nowhere close to the experience of a real device. Certain hardware features, such as multitouch input, accelerometer, vibration, or obtaining location information can't be tested at all on the iOS Simulator because your computer's hardware can't simulate these features. No, it doesn't help to shake your Mac or touch its screen. Try it if you don't believe me.

Tip   The iSimulate app (www.vimov.com/isimulate) is an invaluable development tool, as it allows an iOS device to send accelerometer, GPS, compass, and multi-touch events to an app running in the iOS Simulator.

Runtime Behavior Can Differ

From time to time you may encounter nasty cases where a game runs just fine on the iOS Simulator but crashes on the device or the game slows down for no apparent reason. There may also be graphical glitches that appear only on the iOS Simulator or only on the device. If in doubt, and before delving into a prolonged quest to figure out what's wrong, always try running your game on the device if you're having trouble on the iOS Simulator, or vice versa. Sometimes, the problem may just go away, but if not, you may get a hint about what's going on.

Don't bother figuring out issues that only occur on the Simulator. Likewise, don't ignore any issues that only occur on the device but work fine on the Simulator.

About Performance and Logging

By default, an Xcode project will use the Debug build configuration with code optimizations turned off for debugging purposes, and logging turned on for the same reason.

One NSLog or CCLOG in the wrong place can spam the Debugger Console with logging messages, causing slowdowns and lag. Logging is very slow, and a continuous stream of log messages printed to the Debugger Console can drag your game's performance down to a crawl. If you suspect your game's performance to be particularly slow in Debug builds, always check the Debugger Console for excessive logging activities. In Xcode, click Run ➤ Console to show the Debugger Console window.

The exclusion of logging and typically better code optimization settings are the main reason you should only use Release builds to test your game's performance. You can temporarily set your project to use the Release build configuration by selecting Product ➤ Manage Schemes... from the Xcode menu. Then select your app's target and edit it. Select the Run configuration on the left, as in Figure 2-18. Then just change the Build Configuration to Release.

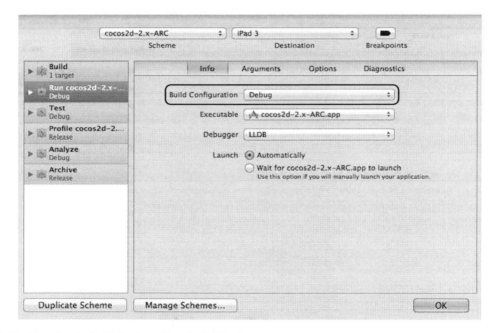

Figure 2-18. Changing the Build Configuration of a build scheme

You can also create a duplicate of the scheme and set one to use the Debug build configuration and the other to use Release. That way you can quickly change between build configurations without having to go through the Manage Schemes menu. Note that you don't need to do the same with the cocos2d-library scheme—it will automatically use the same build configuration as the app.

Summary

Wow, that was a lot for a "Getting Started" chapter! In the first part of this chapter you learned to download and set up all the necessary tools to the point where you had your first cocos2d and Kobold2D template projects running. You also learned how to enable ARC in cocos2d projects.

I then walked you through the basics of the template project to get you up to speed with how an iOS cocos2d application works in principle, and somewhat in detail as well. I do have a pet peeve about proper memory management, which is why I also included those details. I think it's important because it's easy to misunderstand or even completely ignore memory management, and then you might be building your game on a very crumbly foundation.

I did manage to sneak in a short "do it yourself" section to at least show you how touch input is done in cocos2d and how cocos2d objects are stored and retrieved.

Finally, I thought it important to give you the details about the various iOS devices and what you can expect in terms of available memory. I also discussed the iOS Simulator and how it differs for testing your game compared with testing it on a device.

In the next chapter, you'll learn all the essential features of cocos2d, which will bring you closer to making a complete cocos2d game.

Chapter 3

Essentials

This chapter introduces you to the essential building blocks of the cocos2d game engine. You'll be using most of these classes in every game you create, so understanding what's available and how the classes work together will help you write better games. Armed with this knowledge, you'll find it a lot easier to start working with cocos2d.

Accompanying this chapter is an Xcode project called Essentials that includes everything I discuss here, plus additional examples. The source code is full of comments.

This chapter starts with a high-level overview of the cocos2d game engine architecture. Because every game engine is different in the way game objects are managed and presented on the screen, it's best to begin with an understanding of what the individual elements are and how they fit together.

The cocos2d Scene Graph

Sometimes called a scene hierarchy, the scene graph is a hierarchy of every cocos2d node that's currently active.

A cocos2d node is any object derived from the CCNode class. Most nodes, like CCSprite and CCLabelTTF, are displayed on the screen, but a few have no visual representation, including CCNode, CCScene, and CCLayer. They are no less important, though, and they frequently cause confusion for new cocos2d developers.

In the upcoming sections I go into more detail on those classes and explain what they're used for. For now, I focus on the high-level concepts, and it's sufficient for you to know that CCSprite displays a texture on the screen, CCLabelTTF prints arbitrary text, and CCNode, CCScene, and CCLayer are used mainly to group nodes together.

Figure 3-1 depicts the shoot 'em up game that you'll create, starting in Chapter 6, and illustrates what's not immediately noticeable to players of the game but very important for game developers to understand.

Figure 3-1. A shoot 'em up game

The scene in Figure 3-1 is entirely made of CCSprite objects. At least that's what you can see. What you can't see is how the CCScene and CCLayer classes are used to group and order the various sprites—several background layers, the player's ship, the enemies, the bullets, and the virtual joypad and button. To illustrate the layering of this scene's elements, Figure 3-2 shows an exploded view drawing of that scene.

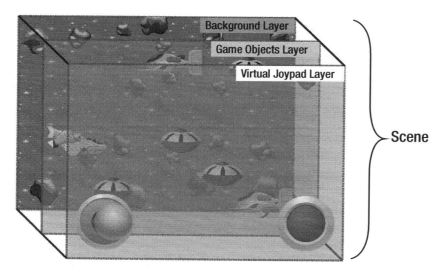

Figure 3-2. An exploded view illustrating a typical cocos2d game scene layout

In this particular case, three layers help maintain the proper draw order of the sprites in relation to each other: the background layer, the game objects layer, and the virtual joypad layer. Using multiple layers in a scene is also helpful if you want to hide an entire layer's nodes, move the layer and thus all the nodes it contains, or reorder the layer so that its nodes are drawn above or behind another layer's nodes. You can even rotate and scale a layer, which would rotate and scale all the nodes contained in that layer. This makes using layers a powerful concept.

In this respect, the game scene is modeled using layers in just the way you edit an image in an image-editing program such as Photoshop, Seashore, or GIMP. However, the nodes (brush strokes) in each layer aren't static and instead remain individual elements.

The actual Scene object is just the container for all the layers (the actual image, so to speak), just like a layer is a container for other nodes. Each of these nodes can run custom game logic, the scene, the layers, the individual nodes, the sprites, the labels, and so on, depending on how you organize your code.

Any node can have any other node as a child, and every node in the hierarchy—except for the scene itself—has one parent object, which is the object the node is a child of. If you remove the node from the scene graph or you haven't added it yet, it won't have a parent object. Note that this parent-child relationship of nodes is not to be confused with inheritance in object-oriented programming. In other words, the parent node is not the node's super class!

This treelike hierarchy of nodes that you can create is what's called the *scene graph*, which I'll sometimes call the *node hierarchy*. For those familiar with programming design patterns, you'll recognize this hierarchical structure as the Composite design pattern. Figure 3-3 shows what the simplified node hierarchy of this scene looks like as a tree structure.

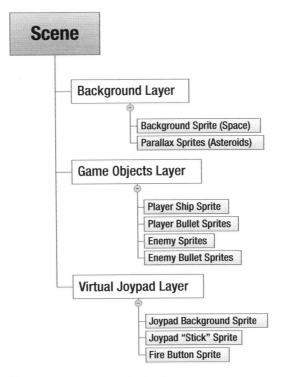

Figure 3-3. The node hierarchy of the scene illustrated in Figure 3-2

Note that this particular scene/layer/nodes structure is not enforced by cocos2d, except that the scene graph always has a CCScene class object as its root node. But other than that, you can use any CCNode class instead of CCLayer to create your "layers." You could even add all of your nodes to the scene itself; if your project has only a small number of nodes, that's perfectly reasonable.

I generally prefer to use the plain CCNode class over CCLayer for layering and grouping objects; in most cases, the CCLayer class adds unnecessary overhead because it contains code to receive touch and accelerometer input in iOS apps and handles keyboard and mouse input in Mac OS X apps. Strip away support for input handling, and the CCLayer class is practically just a CCNode class. The same goes for CCScene, which is also just an abstract concept in order to enforce a common root node class. Otherwise a CCScene class is virtually the same as a CCNode.

Caution   The nodes in a cocos2d node hierarchy are positioned relative to their parent nodes. The child nodes inherit certain properties from their parents, such as scale and rotation but not color and opacity. This may be confusing the first time you experience it.

For example, if the parent of a CCLabelTTF node is a nondrawing node—like the CCNode, CCScene, or CCLayer nodes—and they themselves are the only children of other nondrawing nodes, the position of the label will be relative to the view's lower left-hand corner. So, all is well and as expected. But if you add another CCLabelTTF as a child to this label, the position of the child label will be relative to the parent label.

You would have reason to expect the child label to be centered on the parent label's position. Alas, this is not the case, as you can see in Figure 3-4. You'll find that the child label will be centered on the lower left-hand corner of the parent label's texture instead, which is an unfortunate oddity in cocos2d's design. To correctly position such a node and center it on its parent node, you have to use parent node's contentSize.width / 2 and contentSize.height / 2 as the child node's position.x and position.y.

Figure 3-4. Caution: the default position of a child node is unexpectedly offset from its parent's position

I created the NodeHierarchy project to give you examples of relative positioning and rotation of nodes in a parent-child relationship and to familiarize you with the cocos2d node hierarchy. Consider it a test bed for your own experiments.

The CCNode Class Hierarchy

At this point, you may be wondering what classes derive from CCNode. Figure 3-5 shows the CCNode class hierarchy. The node classes you'll be working with the most are highlighted, and you can make quite impressive games with just these classes. I'll explain the most important classes shortly, and over the course of the book you'll get to know even the more obscure ones in depth.

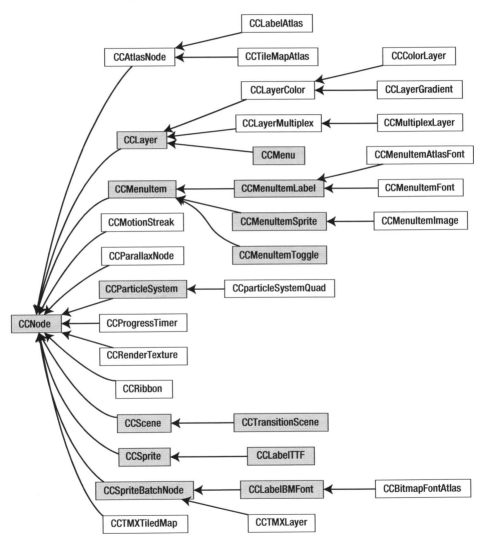

Figure 3-5. The CCNode class hierarchy

CCNode

CCNode is the base class for all nodes. It's an abstract class that has no visual representation and defines all properties and methods common to all nodes.

Working with Nodes

The CCNode class implements all the methods to add, get, and remove child nodes. Here are some of the ways you can work with child nodes:

- You can create a new node:

  ```
  CCNode* childNode = [CCNode node];
  ```

- You can add the new node as a child:

  ```
  [myNode addChild:childNode z:0 tag:123];
  ```

- You can retrieve the child node:

  ```
  CCNode* retrievedNode = [myNode getChildByTag:123];
  ```

- You can remove the child node by tag; cleanup will also stop any running actions:

  ```
  [myNode removeChildByTag:123 cleanup:YES];
  ```

- You can remove the node if you have a pointer to it:

  ```
  [myNode removeChild:retrievedNode];
  ```

- You can remove every child of the node:

  ```
  [myNode removeAllChildrenWithCleanup:YES];
  ```

- You can remove myNode from its parent:

  ```
  [myNode removeFromParentAndCleanup:YES];
  ```

The z parameter in addChild determines the draw order of the node. The node with the lowest z value is drawn first; the one with the highest z value is drawn last. If multiple nodes have the same z value, they're simply drawn in the order they were added. Of course, this applies only to nodes that have a visual representation, such as sprites.

The tag parameter lets you identify and obtain specific nodes at a later time using the getChildByTag method.

> **Note**   If several nodes end up with the same tag number, getChildByTag will return the first node with that tag number. The remaining nodes will be inaccessible. Make sure you use unique tag numbers for your nodes.
>
> Note that actions can have tags, too. Node and action tags don't conflict, however, so an action and a node can have the same tag number without any problem.

Working with Actions

Nodes can also run actions. I'll cover actions more in a bit. For now, just know that actions can move, rotate, and scale nodes—and can do other things with nodes over time.

- Here's an action declaration:

```
CCAction* action = [CCBlink actionWithDuration:10 blinks:20];
action.tag = 234;
```

- Running the action makes the node blink:

```
[myNode runAction:action];
```

    If you need to access the action at a later time, you get it by its tag:

```
CCAction* retrievedAction = [myNode getActionByTag:234];
```

- You can stop the action by tag:

```
[myNode stopActionByTag:234];
```

- Or you can stop it by pointer:

```
[myNode stopAction:action];
```

- Or you can stop all actions running on this node:

```
[myNode stopAllActions];
```

Scheduled Messages

Nodes can schedule messages, which is Objective-C lingo for calling a method. In many cases, you'll want a particular update method to be running on a node in order to do some processing, such as checking for collisions. The simplest way to schedule the particular update method to be called every frame is like this, typically found in the node's init method:

```
[self scheduleUpdate];
```

If a node has the update method scheduled, it will send the update message to your class every frame. You must implement this particular method in your node class:

```
-(void) update:(ccTime)delta
{
    // this method is called every frame
}
```

Dead simple, isn't it? Notice that the update method has a fixed signature, meaning it's always defined exactly this way. The delta parameter is the elapsed time since the method was last called. This is the preferred way to schedule updates that should take place every frame, but there are reasons to use other update methods that give you more flexibility.

If you want a different method to be run, or if you don't want the method to be called every frame but every tenth of a second, you should use this method:

```
[self schedule:@selector(updateTenTimesPerSecond:) interval:0.1f];
```

This will send the updateTenTimesPerSecond message to your node class ten times per second:

```
-(void) updateTenTimesPerSecond:(ccTime)delta
{
    // this method is called according to its interval, ten times per second
}
```

Note that if interval is 0, you should use the scheduleUpdate method instead because it's slightly faster. It's faster because cocos2d has optimizations for the common update selector if it's scheduled with scheduleUpdate, whereas all other scheduled selectors incur an additional overhead because they're stored in lists and prioritized against each other.

The method's signature is still the same: it receives a delta time as its only parameter. But this time the method can be named any way you want, and it's called only every tenth of a second. This may be useful to check for win conditions if they're so complex you don't want to run them every frame. Or if you want something to happen after 10 minutes, you could schedule a selector with an interval of 600.

Each selector can only be scheduled once for each object. If you schedule the same selector for the same object a second time, cocos2d will print out a warning telling you that the selector was already scheduled and its interval has been updated.

Note   The @selector(...) syntax may seem weird. It's the Objective-C way of referring to a specific method by name. The crucial thing here is not to overlook the colon at the end. It tells Objective-C to look for the method with the given name and exactly one parameter. If you forget to add the colon at the end, the program will still compile, but it will crash later. In the Debugger Console, the error log will read "unrecognized selector sent to instance. ..."

The number of colons in @selector(...) must always match the number and names of the parameters of the method. For the following method:

```
-(void) example:(ccTime)delta sender:(id)sender flag:(bool)aBool
```

the corresponding @selector should be written as follows:

```
@selector(example:sender:flag:)
```

There's one major caveat with scheduling your own selectors, and with the @selector(…) keyword in general. By default, the compiler does not complain at allif the method's name doesn't exist. Instead, your app will simply crash with an "unrecognized selector sent to instance" error . Because the message is sent by cocos2d internally, you'll find it hard to figure out the cause of the problem. Luckily, there's a compiler warning you can enable. Figure 3-6 shows the "Undeclared Selector" warning enabled for the NodeHierarchy project, and the Essentials Xcode project for this chapter has it enabled as well.

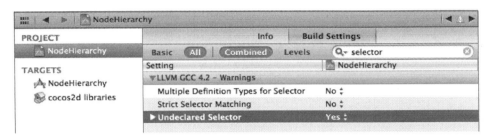

Figure 3-6. *Activating the build setting to warn about undeclared selectors*

What's left is to show how to stop these scheduled methods from being called. You can do so by unscheduling them:

- You can stop all scheduled selectors of the node:

  ```
  [self unscheduleAllSelectors];
  ```

- You can unscheduled the default update method:

  ```
  [self unscheduleUpdate];
  ```

- You can stop a particular selector, in this case the updateTenTimesPerSecond method:

  ```
  [self unschedule:@selector(updateTenTimesPerSecond:)];
  ```

There's also a useful trick for scheduling and unscheduling selectors. Quite often you'll find that in the scheduled method, you want a particular method to no longer be called, without having to replicate the exact name and number of parameters, because they can change. Here's how you'd run a scheduled selector and stop it on the first call:

```
[self scheduleOnce:@selector(tenMinutesElapsed:) delay:600];
```

This is identical to scheduling the selector as usual:

```
[self schedule:@selector(tenMinutesElapsed:) interval:600];
```

And then unscheduling the selector inside the scheduled method by using the _cmd variable as the selector:

```
-(void) tenMinutesElapsed:(ccTime)delta
{
    // unschedule the current method by using the _cmd keyword
    [self unschedule:_cmd];
}
```

The hidden variable _cmd is available in all Objective-C methods. It's the selector of the current method. In the previous code example, _cmd is equivalent to writing @selector(tenMinutesElapsed:). Unscheduling _cmd effectively stops the tenMinutesElapsed method from ever being called again. You can also use _cmd for scheduling the selector in the first place if you want the current method to be rescheduled. Let's assume you need a method called at varying intervals, and this interval is changed each time the method is called. In this case, your code can make use of _cmd like this:

```
-(void) scheduleUpdates
{
    // schedule the first update as usual
    [self schedule:@selector(irregularUpdate:) interval:1];
}


-(void) irregularUpdate:(ccTime)delta
{
    // unschedule the method first so cocos2d won't complain
    [self unschedule:_cmd];

    // I assume you'd have some kind of logic other than random to determine
    // the next time the method should be called
    float nextUpdate = CCRANDOM_0_1() * 10;

    // then re-schedule it with the new interval using _cmd as the selector
    [self schedule:_cmd interval:nextUpdate];
}
```

Using the _cmd keyword will save you a lot of pain in the long run because it avoids the dreaded issue of scheduling or unscheduling the wrong selector, and it decouples the code from having to know the name of the method it's used in.

I'll mention one final scheduling issue, and that's prioritizing updates. Take a look at the following code:

```
// in Node A
[self scheduleUpdate];


// in Node B
[self scheduleUpdateWithPriority:1];


// in Node C
[self scheduleUpdateWithPriority:-1];
```

This may take a moment to sink in. All nodes are still calling the same -(void) update:(ccTime) delta method for themselves. However, scheduling the update methods with a priority causes the one in Node C to be run first. Then the one in Node A is called because, by default, scheduleUpdate uses a priority of 0. Node B's update method is called last because it has the highest number. The update methods are called in the order from lowest-priority number to highest.

You might wonder where that's useful. To be honest, they're rarely needed, but in those cases it's quite useful to be able to prioritize updates, such as when applying forces to physics objects before or after the physics simulation itself is updated or ensuring that the game-over condition is checked only after all game objects have run their update methods. And sometimes, usually late in the project, you may discover an odd bug that turns out to be a timing issue, and it forces you to run the player's update method after all other objects have updated themselves.

Until you need to solve a particular problem by using prioritized updates, you can safely ignore them. Also, keep in mind that each prioritized update method call adds a little overhead because the methods need to be called in a specific order. A quite common implementation for prioritized updates is to have a central object driving the game update of other objects by forwarding the update methods to the objects in the desired order. That way you can also see clearly in the code which object gets called when:

```
-(void) update:(ccTime)delta
{
    [inputHandler update:delta];
    [player update:delta];
    [enemies update:delta];
    [physics update:delta];
    [networkData update:delta];
    [userInterface update:delta];
}
```

A positive benefit of this approach is that it makes selectively pausing certain objects easier. How to pause the game but allow user input on the pause menu is a question that comes up often. The solution is to update your layers individually, and if the game is paused you don't forward the update message to the layers except for the layer that displays the pause menu.

Director, Scenes, and Layers

Like CCNode, the CCScene and CCLayer classes have no visual representation and are used internally as abstract concepts for the starting point of the scene graph, which is always a CCScene-derived object. The CCScene class is the container for all other nodes of the scene. And CCLayer is typically used to group nodes together, particularly to maintain the correct drawing order among multiple layers. But also to receive touch and accelerometer input In iOS, and mouse and keyboard input in Mac OS X.

I start this section with the CCDirector class, however, because it's the class that, among other things, allows you to run and replace scenes.

The Director

The CCDirector class, or simply Director for short, is the heart of the cocos2d game engine. If you recall the "Hello World" application from Chapter 2, you'll remember that a lot of the cocos2d initialization procedure involved calls to [CCDirector sharedDirector].

The CCDirector class is a singleton, which means there can be only one instance of the CCDirector class at any time, and it can be accessed globally by calling the class method sharedDirector. For now that's all you need to know about singletons. Later in this chapter, in the section "A Note on Singletons in cocos2d," I explain what a singleton is and which other singleton classes cocos2d uses.

The CCDirector class stores global configuration settings for cocos2d and also manages the cocos2d scenes. The major responsibilities of the CCDirector class include the following:

- Providing access to the currently running scene
- Changing scenes
- Providing access to cocos2d configuration details
- Providing access to cocos2d's OpenGL view and window
- Modifying certain OpenGL projection and enabling depth tests
- Converting UIKit and OpenGL coordinates
- Pausing, resuming, and ending the game
- Displaying debugging stats
- Counting the total number of frames rendered

In earlier cocos2d versions you could also choose between several Director types. That's no longer the case in cocos2d 2.0. The CCDirector now uses Apple's CADisplayLink class exclusively to synchronize screen updates with the display's refresh rate.

CCScene

A CCScene object is always the first node in the scene graph. In cocos2d, a scene is an abstract concept, and the CCScene class contains virtually no additional code compared to CCNode. But the CCDirector requires a CCScene-derived class to be able to change the currently active scene graph via the CCDirector runWithScene, replaceScene, and pushScene methods. You can also wrap a CCScene class into a class derived from CCSceneTransition to animate the transition between a currently running scene and the new scene.

Normally, the only children of a CCScene are those derived from CCLayer, which in turn contain the individual game objects, although this convention is not enforced by cocos2d. Because the scene object itself in most cases doesn't contain any game-specific code and is rarely subclassed, it's most often created in a static method +(id) scene inside the CCLayer object. I mention this method in Chapter 2, but here it is again to refresh your memory:

```
+(id) scene
{
    CCScene *scene = [CCScene node];
    CCLayer* layer = [HelloWorld node];
    [scene addChild:layer];


    return scene;
}
```

The very first place you'll create a scene is at the end of the app delegate's applicationDidFinishLaunching method. You use Director to start the first scene with the runWithScene method:

```
// only use this to run the very first scene
[[CCDirector sharedDirector] runWithScene:[HelloWorld scene]];
```

For all subsequent scene changes, you must replace the existing scene with the aptly named replaceScene method:

```
// use replaceScene to change all subsequent scenes
[[CCDirector sharedDirector] replaceScene:[HelloWorld scene]];
```

As you'll soon learn in an upcoming section, you can also use transitional effects when replacing scenes. The following is an example that uses the CCTransitionShrinkGrow class as an intermediary scene that manages the transition animation:

```
CCScene* scene = [HelloWorld scene];
CCSceneTransition* tran = [CCTransitionShrinkGrow transitionWithDuration:2 scene:scene];
[[CCDirector sharedDirector] replaceScene:tran];
```

> **Caution**   If you run the preceding code in the HelloWorld scene, it will work just fine, creating a new instance of HelloWorld and replacing the old one, effectively reloading the scene. However, don't try to reload the current scene by passing self as a parameter to replaceScene. This will freeze or crash your game!

Scenes and Memory

Keep in mind that when you replace one scene with another, the new scene is loaded into memory before the old scene's memory is freed. This creates a short spike in memory usage. Replacing scenes is always a crucial point where you can run into memory warnings or straight into a crash related to not enough free memory. You should test scene switching early and often when your app uses a lot of memory.

> **Note**   Cocos2d does a good job of cleaning up its own memory when you replace one scene with another. It removes all nodes, stops all actions, and unschedules all selectors. No extra work is required on your part. I mention this because sometimes I come across code that makes explicit calls to the removeAll and cleanup cocos2d methods. Remember, if in doubt, trust cocos2d's memory management.

This issue becomes even more pronounced when you start using transitions. With transitions, the new scene is created, the transition runs, and only after the transition has done its job is the old scene removed from memory. It's good practice to add log statements to your scene or to the layer that creates the scene:

```
-(id) init
{
    self = [super init];
    if (self)
    {
        CCLOG(@"%@: %@", NSStringFromSelector(_cmd), self);
    }
}
```

```
-(void) dealloc
{
    CCLOG(@"%@: %@", NSStringFromSelector(_cmd), self);
}
```

Keep an eye on these log messages. If you notice that the dealloc log message is never sent when you switch from one scene to another, that's a huge warning sign. In that case, you're leaking the whole scene, not freeing its memory. It's extremely unlikely when using ARC, but it can still happen—for example, if you assign the scene to a custom class's property, such as a view controller or singleton whose lifetime isn't tied to cocos2d scenes. In that case, the scene might be replaced but not removed from memory because the custom class still has a reference to the scene. You're most likely to run into this issue when assigning node objects as delegates for UIKit classes, like Game Center. Be extra careful to set any delegate to nil before replacing the scene.

One thing you should never do is add a node as a child to the scene graph and then pass this node to another node which then keeps a reference to it. Retain cycles—where object A holds on to object B while object B itself holds a reference to object A—are still possible with ARC. In these cases, neither object lets go of the other, keeping them in memory until the app is closed.

Use cocos2d's methods to access node objects instead. As long as you let cocos2d worry about managing the memory of nodes, you'll be fine.

Pushing and Popping Scenes

With regard to changing scenes, the pushScene and popScene methods of Director can be useful tools. They run the new scene without removing the old scene from memory. If you think of your scenes as sheets of paper, pushing a scene means a new sheet of paper is added on top of the currently visible one. The paper underneath stays in place and in memory, unlike in replacing scenes. For each pushed scenes, you then need to call popScene (like removing the topmost sheet of paper) until only the initial scene is left.

The idea is to make changing scenes faster. But there's the conundrum: if your scenes are lightweight enough to share memory with each other, they'll load fast anyway. And if they're complex and thus slow to load, chances are they take away each other's precious memory—and memory usage can quickly climb to a critical level.

The biggest issue with pushScene and popScene is that you need to keep track of how many scenes were pushed in order to pop the exact amount. If you're not very careful about managing your pushes and pops, you'll end up forgetting a pop or popping one scene too many. Besides, all those scenes have to share the same memory.

There are cases where pushScene and popScene are very handy. One is if you have one common scene used in many places, such as the Settings screen where you can change music and sound volume. You can push the Settings scene to display it, and its Back button then simply calls popScene; the game will return to the previous state. Whether you opened the Settings menu from the main menum, from within the game, or from someplace else, this technique works fine and lets you avoid having to keep track of where the Settings menu was opened.

Another case where pushScene and popScene are very useful is if you want to retain the state of the initial scene without having to revert to saving and loading that scene's state. For example, you could push the scene that shows the current leaderboard in a multiplayer game and then pop it again without having to save and load the game state, because the game scene remains in memory. And the game hasn't advanced while the player was inspecting the leaderboard because the game scene was automatically paused while the leaderboard scene was visible.

However, you need to ensure that there's always enough additional free memory available for the pushed scene at any time the scene could be pushed, which is hard to test for. Any scene you may want to push should therefore be very lightweight, consume little memory, and should only pop itself but never push other scenes or even call replaceScene.

For example, to display a Settings scene from anywhere on top of the current scene, use this code:

```
[[CCDirector sharedDirector] pushScene:[Settings scene]];
```

Now inside the Settings scene you need to call popScene when you want to go back to the previous scene that's still in memory:

```
[[CCDirector sharedDirector] popScene];
```

> **Caution**   You can animate only the pushScene with CCSceneTransition and not popScene. This is a drawback of pushing and popping scenes you should be aware of.

CCTransitionScene

Transitions, meaning any class derived from CCTransitionScene, can give your game a really professional look. Figure 3-7 gives you an overview of the CCTransitionScene class hierarchy and shows the available transition classes. Figure 3-7 also complements the CCNode class hierarchy in Figure 3-5, where the CCTransitionScene subclasses were not included for the sake of clarity.

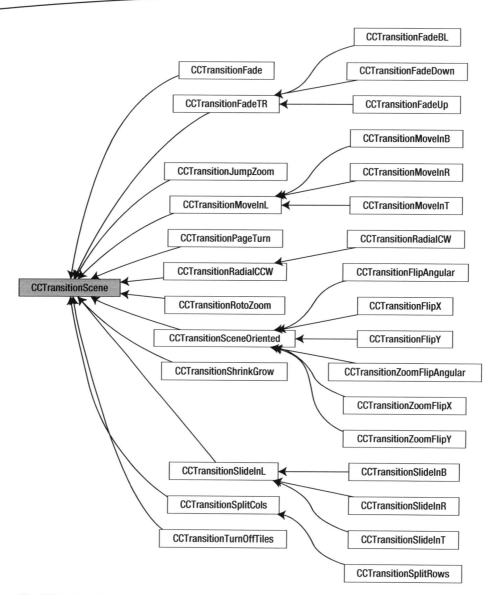

***Figure 3-7.** The CCTransitionScene class hierarchy*

Caution   Not every transition is really useful in a game, even though they all look neat. What players care most about is the speed of a transition. Even waiting two seconds before they can interact with the next scene is quite a strain; I prefer to transition scenes within a second or less, or avoid them altogether if it fits the situation.

What you should certainly try to avoid is picking random transitions when replacing scenes. Players don't care, and game developers know you just got a little over-excited by how cool the transitions are. If you don't know which transition is right for a particular change of scene, don't use any at all. In other words, just because you can doesn't mean you should.

Transitions add only one more line of code to replacing a scene, although admittedly that one line can be a long one, given how long the names of transitions are and how they get even longer with the number of parameters they often require. Here's the very popular fade transition as an example; it fades to white in one second:

```
// initialize a transition scene with the scene we'd like to display next
CCTransitionFade* tran = [CCTransitionFade transitionWithDuration:1
                                    scene:[HelloWorld scene]
                                    withColor:ccWHITE];
// use the transition scene object instead of HelloWorld
[[CCDirector sharedDirector] replaceScene:tran];
```

You can use a CCTransitionScene with replaceScene and pushScene, but as I said earlier, you can't use a transition with popScene (at least not at this time—this may be improved in a future version of cocos2d).

A variety of transitions are available, although most are variations of directions—as in, where the transition moves to or from which side it starts. Here's a list of the currently available transitions, along with a short description for each:

- CCTransitionFade: Fades to a specific color and back. There's also the CCTransitionCrossFade variation.

- CCTransitionFadeTR (three more variations): Tiles flip over to reveal a new scene.

- CCTransitionJumpZoom: Scene bounces and gets smaller; new scene does the reverse.

- CCTransitionMoveInL (three more variations): Scene moves out; new scene moves in at the same time, either from left, right, top, or bottom.

- CCTransitionSceneOriented (six variations): A variety of transitions flipping and optionally zooming the whole scene around on one of its axis.

- CCTransitionPageTurn: An effect like turning a page.

- CCTransitionProgress (six variations): Like a radar screen that reveals the new scene with a radial or axis-aligned wipe animation.

- CCTransitionRotoZoom: Scene rotates and gets smaller; new scene does the reverse.

- CCTransitionShrinkGrow: Current scene shrinks; new scene grows over it.

- CCTransitionSlideInL (three more variations): New scene slides over the current scene, either from left, right, top, or bottom.

- CCTransitionSplitCols (one variation): Columns of scene move up or down to reveal new scene.

- CCTransitionTurnOffTiles: Tiles are randomly replaced by tiles of new scene.

CCLayer

Sometimes you need more than one layer in your scene. In such cases you can add more CCLayer objects to your scene. One way to do so is directly in the scene method:

```
+(id) scene
{
    CCScene* scene = [CCScene node];

    CCLayer* backgroundLayer = [HelloWorldBackground node];
    [scene addChild: backgroundLayer];

    CCLayer* layer = [HelloWorld node];
    [scene addChild:layer];

    CCLayer* userInterfaceLayer = [HelloWorldUserInterface node];
    [scene addChild: userInterfaceLayer];

    return scene;
}
```

This scene now has three distinct layers: the backgroundLayer, the regular game object layer, and on top of that the userInterfaceLayer. Because the layers are added to the scene in the order created, any nodes added to the backgroundLayer will be drawn behind the other layers. Likewise, nodes added to the userInterfaceLayer will always be drawn on top of any nodes in the layer and backgroundLayer.

Tip   Again, strictly speaking, a layer does not have to be derived from the CCLayer class; it could also be a simple CCNode. This is often preferable when you need the layer only to group nodes together and don't require it to handle user input.

One case where you might want to use multiple layers per scene is if you have a scrolling background and a static frame surrounding the background, possibly including user interface elements. Using two separate layers makes it easy to move the background layer by simply adjusting the layer's position while the foreground layer remains in place. In addition, all objects of the same layer will be either in front of or behind objects of another layer, depending on the z-order of the layers. Of course, you can achieve the same effect without layers, but it requires each individual object in the background to be moved separately. That's ineffective, so avoid it if you can.

Like scenes, layers have the same dimension as the cocos2d OpenGL view. For iOS devices, this is almost always the size of the screen; on Mac OS X, it's the size of the window.

Layers are primarily a grouping concept. For example, you can use any action with a layer, and the action will affect all the objects on the layer. That means you can move all layer objects around in unison or rotate and scale them all at once. In general, use a layer if you need a group of objects to perform the same actions and behaviors. Moving all objects to scroll them is one such case; sometimes you might want to rotate them or reorder them so they're drawn on top of other objects. If all these objects are children of a layer, you can simply change the layer's properties or run an action on the layer to affect all its child nodes.

> **Note**   Many recommend not using too many CCLayer objects per scene. This advice is often misunderstood. You can use as many layers as you want without affecting performance any more than using any other node. However, things change if the layer also accepts input, because touch or accelerometer events are costly tasks. Don't use several layers receiving touch or accelerometer input at the same time—one will do. Preferably one layer receives and handles input and, where necessary, informs other nodes or classes about the input events by forwarding them to registered objects. You usually do this via the performSelector method that calls a method with a defined method signature. See cocos2d's CCScheduler class for an example implementation.

Receiving Touch Events

The CCLayer class is designed to receive touch input, but only if you explicitly enable it. To enable receiving touch events, set the property isTouchEnabled to YES:

```
self.isTouchEnabled = YES;
```

This is best done in the class's init method, but you can change it at any time.

Once the isTouchEnabled property is set, a variety of methods for receiving touch input will start to get called. These are the events received when a new touch begins, when a finger is moved on the touchscreen, and when the user lifts the finger off the screen. Canceled touches are rare, and you can safely ignore this method for the most part or simply forward it to the ccTouchesEnded method.

- This is called when a finger just begins touching the screen:

    ```
    -(void) ccTouchesBegan:(NSSet *)touches withEvent:(UIEvent *)event
    ```

- This is called whenever the finger moves on the screen:

  `-(void) ccTouchesMoved:(NSSet *)touches withEvent:(UIEvent *)event`

- This is called when a finger is lifted off the screen:

  `-(void) ccTouchesEnded:(NSSet *)touches withEvent:(UIEvent *)event`

- This is called to cancel a touch:

  `-(void) ccTouchesCancelled:(NSSet *)touches withEvent:(UIEvent *)event`

Cancel events are rare and in most cases should behave just like touches ended.

In many cases, you want to know where a touch occurred. Because the touch events are received by the Cocoa Touch API, the location must be converted to OpenGL coordinates. The following method does this for you:

```
-(CGPoint) locationFromTouches:(NSSet *)touches
{
    UITouch *touch = touches.anyObject;
    CGPoint touchLocation = [touch locationInView:touch.view];
    return [[CCDirector sharedDirector] convertToGL:touchLocation];
}
```

This method works only with a single touch because it uses [touches anyObject]. To keep track of multitouch locations, you have to keep track of each touch individually.

By default, the layer receives the same events as Apple's UIResponder class. Cocos2d also supports targeted touch handlers. The difference is that targeted touches receive only one touch at a time, in contrast to the UIResponder touch events that always receive a set of touches. The targeted touch handler simply splits those touches into separate events that, depending on your game's needs, may be easier to work with. More importantly, the targeted touch handler lets you remove certain touches from the event queue, specifying that you've handled this touch and don't want it to be forwarded to other layers. This makes it easy to sort out if touches are in a specific area of the screen; if they are, you mark the touch as claimed, and all the remaining layers don't need to do this area check again.

To enable the targeted touch handler, add the following method to your layer's class:

```
-(void) registerWithTouchDispatcher
{
    [[CCDirector sharedDirector].touchDispatcher addTargetedDelegate:self
                                    priority:INT_MIN+1
                                    swallowsTouches:YES];
}
```

> **Caution** If you leave the `registerWithTouchDispatcher` method empty, you won't receive any touches at all! If you want to keep the method but also want to use the default handler, you'll have to call [`super registerWithTouchDispatcher`] in this method. It's also worth mentioning that the `registerWithTouchDispatcher` method is only called in `CCLayer` classes. You can also add non-`CCLayer` nodes as touch delegates, but in that case you must call [[`CCDirector sharedDirector].touchDispatcher removeDelegate:self`] at a later time.

Now, instead of using the default touch input methods, you're using a slightly different set of methods. They're almost equivalent with the exception of receiving a (UITouch*) touch instead of a (NSSet*) touches as the first parameter:

```
-(BOOL) ccTouchBegan:(UITouch *)touch withEvent:(UIEvent *)event {}
-(void) ccTouchMoved:(UITouch *)touch withEvent:(UIEvent *)event {}
-(void) ccTouchEnded:(UITouch *)touch withEvent:(UIEvent *)event {}
-(void) ccTouchCancelled:(UITouch *)touch withEvent:(UIEvent *)event {}
```

What's important to note here is that ccTouchBegan returns a BOOL value. If you return YES in that method, it means you don't want this particular touch to be propagated to other targeted touch handlers with a lower priority—you have effectively "swallowed" this touch.

> **Note**   Cocos2d has no built-in support for recognizing gestures, but Kobold2D supports all gesture recognizer types via the KKInput class by writing [KKInput sharedInput].gesturePanEnabled = YES. You can then check the state and properties of the gesture at any time. For cocos2d, this forum thread is a good starting point for a gesture recognizer implementation: www.cocos2d-iphone.org/forum/topic/8929.

Receiving Accelerometer Events

Like touch input, the accelerometer must be specifically enabled to receive accelerometer events:

```
self.isAccelerometerEnabled = YES;
```

Once more, you add a specific method to the layer that receives the accelerometer events:

```
-(void) accelerometer:(UIAccelerometer *)accelerometer
                            didAccelerate:(UIAcceleration *)acceleration
{
    CCLOG(@"acceleration:x:%f/y:%f/z:%f", ↵
    acceleration.x, acceleration.y, acceleration.z);
}
```

You can use the acceleration parameter to determine the acceleration in any of the three directions.

> **Tip**   The KKInput class in Kobold2D not only does accelerometer input, it also provides a simple interface to the gyroscope. For both accelerometer and gyroscope, you can access the high-pass and low-pass filtered values via properties.

Receiving Keyboard Events

If you're creating a Mac OS X app, you want to be able to process keyboard presses. You first have to enable keyboard events:

```
self.isKeyboardEnabled = YES;
```

The callback methods to receive keyboard events are defined in the CCKeyboardEventDelegate protocol as follows:

```
-(BOOL) ccKeyDown:(NSEvent*)event
{
    CCLOG(@"key pressed: %@", event.characters);
}


-(BOOL) ccKeyUp:(NSEvent*)event
{
    CCLOG(@"key released: %@", event.characters);
}


-(BOOL) ccFlagsChanged:(NSEvent*)event
{
    CCLOG(@"flags changed: %@", event.characters);
}
```

The flags changed event is received whenever the user presses or releases a modifier key, regardless of whether any other key is pressed at the same time. You can use it to implement controls that are assigned directly to a modifier key.

A very simplistic keyboard event check to react to presses or releases of the D key would go something like this:

```
NSString* key = event.charactersIgnoringModifiers;
if ([key caseInsensitiveCompare:@"d"] == NSOrderedSame)
{
    CCLOG(@"D key");
}
```

The problem with this approach is that depending on the user's locale, the keys may be in different parts of the keyboard, possibly requiring the Option key as well. Furthermore, in many regions of the world, like Asia, Russia, or the Middle East, users may be unable to (easily) create a D key on their keyboards.

Kobold2D therefore supports locale-independent keyboard input based on key codes. You can check whether the D key was pressed in Kobold2D like this:

```
[[KKInput sharedInput] isKeyDownThisFrame:KKKeyCode_D];
```

This works independently of whether the user has had the Shift key pressed or not. To include the Shift key in the check, simply write:

```
KKInput* input = [KKInput sharedInput];
[input isKeyDownThisFrame:KKKeyCode_D modifierFlags:KKModifierShiftKeyMask];
```

Kobold2D users don't need to delve further into this subject because Kobold2D already provides solid, documented keyboard and mouse input implementation: www.kobold2d.com/ display/KKDOC/Processing+User+Input. But cocos2d users can learn more about keyboard event handling in this forum thread: www.cocos2d-iphone.org/forum/topic/11725. Apple's documentation on handling key events is also very helpful: http://developer.apple.com/library/mac/#documentation/cocoa/conceptual/EventOverview/ HandlingKeyEvents/HandlingKeyEvents.html.

Receiving Mouse Events

Similar to all other input methods, you first have to enable mouse input via the following:

```
self.isMouseEnabled = YES;
```

Then your layer will start receiving CCMouseEventDelegate protocol messages, of which there are quite a few:

```
// received when the mouse moves with no button pressed
-(BOOL) ccMouseMoved:(NSEvent*)event {}


// received when the mouse moves while the corresponding button is held down
-(BOOL) ccMouseDragged:(NSEvent*)event {}
-(BOOL) ccRightMouseDragged:(NSEvent*)event {}
-(BOOL) ccOtherMouseDragged:(NSEvent*)event {}


// received when the corresponding mouse button is pressed (left, right, other)
-(BOOL) ccMouseDown:(NSEvent*)event {}
-(BOOL) ccRightMouseDown:(NSEvent*)event {}
-(BOOL) ccOtherMouseDown:(NSEvent*)event {}


// received when the corresponding mouse button is released (left, right, other)
-(BOOL) ccMouseUp:(NSEvent*)event {}
-(BOOL) ccRightMouseUp:(NSEvent*)event {}
-(BOOL) ccOtherMouseUp:(NSEvent*)event {}


// received when the scroll wheel is turned
-(BOOL) ccScrollWheel:(NSEvent*)event {}
```

Because you get specific events for each mouse button, you mainly use the NSEvent object to get the current mouse cursor position. You have to convert that position to cocos2d coordinates via the Director's convertEventToGL method:

```
CGPoint mousePos = [[CCDirector sharedDirector] convertEventToGL:event];
```

Kobold2D users have to do no such thing. You can check at any time whether a mouse button is pressed:

```
[[KKInput sharedInput] isMouseButtonDown:KKMouseButtonLeft];
```

The mouse position is also readily available and already converted to cocos2d coordinates, so you can simply write this in a scheduled method to use a sprite as the mouse cursor:

```
sprite.position = [KKInput sharedInput].mouseLocation;
```

Apple has a great tutorial on handling mouse events if you want to learn more about It: http://developer.apple.com/library/mac/#documentation/Cocoa/Conceptual/EventOverview/HandlingMouseEvents/HandlingMouseEvents.html.

CCSprite

CCSprite, certainly the most commonly used class, uses an image to display the sprite onscreen. The simplest way to create a sprite is from a file that's loaded into a CCTexture2D texture and assigned to the sprite. You have to add the image file to the Resources group in Xcode; otherwise, the app can't find the file:

```
CCSprite* sprite = [CCSprite spriteWithFile:@"Default.png"];
[self addChild:sprite];
```

Here's a question for you: where do you think this sprite will be positioned on the screen? Contrary to what you might be used to from other game engines, the texture is centered on the sprite's position. The sprite just initialized will be located at position 0,0, so it's positioned at the lower left-hand corner of the screen. Because the sprite's texture is centered on the sprite's position, the texture is only partially visible. Assuming the image is 80×30 pixels in size, you'd have to move the sprite to position 40,15 to make the texture align perfectly with the lower left-hand corner of the screen and be fully visible.

Although unusual at first glance, centering the texture on the sprite does have great advantages. Once you start using the rotation or scale properties of the sprite, the sprite will stay centered on its position.

Warning   Filenames are case-sensitive on iOS devices. While you're on the Simulator, the filename's case doesn't matter, but when you switch to testing on the device it will most likely crash if the filename is actually something like @`"default.PNG"` (from the previous example).

This sensitivity has caused many developers serious headaches, and it's another reason you should test on the device often. Coming up with a naming scheme for filenames and sticking to it is also a good idea. Personally, I keep them in lowercase, using dashes where needed to separate words.

Anchor Points Demystified

Every node has an anchor point, but it only starts to make a difference if the node has a texture, like CCSprite or CCLabelTTF. By default, the anchorPoint property is at 0.5,0.5, or, in other words, at the center of the texture (texture width and height times 0.5).

The anchor point has nothing to do with the node's position, even though changing the anchorPoint will change where the texture is rendered onscreen. By modifying the anchorPoint, you change only where the texture of the node is drawn relative to the node's position. But that also raises the question: why would you want to modify the anchorPoint, and what effects can you achieve by doing so?

For example, setting the anchorPoint to 0,0 effectively moves the texture so that its lower left-hand corner aligns with the node's position. If you set the anchorPoint to 1,1 instead, the top right-hand corner of the texture will align with the node's position. Sometimes this can be useful to align textures with the screen borders or other elements; specifically, it's useful as a way for CCLabel classes to right-align or top-align the text, for example.

Generally, you don't want to modify the anchorPoint unless you have a good reason to do so, because it can have wide-ranging side effects such as offsetting position-based collision checks. It also has an effect on rotation and scaling because the texture will no longer be rotated or scaled around its center position.

I know of three situations where changing the anchor point may be helpful:

1. To align nodes with the screen window borders more easily.

2. To right/left/top/bottom-align a label, button, or image.

3. To align an image whose size was changed without having to modify the sprite's position.

In all other cases use the `position` property of the node.

In the following example code, the sprite image will neatly align with the lower left-hand corner of the screen because its `anchorPoint` is set to 0,0, which causes the texture's lower left-hand corner to align with the sprite's default `position`, which is also 0,0:

```
CCSprite* sprite = [CCSprite spriteWithFile:@"Default.png"];
sprite.anchorPoint = CGPointMake(0, 0);
[self addChild:sprite];
```

CCLabelTTF

CCLabelTTF is the simplest choice when it comes to displaying text on the screen. Here's how to create a CCLabelTTF object to display some text:

```
CCLabelTTF* label = [CCLabelTTF labelWithString:@"text"
                     fontName:@"AppleGothic"
                     fontSize:32];
[self addChild:label];
```

In case you're wondering which TrueType fonts are available on iOS devices, you'll find a list of fonts in the `Essentials` project for this chapter.

Internally, the given TrueType font is used to render the text on a `CCTexture2D` texture. Because this happens every time the text changes, it's not something you should do every frame. Recreating the texture of a `CCLabelTTF` is really slow, and it's done every time the string of the label is modified:

```
[label setString:@"new text"];
```

Also notice that increasing or decreasing the length of the text of a label makes the text behave as if it's center-aligned on the label's position. The following sentences are center-aligned to illustrate this effect:

```
                     Hello World!
                Hello World Once Again!
     Hello Our World and all the other Worlds out there!
```

The center alignment is because of the anchor point and its default position of 0.5,0.5, which causes the center of the texture (in this case the label's text is the texture) to be center-aligned with the label's position. In many cases you want to align labels left, right, up, or down, and you can use the `anchorPoint` property to easily do that. The following code shows how you can align a label by simply changing the `anchorPoint` property:

```
// align label to the right
label.anchorPoint = CGPointMake(1, 0.5f);
// align label to the left
label.anchorPoint = CGPointMake(0, 0.5f);
// align label to the top
label.anchorPoint = CGPointMake(0.5f, 1);
// align label to the bottom
label.anchorPoint = CGPointMake(0.5f, 0);
// use case: place label at top-right corner of the screen
// the label's text extends to the left and down and is always completely on screen
CGSize size = [[CCDirector sharedDirector] winSize];
label.position = CGPointMake(size.width, size.height);
label.anchorPoint = CGPointMake(1, 1);
```

Menus

You'll soon need some kind of button a user can click to perform an action, such as going to another scene or toggling music on and off. This is where the CCMenu class comes into play. CCMenu is a subclass of CCLayer and accepts only CCMenuItem nodes as children. You can see the CCMenuItem class hierarchy in Figure 3-5 and in Figure 3-8 for the sake of clarity.

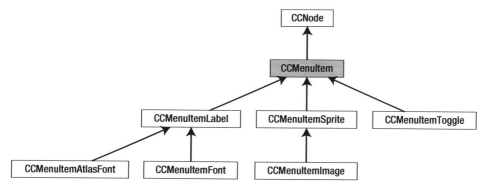

Figure 3-8. The CCMenuItem class hierarchy

Listing 3-1 shows the code for setting up a menu. You can find the menu code in the Essentials project in the MenuScene class.

Listing 3-1. Creating Menus in cocos2d with Text and Image Menu Items

```
CGSize size = [CCDirector sharedDirector].winSize;

// set CCMenuItemFont default properties
[CCMenuItemFont setFontName:@"Helvetica-BoldOblique"];
[CCMenuItemFont setFontSize:26];

// create a few labels with text and selector
CCMenuItemFont* item1 = [CCMenuItemFont itemWithString:@"Go Back!"
                         target:self
                         selector:@selector(menuItem1Touched:)];
```

```
// create a menu item using existing sprites
CCSprite* normal = [CCSprite spriteWithFile:@"Icon.png"];
normal.color = ccRED;
CCSprite* selected = [CCSprite spriteWithFile:@"Icon.png"];
selected.color = ccGREEN;
CCMenuItemSprite* item2 = [CCMenuItemSprite↵
                    itemWithNormalSprite:normal
                        selectedSprite:selected
                            target:self
                            selector:@selector(menuItem2Touched:)];

// create a toggle item using two other menu items (toggle works with images, too)
[CCMenuItemFont setFontName:@"STHeitiJ-Light"];
[CCMenuItemFont setFontSize:18];
CCMenuItemFont* toggleOn = [CCMenuItemFont itemWithString:@"I'm ON!"];
CCMenuItemFont* toggleOff = [CCMenuItemFont itemWithString:@"I'm OFF!"];
CCMenuItemToggle* item3 = [CCMenuItemToggle itemWithTarget:self
                            selector:@selector(menuItem3Touched:)
                            items:toggleOn, toggleOff, nil];

// create the menu using the items
CCMenu* menu = [CCMenu menuWithItems:item1, item2, item3, nil];
menu.position = CGPointMake(size.width/2, size.height/2);
[self addChild:menu];

// aligning is important, so the menu items don't occupy the same location
[menu alignItemsVerticallyWithPadding:40];
```

> **Warning**   The lists of menu items always end with `nil` as the last parameter. This is a technical requirement. If you forget to add `nil` as the last parameter, your app will crash at that particular line.

It takes a fair bit of code to set up a menu. The first menu item is based on `CCMenuItemFont` and simply displays a string. When the menu item is touched, it calls the method `menuItem1Touched`. Internally, `CCMenuItemFont` simply creates a `CCLabel`. If you already have a `CCLabel`, you can use that with the `CCMenuItemLabel` class instead.

Likewise, there are two menu item classes for images: one is `CCMenuItemImage`, which creates an image from a file and uses a `CCSprite` internally, and the other is one I've used here, `CCMenuItemSprite`. This class takes existing sprites as input, which I think is more convenient because you can use the same image and simply tint its color to achieve a highlighting effect when touched.

`CCMenuItemToggle` accepts exactly two `CCMenuItem`-derived objects and, when touched, toggles between the two items. You can use either text labels or images with `CCMenuItemToggle`.

Finally, `CCMenu` itself is created and positioned. Because the menu items are all children of `CCMenu`, they're positioned relative to the menu. To keep them from stacking up on each other, you have to call one of CCMenu's align methods, like `alignItemsVerticallyWithPadding`, as shown at the end of Listing 3-1.

Because CCMenu is a node containing all menu items, you can use actions on the menu to let it scroll in and out. This makes your menu screens appear less static, which is usually a good thing. See the Essentials project for an example. In the meantime, take a look at Figure 3-9 to see what your current menu looks like.

Figure 3-9. This is the menu produced by the code in Listing 3-1

Menu Items with Blocks

Instead of specifying a target and selector, menu items can also use blocks. What now?

A block is like a C function but with the important distinction that the block code can access variables in the scope where the block is declared. You can write a block inside other functions, store it in variables, and pass it as a parameter. Blocks also have access to variables in the scope they're declared in. This makes blocks a very powerful concept, but underused because the syntax is slightly confusing. Apparently Apple also recognized that because they changed the title of the Blocks Programming Guide to A Short Practical Guide to Blocks, which you'll find here: http://developer.apple.com/library/ios/#featuredarticles/Short_Practical_Guide_Blocks/_index.html.

Without going into too much theory, blocks are best explained by example. Let's see how a menu item using a block looks:

```
NSArray* items = [NSArray arrayWithObjects:toggleBlockOn, toggleBlockOff, nil];
CCMenuItemToggle* item4 = [CCMenuItemToggle itemWithItems:items
                               block:^(id sender) {
    // sender is the CCMenuItemToggle
    CCMenuItemToggle* toggleItem = (CCMenuItemToggle*)sender;
    int index = toggleItem.selectedIndex;
    CCLOG(@"item 4 touched with block: %@ - selected index: %i", sender, index);
}];
```

Now look at the same block again, but this time you make use of the fact that the block has access to variables in the scope where the block is declared. In this case, instead of using the sender, which turns out to be the CCMenuItemToggle, you can simply refer to the item4 variable directly. This is called *capturing state*. Even if you assigned a different object to item4 directly after where the block is declared, the block will still refer to the object that was stored in the item4 variable at the time the block was created.

```
NSArray* items = [NSArray arrayWithObjects:toggleBlockOn, toggleBlockOff, nil];
CCMenuItemToggle* item4 = [CCMenuItemToggle itemWithItems:items
                               block:^(id sender) {
    int index = item4.selectedIndex;
    CCLOG(@"item 4 touched with block: %@ - selected index: %i", item4, index);
}];
item4 = nil;//inside the block item4 will still be the menu item object
```

This particular menu item initializer takes a block as a parameter. Unfortunately, cocos2d doesn't document which signature the block function should have, so you'll have to dig up this information from any cocos2d method that accepts a block. Consulting with the CCMenuItem.m file where CCMenuItemToggle is implemented, you can see the block returns void (no return value) and passes an id sender object to the function:

```
block:(void(^)(id sender))block
```

Therefore, the block you need to implement needs to have the following signature:

```
^(id sender) {
  // your code here ...
}
```

By now you'll have noticed the oddly placed caret (^) symbol. That tells the compiler that the following code is a block. Following the caret, you first declare the parameter list in brackets, and following that is your code in curly brackets. So that's pretty straightforward.

One thing you may have noticed is that the block doesn't declare a return type. For void and int parameters, this is optional because the compiler assumes that the return type is void if no return statement is used inside the block. And if there's a return statement returning a value, it defaults to int. Because this leads to compiler errors when you want to return a different value than int, I find it good practice to specify the return type even if you don't have to. The return type always follows the caret symbol:

```
^void(id sender) {
  // your code here ...
}
```

Now you're probably wondering why you'd want to bother with syntactically odd blocks when you can just use target and selector instead? For one, it allows you to write the menu item handling code right where you define the menu item. Moreover, the block has access to local variables. In this example, the message NSString can be used within the block:

```
NSString* message = @"some kind of string";
NSArray* items = [NSArray arrayWithObjects:toggleBlockOn, toggleBlockOff, nil];
CCMenuItemToggle* item4 = [CCMenuItemToggle itemWithItems:items
                               block:^void(id sender) {
    CCLOG(@"message is:%@", message);
}];
```

What's more, you can re-use the same block for multiple menu items by assigning the block to a variable. For clarity, I omit the `NSArray*` items declarations from this example:

```
NSString* message = @"some kind of string";
void (^toggleBlock)(id sender) = ^void(id sender) {
    CCLOG(@"message is: %@ ", message);
};
CCMenuItemToggle* item6 = [CCMenuItemToggle itemWithItems:items
                                block:toggleBlock];
CCMenuItemToggle* item7 = [CCMenuItemToggle itemWithItems:items
                                block:toggleBlock];
message = @"a different string";
CCMenuItemToggle* item8 = [CCMenuItemToggle itemWithItems:items
                                block:toggleBlock];
```

Effectively you have one block that handles three menu items. And because the message string has changed before `item8`, this particular menu item will print out a different string every time you toggle it.

One issue when you start working with blocks is how the implementation and variable declaration differ in subtle but important ways. In the implementation (right-hand side of the equals symbol) you specify the return type following the caret symbol. However, in the variable declaration (left-hand side of the equation), the return type comes first and is never optional. You always have to specify void even if you can omit it on the right-hand side—another reason to always use the return type on the right-hand side as well.

What's more, the variable's name follows the caret symbol, and you have to write both in brackets to avoid compiler errors. Compare the variable declaration on the left-hand side with the block implementation on the right-hand side:

```
void (^toggleBlock)(id sender) = ^void(id sender) { /* block code here */ };
```

These small but subtle differences regarding declaration and implementation are probably what's most off-putting about the block syntax. But once you've seen several example uses, you get used to it, and eventually it becomes second nature. Note that once It's declared as a variable, you can pass the block variable around and you can even call it just as you'd call a C function:

```
toggleBlock(nil);
```

> **Tip** In the Essentials project I've added a method named `-(void) moreBlocksExamples` that contains many examples of how to write blocks. There's also an example using typedef and a preprocessor macro to allow you to write blocks with less syntactic horror. This example declares a block variable whose declaration and implementation were given a readable name:
>
> ```
> NegateBlock Negate = NegateBlockImp{ return !input; }; CCLOG(@"Negate
> returned: %@", Negate(YES) ? @"YES" : @"NO");
> ```

Blocks have a wide variety of uses. For example, they're used as callback mechanisms for Game Center classes, and they're essential for multithreading applications with Grand Central Dispatch and other Cocoa technologies. Internally, cocos2d converts all target/selector menu items to calls with blocks as well. Despite the syntactical oddities, I encourage you to work with blocks because you may be required to understand and use them sooner than you think. And you can start unlocking their powerful secrets sooner as well.

Actions

Actions are lightweight, one-shot classes you use on nodes to perform certain, well, actions. They allow you to move, rotate, scale, tint, fade, and do a lot of other things with a node. Because actions work with every node, you can use them on sprites, labels, and even menus or whole scenes! That's what makes them so powerful.

In Figure 3-10 you can see the CCAction class hierarchy without the many subclasses of CCActionInterval and CCActionInstant. (You'll see their class hierarchies in Figures 3-11 and Figure 3-16.)

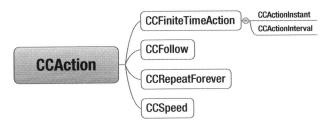

Figure 3-10. The CCAction class hierarchy with subclasses of CCActionInstant and CCActionInterval omitted

Only three actions directly derive from CCAction:

- CCFollow (allows a node to follow another node)
- CCRepeatForever (repeats an action indefinitely)
- CCSpeed (changes the update frequency of an action while it's running)

With the CCFollow action, you can instruct a node to follow another node. For example, to have a label follow the player character sprite, the code might look something like this:

```
[label runAction:[CCFollow actionWithTarget:playerSprite]];
```

You can also have actions or even a whole sequence of actions repeat (loop) forever with CCRepeatForever. You can create endlessly looping animations this way, for example. This code lets a node rotate forever like an endlessly spinning wheel:

```
CCRotateBy* rotateBy = [CCRotateBy actionWithDuration:2 angle:360];
CCRepeatForever* repeat = [CCRepeatForever actionWithAction:rotateBy];
[myNode runAction:repeat];
```

You can use the CCSpeed action to influence the speed of an action while it's running. Let's take the earlier rotation example and wrap it with a CCSpeed action:

```
CCRotateBy* rotateBy = [CCRotateBy actionWithDuration:2 angle:360];
CCRepeatForever* repeat = [CCRepeatForever actionWithAction:rotateBy];
CCSpeed* speedAction = [CCSpeed actionWithAction:repeat speed:0.5f];
speedAction.tag = 1;
[myNode runAction:speedAction];
```

Now the node will take twice as long to make a full revelution because the CCSpeed action's speed is set to 0.5f. You can change the speed property of the CCSpeed action later to influence the speed of the wrapped action while it's running. Without CCSpeed, you'd have to create new CCRotateBy and CCRepeatForever actions to accomplish a change in speed. That would not only waste precious CPU time, it might also cause stutters or jumps in the rotation animation.

To make the node suddenly rotate faster, you only need to get the speed action and modify its speed property:

```
CCSpeed* speedAction = (CCSpeed*)[myNode getActionByTag:1];
speedAction.speed = 2;
```

> **Note**   You can't add a CCSpeed action to a CCSequence action, because you can only use actions derived from CCFiniteTimeAction in a sequence.

Interval Actions

Because most actions happen over time, such as a rotation for three seconds, you'd normally have to write an update method and add variables to store the intermediate results. The CCActionInterval actions shown in Figure 3-11 wrap this kind of logic for you and turn it into simple, parameterized methods:

```
// have myNode move to 100, 200 and arrive there in 3 seconds
CCMoveTo* move = [CCMoveTo actionWithDuration:3 position:CGPointMake(100, 200)];
[myNode runAction:move];
```

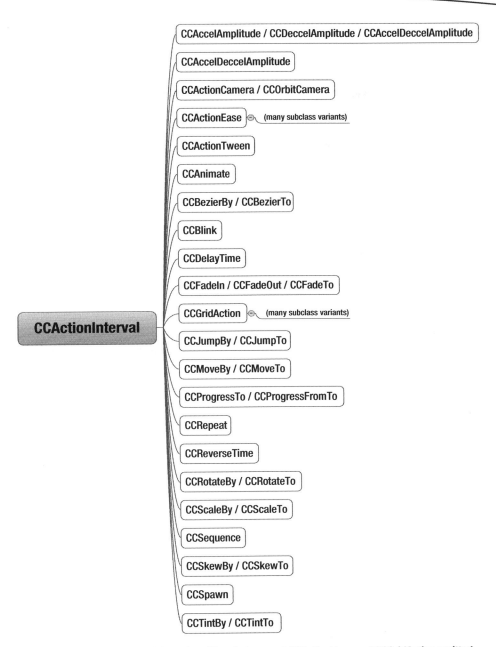

Figure 3-11. The CCActionInterval class hierarchy with subclasses of CCActionEase and CCGridAction omitted

Once you start using this particular code, you'll notice that, depending on the distance myNode has to move, its speed will be different. This very common problem has a simple solution: calculate the distance from the current position to the target position and then divide it by the speed you want the node to move. The result is the correct duration to have the node move to the target position at the same speed, regardless of where the node and target positions are.

```
// have myNode move at a fixed speed to any position
CGPoint targetPos = CGPointMake(100, 200);
float speed = 10; // in pixels per second
float duration = ccpDistance(myNode.position, targetPos) / speed;

CCMoveTo* move = [CCMoveTo actionWithDuration:duration position:targetPos];
[myNode runAction:move];
```

By the way, you don't have to remove an action. Once an action has completed its task, it removes itself from the node automatically and releases the memory it uses. That, unfortunately, is also actions' greatest weakness: you can't re-use them. If you need the same action or action sequence later on, you have to create new instances of the action classes.

Caution   A tip found in the official cocos2d documentation recommends simply "re-initializing" an action by sending it the appropriate `initWith...` message again. But this is dangerous and can lead to memory leaks and possibly crashes because not every action class can be safely re-initialized. And for some actions, it simply doesn't have the desired effect.

If you keep a reference to an action, maybe in an attempt to re-use it later, and then use it in multiple messages to `runAction`, you'll notice that either the action has no effect or the node behaves unexpectedly. The simplest way to provoke this issue is to try to use the same action on two different nodes, like so:

```
CCMoveTo* move = [CCMoveTo actionWithDuration:duration position:targetPos];
[myNode runAction:move];     // this node will stay put
[otherNode runAction:move]; // this node will move
```

Only the `otherNode` will run the action because it was the last node to use it. Actions only act on a single node, and therefore `myNode` won't move at all. If you want both nodes to move, you have to create two instances of the `CCMoveTo` class. There's really no other way around this.

Action Sequences

When you add several actions to the same node, they all perform their duties at the same time. For example, you could have an object rotate and fade out at the same time by adding the corresponding actions. But what if you want to run the actions one after the other?

Sometimes it's more useful to *sequence* actions, meaning as soon as one action has completed its job, the next one starts running. That's where CCSequence comes in. It's so powerful and frequently used, it deserves an extra mention. You can use any number and type of actions in a sequence, which makes it easy to have a node move to a target location and, at arrival, have it rotate around and then fade out, each action followed by the next one until the sequence is complete.

Here's how to cycle a label's colors from red to blue to green while waiting 1 second each after the red and blue tinting actions have run:

```
CCTintTo* tint1 = [CCTintTo actionWithDuration:4 red:255 green:0 blue:0];
CCDelayTime* wait1 = [CCDelayTime actionWithDuration:1];
CCTintTo* tint2 = [CCTintTo actionWithDuration:4 red:0 green:0 blue:255];
CCDelayTime* wait2 = [CCDelayTime actionWithDuration:1];
CCTintTo* tint3 = [CCTintTo actionWithDuration:4 red:0 green:255 blue:0];
CCSequence* sequence = [CCSequence actions:tint1, wait1, tint2, wait2, tint3, nil];
[label runAction:sequence];
```

You can also use a CCRepeatForever action with the sequence:

```
CCSequence* sequence = [CCSequence actions:tint1, tint2, tint3, nil];
CCRepeatForever* repeat = [CCRepeatForever actionWithAction:sequence];
[label runAction:repeat];
```

And being able to modify the speed of the entire repeating sequence can come in handy too:

```
CCSequence* sequence = [CCSequence actions:tint1, tint2, tint3, nil];
CCRepeatForever* repeat = [CCRepeatForever actionWithAction:sequence];
CCSpeed* speedAction = [CCSpeed actionWithAction:repeat speed:0.75f];
[label runAction:speedAction];
```

> **Note** As with menu items, a list of actions always ends with `nil`. If you forget to add `nil` as the last parameter, the line creating the CCSequence will crash!

Ease Actions

Actions become even more powerful when you use actions based on the CCActionEase class. Ease actions allow you to modify the effect of an action over time. For example, if you use a CCMoveTo action on a node, the node will move the whole distance at the same speed until it's arrived. With CCActionEase, you can have the node start slow and speed up toward the target, or vice versa. Or you can let it move past the target location a little and then bounce back. To see easing in action, check out this demo application that runs in a web browser: www.robertpenner.com/easing/easing_demo.html.

Ease actions create very dynamic animations that are normally very time-consuming to implement. The following code shows how to use an ease action to modify the behavior of a regular action. The rate parameter determines how pronounced the effect of the ease action is and should be greater than 1 to see any effect.

```
// I want myNode to move to 100, 200 and arrive there in 3 seconds
CCMoveTo* move = [CCMoveTo actionWithDuration:3 position:CGPointMake(100, 200)];
// this time the node should slowly speed up and then slow down as it moves
CCEaseInOut* ease = [CCEaseInOut actionWithAction:move rate:4];
[myNode runAction:ease];
```

> **Note**   In the preceding example, the ease action is run on the node, not the move action. It's all too easy to forget to change the `runAction` line when you're working with actions—a common mistake by even to the most experienced cocos2d developers. If you notice your actions aren't working as expected or at all, double-check that you're actually running the correct action. And if the correct actions are used, but you're still not seeing the desired result, verify that it's the correct node running the action. That's another common mistake.

Cocos2d implements the following CCActionEase classes:

- CCEaseBackIn, CCEaseBackInOut, CCEaseBackOut
- CCEaseBounceIn, CCEaseBounceInOut, CCEaseBounceOut
- CCEaseElasticIn, CCEaseElasticInOut, CCEaseElasticOut
- CCEaseExponentialIn, CCEaseExponentialInOut, CCEaseExponentialOut
- CCEaseIn, CCEaseInOut, CCEaseOut
- CCEaseSineIn, CCEaseSineInOut, CCEaseSineOut

In Chapter 4, you'll use a number of these ease actions in the DoodleDrop project so you can see what effect they have. The CCActionEase class hierarchy is shown in Figure 3-12 for reference.

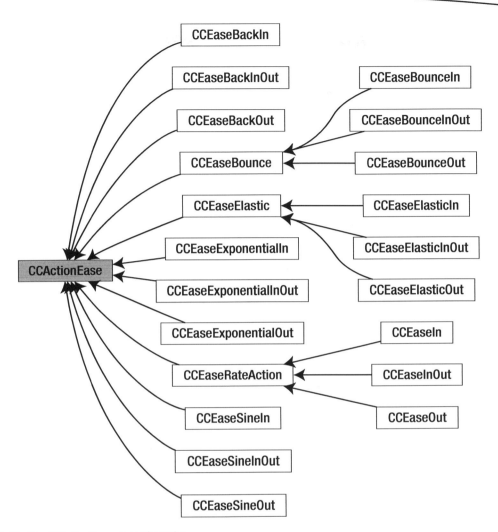

Figure 3-12. The CCActionEase class hierarchy

Grid Actions

Grid actions are purely visual actions derived from CCGridAction and one of its two subclasses, CCGrid3DAction and CCTiledGrid3DAction. Their class hierarchies are shown in Figures 3-13 and 3-14.

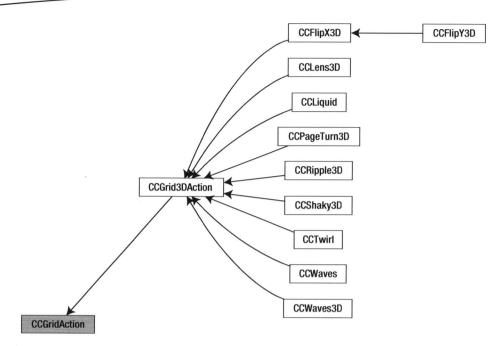

Figure 3-13. *The CCGrid3DAction class hierarchy*

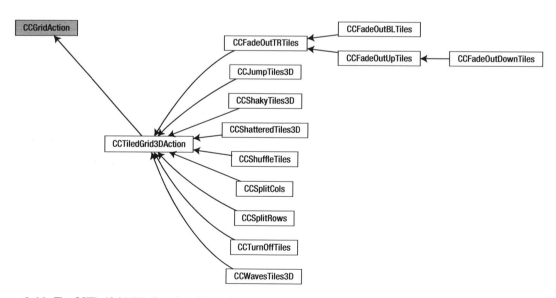

Figure 3-14. *The CCTiledGrid3DAction class hierarchy*

The specialty of the grid actions are three-dimensional effects such as turning a page (CCPageTurn3D; see Figure 3-15) or simulating waves and liquids (CCWaves, CCLiquid). The downside is that the 3D effects may show visual artifacts unless you enable depth buffering, which requires more memory and has a negative impact on rendering performance.

Figure 3-15. The CCPageTurn3D action in action

To enable depth buffering in a cocos2d application, you have to change the line where EAGLView is initialized in your project's AppDelegate.m file. You do this by changing the depthFormat parameter from its default value 0 to either GL_DEPTH_COMPONENT16_OES for a 16-bit depth buffer or GL_DEPTH_COMPONENT24_OES for a 24-bit depth buffer:

```
CCGLView *glView = [CCGLView viewWithFrame:[window_ bounds]
            pixelFormat:kEAGLColorFormatRGB565
            depthFormat:GL_DEPTH_COMPONENT16_OES
        preserveBackbuffer:NO
            sharegroup:nil
            multiSampling:NO
            numberOfSamples:0];
```

Kobold2D users can make this change in the config.lua file by modifying the GLViewDepthFormat parameter as follows:

```
GLViewDepthFormat = GLViewDepthFormat.Depth16Bit,
```

Ideally, you should try the 16-bit depth buffer first; it uses less memory, but in a few cases a 24-bit depth buffer may be necessary if visual artifacts still occur when using 3D actions.

Instant Actions

You may wonder why there are instantaneous actions based on the CCInstantAction class (see Figure 3-16 for the class hierarchy), when you could just as well change the node's property to achieve the same effect. For example, there are instant actions to flip the node, to place it at a specific location, or to toggle its visible property.

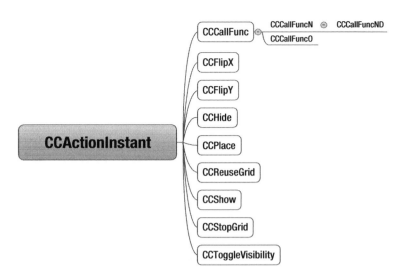

Figure 3-16. The CCActionInstant class hierarchy

The main reason instant actions exist is because they're useful in action sequences. Sometimes in a sequence of actions you have to change a certain property of the node, such as visibility or position, and then continue with the sequence. Instant actions make this possible. True, they're rarely used—with CCCallFunc and its variants being the notable exception.

CCCallFunc Actions

When using an action sequence, you may want to be notified at certain times, for example when the sequence has ended, and then perhaps start another sequence immediately thereafter. To do that, you can make use of several versions of CCCallFunc actions that'll send a message whenever it's their turn in the sequence. Let's rewrite the color cycle sequence so that it calls a method each time one of the CCTintTo actions has done its job:

```
// sends a message to target using selector with this signature:
// -(void) onCallFunc;
CCCallFunc* func = [CCCallFunc actionWithTarget:self
                    selector:@selector(onCallFunc)];


// sends a message to target using selector with this signature:
// -(void) onCallFuncN:(id)sender;
CCCallFuncN* funcN = [CCCallFuncN actionWithTarget:self
                    selector:@selector(onCallFuncN:)];


// Caution: avoid using this due to ARC issues.
// sends a message to target using selector with this signature
// -(void) onCallFuncND:(id)sender data:(void*)data;
CCCallFuncO* funcO = [CCCallFuncO actionWithTarget:self
                    selector:@selector(onCallFuncO:)
                      object:self];
```

```
// sends a message to target using selector with this signature:
// -(void) onCallFunc0:(id)object;
void* someDataPointer = nil;
CCCallFuncND* funcND = [CCCallFuncND actionWithTarget:self
                        selector:@selector(onCallFuncND:data:)
                          data:someDataPointer];


CCSequence* seq = [CCSequence actions: ↵
  tint1, func, tint2, funcN, tint3, funcO, funcND, nil];
[label runAction:seq];
```

The difference between these variants of CCCallFunc is in which selector they call and thus which context is available to the method they call. For example, when CCCallFunc calls the onCallFunc method, you have no way of knowing who called the method or why. There's no context, but in many cases that context isn't needed.

Caution   Never use an Objective-C class (any id type) as the data parameter of CCCallFuncND. Doing so runs the risk of leaking memory or crashing your app in an ARC-enabled project. For id types, always use the CCCallFuncO action or consider using the CCCallBlock actions later in this section because the block can use any variable that's in scope where the block is declared.

The action sequence seq will call the methods in the following code one after another. The sender parameter will always be derived from CCNode—it's the node that's running the actions. You can use the data parameter any way you want, including passing values, structs, or other pointers. You only have to properly cast the data pointer.

```
-(void) onCallFunc
{
    CCLOG(@"end of tint1!");
}


-(void) onCallFuncN:(id)sender
{
    CCLOG(@"end of tint2! sender: %@", sender);
}


-(void) onCallFuncO:(id)object
{
    // object is the object you passed to CCCallFuncO
    CCLOG(@"call func with object %@", object);
}


-(void) onCallFuncND:(id)sender data:(void*)data
{
    CCLOG(@"end of sequence! sender: %@ - data: %p", sender, data);
}
```

Of course, the CCCallFunc actions also work with CCRepeatForever sequences. Your methods will be called repeatedly at the appropriate time.

CCCallBlock Actions

For all intents and purposes, you can replace the CCCallFunc actions with CCCallBlock actions. The only thing block actions don't allow is passing an arbitrary void* pointer—mainly because doing so conflicts with ARC (see the previous Caution box).

The CCCallBlock, CCCallBlockN, and CCCallBlockO classes are initialized and used as follows:

```
CCCallBlock* blockA = [CCCallBlock actionWithBlock:^void(){
  CCLOG(@"action with block got called");
}];


CCCallBlock* blockB = [CCCallBlock actionWithBlock:^{
  CCLOG(@"action with block got called");
}];


CCCallBlockN* blockN = [CCCallBlockN actionWithBlock:^void(CCNode* node){
  CCLOG(@"action with block got called with node %@", node);
}];


CCCallBlockO* blockO = [CCCallBlockO actionWithBlock:^void(id object){
  CCLOG(@"action with block got called with object %@", object);
}
                        object:background];


CCSequence* sequence = [CCSequence actions:block, blockN, blockO, nil];
[label runAction:sequence];
```

The blockA and blockB instances of the CCCallBlock class only differ in the way the block is declared. Because that particular block has no return value, you can omit void. And because it takes no parameters, you can also omit the brackets as well. This means ^void(){ .. } and ^{ .. } declare exactly the same type of block, the latter simply being a shorthand for the former.

The block used in the CCCallBlockN class must take a single parameter of type CCNode*. The node is the node that's running the CCCallBlockN action. The block used by CCCallBlockO requires a single parameter of type id. That's the object passed as the second parameter to CCCallBlockO. It's easy to miss, unfortunately, because the object parameter follows the block parameter and therefore causes some syntactical awkwardness because it's either dangling at the end of the block or floating by itself after what seems to be an empty line.

It's syntactically cleaner and easier to read if you assign the block to a variable and rewrite the CCCallBlockO initialization like this:

```
void (^callBlock)(id object) = ^void(id object){
    CCLOG(@"action with block got called with object %@", object);
    [label setString:@"label string changed by block"];
};
```

```
CCCallBlockO* blockO2 = [CCCallBlockO actionWithBlock:callBlock
                               object:background];
```

Which reminds me: you can assign blocks to variables—and what that looks like. I'm hoping that maybe now, after a few pages, blocks are starting to click with you. If not, don't worry. I'll be revisiting them a couple more times over the course of the book.

In case you're missing the potentially useful CCCallBlockNO class, whose block would take both the sending node and a user-supplied object as a parameter, remember that blocks have access to the local scope. Essentially, you won't even need to use either CCCallBlockN or CCCallBlockO in most cases because you can just access the variables label and background from inside the block without their being passed as block parameters:

```
// assuming label and background are already declared & initialized at this point ...
CCCallBlock* block = [CCCallBlock actionWithBlock:^void(){
  CCLOG(@"label: %@  --  background object: %@", label, background);
}];
```

Writer's block may be a bad thing, but coder's block is nothing but awesome!

Orientation, Singletons, Tests, and API References

This section summarizes three aspects of cocos2d that don't receive the attention they deserve—or in the case of the Singleton pattern, perhaps they receive too much. Singletons are often singled out as bad practice, with some developers even going as far as stating that no project should ever use them. Pragmatists like me, though, have yet to see a game engine or game project that didn't use singletons, and reasonably so.

Then there are cocos2d test cases and the API references, both helpful resources that can help answer your questions—if only you knew where to look for them. But I'd like to start off by explaining how to get your app locked to a certain device orientation.

Orientation Course in Device Orientation

More often than not, you want to lock your app to be used only in one of the four possible device orientations, or at least in either Landscape or Portrait modes.

I'll start with Kobold2D because it just works like any other Cocoa Touch app. Kobold2D respects the Supported Device Orientations setting of the target. Select your project's target, go to the Summary tab, and you'll find the Supported Device Orientations setting under the iPhone / iPad Deployment Info heading. By default, all four device orientations are supported. To restrict the app to Landscape orientations, simply deselect the Portrait orientations as shown in Figure 3-17. That's really all you need to do.

If you can't see the device orientation setting, make sure you've selected the iOS target. After all, almost all Kobold2D projects also include a Mac build target.

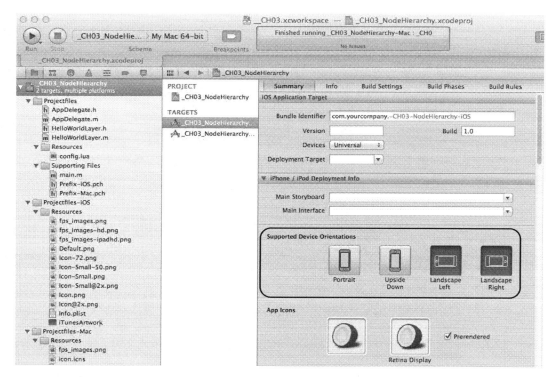

Figure 3-17. Kobold2D recognizes the Supported Device Orientations setting in Xcode

In a purely cocos2d app, you have to open AppDelegate.m and locate the
shouldAutorotateToInterfaceOrientation method. Kobold2D users can also add this method to
the AppDelegate class to change the supported orientations while the app is running. The default
implementation allows autorotation to both Landscape orientations and is similar to this one,
except for the method parameter which I changed from interfaceOrientation to orientation to
make the source code in the book more readable:

```
-(BOOL)shouldAutorotateToInterfaceOrientation:(UIInterfaceOrientation)orientation
{
    return UIInterfaceOrientationIsLandscape(orientation);
}
```

The system queries this method frequently to determine whether it's allowed to autorotate the
app to a certain interface orientation. The method should return YES if the app supports the
orientation it was passed in, and NO otherwise. You should return YES for at least one interface
orientation—otherwise iOS defaults to Portrait mode.

The iOS SDK offers two macros to test whether an interface orientation is either one of the two
Portrait modes or one of the two Landscape modes:

```
BOOL isLandscape = UIInterfaceOrientationIsLandscape(orientation);
BOOL isPortrait = UIInterfaceOrientationIsPortrait(orientation);
```

Allowing your app to rotate to both Landscape or both Portrait orientations Is recommended
because some users prefer the home button on the left side, others on the right side, and others

just want to use the app in the orientation they're currently holding the device in. Therefore the decision should be left up to the user where possible.

However, there are reasons to restrict your app to one particular device orientation. For example, if your app is accelerometer controlled, like the popular Labyrinth game, tilting the device too far in one direction could trigger autorotation inadvertently. That could make the game unplayable. To force your app to use only a specific orientation, compare the orientation parameter with one of the four UIInterfaceOrientation types. In this example, only the Landscape Left orientation is allowed:

```
-(BOOL)shouldAutorotateToInterfaceOrientation:(UIInterfaceOrientation)orientation
{
    return interfaceOrientation == UIInterfaceOrientationLandscapeLeft;
}
```

> **Note**   The UIInterfaceOrientationLandscapeLeft orientation is the orientation as
> depicted by the Landscape Left icon in Figure 3-17. That means the home button is on the
> left side. This is important to note in case you've been using an earlier cocos2d version where
> the device orientation was used instead of the interface orientation. Whereas the device
> orientation used to be set to UIDeviceOrientationLandscapeRight, you now have to use
> UIInterfaceOrientationLandscapeLeft, and where UIDeviceOrientationLandscapeLeft
> was used, you have to use UIInterfaceOrientationLandscapeRight.

In the rare case where you want to support all four orientations, just return YES in the shouldAutorotateToInterfaceOrientation method.

Singletons in cocos2d

Cocos2d makes good use of the Singleton design pattern, which is regularly and hotly debated. In principle, a *singleton* is a regular class that's instantiated only once during the lifetime of the application. To ensure that this is the case, you use a static method to both create and access the instance of the object. So, instead of using alloc/init or a static autorelease initializer, you gain access to a singleton object via methods that begin with shared. The most prominent singleton class in cocos2d is the CCDirector class:

```
CCDirector* director = [CCDirector sharedDirector];
```

The director itself hosts other singleton classes, which in cocos2d v1.x are separate classes. Starting with cocos2d v2.0 you can access the CCScheduler, CCActionManager, and CCTouchDispatcher as properties of the CCDirector class.

```
CCDirector* director = [CCDirector sharedDirector];

CCScheduler* scheduler = director.scheduler;
CCActionManager* actionManager = director.actionManager;
// only when building for iOS
CCTouchDispatcher* touchDispatcher = director.touchDispatcher;
// only when building for Mac OS X
CCEventDispatcher* eventDispatcher = director.eventDispatcher;
```

The four cache classes in cocos2d are also implemented as Singleton classes:

```
CCAnimationCache* animCache = [CCAnimationCache sharedAnimationCache];
CCShaderCache* shaderCache = [CCShaderCach sharedShaderCache];
CCSpriteFrameCache* sfCache = [CCSpriteFrameCache sharedSpriteFrameCache];
CCTextureCache* textureCache = [CCTextureCache sharedTextureCache];
```

Each of these classes caches specific resources. *Caching* here means that loaded resources are kept in memory even if they're no longer in use. This prevents the resources from having to be reloaded from flash memory, which is relatively slow. But the caches also prevent you from loading the same resource twice. Whether you create a single sprite or a thousand sprites using the same texture, the texture will only be loaded and stored in memory once.

There are a few more (but rarely used) singleton classes in cocos2d:

```
CCConfiguration* config = [CCConfiguration sharedConfiguration];
CCProfiler* profiler = [CCProfiler sharedProfiler];
```

To complete the list, the CocosDenshion audio engine also provides two singleton classes to the CDAudioManager and its easier-to-use cousin SimpleAudioEngine:

```
CDAudioManager* sharedManager = [CDAudioManager sharedManager];
SimpleAudioEngine* sharedEngine = [SimpleAudioEngine sharedEngine];
```

The upside of a singleton is that it can be used anywhere by any class at any time. It acts almost like a global class, much like global variables. Singletons are very useful if you have a combination of data and methods you need to use in many different places.

Caching and audio are good examples of this, because any of your classes—whether the player, an enemy, a menu button, or a cutscene—might want to play a sound effect or change the background music. So it makes a lot of sense to use a singleton for playing audio. Likewise, if you have global game stats—perhaps the size of the player's army and each platoon's number of troops—you might want to store that information in a singleton so you can carry it over from one level to another.

Implementing a singleton is straightforward, as Listing 3-2 shows. This code implements the class MyManager as a singleton with minimal code. The sharedManager static method grants access to the single instance of MyManager. The first time the sharedManager method runs, the sharedManager instance is allocated and initialized; from then on the existing instance is returned.

Listing 3-2. Implementing the Exemplary Class MyManager as a Singleton

```
static MyManager *sharedManager = nil;

+(MyManager*) sharedManager
{
  static dispatch_once_t once;
  static MyManager* sharedManager;
  dispatch_once(&once, ^{ sharedManager = [[self alloc] init]; });
  return sharedManager;
}
```

Note   Listing 3-2 is not only Apple's recommended way to write a singleton, it's also the fastest and safest with only four lines of code. Yet singletons have a long history, and you're bound to run into a number of solutions, most of which basically do the exact same thing but with subtle differences. The Q&A site Stackoverflow.com has a great discussion about Objective-C singletons in which a great variety of implementations and their pros and cons are debated: `http://stackoverflow.com/questions/145154/what-does-your-objective-c-singleton-look-like`

Singletons also have ugly sides. Because they're simple to use and implement and can be accessed from any other class, there's a tendency to overuse them. They're like global variables, which most programmers agree should be used scarcely and judiciously.

For example, you might think you have only one player object, so why not make the player class a singleton? Everything seems to be fine—until you realize that whenever the player advances from one level to another, the singleton not only keeps the player's score but also his last animation frame, his health, and all the items he's picked up, and then he might even begin the new level in Berserk mode because that mode was active when he left the previous level.

To fix that, you add another method to reset certain variables when changing levels. So far, so good. But as you add more features to the game, you end up having to add and maintain more and more variables when switching a level. What's worse, suppose one day a friend suggests you give the iPad version a two-player mode. But, wait, your player is a singleton; you can have only one player at any time! This gives you a major headache: refactor a lot of code or miss out on the cool two-player mode?

Or why not make the second player a singleton, too? And whenever the second player needs to know something of the first player, it'll just use that singleton. So, they keep a reference to each other, which means you can't have a single-player game without initializing the other players as well. This is one side effect of classes strongly dependent on each other, also known as *tight coupling*. The more classes are tightly coupled with each other, the harder it is to make changes to any part of your code. It's like mixing cement that's slowly drying up until it's so hard that any change is easier to do by hacking it instead of improving the code. That's the point where bugs seem to occur everywhere, at random, with no connection to a recent change. In one word: frustrating.

The more you rely on singletons, the more likely such issues will arise. Before creating a singleton class, always consider whether you really need only one instance of this class and its data and whether that might change later.

I understand it's hard for a beginner to judge when and where to use a singleton, particularly if you haven't had much experience with object-oriented programming. The Q&A web site Stackoverflow.com hosts a discussion with additional links that illustrates the controversy around the Singleton design pattern and gives some food for thought: `http://stackoverflow.com/questions/137975/what-is-so-bad-about-singletons`.

My advice is to study popular uses of singletons. The use of singletons in the cocos2d game engine for resource management is perfectly fine, because it simplifies the overall design of the game engine. Most other game engines use singletons for similar purposes as well, and I've rarely heard anyone complain about that. You'll even find singletons in the iOS SDK. Singletons are generally not as bad as some make them sound like, although they do tend to be very problematic by introducing strong dependencies, and the problems grow exponentially with the size of the code base.

Cocos2d Test Cases

Did you know that cocos2d comes with a lot of sample code? In your cocos2d-iphone folder, you'll find a project aptly named cocos2d-ios.xcodeproj that contains a lot of test targets you can build and run. You can see how things work and then check the code to see how it's implemented.

But I'm also somewhat hesitant to recommend the test cases because you'll see a lot of nonstandard code. Some of the tests are downright sloppy. After all, the code was written just to test that the code is working. It wasn't written to teach best programming practices. So take everything you see in the test cases with a grain of salt.

Nevertheless, the test cases document practically every feature of cocos2d. It can't hurt to run each of the test cases once to see what's in them, or at least those that seem interesting to you. For example, the test cases show off all the actions that cocos2d supports, including the 3D actions with ripple, wave, or page turn effects.

Cocos2d API Reference

The cocos2d API reference describes every class, every method, every property in cocos2d. Finding out, for example, which varieties of initializer methods a class supports, or what properties it has, is very helpful. This is valuable information that can help you plan your code ahead of time and learn more about the cocos2d API as you stumble across methods and parameters you didn't know existed.

Whenever you have a question like "Can I do x with this class y?" you should consult the API reference, look for class y, and see what properties and methods it has available to you. Take, for example, the CCNode class reference here: `www.learn-cocos2d.com/api-ref/latest/cocos2d-iphone/html/interface_c_c_node.html`. When you glance over it, you may notice how it reads like a condensed version of the CCNode section of this chapter. The API reference doesn't tell you the why's and how's, but it does show you what's available.

The official cocos2d API reference is hosted here: `www.cocos2d-iphone.org/api-ref`. Be sure to select the API reference for the cocos2d version you're using, as there is at least one API reference for each minor version of cocos2d. Sadly, the cocos2d API reference is incomplete and missing several classes, methods, and properties. In particular, most of the Mac OS X features are absent.

On the Learn Cocos2D web site, I host API references for all the libraries used in Kobold2D, including cocos2d-iphone, the cocos2d-iphone-extensions project, Box2D, and Chipmunk. The cocos2d API reference on my web site is a cleaned-up version of the official API reference and includes all the undocumented classes, methods, and properties not found in the official API reference. The cocos2d API reference and many others are also split into iOS and Mac OS X versions, so you won't be confused by references to code that's not available on your target platform.

In addition, I find the Kobold2D API references easier to browse because they use a tree-like class index and keep the relatively large class collaboration and inheritance diagrams hidden by default. You can find the Kobold2D API references either at `www.learn-cocos2d.com/api-ref` or directly from the Kobold2D website: `www.kobold2d.com/x/xgMO`. Again, use the link for the appropriate version, which for this book is Kobold2D 2.0.

API References in Xcode and elsewhere

If you install Kobold2D from the installer package, it also installs the API references of all libraries used in Kobold2D (including cocos2d of course) as documentation sets. These so-called docsets are available from within Xcode. Choose Help > Xcode Help to browse the available documentation sets. Even if you don't plan to use Kobold2D, you should install it for this reason alone.

The alternative for cocos2d users—and in fact this is generally recommended—is to install the Dash (Docs & Snippets) app from the Mac App Store. Dash remains resident and waits for you to press a keyboard shortcut to bring its window to the front. Then just type in whatever function, property, or class name you want to search for, and it shows you the results not just for Xcode documentation but for a number of other documentation sets like PHP, HTML, Java, and so on.

I mention Dash as an alternative because one of the optionally downloadable docsets is for cocos2d. Simply go to Dash's Preferences screen and download the cocos2d docset if you want an offline version. Kobold2D users, however, shouldn't do so since you already have the cocos2d docset.

You can download Dash (Docs & Snippets) from the Mac App Store via this link:

`http://itunes.apple.com/app/dash-docs-snippets/id458034879.`

Summary

Wow! That was a lot to take in! I don't expect you to remember all of this chapter's content at once. Feel free to come back at any time to look again at cocos2d's scene graph and how to use the various CCNode classes. I wrote this chapter to be a good reference whenever you need it, as well as the accompanying NodeHierarchy and Essentials Xcode projects.

Armed with this chapter's knowledge and a fair bit of motivation on your side, you could be starting to write your own games now.

You know what, let's do that together. Read on to the next chapter, and I'll walk you through your first complete game project!

Chapter 4

Your First Game

In this chapter you'll build your first complete game. It won't win any awards, but you'll learn how to get the essential elements of cocos2d to work together, and the game can be easily adapted. In fact, several variations of this game were released to the App Store by readers of earlier editions of this book.

The game is the inversion of the famous Doodle Jump game, aptly named DoodleDrop. The player's goal is to avoid falling obstacles for as long as possible by rotating the device to move the player sprite. Take a look at the final version in Figure 4-1 to get an idea of what you'll be creating in this chapter.

Figure 4-1. *The final version of the DoodleDrop game*

Create the DoodleDrop Project

In Chapter 2 you learned how to create a Kobold2D and a cocos2d project with ARC enabled.

Kobold2D users should run the Kobold2D Project Starter app and choose the Empty-Project template (see Figure 2-2 in Chapter 2) to start from scratch. Use DoodleDrop as the name for the project and you're all set. The only thing left to do is to select the app's target and select the portrait mode icons under Supported Device Orientation, as shown in Figure 3-17 in Chapter 3. The landscape icons should be deselected because DoodleDrop is designed to be played in Portrait mode.

The next section is for cocos2d users only—Kobold2D users may want to skip it.

Start with an ARC-enabled cocos2d Project

Cocos2d users should follow the instructions in Chapter 2 to create an ARC-enabled cocos2d project. If you've already done so then just make a copy of the project you've created. Here's an important time-saver: keep an unmodified version of such an original cocos2d project template converted to ARC enabled around, so you can create new projects easily and quickly.

Tip   In the book's source code you'll find ARC-enabled cocos2d template projects in the `Cocos2D_ARC_Template_Projects` folder.

After following the instructions in Chapter 2, you'll have an ARC-enabled cocos2d project. Mine is named `cocos2d-2.x-ARC-iOS`. Simply make a copy of the folder that contains the `.xcodeproj` file before opening it in Xcode. Don't rename the `.xcodeproj` file itself, though, because doing so would render it unusable.

Now you can rename the project from within Xcode, which will also rename the `.xcodeproj` file. In the Project Navigator select the cocos2d-2.x-ARC-iOS project (the first entry, see Figure 2-5 in Chapter 2) and edit it with a delayed double-click. That means click it once to select it, wait a second or two, then click it again, and the project's name will become editable. Enter *DoodleDrop* as the name for the project.

After you press Enter to confirm the change, Xcode will ask you to confirm renaming several items, as seen in Figure 4-2. You should confirm by clicking Rename. If you click Don't Rename, Xcode will still have renamed the project but all other items are not. So even if you recognize a typo or don't like the name, click Rename anyway. You may also see a warning, "New name for file can not be the same," regarding the `Prefix.pch` file after renaming. You can safely ignore that warning.

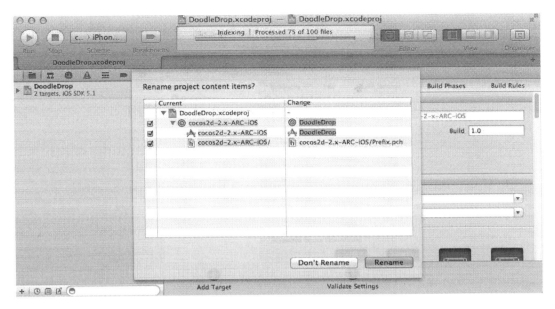

Figure 4-2. *Confirm renaming the project and related files*

There's one last item you need to rename manually: the app's scheme. It will still be named cocos2d-2.x-ARC-iOS, or whichever name you gave your ARC-enabled cocos2d project. Select Product ➤ Manage Schemes… to view the list of schemes. Select and edit the scheme's name by delay-clicking it to make its name editable and then renaming it to DoodleDrop. Once done, close the scheme list.

Because DoodleDrop is going to be a Portrait mode application, you must edit the AppDelegate.m file and change the shouldAutorotateToInterfaceOrientation method to return YES only for portrait modes:

```
return UIInterfaceOrientationIsPortrait(interfaceOrientation);
```

Now select the DoodleDrop scheme from the drop-down menu to the right of the Run and Stop buttons and run it to verify that everything is in working order.

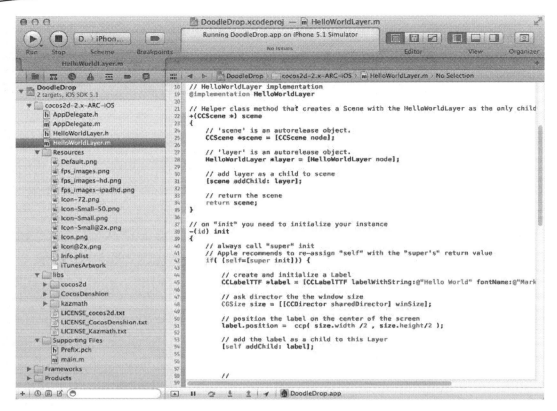

Figure 4-3. *Let the games begin! The DoodleDrop project here is based on the cocos2d ARC project from Chapter 2, but the Kobold2D Empty-Project template isn't much different*

Create the DoodleDrop Scene

The next step you're faced with is a decision: do you start working with the existing HelloWorldLayer because it's there already, possibly renaming it later? Or do you go through the extra steps to create your own scene to replace the HelloWorldLayer? I chose the latter because eventually you'll have to add new scenes anyway, so it's a good idea to learn the ropes here and now and start with a clean slate.

Make sure the group where you want to add the new scene class is selected and then select File ➤ New ➤ New File… or right-click in the appropriate location in the Project Navigator tree and select New File… to open the New File dialog shown in Figure 4-4.

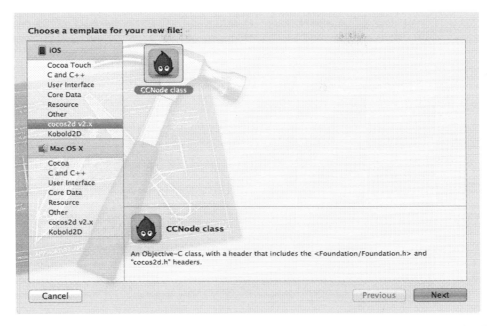

Figure 4-4. *Adding new CCNode-derived classes is best done using the class templates provided by cocos2d or Kobold2D. In this case, you want the CCNode class to be a subclass of CCLayer because you're setting up a new scene and layer*

Because Cocos2d and Kobold2D provide class templates for the most important nodes and classes, it'd be a shame not to use them. On the other hand, Xcode's own Objective-C class template is also a very good template for new classes—you only need to change the base class from NSObject to CCLayer manually. From the cocos2d v2.x templates section, select the CCNode class, click Next, and make sure it's set to Subclass of CCLayer before clicking Next again to bring up the Save File dialog in Figure 4-5.

I'm going to name the new file GameLayer.m. It's going to be the class where all of the DoodleDrop game play logic takes place, so that name seems appropriate. Be sure that the DoodleDrop target check box is checked (see Figure 4-5).

> **Note**   Not reviewing the target check boxes may incorrectly assign the newly added file to the wrong target. This can lead to all kinds of issues—compile or "file not found" errors are the typical result. Sometimes the game may crash during game play when a file hasn't been added to the app's target. Or you might simply waste space by adding files to targets that don't need them at all.

Figure 4-5. *Naming the new scene and making sure it's added to the appropriate group and targets*

At this point, the GameLayer class is empty, and the first thing you need to do, to set it up as a scene, is to add the +(id) scene method to it. The code to plug in is essentially the same as in Chapter 3, with only the layer's class name changed. What you'll almost always need in any class is the -(id) init method. Adding the -(void) dealloc method also can't hurt, if only to be able to log that an object has been properly disposed of. Monitoring the dealloc method can be an effective early warning system for detecting memory leaks.

I'm also a very cautious programmer and decided to add the logging statements introduced in Chapter 3. The resulting GameLayer.h is shown in Listing 4-1, and GameLayer.m is in Listing 4-2.

Listing 4-1. GameLayer.h with the Scene Method

```
#import < Foundation/Foundation.h>
#import "cocos2d.h"

@interface GameLayer : CCLayer
{
}
+(id) scene;

@end
```

Listing 4-2. GameLayer.m with the Scene Method and Standard Methods Added, Including Logging

```
#import "GameLayer.h"

@implementation GameLayer

+(id) scene
{
    CCScene *scene=[CCScene node];
    CCLayer* layer=[GameLayer node];
    [scene addChild:layer];
    return scene;
}

-(id) init
{
    if ((self=[super init]))
    {
        CCLOG(@"%@: %@", NSStringFromSelector(_cmd), self);
    }

    return self;
}

-(void) dealloc
{
    CCLOG(@"%@: %@", NSStringFromSelector(_cmd), self);
}

@end
```

Now you can safely delete the HelloWorldLayer class. When asked, select the Move to Trash option to remove the file from the hard drive as well, not just from the Xcode project. Select both HelloWorldLayer files and choose Edit ➤ Delete, or right-click the files and choose Delete from the context menu.

Kobold2D users now only need to open the config.lua file in the Resources group and change the FirstSceneClassName entry to read:

```
FirstSceneClassName="GameLayer",
```

That's all. But in a purely cocos2d app, you have to modify AppDelegate.m and replace any references to HelloWorldLayer with GameLayer. Listing 4-3 highlights the necessary changes to the #import and pushScene statements if you're not using Kobold2D.

Listing 4-3. Changing the AppDelegate.m Fil to Use the GameLayer Class Instead of HelloWorldLayer

```
// replace the line #import "HelloWorldLayer.h" with this one:
#import "GameLayer.h"
- (BOOL)application:(UIApplication *)application ↵
    didFinishLaunchingWithOptions:(NSDictionary *)launchOptions
{
    ...
```

```
    // replace HelloWorldLayer with GameLayer
    [director_ pushScene:[GameLayer scene]];
}
```

Compile and run, and you should end up with…a blank scene. Success! If you run into any problems, compare your project with the DoodleDrop01 project that accompanies this book.

Tip   The app builds successfully but it won't run? Remember that there can be multiple targets in an Xcode project, and even multiple schemes for a single target. Check the scheme selection / deployment target drop-down menu located in the Xcode toolbar right next to the Run and Stop buttons (see Figure 2-6). The left half of the drop-down menu allows you to choose the active scheme. Make sure it's the one with the name DoodleDrop in it. Most other schemes like cocos2d-library will be static libraries. You can only build static libraries, but you can't run them. Unfortunately deleting, hiding or selecting schemes is a per-user setting and must be done by each user individually. If not for that I would have cleaned up the projects for you.

Adding the Player Sprite

Next you'll add the player sprite and use the accelerometer to control the player's actions. To add the player image, select the Resources group in Xcode and select File ➤ Add Files to "DoodleDrop"… or, alternatively, right-click and from the context menu pick Add Files to "DoodleDrop"… to open the File Picker dialog. If you accidentally add files to the wrong group, you can also drag the file in the Project Navigator. There's also nothing special about the Resources group—it's merely by definition supposed to contain the files that are not source code.

The player images `alien.png` and `alien-hd.png` are located in the Resources folder of the DoodleDrop project supplied with the book. You can also choose your own image, as long as it's 64 × 64 pixels in size and 128 × 128 pixels in the high-resolution (HD) format, the file with the -hd suffix. The HD files are used automatically by cocos2d on iPhone and iPod touch devices with Retina display; the regular standard-definition (SD) files are used only on the iPhone 3GS. Cocos2d recognizes two other file suffixes: -ipad for iPad and iPad 2 and -ipadhd for 3rd-generation iPads (and newer) with Retina displays.

The -hd, -ipad, and -ipadhd extensions are the default file extensions used by cocos2d for Retina and iPad-specific assets. These file extensions aren't used by regular iOS apps. Such apps have to use Apple's @2x file extension for high-resolution images. Although the @2x extension does work with cocos2d apps as well, the cocos2d documentation warns users not to use the @2x file extension.

> **Tip**   A very frequently asked question is whether it wouldn't be appropriate to simply downscale HD images on non-Retina devices. It's not, and there's two reasons for that. One is memory constraints. The non-Retina devices have only half the memory (or even less) than what's available even on the earliest Retina devices. Requiring a non-Retina device to load an HD image will use up four times as much memory compared to an already downscaled and bundled SD image. Second, it takes noticably longer to load a Retina image, more so on older and slower devices like those without Retina displays.
>
> The alternative, to use standard-resolution assets throughout, isn't very appealing either. You simply won't be able to take advantage of the Retina resolution, and your app's image quality will never look appropriately high-resolution on Retina devices. No amount of upscaling and clever image-processing algorithms will be able to generate a crisp and clear look on Retina devices from standard-resolution images. That's why you should design all your game's assets in high resolution and then downscale if needed. The only thing to watch out for is to use dimensions that are divisible by two with no remainder.

Xcode asks you details about how and where to add the files, as in Figure 4-6. Make sure the Add To Targets check boxes are set for each target that will use the files, which in the figure is only the DoodleDrop target, but in Kobold2D you may want to add the file to the Mac OS X target as well. The check box "Copy items into destination group's folder (if needed)" should be checked if the file isn't already located in the project's folder. If in doubt make sure it's checked, at worst you will have duplicate versions of the same file. If you don't check it, at worst files may be missing if you add the project to source control or if you zip and share the project.

> **Tip**   The preferred image format for iOS games is PNG (Portable Network Graphics). It's a compressed file format, but unlike JPG's, its compression is lossless, retaining all pixels of the original image unchanged. Although you can also save JPEG files without compression, the same image in PNG format is typically smaller than an uncompressed JPEG file. This affects only the app size, not the memory (RAM) usage of the textures. Another reason not to use JPEG files is that they're particularly slow to load with cocos2d on iOS devices—about a factor of 8 times slower than PNGs, the last time I measured. In Chapter 6 you'll also learn about TexturePacker, a tool that manages images for you. It allows you to convert images into various compressed formats or reduce the color depth while retaining the best possible image quality through dithering and other techniques.

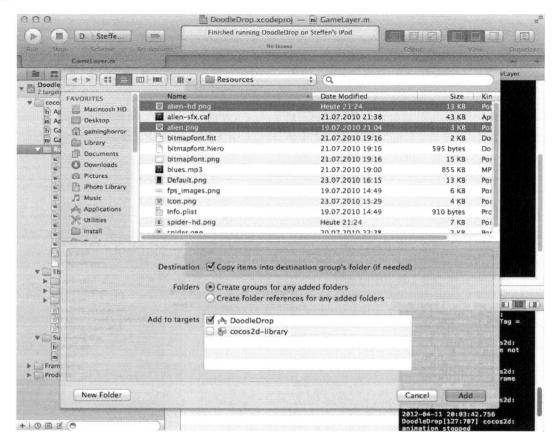

Figure 4-6. *You'll see this dialog whenever you add resource files. In most cases you should use these default settings*

Now add the player sprite to the game scene. I decided to add it as a CCSprite* member variable to the GameLayer class That's easier for now, and the game is simple enough for everything to go into the same class. Generally, that's not the recommended approach, so the projects in later chapters will create separate classes for individual game components as a matter of good code design.

Listing 4-4 shows the addition of the CCSprite* member to the GameLayer header file.

Listing 4-4. The CCSprite Player Is Added as a Member Variable to the GameLayer Class*

```
#import <Foundation/Foundation.h>
#import "cocos2d.h"

@interface GameLayer : CCLayer
{
    CCSprite* player;
}
+(id) scene;

@end
```

Listing 4-5 contains the code I've added to the init method to initialize the sprite, assign it to the member variable, and position it at the bottom center of the screen. I've also enabled accelerometer input

Listing 4-5. Enabling Accelerometer Input and Creating and Positioning the Player Sprite

```
-(id) init
{
    if ((self=[super init]))
    {
        CCLOG(@"%@: %@", NSStringFromSelector(_cmd), self);

        self.isAccelerometerEnabled=YES;

        player=[CCSprite spriteWithFile:@"alien.png"];
        [self addChild:player z:0 tag:1];

        CGSize screenSize=[CCDirector sharedDirector].winSize;
        float imageHeight=player.texture.contentSize.height;
        player.position=CGPointMake(screenSize.width / 2, imageHeight / 2);
    }

    return self;
}
```

The player sprite is added as a child with a tag of 1, which will later be used to identify and separate the player sprite from all other sprites. For the filename, the standard resolution image filename is used, in this case alien.png. Cocos2d will automatically load the alien-hd.png on Retina devices. If there's no accompanying –hd file, cocos2d will simply load the standard-resolution image instead. In that case the image will appear smaller on Retina devices than it will be on non-Retina devices. It's good practice to provide –hd variants of all image assets.

> **Caution** Filenames on iOS devices are case-sensitive. If you try to load Alien.png or
> ALIEN.PNG, it will work in the simulator but not on any iOS device because the real name is
> alien.png in all lowercase. That's why it's a good idea to stick to a naming convention like
> consistently keeping all filenames in all lowercase. Why lowercase? Because filenames in all
> uppercase are typically harder to read, and they speak to you quite loudly.

You set the initial position of the player sprite by centering the x position at half the screen width, which puts the sprite in the center horizontally. Vertically you want the bottom of the player sprite's texture to align with the bottom of the screen. If you remember from Chapter 3, you know that the sprite texture is centered on the node's position. Positioning the sprite vertically at 0 would cause the bottom half of the sprite texture to be below the screen. That's not what you want—you want to move it up by half the texture height.

You do that with the call to player.texture.contentSize.height, which returns the sprite texture's content size. What exactly is the content size? In Chapter 3, I mentioned that the texture dimensions of iOS devices can only be powers of two. But the actual image size may be less than the texture size—for example, the case of the image being 100 × 100 pixels while the texture has to be 128×128 pixels. The `contentSize` property of the texture returns the original image's size of 100×100 pixels. In most cases, you'll want to work with the content size, not the texture size. Even if your image is a power of two, you should use `contentSize` because the texture might be a texture atlas containing multiple images. Texture atlases are covered in Chapter 6.

By taking half the image height and setting this as the position on the y-axis, the sprite image will align neatly with the bottom of the screen.

Tip   Avoiding using fixed positions wherever you can is good practice. If you simply set the player position to 160,32, you're making two assumptions you should avoid. First, you're assuming the screen width will be 320 pixels, but that will not hold true for every iOS device. Second, you're assuming that the image height is 64 pixels, but that might change too. Once you start to make assumptions like these, your code will be less flexible, and it takes more time to make changes.

The way I wrote the positioning code involves a bit more typing, but in the long run this pays off big time. You can deploy to different devices and it'll work, and you can use different image sizes and it'll work. There's no need to change this particular code anymore. One of the most time-consuming tasks a programmer faces is having to change code that's based on assumptions.

Simple Accelerometer Input

One last step, and then you're done tilting the player sprite around. As I demonstrated in Chapter 3, you have to add the accelerometer method to the layer that receives accelerometer input. Here I use the `acceleration.x` parameter and add it to the player's position; multiplying by 10 is to speed up the player's movement.

```
-(void) accelerometer:(UIAccelerometer *)accelerometer
    didAccelerate:(UIAcceleration *)acceleration
{
   CGPoint pos=player.position;
   pos.x+= acceleration.x * 10;
   player.position=pos;
}
```

Notice something odd? I wrote three lines where one might seem to suffice:

```
// ERROR: lvalue required as left operand of assignment
player.position.x += acceleration.x * 10;
```

Unlike other programming languages such as Java, C++, and C#, writing something like `player.position.x += value` won't work with Objective-C properties. The `position` property is a CGPoint, which is a regular C struct data type. Objective-C properties simply can't assign a value to a field in a struct directly. The problem lies in how properties work in Objective-C and also how assignment works in the C language, on which Objective-C is based.

The statement `player.position.x` is actually a call to the position getter method `[player position]`, which means you're actually retrieving a temporary position and then trying to change the x member of the temporary `CGPoint`. But the temporary `CGPoint` would then get thrown away. The position setter `[player setPosition]` simply will not be called automagically. You can only assign to the `player.position` property directly—in this case, a new `CGPoint`. In Objective-C you have to live with this unfortunate issue—and possibly change programming habits if you come from a Java, C++, or C# background.

This is why the previous code has to create a temporary `CGPoint` object, change the point's x field, and then assign the temporary `CGPoint` to `player.position`. Unfortunately, this is how you have to do it in Objective-C.

First Test Run

Your project should now be at the same level as the one in the DoodleDrop02 folder of the code provided with this chapter. Give it a try now. Make sure you choose to run the app on the device, because you won't get accelerometer input from the simulator. Test how the accelerometer input behaves in this version.

If you haven't installed your development provisioning profiles in Xcode for this particular project yet, you'll get a "code sign" error. Code signing is required to run an app on an iOS device. Refer to Apple's documentation to learn how to create and install the necessary development provisioning profiles (`http://developer.apple.com/ios/manage/provisioningprofiles/howto.action`).

Player Velocity

Notice how the accelerometer input isn't quite right? It's reacting slowly, and the motion isn't fluid. That's because the player sprite doesn't experience true acceleration and deceleration. Let's fix that now. You'll find the accompanying code changes in the DoodleDrop03 project.

The concept for implementing acceleration and deceleration is not to change the player's position directly but to use a separate `CGPoint` variable as a velocity vector. Every time an accelerometer event is received, the velocity variable accumulates input from the accelerometer. Of course, that means you also have to limit the velocity to an arbitrary maximum; otherwise, it'll take too long to decelerate. The velocity is then added to the player position every frame, regardless of whether accelerometer input was received.

> **Note** Why not use actions to move the player sprite? Well, move actions are a bad choice whenever you want to change an object's speed or direction very often—say, multiple times per second. Actions are designed to be relatively long-lived, one-shot objects; creating new ones frequently creates additional overhead in terms of allocating and releasing memory. This can quickly drain a game's performance.
>
> Worse yet, actions don't work at all if you don't give them any time to do their work. That's why adding a new action to replace the previous one every frame won't show any effect whatsoever. Many cocos2d developers have stumbled across this seemingly odd behavior.

For example, stopping all actions and then adding a new MoveBy action to an object every frame won't make it move at all! The MoveBy action will change the object's position only in the next frame. But that's when you're already stopping all actions again and adding another new MoveBy action. Repeat *ad infinitum*, but the object will simply not move at all. It's like the clichéd donkey: push it too hard, and it'll become a stubborn, immobile object.

Let's go through the code changes. Add the `playerVelocity` variable to the header:

```
@interface GameLayer : CCLayer
{
    CCSprite* player;

    CGPoint playerVelocity;
}
```

If you wonder why I'm using a CGPoint instead of float, who's to say you'll never want to accelerate up or down a little? So, it doesn't hurt to be prepared for future expansions.

Listing 4-6 shows the accelerometer code, which I changed to use the velocity instead of updating the player position directly. It introduces three new design parameters for the amount of deceleration, the accelerometer sensitivity, and the maximum velocity. Those are values that don't have an optimum; you need to tweak them and find the right settings that work best with your game's design (which is why they're called *design parameters*).

Deceleration works by reducing the current velocity before adding the new accelerometer value multiplied by the sensitivity. The lower the deceleration, the quicker the player can change the alien's direction. The higher the sensitivity, the more responsive the player will react to accelerometer input. These values interact with each other because they modify the same value, so be sure to tweak only one value at a time.

Listing 4-6. GameLayer Implementation Gets playerVelocity

```
-(void) accelerometer:(UIAccelerometer *)accelerometer
        didAccelerate:(UIAcceleration *)acceleration
{
    // controls how quickly velocity decelerates (lower=quicker to change direction)
    float deceleration=0.4f;
    // determines how sensitive the accelerometer reacts (higher=more sensitive)
    float sensitivity=6.0f;
    // how fast the velocity can be at most
    float maxVelocity=100;

    // adjust velocity based on current accelerometer acceleration
    playerVelocity.x=playerVelocity.x * deceleration+acceleration.x * sensitivity;

    // we must limit the maximum velocity of the player sprite, in both directions
    if (playerVelocity.x>maxVelocity)
```

```
    {
        playerVelocity.x=maxVelocity;
    }
    else if (playerVelocity.x <- maxVelocity)
    {
        playerVelocity.x =- maxVelocity;
    }
}
```

Now playerVelocity will be changed, but how do you add the velocity to the player's position? By scheduling the update method in the GameLayer init method, adding this line:

```
// schedules the -(void) update:(ccTime)delta method to be called every frame
[self scheduleUpdate];
```

You also need to add the -(void) update:(ccTime)delta method as shown in Listing 4-7. The scheduled update method is called every frame, and that's where you add the velocity to the player position. This way, you get a smooth constant movement in either direction regardless of the frequency of accelerometer input.

Listing 4-7. Updating the Player's Position with the Current Velocity

```
-(void) update:(ccTime)delta
{
    // Keep adding up the playerVelocity to the player's position
    CGPoint pos=player.position;
    pos.x+= playerVelocity.x;

    // The Player should also be stopped from going outside the screen
    CGSize screenSize=[CCDirector sharedDirector].winSize;
    float imageWidthHalved=player.texture.contentSize.width * 0.5f;
    float leftBorderLimit=imageWidthHalved;
    float rightBorderLimit=screenSize.width - imageWidthHalved;

    // preventing the player sprite from moving outside the screen
    if (pos.x<leftBorderLimit)
    {
        pos.x=leftBorderLimit;
        playerVelocity=CGPointZero;
    }
    else if (pos.x>rightBorderLimit)
    {
        pos.x=rightBorderLimit;
        playerVelocity=CGPointZero;
    }

    // assigning the modified position back
    player.position=pos;
}
```

A boundary check prevents the player sprite from leaving the screen. Once again, you have to take the player texture's `contentSize` into account, because the player position is at the center of the sprite image, but you don't want either side of the image to be off the screen. For this, you calculate `imageWidthHalved` and then use it to check whether the newly updated player position is within the left and right border limits. The code may be a bit verbose at this point, but that makes it easier to understand. Build and run the project now to see how controlling the player feels like.

Tip   You'll notice that this straightforward implementation of accelerometer control doesn't give you the same dynamic feeling that you may be used to from games like Tilt to Live. The reason is that smooth, dynamic accelerometer controls require accelerometer filtering. The KKInput class in Kobold2D allows you to obtain high-pass (instantaneous) and low-pass (smooth) filtered accelerometer values as properties, for example:

```
float smoothed = [KKInput sharedInput].acceleration.smoothedX;
```

Typically accelerometer-controlled games use a low-pass filter; *low-pass* means filtering out sudden, extreme changes of acceleration and thereby smoothing the resulting values. The following is a low-pass filter that generates new smoothedX/smoothedY values (instance variables) from the accelerometer input values (rawX/rawY) and a constant filterFactor in the range from 0.0 to 1.0. A good filter factor would be 0.1, which means only 10% of the current raw acceleration values are factored into the new smoothed values:

```
smoothedX = (rawX * filterFactor) + (smoothedX * (1.0 - filterFactor));

smoothedY = (rawY * filterFactor) + (smoothedY * (1.0 - filterFactor));
```

Adding Obstacles

This game isn't any good until we add something for the player to avoid. Let's introduce an abomination of nature: a six-legged man-spider. Who wouldn't want to avoid that?

As with the player sprite, you should add the `spider.png` and `spider-hd.png` files to the Resources group. Then the GameLayer.h file gets three new member variables added to its interface: a spiders NSMutableArray, whose class reference is shown in Listing 4-9, and the spiderMoveDuration and numSpidersMoved, which are used in Listing 4-12:

```
@interface GameLayer : CCLayer
{
    CCSprite* player;
    CGPoint playerVelocity;

    NSMutableArray* spiders;
    float spiderMoveDuration;
    int numSpidersMoved;
}
```

> **Caution** Avoid using CCArray in your own code. CCArray is a faster replacement for NSArray
> and NSMutableArray. But it's only marginally faster and using it will hardly affect framerate
> in almost all cases. Some methods like insertAtIndex or removeObjects are significantly
> slower than the same methods of NSMutableArray. The biggest problem with CCArray is that
> it's been shown to have critical bugs in the past, including ARC-compatibility issues. It also doesn't
> support all the features of NSArray/NSMutableArray. For example, you can't enumerate a
> CCArray with blocks, which makes it unsuitable for concurrent processing (via Grand Central
> Dispatch, for example). Overall, CCArray is simply not as reliable, compatible, or defect-free as
> NSMutableArray is. I would trade performance any time for reliability. Cocos2d uses CCArray
> internally, and for internal uses CCArray has been proven and well tested. I would leave it at that.

And in the GameLayer init method, add the call to the initSpiders method discussed next, right
after scheduleUpdate:

```
-(id) init
{
    if ((self=[super init]))
    {
        ...

        [self scheduleUpdate];

        [self initSpiders];
    }
    return self;
}
```

After that you add a fair bit of code to the GameLayer class, beginning with the initSpiders
method in Listing 4-8, which is creating the spider sprites.

Listing 4-8. For Easier Access, Spider Sprites Are Initialized and Added to a CCArray

```
-(void) initSpiders
{
    CGSize screenSize=[CCDirector sharedDirector].winSize;

    // using a temporary spider sprite is the easiest way to get the image's size
    CCSprite* tempSpider=[CCSprite spriteWithFile:@"spider.png"];

    float imageWidth=tempSpider.texture.contentSize.width;

    // Use as many spiders as can fit next to each other over the whole screen width.
    int numSpiders=screenSize.width / imageWidth;

    // Initialize the spiders array using alloc.
    spiders=[NSMutableArray arrayWithCapacity:numSpiders];
```

```
for (int i=0; i<numSpiders; i++)
{
    CCSprite* spider=[CCSprite spriteWithFile:@"spider.png"];
    [self addChild:spider z:0 tag:2];

    // Also add the spider to the spiders array.
    [spiders addObject:spider];
}

// call the method to reposition all spiders
[self resetSpiders];
}
```

There are a few things to note. You create a tempSpider CCSprite only to find out the sprite's image width, which you then use to decide how many spider sprites can fit next to each other. The easiest way to get an image's dimensions is by simply creating a temporary CCSprite. Note that you didn't add the tempSpider as child to any other node, nor assign it to an instance variable. This means that once execution leaves the initSpiders method, ARC will recognize that the tempSpider object is no longer in use and will automatically release its memory.

This is in contrast to the spiders array you're using to hold references to the spider sprites. The array is assigned to the instance variable spiders; therefore, ARC won't release the object until the GameLayer object itself is released. Under ARC, you don't have to release the spiders array in any way or form.

At the end of Listing 4-8, the method [self resetSpiders] is called; this method is shown in Listing 4-9. The reason for separating the initialization of the sprites and positioning them is that eventually there will be a game over, after which the game will need to be reset. The most efficient way to do so is to simply move all game objects to their initial positions. However, that may stop being feasible once your game scene gets to a certain complexity. Eventually, it may be easier to simply reload the whole scene, at the cost of having the player wait for the scene to reload.

Caution   Speaking of reloading a scene, you may be tempted to write [[CCDirector sharedDirector] replaceScene:self];, to reload the same scene. This will cause a crash because self is the currently running scene, and trying to replace a running scene with itself is something cocos2d doesn't like and causes the app to crash. Instead, you must create a new instance of the GameLayer class: [[CCDirector sharedDirector] replaceScene:[GameLayer scene]];.

Listing 4-9. Resetting Spider Sprite Positions

```
-(void) resetSpiders
{
    CGSize screenSize=[CCDirector sharedDirector].winSize;

    // Get any spider to get its image width
    CCSprite* tempSpider=[spiders lastObject];
    CGSize size=tempSpider.texture.contentSize;
```

```
int numSpiders = [spiders count];
for (int i = 0; i < numSpiders; i++)
{
    // Put each spider at its designated position outside the screen
    CCSprite* spider = [spiders objectAtIndex:i];
    spider.position = CGPointMake(size.width * i + size.width * 0.5f,↵
        screenSize.height + size.height);

    [spider stopAllActions];
}
// Schedule the spider update logic to run at the given interval.
[self schedule:@selector(spidersUpdate:) interval:0.7f];

// reset the moved spiders counter and spider move duration (affects speed)
numSpidersMoved = 0;
spiderMoveDuration = 4.0f;
}
```

Once again you obtain a reference to one of the existing spiders temporarily to get its image size via the texture's contentSize property. You don't create a new sprite here because there are already existing sprites of the same kind, and because all spiders use the same image with the same size, you shouldn't even care which sprite you're getting. So, simply get the last spider from the array.

You then modify each spider's position so that together they span the entire width of the screen. You add half the image size's width—once again, this is because of the sprite's texture being centered on the node's position. As for the height, also set each sprite to be one image size above the upper screen border. This is an arbitrary distance, as long as the image isn't visible, which is all you want to achieve. Because the spider might still be moving when the reset occurs, you also stop all of its actions at this point.

> **Tip** To save a few CPU cycles, it's good practice not to use method calls in the conditional block of for or other loops if it's not strictly necessary. In this case, I created a variable numSpiders to hold the result of [spiders count] and I use that in the conditional check of the for loop. The count of the array remains the same during the for loop's iterations because the array itself isn't modified in the loop. That's why I can cache this value and save the repeated calls to [spiders count] during each iteration of the for loop.

I'm also scheduling the spidersUpdate: selector to run every 0.7 seconds, which is how often another spider will drop down from the top of the screen. If the selector is already scheduled, then cocos2d will acknowledge that with a log message you can ignore. Cocos2d doesn't schedule the selector a second time, but merely updates the scheduled selector's interval. The spidersUpdate: method, shown in Listing 4-10, randomly picks one of the existing spiders, checks whether it's idle, and lets it fall down the screen by using a sequence of actions.

Listing 4-10. The spidersUpdate: Method Frequently Lets a Spider Fall

```
-(void) spidersUpdate:(ccTime)delta
{
    // Try to find a spider which isn't currently moving.
    for (int i=0; i<10; i++)
    {
        int randomSpiderIndex=CCRANDOM_0_1() * spiders.count;
        CCSprite* spider=[spiders objectAtIndex:randomSpiderIndex];

        // If the spider isn't moving it won't have any running actions.
        if (spider.numberOfRunningActions == 0)
        {
            // This is the sequence which controls the spiders' movement
            [self runSpiderMoveSequence:spider];

            // Only one spider should start moving at a time.
            break;
        }
    }
}
```

I don't let any listing pass without some curiosity, do I? In this case, you might wonder why you're iterating exactly ten times to get a random spider. The reason is that you don't know if the randomly generated index will get you a spider that isn't moving already, so you want to be reasonably sure it eventually picks a spider that's currently idle. If after ten tries—and this number is arbitrary—you didn't have the luck to get an idle spider chosen randomly, simply skip this update and wait for the next.

You could brute-force your way and just keep trying to find an idle spider using a do/while loop. However, it's possible that all spiders could be moving at the same time, because this depends on design parameters such as the frequency with which new spiders are being dropped. In that case, the game would simply lock up, looping endlessly trying to find an idle spider. Moreover, I'm not so keen on trying too hard; it really doesn't matter much for this game if you're unable to send another spider falling down for a few seconds. That said, if you check out the DoodleDrop03 project, you'll see I added a logging statement that will print out how many retries it took to find an idle spider.

Because the movement sequence is the only action the spiders perform, you simply check whether the spider is running any actions at all, and if not, assume it's idle. And that brings us to the runSpiderMoveSequence in Listing 4-11.

Listing 4-11. Spider Movement Is Handled by an Action Sequence

```
-(void) runSpiderMoveSequence:(CCSprite*)spider
{
    // Slowly increase the spider speed over time.
    numSpidersMoved++;
    if (numSpidersMoved % 8 == 0 && spiderMoveDuration > 2.0f)
```

```
{
    spiderMoveDuration -= 0.1f;
}

// This is the sequence which controls the spiders' movement.
CGPoint belowScreenPosition=CGPointMake(spider.position.x,↲
    -spider.texture.contentSize.height);
CCMoveTo* move=[CCMoveTo actionWithDuration:spiderMoveDuration
                              position:belowScreenPosition];

CCCallBlock* callDidDrop=[CCCallBlock actionWithBlock:^void(){
  // move the droppedSpider back up outside the top of the screen
  CGPoint pos=spider.position;
  CGSize screenSize=[CCDirector sharedDirector].winSize;
  pos.y=screenSize.height+spider.texture.contentSize.height;
  spider.position=pos;
}];

CCSequence* sequence=[CCSequence actions:move, callDidDrop, nil];
[spider runAction:sequence];
}
```

The runSpiderMoveSequence method keeps track of the number of dropped spiders. Every eighth spider, the spiderMoveDuration decreases, and thus any spider's speed increases. In case you're wondering about the % operator, it's called the *modulo* operator. The result is the remainder of the division operation, meaning that if numSpidersMoved is divisible by 8, the result of the modulo operation will be 0.

The action sequence consists only of a CCMoveTo action and a CCCallBlock action. You could improve it to let spiders drop down a bit, wait, and then drop all the way, as evil six-legged man-spiders would normally do. I leave this improvement to you, and you can find an example implementation in the final DoodleDrop project.

For now it's only important to know that I chose to reset the spider's position in a block function passed to the CCCallBlock action. The block function can simply use the same spider variable passed to the runSpiderMoveSequence method. The block is called after the spider's movement is done, meaning it dropped past the player character. Thanks to the block you don't have to jump through hoops to find the right spider. The spider's position is then reset to just above the top of the screen. Listing 4-12 shows the same block from Listing 4-11 again, in isolation.

Listing 4-12. Resetting the Spider Position So It Can Fall Back Down Again is done in a CCCallBlock block

```
CCCallBlock* callDidDrop=[CCCallBlock actionWithBlock:^void(){
  // move the droppedSpider back up outside the top of the screen
  CGPoint pos=spider.position;
  CGSize screenSize=[CCDirector sharedDirector].winSize;
  pos.y=screenSize.height+spider.texture.contentSize.height;
  spider.position=pos;
}];
```

So far, so good. You may want to build and run the game now and play it a little. I think you'll quickly notice what's still missing. Hint: read the next headline.

Collision Detection

You may be surprised to see that collision detection can be as simple as Listing 4-13. Admittedly, this only checks the distance between the player and all spiders, which makes this type of collision detection a *radial check*. For this type of game, it's sufficient. Add the call to [self checkForCollision] to the end of the -(void) update:(ccTime)delta method, along with the resetGame method, which resets the spiders.

Listing 4-13. A Simple Range-Check or Radial Collision-Check Suffices

```
-(void) checkForCollision
{
    // Assumption: both player and spider images are squares.
    float playerImageSize=player.texture.contentSize.width;
    CCSprite* spider=[spiders lastObject];
    float spiderImageSize=spider.texture.contentSize.width;
    float playerCollisionRadius=playerImageSize * 0.4f;
    float spiderCollisionRadius=spiderImageSize * 0.4f;

    // This collision distance will roughly equal the image shapes.
    float maxCollisionDistance=playerCollisionRadius+spiderCollisionRadius;

    int numSpiders=spiders.count;
    for (int i=0; i<numSpiders; i++)
    {
        spider=[spiders objectAtIndex:i];

        if (spider.numberOfRunningActions == 0)
        {
            // This spider isn't even moving so we can skip checking it.
            continue;
        }

        // Get the distance between player and spider.
        float actualDistance=ccpDistance(player.position, spider.position);

        // Are the two objects closer than allowed?
        if (actualDistance<maxCollisionDistance)
        {
            // Game Over (just restart the game for now)
            [self resetGame];
            break;
        }
    }
}
-(void) resetGame
{
    [self resetSpiders];
}
```

The image sizes of the player and spider are used as hints for the collision radii (or radiuses, if you prefer). The approximation is good enough for this game. If you check the DoodleDrop03 project, you'll also notice that I've added a debug drawing method (see Listing 4-14) that renders the collision radii for each sprite.

You're iterating over all the spiders but ignoring those that aren't moving at the moment because they'll definitely be out of range. The ccpDistance method calculates the distance between the current spider and the player. This is another undocumented but fully supported cocos2d method. You can find these and other useful math functions in the CGPointExtension filesin the cocos2d/Support group in the Xcode project and in the amended cocos2d API reference hosted on the Learn Cocos2D web site: www.learn-cocos2d.com/api-ref.

The resulting distance is then compared to the sum of the player's and spider's collision radius. If the actual distance is smaller than that, a collision has occurred. Because you've not implemented a game-over, you can just reset all the spiders to restart the game.

Listing 4-14. Drawing Collision Radii in Debug Builds

```
#if DEBUG
-(void) draw
{
    [super draw];

    // Iterate through all nodes of the layer.
    for (CCNode* node in [self children])
    {
        // Make sure the node is a CCSprite and has the right tags.
        if ([node isKindOfClass:[CCSprite class]] && (node.tag == 1 || node.tag == 2))
        {
            // The sprite's collision radius is a percentage of its image width.
            // The same factor is used in the checkForCollision method.
            CCSprite* sprite = (CCSprite*)node;
            float radius = sprite.texture.contentSize.width * 0.4f;
            float angle = 0;
            int numSegments = 10;
            bool drawLineToCenter = NO;
            ccDrawCircle(sprite.position, radius, angle, numSegments, drawLineToCenter);
        }
    }
}
#endif
```

Labels and Bitmap Fonts

Labels are the second-most important graphical element of cocos2d games, right after sprites. The easiest and most flexible solution seems to be the CCLabelTTF class, but its performance is terrible if you need to change the displayed text frequently. The alternative is the CCLabelBMFont class, which renders bitmap fonts instead of TrueType fonts. Along with that I'll introduce you to Glyph Designer, an elegant tool for converting TrueType fonts into bitmap fonts and enhancing them along the way with effects like shadows, color gradients, and so on.

Adding the Score Label

The game needs some kind of scoring mechanism. Let's add a simple time-lapse counter as the score. Start by adding the score's Label in the init method of the GameLayer class:

```
scoreLabel=[CCLabelTTF labelWithString:@"0" fontName:@"Arial" fontSize:48];
scoreLabel.position=CGPointMake(screenSize.width / 2, screenSize.height);

// Adjust the label's anchorPoint's y position to make it align with the top.
scoreLabel.anchorPoint=CGPointMake(0.5f, 1.0f);

// Add the score label with z value of -1 so it's drawn below everything else
[self addChild:scoreLabel z:-1];
```

You also need to declare the score and scoreLabel instance variables in the GameLayer.h file. Instead of adding a CCLabelTTF object, however, use a CCNode object that implements the CCLabelProtocol. That way, later you can change the implementation from CCLabelTTF to CCLabelBMFont without having to change the instance variable's declaration. Using the protocol instead of a concrete class is an example of interface-based programming, which makes programs easier to modify and maintain. The scoreLabel is now oblivious to whether it's a CCLabelTTF or CCLabelBMFont object.

```
@interface GameLayer : CCLayer
{
  CCSprite* player;
  CGPoint playerVelocity;

  NSMutableArray* spiders;
  float spiderMoveDuration;
  int numSpidersMoved;

  int score;
  CCNode<CCLabelProtocol>* scoreLabel;
}
```

I consciously chose a CCLabelTTF object for now because it would likely be the first choice for most beginning cocos2d programmers. And that's where things might get ugly pretty fast. In Chapter 3, I mentioned that updating a CCLabelTTF's text is slow. The whole texture is re-created using iOS font-rendering methods, and they take their time, besides allocating a new texture and releasing the old one. On current-generation devices and with a single label, you probably won't notice it. But use several frequently updating devices and run the game on an iPhone 3GS and perhaps you'll notice a severe drop in framerate.

But keep in mind that CCLabelTTF is slow only when changing its string frequently. If you create the CCLabelTTF once when the scene begins and never or rarely change it, it's just as fast as any other CCSprite of the same dimensions.

You should also update the resetGame method so that it resets the score and scoreLabel variables:

```
-(void) resetGame
{
  [self resetSpiders];
```

```
score = 0;
[scoreLabel setString:@"0"];

}
```

To frequently change the label for testing, you can add the following line to the update method. It simply prints the number of total frames rendered so far:

```
score = [CCDirector sharedDirector].totalFrames;
[scoreLabel setString:[NSString stringWithFormat:@"%i", score]];
```

Introducing CCLabelBMFont

Labels that update fast at the expense of more memory usage, like any other CCSprite, are the specialty of the CCLabelBMFont class. I've replaced the CCLabelTTF with a CCLabelBMFont in DoodleDrop04. The code change is relatively straightforward; you have to change the line in the init method, as shown here:

```
scoreLabel = [CCLabelBMFont labelWithString:@"0" fntFile:@"bitmapfont.fnt"];
```

> **Note**   Bitmap fonts are a great choice for games because they're fast, but they do have one disadvantage: the size of any bitmap font is fixed. If you need the same font but larger or smaller in size, you can scale the CCLabelBMFont—but you lose image quality scaling up, and you're wasting memory when scaling down. The other option is to create a separate font file with the new size, but this uses up more memory because each variation of a bitmap font uses its own texture.

You also need to add the bitmapfont.fnt and bitmapfont-hd.fnt files as well as the accompanying bitmapfont.png and bitmapfont-hd.png, which are all in the DoodleDrop04 project's Resources folder. Don't add the .GlyphProject files, though—those files are used by, and useful only to, Glyph Designer.

The tool to create bitmap fonts used to be Hiero, but by now Hiero is only the tool of choice if you really don't want to spend any money. Written by Kevin James Glass, Hiero is a free Java Web application, available from http://slick.cokeandcode.com/demos/hiero.jnlp.

The downside is, it's a free Java web application. It asks you to trust the application because of a missing security certificate. On the other hand, many developers use the tool, and so far there's been no evidence that the application is untrustworthy. Hiero also "features" several odd and downright annoying bugs, including an obnoxious one that has the resulting image file flipped upside-down. If you see only garbage instead of a bitmap font text in your app, you may have to flip the bitmap font PNG image upside down with an image-editing program. I've documented these issues and how to fix them in my Hiero tutorial: www.learn-cocos2d.com/knowledge-base/tutorial-bitmap-fonts-hiero.

Some developers also swear by BMFont. But as a Windows program, it requires a Windows computer or Windows installed in a virtual machine on your Mac. That's why it's not more widely used in the Mac developer community. You can download BMFont from www.angelcode.com/products/bmfont.

For everyone else, there's Glyph Designer.

Creating Bitmap Fonts with Glyph Designer

The guys at `www.71squared.com` released the Hiero replacement tool called Glyph Designer. Although it's not free, it's definitely worth every cent.

You can download a trial version at `http://glyphdesigner.71squared.com`, and if you're already familiar with Hiero, you'll notice a striking similarity in features, although the user interface is a lot easier to use and encourages experimentation. Mike Daley also mentioned in an episode of the Cocos2D Podcast (available at `http://cocos2dpodcast.wordpress.com`) that Glyph Designer will get a new feature that allows you to share font designs with other users of the tool.

Figure 4-7 shows Glypgh Designer in action. The process of creating a bitmap font is relatively playful, and it doesn't hurt to change the various knobs, buttons, and colors as you please. I outline just the basic editing areas for you.

Figure 4-7. Glyph Designer lets you create bitmap fonts from any TrueType font and can export FNT and PNG files compatible with the CCLabelBMFont class of cocos2d

On the left-hand side you have the list of TrueType fonts, and if those aren't enough, you can use the Load Font icon to load any TTF file. Below the list you can change the size of the font with the slider and also switch to bold, italic, and other font styles.

> **Tip**   Creating Retina-enabled bitmap fonts is easy. Create your font as usual and export it. This will be your non-Retina or SD font. Then simply change the size of the font in Glyph Designer to twice its normal size; for example, move the slider from a font size of 30 to a font size of 60. Then reexport the font using the same name but adding the -hd suffix. Now you have the same font in regular/SD and Retina/HD sizes.
>
> Cocos2d will automatically recognize and use the font with the -hd suffix if Retina support is enabled and the game is running on a Retina device.

In the center of the screen, you see the resulting texture atlas used for your current font settings. Notice that the texture atlas size and the order of the glyphs frequently change as you modify the font settings. You can also select a glyph and see its info on the right-hand pane under Glyph Info.

Further down on the right-hand pane you can change the texture atlas settings, although in most cases you don't have to. Glyph Designer makes sure the texture atlas size is always large enough to contain all the glyphs in a single texture.

With the Glyph Fill settings, you can change the color and the way glyphs are filled, including a gradient setting. Alongside that you have the option to change the Glyph Outline, which is a black thin line around each glyph, and the Glyph Shadow, which allows you to create a 3D-ish look of the font.

At the very bottom of the right-hand pane you find the Included Glyphs section. With that you can choose from a predefined selection of glyphs to include in the atlas. If you absolutely know for sure that you won't be needing certain characters, you can also enter your own list of characters to reduce the size of the texture. This is especially helpful for score strings, where you may only need digits plus very few extra characters. For example, the bitmap font used in the DoodleDrop project only contains letters to minimize the font's memory usage.

Once you're satisfied with your bitmap font, you can save the entire project so that you can restore previous settings. To save the font in a format usable by cocos2d, you have to save it via File ➤ Export in the .fnt (Cocos2d Text) format. You can then add the FNT and PNG files created by Glyph Designer to your Xcode project and use the FNT file with the `CCLabelBMFont` class.

> **Caution**   If you try to display characters using a `CCLabelBMFont`, which aren't available in the .fnt file, they'll simply be skipped and not displayed. For example, if you do `[label setString:@"Hello, World!"]`, but your bitmap font contains only lowercase letters and no punctuation characters, you'll see the string "ello orld" displayed instead.

Simply Playing Audio

I've added some audio files to complete this game. In the Resources folder of the DoodleDrop04 project, you'll find the audio files named blues.mp3 and alien-sfx.caf that you can add to your project. The first choice and the easiest way to play audio files in cocos2d is by using the SimpleAudioEngine. Audio support is not an integral part of cocos2d; this is the domain of CocosDenshion, a third-party addition to cocos2d and fortunately distributed with cocos2d.

Tip   If you're looking for an alternative sound engine, I recommend ObjectAL, available from http://kstenerud.github.com/ObjectAL-for-iPhone, which is readily available in Kobold2D (see Chapter 16). ObjectAL has a cleanly written API and excellent documentation but is only compatible with iOS.

Because CocosDenshion is treated as separate code from cocos2d, you have to add the corresponding header files whenever you use the CocosDenshion audio functionality, like so:

```
#import "GameLayer.h"

#import "SimpleAudioEngine.h"
```

You'll find playing music and audio using the SimpleAudioEngine is straightforward, as shown here:

```
[[SimpleAudioEngine sharedEngine] playBackgroundMusic:@"blues.mp3" loop:YES];
[[SimpleAudioEngine sharedEngine] playEffect:@"alien-sfx.caf"];
```

You may want to preload sound effects especially when the game starts, to avoid a small delay when each sound effect is first played. This is also easily accomplished:

```
[[SimpleAudioEngine sharedEngine] preloadEffect:@"alien-sfx.caf"];
```

For music and longer speech files, playing MP3 files is the preferred choice. Note that you can play only one MP3 file in the background at a time. Technically, it's possible to play two or more MP3 files, but only one can be decoded in hardware. The extra strain on the CPU is undesirable for games, so playing multiple MP3 files at the same time, or merely crossfading two music tracks, is something you might want to avoid unless your app's design calls for it.

This also means that short-lived sound effects should not be in MP3 format. For those audio effects, I've had good experiences with 16-bit PCM (uncompressed) audio in either the WAV or CAF file format. The sampling rate can be 22.5 kHz for most game sound effects, unless you need or want crystal-clear audio quality, in which case use 44.1 kHz.

A good and complete audio-editing tool for Mac OS X is Audacity, which you can download for free from http://audacity.sourceforge.net. If you need only to quickly convert audio files from one format to another, possibly changing some basic settings such as sampling rate, I recommend SoundConverter, which was developed by Steve Dekorte. The tool is free to use for files up to 500KB in size, and the license to use SoundConverter without restrictions is just $15. You can download SoundConverter from http://dekorte.com/projects/ shareware/ SoundConverter/.

A free alternative to SoundConverter is the command-line tool afconvert. Familiarity with Terminal is recommended. You can do a lot with afconvert, but being a command-line tool, you'll also have to type a lot. To get help for afconvert, open the Terminal app and type the following:

```
afconvert -h
```

The preferred audio format for iOS devices is 16-bit, little endian, linear PCM packaged as CAF file (Apple CAF audio format code: LEI16), according to Apple's Audio Coding How To, which contains generally helpful advice for audio programming: http://developer.apple.com/library/ios/#codinghowtos/AudioAndVideo/_index.html.

To convert any audio file that afconvert supports to the preferred iOS audio format, run the afconvert command like this:

```
afconvert -f caff -d LEI16 myInputFile.mp3 myOutputFile.caf
```

The -f (or -file) switch denotes the file format, which is caff for CAF files. With the -d switch, you specify the audio data format, here LEI16. You can get a list of the audio data formats supported by afconvert by running afconvert with the -hf switch.

Note If you're ever in the situation where an audio file just won't play or results in a garbled mess of noise, there's probably nothing wrong with your code or your device. There are countless audio applications and numerous audio codecs, and they all create their own variations of the respective formats. Some can't play on iOS devices but play fine otherwise. Particularly, WAV files seem to be affected, which is why I prefer to use Apple's more native audio container format CAF. Typically, the way you can fix broken audio files is to open the audio file in an audio-editing program that you know is capable of saving iOS-compatible audio files and then save it again. You can do this with the aptly named SoundConverter or the audio application of your choice. Usually, after this resave, the file will play just fine on the iOS device. Also sound issues are common in the iOS Simulator. If the issue only occurs in the Simulator, you can ignore it and maybe fix it by rebooting your computer.

---

iPad Considerations

With all coordinates taking the screen's size into account, the game should simply scale up without any problems when running it on the iPad's bigger screen. And it does. Just like that. In contrast, if you had been using fixed coordinates, you'd be facing a serious rework of your game.

You can try this out by deploying the DoodleDrop project to an iPad device or by selecting the iPad Simulator from the scheme drop-down menu.

Supporting the Retina iPad

The 3rd-generation iPad features a Retina display with four times as many pixels as its predecessors. But if you run the DoodleDrop project as is, you may notice that the images are too small on a Retina iPad.

When running your app on an iPad, cocos2d will try to load assets with the suffix -ipad and -ipadhd. If they don't exist, cocos2d reverts back to loading the standard-resolution asset with no suffix. In this case the Retina iPad won't find the -ipadhd versions of any assets and displays the smaller SD assets.

You can either provide both -ipad and -ipadhd variants of all your assets or you can change which type of suffix cocos2d should look for. For the DoodleDrop project it's sufficient to use the regular Retina assets on a Retina iPad. Do that by changing the iPad and iPad Retina suffixes to the empty string and -hd respectively:

```
[CCFileUtils setiPadSuffix:@""];
[CCFileUtils setiPadRetinaDisplaySuffix:@"-hd"];
```

Run this code as early as possible—for example, in the init method of the first scene or directly in the AppDelegate class. From then on, the 1st- and 2nd-generation iPads will load the assets without suffixes, whereas the Retina iPads will load the -hd assets.

One Universal App or Two Separate Apps?

When porting your app to iPad, you generally have to decide whether your app will be treated as a single (Universal) app on the App Store or whether it should be treated as two separate apps. Both options have their pros and cons, and generally you could say that Universal apps are better and fairer for customers, whereas separate apps may be better for developers.

Universal apps include code and assets for both iPhone/iPod touch and iPad devices. This has the drawback that all assets are added to the same Xcode target, increasing the app's size—possibly beyond the over-the-air download limit of (currently) 50 MB. That's the technical drawback; there are no performance penalties.

With a Universal app, you can't set different prices for iPhone/iPod touch and iPad versions. That's probably the biggest bummer, knowing that iPad users tend to be more willing to pay more for an app. Moreover, you won't know which percentage of your download's respective purchases were made by iPad users. You'd have to have the app "call home" to determine that.

Regardless of that, Universal apps will still be ranked separately by device in the App Store charts. If the user downloads or purchases the app on an iPhone or iPod touch device, it's accounted for in the iPhone charts. The same goes for downloads/purchases on the iPad, which add to your app's ranking in the iPad charts. That leaves the question of how iTunes downloads/purchases are accounted for. They're simply accounted for in the iPhone rankings. That makes it impossible to even estimate how many of your users are iPad users, unless you add analytics tracking code to your app.

Splitting your app into two separate apps for iPhone/iPod touch and iPad allows you to keep the game assets separate. But the biggest drawback is if iOS users want both the iPhone and iPad versions, they'll have to buy both. That's good for you, but bad for the customer. And some won't hesitate to give your app a bad rating just because of that.

Because your app will be treated as two entirely separate apps in the App Store, at least the customer reviews and comments will be specific to the particular app version. You'll also be able to optimize each app's description and screenshots for the target platform and update each version separately. Splitting your app is also a good choice if your app has been on the App

Store for a while, because adding support for new devices in a Universal app won't have your app appear in the What's New section of the App Store.

Restricting Device Support

By default all cocos2d projects are set to be Universal apps that run natively on iPhone, iPod touch, and iPad devices. But you can change your app to work only on iPhone and iPod touch or iPads.

First, select the project DoodleDrop in the Project Navigator. This brings up the list of targets where you select the DoodleDrop target and then choose the Summary tab. Under the iOS Application Target section, there's a pop-up control labeled Devices that gives you three choices: iPhone, iPad, and Universal.

In Figure 4-8 the target is set to build a Universal app. Changing this setting to either iPhone or iPad will restrict your app to users of that device. Of course, iPad users can still buy and download iPhone apps, but they're displayed on the iPad as an iPhone screen-sized app that iPad users can optionally zoom up with the 2x button.

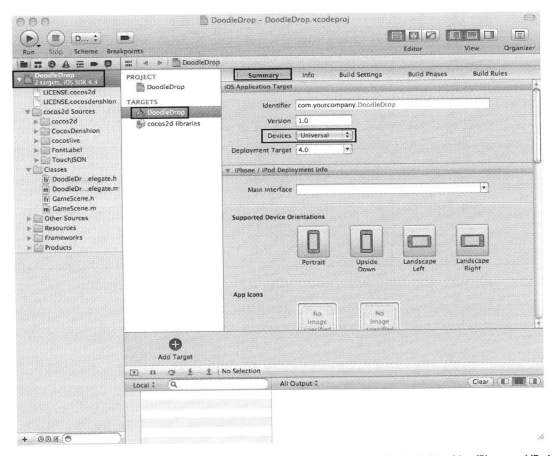

Figure 4-8. *Changing the application target to build either a Universal app or one that's limited to either iPhone and iPod touch or iPads*

Now you may be wondering, what if I want two separate targets for iPhone and iPad? This can be useful to charge different prices for iPhone and iPad versions or simply to reduce the download size of either version.

In that case, all you have to do is to select the target—DoodleDrop in this case—and choose Edit ➤ Duplicate. Or just right-click the target and select Duplicate. This creates a duplicate of the target, which allows you to set one target's Devices setting to iPhone and the other target's Devices setting to iPad. Now you have a separate target for each device type, and you might want to rename both targets and their schemes accordingly to avoid confusion.

Summary

I hope you had fun building this first game. It was surely a lot to take in, but I'd rather err on the side of too much information than too little.

At this point, you've learned how to create your own game-layer class and how to work with sprites. You've used the accelerometer to control the player and added velocity to allow the player sprite to accelerate and decelerate, giving it a more dynamic feel.

Simple radial collision detection using the distance check method from the likewise undocumented CGPointExtensions was also on the menu. And for dessert you had a potpourri of labels, bitmap fonts, and the Glyph Designer tool, garnished with some audio programming.

What's left? Maybe going through the source code for this chapter. I've added a finalized version of this game that includes some game-play improvements, a startup menu, and a game-over message.

There's just one thing about the DoodleDrop project I haven't mentioned yet: it's all in one class. For a small project, this may suffice, but it'll quickly get messy as you move on to implement more features. You need to add some structure to your code design. The next chapter will arm you with cocos2d programming best practices, show you how to lay out your code, and discuss the various ways you can pass information between objects if they're no longer in the same class.

In the meantime, you may want to check out the DoodleDrop05 game, which I improved with a game-over screen and additional visual effects.

Chapter 5

Game Building Blocks

The game DoodleDrop in Chapter 4 was written to be easy to understand if you're new to cocos2d. If you're a more experienced developer, though, you probably noticed that there's no separation of code—everything is in just one file. Clearly, that doesn't scale, and if you're going to make bigger, more exciting games than DoodleDrop, you'll have to find a suitable way to structure your code. Otherwise, you might end up with one class driving your game's logic. The code size can quickly grow to thousands of lines, making it hard to navigate and tempting to change anything from anywhere, very likely introducing subtle and hard-to-find bugs.

Each new project demands its own code design. In this chapter, I introduce you to some of the building blocks for writing more complex cocos2d games. You can then use the code foundation laid out in this chapter to create the side-scrolling shooter game you'll be building in the next few chapters.

Because this chapter contains lots of reference material, I concentrate on the relevant code and omit the details of creating new cocos2d classes as shown in earlier chapters. You may want to download the book's source code at this point to see this chapter's projects in action. You can download the book's source code from the book's page on www.apress.com or from the Learn Cocos2D web site at www.learn-cocos2d.com/store/book-learn-cocos2d.

Working with Multiple Scenes

The DoodleDrop game had only one scene and one layer. More complex games need several scenes and multiple layers. How and when to use them will become second nature for you. Let's see what's involved.

Adding More Scenes

In Listings 4-1 and 4-2 in the previous chapter, I outlined the basic code needed to create a scene. Those basics still apply. Adding more scenes is a matter of adding more classes built on that same basic code. It's when you're transitioning between scenes that things get a little more interesting. There's a set of three methods in CCNode that are sent to each node object (sprite, label, menu item, and so on) in the current scene hierarchy when you're replacing a scene via the CCDirector replaceScene method. You can use these methods to react to scene changes, remove some memory, or load additional assets in the new scene.

The onEnter and onExit methods get called at certain times during a scene change, depending on whether a CCTransitionScene is used. You must always call the super implementation of these methods to avoid input problems and memory leaks. Take a look at Listing 5-1 and note that all these methods call the super implementation.

Listing 5-1. The onEnter and onExit Methods

```
-(void) onEnter
{
    // Sent to new scene right after its init method was run.
    // If using a CCTransitionScene: sent when the transition begins.

    [super onEnter];
}

-(void) onEnterTransitionDidFinish
{
    // Sent to the new scene right after onEnter.
    // If using a CCTransitionScene: sent when the transition has ended.

    [super onEnterTransitionDidFinish];
}

-(void) onExit
{
    // Sent to the previous scene right before its dealloc method is run.
    // If using a CCTransitionScene: sent when the transition has ended.

    [super onExit];
}

-(void) onExitTransitionDidStart
{
    // Sent to the previous scene only when using a CCTransitionScene.
    // It's sent when the transition begins, at the same time as the
    // new scene's onEnter method is run.

    [super onExitTransitionDidStart];
}
```

> **Note** If you don't make the call to the super implementation in the onEnter methods, your new scene won't react to touch or accelerometer input. If you don't call super in onExit, the current scene won't be released from memory. Similar issues may occur if you don't call the super implementation in the other two methods. Because it's easy to forget this, and the resulting behavior doesn't lead you to realize that it may be related to these methods, it's important to stress this point.

These methods are useful whenever you need to do something in any node (CCNode, CCLayer, CCScene, CCSprite, CCLabelTTF, and so on) right before a scene is changed or right after. The difference from simply writing the same code in a node's init or dealloc method is that the scene is already fully set up during onEnter, and it still contains all nodes during onExit.

That can be important. For example, if you perform a transition to change scenes, you may want to pause certain animations or hide user interface elements until the transition finishes. Here's the sequence in which these methods get called when using a scene transition from FirstLayer to SecondLayer, based on the logging information from the ScenesAndLayers01 project:

1. scene: SecondLayer

2. init: SecondLayer

3. onExitTransitionDidStart: FirstLayer

4. onEnter: SecondLayer

5. // Transition is running here for a few seconds ...

6. onExit: FirstLayer

7. onEnterTransitionDidFinish: SecondLayer

8. dealloc: FirstLayer

At first, SecondLayer's +(id) scene method is called to initialize a CCScene. This also adds a CCLayer to the scene. The SecondLayer's init method is then called, directly followed by the onEnter method in line 4. Just before that, all the nodes in FirstLayer receive the onExitTransitionDidStart message as a hint that the scene has started to transition to another scene.

In line 5, the transition is animating the new scene, and when it's done, the FirstLayer and all its nodes receive the onExit message before the FirstLayer is deallocated in line 8. At the same time the SecondLayer receives the onEnterTransitionDidFinish message in line 7.

If you're not using a scene transition to change scenes, the process changes slightly. Most notably the FirstLayer and its nodes receive the onExit message right away, and are also deallocated immediately following onExit. The SecondLayer and its nodes receive both onEnter and onEnterTransitionDidFinish messages consecutively, making them interchangeable. Receiving the onEnterTransitionDidFinish method in this case is superfluous; I would consider this a bug and wouldn't rely on that behavior to stay.

The following is the sequence of messages sent to FirstLayer and SecondLayer in the order they will occur during the scene change without using a transition:

1. scene: SecondLayer

2. init: SecondLayer

3. onExit: FirstLayer

4. dealloc: FirstLayer

5. onEnter: SecondLayer

6. onEnterTransitionDidFinish: SecondLayer

Note that the `FirstScene` `dealloc` method is always called after the other scene was initialized. This means that during a transition the previous scene is still in memory until the transition has ended.

If you want to allocate memory-intensive nodes only after the previous scene is guaranteed to be deallocated, you have to schedule a selector to wait at least one frame before doing the memory allocations, to be certain that the previous scene's memory is released. You can schedule a method that's guaranteed to be called during the next frame by setting the `delay` parameter to 0 when scheduling the method:

```
[self scheduleOnce:@selector(waitOneFrame:) delay:0.0f];
```

The drawback to this solution is that all nodes you add after the delay will not be seen for one frame, and during the entire transition. So it's best to save this for assets that are initially outside the visible area or general memory allocations, such as arrays, collision maps, or other game data.

Loading Next Paragraph, Please Stand By

Sooner or later you'll face noticeable loading times during scene transitions. As you add more content, loading times correspondingly increase. As I just explained, a new scene is allocated before the scene transition starts. If you have very complex code or load a lot of assets in the new scene's `init` or `onEnter` methods, there will be an obvious delay before the transition begins. This is especially problematic if the new scene takes more than fractions of a second to load, and the user initiated the scene change by clicking a button. The user may get the impression that the game has locked up or frozen. The way to alleviate this problem is to add another scene in between: a loading scene. You'll find the example implementation of the `LoadingScene` class in the ScenesAndLayers01 project.

In effect, the `LoadingScene` class acts as an intermediate scene. It's derived from the cocos2d `CCScene` class. You don't have to create a new `LoadingScene` for each transition; you can use one scene for which you simply specify the target scene you'd like to be loaded. An enum works best for this; it's defined in the `LoadingScene` header file shown in Listing 5-2.

Listing 5-2. LoadingScene.h

```
typedef enum
{
    TargetSceneINVALID = 0,
    TargetSceneFirst,
    TargetSceneSecond,
    TargetSceneMAX,

} TargetSceneTypes;

// LoadingScene is derived directly from Scene. We don't need a CCLayer for this scene.
@interface LoadingScene : CCScene

{
    TargetSceneTypes targetScene;
}

+(id) sceneWithTargetScene:(TargetSceneTypes)sceneType;
-(id) initWithTargetScene:(TargetSceneTypes)sceneType;
```

> **Tip**   It's good practice to set the first enum value to be an `INVALID` value, unless you intend to make the first the default. Variables in Objective-C are initialized to 0 automatically unless you specify a different value.
>
> You can also also add a `MAX` or `NUM` entry at the end of the enum if you intend to iterate over every enum value, as in:
>
> ```
> for (int i=TargetSceneINVALID+1; i<TargetScenesMAX; i++) { .. }
> ```
>
> In the case of the `LoadingScene`, it's not necessary, but I tend to add these entries merely out of habit, even if I don't need them.

This brings me to the LoadingScene class implementation of the ScenesAndLayers01 project in Listing 5-3. You'll notice that the scene is initialized differently and that it uses scheduleUpdate to delay replacing the LoadingScene with the actual target scene.

Listing 5-3. The LoadingScene Class Uses a Switch to Decide Whether to Load the Target Scene

```objectivec
+(id) sceneWithTargetScene:(TargetSceneTypes)sceneType;
{
    return [[self alloc] initWithTargetScene:sceneType];
}

-(id) initWithTargetScene:(TargetSceneTypes)sceneType
{
    if ((self = [super init]))
    {
        targetScene = sceneType;

        CCLabelTTF* label = [CCLabelTTF labelWithString:@"Loading ..."
                                    fontName:@"Marker Felt"
                                    fontSize:64];
        CGSize size = [CCDirector sharedDirector].winSize;
        label.position = CGPointMake(size.width / 2, size.height / 2);
        [self addChild:label];

        // Must wait one frame before loading the target scene!
        [self scheduleOnce:@selector(loadScene:) delay:0.0f];
    }

    return self;
}

-(void) loadScene:(ccTime)delta
{
    // Decide which scene to load based on the TargetScenes enum.
    switch (targetScene)
    {
        case TargetSceneFirstScene:
            [[CCDirector sharedDirector] replaceScene:[FirstLayer scene]];
            break;
```

```
        case TargetSceneOtherScene:
            [[CCDirector sharedDirector] replaceScene:[SecondLayer scene]];
            break;

        default:
            // Always warn if an unspecified enum value was used
            NSAssert2(nil, @"%@: unsupported TargetScene %i", ↵
             NSStringFromSelector(_cmd), targetScene);
            break;
    }
}
```

Because the LoadingScene is derived from CCScene and requires a new parameter passed to it, it's no longer sufficient to call [CCScene node]. The sceneWithTargetScene method first allocates self, calls the initWithTargetScene method, and returns the new instance. The sceneWithTargetScene class method isn't strictly necessary but is good style. It makes the calling code shorter because you can avoid calling alloc. Also, most cocos2d and Cocoa classes have such initializing class methods, and many developers expect classes to offer them.

The init method of the LoadingScene class simply stores the target scene in a member variable, creates the "Loading…" label, and calls scheduleOnce with a 0.0f delay to ensure the loadScene method is called one frame after init.

Caution   Why not just call replaceScene right inside the init method? Two reasons. Reason number 1 is never call CCDirector's replaceScene in a node's init method. It will cause a crash. The Director can't cope with replacing a scene from a node that's currently being initialized. Reason number 2 is that you need to give the LoadingScene class time to draw itself—otherwise it won't be visible and it would appear as if the previous scene just froze.

The update method then uses a simple switch statement based on the provided TargetSceneTypes enum to determine which scene is to be replaced. The default switch contains an NSAssert, which always triggers when the default case is hit. This is good practice because you'll be editing and expanding this list several times, and if you forgot to update the switch statement with a new case, you'll be notified of that.

This is a very simple LoadingScene implementation that you can use in your own games. Simply extend the enum and switch statement with more target scenes or use the same target scene multiple times but with different transitions. But as I mentioned, don't overdo the transitions just because they're cool-looking.

Using the LoadingScene has an important effect regarding memory. Because you're replacing the existing scene with the lightweight LoadingScene and then replacing the LoadingScene with the actual target scene, you're giving the previous scene enough time to remove itself from memory. Effectively there's no longer any overlap of two potentially memory-hungry scenes at the same time, thereby reducing spikes in memory usage during scene changes.

Working with Multiple Layers

The project ScenesAndLayers02 illustrates how you can use multiple layers to scroll the contents of a game's objects layer while the content of the user interface layer, where it says "Here be your Game Scores" (see Figure 5-1), remains static. You'll learn how multiple layers can cooperate and react only to their own touch input, as well as how to access the various layers from any node.

Figure 5-1. *The ScenesAndLayers04 project. So far, so normal*

Start by putting the MultiLayerScene together in the init method. If you skim over the code in Listing 5-4, you'll barely notice anything different from what we've done so far.

Listing 5-4. Initializing the MultiLayerScene

```
-(id) init
{
    if ((self = [super init]))
    {
        sharedMultiLayerScene = self;

        // The GameLayer will be moved, rotated and scaled independently
        GameLayer* gameLayer = [GameLayer node];
        [self addChild:gameLayer z:1 tag:LayerTagGameLayer];
        gameLayerPosition = gameLayer.position;

        // The UserInterfaceLayer remains static and relative to the screen area.
        UserInterfaceLayer* uiLayer = [UserInterfaceLayer node];
        [self addChild:uiLayer z:2 tag:LayerTagUserInterfaceLayer];
    }

    return self;
}
```

> **Tip**   It's worth mentioning that I've started using enum values for tags, like
> LayerTagGameLayer. Doing so has the advantage over using numbers in that you can actually
> read whose tag it is instead of having to remember which layer had tag 7 assigned to it. It also
> shows that the actual tag values aren't important—what's important is that you use the same
> value consistently for the same node. Using a human-readable tag makes that task easier and less
> error prone. The same goes for action tags, of course.

You may have noticed the variable multiLayerSceneInstance and that it gets self assigned.
A bit strange, isn't it? What would that be good for? Recall how to create a singleton class
from Chapter 3. In this case, I'll turn the MultiLayerScene class into a singleton by giving other
classes the ability to access the current instance via a class method. See Listing 5-5 and, if
you want, compare it with Listing 3-1 to spot the differences. In this case the class is already
initialized—not initialized on demand within the sharedLayer method.

Listing 5-5. Turning the MultiLayerScene into a Semi-Singleton Object

```
static MultiLayerScene* sharedMultiLayerScene;

+(MultiLayerScene*) sharedLayer
{
  NSAssert(sharedMultiLayerScene! = nil, @"MultiLayerScene not available!");
  return sharedMultiLayerScene;
}

-(void) dealloc
{
  // MultiLayerScene will be deallocated now, you must set it to nil manually
  sharedMultiLayerScene = nil;
}
```

Simply put, the sharedMultiLayerScene is a static global variable that will hold the
current MultiLayerScene object during its lifetime. The static keyword denotes that the
sharedMultiLayerScene variable is accessible only within the implementation file it's defined in.
At the same time, it's not an instance variable; it lives outside the scope of any class. That's why
it is defined outside any method, and it can be accessed in class methods like sharedLayer.

When the layer is deallocated, the sharedMultiLayerScene variable is set back to nil to avoid
crashes, because the sharedMultiLayerScene variable would be pointing to an already released
object after the dealloc method has run. Variables declared static live on past the deallocation
of a class. Using static variables to store pointers to dynamically allocated classes requires
great care to ensure that the static variable always points to a valid object and is nil otherwise.

The reason for this semi-singleton is that you'll be using several layers, each with its own child
nodes, but you still need to somehow access the main layer. It's a very comfortable way to give
other layers and nodes of the current scene access to the main layer.

> **Caution** This semi-singleton works only if there is only ever one instance of MultiLayerScene allocated at any one time. It also can't be used to initialize MultiLayerScene, unlike a regular singleton class.

You grant access to the GameLayer and UserInterfaceLayer through property getter methods, for ease of use. The properties are defined in Listing 5-6, which shows the relevant part from MultiLayerScene.h.

Listing 5-6. Property Definitions for Accessing the GameLayer and UserInterfaceLayer

```
@property (readonly) GameLayer* gameLayer;
@property (readonly) UserInterfaceLayer* uiLayer;
```

The properties are defined as readonly, because we only ever want to retrieve the layers, never set them through the property. Their implementation in Listing 5-7 is a straightforward wrapper to the getChildByTag method, but they also perform a safety check just in case, verifying that the retrieved object is of the correct class.

Listing 5-7. Implementation of the Property Getters

```
-(GameLayer*) gameLayer
{
   CCNode* layer = [self getChildByTag:LayerTagGameLayer];
   NSAssert([layer isKindOfClass:[GameLayer class]], @"%@: not a GameLayer!", ⏎
     NSStringFromSelector(_cmd));
   return (GameLayer*)layer;
}
-(UserInterfaceLayer*) uiLayer
{
   CCNode* layer = [[MultiLayerScene sharedLayer] getChildByTag:LayerTagUILayer];
   NSAssert([layer isKindOfClass:[UserInterfaceLayer class]], @"%@: not a UILayer!", ⏎
     NSStringFromSelector(_cmd));
   return (UserInterfaceLayer*)layer;
}
```

This makes it easy to access the various layers from any node of the MultiLayerScene.

■ You can access the "scene" layer of MultiLayerScene:

```
MultiLayerScene* sceneLayer = [MultiLayerScene sharedLayer];
```

■ You can access the other layers through the scene layer:

```
GameLayer* gameLayer = [sceneLayer gameLayer];
UserInterfaceLayer* uiLayer = [sceneLayer uiLayer];
```

■ As an alternative, because of the @property definition, you can also use the dot accessor. Whichever you prefer is up to you, as long as you stick to it consistently. Technically and performance-wise, there's absolutely no difference.

```
GameLayer* gameLayer = sceneLayer.gameLayer;
UserInterfaceLayer* uiLayer = sceneLayer.uiLayer;
```

The UserInterfaceLayer and GameLayer classes both handle touch input, but independently. To achieve the correct results, you need to use TargetedTouchHandlers, and by using the priority parameter, you can make sure that the UserInterfaceLayer gets to look at a touch event before the GameLayer. The UserInterfaceLayer uses the isTouchForMe method to determine whether it should handle the touch, and it returns YES from the ccTouchBegan method if it did handle the touch. This keeps other targeted touch handlers from receiving this touch. Listing 5-8 illustrates the important bits of the touch event code for the UserInterfaceLayer.

Listing 5-8. Touch Input Processing Using TargetedTouchDelegate

```
// Register TargetedTouch handler with higher priority than GameLayer
-(void) registerWithTouchDispatcher
{
    [[CCDirector sharedDirector].touchDispatcher addTargetedDelegate:self
                                    priority:-1
                                swallowsTouches:YES];
}

// Checks if the touch location was in an area that this layer wants to handle as input.
-(BOOL) isTouchForMe:(CGPoint)touchLocation
{
    CCNode* node = [self getChildByTag:UILayerTagFrameSprite];
    return CGRectContainsPoint([node boundingBox], touchLocation);
}

-(BOOL) ccTouchBegan:(UITouch*)touch withEvent:(UIEvent *)event
{
    CGPoint location = [MultiLayerScene locationFromTouch:touch];
    BOOL isTouchHandled = [self isTouchForMe:location];
    if (isTouchHandled)
    {
        CCNode* node = [self getChildByTag:UILayerTagFrameSprite];
        NSAssert([node isKindOfClass:[CCSprite class]], @"node is not a CCSprite");

        // Highlight the UI layer's sprite for the duration of the touch
        ((CCSprite*)node).color = ccRED;

        // Access the GameLayer via MultiLayerScene.
        GameLayer* gameLayer = [MultiLayerScene sharedLayer].gameLayer;

        // Run Actions on GameLayer ... (code removed for clarity)
    }

    return isTouchHandled;
}
```

```
-(void) ccTouchEnded:(UITouch*)touch withEvent:(UIEvent *)event
{
    CCNode* node = [self getChildByTag:UILayerTagFrameSprite];
    NSAssert([node isKindOfClass:[CCSprite class]], @"node is not a CCSprite");
    ((CCSprite*)node).color = ccWHITE;
}
```

In registerWithTouchDispatcher, the UserInterfaceLayer registers itself as a targeted touch handler with a priority of −1. Because GameLayer uses the same code but with a priority of 0, the UserInterfaceLayer is the first layer to receive touch input.

In ccTouchBegan, the first thing to do is to check whether this touch is of relevance to the UserInterfaceLayer. The isTouchForMe method implements a simple "point in boundingBox" check via CGRectContainsPoint to see whether the touch began on the uiframe sprite. More useful methods are available in CGGeometry to test intersection, containing points, or equality. Refer to Apple's documentation to learn more about the CGGeometry methods (http://developer.apple.com/mac/library/documentation/GraphicsImaging/Reference/CGGeometry/Reference/reference.html).

If the touch location check determines that the touch is on the sprite, ccTouchBegan returns YES, signaling that this touch event was used and should not be processed by other layers with a targeted touch delegate of lower priority.

Only if the isTouchForMe check fails will the GameLayer receive the touch input and use it to scroll itself when the user moves a finger over the screen. You can compare GameLayer's input handling code in Listing 5-9.

Listing 5-9. GameLayer Receives the Remaining Touch Events and Uses Them to Scroll Itself

```
-(void) registerWithTouchDispatcher
{
    [[CCDirector sharedDirector].touchDispatcher addTargetedDelegate:self
                                priority:0
                                swallowsTouches:YES];
}
-(BOOL) ccTouchBegan:(UITouch*)touch withEvent:(UIEvent *)event
{
    lastTouchLocation = [MultiLayerScene locationFromTouch:touch];

    // Stop the move action so it doesn't interfere with the user's scrolling.
    [self stopActionByTag:ActionTagGameLayerMovesBack];

    // Always swallow touches, GameLayer is the last layer to receive touches.
    return YES;
}
-(void) ccTouchMoved:(UITouch*)touch withEvent:(UIEvent *)event
{
    CGPoint currentTouchLocation = [MultiLayerScene locationFromTouch:touch];
```

```
    // Take the difference of the current to the last touch location.
    CGPoint moveTo = ccpSub(lastTouchLocation, currentTouchLocation);

    // Then reverse to give the impression of moving the background
    moveTo = ccpMult(moveTo, -1);

    lastTouchLocation = currentTouchLocation;

    // Adjust the layer's position accordingly, and with it all child nodes.
    self.position = ccpAdd(self.position, moveTo);
}

-(void) ccTouchEnded:(UITouch*)touch withEvent:(UIEvent *)event
{
    // Move the game layer back to its designated position.
    CCMoveTo* move = [CCMoveTo actionWithDuration:1 position:gameLayerPosition];
    CCEaseIn* ease = [CCEaseIn actionWithAction:move rate:0.5f];
    ease.tag = ActionTagGameLayerMovesBack;
    [self runAction:ease];
}
```

Because GameLayer is the last layer to receive input, it doesn't need to do any isTouchForMe checks and simply swallows all touches.

Tip   Instead of handling user input in multiple layers, consider having one layer dedicated to all input handling. It can decide what to do, forward touches to other layers, and call methods on other nodes. The advantage of this is shorter and less error-prone input handling code, because all the decisions are made in one class instead of being spread out to a variety of classes.

The ccTouchMoved event calculates the difference between the previous and current touch location. It's then reversed by multiplying it by –1 to change the effect from moving the camera over the background to moving the background under the camera. If you have a hard time imagining what I mean by that, try the ScenesAndLayers02 project and then try it a second time, commenting out the moveTo=ccpMult(moveTo, -1); line. You'll notice the second time that every finger movement moves the layer in the opposite direction.

ccTouchEnded simply moves the layer back to its center position automatically when the user lifts the finger off the screen. Figure 5-2 shows this project in action with the whole GameLayer rotated and zoomed out. Every game object on the GameLayer abides by every movement, rotation, and scaling of the GameLayer automatically, whereas the UserInterfaceLayer always stays put.

Figure 5-2. The utility of multiple layers becomes clear once the GameLayer is zoomed out and rotated, with all its nodes adhering to the layer's behavior, while the UserInterfaceLayer on top remains in place, unaffected

How to Best Implement Levels

So far you've examined multiple scenes and multiple layers. Now you want to cover what—levels?

Well, the concept of levels is common in many games, so I don't think I need to explain that. What's much harder is deciding which approach best serves a level-based game. In cocos2d you can go either way—choosing a new scene for each level or using separate layers to manage multiple levels. Both have their uses, and which one to choose depends mostly on what purpose levels serve in your game.

Scenes as Levels

The most straightforward approach is to run each level as a separate scene. You can either create a new Scene class for each level or choose to initialize one common LevelScene class and pass as a parameter the level number or other information necessary to load the correct level data.

This approach works best if you have clearly separated levels and most everything that happens within a level is no longer relevant or needed after the player has progressed through that level. Maybe you keep the player's score and the number of lives left, but that's about it. The user interface is probably minimal, noninteractive, and purely informative without any interactive elements other than a pause button.

I imagine this approach works best for twitch-based action game levels.

Layers as Levels

Using separate layers in the same scene to load and display levels is an approach I recommend if you have a complex user interface that should not be reset when a level changes. You may even want to keep the player and other game objects in the exact same positions and states when changing levels.

You probably have a number of variables that keep the current game state and user interface settings, such as an inventory. It's more work to save and restore these game settings and reset all visual elements than to switch out one layer with another within the same scene.

This may be the ideal solution for a hidden object or adventure game, where you move from room to room, especially if you want to replace the level contents using an animation that moves in or out beneath the user interface.

The CCLayerMultiplex class may be the ideal solution for such an approach. It can contain multiple nodes, but only one is active at any given time. Listing 5-10 shows an example of using the CCLayerMultiplex class. The only drawback is that you can't transition between the layers. There's only one layer visible at a time, which makes any transition effects impossible.

Listing 5-10. Using the CCMultiplexLayer Class to Switch Between Multiple Layers

```
CCLayer* layer1 = [CCLayer node];
CCLayer* layer2 = [CCLayer node];
CCLayerMultiplex* mpLayer = [CCLayerMultiplex layerWithLayers:layer1, layer2, nil];

// Switches to layer2 but keeps layer1 as child of mpLayer.
[mpLayer switchTo:1];

// Switches to layer1, removes layer2 from mpLayer and releases its memory.
// After this call you must not switch back to layer2 (index: 1) anymore!
[mpLayer switchToAndReleaseMe:0];
```

CCLayerColor and CCLayerGradient

In the ScenesAndLayers project, so far the background is simply a black screen. You can see it when you scroll to the edge of the grassy background image or tap the "user interface" to have the GameLayer zoom out. To change the background color, cocos2d provides a CCLayerColor, which is added to the ScenesAndLayers02 project and works like this:

```
// Set background color to magenta. The most unobtrusive color imaginable.
CCLayerColor* colorLayer = [CCLayerColor layerWithColor:ccc4(255, 0, 255, 255)];
[self addChild:colorLayer];
```

In the same way, you can create a much more vibrant background using CCLayerGradient. It allows you to specify two colors between which cocos2d will smoothly interpolate. And you can adjust the gradient's direction.

```
CCLayerGradient* gradient = [CCLayerGradient layerWithColor:ccc4(0, 150, 255, 255)
                    fadingTo:ccc4(255, 150, 50, 255)
                    alongVector:CGPointMake(1.0f, 1.0f)];
[self addChild:gradient];
```

The gradient direction is given by a vector. In this case the vector points one unit to the right and one unit up, which has the gradient rotated at a perfect 45° angle. The vector points in the direction of the fadingTo color, which means the blue-ish color is at the bottom left whereas the orange-ish color is more to the upper right. To reverse the orientation of the color, you can either switch colors or simply reverse the signs of the vector.

Note that you can also change the width and height of CCLayerColor and CCLayerGradient and thus the area they fill with a color:

```
[gradientLayer changeWidth:400 height:200];
```

Subclassing Game Objects from CCSprite

Very often your game objects implement logic of their own. It makes sense to create a separate class for each type of game object. This could be your player character, various enemy types, bullets, missiles, platforms, and just about everything else that can be individually placed in a game's scene and needs to run logic of its own.

The question then is, where to subclass from?

A lot of developers choose the seemingly obvious route of subclassing CCSprite. I don't think that's a good idea. The relationship of subclassing is a "is a" relationship. Think closely: is your player character a CCSprite? Are all your enemy characters CCSprites?

At first the answer seems logical: of course they're sprites! That's what they use to display themselves. But wait a second. For all we know, game characters can also be characters in the literal sense. In Rogue-like games, your player character is an @. So, would that character be a CCLabelTTF then?

I think the confusion comes from CCSprite being the most widely used class to display anything onscreen. But the true relationship of your game characters to CCNode classes is a "has a" relationship. Your player class "has a" CCSprite that it uses to display itself, and it may even have to use multiple sprites for weapons, armor, and so on—and maybe even particle effects for running at high speed, a health bar, and a label to display the player's name in multiplayer modes.

The distinction becomes even clearer when you think of why you'd normally subclass the CCSprite class: in general, to add new features to the CCSprite class—for example, to have a CCSprite class that uses a CCRenderTexture to modify how it's displayed based on what's beneath it on the screen. Essentially you'd want to subclass CCSprite to change the behavior of the CCSprite class itself and how the sprite is displayed—not to add gameplay code to it.

Input handling, animating the player, collision detection, physics—in general, game logic. None of these things belongs to a CCSprite class because this code is about how an object behaves and how you interact with it, not how a sprite is drawn on the screen. Another way to look at it is to consider which of the code you add to a subclassed CCSprite is generally useful and usable by all sprites. Most game code is very specific to an individual game object, be it player, boss monster, or collectible item.

Consider the case where you want your player to have several visual representations that it should be able to switch to seamlessly. If the player needs to morph from one sprite to another using FadeIn/FadeOut actions, you're going to have to use two sprites—or if you want your game objects to appear on different parts of the screen at the same time, as in a game like Asteroids where the asteroid leaving the top of the screen should also show up partially at the bottom of the screen. You need two sprites to do this, and that's just one reason why composition (or aggregation) is preferable to subclassing (or inheritance). Inheritance causes tight coupling between classes, with changes to parent classes potentially introducing bugs and anomalies in subclasses. The deeper the class hierarchy, the more code will reside in base classes, which amplifies the problem.

Another good reason is that a game object encapsulates its visual representation. If the logic is self-contained, only the game object itself should ever change any of the CCNode properties, such as position, scale, rotation, or even running and stopping actions. One of the core problems many game developers face sooner or later is that their game objects are directly manipulated by outside influences. For example, you may inadvertently create situations where the scene's layer, the user interface, and the player object itself all change the player sprite's position. This is undesirable. You want all the other systems to notify the player object to change its position, giving the player object itself the final say about how to interpret these commands—whether to apply them, modify them, or ignore them.

Composing Game Objects Using CCSprite

Let's try this. Instead of creating a new class derived from a CCSprite class, create it from cocos2d's base class CCNode. Although you can also base your class on the Objective-C base class NSObject, it's easier to stick to CCNode because it's generally easier to work with CCNode as your base class within cocos2d. Otherwise you can't use convenience features like CCNode's scheduling methods.

I decided to turn the spiders in the ScenesAndLayers02 project into a class of their own. The class is simply called Spider. Listing 5-11 reveals the Spider class's header file.

Listing 5-11. The Spider Class Interface

```
#import "cocos2d.h"

@interface Spider : CCNode
{
 CCSprite* spiderSprite;
 int numUpdates;
}

+(id) spiderWithParentNode:(CCNode*)parentNode;
-(id) initWithParentNode:(CCNode*)parentNode;

@end
```

You can see that the CCSprite is added as a member variable to the class and is named spiderSprite. This is called *composition* because you compose the Spider class of a CCSprite used to display it and later, possibly, other objects (including additional CCSprite classes) and variables.

The Spider class in Listing 5-12 has a spiderWithParentNode class method to create an instance of the Spider class. Another convenient feature I added is to pass a parentNode as a parameter to the initWithParentNode method. By doing that, the Spider class can add itself to the node hierarchy by calling [parentNode addChild:self], which makes creating an instance of a Spider class a one-liner in GameLayer.m because you only need to write [Spider spiderWithParentNode:self].

On the other hand, the spiderSprite should be self-contained because it's created and managed by the Spider class. The spiderSprite is added via [self addChild:spiderSprite] to the Spider class and not the parentNode. Although you could do that, I don't recommend it because it breaks encapsulation. For one, the parentNode code could possibly remove the spiderSprite from its hierarchy, and moving the Spider object would no longer move the spiderSprite.

Listing 5-12. The Spider Class Implementation

```
#import "Spider.h"

@implementation Spider

// Static initializer, mimics cocos2d's memory allocation scheme.
+(id) spiderWithParentNode:(CCNode*)parentNode
{
  return [[self alloc] initWithParentNode:parentNode];
}

-(id) initWithParentNode:(CCNode*)parentNode
{
   if ((self = [super init]))
   {
      [parentNode addChild:self];

      CGSize screenSize = [CCDirector sharedDirector].winSize;

      spiderSprite = [CCSprite spriteWithFile:@"spider.png"];
      spiderSprite.position = CGPointMake(CCRANDOM_0_1() * screenSize.width, ↵
        CCRANDOM_0_1() * screenSize.height);
      [self addChild:spiderSprite];

      [self scheduleUpdate];
   }

    return self;
}

-(void) update:(ccTime)delta
{
    numUpdates++;
    if (numUpdates > 60)
    {
        numUpdates = 0;
        [spiderSprite stopAllActions];

        // Let the Spider move randomly.
        CGPoint moveTo = CGPointMake(CCRANDOM_0_1() * 200-100, ↵
          CCRANDOM_0_1() * 100-50);
        CCMoveBy* move = [CCMoveBy actionWithDuration:1 position:moveTo];
        [spiderSprite runAction:move];
    }
}

@end
```

The Spider class now uses its own game logic to move the spiders around on the screen. Granted, it won't win any prizes at this year's Artificial Intelligence Symposium; it's just meant as an example.

Up to this point you know you can receive touch input using CCLayer nodes, but in fact any class can receive touch input by using the CCTouchDispatcher class directly. Your class only needs to implement either the CCStandardTouchDelegate or CCTargetedTouchDelegate protocol. You add the appropriate protocol definition in angle brackets following the parent class in the @interface definition, as shown in Listing 5-13.

Listing 5-13. The CCTargetedTouchDelegate Protocol

```
@interface Spider : CCNode<CCTargetedTouchDelegate>
{
    ...
}
```

The implementation in Listing 5-14 highlights the changes made to the Spider class. The Spider class now reacts to targeted touch input. Whenever you tap a spider, it quickly moves away from your finger. (Contrary to common perceptions, spiders are usually more afraid of humans than the other way around, exceptions notwithstanding.)

The Spider class is registered with CCTouchDispatcher to receive input as a touch delegate, but this delegate association must also be removed on cleanup. Otherwise, the scheduler or touch dispatcher would still keep a reference to the Spider class even though it was released from memory, and that would likely cause a crash shortly thereafter. And it must be in the cleanup method, not dealloc, for the simple reason that the touch dispatcher holds (retains) a reference to your class. If you don't instruct the touch dispatcher to remove your class, it will never be deallocated.

Listing 5-14. The Changed Spider Class

```
-(id) initWithParentNode:(CCNode*)parentNode
{
    if ((self = [super init]))
    {
        ...

        // Manually add this class as receiver of targeted touch events.
        [[CCDirector sharedDirector].touchDispatcher addTargetedDelegate:self
                                        priority:-1
                                        swallowsTouches:YES];
    }

    return self;
}
-(void) cleanup
{
    // Must manually remove this class as touch input receiver!
    [[CCTouchDispatcher sharedDispatcher] removeDelegate:self];

    [super cleanup];
}
```

```
// Extract common logic into a separate method accepting parameters.
-(void) moveAway:(float)duration position:(CGPoint)moveTo
{
    [spiderSprite stopAllActions];
    CCMoveBy* move = [CCMoveBy actionWithDuration:duration position:moveTo];
    [spiderSprite runAction:move];
}

-(void) update:(ccTime)delta
{
    numUpdates++;
    if (numUpdates > 50)
    {
        numUpdates = 0;

        // Move at regular speed.
        CGPoint moveTo = CGPointMake(CCRANDOM_0_1() * 200-100, ↵
        CCRANDOM_0_1() * 100-50);
        [self moveAway:2 position:moveTo];
    }
}

-(BOOL) ccTouchBegan:(UITouch *)touch withEvent:(UIEvent *)event
{
    // Check if this touch is on the Spider's sprite.
    CGPoint touchLocation = [MultiLayerScene locationFromTouch:touch];
    BOOL isTouchHandled = CGRectContainsPoint([spiderSprite boundingBox], ↵
    touchLocation);
    if (isTouchHandled)
    {
        // Reset move counter.
        numUpdates = 0;

        // Move away from touch loation rapidly.
        CGPoint moveTo;
        float moveDistance = 40;
        float rand = CCRANDOM_0_1();

        // Randomly pick one of four corners to move away to.
        if (rand < 0.25f)
            moveTo = CGPointMake(moveDistance, moveDistance);
        else if (rand < 0.5f)
            moveTo = CGPointMake(-moveDistance, moveDistance);
        else if (rand < 0.75f)
            moveTo = CGPointMake(moveDistance, -moveDistance);
        else
            moveTo = CGPointMake(-moveDistance, -moveDistance);

        // Move quickly:
        [self moveAway:0.1f position:moveTo];
    }

    return isTouchHandled;
}
```

I decided to improve the move logic by extracting the functionality into a separate method. The straightforward way would have been to just copy the existing code from the update method to the ccTouchBegan method. However, copy-and-paste is evil. If you join the Cult of Programmology, be aware that it's considered a deadly sin to duplicate existing code.

Caution   Using copy-and-paste is very easy, and everyone knows how to do it, which makes it so tempting. But whenever you duplicate code, you duplicate the effort needed to change that code later. Consider the case where you duplicate the same sequence of actions ten times and you need to change the duration of the action sequence. You can't change it just once; you have to change it ten times now, and more importantly you have to test the change ten times because you might have forgotten to apply the change to one of the ten places. More code also means more chances of introducing a bug, and since this bug will possibly happen in only one of ten cases, it'll be harder to find as well. I've had the pleasure to work with a project that was 30,000 lines of pretty much identical code copied and pasted hundreds of times. All in one file. Don't go there, or I will haunt you! To avoid copy & paste style programming, I suggest to take the DRY principle to heart. DRY stands for "Don't repeat yourself," and the principle is described at http://c2.com/cgi/wiki?DontRepeatYourself.

Using methods to extract common functionality, exposing what needs to be flexible as parameters, is a very simple task. I hope that the moveAway method in Listing 5-14 illustrates my point well. It doesn't contain much code, but even the smallest amount of duplicated code increases the time you spend maintaining It.

The ccTouchBegan method takes the touch location and checks via the CGRectContainsPoint whether the touch location is inside the spider sprite's boundingBox. If so, it handles the touch and runs the code that lets the spider move away quickly in one of four directions.

In summary, using a CCNode as a base class for your game objects makes a few things more inconvenient at first glance. The benefits do become visible when you start creating larger projects, however, like when you're dealing with more than a dozen of classes for game objects. It's okay if you prefer to subclass CCSprite for now. But when you get more proficient—and more ambitious—please come back to this chapter and try this approach. It leads to a better code structure and more clearly separated boundaries and responsibilities of the individual game elements.

Curiously Cool CCNode Classes

Please remain seated as I walk you through a few more CCNode-derived classes that fulfill very specific purposes. They are CCProgressTimer, CCParallaxNode, and CCMotionStreak.

CCProgressTimer

In the ScenesAndLayers07 project, I've added a CCProgressTimer node to the
UserInterfaceLayer class. You can see how it cuts off chunks from a sprite in a radial fashion in
Figure 5-3.

Figure 5-3. The CCProgressTimer in action. I would say it's about 10 past 12

The progress timer class is useful for any kind of progress display, like a loading bar or the time
it takes an icon to become available again. Think of the action buttons in World of Warcraft and
their recast timer. The progress timer takes a sprite and, based on a percentage, displays only
part of it to visualize some kind of progress in your game. Listing 5-15 shows how to initialize the
CCProgressTimer node.

Listing 5-15. Initializing a CCProgressTimer Node

```
// Progress timer is a sprite that is only partially displayed
// to visualize some kind of progress.
CCSprite* fireSprite = [CCSprite spriteWithFile:@"firething.png"];
CCProgressTimer* timer = [CCProgressTimer progressWithSprite:fireSprite];
timer.type = kCCProgressTimerTypeRadial;
timer.percentage = 0;
[self addChild:timer z:1 tag:UILayerTagProgressTimer];

// The update is needed for the progress timer.
[self scheduleUpdate];
```

The timer type is from the CCProgressTimerType enum defined in CCProgressTimer.h. You can
choose between radial and rectangular progress timers—the latter requires the timer type to be
set to kCCProgressTimerTypeBar. There's one caveat: the timer doesn't update itself. You have to
change the timer's percentage value frequently to update the progress. That's why I called the
scheduleUpdate method in Listing 5-15. Listing 5-16 shows the implementation of the update
method that does the actual progressing.

Listing 5-16. The Implementation of the update Method

```
-(void) update:(ccTime)delta
{
    CCNode* node = [self getChildByTag:UILayerTagProgressTimer];
    NSAssert([node isKindOfClass:[CCProgressTimer class]], @"node is not a ↵
      CCProgressTimer");

    // Updates the progress timer
    CCProgressTimer* timer = (CCProgressTimer*)node;
    timer.percentage += delta * 10;
    if (timer.percentage >= 100)
    {
        timer.percentage = 0;
    }
}
```

You must frequently update the CCProgressTimer node's percentage property as needed—it won't progress by itself automatically. The progress here is simply the passing of time. Isn't that what games are all about?

CCParallaxNode

Parallaxing is an effect used in 2D games to give the impression of depth, created by using layered images that move at different rates. The images in the foreground move faster relative to the images in the background. Although you can't see the parallax effect in a static image, Figure 5-4 at least gives you a first impression of a background made up of individual layers. The clouds are at the very back; the mountains are in front of the clouds but behind the (ugly) trees. At the very bottom is the road where you might typically add a player character moving left and right along this scenery.

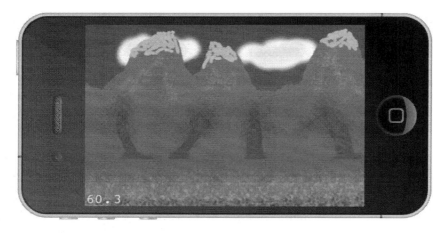

Figure 5-4. The CCParallaxNode lets you create an illusion of depth

> **Note** Why does parallaxing create the illusion of depth? Because our minds are trained to this effect. Imagine you're traveling in a car at high speed and looking out a side window. You notice the trees next to the road (closest to you) zipping by so fast you can hardly focus on a single one. Look a little further, and you'll see the barnyard passing you by at a seemingly much slower rater. Then look to the mountains at the horizon, and you'll hardly notice you're moving past them at all. This is the parallax effect in a three-dimensional world, where there are an infinite number of parallax layers. In a 2D game we have to (very roughly) simulate the same effect with around two to eight parallax layers. Each layer tries to fool your mind into thinking that it's a certain distance away from your viewpoint, simply because it's moving at certain speeds relative to other layers. It works surprisingly well.

Cocos2d has a specialized node you can use to create this effect. The code to create a CCParallaxNode in Listing 5-17 is found in the Parallax01 project.

Listing 5-17. The CCParallaxNode Requires a Lot of Setup Work, but the Results Are Worth It

```
// Load the sprites for each parallax layer, from background to foreground.
CCSprite* para1 = [CCSprite spriteWithFile:@"parallax1.png"];
CCSprite* para2 = [CCSprite spriteWithFile:@"parallax2.png"];
CCSprite* para3 = [CCSprite spriteWithFile:@"parallax3.png"];
CCSprite* para4 = [CCSprite spriteWithFile:@"parallax4.png"];

// Set the correct offsets depending on the screen and image sizes.
para1.anchorPoint = CGPointMake(0, 1);
para2.anchorPoint = CGPointMake(0, 1);
para3.anchorPoint = CGPointMake(0, 0.6f);
para4.anchorPoint = CGPointMake(0, 0);

CGPoint topOffset = CGPointMake(0, screenSize.height);
CGPoint midOffset = CGPointMake(0, screenSize.height / 2);
CGPoint downOffset = CGPointZero;
// Create a parallax node and add the sprites to it.
CCParallaxNode* paraNode = [CCParallaxNode node];
[paraNode addChild:para1
        z:1
    parallaxRatio:CGPointMake(0.5f, 0)
    positionOffset:topOffset];

[paraNode addChild:para2 z:2 parallaxRatio:CGPointMake(1, 0) positionOffset:topOffset];
[paraNode addChild:para3 z:4 parallaxRatio:CGPointMake(2, 0) positionOffset:midOffset];
[paraNode addChild:para4 z:3 parallaxRatio:CGPointMake(3, 0) positionOffset:downOffset];
[self addChild:paraNode z:0 tag:ParallaxSceneTagParallaxNode];

// Move the parallax node to show the parallaxing effect.
CCMoveBy* move1 = [CCMoveBy actionWithDuration:5 position:CGPointMake(-160, 0)];
CCMoveBy* move2 = [CCMoveBy actionWithDuration:15 position:CGPointMake(160, 0)];
CCSequence* sequence = [CCSequence actions:move1, move2, nil];
CCRepeatForever* repeat = [CCRepeatForever actionWithAction:sequence];
[paraNode runAction:repeat];
```

To create a CCParallaxNode, you first create the desired CCSprite nodes that make up the individual parallaxing images and then you have to properly position them on the screen. In this case, I chose to modify their anchor points instead because it was easier to align the sprites with the screen borders. You create the CCParallaxNode as you do any other node, but you add its children using a special initializer. With it you specify the parallaxRatio, which is a CGPoint used as a multiplier for any movement of the CCParallaxNode. In this case, the CCSprite para1 would move at half the speed, para2 at normal speed, para3 at double the speed of the CCParallaxNode, and so on.

Using a sequence of CCMoveBy actions, the CCParallaxNode is moved from left to right and back. Notice how the clouds in the background move slowest, and the trees and gravel in the foreground scroll by the fastest. This gives the illusion of depth.

> **Note** You can't modify the positions of individual child nodes once they're added to the CCParallaxNode. You can only scroll as far as the largest and fastest-moving image before the background shows through. You can see this effect if you modify the CCMoveBy actions to scroll a lot farther. You can increase the scrolling distance by adding more of the same sprites with the appropriate offsets. But if you require endless scrolling in one or both directions, you'll have to implement your own parallax system. In fact, this is what you're going to do in Chapter 7.

CCMotionStreak

CCMotionStreak is essentially a wrapper around CCRibbon. It causes the CCRibbon elements to more or less slowly fade out and disappear after you've drawn them. Try it in the ScenesAndLayers10 project and take a look at Figure 5-5 to get an impression how the fade-out effect might look.

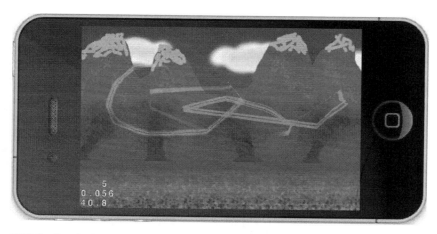

Figure 5-5. The CCMotionStreak class lets you draw a slowly fading line

As you can see in Listing 5-18, you can use CCMotionStreak to draw a slowly fading line, where a texture is stretched to the entire length of the line. For example, you can use this to create high-speed bullets that stretch out the faster they move. Listing 5-19 shows the code to create and move a CCMotionStreak node to the location of a touch. In the Parallax01 project, you can touch the screen to draw a motion streak line.

Listing 5-18. The CCMotionStreak Creates a Line Stroke Effect

```
-(void) resetMotionStreak
{
    // Removes the CCMotionStreak and creates a new one.
    [self removeChildByTag:ParallaxSceneTagMotionStreak cleanup:YES];
    CCMotionStreak* streak = [CCMotionStreak streakWithFade:0.99f
                                    minSeg:8
                                     width:32
                                     color:ccc3(255, 0, 255)
                           textureFilename:@"spider.png"];

    [self addChild:streak z:5 tag:ParallaxSceneTagMotionStreak];

    streak.blendFunc = (ccBlendFunc){GL_ONE, GL_ONE};
}

-(CCMotionStreak*) getMotionStreak
{
    CCNode* node = [self getChildByTag:ParallaxSceneTagMotionStreak];
    NSAssert([node isKindOfClass:[CCMotionStreak class]], @"not a CCMotionStreak");

    return (CCMotionStreak*)node;
}

-(CGPoint) locationFromTouch:(UITouch*)touch
{
    CGPoint touchLocation = [touch locationInView: [touch view]];
    return [[CCDirector sharedDirector] convertToGL:touchLocation];
}

-(void) moveMotionStreakToTouch:(UITouch*)touch
{
    CCMotionStreak* streak = [self getMotionStreak];
    streak.position = [self locationFromTouch:touch];
}

-(BOOL) ccTouchBegan:(UITouch*)touch withEvent:(UIEvent *)event
{
    [self moveMotionStreakToTouch:touch];
    // Always swallow touches.
    return YES;
}

-(void) ccTouchMoved:(UITouch*)touch withEvent:(UIEvent *)event
{
    [self moveMotionStreakToTouch:touch];
}
```

The fade parameter of CCMotionStreak determines how fast ribbon elements fade out—the smaller the number, the quicker they disappear, and the shorter the line will be. The minSeg parameter apparently modifies how many segments the line consists of at a minimum. However, it has almost no discernable effect, though it shouldn't be too low to prevent graphical glitches like gaps in the streak, nor too high (dozens or more) to avoid performance issues. The color is used to tint the texture.

Tip   If you're interested in creating a line-drawing game similar to Flight Control or Harbor Master, then CCMotionStreak won't help you draw the line—literally speaking, of course. The problem is that motion streak lines disappear quickly. Instead you should check out the Line-Drawing Game Starterkit that I'm selling: www.learn-cocos2d.com/store/line-drawing-game-starterkit. It contains all the code necessary to draw paths with your finger, drawing lines with OpenGL and having an object follow that line—among other things.

Summary

In this chapter, you learned more about scenes and layers—how and when to use them and for what. I explained why it's usually not a good idea to subclass game objects directly from CCSprite, and I showed you how to create a fully self-contained game object class that derives from CCNode instead and contains a sprite. That way it it's easier to extend should the object need multiple sprites, particle effects, or what have you.

Finally, you learned how to use some of the more specialized CCNode classes like CCProgressTimer, CCParallaxNode, and CCMotionStreak.

You now have enough knowledge about cocos2d to start creating more complex games, like the side-scrolling shooter I'm preparing you for. And with complex games come complex graphics, including animations. How to handle all these sprites efficiently, both in terms of memory and performance, is the topic of the next chapter.

Chapter 6

Sprites In-Depth

In this chapter, I focus on working with sprites. You can create sprites in numerous ways from individual image files and texture atlases. I also explain how to create and play sprite animations.

A *texture atlas* is a regular texture that contains more than one image. Often it's used to store all animation frames of a single character in one texture, but it's not limited to that—in fact, you can place any image into a texture atlas. The goal is to get as many images as possible into each texture atlas. To help create a texture atlas, you have a great tool to rely on called TexturePacker, also introduced in this chapter.

Sprite batching is a technique for speeding up the drawing of sprites. As the name implies, batching sprites allows the GPU to render all the sprites in one go (or in technical terms, in one draw call). It speeds up drawing identical sprites but is most effective when using a texture atlas. If you use a texture atlas along with sprite batching, you can draw all the images in that texture atlas in one draw call.

A *draw call* is the process of transmitting the necessary information to the graphics hardware in order to render a texture or parts of it. For example, when you're using the `spriteFromFile` method to create a `CCSprite` node, that sprite creates one draw call. The CPU overhead for issuing each draw call can add up so much that it can decrease the framerate, particularly when you want to display more sprites.

`CCSpriteBatchNode` functions like an extra layer to which you can add sprite nodes, as long as they all use the same texture. From then on, all the sprite children of the `CCSpriteBatchNode` are drawn with a single draw call. Effectively, the CPU tells the GPU what texture it should draw from but also passes a long list of frames and positions to the GPU so it can render a large number of sprites from that texture all by itself.

To summarize: sprite batching speeds up drawing identical sprites using the same texture and is most effective when using a texture atlas created with TexturePacker. The more sprites you display onscreen, and the bigger the sprites are (and particularly if they're rotated and scaled too), the greater the benefit of using sprite batching.

The lessons you'll learn in this chapter will become the foundation for the parallax-scrolling shoot-'em-up game in Chapters 7 and 8.

Retina Display

The newer iPhone models starting with iPhone 4 use a high-resolution display called the Retina display. It has a resolution of 960×640 pixels, which doubles the number of pixels in each direction (previous-generation devices were 480×320 pixels). The 3rd-generation iPad also has a Retina display, doubling the resolution of previous iPads from 1024×768 pixels to 2048×1536 pixels.

To make this distinction, the Retina display graphics are commonly called high-definition (HD) graphics, whereas non-Retina graphics are standard-definition (SD) graphics. HD is not limited to image files. Cocos2d also supports HD resolution versions of particle effects, bitmap fonts, and tilemaps. For each of those, you should create the HD version first and then downscale the asset for SD resolution.

Table 6-1 sketches a brief overview of the technical specifications of iOS devices. If you recall from Chapter 2, cocos2d 2.0 doesn't support 1st- and 2nd-generation devices, but they're in the table for comparison. One thing to keep in mind: the maximum texture size for iPad 2 has been increased to 4096×4096 but only if the device is running iOS 5.1 or newer.

Table 6-1. *The Technical Specifications of iOS Devices*

Device	Processor	Max. Texture Size	Display Resolution	Memory
iPhone	ARMv6	1024×1024	480×320	128MB
iPhone 3G	ARMv6	1024×1024	480×320	128MB
iPhone 3GS	Cortex-A8	2048×2048	480×320	256MB
iPhone 4	Cortex-A8 (Apple A4)	2048×2048	960×640	512MB
iPhone 4S	Cortex-A9 Dual-Core (Apple A5)	4096×4096	960×640	512MB
iPad	Cortex-A8 (Apple A4)	2048×2048	1024×768	256MB
iPad 2	Cortex-A9 Dual-Core (Apple A5)	2048×2048 4096×4096 iOS 5.1	1024×768	512MB
iPad 3	Cortex-A9 Dual-Core (Apple A5X)	4096×4096	2048×1536	1024MB

Cocos2d uses a resolution-independent coordinate system using points instead of pixels. One point is exactly one pixel on the SD devices, but one point is two pixels on Retina display devices. By writing all positions in points, the coordinates will remain the same on both devices! On a Retina iPhone the pixel resolution is 960×640, but the point resolution remains 480×320, which makes it a lot easier to develop apps for both Retina and non-Retina devices.

> **Tip** To set an object to an exact pixel location on Retina devices, express the points in fractions. For example, the point 100.5,99.5 will set an object to the pixel coordinate 201,200 on a Retina device. However, this also sets the pixel position to 100.5,99.5 on a non-Retina device, which is referred to as *subpixel* rendering. Because the image is not on an exact pixel location, some blending can occur, which can cause objects to not align properly or to leave gaps. Avoiding this kind of situation is generally recommended.

Cocos2d is smart when it comes to loading images. If your code has Retina support enabled, and the app is running on an iPhone or iPod touch device that has a Retina display, cocos2d tries to load a sprite with the -hd suffix first. When the app is running on a Retina iPad, cocos2d looks for the sprite with the –ipadhd suffix instead. These suffixes are not fixed and can be changed through the CCFileUtils singleton class, although I recommended sticking with the defaults as they're most widely supported by third-party tools. You can find this code with explanations in newly created cocos2d projects in the AppDelegate.m file:

```
// If the 1st suffix is not found and if fallback is enabled then fallback suffixes
// are searched. If no fallback file is found, it will try the file without any suffix.
// On iPad Retina  : "-ipadhd", fallback: "-ipad", second fallback: "-hd"
// On iPad         : "-ipad", fallback: "-hd"
// On iPhone Retina: "-hd"

CCFileUtils *sharedFileUtils = [CCFileUtils sharedFileUtils];
[sharedFileUtils setEnableFallbackSuffixes:NO];
[sharedFileUtils setiPhoneRetinaDisplaySuffix:@"-hd"];
[sharedFileUtils setiPadSuffix:@"-ipad"];
[sharedFileUtils setiPadRetinaDisplaySuffix:@"-ipadhd"];
```

So if you specify in your code to load a file named ship.png, then on a Retina display device it will first try to load ship-hd.png, and if that file doesn't exist or the device isn't a Retina display device, the SD image ship.png is loaded. On the iPad it tries to load the ship-ipad.png file and, if fallback is enabled, it also tries loading ship-hd.png before trying to load ship.png. On the Retina iPad cocos2d first looks for ship-ipadhd.png and, if fallback is enabled, it also tries ship-ipad.png, followed by ship-hd.png, before finally reverting to load ship.png.

Because those fallback mechanisms can be quite tricky to get right, I strongly recommend that you provide assets for all variants. For iPhone and iPod touch apps, you need standard resolution files with no suffix and the Retina resolution with the –hd suffix. For iPad apps, you will want to supply -ipad and -ipadhd assets. And for a universal app, you should really provide all four variants.

Of course, this makes sense only if all HD images have exactly twice the resolution of the SD ones. Otherwise, you'll notice that HD images which are not exactly twice the resolution are more or less offset when displayed in your app. In general, you should avoid using HD images, whose pixel resolution is not divisible by two without a remainder. If you do support Retina displays, you should create all images in HD resolution first and then scale them down by 50 percent and save them as the SD images. Upscaling SD images doesn't give you Retina display quality with more image details—that can only be done by the computer experts on *CSI*. The programming community at large is still perplexed about how they do that.

The nice thing about cocos2d's HD image support is that your game doesn't even have to know if it's running on a Retina device. The code is the same. The only thing you do need to care about is that you need two images instead of one, or four if you create a universal app.

In theory, it's also possible to use only HD graphics and then scale them down at runtime using the scale property of sprites to match the display resolution. But this comes with a major drawback: memory usage! The HD image in Figure 6-1 uses 128 KB of texture memory, assuming 32-bit color quality. The SD version consumes only 32 KB of memory. The non-Retina devices have generally half the memory (or less) than Retina devices and quickly run out of memory when you have them load textures taking up four times as much memory as needed.

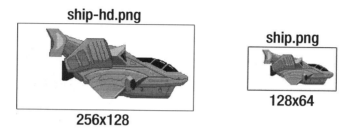

Figure 6-1. *Sprites in two resolutions for HD (Retina) and SD (non-Retina) displays*

Displaying a scaled-down version of an image also incurs a performance penalty because four times more pixels must be processed each frame to display a scaled-down version of the image. On the other hand, upscaling standard resolution images for Retina devices simply provides no visual improvement, so you could just as well disable Retina mode in cocos2d altogether and simply provide only SD assets.

To enable support for Retina display resolutions in cocos2d, you must call the CCDirector method enableRetinaDisplay. Typically this is already done as part of the AppDelegate initialization code, so you only need to change this if you absolutely don't plan to have Retina assets in your app and want to disable Retina mode.

```
if (![director enableRetinaDisplay:YES])
{
    CCLOG(@"Retina Display Not supported");
}
```

Caution   If you enable Retina display support, you should supply HD images for all your sprites, bitmap fonts, particle effects, and so on. If you don't, the resulting effect will be that your app looks normal on SD devices, but all the visuals that don't have an HD version will be drawn in half the size on Retina displays. Always test your app on standard and Retina resolution devices. If you don't have both, you can also change the iOS Simulator via Hardware ➤ Device to emulate a Retina device. Note that iOS Simulator set to emulate a Retina device runs a lot slower than usual. And the iPad Retina Simulator may even be unplayable if the 2048x1536 window doesn't fit entirely on your screen.

CCSpriteBatchNode

Every time a texture is drawn on the screen, the graphics hardware has to prepare the rendering, render the graphics, and clean up after rendering. There's an inherent overhead caused by starting and ending the rendering of a single texture. You can alleviate it by letting the graphics hardware know that you have a group of sprites that should be rendered using the same texture. In that case, the graphics hardware will perform the preparation and cleanup steps only once for a group of sprites.

Figure 6-2 shows an example of this kind of batch rendering. You can see the hundreds of identical bullets on the screen. If you rendered them each one at a time, your framerate would drop by at least 15 percent in this case, and by a lot more if the bullet texture were larger and the sprites were rotated and scaled. With a CCSpriteBatchNode, you can keep your app running at top speed. To test the effect of sprite batching, try out the Kobold2D template project named Sprite-Performance and read my blog post about sprite batch performance here: www.learn-cocos2d.com/2011/09/cocos2d-spritebatch-performance-test.

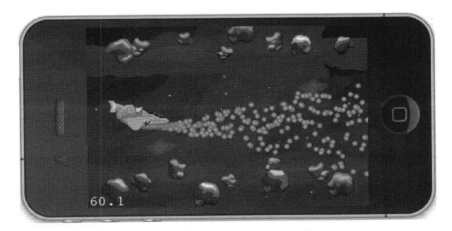

Figure 6-2. *Drawing many CCSprite nodes using the same texture is more efficient when they're added to a CCSpriteBatchNode*

As a refresher, here's how to create a CCSprite the normal way:

```
CCSprite* sprite = [CCSprite spriteWithFile:@"bullet.png"];
[self addChild:sprite];
```

Listing 6-1 changes the creation of the same CCSprite to use a CCSpriteBatchNode instead. Of course, just adding one CCSprite to it won't give you any benefit, so I'll be adding a number of sprites using the same texture to the CCSpriteBatchNode.

Listing 6-1. Creating Multiple CCSprites and Adding Them to a CCSpriteBatchNode to Render Them Faster

```
CCSpriteBatchNode* batch = [CCSpriteBatchNode batchNodeWithFile:@"bullet.png"];
[self addChild:batch];

for (int i = 0; i < 100; i++)
{
    CCSprite* bullet = [CCSprite spriteWithFile:@"bullet.png"];
    [batch addChild:bullet];
}
```

Notice that in Listing 6-1 the CCSpriteBatchNode takes a file as an argument, even though the CCSpriteBatchNode itself isn't displayed. It's more like a CCLayer in that regard, except that you can add only CCSprite nodes to it. The reason it takes an image file as an argument is that all CCSprite nodes added to the CCSpriteBatchNode must use the same texture. If you accidentally add a sprite with a different texture, or a non-sprite node to the batch node, you'll see one of these two error messages in the Debug Console:

```
'NSInternalInconsistencyException', reason: 'CCSprite is not using the same texture id'
'NSInternalInconsistencyException', reason: 'CCSpriteBatchNode only supports CCSprites as
children'
```

When to Use CCSpriteBatchNode

You can use CCSpriteBatchNode whenever you display two or more CCSprites of the same kind. The more CCSprites you can group together, the greater the benefit of using CCSpriteBatchNode.

There are limitations, though. Because all the CCSprite nodes are added to the CCSpriteBatchNode, all CCSprite nodes added to it will be drawn at the same z-order (depth). If your game is supposed to have bullets flying behind and in front of enemies, you would have to use two CCSpriteBatchNodes to group the bullet sprites of the lower and the higher z-order independently.

Another drawback is that all CCSprites added to the CCSpriteBatchNode need to use the same texture. But that also means the CCSpriteBatchNode becomes most important when you're using a texture atlas. With a texture atlas, you're not limited to drawing only one image; instead, you can add a number of different images to the same texture atlas and draw all of them using the same CCSpriteBatchNode—speeding up the rendering of all the images of the same texture atlas.

If all your game's images could fit into the same texture atlas, you could compose almost your entire game using just a single CCSpriteBatchNode (although this would be the rare exception).

Think of the CCSpriteBatchNode as similar to a CCLayer, except that it only accepts CCSprite nodes using the same texture. With that mind-set, I'm sure you'll find the right places to use the CCSpriteBatchNode.

The Sprites01 Demo Project

This project demonstrates how to use CCSpriteBatchNode. Let's take the first steps toward the scrolling shoot-'em-up game in Chapters 7 and 8. Because developers often start by using just the CCSprite node and then improve the code to support CCSpriteBatchNode, I found it interesting to show this process exactly and how the code changes along the way.

The project uses two classes—Ship and Bullet, both derived from CCSprite—to illustrate how you can change a project from using regular CCSprite objects to a CCSpriteBatchNode.

A Common and Fatal Mistake

Before I begin, I want you to know about a common trap developers new to Objective-C can quickly find themselves in. It's easy to make this mistake but hard to figure out the cause and how to fix it. I fell into this trap myself once. Take a look at Listing 6-2; do you see what's wrong with this code?

Listing 6-2. A Commonly Made Fatal Mistake When Subclassing CCSprite (or Other Classes for That Matter)

```
-(id) init
{
    if ((self = [super initWithFile:@"ship.png"]))
    {
        [self scheduleUpdate];
    }
    return self;
}
```

No, it's not about scheduleUpdate; that's just to throw you off guard. The problem lies in the fact that the -(id) init method is the default initializer, which is eventually called by any other specialized initializer like initWithFile. Can you imagine now what's wrong with the code?

Well, initWithFile will eventually call the default initializer, -(id) init. Then, because this class's implementation overrides it, it will call [super initWithFile: ..] again. Repeat *ad infinitum*.

The solution is very simple. As shown in Listing 6-3, just give the initializer method a different name—something other than -(id) init.

Listing 6-3. Fixing the Infinite Loop Caused by the Code in Listing 6-2

```
-(id) initWithShipImage
{
    if ((self = [super initWithFile:@"ship.png"]))
    {
        [self scheduleUpdate];
    }
    return self;
}
```

Bullets Without a SpriteBatch

The Sprites01 project creates a new CCSprite for each Bullet. Notice how in Listing 6-4 the ship sprite is adding the bullets to its parent node. It doesn't add them to itself—otherwise, all the flying bullets would be positioned relative to the ship and mimic the ship's movement.

Listing 6-4. The Ship Shooting the Bullets

```
-(void) update:(ccTime)delta
{
    // Keep creating new bullets
    Bullet* bullet = [Bullet bulletWithShip:self];

    // Add the bullets to the ship's parent
    CCNode* gameScene = [self parent];
    [gameScene addChild:bullet z:0 tag:GameSceneNodeTagBullet];
}
```

The Bullet sprites are added to the ship's parent for the simple reason that adding them to the ship would position all flying bullets at an offset to the ship. This means that if the ship were to move—if it didn't, this would be a really boring game—all the flying bullets would change their positions relative to the ship, as if they were somehow attached to it.

> **Tip**   The bullets are all added with the same z-order, 0. All nodes using the same z-order are drawn in the order in which they're added to the scene hierarchy, meaning the node added last will be drawn in front of all other previously added nodes with the same z-order.
>
> In addition, all bullets use the same tag. Tags don't need to be unique, and sometimes it can be helpful to use a tag to denote group membership of nodes. You could then loop through all children of a node and perform different code based on the node tag.

The bullets also use an update method to update their position and to remove themselves at some point. Although sprites aren't drawn if they're outside the screen, they still consume memory and CPU power, so it's good practice to remove any stray objects that leave the screen area at some point in time. In this case, you simply check the bullet's position against the right-hand side of the screen, as shown in Listing 6-5.

Listing 6-5. Moving and Removing the Bullets

```
-(void) update:(ccTime)delta
{
    // update position of the bullet
    // multiply the velocity by the time since the last update was called
    // this ensures same bullet velocity even if framerate drops
    self.position = ccpAdd(self.position, ccpMult(velocity, delta));

    // delete the bullet if it leaves the screen
    if (self.position.x > outsideScreen)
    {
        [self removeFromParentAndCleanup:YES];
    }
}
```

The bullet position is updated by multiplying its velocity (speed and direction given by a CGPoint) and then adding the result to the bullet's position. The velocity simply determines how many pixels to move in each direction every second. Multiplying the velocity by the time gives the distance the bullet traveled. The reason for using the delta time when updating the position is that this makes the movement of the bullets independent from the framerate. If you don't do that for all moving objects, your game would slow down proportionally with a decreasing framerate — for example, when there's a boss fight with lots of sprites on the screen.

Calculating the movement in the aptly named update method update is much more effective than using CCMoveTo or CCMoveBy actions in this case. It avoids some overhead and the problem that actions run for a given duration. If the ship were to move closer to the right-hand side of the screen, the move actions would cause the bullets to move more slowly because they need to travel a shorter distance in the same time.

> **Tip**   You can have the CCMoveTo and CCMoveBy actions move a node at a fixed speed to any position. To do so, you would first have to calculate the distance between the node's current position to its desired destination by using the ccpDistance method. Then divide the distance by the desired speed (in pixels per frame). This works well enough, but the drawback is that ccpDistance calls the sqrtf (square root) method, which is computationally expensive. You should avoid doing this regularly. For something as simple as updating node positions every frame, avoid using move actions for continuously moving nodes.

Introducing the CCSpriteBatchNode

In the Sprites01 project, I decided to add the CCSpriteBatchNode for bullets to the GameScene itself, because bullets aren't supposed to be added to the Ship class. Because the Ship class has no access to the GameScene, I also needed to add the singleton accessor sharedGameLayer to allow the ship to get to the CCSpriteBatchNode, as shown in Listing 6-6.

Listing 6-6. The GameScene Gets a CCSpriteBatchNode for Bullets and Accessors for the Ship Class

```
static GameScene* sharedGameLayer;
+(GameScene*) sharedGameLayer
{
    NSAssert(sharedGameLayer ! = nil, @" instance not yet initialized!");
    return sharedGameLayer;
}

-(id) init
{
    if ((self = [super init]))
    {
        sharedGameLayer = self;

        . . .

        CCSpriteBatchNode* batch = [CCSpriteBatchNode batchNodeWithFile:@"bullet.png"];
        [self addChild:batch z:1 tag:GameSceneNodeTagBulletSpriteBatch];
    }
    return self;
}
```

```
-(void) dealloc
{
    sharedGameLayer = nil;
}
-(CCSpriteBatchNode*) bulletSpriteBatch
{
    CCNode* node = [self getChildByTag:GameSceneNodeTagBulletSpriteBatch];
    NSAssert([node isKindOfClass:[CCSpriteBatchNode class]], @"not a SpriteBatch");
    return (CCSpriteBatchNode*)node;
}
```

> **Caution**   I know this singleton and the additional accessor method `bulletSpriteBatch` may not be to everyone's liking. Why don't you simply pass the `CCSpriteBatchNode` as a pointer to the `Ship` class, either in the initializer or via a property?
>
> One reason is that `Ship` doesn't own the bullet sprite batch, and therefore it shouldn't keep a reference to it. Moreover, if the `Ship` class also holds a reference to the sprite batch, it could cause your whole scene to not be deallocated if you're not careful. Nodes should never hold references to nodes that are not children or grandchildren of itself.
>
> A node that holds a reference to its parent or any of its grandparents would cause the parent to not get deallocated. And the child nodes won't be deallocated unless its parent gets deallocated. That means a node holding a strong reference to one of its parents will create a so-called retain cycle. This vicious circle causes a memory leak and potentially weird side effects because some nodes may remain in memory. Therefore it's good practice to monitor the execution of a scene's dealloc method. Whenever it doesn't get called when changing scenes, you should investigate the cause.,

Now the `Ship` class can add the bullets to the sprite batch directly using the `sharedGameLayer` and `bulletSpriteBatch` accessors, as shown in Listing 6-7.

Listing 6-7. GameScene Gets a CCSpriteBatchNode for Bullets and Accessors for the Ship Class

```
-(void) update:(ccTime)delta
{
    Bullet* bullet = [Bullet bulletWithShip:self];
    [[[GameLayer sharedGameLayer] bulletSpriteBatch] addChild:bullet
                                               z:0
                                             tag:GameSceneNodeTagBullet];
}
```

Optimizations

While you're optimizing this code, why not get rid of the unnecessary memory allocations and releases caused by the `Bullet` class? Allocating and releasing memory is an expensive operation you should aim to minimize during game play. A common solution is to instantiate a fixed number of objects when the game starts and then simply enable or disable/hide the objects as needed. This is called *object pooling*.

Because you can safely define an upper limit for the number of bullets that can be on the screen at the same time, bullets are an excellent candidate for pooling to avoid allocating and releasing bullets during game play. Because the bullets share the same texture, the additional memory used by having a greater number of bullets that resides in memory at all times is negligible. Listing 6-8 shows the changes to GameScene's init method implemented in the Sprites01 project.

Listing 6-8. Creating a Reasonable Number of Bullet Sprites Up Front Avoids Unnecessary Memory Allocations During Game Play

```
CCSpriteBatchNode* batch = [CCSpriteBatchNode batchNodeWithFile:@"bullet.png"];
[self addChild:batch z:0 tag:GameSceneNodeTagBulletSpriteBatch];

// Create a number of bullets up front and reuse them whenever necessary.
for (int i = 0; i < 400; i++)
{
    Bullet* bullet = [Bullet bullet];
    bullet.visible = NO;
    [batch addChild:bullet];
}
```

All the bullets are made invisible because you don't use them just yet. The GameScene class gets a new method in Listing 6-9 that allows it to shoot bullets from the ship by reactivating inactive bullets in sequence. This process is often called *object pooling*. Shooting is now rerouted through the GameScene because it contains the CCSpriteBatchNode used for the bullets. Once an inactive bullet has been selected, it's instructed to shoot itself.

Listing 6-9. Shooting Is Now Rerouted

```
-(void) shootBulletFromShip:(Ship*)ship
{
    CCArray* bullets = [self.bulletSpriteBatch children];

    CCNode* node = [bullets objectAtIndex:nextInactiveBullet];
    NSAssert([node isKindOfClass:[Bullet class]], @"not a bullet!");

    Bullet* bullet = (Bullet*)node;
    [bullet shootBulletFromShip:ship];

    nextInactiveBullet++;
    if (nextInactiveBullet >= bullets.count)
    {
        nextInactiveBullet = 0;
    }
}
```

By keeping the reference counter nextInactiveBullet, each shot uses the sprite-batched bullet from that index. Once all bullets have been shot once, the index is reset. This works fine as long as the number of bullets in the pool is always greater than the maximum number of bullets on the screen.

The Bullet class's shoot method in Listing 6-10 only performs the necessary steps to reinitialize a bullet, including rescheduling its update selector by first unscheduling the update selector in case it's already running. Most importantly, the Bullet is set to be visible again. Its position and velocity are also reset. The Bullet class's shoot method simply resets the relevant variables such as position and velocity and then sets the bullet to be visible. Once the bullet has reached the end of its lifetime, it's simply set to not be visible again.

Listing 6-10. The Bullet Class's Shoot Method Reinitializing a Bullet

```
-(void) shootBulletFromShip:(Ship*)ship
{
    float spread = (CCRANDOM_0_1() - 0.5f) * 0.5f;
    velocity = CGPointMake(1, spread);

    outsideScreen = [CCDirector sharedDirector].winSize.width;

    self.position = CGPointMake(ship.position.x+ship.contentSize.width * 0.5f, ↵
        ship.position.y;
    self.visible = YES;

    [self scheduleUpdate];
}
-(void) update:(ccTime)delta
{
    self.position = ccpAdd(self.position, velocity);

    if (self.position.x > outsideScreen)
    {
        self.visible = NO;
        [self unscheduleUpdate];
    }
}
```

Sprite Animations the Hard Way

Now brace yourself. I'd like to show you how sprite animations work. Figure 6-3 shows the ship's animation frames. Remember that you have the entire animation in both HD and SD resolution.

Figure 6-3. The ship's animation—five frames with different flames

Sprite animations are another good reason to use CCSpriteBatchNode, because you can put all animation frames into the same texture to conserve memory. It's quite a bit of code actually, as you'll see in Listing 6-11 and in the Sprites01 project. After that, I show you how to create the same animation using a texture atlas, which cuts down the amount of code you have to write.

Listing 6-11. Adding an Animation to the Ship Without Using a Texture Atlas Requires Quite a Bit of Code

```
// Load the ship's animation frames as textures and create a sprite frame
NSMutableArray* frames = [NSMutableArray arrayWithCapacity:5];
```

```
for (int i = 0; i<5; i++)
{
    // Create a texture for the animation frame
    NSString* file = [NSString stringWithFormat:@"ship-anim%i.png", i];
    CCTexture2D* texture = [[CCTextureCache sharedTextureCache] addImage:file];

    // The whole image should be used as the animation frame
    CGSize texSize = texture.contentSize;
    CGRect texRect = CGRectMake(0, 0, texSize.width, texSize.height);

    // Create a sprite frame from the texture
    CCSpriteFrame* frame = [CCSpriteFrame frameWithTexture:texture rect:texRect];
    [frames addObject:frame];
}

// Create an animation object from all the sprite animation frames
CCAnimation* anim = [CCAnimation animationWithSpriteFrames:frames delay:0.08f];

// Run the animation by using the CCAnimate action and loop it with CCRepeatForever
CCAnimate* animate = [CCAnimate actionWithAnimation:anim];
CCRepeatForever* repeat = [CCRepeatForever actionWithAction:animate];
[self runAction:repeat];
```

All that just to create a sprite animation with five frames? I'm afraid so. I'll walk you through the code backward this time, which may explain the setup better. At the very end you're using a CCAnimate action to play an animation. In this case, you're also using a CCRepeatForever action to loop the animation.

The CCAnimate action uses a CCAnimation object (which is a container for animation frames) that defines the delay between each individual frame. In many cases, you'll later want to refer to a previously created animation. For that purpose, cocos2d has a CCAnimationCache class that stores CCAnimation instances by name, as shown in Listing 6-12. Using the CCAnimationCache, you can access a particular animation by name later.

Listing 6-12. *The CCAnimationCache Class Can Store Animations for You, Which Can Be Retrieved by Name*

```
CCAnimation* anim = [CCAnimation animationWithSpriteFrames:frames delay:1];

// Store the animation in the CCAnimationCache
[[CCAnimationCache sharedAnimationCache] addAnimation:anim name:@"move"];

// Sometime later: retrieve the move animation from the CCAnimationCache
CCAnimation* move = [[CCAnimationCache sharedAnimationCache] animationByName:@"move"];
```

Going back to Listing 6-11, notice the for loop. This is where it gets complicated. The CCAnimation class must be initialized with an NSArray containing CCSpriteFrame objects. A *sprite frame* consists only of a reference to a texture and a rectangle that defines the area of the texture that should be drawn. The texture rectangle equals the texture's contentSize property—in other words, the size of the actual image contained in the texture. Keep in mind that the texture can be bigger than the image it contains because textures can only have dimensions that are powers of two.

Now, unfortunately the CCSpriteFrame doesn't take an image filename as input; it only accepts existing CCTexture2D objects. You create the texture using the CCTextureCache singleton's addImage method, normally used to preload images as textures into memory without having to create a CCSprite or other object. You construct the filename using NSString's stringWithFormat method, which allows you to use the loop variable i to be appended to the filename, instead of having to write out all five filenames.

To recap, from top to bottom, here's how you can create and run a sprite animation:

1. Create NSMutableArray.

2. For each animation frame:

    a. Create a CCTexture2D for each image.

    b. Create a CCSpriteFrame using the CCTexture2D.

    c. Add each CCSpriteFrame to the NSMutableArray.

3. Create a CCAnimation using the frames in the NSMutableArray.

4. Optionally, add the CCAnimation to the CCAnimationCache with a name.

5. Use a CCAnimate action to play the animation.

Shh, calm down—no need to take that Valium. If you pack your animation frames into a texture atlas, things will get a bit easier and more efficient at the same time. More helpful is to encapsulate all this code into a helper method and stick to a naming convention for your animation files.

Animation Helper Category

Because the code to create the animation frames and the animation is common to all animations, you should consider encapsulating this into a helper method. I've done so by adding the CCAnimationHelper class to the project Sprite01. Instead of using static methods, I extend the CCAnimation class using an Objective-C feature called a *category*. Categories offer a way to add methods to an existing class without having to modify the original class. The only downside is that with a category you can't add member variables to the class; you can only add methods. The following code is the @interface for the CCAnimation category, which I informally named Helper:

```
@interface CCAnimation (Helper)
+(CCAnimation*) animationWithFile:(NSString*)name
                  frameCount:(int)frameCount
                       delay:(float)delay;
@end
```

The @interface for an Objective-C category uses the same name as the class it extends and adds a category name within parentheses. The category name is like a variable name and thus cannot contain spaces or other characters you can't use in variables—punctuation characters, for example. The @interface also must not contain curly brackets, because adding member variables to a category isn't possible or allowed.

The actual @implementation for the CCAnimation category uses the same schema as the @interface by appending the category name in parentheses after the class name. Everything else is just like writing regular class methods; in this case, my extension method is named animationWithFile and takes the filename, the number of frames, and the animation delay as input:

```
@implementation CCAnimation (Helper)

// Creates an animation from single files
+(CCAnimation*) animationWithFile:(NSString*)name
                    frameCount:(int)frameCount
                         delay:(float)delay
{
    // Load the animation frames as textures and create the sprite frames
    NSMutableArray* frames = [NSMutableArray arrayWithCapacity:frameCount];
    for (int i = 0; i< frameCount; i++)
    {
        // Assuming all animation files are named "nameX.png"
        NSString* file = [NSString stringWithFormat:@"%@%i.png", name, i];
        CCTexture2D* texture = [[CCTextureCache sharedTextureCache] addImage:file];

        // Assuming that image file animations always use the whole image
        CGSize texSize = texture.contentSize;
        CGRect texRect = CGRectMake(0, 0, texSize.width, texSize.height);
        CCSpriteFrame* frame = [CCSpriteFrame frameWithTexture:texture rect:texRect];
        [frames addObject:frame];
    }

    // Return a CCAnimation object using all the sprite animation frames
    return [CCAnimation animationWithSpriteFrames:frames delay:delay];
}
@end
```

Here's how the naming convention comes into play. The Ship's animations have the base name ship-anim followed by a consecutive number starting with 0 and ending in the .png file extension. For example, the filenames for the Ship's animation are named ship-anim0.png through ship-anim4.png. If you create all your animations using that naming scheme, you can use the preceding CCAnimation extension method for all your animations.

Tip   I can't help but notice that a lot of developers and artists have a habit of consecutively naming files with a fixed number of digits, by adding leading zeros where necessary. For example, you might be tempted to name your files my-anim0001 through my-anim0024. I think this habit goes back to the good ol' computer operating systems that were incapable of natural sorting and thus incorrectly sorted filenames with consecutive numbers, with file1 followed by file10 and then file2. Those days are long gone, and you'll actually make it harder for the programmer to load files named like that in a for loop, because you'll have to take into account how many leading zeros should be prepended. There is a nice formatting shortcut, %03i, to prepend zeros so that the number is always at least three digits long. However, I think it's better in our modern world to just name filenames consecutively without prepending any leading zeros. You gain a little bit of simplicity and peace of mind.

This greatly simplifies the code used to create an animation from individual files:

```
// The whole shebang is now encapsulated into a Category extension method
CCAnimation* anim = [CCAnimation animationWithFile:@"ship-anim"
                    frameCount:5
                    delay:0.08f];
```

Essentially this cuts down the number of lines from nine to just this one. As for the filename, you only need to pass the base name of your animation—in this case `ship-anim`. The helper method adds the consecutive numbers based on the `frameCount` parameter and also appends the `.png` file extension. You can also use the base name for the animation as the name for the animation when you add it to the `CCAnimationCache` so you don't have to remember alternate names for the same animation. Previously I named the ship's animation `move`. Now it's called `ship-anim`, in line with the filenames. You could store and access the animation from the `CCAnimationCache` by using its base name like so:

```
NSString* shipAnimName = @"ship-anim";

CCAnimation* anim = [CCAnimation animationWithFile:shipAnimName
                    frameCount:5
                    delay:0.08f];
[[CCAnimationCache sharedAnimationCache] addAnimation:anim name:shipAnimName];

// sometime later:
CCAnimation* shipAnim = [shipSprite animationByName:shipAnimName];
```

The `animationWithFile` helper method makes two assumptions: animation image filenames are consecutively numbered beginning with 0, and the files must have the `.png` file extension. It's up to you whether to stick to this exact naming convention or change it to accommodate your own needs. For example, you might find it more convenient to start numbering your animations starting with 1 instead of 0. In that case, you'll have to change the `for` loop so that the name string is formatted with `i + 1`. The important part is to stick to whatever naming convention you choose to make your life (and your code) easier.

You should take away three things from this:

- Encapsulate commonly used code by defining your own methods.
- Use Objective-C categories to add methods to existing classes.
- Define resource filenaming conventions to support your code.

Working with Texture Atlases

Texture atlases help conserve precious memory and speed up the rendering of sprites. Because a texture atlas is nothing but a big texture, you can render all the images it contains using a `CCSpriteBatchNode`, thus reducing the draw call overhead. Using texture atlases is a win-win for both memory usage and performance.

What Is a Texture Atlas?

So far, for all the sprites used, I simply loaded the image file they need to display. Internally, this image becomes the sprite's texture, which contains the image, but the texture width and height always have to be a power of two—for example, 1024×128 or 256×512. The texture size is increased automatically to conform to this rule, possibly taking up more memory than the image size would suggest. For example, an image with dimensions of 140×600 becomes a texture with dimensions of 256×1024 in memory. This texture is wasting a lot of precious memory, and the amount of wasted memory becomes significant if you have several such images and you load them each into individual textures.

That's where the texture atlas comes in. It's simply an image that is already aligned to a power-of-two dimension and contains multiple images. Each image contained in the texture atlas has a sprite frame that defines the rectangle area where the image is within the texture atlas. In other words, a sprite frame is a CGRect structure that defines which part of the texture atlas should be used as the sprite's image. These sprite frames are saved in a separate .plist file so that cocos2d can render very specific images from a large texture atlas texture.

Introducing TexturePacker

Packing images into a texture atlas and noting the rectangular sprite frames they occupy would be a monumental task if it weren't for TexturePacker, a 2D sprite-packing tool (shown in Figure 6-4). The TexturePacker app is available in both free and paid versions and can be downloaded from www.texturepacker.com.

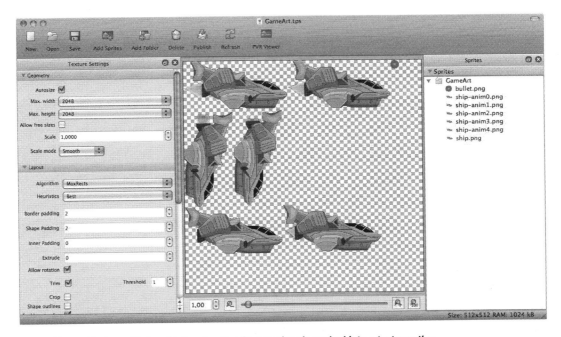

Figure 6-4. TexturePacker with the ship's animation frames already packed into a texture atlas

The free version TexturePacker Essential is sufficient for basic needs and you can use it to create commercial apps. It doesn't have the Pro version's more advanced features, such as saving high-resolution data for Retina displays, scaling down images for non-Retina displays on the fly, or optimizing the graphics to save memory. The Pro version requires a paid license that comes at a reasonably low price.

You can also run TexturePacker as a command-line tool via the Terminal app, allowing it to be integrated in your Xcode build process. You can find more information on the TexturePacker command-line tool and how to use it on the TexturePacker web site.

In this chapter, I use TexturePacker Pro because it can also export to the PVR image format, the native image format for iPhone's PowerVR graphics chip. The Pro version also conveniently creates the SD and HD textures you need to be able to run the project on all variants of the iPhone.

Preparing the Project for TexturePacker

To use TexturePacker, the project Sprites02 need a little reorganizing. Currently all images in the HD and SD variants are in the Resources folder. Because you're going to use a texture atlas that contains all the images in one texture, the individual images don't need to be copied onto the device anymore.

First create a new folder called Assets that keeps all the source images and the save file for the texture atlases. You don't need to have both HD and SD versions of each image anymore because TexturePacker will scale down the images for you. So, with TexturePacker you're working only with the HD variants, and the image files don't need to have the -hd suffix anymore. Figure 6-5 shows the Assets folder of the Sprites02 project.

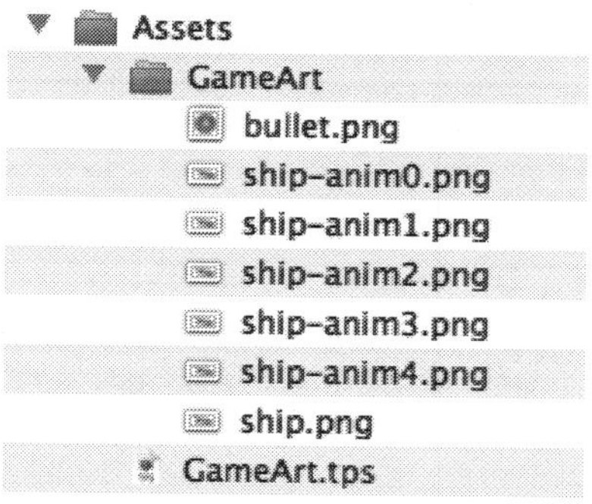

Figure 6-5. *The folder contents of the Assets folder*

Another tip that makes handling image files easier is to put all image files that should be packed into the same texture atlas in the same subfolder. In the case of the Sprites02 project, the Assets folder has a subfolder called GameArt that contains all the image files that are packed into the game-art texture atlas.

TexturePacker simply adds new image files in that folder when you're refreshing the texture atlas in TexturePacker, so you don't have to add individual images manually anymore. TexturePacker will create one `.tps` (TexturePacker Save) file for each folder.

Caution   If you have an individual image file called `bullet.png`, the HD version must be named `bullet-hd.png`, and in cocos2d you have to load the file with the string @`"bullet.png"`.

A common mistake that happens when you move from individual images to a texture atlas is to add images to the texture atlas that have the –hd prefix in their filename. In that case, the resulting texture atlas for SD and HD versions might be named `bulletatlas.pvr.czz` and `bulletatlas-hd.pvr.czz`. But the images contained in the texture atlas, now called sprite frames, will all have the name `bullet-hd.png` even in the SD texture atlas. Thus, you'd have to change all references in cocos2d from @`"bullet.png"` to @`"bullet-hd.png"`. To avoid this issue, for creating a texture atlas I recommend using HD version images without the –hd suffix in the filename.

Even worse would be to manually create two texture atlases, one for SD images containing only image files without the –hd suffix and one for HD images containing only image files with the –hd suffix. If you then loaded @`"bullet.png"` in cocos2d, it wouldn't be able to find the –hd image on Retina devices. If you loaded @`"bullet-hd.png"`, the SD images wouldn't load. That's because the distinction between SD and HD is done at the texture atlas level; you will have a texture atlas with the –hd suffix and one without. The names of the sprite frames inside a texture atlas must be identical for both SD and HD texture atlases.

Creating a Texture Atlas with TexturePacker

Working with TexturePacker is very straightforward and involves only a few steps, as illustrated in Figure 6-6. In most cases you're fine using the default settings.

First add the images you want to add to the texture atlas. You can always add more at a later time or remove existing ones. Click the Add Sprites or Add Folder button, or simply drag and drop sprites or folders on the right pane. TexturePacker can load images from the most common graphics formats. In this case, you add all ship images and animation frames, as well as the bullet image. You can find them in the Assets folder in the Sprites02 example.

Simply drop the GameArt folder on the right pane. After doing so, the sprites immediately appear in the center pane, which is the real-time preview of our texture atlas. It updates immediately whenever you change any setting, including image optimizations and image layout.

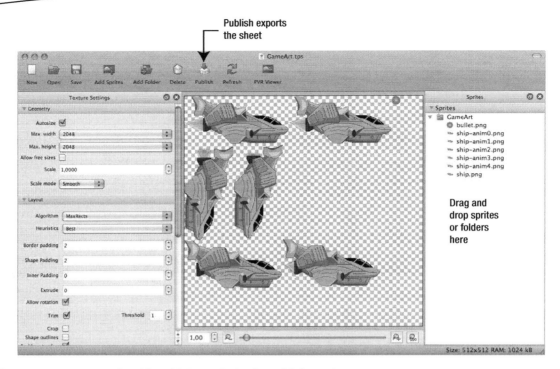

Figure 6-6. *The process of working with TexturePacker is straightforward*

In the status bar at the bottom right-hand corner, you also see how big the resulting texture will be and how much memory it will use on the device. In this case, the texture atlas is 1024×1024 pixels and will use up 4MB of texture memory. This information is for the HD texture. The SD texture will be about 512×512 pixels in size and consume a quarter of the memory, which is 512KB. Note that the SD texture atlas may not always be exactly half the width and height of the HD atlas. That's because some layout features such as padding don't scale when the SD texture is created.

> **Caution**   Unless you develop your game exclusively for the latest generation of devices, you shouldn't use a texture width or height above 2048 pixels. All devices supported by cocos2d 2.0 support texture dimensions of 2048×2048 pixels—only iPhone 4S and iPad 2 and newer support 4096×4096 texture dimensions. You can limit the maximum texture size that TexturePacker should generate in the left-hand pane's Geometry section.

TexturePacker uses several tricks to optimize the texture space to create an optimal packing rate. First it trims the transparent border pixels of each image. Cocos2d compensates for this by adding the trimmed area as an offset to the sprite's position when drawing it. This has two advantages: it reduces the texture size and speeds up the rendering of the sprites.

You may also notice that some images are rotated. TexurePacker rotates them to optimize how the texture atlas space is used. Again, cocos2d compensates by restoring the original orientation when loading the image into memory. If you add two or more exactly identical images, TexturePacker will add only one image to further save texture atlas space. If the images are referenced by different filenames, then you can load the image in cocos2d by using any of the image's source filenames. Whenever an image in a texture atlas has multiple source files containing the same image, TexturePacker will draw a small overlay (a stack of paper) over the image in the center pane.

In case you're wondering about the Border Padding and Shape Padding settings, they determine how many pixels of space are left between all images and the border of the atlas. The default of 2 pixels ensures that all the images in the texture atlas can be drawn without any artifacts. With less padding, images can show stray pixels around their borders when displayed in your game. The amount and color of these stray pixels depend on the surrounding pixels from other images in the texture atlas. This is a technical issue that has to do with how the graphics hardware filters textures, and the only solution is to leave a certain amount of padding between all images in a texture atlas.

Before you can save the texture atlas, you need to make adjustments to the TexturePacker Output settings depicted in Figure 6-7.

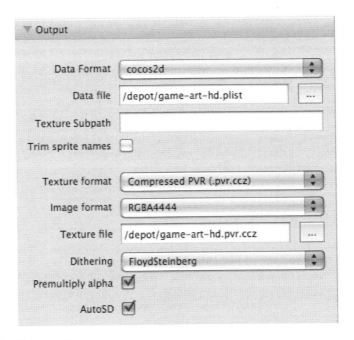

Figure 6-7. TexturePacker Output settings

First make sure that the data format is set to cocos2d because TexturePacker can be used with other game engines as well.

For the data file, specify a file located in the project's Resources folder. Make sure the file has the -hd suffix. In the Sprites02 project, the file is named game-art-hd.plist. TexturePacker will save the HD texture to the given filename but will omit the -hd suffix for the SD version, which is exactly how cocos2d wants the data. To have TexturePacker automatically create the SD version of the texture atlas, you also need to check the AutoSD check box at the bottom.

Finally, choose Texture Format and Image Format for the exported texture atlas. The recommended Texture Format setting is Compressed PVR (.pvr.ccz), which is a compressed version of the iPhone's native PVR format. This format typically loads a lot faster than PNG, and if you have images with a 16-bit color depth, the compressed PVR format will create smaller files than PNG. The PNG file format will always store 32-bit color values, regardless of the actual color bit depth of the image.

Note   Color depth, bit depth, or bits per pixel is the number of bits that are stored to represent a pixel's color information. A color depth of 4 bits allows each pixel in the image to have one of 16 possible colors. With a color depth of 16 bits, an image's pixel can display a range of 65,536 colors. And with a 24-bit color depth it can have millions of colors—so many, in fact, that an image with 24-bit color depth is sometimes referred to as a true-color image. Why is this format commonly referred to as 32-bit? Because the additional 8 bits in the most common file formats are used to store the opacity of each pixel.

I encourage you to read the Wikipedia articles on color depth (http://en.wikipedia.org/wiki/Color_depth) and the RGB color model (http://en.wikipedia.org/wiki/RGB) to learn more about how computing devices display color.

When using the PVR format, you should also enable the Premultiply alpha check box to avoid dark borders around sprites in some cases. In your project's app delegate, after cocos2d has been initialized and shortly before running the first scene, you should also let cocos2d know that your PVR images uses premultiplied alpha. In cocos2d project templates this is already set in the AppDelegate.m file.

```
// Enable pre multiplied alpha for PVR textures to avoid artifacts
[CCTexture2D PVRImagesHavePremultipliedAlpha:YES];
```

For the Image Format setting, you have a variety of options. The default format is RGBA8888, which gives the best-looking results. It provides 24-bit color depth and an 8-bit alpha channel. The downside is that it's also the slowest to render, and particularly on 1st- and 2nd-generation devices, falling back to a lower-quality image format and favoring rendering speed are recommended. However, providing device-specific variants of texture atlases is cumbersome to work with. You may want to simply render fewer sprites on older devices or possibly even drop support for those devices altogether.

The best compromise between quality, memory usage, and rendering speed is provided by the RGBA4444 format. It uses 4 bits per color and 4 bits for the alpha channel. This is the most commonly used image format for sprites.

If transparency isn't important to you, and you'd like to have more color variations, you should use the RGB5551 format, which provides 5 bits per color and only 1 bit for the alpha channel. The 1 bit for the alpha channel can be either set or not, which means your image can have only fully transparent or fully opaque pixels. In other words, RGB5551 sprites can't blend with pixels in the background.

If you don't need any transparency at all, like for background images, you can use the RGB565 format, which provides 5 bits for red, 6 bits for green, and 5 bits for the blue color channel. It doesn't use an alpha channel. The fact that there are 6 bits for green colors and only 5 bits for the other two color channels has something to do with our hunter-gatherer background. Our retina is simply trained to differentiate better between green color tones, so that extra bit is provided to the green channel where we would notice a "missing color bit" more easily.

The PVRTC2 and PVRTC4 image formats provide 2 and 4 bits per pixel, respectively, and no alpha channel. Only use this format for monotonous or dark background images and if you really need to squeeze out some memory and rendering speed because they come with a severe impact on image quality. Think of the artifacts seen in JPEG images with a relatively low-quality setting.

The Dithering option allows you to optimize the image quality whenever the image format requires the image's color depth to be reduced. Dithering emulates gradients by randomly distributing pixels with similar color tones across a larger area. This effectively reduces the "banding" effect when the color depth of an image is reduced. Because all the dithering options are applied in real time in the TexturePacker preview without affecting your source images, you can just try the various dithering algorithms to find out which provides the best quality.

> **Tip**   While evaluating dithering algorithms, keep in mind that the ultimate quality test is of course your game running on a device. Some artifacts that are clearly visible on your computer screen may not be noticeable on the device. In particular, that's because the color profile of your computer screen is different from the device's color profile, either through manual adjustments (brightness, contrast, color tone), limitations imposed by the display technology, or a change in color vibrancy as the display ages. That also means a single device isn't representative for the final look of the game. At the very least, you should test the game with the device brightness set to minimum and maximum levels.

When you're done with the Output settings, simply click Publish, and TexturePacker will write the HD and SD textures and the accompanying `plist` files to your `Resources` folder.

Using the Texture Atlas with cocos2d

The next thing you should do is add the new texture atlas to the Xcode project's Resource group. Cocos2d only needs the `game-art-hd.pvr.ccz`, `game-art.pvr.ccz`, `game-art-hd.plist`, and `game-art.plist` files for the texture atlas. Don't add the TexturePacker `.tps` files and individual source image files to your project. The code in Listing 6-13 now replaces the code in Listing 6-11.

Listing 6-13. The Ship Class Now Uses the Texture Atlas for Its Initial Frame and the Animation

```
// Load the texture atlas sprite frames; this also loads the Texture with the same name
CCSpriteFrameCache* frameCache = [CCSpriteFrameCache sharedSpriteFrameCache];
[frameCache addSpriteFramesWithFile:@"game-art.plist"];

// Loading the ship's sprite using a sprite frame name (e.g., the file name)
if ((self = [super initWithSpriteFrameName:@"ship.png"]))
{
    // Load the ship's animation frames
    NSMutableArray* frames = [NSMutableArray arrayWithCapacity:5];
    for (int i = 0; i<5; i++)
    {
        NSString* file = [NSString stringWithFormat:@"ship-anim%i.png", i];

        CCSpriteFrame* frame = [frameCache spriteFrameByName:file];
        [frames addObject:frame];
    }

    // Create an animation object from all the sprite animation frames
    CCAnimation* anim = [CCAnimation animationWithSpriteFrames:frames delay:0.08f];

    // Run the animation by using the CCAnimate action
    CCAnimate* animate = [CCAnimate actionWithAnimation:anim];
    CCRepeatForever* repeat = [CCRepeatForever actionWithAction:animate];
    [self runAction:repeat];
}
```

At the very beginning of the code, I assigned the sharedSpriteFrameCache to a local variable. The only reason to do so is that the [CCSpriteFrameCache sharedSpriteFrameCache] singleton accessor is pretty lengthy to write.

To load a texture atlas, use the CCSpriteFrameCache's method addSpriteFramesWithFile and pass it the name of the .plist file for this texture atlas. The CCSpriteFrameCache will load the sprite frames and will also try to load the texture. Cocos2d automatically tries to load the -hd suffixed files on Retina display devices.

> **Note**   If you're using a large texture atlas texture—with dimensions of 1024×1024 or higher—you should load this texture before game play begins. It will take a moment to load such a large texture (in the worst case it will freeze the game for a few seconds). You may not notice the delay when testing on a Retina iPad, but users with an iPhone 3GS will surely notice the delay.

Because the Ship class derives from CCSprite, and because I wanted it to use the ship.png image from the texture atlas, I changed its initialization to use the initWithSpriteFrameName method. This is identical to the code that initializes a regular CCSprite from a texture atlas using a sprite frame name.

```
CCSprite* sprite = [CCSprite spriteWithSpriteFrameName:@"ship.png"];
```

If you load several texture atlases, and only one contains the sprite frame with the name ship. png, cocos2d will still find that frame and use the correct texture for the sprite. In essence, you work with the sprite frames by name as if they were the image's filenames, but you don't need to know which texture contains the actual image (unless you use a CCSpriteBatchNode, of course, which requires that all its children use the same texture).

In Listing 6-13 you could get rid of most of the extra code required to initialize a CCSpriteFrame object. There's no need any more to load a Texture2D and define the texture's dimensions. Instead, simply call [CCSpriteFrame spriteFrameByName:file] to create the sprite frame with the corresponding name.

Updating the CCAnimation Helper Category

Although you could significantly reduce the code to create a CCAnimation by using a texture atlas, it's still worthwhile to encapsulate this code into the CCAnimationHelper class. After all, one line of code is still less than five lines, especially if you would otherwise use the same five lines of code everywhere. Without further ado, Listing 6-14 shows the extended CCAnimation Helper interface declaration, which adds the animationWithFrame method.

Listing 6-14. The @interface for the CCAnimation Helper Category

```
interface CCAnimation (Helper)
+(CCAnimation*) animationWithFile:(NSString*)name
                    frameCount:(int)frameCount
                        delay:(float)delay;

+(CCAnimation*) animationWithFrame:(NSString*)frame
                    frameCount:(int)frameCount
                        delay:(float)delay;

@end
```

This code is essentially the same method using the same parameters, except that this method uses sprite frames instead of filenames. The implementation is nothing spectacular and is very similar to the animationWithFile method shown in Listing 6-15.

Listing 6-15. The animationWithFrame Helper Method Makes It Easier to Create an Animation

```
// Creates an animation from sprite frames
+(CCAnimation*) animationWithFrame:(NSString*)frame
                    frameCount:(int)frameCount
                        delay:(float)delay
{
    // load the ship's animation frames as textures and create a sprite frame
    NSMutableArray* frames = [NSMutableArray arrayWithCapacity:frameCount];
    for (int i = 0; i<frameCount; i++)
    {
        NSString* file = [NSString stringWithFormat:@"%@%i.png", frame, i];
        CCSpriteFrameCache* frameCache = [CCSpriteFrameCache sharedSpriteFrameCache];
        CCSpriteFrame* frame = [frameCache spriteFrameByName:file];
        [frames addObject:frame];
    }

    // Return an animation object from all the sprite animation frames
    return [CCAnimation animationWithSpriteFrames:frames delay:delay];
}
```

The big plus is now, once again, that you can create an animation from a texture atlas using sprite frame names with just one line of code:

```
// Create an animation object from all the sprite animation frames
CCAnimation* anim = [CCAnimation animationWithFrame:@"ship-anim"
                    frameCount:5
                    delay:0.08f];
```

The much, much bigger plus, though, is that you can now work with your animations as single files and only later create a texture atlas. All you have to do is to change one line of code from using `animationWithFile` to the `animationWithFrame` method. This allows you to quickly prototype animations using individual files, and only when you're satisfied do you pack the animation frames into a texture atlas and load the animation images from it.

You'll also find this updated `CCAnimationHelper` code in the Sprites02 project.

All into One and One for All

Whenever possible, you should add all your game's images into one texture atlas or as few as possible, and preferably use one `CCSpriteBatchNode` to draw all the sprites from the same texture atlas. It's more effective both from a workflow perspective and for performance to use one texture atlas with dimensions of 2048×2048 than 10 smaller ones, and you will have to use at least 10 sprite batch nodes instead of just one. That means 10 draw calls at a minimum, which is less than ideal. Organizing your images may require some thought, but it's well worth it.

Unlike code, which you should separate into distinct logical components, with a texture atlas your goal should be to put as many images as possible into the same texture atlas while trying to reduce the wasted space of each texture atlas as much as possible.

It may seem logical to use one texture atlas for your player's images; another for monster A, B, and C and their animations; and so on. But that would mean more draw calls. However, that's helpful only if you have a huge number of images for each game object and you want to be selective about which images to load into memory at any one time. One such scenario might be a shoot-'em-up game with different worlds where you know that each world has separate types of enemies. In that case, it makes sense to not mix and match enemies of different worlds into the same texture atlas. Otherwise, just for organization's sake, you shouldn't split up your texture atlases by game objects but rather fill each texture atlas as much as possible.

Don't fall into the habit of creating one texture atlas per graphical object because it seems logical to do so. The best-performing texture atlases are full to the brim with a great variety of images that can all be rendered with a single sprite batch node.

As long as your game's images can fit into two or three texture atlases of 2048×2048 size, you should just put all the images into those texture atlases and load them up front. This will use 32MB to 48MB of memory for your textures. Your actual program code and other assets such as audio files don't take up that much space, so you should be able to keep these texture atlases in memory even on iOS devices with just 256MB of memory.

Once you pass that point, however, you need a better strategy to handle your texture memory. One such strategy, as mentioned earlier, could be to divide your game's images into worlds and load only the texture atlases needed for the current world. This will introduce a short delay when a new world is loaded and would be a good use for the `LoadingScene` described in Chapter 5.

Because cocos2d automatically caches all images, you need a way to specifically unload textures that you know you don't need. You can rely on cocos2d to do that for you:

```
[[CCSpriteFrameCache sharedSpriteFrameCache] removeUnusedSpriteFrames];
[[CCTextureCache sharedTextureCache] removeUnusedTextures];
```

Obviously you should call these methods only when you want to remove unused textures. You typically do that after changing scenes—not during game play. Keep in mind that changing scenes causes the previous scene to be deallocated only after the new scene has been initialized. This means you can't use the removeUnused methods in the init method of a scene because the textures will still be in use—that is, unless you use the LoadingScene from Chapter 5 in between two scenes, in which case you should extend it so that it removes unused textures before replacing itself with the new scene.

If you absolutely want to remove all textures from memory before loading new ones, you should use the purge methods instead:

```
[CCSpriteFrameCache purgeSharedSpriteFrameCache];
[CCTextureCache purgeSharedTextureCache];
```

Summary

In this chapter, you learned how to use a CCSpriteBatchNode to render multiple sprites using the same texture faster, whether that texture is a single image or a sprite frame of a texture atlas.

Subclassing your game objects from CCSprite also introduces a few subtle differences and stumbling blocks, which I demonstrated earlier in this chapter, before moving on to show you how to create sprite animations. Because the code to create animations is very complex, I gave you the solution in the form of a CCAnimationHelper category.

I also showed you how to work with texture atlases and why and how you should use them. Of course, one can't say "texture atlas" without mentioning TexturePacker in the same sentence. It's hands down the best tool to create and modify texture atlases, and if you don't want to spend money on it, you can still use the free command-line version without the advanced features.

In the next chapter, you'll be working on your next game, as we work on making the shooter game playable.

Chapter 7

Scrolling with Joy

Continuing with the beginnings of the game from Chapter 6, you'll now turn it into something resembling an actual shoot-'em-up game. The very first thing will be to make the player's ship controllable. Accelerometer controls don't make sense in this case; a virtual joypad would be much more appropriate. But instead of reinventing the wheel, you'll use a cool source code package called SneakyInput to add a virtual joypad to this cocos2d game.

Moving the player's ship around is one thing. You also want the background to scroll, to give the impression of moving into a certain direction. To make that happen, you'll implement your own solution for parallax scrolling, because `CCParallaxNode` is too limited—it doesn't allow an infinitely scrolling parallax background.

In addition, in this chapter I illustrate what you've learned about texture atlases and sprite batching in Chapter 6. There's one texture atlas containing all the game's graphics because there's no need to group the images separately when using a texture atlas.

Advanced Parallax Scrolling

Because `CCParallaxNode` doesn't allow infinite scrolling, for this shooting game you'll add a `ParallaxBackground` node, which does just that. Moreover, it uses a `CCSpriteBatchNode` to speed up the rendering of the background images.

Creating the Background as Stripes

First, I want to illustrate how I made the background stripes that will create the parallaxing effect. This is crucial to understanding how the texture atlas TexturePacker creates can help you save memory and performance and also save time positioning the individual stripes. Figure 7-1 shows the background layer as a Seashore image composed of individual parallax layers. This image is also in the Assets folder of the ScrollingWithJoy01 project, as `background-parallax.xcf`.

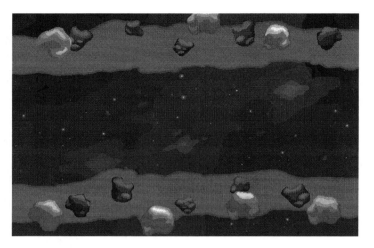

Figure 7-1. *The source image for the parallax scrolling background*

Each stripe is on its own layer in the image-editing program Seashore. In Figure 7-2 you can see the various layers, and the Assets folder holds images named bg0.png through bg6.png, which correspond to the seven individual stripes making up the background.

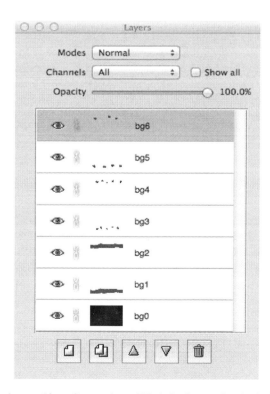

Figure 7-2. *Each stripe of the background is on its own layer. This helps in creating the individual images and positioning them in the game*

I recommend creating the parallax background image this way for several reasons. You can create the image as a whole, but you're able to save each layer to an individual file. All these files are 960×640 pixels in size, which may seem wasteful at first, but you're not adding the individual images to the game—instead, you're adding them to a texture atlas. Because TexturePacker removes the surrounding transparent space of each image, it shrinks the individual stripes down to a bare minimum. You can see this in Figure 7-3.

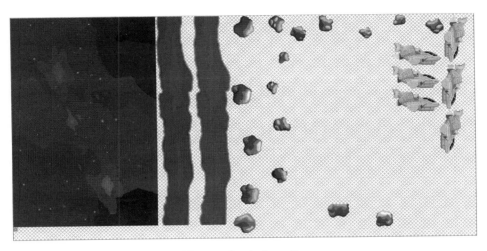

Figure 7-3. The background stripes as they would appear in a texture atlas

Splitting the stripes into individual images is not only helpful for drawing the images at the correct z-order. Strictly speaking, the images bg5.png and bg6.png can be at the same z-order because they don't overlap, yet I chose to save them into separate files. In Figure 7-3 you can see these two files as the two topmost stripes. Notice how little space they actually use up in the texture atlas; that's because TexturePacker removed most of the surrounding transparent parts of these images.

Now suppose I left both these stripes in the same 960×640 image—one would be at the top and the other at the bottom of the image, with a big gaping hole of transparency in between them. TexturePacker can't remove the transparent part between the two sprites, so they would have remained as a 960×640 image in the texture atlas, which is a lot more space than they take up as individual images.

Splitting the stripes into individual images also helps maintain a high framerate. The iOS devices are very limited in *fill rate* (that is, the number of pixels they can draw every frame). Because images frequently overlap each other, the iOS device often has to draw the same pixel several times in every frame. The extreme scenario would be a full-screen image on top of another full-screen image. You can see only one of the two images, but the device actually has to draw both. The technical term for that is *overdraw*. Separating the background into individual stripes with as little overlap as possible reduces the number of pixels drawn.

> **Tip** By using 16-bit textures (RGB565, RGBA5551, and RGBA4444) or even PVR compressed textures, you can improve the rendering performance of your game. Of course, you lose some image quality, but in many cases it's hardly noticeable on the iPhone screen, even if you do see some artifacts on your computer's screen. TexturePacker lets you reduce the color depth of your images while retaining most of the image quality through dithering techniques. And if you experience long load times, saving images in the compressed `pvr.czz` format is worth a try because this particular image file format loads noticeably faster than other ones.

Re-creating the Background in Code

You may be wondering by now how you can put these images back together in the source code without spending a lot of time properly positioning these stripped-down images. The answer is you don't have to. Because all these images were saved as full-screen images, TexturePacker stores the image offsets, and cocos2d then uses these offsets when rendering the sprites. All you really have to do is center each of these images on the screen, and they will be at the correct place.

Look at the code for the `ParallaxBackground` node newly added to the `ScrollingWithJoy01` project. The header file is pretty straightforward:

```
@interface ParallaxBackground : CCNode
{
    CCSpriteBatchNode* spriteBatch;
    int numSprites;
}
@end
```

I only kept a reference to the `CCSpriteBatchNode` around because I'll be accessing it in the code frequently. Storing a node as an instance variable is faster than asking cocos2d for the node via the `getNodeByTag` method, and more so the more children the node has. Keeping a reference to a node by storing it as an instance variable saves you a few CPU cycles. It's nothing too dramatic, and it's certainly not worth keeping several hundreds of member variables around. But it's very convenient in cases where you need to access a particular node frequently.

In the `init` method of the `ParallaxBackground` class, the `CCSpriteBatchNode` is created, and all seven background images are added from the texture atlas, as shown in Listing 7-1.

Listing 7-1. Loading the Background Images

```
-(id) init
{
    if ((self=[super init]))
    {
        CGSize screenSize=[CCDirector sharedDirector].winSize;

        // Get the game's texture atlas texture by adding it to the cache
        CCTexture2D* gameArtTexture=[[CCTextureCache sharedTextureCache] ↵
            addImage:@"game-art.pvr.ccz"];
```

```
    // Create the background spritebatch
    spriteBatch = [CCSpriteBatchNode batchNodeWithTexture:gameArtTexture];
    [self addChild:spriteBatch];

    // Add the 6 different layer objects and position them on the screen
    for (int i=0; i<7; i++)
    {
        NSString* frameName = [NSString stringWithFormat:@"bg%i.png", i];
        CCSprite* sprite = [CCSprite spriteWithSpriteFrameName:frameName];
        sprite.position = CGPointMake(screenSize.width / 2, ↵
            screenSize.height / 2);
        [spriteBatch addChild:sprite z:i];
    }

    scrollSpeed = 1.0f;
    [self scheduleUpdate];
    }
    return self;
}
```

First you're getting the game-art.pvr.czz texture from the CCTextureCache. Normally you'd use the textureForKey method to access the already loaded texture. But if you're not sure whether the texture is already in the cache, you can also use the addImage method instead of textureForKey. That also loads the texture if it wasn't cached—otherwise addImage just returns the cached texture. As long as the image is included in the app bundle, addImage is guaranteed to return a valid texture.

With the CCSpriteBatchNode created and set up, the next step is to load the seven individual background images. I deliberately chose to number them from 0 to 6 so you can use stringWithFormat to create the filenames as strings in a very effective way:

```
NSString* frameName = [NSString stringWithFormat:@"bg%i.png", i];
```

With that sprite frameName, create a CCSprite as usual and then position it at the center of the screen:

```
sprite.position = CGPointMake(screenSize.width / 2, screenSize.height / 2);
```

Of course, once you create an iPad version of this project, the images won't fit perfectly anymore because they were designed for a screen of 960 × 640 resolution. To create an iPad version, follow the exact same steps except make your original image 1024 × 768 in size, or even double that if you also want to support Retina iPad resolutions. You can then downscale the 960 × 640 images from the higher resolution images easily just by cropping the borders.

Tip It takes surprisingly little effort to re-create the source image from individual sprite frames in cocos2d, and it's all thanks to TexturePacker saving the image offsets for you. It's also a great way to create your game screen layouts. You can have an artist design each screen as separate layers, as many as needed, using the native screen resolution (960 × 640 for iPhone and 2048 × 1536 for iPad). Then export each layer as an individual full-screen file with transparency. Next create a texture atlas from these files and you'll have the artist-envisioned screen design in cocos2d with no hassle of positioning individual files and no wasted memory either. TexturePacker takes care of scaling down the images to standard resolution, if needed.

Because the ParallaxBackground class is derived from CCNode, you only need to add it to the GameLayer init method after the sprite frames are loaded to add the ParallaxBackground to the game, like this:

```
-(id) init
{
    if ((self=[super init]))
    {
        sharedGameLayer=self;

        // if the background shines through we want to be able to see it!
        glClearColor(1, 1, 1, 1);

        // Load all of the game's artwork up front.
        CCSpriteFrameCache* frameCache=[CCSpriteFrameCache sharedSpriteFrameCache];
        [frameCache addSpriteFramesWithFile:@"game-art.plist"];

        CGSize screenSize=[CCDirector sharedDirector].winSize;

        ParallaxBackground* background=[ParallaxBackground node];
        [self addChild:background z:-1];

        /*
        // add a background image
        CCSprite* background=[CCSprite spriteWithSpriteFrameName:@"background.png"];
        background.position=CGPointMake(screenSize.width / 2, screenSize.height / 2);
        [self addChild:background];
        */

        ...
```

You also need to import the ParallaxBackground.h header file at the top of the GameLayer.m file:

```
#import "ParallaxBackground.h"
```

The parallax background replaces the CCLayerColor and the background CCSprite, which were placeholders from Chapter 6, so you also want to remove or comment out any reference to the background sprite or CCLayerColor. In addition, I set the OpenGL clear color to white—later this will help you see a visual artifact that occurs in the early versions of the parallax scrolling code.

Moving the ParallaxBackground

In the ScrollingWithJoy01 project, I also added a quick-and-dirty scrolling of the background stripes. It does show a parallax effect, although the images quickly leave the screen, revealing the blank background behind them. Figure 7-4 isn't exactly what I had in mind, but I'm getting there.

Figure 7-4. The background stripes are moving, but they're also leaving the screen forever

> **Note**   You'll also notice that Figure 7-4 doesn't look at all like Figure 7-1 or the game project.
> Figure 7-4 uses dummy graphics to better illustrate the parallax images "leaving" the screen.
> It's much harder to see with the star background stripes. You'll notice this effect much better in
> motion. What you can see in the image is that the individual stripes have moved at different rates,
> which is what parallax scrolling is all about.

Listing 7-2 shows that the code to make the background scroll is surprisingly simple if you
ignore for a moment the flaw seen in Figure 7-4.

Listing 7-2. Moving the Background Stripes

```
-(void) update:(ccTime)delta
{
    for (CCSprite* sprite in spriteBatch.children)
    {
        CGPoint pos=sprite.position;
        pos.x -=(scrollSpeed+sprite.zOrder) * (delta * 20);
        sprite.position=pos;
    }
}
```

Every background image's x position gets subtracted a bit every frame to scroll it from right
to left. How much an image moves depends on the predefined scrollSpeed plus the sprite's
zOrder. The delta multiplier is used to make the scrolling speed independent of the framerate,
which is then multiplied by 20 to make the scrolling reasonably fast. Images that are closer to the
screen scroll faster. However, using the zOrder property causes the stripes that should be at the
same visual depth to scroll at different speeds.

The position is also multiplied by the *delta time* to make the scrolling speed independent of the framerate. The delta time itself is just a tiny fraction—it's the time between two calls to the update method. At exactly 60 frames per second (FPS), it's 1/60 of a second, which is a delta time of 0.167 seconds. For that reason, I multiply delta by 20 just to get a reasonably fast scroll; otherwise the images move too slowly.

Parallax Speed Factors

Somehow the stripes of the same color need to scroll at the same speed, and the stripes should repeat so that the background doesn't show up. My solutions to these issues are in the ScrollingWithJoy02 project.

The first change has to do with scrolling speed. I decided to use a NSMutableArray to store the speed factor with which individual stripes move. Other solutions are available, but this allows me to illustrate a key issue of NSMutableArray and, in fact, all iOS SDK collection classes: they can store only objects, never values such as integers and floating-point numbers.

The way around this is to box numbers into an NSNumber object. The following code is the newly added NSMutableArray* speedFactors, which stores floating-point values. The array is defined in the ParallaxBackground class header:

```
@interface ParallaxBackground : CCNode
{
    CCSpriteBatchNode* spriteBatch;
    int numStripes;

    NSMutableArray* speedFactors;
    float scrollSpeed;
}
@end
```

Then it's filled with factors in the init method of the ParallaxBackground class. Notice how NSNumber numberWithFloat is used to store a float value inside the array. I explain the code that adds additional background sprites in the next section. I added the following code just above the scheduleUpdate line in the init method:

Listing 7-3. Modified init method of the ParallaxBackground class

```
...
numStripes=7;

// Add 7 more stripes, flip them and position them next to their neighbor stripe
for (int i=0; i<numStripes; i++)
{
    NSString* frameName=[NSString stringWithFormat:@"bg%i.png", i];
    CCSprite* sprite=[CCSprite spriteWithSpriteFrameName:frameName];

    // Position the new sprite one screen width to the right
    sprite.position=CGPointMake(screenSize.width+screenSize.width / 2, ↵
        screenSize.height / 2);

    // Flip the sprite so that it aligns perfectly with its neighbor
    sprite.flipX=YES;
```

```
    // Add the sprite using the same tag offset by numStripes
    [spriteBatch addChild:sprite z:i tag:i+numStripes];
}

// Initialize the array that contains the scroll factors for individual stripes.
speedFactors=[NSMutableArray arrayWithCapacity:numStripes];
[speedFactors addObject:[NSNumber numberWithFloat:0.3f]];
[speedFactors addObject:[NSNumber numberWithFloat:0.5f]];
[speedFactors addObject:[NSNumber numberWithFloat:0.5f]];
[speedFactors addObject:[NSNumber numberWithFloat:0.8f]];
[speedFactors addObject:[NSNumber numberWithFloat:0.8f]];
[speedFactors addObject:[NSNumber numberWithFloat:1.2f]];
[speedFactors addObject:[NSNumber numberWithFloat:1.2f]];
NSAssert(speedFactors.count == numStripes,
    @"speedFactors count does not match numStripes!");
```

```
scrollSpeed=1.0f;
[self scheduleUpdate];
```

The final assert is simply a safety check for human error. Consider that you may be adding or removing stripes from the background for whatever reason but might forget to adjust the number of values you're adding to the speedFactors array. If you forget to modify the speedFactors initialization, the assert will remind you of it, instead of potentially crashing the game seemingly at random at a later time.

In Figure 7-5 you can see which speed factor is applied to which stripe. Stripes with higher speed factors move faster than those with slower ones, which creates the parallax effect. Once again, I use dummy graphics to make each individual stripe clearly visible.

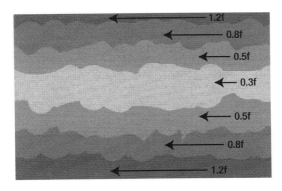

Figure 7-5. The speed factors applied to each background stripe

To use the newly introduced speed factors, change the update method to this:

```
-(void) update:(ccTime)delta
{
    for (CCSprite* sprite in spriteBatch.children)
    {
        NSNumber* factor=[speedFactors objectAtIndex:sprite.zOrder];

        CGPoint pos=sprite.position;
```

```
        pos.x -=(scrollSpeed * factor.floatValue) * (delta * 50);
        sprite.position=pos;
    }
}
```

Based on the sprite's zOrder property, a speed factor NSNumber is obtained from the speedFactors array. This is multiplied by the scrollSpeed to speed up or slow down the movement of individual stripes. You can't multiply the NSNumber object directly because it's a wrapper class storing a primitive data type such as float, int, char, or others. NSNumber has a floatValue property that returns the floating-point value stored in it, and it has a number of other properties to retrieve different data types as well. You could also use intValue, even though this NSNumber stores a floating-point value. It's essentially the same as casting a float to an int. Once again, the delta time is also factored in to make the scrolling speed independent of the framerate.

By using the speedFactors array and giving the same-colored stripes the same factor, the background stripes will now move as expected. But there's still the issue of making endless scrolling.

Scrolling to Infinity and Beyond

Also in ScrollingWithJoy02 is the first step toward endless scrolling. You'll find in Listing 7-4, which repeats the snippet of code first introduced in Listing 7-3, seven more background stripes to the CCSpriteBatchNode, although with a slightly different setup.

Listing 7-4. Adding Off-Screen Background Images

```
// Add seven more stripes, flip them, and position them next to their neighbor stripe
for (int i=0; i<numStripes; i++)
{
    NSString* frameName=[NSString stringWithFormat:@"bg%i.png", i];
    CCSprite* sprite=[CCSprite spriteWithSpriteFrameName:frameName];

    // Position the new sprite one screen width to the right
    sprite.position=CGPointMake(screenSize.width+screenSize.width / 2, ↵
        screenSize.height / 2);

    // Flip the sprite so that it aligns perfectly with its neighbor
    sprite.flipX=YES;

    // Add the sprite using the same tag offset by numStripes
    [spriteBatch addChild:sprite z:i tag:i+numStripes];
}
```

The idea is to add one more stripe of the same type each. They're positioned so that they align with the right end of the original stripe's position. In effect, this doubles the total width of the background stripes, and that's enough for endless scrolling. But I'll get to that shortly.

First I need to point out that the new neighboring images' x coordinates are flipped (mirrored along the y-axis) so that the images match visually where they're aligned, to avoid any sharp edges. The new images also get a different tag number, one that's offset by the number of stripes in use. This way it's easy to get to the neighboring stripe by either adding or deducting numStripes from the tag number.

Right now, the background image scrolls just a bit longer before showing the blank canvas behind the images. But you're not stopping there; instead you'll complete the effort and add seamless infinite scrolling.

First change the anchorPoint property of the original stripes to make things a little easier. The x position is set to 0, and the stripes are left-aligned with the anchorPoint's x coordinate also set to 0. The same goes for the additional, flipped stripes, which now only need to be offset by the screen width to make them align with the original stripes. The changes to the init method of the ParallaxBackground class are highlighted in Listing 7-5.

Listing 7-5. Adding Off-Screen Background Images

```
numStripes=7;

// Add the 7 different stripes and position them on the screen
for (int i=0; i<numStripes; i++)
{
    NSString* frameName=[NSString stringWithFormat:@"bg%i.png", i];
    CCSprite* sprite=[CCSprite spriteWithSpriteFrameName:frameName];
    sprite.anchorPoint=CGPointMake(0, 0.5f);
    sprite.position=CGPointMake(0, screenSize.height / 2);
    [spriteBatch addChild:sprite z:i tag:i];
}

// Add 7 more stripes, flip them and position them next to their neighbor stripe
for (int i=0; i<numStripes; i++)
{
    NSString* frameName=[NSString stringWithFormat:@"bg%i.png", i];
    CCSprite* sprite=[CCSprite spriteWithSpriteFrameName:frameName];

    // Position the new sprite one screen width to the right
    sprite.anchorPoint=CGPointMake(0, 0.5f);
    sprite.position=CGPointMake(screenSize.width, screenSize.height / 2);

    // Flip the sprite so that it aligns perfectly with its neighbor
    sprite.flipX=YES;

    // Add the sprite using the same tag offset by numStripes
    [spriteBatch addChild:sprite z:i tag:i+numStripes];
}
```

The stripes' anchorPoint is changed from its default (0.5f, 0.5f) to (0, 0.5f) to make them left-aligned. Doing that makes it easier to work with the parallax sprites, because in this particular case you don't want to have to take into account that that texture's origin and the sprite's x position aren't at the same location. Figure 7-6 shows how this makes it easier to calculate the x position.

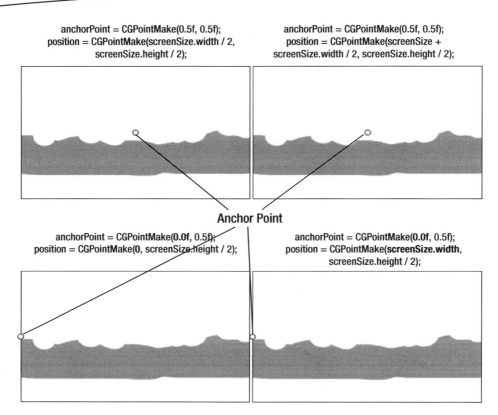

anchorPoint = CGPointMake(0.5f, 0.5f);
position = CGPointMake(screenSize.width / 2, screenSize.height / 2);

anchorPoint = CGPointMake(0.5f, 0.5f);
position = CGPointMake(screenSize + screenSize.width / 2, screenSize.height / 2);

Anchor Point

anchorPoint = CGPointMake(0.0f, 0.5f);
position = CGPointMake(0, screenSize.height / 2);

anchorPoint = CGPointMake(0.0f, 0.5f);
position = CGPointMake(**screenSize.width**, screenSize.height / 2);

Figure 7-6. *Anchor point moved to the left for simplicity*

You can see in Listing 7-6 how this is helpful in the changed update method, which now gives us endless scrolling.

Listing 7-6. Moving the Image Pairs Seamlessly

```
-(void) update:(ccTime)delta
{
    for (CCSprite* sprite in spriteBatch.children)
    {
        NSNumber* factor=[speedFactors objectAtIndex:sprite.zOrder];

        CGPoint pos=sprite.position;
        pos.x -=(scrollSpeed * factor.floatValue) * (delta * 50);

        // Reposition stripes when they're out of bounds
        CGSize screenSize=[CCDirector sharedDirector].winSize;
        if (pos.x<-screenSize.width)
        {
            pos.x+= screenSize.width * 2;
        }

        sprite.position=pos;
    }
}
```

The stripes' x position now only needs to be checked if it's less than negative screen width and, if it is, multiplied by twice the screen width. Essentially, this moves the sprite that has just left the screen on the left side to the right side, just outside the screen. This repeats forever with the same two sprites, giving the effect of endless scrolling.

> **Tip**   Notice that the background of the screen scrolls, but the ship stays in place. Inexperienced game developers often have the misconception that everything on the screen needs to be scrolling to achieve the effect of game objects passing by the player character as he progresses through the game world. Instead, you can much more easily create the illusion of objects moving on the screen by moving the background layers but keeping the player character fixed in place. Popular examples of games that make use of this visual illusion are Super Turbo Action Pig, Canabalt, Super Blast, DoodleJump, and Zombieville USA. Typically, the game objects scrolling into view are randomly generated shortly before they appear, and when they leave the screen they're removed from the game. Chapter 11 makes use of the same effect where the player character remains in the center of the screen while only the game world underneath the player is actually moving, giving the impression that the player moves around in the world.

Fixing the Flicker

So far, so good. Only one issue remains. If you look closely, you'll notice a vertical, flickering line appearing where the two background stripes meet. That's where they align with each other. This line appears because of rounding errors in their positions in combination with subpixel rendering. From time to time, a 1-pixel-wide gap can appear for just a fraction of a second. Sometimes it may appear every other frame, other times only occasionally; it depends on the scrolling speed. It's still noticeable and is something you should get rid of for a commercial-quality game.

The simplest solution is to overlap the stripes by just 1 pixel. In the ScrollingWithJoy02 project change the initial positions for the flipped background stripes in the `init` method by subtracting 1 pixel from the x position:

```
sprite.position=CGPointMake(screenSize.width - 1, screenSize.height / 2);
```

This also requires updating the stripe-repositioning code in the `update` method so that the stripe is positioned 2 pixels farther to the left than before:

```
// Reposition stripes when they're out of bounds
if (pos.x<-screenSize.width)
{
    pos.x+= (screenSize.width * 2) - 2;
}
```

Why 2 pixels? Well, because the initial position of the flipped stripes is already moved to the left by 1 pixel, we have to move all of them 2 pixels to the left each time they flip around to maintain the same distance and to keep the overlap of 1 pixel.

An alternative solution would be to update only the position of the currently leftmost sprite and then find the sprite that is aligned to the right of it and offset it by exactly the screen width. This way, you also avoid the rounding errors. Figure 7-7 shows the finished result with the final graphics.

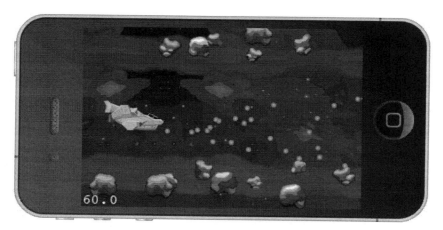

Figure 7-7. The result: an infinitely scrolling parallax background

Repeat, Repeat, Repeat

Another neat trick deserves mention. You can set any texture to repeat over a certain rectangular area. If you make this area big enough, you can have this texture repeat nearly endlessly. At least several thousand pixels or dozens of screen areas can be covered with a repeating texture, with no penalty to memory usage.

The trick is to use the GL_REPEAT texture parameter supported by OpenGL. But it only works with square images that are exactly a power of 2, like 32×32 or 512×512 pixels. Listing 7-7 shows the code.

Listing 7-7. Repeating Background with GL_REPEAT

```
CGRect repeatRect=CGRectMake(-5000, -5000, 5000, 5000);
CCSprite* sprite=[CCSprite spriteWithFile:@"square.png" rect:repeatRect];
ccTexParams params =
{
    GL_LINEAR, // texture minifying function
    GL_LINEAR, // texture magnification function
    GL_REPEAT, // how texture should wrap along X coordinates
    GL_REPEAT  // how texture should wrap along Y coordinates
};
[sprite.texture setTexParameters:&params];
```

In this case, you must initialize the sprite with a rect that determines the area the sprite will occupy. The ccTexParams struct is initialized with the wrap parameters for the texture coordinates set to GL_REPEAT. Don't worry if that doesn't mean anything to you. These OpenGL parameters are then set on the sprite's texture using the CCTexture2D method setTexParameters.

The result is a tiled area repeating the same square.png image over and over again. If you move the sprite, the whole area covered by the repeatRect is moved. You could use this trick to remove the bottommost background stripe and replace it with a smaller image that simply repeats. I'll leave that up to you as an exercise.

A Virtual Joypad

Because the iOS devices all use a touchscreen for input and have no buttons, D-pads, or analog joypads like conventional mobile gaming devices do, you need something called a *virtual joypad*. This emulates the behavior of digital or analog thumbsticks by allowing you to touch the screen where the digipad or thumbstick is displayed and move your finger over it to control the action on the screen. Buttons are also designated areas of the touchscreen that you can tap or hold to cause actions on the screen. Figure 7-8 shows a virtual joypad in action.

Figure 7-8. A skinned analog thumbstick and fire button created with SneakyInput

Caution Virtual joypads resemble joypad controllers in looks but never in feel. The user is still touching a flat surface with no feedback to the fingers as to how far the virtual analog stick was moved or whether the virtual button has actually been pressed or was missed. A number of players feel uneasy controlling a game with virtual joypads. It has become more or less common wisdom that a virtual joypad should have no more than two or three controller elements, usually a stick/pad (sometimes limited to two directions) and one or two buttons. Adding more can make your game exponentially harder to control. Also consider that you can often replace at least one axis of the directional buttons with input from the accelerometer, so that the user can tilt the device to move left or right instead of holding the corresponding virtual buttons.

Introducing SneakyInput

Over time, many a developer has faced the problem of implementing a virtual joypad. There are many ways to go about it, and even more ways to fail at it. But why spend time on that if there's a ready-to-use solution?

This is generally sound advice. Before you program anything that seems reasonably common, which others have probably worked on before, always check to see whether a general-purpose solution is available that you can just use instead of having to spend a lot of time creating it yourself. In this case, SneakyInput is just too good to be ignored.

SneakyInput was created by Nick Pannuto, with skinning examples by CJ Hanson. SneakyInput is open source software and free to download, but if you like this product, please consider making a donation to Nick Pannuto here: `http://pledgie.com/campaigns/9124`.

Kobold2D users don't need to concern themselves—SneakyInput is already part of the Kobold2D distribution. Kobold2D users can skip the next two sections.

Download SneakyInput

The SneakyInput source code is hosted on GitHub, a social coding web site: `http://github.com/sneakyness/SneakyInput`.

It may not be immediately obvious what you have to do to download the source code from GitHub. When you click a file, you see the actual source code displayed in your browser. But you want the full source code project, not individual files. What you do is locate either the Downloads tab below the upper right-hand corner of the web site, or the ZIP button on the left side of the page just between the Clone in Mac and HTTP|Git Read-Only buttons. Then save the file to your computer and extract it.

Because SneakyInput comes with an example project that has cocos2d integrated, it's likely that the cocos2d version used by the SneakyInput demo project may not be the most current version, or may not even compile. For the rest of the chapter that doesn't matter, as I'll cherry-pick the code that works with cocos2d 2.0.

Integrating SneakyInput

You already have a working project and you don't want to use the project provided by SneakyInput. So how do you get it to work with your project?

This issue isn't limited to SneakyInput but possibly any source code project you can download that comes already bundled with its own version of cocos2d. In most cases, and as long as the programming language of that source code is Objective-C, you only have to figure out which of the project's files are necessary and add them to your own project. There's no clear guideline, however, because every project is different.

I can tell you which files you need to add to your project regarding SneakyInput, however. It consists at its core of four classes:

- SneakyButton and SneakyButtonSkinnedBase
- SneakyJoystick and SneakyJoystickSkinnedBase

The remaining files aren't needed but may serve as references, except for the ColoredCircleSprite and ColoredSquareSprite classes, which are incompatible with cocos2d 2.0. Figure 7-9 shows the selection in the Add Files To … dialog.

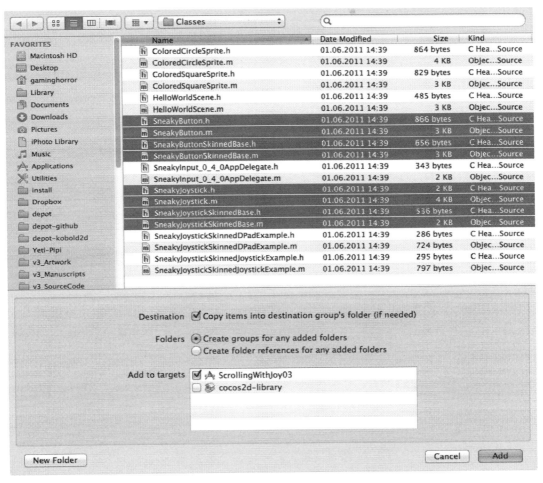

Figure 7-9. You need these files to get SneakyInput to work in your own project; the other files are used only for example code

The HelloWorldScene class is created by a cocos2d project template and most likely doesn't contain anything but example code. Of course, I already have an AppDelegate in my project, so I don't need to be adding SneakyInput's AppDelegate class—it might be in conflict with the existing AppDelegate. Then there are two classes explicitly suffixed with Example, which indicates that these files are not core classes for SneakyInput but further example code.

After adding the SneakyInput button and joystick classes, your project won't compile anymore. That's because SneakyInput classes haven't been converted to ARC. You should do so now by selecting Edit ➤ Refactor ➤ Convert to Objective-C ARC … from Xcode's menu. Make sure only the ScrollingWithJoy03 project is selected before running the ARC conversion check. When Xcode is done checking you'll see a preview; click Save to accept all changes.

> **Tip** If you ever run into third-party code that can't be refactored to ARC, you can do one of two things. One is to compile that code as a separate static library with ARC disabled and linking that library with your app, just like what you did with cocos2d in Chapter 2. The alternative is to add the compiler flag `-fobjc-no-arc` to every file that should be compiled without ARC. To add the flag, in the target's Build Phases tab expand the Compile Sources section and enter the flag on the right-hand side to the Compiler Flags column. Note that code requiring either of these approaches may be generally incompatible with ARC. Consult with the author or other users of the code to find out whether the code is safe to use with ARC.

Now the code will compile but not without four warnings complaining about sharedDispatcher being deprecated. You can choose to ignore the warnings but eventually you're going to have to fix them, so you may as well do it now. The lines in question all start with [CCTouchDispatcher sharedDispatcher], for example:

```
[[CCTouchDispatcher sharedDispatcher] removeDelegate:self];
```

To fix the warning, change the lines so that they use the touch dispatcher provided by CCDirector instead:

```
[[CCDirector sharedDirector].touchDispatcher removeDelegate:self];
```

Touch Button to Shoot

Let's try this. With the SneakyInput source code added to the project ScrollingWithJoy03, the first goal is to add a button that allows the player to shoot bullets from the player's ship. You're going to add a separate InputLayer class to the project by adding an Objective-C class template file and making sure it's derived from CCLayer. Add the InputLayer class instance to the GameLayer class. Listing 7-8 updates the scene method to add the new InputLayer to it, and both layers get a tag just in case you need to identify them later.

Listing 7-8. Adding the InputLayer to the GameScene

```
#import "InputLayer.h"

...

+(id) scene
{
    CCScene* scene = [CCScene node];
    GameScene* layer = [GameScene node];
    [scene addChild:layer z:0 tag:GameSceneLayerTagGame];
    InputLayer* inputLayer = [InputLayer node];
    [scene addChild:inputLayer z:1 tag:GameSceneLayerTagInput];
    return scene;
}
```

The new tags are defined in the GameLayer header file just above the existing GameSceneNodeTags enum as follows:

```
typedef enum
{
    GameSceneLayerTagGame = 1,
    GameSceneLayerTagInput,
} GameSceneLayerTags;
```

With the InputLayer in place, the next step is to add the header files for the SneakyInput files you want to use to the InputLayer.h header file. I'm not picky, and you're probably going to use most of the classes, so just add all the SneakyInput header files:

```
#import <Foundation/Foundation.h>
#import "cocos2d.h"
#import "GameLayer.h"
#import "Ship.h"

// SneakyInput headers
#import "SneakyButton.h"
#import "SneakyButtonSkinnedBase.h"
#import "SneakyJoystick.h"
#import "SneakyJoystickSkinnedBase.h"

@interface InputLayer : CCLayer
{
    SneakyButton* fireButton;
    SneakyJoystick* joystick;

    ccTime totalTime;
    ccTime nextShotTime;
}
@end
```

In addition, you want to add a SneakyButton member variable for easier access to the button you're going to create now. The addFireButton method does this in Listing 7-9. I explain the totalTime and nextShotTime variables as well as the SneakyJoystick later.

Listing 7-9. Creating a SneakyButton

```
-(id) init
{
    if ((self = [super init]))
    {
        [self addFireButton];
        [self scheduleUpdate];
    }
    return self;
}

-(void) addFireButton
{
    float buttonRadius = 80;
    CGSize screenSize = [CCDirector sharedDirector].winSize;

    fireButton = [[SneakyButton alloc] initWithRect:CGRectZero];
    fireButton.radius = buttonRadius;
```

```
    fireButton.position=CGPointMake(screenSize.width - buttonRadius, buttonRadius);
    [self addChild:fireButton];
}
```

SneakyButton doesn't use the CGRect parameter of the button's initWithRect method, which is why you're simply passing CGRectZero. The actual touch code uses the radius property to determine whether the button should react to the touch. The button in this case should be neatly tucked into the lower right-hand corner. Subtracting the buttonRadius from the screen width and setting its height to buttonRadius places it exactly at the desired location.

> **Tip**   The use of the buttonRadius variable lets you change the radius of the button in one place. Otherwise, you'd have to update several values in several places. This is not only extra work for a value you might want to tweak several times before you get it exactly the way you want, but it can also introduce subtle bugs, because you're a human and you tend to forget things, such as changing that one value over there. Suddenly the button is offset—or worse, the input doesn't match the button's location.

The InputLayer class also schedules the update method. For now, the update method is used only to log whether the fire button was touched:

```
-(void) update:(ccTime)delta
{
    if (fireButton.active)
    {
        CCLOG(@"FIRE!!!");
    }
}
```

Instead of shooting a bullet, keep things simple for now and simply log a successful button press. If you try the ScrollingWithJoy03 project now, you'll notice that there isn't any button drawn. Yet when you touch the screen at the lower right-hand corner, you'll see the "FIRE!!!" message appear in the Debugger Console window. So, all is well and right, except that the button can't be seen—which you need to fix.

Skinning the Button

Eeeww! No, it's not what you think. *Skinning* in computer graphics refers to giving an otherwise featureless object a texture or simply a different look. In this case, you want to actually see your button, so you need an image for that.

I created four button images that are 100 × 100 pixels in size—twice the final button radius of 50. The button images come in four variations: Default, Pressed, Activated, and Disabled. The default state is what the button looks like when it isn't pressed, which should make it obvious what the Pressed state is. The Activated state comes into play only for toggle buttons, meaning the toggle button is *active*, or *on*. The Disabled image is used if the button currently has no function. For example, when the ship's weapons are overheated and you can't shoot for a few seconds, you could disable the button, and it would show the Disabled image.

For the shoot button, you only need the Default and Pressed images. Listing 7-11 shows the updated addFireButton method of the InputLayer class.

Listing 7-11. Replacing Listing 7-9 with a Skinned Button

```
float buttonRadius = 50;
CGSize screenSize = [CCDirector sharedDirector].winSize;

CCSprite* idle = [CCSprite spriteWithSpriteFrameName:@"fire-button-idle.png"];
CCSprite* press = [CCSprite spriteWithSpriteFrameName:@"fire-button-pressed.png"];

fireButton = [[SneakyButton alloc] initWithRect:CGRectZero];
fireButton.isHoldable = YES;

SneakyButtonSkinnedBase* skinFireButton = [[SneakyButtonSkinnedBase alloc] init];
skinFireButton.button = fireButton;
skinFireButton.defaultSprite = idle;
skinFireButton.pressSprite = press;
skinFireButton.position = CGPointMake(screenSize.width - buttonRadius, buttonRadius);
[self addChild:skinFireButton];
```

The code initializes the fireButton as usual except that I made it holdable, which means you can keep it pressed down for a continuous stream of bullets. It also doesn't set the radius property anymore, because the images of the SneakyButtonSkinnedBase class determine the radius now. The fireButton is later assigned to the skinFireButton.button property, so that the two work together.

Instead of positioning the fireButton, the skinned button is now determining the position of the button on the screen; the actual fireButton is updated accordingly by the SneakyButtonSkinnedBase class.

At this point, it makes sense to also write the firing code; Listing 7-12 shows the update method now sending the fire message to the GameScene class. This is also where the totalTime and nextShotTime variables come into play.

Listing 7-12. Shooting Bullets Whenever the Fire Button Is Active

```
-(void) update:(ccTime)delta
{
    totalTime += delta;

    GameLayer* game = [GameLayer sharedGameLayer];
    Ship* ship = [game defaultShip];

    if (fireButton.active && totalTime > nextShotTime)
    {
        nextShotTime = totalTime + 0.5f;
        [game shootBulletFromShip:ship];
    }

    // Allow faster shooting by quickly tapping the fire button
    if (fireButton.active == NO)
    {
        nextShotTime = 0;
    }
}
```

The two ccTime variables, totalTime and nextShotTime, are used to limit the number of bullets the ship will emit to two per second. If the fire button isn't active (meaning it isn't pressed), the nextShotTime is set to 0 so that the next time you press the button a shot is guaranteed to be fired. Tap the button quickly, and you should be able to shoot more bullets than with continuous fire.

You have to make a few minor changes in order to have the ship shoot bullets when pressing the fire button. Add the declaration of the defaultShip method to the GameLayer interface as well as the GameSceneNodeTagShip enum:

```
typedef enum
{
        GameSceneNodeTagBullet=1,
        GameSceneNodeTagBulletSpriteBatch,
        GameSceneNodeTagShip,

} GameSceneNodeTags;

@interface GameLayer : CCLayer
{
    NSUInteger nextInactiveBullet;
}

+(id) scene;
+(GameLayer*) sharedGameLayer;
-(CCSpriteBatchNode*) bulletSpriteBatch;
-(void) shootBulletFromShip:(Ship*)ship;
-(Ship*) defaultShip;
@end
```

In the implementation file of GameLayer, find the lines where the ship class is created in the init method and assign the ship the GameSceneNodeTagShip tag so that it's easily accessed later on. Alternatively you can also use an instance variable to store the reference to the ship object.

```
// add the ship
Ship* ship=[Ship ship];
ship.position=CGPointMake(80, screenSize.height / 2);
ship.tag=GameSceneNodeTagShip;
[self addChild:ship z:10];
```

Then add the new defaultShip method anywhere in the @implementation section of the GameLayer class.

```
-(Ship*) defaultShip
{
    CCNode* node=[self getChildByTag:GameSceneNodeTagShip];
    NSAssert([node isKindOfClass:[Ship class]], @"node is not a Ship!");
    return (Ship*)node;
}
```

What's left is to stop the ship from automatically shooting bullets all the time. To do that, open the Ship implementation file and comment out or remove the shootBulletFromShip line in the update method:

```
-(void) update:(ccTime)delta
{
    // Shooting is relayed to the game scene
    //[[GameLayer sharedGameLayer] shootBulletFromShip:self];
}
```

Now you can shoot bullets on demand whenever you press or hold the fire button. If you tap the button repeatedly in quick succession, you should be able to shoot bullets more rapidly.

Controlling the Action

You can't fly a ship without some form of input. This is where SneakyJoystick lends a helping hand, I mean, a helping virtual thumbstick. For the joystick, go right ahead and create a skinned one in the addJoystick method in Listing 7-13. You should add this method to the InputLayer class.

Listing 7-13. Adding a Skinned Joystick

```
-(void) addJoystick
{
    float stickRadius = 50;

    joystick = [[SneakyJoystick alloc] initWithRect:
        CGRectMake(0, 0, stickRadius, stickRadius)];
    joystick.autoCenter = YES;
    joystick.hasDeadzone = YES;
    joystick.deadRadius = 10;

    CCSprite* back = [CCSprite spriteWithSpriteFrameName:@"joystick-back.png"];
    CCSprite* thumb = [CCSprite spriteWithSpriteFrameName:@"joystick-stick.png"];

    SneakyJoystickSkinnedBase* skinStick = [[SneakyJoystickSkinnedBase alloc] init];
    skinStick.joystick = joystick;
    skinStick.backgroundSprite.color = ccYELLOW;
    skinStick.backgroundSprite = back;
    skinStick.thumbSprite = thumb;
    skinStick.position = CGPointMake(stickRadius * 1.5f, stickRadius * 1.5f);
    [self addChild:skinStick];
}
```

The SneakyJoystick is initialized with a CGRect, and contrary to the SneakyButton, the CGRect is actually used to determine the joystick's radius. I set the joystick to autoCenter so that the thumb controller jumps back to the neutral position, like most real-world game controllers. The dead zone is also enabled; this is a small area defined by the deadRadius in which you can move the thumb controller without any effect. This gives users a certain radius where they can keep the thumb controller centered. Without the dead zone, it would be almost impossible to center the thumb controller manually.

The SneakyJoystickSkinnedBase is positioned a small distance away from the edge of the screen. The button's position and size may not be ideal for the game, but it demonstrates the controls better. If you align the thumb controller with the screen edges, it's too easy to inadvertently move your finger off the touchscreen and thus lose control of the ship.

Before you can test the joystick you also have to send the addJoystick message to the InputLayer class. Just add this next to the addFireButton in the init method:

```
-(id) init
{
    if ((self=[super init]))
    {
        [self addFireButton];
        [self addJoystick];
        [self scheduleUpdate];
    }
    return self;
}
```

> **Tip**   Gray areas are useful! I mean gray images like joystick-back.png. By using just grayscale colors, you can colorize (tint) the image using the color property of the sprite. You can create red, green, yellow, blue, magenta, and other colored versions of the same image, saving both download size and in-game memory. The only drawback is that its's a flat color, so instead of shades of gray, your image uses shades of red. This trick works best with images that are supposed to be shades of a single color.

You want the thumbstick on the screen to be used to control the ship, of course. As usual, the update method processes the input, as shown in Listing 7-14. You can add the changes at the end of the method.

Listing 7-14. Moving the Ship Based on Joystick Input

```
-(void) update:(ccTime)delta
{
    ...
    // Velocity must be scaled up by a factor that feels right
    CGPoint velocity=ccpMult(joystick.velocity, 7000 * delta);
    ship.position=CGPointMake(ship.position.x+velocity.x * delta,↩
        ship.position.y+velocity.y * delta);
}
```

You use the velocity property of the joystick to change the ship's position, but not without scaling it up. The velocity values are a tiny fraction of a pixel, so you need to multiply the velocity using cocos2d's ccpMult method, which takes a CGPoint and a float factor, for the joypad velocity to have a noticeable effect. The scale factor is arbitrary; it's just a value that feels good for this game.

To ensure smooth movement even if the update method is called at uneven intervals, factor in the update method's delta parameter as well. The delta parameter is passed by cocos2d and contains the time elapsed since the update method was last called. This isn't strictly necessary, but it's good practice. If you don't do it, you run the risk that the ship will move more slowly whenever the framerate drops below 60 fps. Tiny things like these can be pretty annoying to players, and as a game developer your goal is the exact opposite of annoying players.

At this point, moving the ship outside the screen area is still possible. I bet you'd like for the ship to stay on the screen as much as I do. And you may be tempted to add this code directly to the InputLayer where the ship's position is updated. That brings up a question: do you want to prevent the joystick input from moving the ship outside the screen, or do you want to prevent the ship from ever being able to move outside the screen, regardless of who or what changes its position? The latter is the more general solution and preferable in this case. To do so, you only need to override the setPosition method in the Ship class by adding the code shown in Listing 7-15 to the Ship class.

Listing 7-15. Overriding the Ship's setPosition Method

```
// Override setPosition to keep the ship within bounds
-(void) setPosition:(CGPoint)pos
{
    CGSize screenSize = [CCDirector sharedDirector].winSize;
    float halfWidth = contentSize_.width * 0.5f;
    float halfHeight = contentSize_.height * 0.5f;

    // Cap the position so the ship's sprite stays on the screen
    if (pos.x < halfWidth)
    {   pos.x = halfWidth;

    }
    else if (pos.x > (screenSize.width - halfWidth))
    {
        pos.x = screenSize.width - halfWidth;
    }

    if (pos.y < halfHeight)
    {
        pos.y = halfHeight;
    }
    else if (pos.y > (screenSize.height - halfHeight))
    {
        pos.y = screenSize.height - halfHeight;
    }

    // Must call super with the new position
    [super setPosition:pos];
}
```

Every time the ship's position property changes, the preceding code performs the check to see whether the ship's sprite is still inside the screen boundaries. If not, then the x or y coordinate is set to a distance of half the contentSize away from the respective screen border. This prevents any part of the player ship's sprite from leaving the screen.

Because position is a property, the setPosition method gets called by this code:

```
ship.position = CGPointMake(200, 100);
```

You can override other base class methods in this way to change the behavior of your game objects. For example, if an object is allowed to be rotated only between 0 and 180 degrees, you'd override the setRotation:(float)rotation method and add the code to limit the rotation.

Digital Controls

You can turn the SneakyJoystick class into a digital controller as well, often referred to as a *D-pad*. The necessary code changes are minimal:

```
joystick=[SneakyJoystick joystickWithRect:CGRectMake(0, 0, stickRadius, stickRadius)];
joystick.autoCenter=YES;

// Now with fewer directions
joystick.isDPad=YES;
joystick.numberOfDirections=8;
```

The dead zone properties can be removed—they're not needed for a digital controller. The joystick is set to digital controls by setting the isDPad property to YES.

You can also define the number of directions. While D-pads regularly have four directions, in many games you can keep two directions pressed at the same time to have the character move in a diagonal direction. To achieve the same effect, set the numberOfDirections property to 8. SneakyJoystick automatically ensures that these directions are evenly divided onto the thumbpad controller. Of course, you'll get strange results if you set the number of directions to 6, but then again, maybe that's exactly what you need to travel across a hexagonal tile map.

Summary

In this chapter you learned several tricks to make an effective parallax scrolling background. Not only can you scroll the background infinitely and without flickering edges, you also learned how to properly separate the parallax layers so TexturePacker can cut down on unnecessary transparent areas while keeping the image's offset so you don't have to fumble with positioning the parallax layers.

The second half of this chapter introduced you to SneakyInput, an open source project to add virtual thumbsticks and buttons to any cocos2d game. It may not be perfect, as it needs a few tweaks to work with ARC and the latest cocos2d 2.0 version—unless you're using Kobold2D, of course—but it's good enough for most games, and it definitely beats writing your own virtual thumbstick code.

The ship is now controllable with a virtual joypad and stays within the screen's boundaries while moving, and it's able to shoot with the press of a button—but the game is still lacking something. A shoot-'em-up isn't a shoot-'em-up without something to shoot down, is it? The next chapter addresses that issue.

Chapter **8**

Shoot 'em Up

What does a game of this kind need above all else? Something to shoot up and bullets to evade. In this chapter, you'll be adding enemies to the game and even a boss monster.

Both enemies and player will use the new BulletCache class to shoot a variety of bullets from the same pool. The cache class reuses inactive bullets to avoid constantly allocating and releasing bullets from memory. Likewise, enemies will use their own EnemyCache class because they, too, will appear in greater numbers on the screen.

Obviously the player will be able to shoot these enemies. I also introduce the concept of component-based programming, which allows you to extend the game's actors in a modular way. Besides shooting and moving components, you also create a healthbar component for the boss monster. After all, a boss monster should not be an ins tant kill but require several hits before it is destroyed.

Adding the BulletCache Class

The BulletCache class is the one-stop shop for creating new bullets in the ShootEmUp01 project. Previously all this code was in the GameLayer class, but it shouldn't be the responsibility of the GameLayer to manage and create new bullets. Listing 8-1 shows the new BulletCache header file, and it now contains the CCSpriteBatchNode and the inactive bullets counter.

Listing 8-1. The @interface of the BulletCache Class

```
#import <Foundation/Foundation.h>
#import "cocos2d.h"

@interface BulletCache : CCNode
{
    CCSpriteBatchNode* batch;
    NSUInteger nextInactiveBullet;
}
```

```
-(void) shootBulletFrom:(CGPoint)startPosition
             velocity:(CGPoint)velocity
            frameName:(NSString*)frameName;
@end
```

To refactor the bullet-shooting code out of the GameLayer class, you need to move both the initialization and the method to shoot bullets to the new BulletCache class.

Therefore remove the declaration and implementation of the shootBulletFromShip:(Ship*)ship method from the GameLayer class. Also remove the nextInactiveBullet instance variable from the interface and remove the bullet initialization code from the init method, as seen in Listing 8-2. All this code will be moved over to the new BulletCache class, the implementation of which is in Listing 8-4.

Listing 8-2. Remove This Code from the GameLayer class's init Method

```
// Now uses the image from the Texture Atlas.
CCSpriteFrame* bulletFrame=[[CCSpriteFrameCache sharedSpriteFrameCache]
spriteFrameByName:@"bullet.png"];
CCSpriteBatchNode* batch=[CCSpriteBatchNode batchNodeWithTexture:bulletFrame.texture];
[self addChild:batch z:1 tag:GameSceneNodeTagBulletSpriteBatch];

// Create a number of bullets up front and re-use them whenever necessary.
for (int i=0; i<400; i++)
{
    Bullet* bullet=[Bullet bullet];
    bullet.visible=NO;
    [batch addChild:bullet];
}

// call bullet countrer from time to time
[self schedule:@selector(countBullets:) interval:3];

BulletCache* bulletCache=[BulletCache node];
[self addChild:bulletCache z:1 tag:GameSceneNodeTagBulletCache];
```

You should then add the initialization of the BulletCache class in place of the removed code from Listing 8-2 and also import the BulletCache.h header file at the top of the GameLayer.m implementation file.

Listing 8-3. Import the BulletCache Header and Add the BulletCache Initialization to the init Method

```
#import "BulletCache.h"

...

-(id) init
{
    if ((self=[super init]))
    {

        ...

        BulletCache* bulletCache=[BulletCache node];
```

```
        [self addChild:bulletCache z:1 tag:GameSceneNodeTagBulletCache];
    }
    return self;
}
```

You will also have to add GameSceneNodeTagBulletCache to the GameSceneNodeTags enum in the GameLayer.h file, and you have to add a bulletCache accessor method so other classes can access the BulletCache instance through the GameLayer. You can add this method just next to the defaultShip method:

```
-(BulletCache*) bulletCache
{
    CCNode* node=[self getChildByTag:GameSceneNodeTagBulletCache];
    NSAssert([node isKindOfClass:[BulletCache class]], @"not a BulletCache");
    return (BulletCache*)node;
}
```

Finally, this is the refactored GameLayer interface with the changes highlighted. Most notably a @class forward for the BulletCache class was added, and both defaultShip and bulletCache accessor methods are declared as properties, so from now on you can alternatively access them with dot notation.

```
...
@class Ship;
@class BulletCache;

@interface GameLayer : CCLayer
{
}

@property (readonly) Ship* defaultShip;
@property (readonly) BulletCache* bulletCache;

+(id) scene;
+(GameLayer*) sharedGameLayer;
-(CCSpriteBatchNode*) bulletSpriteBatch;
@end
```

For the new BulletCache class, I decided to keep the CCSpriteBatchNode in a member variable instead of using the CCNode getChildByTag method every time you need the sprite batch object. It's a minor performance optimization. Because you'll be adding the BulletCache class as child to the GameLayer, you can simply add the sprite batch node to the BulletCache class.

> **Note** There's little harm in increasing the depth of the scene hierarchy by adding an in-between CCNode like BulletCache. If you're concerned about scene hierarchy depth, the alternative would be to add the sprite batch node to the GameLayer class as usual and use an accessor method to get to the sprite batch node in the BulletCache class. But the additional function call overhead could possibly void any performance gain. If in doubt, always prefer to make your code more readable and then refactor later to improve performance where necessary, and only where necessary. And make no performance optimizations based on assumptions alone. Always measure performance before and after making supposedly performance-enhancing changes!

Listing 8-4. The BulletCache Maintains a Pool of Bullets for Reuse

```
#import "BulletCache.h"
#import "Bullet.h"

@implementation BulletCache

-(id) init
{
    if ((self=[super init]))
    {
        // get any bullet image from the texture atlas we're using
        CCSpriteFrame* bulletFrame=[[CCSpriteFrameCache sharedSpriteFrameCache]↵
            spriteFrameByName:@"bullet.png"];

        // use the bullet's texture
        batch=[CCSpriteBatchNode batchNodeWithTexture:bulletFrame.texture];
        [self addChild:batch];

        // Create a number of bullets up front and re-use them
        for (int i=0; i<200; i++)
        {
            Bullet* bullet=[Bullet bullet];
            bullet.visible=NO;
            [batch addChild:bullet];
        }
    }

    return self;
}

-(void) shootBulletFrom:(CGPoint)startPosition
              velocity:(CGPoint)velocity
             frameName:(NSString*)frameName
{
    CCArray* bullets=batch.children;
    CCNode* node=[bullets objectAtIndex:nextInactiveBullet];
    NSAssert([node isKindOfClass:[Bullet class]], @"not a Bullet!");

    Bullet* bullet=(Bullet*)node;
    [bullet shootBulletFrom:startPosition velocity:velocity frameName:frameName];

    nextInactiveBullet++;
    if (nextInactiveBullet>= bullets.count)
    {
        nextInactiveBullet=0;
    }
}
@end
```

The shootBulletFrom method has changed the most, as you can see. It now takes three
parameters—startPosition, velocity, and frameName—instead of a pointer to the Ship class.
It then passes on these parameters to the Bullet class's shootBulletFrom method, which I had
to refactor as well. This is the new implementation that replaces the original shootBulletFrom
method:

```
-(void) shootBulletFrom:(CGPoint)startPosition
              velocity:(CGPoint)vel
             frameName:(NSString*)frameName
{
    self.velocity=vel;
    self.position=startPosition;
    self.visible=YES;

    // change the bullet's texture by setting a different SpriteFrame to be displayed
    CCSpriteFrame* frame=[[CCSpriteFrameCache sharedSpriteFrameCache]↵
        spriteFrameByName:frameName];
    [self setDisplayFrame:frame];

    [self unscheduleUpdate];
    [self scheduleUpdate];
}
```

You also need to replace the method declaration in the Bullet.h interface. No surprises there:

```
-(void) shootBulletFrom:(CGPoint)startPosition
              velocity:(CGPoint)vel
             frameName:(NSString*)frameName;
```

Both velocity and position are now directly assigned to the bullet. This means the code calling the shootBulletFrom method has to determine the position, direction, and speed of the bullet. This is exactly what you want: full flexibility for shooting bullets, including changing the bullet's sprite frame by using the setDisplayFrame method. Because the bullets are all in the same texture atlas and thus use the same texture, all it needs to do to change which bullet is displayed is set the desired sprite frame. In effect, this simply renders a different part of the texture and comes at no extra cost.

While in the Bullet class, I also fixed the boundary issues the bullets would have had—that only bullets moving outside the right-hand side of the screen would have been set invisible and put back on the waiting list. By using the CGRectIntersectsRect check with the bullet's boundingBox and the screenRect in the update method, any bullet having moved completely outside the screen area will be marked for reuse. Shown in Listing 8-5 are the improved init and update methods of the Bullet class.

Listing 8-5. The Bullet Class Code Is Changed to Test if a Bullet Left the Screen

```
static CGRect screenRect;
-(id) initWithBulletImage
{
    if ((self=[super initWithSpriteFrameName:@"bullet.png"]))
    {
        // make sure to initialize the screen rect only once
        if (CGRectIsEmpty(screenRect))
        {
            CGSize screenSize=[CCDirector sharedDirector].winSize;
            screenRect=CGRectMake(0, 0, screenSize.width, screenSize.height);
        }
    }
```

```
        return self;
    }

    ...

    -(void) update:(ccTime)delta
    {
        self.position = ccpAdd(self.position, ccpMult(velocity, delta));

        // When the bullet leaves the screen, make it invisible
        CGSize screenSize = [CCDirector sharedDirector].winSize;
        CGRect screenRect = CGRectMake(0, 0, screenSize.width, screenSize.height);
        if (CGRectIntersectsRect(self.boundingBox, screenRect) == NO)
        {
            self.visible = NO;
            [self unscheduleUpdate];
        }
    }
}
```

The screenRect variable itself is now stored for convenience and performance reasons as a static variable, so it can be accessed by other instances of the Bullet class and doesn't need to be re-created for each use. Static variables like screenRect are available in the class implementation file where they're declared. They're like global variables to the class; any class instance can read and modify the variable, as opposed to class member variables, which are local to every class instance. Because the screen size never changes during game play, and all Bullet instances need to use this variable, it makes sense to store it in a static variable for all class instances. The first bullet to be initialized sets the screenRect variable. The CGRectIsEmpty method checks whether the screenRect variable is still uninitialized; because the variable is static, it needs to be initialized only once.

In fact screenRect is useful to other classes, so it may be a good idea to move it to where you can access it from other classes. One way to do that is to add a property to the GameLayer class. You add the same init code as in Listing 8-5 to the GameLayer init method, and a method to return the static variable with the same name:

```
static CGRect screenRect;
-(CGRect) screenRect

{
    return screenRect;
}
```

And to the interface of GameLayer add the readonly property declaration for screenRect:

```
@property (readonly) CGRect screenRect;
```

By the way, whether screenRect is a static variable or an instance variable of the GameLayer class makes no difference in this instance. You can now import the GameLayer.h header file in another class and access screenRect via:

```
CGRect rect = [GameLayer sharedGameLayer].screenRect;
```

The InputLayer can now use the new BulletCache class and use it to shoot the player's bullets. The bullet properties, such as starting position, velocity, and the sprite frame to use, are now passed by the shooting code in the update method of the InputLayer in Listing 8-6.

Listing 8-6. The InputLayer Class Is Modified to Let the BulletCache Class Handle All the Action

```
#import "BulletCache.h"

...

-(void) update:(ccTime)delta
{
    totalTime += delta;

    GameLayer* game = [GameLayer sharedGameLayer];
    Ship* ship = game.defaultShip;
    BulletCache* bulletCache = game.bulletCache;

    if (fireButton.active && totalTime > nextShotTime)
    {
        nextShotTime = totalTime + 0.4f;

        // Set the position, velocity and spriteframe before shooting
        CGPoint shotPos = CGPointMake(ship.position.x+45, ship.position.y - 19);

        float spread = (CCRANDOM_0_1() - 0.5f) * 0.5f;
        CGPoint velocity = CGPointMake(200, spread * 50);
        [bulletCache shootBulletFrom:shotPos velocity:velocity frameName:@"bullet.png"];
    }
    // Allow faster shooting by quickly tapping the fire button.
    if (fireButton.active == NO)
    {
        nextShotTime = 0;
    }
    CGPoint velocity = ccpMult(joystick.velocity, 7000 * delta);
    ship.position = CGPointMake(ship.position.x+velocity.x * delta,
                                ship.position.y+velocity.y * delta);
}
```

This short refactoring session adds much-needed flexibility to shooting bullets. I'm sure you can imagine how enemies can now use the very same code to shoot their own bullets.

Let's Make Some Enemies

At this point, maybe you have only a fuzzy idea about what the enemies are, what they do, and what their behavior will be. That's the thing with enemies—you never quite know what they're up to.

In the case of games, that means going back to the drawing board, planning out what you want the enemies to do, and then deducing from that plan what you need to program. Contrary to real life, you have full control over the enemies. Doesn't that make you feel powerful? But before you or anyone else can have fun, you need to come up with a plan for world domination.

I already created the graphics for three different types of enemies. At this point, I know only that at least one of them is supposed to be a boss monster. Take a look at Figure 8-1 and try to imagine what these enemies could be up to.

Figure 8-1. The graphics used as the game's enemy characters

Before you start programming, you should have a good understanding of which behaviors the enemies will have in common so that you program those parts only once. Eliminating code duplication is the single most important goal of clean code design.

Let's see what we know for sure is common to all enemies:

- Shoots bullets

- Has logic that determines when and where to shoot what bullet

- Can be hit by player's bullets

- Cannot be hit by other enemy's bullets

- Can take one or more hits (has health)

- Has a specific behavior and movement pattern

- Has a specific behavior or animation when destroyed

- Will appear outside the screen area and move inside

- Will not leave the screen area once inside

When you look at that list, you may notice that some of these attributes also apply to the player's ship. It certainly can shoot bullets, we may want it to sustain multiple hits, and it should have a specific behavior or animation when destroyed. It makes sense to consider the player's ship as just a special type of enemy and take it into consideration as well.

Looking at this feature set, I see three possible approaches. You could create one class that contains all the code for the ship, the enemies, and the boss monster. Certain parts of the code would run conditionally, depending on the type of enemy. For example, the shooting code may have different code paths for each type of game object. With a limited number of different objects, this approach works reasonably well—but it doesn't scale. As you add more and more types of game objects, you end up with a bigger and fatter class containing all the game logic code. Any change to any part of that class has the potential to cause undesirable side effects in enemies' or even the player ship's behavior. Determining which code path to execute depending on a type variable is quite reminiscent of pure C programming and doesn't make use of the object-oriented nature of Objective-C. But if used judiciously, it's a very powerful concept even today.

The second approach is to create a class hierarchy with the `Entity` class as the base class and then derive a ship, two monsters, and a boss monster class from it. This is what a lot of programmers actually do, and it also works reasonably well for a small number of game objects. But in essence, it's little different from the first approach, in that common code often ends up piling up in the base `Entity` class when it's needed by some of the subclasses, but not all of them. It takes a turn for the worse as soon as that code in the `Entity` class starts to add switches based on the type of the enemy, to skip parts of the code or execute code paths specific to that type of enemy. That's the same problem of the first C-style programming approach. With a little care, you can make sure the code specific to an enemy is part of that enemy's class, but it's all too easy to end up making most changes in the `Entity` class itself.

The third option is to use a component system, also called *composition* or *aggregation*. This means that individual code paths are separated from the class hierarchy and only added to the subclasses that need the components, such as a healthbar component. Because component-based development could be a book on its own and is likely overkill for a small project like this shoot-'em-up game, you'll use a mixture of the class hierarchy approach and component design to at least give you an idea how compositing game objects out of individual parts works in principle and what the benefits are.

I do want to point out that there is no one best approach to code design. Certain choices are entirely subjective and depend on personal preferences and experience. Working code is often preferable to clean code if you're willing to refactor your codebase often as you learn more about the game you're making. Experience allows you to make more of these decisions up front in the planning stage and enables you to create more complex games faster. So if that's your goal, start by making and completing smaller games and slowly push yourself to new limits and new challenges. It's a learning process, and unfortunately the easiest way to kill your motivation is to be over-ambitious. There's a reason why every seasoned game programmer will tell a beginner to start simple and to re-create classic arcade games like Tetris, Pac-Man, or Asteroids first.

Tip   About beginner's enthusiasm: it's good to have it. You'll need it! But also be realistic about your expectations and what you'll be able to pull off on your own or with a very small team. The web site "Your Game Idea Is Too Big" offers one very simple, fun, and thought-provoking way to make sure your game idea remains realistic. Test yourself: `http://yourgameideaistoobig.com`. Don't miss the But... link at the bottom for excellent and inspirational advice.

The Enemy Class

Whether you create one class for each enemy type or write all the enemy code in one class depends a lot on the number of enemies. Typically neither approach is ideal because many classes may mean a lot of duplicate code or a deep class hierarchy. All enemy code in one class, however, can easily bloat that class and make it cumbersome to work with, especially if enemies have very diverse abilities. Using components to extend and modify classes is one solution to this problem, as I explain later. For now, because there will only be three enemy types and they aren't very different in their behavior, a single class is just fine.

The Enemy class introduced in the ShootEmUp02 project derives from `CCSprite` for simplicity's sake, and that will make it easier to work with sprite batching. And it declares an enum for the three enemy types that it should control. The interface in the header file is shown in Listing 8-7.

Listing 8-7. The @interface of the Enemy Class

```
#import <Foundation/Foundation.h>
#import "cocos2d.h"

typedef enum
{
    EnemyTypeUFO=0,
    EnemyTypeCruiser,
    EnemyTypeBoss,

    EnemyType_MAX,
} EnemyTypes;

@interface Enemy : CCSprite
{
    EnemyTypes type;
    int initialHitPoints;
    int hitPoints;
}

@property (readonly, nonatomic) int initialHitPoints;
@property (readonly, nonatomic) int hitPoints;

+(id) enemyWithType:(EnemyTypes)enemyType;
+(int) getSpawnFrequencyForEnemyType:(EnemyTypes)enemyType;
-(void) spawn;
@end
```

There is nothing too exciting here. The EnemyTypes enum is used to differentiate between the three different types of enemies currently supported, with EnemyType_MAX used as the upper limit for loops, as you'll soon see. The Enemy class has a member variable that stores the type so that you can use switch statements to branch the code depending on the type of enemy as needed.

The implementation of Enemy contains a lot of code I'd like to discuss, so I'll split the discussion into several topics and present only the relevant code, beginning with the initWithType method in Listing 8-8.

Listing 8-8. Initializing an Enemy with a Type

```
#import "Enemy.h"
#import "GameLayer.h"
#import "StandardMoveComponent.h"
#import "StandardShootComponent.h"

...

@synthesize initialHitPoints, hitPoints;

-(id) initWithType:(EnemyTypes)enemyType
{
    type=enemyType;

    NSString* enemyFrameName;
    NSString* bulletFrameName;
    float shootFrequency=6.0f;
```

```
    initialHitPoints = 1;

    switch (type)
    {
        case EnemyTypeUFO:
            enemyFrameName = @"monster-a.png";
            bulletFrameName = @"shot-a.png";
            break;
        case EnemyTypeCruiser:
            enemyFrameName = @"monster-b.png";
            bulletFrameName = @"shot-b.png";
            shootFrequency = 1.0f;
            initialHitPoints = 3;
            break;
        case EnemyTypeBoss:
            enemyFrameName = @"monster-c.png";
            bulletFrameName = @"shot-c.png";
            shootFrequency = 2.0f;
            initialHitPoints = 15;
            break;

        default:
            [NSException exceptionWithName:@"Enemy Exception"
                                    reason:@"unhandled enemy type"
                                  userInfo:nil];
    }

    self = [super initWithSpriteFrameName:enemyFrameName];
    if (self)
    {
        // Create the game logic components
        [self addChild:[StandardMoveComponent node]];

        StandardShootComponent* shootComponent = [StandardShootComponent node];
        shootComponent.shootFrequency = shootFrequency;
        shootComponent.bulletFrameName = bulletFrameName;
        [self addChild:shootComponent];

        // enemies start invisible
        self.visible = NO;

        [self initSpawnFrequency];
    }

    return self;
}

+(id) enemyWithType:(EnemyTypes)enemyType
{
    return [[self alloc] initWithType:enemyType];
}
```

The code begins by setting variables, depending on the enemy type, using a `switch` statement to provide default values for each type of enemy—the sprite frame name to use, the name of the bullet sprite frame, and the shooting frequency. The default case of the `switch` statement throws an exception because that option usually results from adding a new enemy type to the EnemyTypes enum without extending this switch statement accordingly. Safeguarding your switch statements in this way so that no default case will be accepted is a good strategy to avoid spending too much debugging time on simple human errors. And you are a human being, right? So, you're prone to forget these things. I know I am. Instead of wondering why your new enemy doesn't move or shoots the wrong bullets, you'll get a crash that waves a big red flag saying, "Hey, you forgot to update me!"

It's also perfectly fine to run code before the assignment to self, as long as you don't forget to call a [super init...] method eventually. Otherwise, the superclass won't be properly initialized, and that can lead to strange bugs and crashes.

The component classes created and added to Enemy contain exchangeable code used to extend the behavior and looks of the enemies. I'll get to components soon; for the moment, just know that the StandardMoveComponent class allows the enemy to move, whereas the StandardShootComponent allows it to—you guessed it—shoot. The necessary import statements are at the beginning of Listing 8-8.

Focus your attention now on the initSpawnFrequency method in the Enemy class. The relevant code is shown in Listing 8-9.

Listing 8-9. Controlling the Spawning of Enemies

```
static NSMutableArray* spawnFrequency = nil;

-(void) initSpawnFrequency
{
    // initialize how frequently the enemies will spawn
    if (spawnFrequency == nil)
    {
        spawnFrequency = [NSMutableArray arrayWithCapacity:EnemyType_MAX];
        [spawnFrequency insertObject:[NSNumber numberWithInt:80]
                                                    atIndex:EnemyTypeUFO];
        [spawnFrequency insertObject:[NSNumber numberWithInt:260]
                                                    atIndex:EnemyTypeCruiser];
        [spawnFrequency insertObject:[NSNumber numberWithInt:1500]
                                                    atIndex:EnemyTypeBoss];

        // spawn one enemy immediately
        [self spawn];
    }
}

+(int) getSpawnFrequencyForEnemyType:(EnemyTypes)enemyType
{
    NSAssert(enemyType < EnemyType_MAX, @"invalid enemy type");
    NSNumber* number = [spawnFrequency objectAtIndex:enemyType];
    return number.intValue;
}
```

You store the spawn frequency values for each type of enemy in a static spawnFrequency NSMutableArray. It's a static variable because the spawn frequency isn't needed for each enemy but only for each enemy type. The first Enemy instance that executes the initSpawnFrequency method will find that the spawnFrequency NSMutableArray is nil and so initializes it.

Because an NSMutableArray can store only objects and not primitive data types like integers, the values have to be wrapped into an NSNumber class using the numberWithInt initializer. I chose to use insertObject here instead of addObject because it not only ensures that the values will have the same index as the enemy type defined in the enum, but it also tells any other programmer looking at this code that the index used has a meaning. In this case, the index is synonymous with the enemy type. Although it's technically unnecessary to specify the index here, it helps to show which value is used for which enemy type.

Because you're using ARC, you don't need to consider freeing the memory of the spawnFrequency array. Its memory will be released when it's no longer used. Which in the case of static variables is when the app shuts down.

> **Note**   This reminds me of a misconception about memory leaks—fact is, when an iOS app is leaking memory, then less free memory is available for the app, and that's all there is to it. But when an app terminates or is terminated by the system, iOS frees all of the memory that was in use by the app, leaked or not. This behavior is unlike desktop operating systems. Memory leaks in iOS apps won't affect other apps or decrease available memory for other apps if the leaking app was terminated.
>
> The reason why rebooting your device helps free up memory is caused by either memory leaks in iOS itself or iOS loading additional subsystems and spawning new processes as part of the app's interaction with iOS.

You spawn an enemy with the spawn method:

```
-(void) spawn
{
    // Select a spawn location just outside the right side of the screen
    CGSize screenSize=[CCDirector sharedDirector].winSize;
    CGSize spriteSize=self.contentSize;
    float xPos=screenSize.width+spriteSize.width * 0.5f;
    float yPos=CCRANDOM_0_1() * (screenSize.height - spriteSize.height)+↵
        spriteSize.height * 0.5f;
    self.position=CGPointMake(xPos, yPos);

    // reset health
    hitPoints=initialHitPoints;

    // Finally set yourself to be visible, this also flag the enemy as "in use"
    self.visible=YES;
}
```

Because an EnemyCache is used to create all instances of enemies up front, the whole spawning process is limited to choosing a random y position just outside the right-hand side of the screen and then setting the Enemy sprite to be visible. The visible status is used elsewhere in the project, specifically by component classes, to determine whether the Enemy is currently in use. If it's not visible, it can be spawned to make it visible, but it should run its game logic code only while it's visible.

The EnemyCache Class

I just mentioned the EnemyCache class, which is also new in the ShootEmUp02 project. By its name, it should remind you of the BulletCache class, which also holds a number of pre-initialized objects for fast and easy reuse. This avoids creating and releasing objects during game play that can be a source of minor performance hiccups. Especially for action games, those small glitches can have a devastating effect on the player's experience. With that said, look at the unspectacular header file of the EnemyCache in Listing 8-10.

Listing 8-10. The @interface of the EnemyCache Class

```
#import <Foundation/Foundation.h>
#import "cocos2d.h"

@interface EnemyCache : CCNode
{
    CCSpriteBatchNode* batch;
    NSMutableArray* enemies;

    int updateCount;
}
@end
```

After the spriteBatch, which contains all the enemy sprites, there's an enemies NSMutableArray that stores a list of enemies of each type. The updateCount variable is increased every frame and used to spawn enemies at regular intervals. The init method of the EnemyCache is quite similar to the BulletCache init with its initialization of the CCSpriteBatchNode:

```
-(id) init
{
    if ((self=[super init]))
    {
        // get any image from the texture atlas we're using
        CCSpriteFrame* frame=[[CCSpriteFrameCache sharedSpriteFrameCache]↵
            spriteFrameByName:@"monster-a.png"];
        batch=[CCSpriteBatchNode batchNodeWithTexture:frame.texture];
        [self addChild:batch];

        [self initEnemies];
        [self scheduleUpdate];
    }

    return self;
}
```

But because the code for initializing the enemies is a bit more complex, I extracted it into its own method, as shown in Listing 8-11.

Listing 8-11. Initializing the Pool of Enemies for Later Reuse

```
-(void) initEnemies
{
    // create the enemies array containing further arrays for each type
    enemies=[NSMutableArray arrayWithCapacity:EnemyType_MAX];
```

```
// create the arrays for each type
for (NSUInteger i=0; i<EnemyType_MAX; i++)
{
    // depending on enemy type the array capacity is set
    // to hold the desired number of enemies
    NSUInteger capacity;
    switch (i)
    {
        case EnemyTypeUFO:
            capacity=6;
            break;
        case EnemyTypeCruiser:
            capacity=3;
            break;
        case EnemyTypeBoss:
            capacity=1;
            break;

        default:
            [NSException exceptionWithName:@"EnemyCache Exception"
                                    reason:@"unhandled enemy type"
                                  userInfo:nil];
            break;
    }

    // no alloc needed since the enemies array will retain anything added to it
    NSMutableArray* enemiesOfType=[NSMutableArray arrayWithCapacity:capacity];
    [enemies addObject:enemiesOfType];

    for (NSUInteger j=0; j<capacity; j++)
    {
        Enemy* enemy=[Enemy enemyWithType:i];
        [batch addChild:enemy z:0 tag:i];
        [enemiesOfType addObject:enemy];
    }
}
}
```

The interesting part here is that the NSMutableArray* enemies itself contains NSMutableArray* objects, one per enemy type. It's what's called a two-dimensional array—an array of arrays.

The initial capacity of each enemiesOfType NSMutableArray also determines how many enemies of that type can be on the screen at once. In this way, you can keep the maximum number of enemies on the screen under control. Each enemiesOfType NSMutableArray is then added to enemies NSMutableArray using addObject, just like any other object. If you want, you can create deep hierarchies in this way. As a matter of fact, the cocos2d node hierarchy is built on CCNode classes containing a children instance variable of an array that can contain more CCNode classes, and so on. I mentioned earlier that cocos2d uses the CCArray class internally. It's an optimized replacement class for NSMutableArray, but as with all optimizations there are some drawbacks and compatibility issues. With NSMutableArray you're always on the safe side.

Based on the initial capacity set for enemiesOfType, the desired number of enemies is created, added to the CCSpriteBatchNode, and also added to the corresponding enemiesOfType NSMutableArray. While the enemies could also be accessed through the CCSpriteBatchNode, keeping references to the enemy entities in separate arrays makes it easier to process them during later activities such as spawning, as shown in Listing 8-12.

Listing 8-12. Spawning Enemies

```
-(void) spawnEnemyOfType:(EnemyTypes)enemyType
{
    NSMutableArray* enemiesOfType=[enemies objectAtIndex:enemyType];
    for (Enemy* enemy in enemiesOfType)
    {
        // find the first free enemy and respawn it
        if (enemy.visible == NO)
        {
            CCLOG(@"spawn enemy type %i", enemyType);
            [enemy spawn];
            break;
        }
    }
}

-(void) update:(ccTime)delta
{
    updateCount++;

    for (int i=(EnemyType_MAX - 1); i>= 0; i--)
    {
        int spawnFrequency=[Enemy getSpawnFrequencyForEnemyType:i];

        if (updateCount % spawnFrequency == 0)
        {
            [self spawnEnemyOfType:i];
            break;
        }
    }
}
```

The update method increases a simple update counter. It doesn't take into effect the actual time passed, but because the variances are typically minimal, it's a fair trade-off to make life a bit easier. This for loop oddly starts at (EnemyType_MAX - 1) and runs until i is negative. The only purpose for this is that higher-numbered EnemyTypes have spawn precedence over lower-numbered EnemyTypes. If a boss monster is scheduled to appear at the same time as a cruiser, the boss will be spawned. Otherwise, it could happen that the cruiser takes the boss's spawn slot by trying to spawn at the same time, blocking the boss from ever spawning. It's a side effect of the spawning logic, and I leave it up to you to extend and improve this code, because you'll probably have to do anyway if you decide to write your own version of a classic shoot-'em-up game.

The spawnFrequency is obtained from Enemy's getSpawnFrequencyForEnemyType method:

```
+(int) getSpawnFrequencyForEnemyType:(EnemyTypes)enemyType
{
    NSAssert(enemyType<EnemyType_MAX, @"invalid enemy type");
    NSNumber* number=[spawnFrequency objectAtIndex:enemyType];
    return number.intValue;
}
```

First the method asserts that the enemyType number is actually within the defined range. Then the NSNumber object for that enemy type is obtained and returned as intValue.

The modulo operator % returns the remainder left after the division of the two operands updateCount and spawnFrequency. This means an enemy is spawned only when updateCount can be evenly divided by spawnFrequency, resulting in a remainder of 0.

The spawnEnemyOfType method then gets the NSMutableArray from the enemies NSMutableArray, which contains the list of enemiesOfType, another NSMutableArray. You can now iterate over only the desired enemy types, rather than having to go through all sprites added to the CCSpriteBatchNode. As soon as one enemy is found that isn't visible, its spawn method is called. If all enemies of that type are visible, the maximum number of enemies is currently onscreen, and no further enemies are spawned, effectively limiting the number of enemies of a type on the screen at any time.

Finally, to have enemies appear on screen, open the GameLayer.m file and extend the init method with the code that initializes the EnemyCache. Add this code just above the BulletCache initialization, and don't forget to import the EnemyCache.h header file at the top of GameLayer.m:

```
#import "EnemyCache.h

...

-(id) init
{
    if ((self=[super init]))
    {
        ...

        EnemyCache* enemyCache=[EnemyCache node];
        [self addChild:enemyCache z:0];

        BulletCache* bulletCache=[BulletCache node];
        [self addChild:bulletCache z:1 tag:GameSceneNodeTagBulletCache];
    }
    return self;
}
```

The Component Classes

Component classes are intended as plug-ins for game logic. If you add a component to a node, the node will execute the behavior of the component: moving, shooting, animating, showing a healthbar, and so on. The big benefit is that you program these components to work generically and can use them with a great number of game objects. The components interact with their parent and should make as few assumptions about the parent class as possible. Of course, in some cases a component requires the parent to be a CCSprite or even an Enemy class, but then you can still use it with any type of CCSprite or Enemy class.

You can also configure component classes depending on the class that's using the component. As an example for component classes, take a look at the StandardShootComponent initialization in the Enemy class:

```
StandardShootComponent* shootComponent = [StandardShootComponent node];
shootComponent.shootFrequency = shootFrequency;
shootComponent.bulletFrameName = bulletFrameName;
[self addChild:shootComponent];
```

The variables shootFrequency and bulletFrameName were set previously based on the EnemyType. By adding the StandardShootComponent to the Enemy class, the enemy will shoot specific bullets at certain intervals. Because this component makes no assumptions about the parent class, you can even add an instance of it to the Ship class and have your player's ship shoot automatically at specific intervals! Or by simply activating and deactivating specialized shooting components, you can create the effect of changing weapons for the player with very little code. You just program the shooting code in isolation and then add it to a node and add some parameters to it. The only logic left for programming the switching of weapons is simply when to deactivate which components.

What's more, you can reuse components in other games where they make sense, just by adding them to the new project. There should be no need to modify the component class behavior, therefore components are great for writing reusable code and are a standard mechanism in many, many game engines. To learn more about game components, see this blog post on my web site: www.learn-cocos2d.com/2010/06/prefer-composition-inheritance.

Look at the StandardShootComponent's source code, starting with the header file:

```
#import < Foundation/Foundation.h>
#import "cocos2d.h"

@interface StandardShootComponent : CCSprite
{
    float updateCount;
    float shootFrequency;
    NSString* bulletFrameName;
}

@property (nonatomic) float shootFrequency;
@property (nonatomic) NSString* bulletFrameName;

@end
```

There's one notable thing about this class. The StandardShootComponent inherits from CCSprite, even though it doesn't use any texture, nor does it need to be displayed on screen in any way. That's a workaround because all Enemy objects are added to a CCSpriteBatchNode, which can contain only CCSprite-based objects. This also extends to any child node of the Enemy class; thus, the StandardShootComponent needs to inherit from CCSprite to satisfy the requirement of the CCSpriteBatchNode.

The implementation of the StandardShootComponent is shown in Listing 8-13.

Listing 8-13. The StandardShootComponent Implementation in Its Entirety

```
#import "StandardShootComponent.h"
#import "BulletCache.h"
#import "GameLayer.h"

@implementation StandardShootComponent
```

```
@synthesize shootFrequency;
@synthesize bulletFrameName;

-(id) init
{
    if ((self=[super init]))
    {
        [self scheduleUpdate];
    }

    return self;
}

-(void) update:(ccTime)delta
{
    if (self.parent.visible)
    {
        updateCount += delta;

        if (updateCount >= shootFrequency)
        {
            updateCount = 0;

            GameLayer* game = [GameLayer sharedGameLayer];
            CGPoint startPos = ccpSub(self.parent.position, ↵
                CGPointMake(self.parent.contentSize.width * 0.5f, 0));
            [game.bulletCache shootBulletFrom:startPos
                                    velocity:CGPointMake(-200, 0)
                                   frameName:bulletFrameName];
        }
    }
}
@end
```

The actual shooting code first checks whether the parent is visible, because if the parent isn't
visible, the code obviously shouldn't shoot. The BulletCache is what shoots the bullet, using
the bulletFrameName provided to the component and a fixed velocity. For the start position, the
component's position itself is irrelevant. Instead, the parent position and contentSize properties are
used to calculate the correct starting position—in this case, at the left side of the enemy's sprite.

This bullet startPos works reasonably well for regular enemies but may need tweaking for the boss
enemy. I'll leave it up to you to add another property to this component to set the bullet startPosition
with. Alternatively, you could also create a separate BossShootComponent and add this only to boss
enemies to create more complex shooting patterns. The same goes for StandardMoveComponents,
which for the boss might require hovering at a certain position at the right-hand side of the screen.

Speaking of which, the interface for the StandardMoveComponent is pretty lightweight:

```
#import <Foundation/Foundation.h>
#import "cocos2d.h"

@interface StandardMoveComponent : CCSprite
{
    CGPoint velocity;
}
@end
```

And the implementation doesn't do anything fancy either, as you can see in Listing 8-14.

Listing 8-14. The Implementation of the StandardMoveComponent

```
#import "StandardMoveComponent.h"
#import "GameLayer.h"

@implementation StandardMoveComponent

-(id) init
{
    if ((self=[super init]))
    {
        velocity=CGPointMake(-100, 0);
        [self scheduleUpdate];
    }

    return self;
}

-(void) update:(ccTime)delta
{
    if (self.parent.visible)
    {
        CGSize screenSize=[CCDirector sharedDirector].winSize;
        if (self.parent.position.x>screenSize.width * 0.5f)
        {
            self.parent.position=ccpAdd(self.parent.position, ↵
                ccpMult(velocity, delta));
        }
    }
}
@end
```

The StandardMoveComponent initializes its velocity so that whatever node is using it, it will move at a fixed speed to the left. The update method first checks whether the parent is visible, because if not, it's implied that the parent is currently inactive. The parent is moved until it crosses the center position of the screen with the given velocity multiplied by the delta time, to move the same distance regardless of framerate.

As you can see, component code is usually very simple. That makes it easy to find and fix flaws in components as well. Over time, you can accumulate a number of such components for re-use in other apps, and you'll need to write fewer of the commonly used code and more of the application-specific code—code that's new and challenging and fun to write.

Shooting Things

I almost forgot—you actually want to shoot the enemies, right? Well, in the ShootEmUp03 project, you can!

The ideal starting point to check whether a bullet has hit something is in the BulletCache class. I've added just the method to do that. Actually, I've added three methods, two of them public; the third is private to the class and combines the common code (see Listing 8-15).

Listing 8-15. Checking for Collisions with Bullets

```
-(BOOL) isPlayerBulletCollidingWithRect:(CGRect)rect
{
    return [self isBulletCollidingWithRect:rect usePlayerBullets:YES];
}
-(BOOL) isEnemyBulletCollidingWithRect:(CGRect)rect
{
    return [self isBulletCollidingWithRect:rect usePlayerBullets:NO];
}
-(BOOL) isBulletCollidingWithRect:(CGRect)rect usePlayerBullets:(bool)usePlayerBullets
{
    BOOL isColliding = NO;

    for (Bullet* bullet in batch.children)
    {
        if (bullet.visible && usePlayerBullets == bullet.isPlayerBullet)
        {
            if (CGRectIntersectsRect([bullet boundingBox], rect))
            {
                isColliding = YES;

                // remove the bullet
                bullet.visible = NO;
                break;
            }
        }
    }

    return isColliding;
}
```

You will also need to add the method declarations to the `BulletCache` interface:

```
-(BOOL) isPlayerBulletCollidingWithRect:(CGRect)rect;
-(BOOL) isEnemyBulletCollidingWithRect:(CGRect)rect;
```

The idea behind using the two wrapper methods, isPlayerBulletCollidingWithRect and isEnemyBulletCollidingWithRect, is to hide the internal detail of determining which kinds of bullets to use for collision checks. You could also expose the usePlayerBullets parameter to other classes, but doing so would only make it harder to eventually change the parameter from a BOOL to an enum, in case you want to introduce a third type of bullet.

Only visible bullets can collide, of course, and by checking the bullet's new isPlayerBullet property, you ensure that enemies can't shoot themselves. The actual collision test is a simple CGRectIntersectsRect test, and if the bullet has actually hit something, the bullet itself is also set to be invisible to make it disappear. The Bullet class is extended to include the isPlayerBullet property:

```
#import <Foundation/Foundation.h>
#import "cocos2d.h"

@class Ship;
```

```objc
@interface Bullet : CCSprite
{
    CGPoint velocity;
    float outsideScreen;
    BOOL isPlayerBullet;
}

@property (readwrite, nonatomic) CGPoint velocity;
@property (readwrite, nonatomic) BOOL isPlayerBullet;

+(id) bullet;
-(void) shootBulletFrom:(CGPoint)startPosition
                velocity:(CGPoint)vel
               frameName:(NSString*)frameName
           isPlayerBullet:(BOOL)playerBullet;
@end
```

Accordingly the shootBulletFrom method in the Bullet class implementation has been extended to receive the isPlayerBullet parameter:

```objc
@synthesize velocity, isPlayerBullet;

...

-(void) shootBulletFrom:(CGPoint)startPosition
                velocity:(CGPoint)vel
               frameName:(NSString*)frameName
           isPlayerBullet:(BOOL)playerBullet;
{
    self.velocity = vel;
    self.position = startPosition;
    self.visible = YES;
    self.isPlayerBullet = playerBullet;

    ...
}
```

In the exact same fashion, the shootBulletFrom method in the BulletCache class needs to be extended to receive the isPlayerBullet parameter and then pass it on to the Bullet class. Both InputLayer and StandardShootComponent make use of the shootBulletFrom method, and they need to pass in the isPlayerBullet parameter. The one in InputLayer sets it to YES, because that code is responsible for shooting with the ship. The StandardShootComponent sets isPlayerBullet to NO because the component is used for enemies.

The EnemyCache class holding all Enemy objects is the perfect place to call the new collision-detection methods to check whether any enemy was hit by a player bullet. The class has a new checkForBulletCollisions method, which is called from its update method as seen in Listing 8-16.

Listing 8-16. Performing the Collision Checks in the EnemyCache Class

```objc
#import "BulletCache.h"
#import "GameLayer.h"

...
```

```
-(void) update:(ccTime)delta
{

    . . .

    [self checkForBulletCollisions];
}
-(void) checkForBulletCollisions
{
    for (Enemy* enemy in batch.children)
    {
        if (enemy.visible)
        {
            BulletCache* bulletCache=[GameLayer sharedGameLayer].bulletCache;
            CGRect bbox=enemy.boundingBox;
            if ([bulletCache isPlayerBulletCollidingWithRect:bbox])
            {
                // This enemy got hit . . .
                [enemy gotHit];
            }
        }
    }
}
```

Here again it's convenient to be able to iterate over all the enemy entities in the game, skipping those that are currently not visible. Using each enemy's boundingBox to check with the BulletCache isPlayerBulletCollidingWithRect method, you can quickly find whether an enemy got hit by a player bullet. If so, the Enemy method gotHit is called, which simply sets the enemy to be invisible for now if there are no more remaining hitpoints:

```
-(void) gotHit
{
    hitPoints--;
    if (hitPoints<=0)
    {
        self.visible=NO;
    }
}
```

Consider it an exercise for you to implement the player's ship being hit by enemy bullets. You'll have to schedule an update method in Ship and then implement the checkForBulletCollisions method and call it from the update method. You'll have to change the call to isPlayerBulletCollidingWithRect to isEnemyBulletCollidingWithRect and decide how you want to react to being hit by a bullet—for example, by playing a sound effect and maybe displaying a "game over" message.

A Healthbar for the Boss

The boss monster isn't an easy, one-hit kill. It should give the player visual feedback about its health by displaying a healthbar that decreases with each hit. The first step toward a healthbar is utilizing the hitPoints member variable of the Enemy class, which tells you how many hits the enemy can take before being destroyed. The initialHitPoints variable stores the maximum hit points, because after an enemy gets killed you need to be able to restore the original hit points. You're going to need both.

To display the healthbar, another component class is ideal because it provides a plug-and-play solution and can be re-used for other enemies if needed. The header file for the HealthbarComponent proves to be highly unspectacular:

```
#import <Foundation/Foundation.h>
#import "cocos2d.h"

@interface HealthbarComponent : CCSprite
{
}

-(void) reset;

@end
```

The implementation of the HealthbarComponent class is more interesting, as Listing 8-17 shows.

Listing 8-17. The HealthBarComponent Updates Its scaleX Property Based on the Enemy's Remaining Hit Points

```
#import "HealthbarComponent.h"
#import "Enemy.h"

@implementation HealthbarComponent

-(void) onEnter
{
    [super onEnter];

    [self scheduleUpdate];
}

-(void) reset
{
    float parentWidthHalf = self.parent.contentSize.width / 2;
    float parentHeight = self.parent.contentSize.height;
    float selfHeight = self.contentSize.height;
    self.position = CGPointMake(parentWidthHalf, parentHeight + selfHeight);
    self.scaleX = 1.0f;
    self.visible = YES;
}

-(void) update:(ccTime)delta
{
    if (self.parent.visible)
    {
        NSAssert([self.parent isKindOfClass:[Enemy class]], @"not a Enemy");
        Enemy* enemy = (Enemy*)self.parent;
        self.scaleX = enemy.hitPoints / (float)enemy.initialHitPoints;
    }
    else if (self.visible)
    {
        self.visible = NO;
    }
}
}
@end
```

The healthbar turns its visible state on and off to be in line with its parent Enemy object. The reset method places the healthbar sprite at the proper location just above the head of the Enemy's sprite. Because the healthbar is a child of the enemy, it only needs to be offset from the enemy sprite's 0,0 position (lower left-hand corner by default). And because a decrease in health is displayed by modifying the scaleX property, it, too, needs to be reset to its default scale.

In the update method, and only when its parent is visible, the HealthbarComponent first asserts that the parent is of the class Enemy. Because this component relies on certain properties only available in the Enemy class and its subclasses, you need to make sure that it's the right parent class. Modify the scaleX property as a percentage of the current hit points divided by the initial hit points. Because there's currently no way of telling when exactly the hit points changed, the calculation is done every frame, regardless of whether it's needed. The overhead here is minimal, but for more complex calculations, a call to the HealthbarComponent from the onHit method of the Enemy class would be preferable.

> **Caution** The enemy.initialHitPoints divisor is cast to float. Otherwise, the division would be an integer division that would always result in 0 because integers can't represent fractional numbers and are always rounded down. Casting the divisor to a float data type ensures that the division is done with floating-point precision, and therefore the result is a floating-point value.

In the init method of the Enemy class, the HealthbarComponent is added alongside the other components, but only if the enemy type is EnemyTypeBoss:

```
// Create the game logic components
[self addChild:[StandardMoveComponent node]];

StandardShootComponent* shootComponent = [StandardShootComponent node];
shootComponent.shootFrequency = shootFrequency;
shootComponent.bulletFrameName = bulletFrameName;
[self addChild:shootComponent];

if (type == EnemyTypeBoss)
{
    HealthbarComponent* healthbar = [HealthbarComponent •
        spriteWithSpriteFrameName:@"healthbar.png"];
    [self addChild:healthbar];
}
```

In addition, the spawn method has been extended to include resetting the hit points to their initial values and calling the reset method of any possible HealthbarComponent added to the enemy. I omitted the explicit check if the enemy is a boss type here simply because the HealthbarComponent is universal and could be used by any type of enemy.

```
-(void) spawn
{
    // Select a spawn location just outside the right side of the screen
    CGSize screenSize = [CCDirector sharedDirector].winSize;
    CGSize spriteSize = self.contentSize;
```

```
float xPos = screenSize.width + spriteSize.width * 0.5f;
float yPos = CCRANDOM_0_1() * (screenSize.height - spriteSize.height) +↵
    spriteSize.height * 0.5f;
self.position = CGPointMake(xPos, yPos);

// reset health
hitPoints = initialHitPoints;

// Finally set yourself to be visible, this also flag the enemy as "in use"
self.visible = YES;

// reset certain components
for (CCNode* node in self.children)
{
    if ([node isKindOfClass:[HealthbarComponent class]])
    {
        HealthbarComponent* healthbar = (HealthbarComponent*)node;
        [healthbar reset];
    }
}
}
```

You can now run the app and wait for a boss to appear. Each boss will have a red healthbar on top that decreases in width the more bullets it's hit with.

Summary

Creating a complete and polished game is quite an effort—one that involves a lot of refactoring, changing working code to improve its design and to allow for more features existing in harmony with each other.

In this chapter, you learned the value of classes like BulletCache and EnemyCache, which manage all instances of certain classes so that you have easy access to them from one central point. And pooling objects together helps improve performance.

By using component classes and cocos2d's node hierarchy to your advantage, you can create plug-and-play classes with very specific functionality. This helps you construct your game objects using composition rather than inheritance. It's a much more flexible way to write game logic code and leads to better code reuse.

Finally, you learned how to shoot enemies and how the BulletCache and EnemyCache classes help perform such tasks in a straightforward manner. And the HealthbarComponent provided the perfect example of the component system at work.

The game to this point leaves a couple things open for you to build on. First and foremost, the player doesn't get hit yet. And you might want to add a healthbar to the cruiser monster and write specialized move and shoot components for the boss monster's behavior. Overall, it's an excellent starting point for your own side-scrolling game, just waiting for you to improve on it.

In the next chapter, I show you how to add visual eye candy to the shoot-'em-up game by using particle effects.

Chapter 9

Particle Effects

To create special visual effects, game programmers often make use of particle systems. *Particle systems* work by emitting vast numbers of tiny particles and rendering them efficiently—much more efficiently than if they were sprites. This allows you to simulate effects such as rain, fire, snow, explosions, vapor trails, and many more.

Particle systems are driven by a great number of properties. By *great* I mean about 30 properties, which all influence not only the appearance and behavior of individual particles but the whole particle effect. The *particle effect* is the totality of all particles working together to create a particular visual outcome. One particle alone does not make a fire effect; ten still don't get close enough. You would want several dozens, if not hundreds, of particles to work together in just the right way to create the fire effect.

Creating convincing particle effects is a trial-and-error process. Trying all the various properties in source code and tweaking a particle system by compiling the game, seeing what it looks like, and then making changes and repeating this process is cumbersom to say the least. That's where a particle design tool comes in handy, and I know just the right one: it's called Particle Designer, and I explain how it works in this chapter.

Example Particle Effects

Cocos2d comes with a number of built-in particle effects that give you a good idea of the kinds of effects they'll produce. You can use them as placeholders in your game or subclass and modify the examples defined in the CCParticleExamples.m file if you just want to apply some minor tweaks. The good thing about them is that you don't need any outside help; you create the example particle effects as if they were simple CCNode objects. As a matter of fact, they are actually derived from CCNode.

I created a project called ParticleEffects01 that shows all the cocos2d example particle effects. You can cycle through the examples by quickly tapping the screen, and you can also drag and move them with your finger. Many particle effects look totally different as soon as they start moving, as you can see in Figure 9-1. What seems like just a huge blob of particles may well work as an engine exhaust effect if the particle effect is moving.

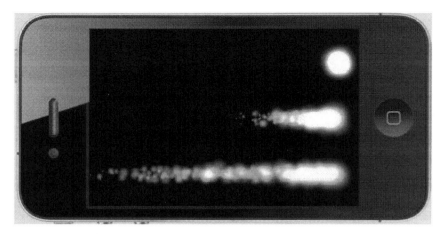

Figure 9-1. *The same particle effect from top to bottom: motionless, moving slowly, moving fast*

There's only one type of effect that can't be moved once started—one-time effects like the CCParticleExplosion shown in Figure 9-2. What's special about this effect is that it emits all its particles at once and stops emitting new particles instantly. All other particle effects run continuously, always creating new particles while those that have exceeded their lifetime are removed. The challenge in that situation is to balance the total number of particles that are on the screen.

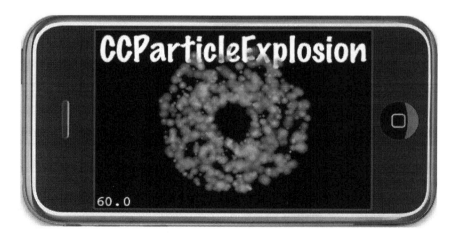

Figure 9-2. *The CCParticleExplosion is an example effect provided by cocos2d*

Listing 9-1 shows the relevant methods used in the ParticleEffects01 example project. By using the current particleType variable in the switch statement, the corresponding built-in particle effect is created. Note that a CCParticleSystem pointer is used to store the particles, so you need to use the addChild code only once at the end of the runEffect method. Every example particle effect is derived from CCParticleSystem.

Listing 9-1. Using the Built-in Effects

```objc
-(void) runEffect
{
    // remove any previous particle FX
    [self removeChildByTag:1 cleanup:YES];

    CCParticleSystem* system;

    switch (particleType)
    {
        case ParticleTypeExplosion:
            system=[CCParticleExplosion node];
                      break;
        case ParticleTypeFire:
            system=[CCParticleFire node];
            break;
        case ParticleTypeFireworks:
            system=[CCParticleFireworks node];
            break;
        case ParticleTypeFlower:
            system=[CCParticleFlower node];
            break;
        case ParticleTypeGalaxy:
            system=[CCParticleGalaxy node];
            break;
        case ParticleTypeMeteor:
            system=[CCParticleMeteor node];
            break;
        case ParticleTypeRain:
            system=[CCParticleRain node];
            break;
        case ParticleTypeSmoke:
            system=[CCParticleSmoke node];
            break;
        case ParticleTypeSnow:
            system=[CCParticleSnow node];
            break;
        case ParticleTypeSpiral:
            system=[CCParticleSpiral node];
            break;
        case ParticleTypeSun:
            system=[CCParticleSun node];
            break;

        default:
            // do nothing
            break;
    }
```

```
        CGSize winSize = [CCDirector sharedDirector].winSize;
        system.position = CGPointMake(winSize.width / 2, winSize.height / 2);

        [self addChild: system z:1 tag:1];

        [label setString:NSStringFromClass([system class])];
}

-(void) setNextParticleType
{

    particleType++;
    if (particleType == ParticleTypes_MAX)
    {
        particleType = 0;
    }
}
```

> **Note**   The NSStringFromClass method is very helpful in this example for printing out
> the name of the class without having to enter dozens of matching strings. It's one of the cool
> runtime features of the Objective-C language that you're able to get a class's name as a string.
> Try to do that in C++, and you'll be biting your toenails. The Objective-C Runtime Programming
> Guide is a good starting point if you'd like to dive into this advanced topic or if you just want to
> learn how Objective-C works on a lower level: http://developer.apple.com/library/
> mac/#documentation/Cocoa/Conceptual/ObjCRuntimeGuide/Introduction/
> Introduction.html.
>
> For game-play code, the NSStringFromClass and related methods hardly play any role, but
> they're very helpful debugging and logging tools. You can find a complete list and description of
> these methods in Apple's Foundation Function Reference: http://developer.apple.com/
> mac/library/documentation/Cocoa/Reference/Foundation/Miscellaneous/
> Foundation_Functions/Reference/reference.html.

If you use one of these example effects in your own project, you might be shocked to see ugly, square pixels. Figure 9-3 shows this effect very clearly. This occurs because all the built-in particle effects try to load a specific texture named fire.png, which is distributed with cocos2d-iphone in the Resources/Images folder. You can still create very good particle effects even without a texture, provided that the particle sizes remain fairly small. But to see the built-in particle effects as they were intended, you need to add the fire.png image to your Xcode project.

Figure 9-3. If your example particle effects, like this CCParticleFireworks, display huge, square particles, you forgot to add the fire.png image to your Xcode project

Creating a Particle Effect the Hard Way

You can easily create your own subclass of the CCParticleSystem class. What's not so easy is creating a convincing particle effect with it, let alone one that comes close to what you originally envisioned. The following is the list of properties grouped by function that determine the particle system's look and behavior:

- emitterMode = gravity
    - sourcePosition
    - gravity
    - radialAccel, radialAccelVar
    - speed, speedVar
    - tangentialAccel, tangentialAccelVar
- emitterMode = radius
    - startRadius, startRadiusVar, endRadius, endRadiusVar
    - rotatePerSecond, rotatePerSecondVar
- duration
- posVar
- positionType
- startSize, startSizeVar, endSize, endSizeVar
- angle, angleVar
- life, lifeVar

- ▓ emissionRate

- ▓ startColor, startColorVar, endColor, endColorVar

- ▓ blendFunc, blendAdditive

- ▓ texture

As you can imagine, there's a lot to tweak here, and that's the main problem of achieving what you want: you don't see the effect of your changes until you rebuild and run your project. When you read about Particle Designer later in this chapter, you'll learn how much it streamlines the creation of new particle effects.

For now you'll do it the hard way first and start at the beginning to gain an understanding about how the cocos2d particle system works. To program a particle effect from scratch, you first learn how to subclass the CCParticleSystem class and how to initialize it. A detailed description of the particle system's properties follows.

Subclassing CCParticleSystem

To create your own particle effect without Particle Designer, you should subclass from CCParticleSystemQuad. The quad particle system is not only faster than CCParticleSystem, it can also be batched. Using the CCParticleBatchNode class allows you to have the same effect multiple times on the screen while only using one draw call.

For the customized particle effect in the ParticleEffects01 project, I've created the ParticleEffectSelfMade class. The interface of this class is in Listing 9-2.

Listing 9-2. Subclassing from the Optimal Particle System Class

```
#import < Foundation/Foundation.h>
#import "cocos2d.h"

@interface ParticleEffectSelfMade : CCParticleSystemQuad
{
}
@end
```

Now you'll look at the implementation of the self-made particle effect, which uses all the available properties. I'll attempt to explain each of them, but it's much better to see it for yourself and experiment with the parameters, so I encourage you to tweak the properties in this project. In the ParticleEffects01 project (Listing 9-3), you'll also find comments describing each parameter in brief.

Listing 9-3. Manually Setting a Particle System's Properties

```
#import "ParticleEffectSelfMade.h"

@implementation ParticleEffectSelfMade
-(id) init
{
    return [self initWithTotalParticles:250];
}
```

```objc
-(id) initWithTotalParticles:(int)numParticles
{
    self=[super initWithTotalParticles:numParticles];
    if (self)
    {
        self.duration=kCCParticleDurationInfinity;
        self.emitterMode=kCCParticleModeGravity;

        // some properties must only be used with a specific emitterMode!
        if (self.emitterMode == kCCParticleModeGravity)
        {
            self.sourcePosition=CGPointMake(-15, 0);
            self.gravity=CGPointMake(-50, -90);
            self.radialAccel=-90;
            self.radialAccelVar=20;
            self.tangentialAccel=120;
            self.tangentialAccelVar=10;
            self.speed=15;
            self.speedVar=4;
        }
        else if (self.emitterMode == kCCParticleModeRadius)
        {
            self.startRadius=100;
            self.startRadiusVar=0;
            self.endRadius=10;
            self.endRadiusVar=0;
            self.rotatePerSecond=-180;
            self.rotatePerSecondVar=0;
        }

        self.position=CGPointZero;
        self.posVar=CGPointZero;
        self.positionType=kCCPositionTypeFree;

        self.startSize=40.0f;
        self.startSizeVar=0.0f;
        self.endSize=kCCParticleStartSizeEqualToEndSize;
        self.endSizeVar=0;

        self.angle=0;
        self.angleVar=0;

        self.life=5.0f;
        self.lifeVar=1.0f;

        self.emissionRate=30;
        self.totalParticles=250;

        startColor.r=1.0f;
        startColor.g=0.25f;
```

```
        startColor.b = 0.12f;
        startColor.a = 1.0f;
        startColorVar.r = 0.0f;
        startColorVar.g = 0.0f;
        startColorVar.b = 0.0f;
        startColorVar.a = 0.0f;
        endColor.r = 0.0f;
        endColor.g = 0.0f;
        endColor.b = 0.0f;
        endColor.a = 1.0f;
        endColorVar.r = 0.0f;
        endColorVar.g = 0.0f;
        endColorVar.b = 1.0f;
        endColorVar.a = 0.0f;

        self.blendFunc = (ccBlendFunc){GL_SRC_ALPHA, GL_DST_ALPHA};
        // or use this shortcut to set the blend func to: GL_SRC_ALPHA, GL_ONE
        //self.blendAdditive = YES;

        self.texture = [[CCTextureCache sharedTextureCache] addImage:@"fire.png"];
    }
    return self;
}
@end
```

CCParticleSystem Properties

In Listing 9-3 you will have noticed how verbose the code is simply because so many particle system properties can be initialized. And most of them need to be set to acceptable values in order to display a reasonably meaningful particle effect onscreen. Some properties are even mutually exclusive and can't be used together. It's time to take a close look at what these particle system properties actually do.

Variance Properties

You'll notice that many properties have companion properties suffixed with Var. These are variance properties, and they determine the range of fuzziness allowed for the corresponding property. Take, for example, the properties life = 5 and lifeVar = 1. These values mean that on average each particle will live for five seconds. The variance allows a range of 5–1 to 5 + 1. So, each particle gets a random lifetime between four to six seconds.

If you don't want any variation, set the Var variable to 0. Variation is what gives particle effects their organic, fuzzy behavior and appearance. But variation can also be confusing when you design a new effect, so unless you have some experience, I recommend starting with a particle effect that has little or no variance.

Number of Particles

It's time for you to get acquainted with particles by starting with the total number of particles in the particle effect, controlled by the `totalParticles` property. The `totalParticles` variable is usually set by the `initWithTotalParticles` method but can be changed later. The number of particles has a direct impact both on the look of the effect and on performance.

```
-(id) init
{
    return [self initWithTotalParticles:250];
}
```

Use too few particles and you won't get a nice glow, but it may be sufficient to sprinkle a few stars around the player's head when he runs into a wall. Use too many particles and it might not be what you want either, because many particles are rendered on top of one another and possibly blended, so you basically end up with a white blob. Furthermore, using too many particles easily kills your framerate. There's a reason why the Particle Designer tool won't let you create effects with more than 2,000 particles.

> **Tip** In general, you should aim to achieve the desired effect with the smallest number of particles. Particle size also plays an important role—the smaller the size of individual particles, the better the performance will be. Especially with particle effects, it's important to test on older devices because they can have a severely negative impact on performance.

Emitter Duration

The `duration` property determines how long particles will be emitted. If set to 2, it will create new particles for two seconds and then stop. It's that simple:

```
self.duration=2.0f;
```

If you'd like the particle effect node to be automatically removed from its parent node once the particle system has stopped emitting particles and the last particles have vanished, set the `autoRemoveOnFinish` property to YES:

```
self.autoRemoveOnFinish=YES;
```

The `autoRemoveOnFinish` property is a convenience feature that's meaningful only if used in conjunction with particle systems that don't run infinitely, like one-time explosion effects. Cocos2d defines a constant `kCCParticleDurationInfinity` (equals: -1) for infinitely running particle effects.

```
self.duration=kCCParticleDurationInfinity;
```

The majority of particle effects are infinitely running, and you can only stop them by removing them from the node hierarchy. Infinitely running particle effects ignore the `autoRemoveOnFinish` property.

Emitter Modes

There are two emitter modes: gravity and radius, controlled by the emitterMode property. These two modes create fundamentally different effects even if most of the parameters are the same, as you can see when you compare Figure 9-4 with Figure 9-5. Both modes use several exclusive properties (see Listing 9-3) that must not be set if they are not supported by the current mode; otherwise, you'll receive a runtime exception from cocos2d like this:

```
ParticleEffects[6332:207] *** Terminating app due to uncaught exception
        'NSInternalInconsistencyException', reason: 'Particle Mode should be Radius'
```

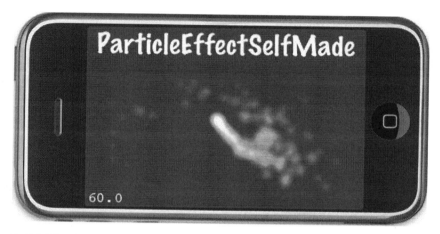

Figure 9-4. *The ParticleEffectSelfMade from the ParticleEffects01 project in gravity mode*

Figure 9-5. *The very same effect using radius mode looks completely different*

Emitter Mode: Gravity

Gravity mode lets particles fly toward or away from a center point. Its strength is that it allows very dynamic, organic effects. You set gravity mode with this line:

```
self.emitterMode = kCCParticleModeGravity;
```

Gravity mode uses the following exclusive properties, which can be used only when emitterMode is set to kCCParticleModeGravity:

```
self.sourcePosition = CGPointMake(-15, 0);
self.gravity = CGPointMake(-50, -90);
self.radialAccel = -90;
self.radialAccelVar = 20;
self.tangentialAccel = 120;
self.tangentialAccelVar = 10;
self.speed = 15;
self.speedVar = 4;
```

The sourcePosition determines the offset as a CGPoint from the node's position where new particles appear. The name is a bit misleading in that the actual center of gravity is the node's position, and sourcePosition is an offset to that center of gravity. The gravity property then determines the speed with which particles accelerate in the x and y directions. In this case, the negative values indicate that the gravitational force will accelerate particles toward the left (−50) and downward (−90). But this acceleration is relative to the particle node's position. Because particles start out at a sourcePosition offset of −15 (slightly offset to the left), they perform a counterclockwise movement around the particle node's position. You can see this effect in Figure 9-4, and tweaking the values in the ParticleEffects01 project helps to understand how sourcePosition and gravity affect the movement of particles.

For the center of gravity to have any impact, the gravity of the particles shouldn't be too high, and the sourcePosition should not be offset too far. The previous values give you a good working example that you can tweak.

The radialAccel property defines how fast particles accelerate the farther they move away from the emitter. This parameter can also be negative, which makes particles slow down as they move away. The tangentialAccel property is similar in that it lets particles rotate around the emitter and speed up as they move away. Negative values let the particles spin clockwise, and positive values spin them counterclockwise.

The speed property should be fairly obvious—it's simply the speed of the particles. It has no particular unit of measurement. Figure 9-4 shows an example particle effect using gravity mode. Particles are attracted by the particle node's position and start out slightly to the left of the particle node's position, so they perform a counterclockwise radial movement.

Emitter Mode: Radius

Radius mode causes particles to rotate in a circle. It also allows you to create spiral effects with particles either rushing inward or rotating outward. You set radius mode with this line:

```
self.emitterMode = kCCParticleModeRadius;
```

Like gravity mode, radius mode has exclusive properties. The following properties can be used only when emitterMode is set to kCCParticleModeRadius:

```
self.startRadius = 100;
self.startRadiusVar = 0;
self.endRadius = 10;
self.endRadiusVar = 0;
self.rotatePerSecond = -180;
self.rotatePerSecondVar = 0;
```

The startRadius property determines how far away from the particle effect node's position the particles will be emitted. Likewise, endRadius determines the distance from the node's position the particles will rotate toward. If you want to achieve a perfect circle effect, you can set endRadius to the same as the startRadius using this constant:

```
self.endRadius = kCCParticleStartRadiusEqualToEndRadius;
```

Using the rotatePerSecond property, you can influence the direction the particles move and the speed with which they move, and thus the number of times they rotate around if startRadius and endRadius are different.

The same particle effect that was shown in Figure 9-4 using gravity mode is shown in Figure 9-5 using radius mode, and you'll notice how different it looks, despite all other properties—except for the exclusive ones—being the same. To test this, uncomment the following line in the ParticleEffects01 project:

```
//self.emitterMode = kCCParticleModeRadius;
```

Particle Position

By moving the node, you also move the effect. But the effect also has a posVar property that determines the variance in the position where new particles will be created. By default, both are at the center of the node:

```
self.position = CGPointZero;
self.posVar = CGPointZero;
```

A very important aspect of particle positions is whether existing particles should move relative to the node's movement or whether they should not be influenced at all by the node's position. For example, if you have a particle effect that creates stars around your player-character's head, you'd want the stars to follow the player as he moves around. You can achieve this effect by setting this property:

```
self.positionType = kCCPositionTypeGrouped;
```

On the other hand, if you want to set your player on fire and you want the particles to create a trail-like effect as the player moves around, you should set the positionType property like this:

```
self.positionType = kCCPositionTypeFree;
```

The free movement is best used with steam, fire, engine exhaust smoke, and similar effects that move around with the object they are attached to and should give the impression of not being connected to the object that emits these particles.

Particle Size

The size of particles is given in pixels using the startSize and endSize properties, which determine the size of the particles when they're emitted and how big they are when they're removed. The size of the particle gradually scales from startSize to endSize.

```
self.startSize=40.0f;
self.startSizeVar=0.0f;
self.endSize=kCCParticleStartSizeEqualToEndSize;
self.endSizeVar=0;
```

You can use the constant kCCParticleStartSizeEqualToEndSize to ensure that the particle size does not change during a particle's lifetime.

Particle Direction

You set the direction in which particles are initially emitted with the angle propert, measured in degrees from 0 to 360. A value of 0 means that particles will be emitted upward, but this is true only for the gravity emitterMode. In radius emitterMode, the angle property determines where on the startRadius the particles will be emitted; higher values will move the emission point counterclockwise along the radius.

```
self.angle=0;
self.angleVar=0;
```

Particle Lifetime

A particle's lifetime determines how many seconds it will take to transition from start to end, where the particle will simply fade out and disappear. The life property sets the lifetime of individual particles. Keep in mind that the longer particles live, the more particles will be onscreen at any given time. If the total number of particles is reached, no new particles will be spawned until some existing particles have died.

```
self.life=5.0f;
self.lifeVar=1.0f;
```

The emissionRate property directly influences how many particles are created per second. Together with the totalParticles property, it has a big impact on what the particle effect looks like.

```
self.emissionRate=30;
self.totalParticles=250;
```

In general, you will want to balance the emissionRate so that it matches the particle lifetime with the totalParticles allowed in the particle effect. You can do so by dividing totalParticles by life and set the result as the emissionRate:

```
self.emissionRate=self.totalParticles / self.life;
```

> **Tip**   By tweaking particle lifetime, the total number of particles allowed in the system, and the `emissionRate`, you can create burst effects by allowing the stream of particles to be frequently interrupted just because the number of particles onscreen is limited and new particles are emitted relatively quickly. On the other hand, if you notice undesirable gaps in your particle stream, you need to either increase the number of allowed particles or preferably reduce the lifetime and/or emission rate. In that case, you should use `emissionRate = totalParticles / life`.

Particle Color

Each particle can transition from a starting color to an end color, creating the vibrant colors particle effects are known for. You should at least set the `startColor` in a particle effect; otherwise, the particles may not be visible at all because the default color is black. The colors are of type `ccColor4F`, a struct with four floating-point members: `r`, `g`, `b`, and a, corresponding to the colors red, green, and blue, as well as the alpha channel, which determines the color's opacity. The value range for each of these members goes from 0 to 1, with 1 being the full color.

If you want a completely white particle color, you'd set all four `r`, `g`, `b`, and a members to 1. If you want a red color, you only need to set the `r` and a values to `1.0f`. If you want blue, then set b and a to `1.0f`. Note that the a value is the alpha transparency of the color. If you leave it at the default value of `0.0f`, the color will be completely translucent and thus not visible.

```
// startColor is mostly red and fully opaque
startColor.r = 1.0f;
startColor.g = 0.25f;
startColor.b = 0.12f;
startColor.a = 1.0f;
// startColor has no variance (plus/minus 0.0f)
startColorVar.r = 0.0f;
startColorVar.g = 0.0f;
startColorVar.b = 0.0f;
startColorVar.a = 0.0f;
// endColor is a fully opaque black color
endColor.r = 0.0f;
endColor.g = 0.0f;
endColor.b = 0.0f;
endColor.a = 1.0f;
// endColorVar specifies a full variance range for color blue
// the end of lifetime color of a particle will be randomly between black and blue
endColorVar.r = 0.0f;
endColorVar.g = 0.0f;
endColorVar.b = 1.0f;
endColorVar.a = 0.0f;
```

Particle Blend Mode

Blending refers to the computation a particle's pixels go through before being displayed onscreen. The property blendFunc takes a ccBlendFunc struct as input, which provides the source and destination blend modes:

```
self.blendFunc = (ccBlendFunc){GL_SRC_ALPHA, GL_DST_ALPHA};
```

Blending works by taking the red, green, blue, and alpha of the source image (the particle) and mixing it with the colors of any images that are already onscreen when the particle is rendered. In effect, the particle blends in a certain way with its background, and blendFunc determines how much and what colors of the source image are blended with how much and with which colors of the background.

The formula to determine the final pixel color onscreen is as follows:

```
(source color * source blend function)+(destination color * destination blend function)
```

Let's assume your example source pixel has the RGB values (0.1, 0.2, 0.3), and the destination pixel has the RGB values (0.4, 0.5, 0.6). Both color values are multiplied by the blend function, the simplest being GL_ONE, which equals 1.0. That means the resulting pixel's color will be as follows:

```
(0.1 * 1+0.4 * 1, 0.2 * 1+0.5 * 1, 0.3 * 1+0.6 * 1)=(0.5, 0.7, 0.9)
```

The blendFunc property has a very profound effect on how particles are displayed. By using a combination of the following blend modes for both source and target, you can create rather bizarre effects or simply cause the effect to render as black squares. There's lots of room for experimentation.

- GL_ZERO
- GL_ONE
- GL_SRC_COLOR
- GL_ONE_MINUS_SRC_COLOR
- GL_SRC_ALPHA
- GL_ONE_MINUS_SRC_ALPHA
- GL_DST_ALPHA
- GL_ONE_MINUS_DST_ALPHA

You'll find more information on the OpenGL blend modes and details about the blend calculations in the OpenGL ES documentation at www.khronos.org/opengles/documentation/opengles1_0/html/glBlendFunc.html.

> **Tip**   Because it's hard to imagine which blend functions will create which results with varying images, I'd like to point you to an article that describes the most common blend operations with example images: www.machwerx.com/2009/02/11/glblendfunc/.
>
> Even more interesting is the Visual glBlendFunc tool developed by Anders Riggelsen: www.andersriggelsen.dk/OpenGL/. With any HTML5-compatible browser, you can play with various images and blend functions to see the results instantly.
>
> Note that you can also modify the blendFunc property of other cocos2d nodes, namely, all nodes that conform to the CCBlendProtocol such as the classes CCSprite, CCSpriteBatchNode, CCLabelTTF, CCLayerColor, and CCLayerGradient.

The source and target blend modes GL_SRC_ALPHA and GL_ONE are frequently combined to create additive blending, resulting in very bright or even white colors where many particles are drawn on top of each other:

```
self.blendFunc = (ccBlendFunc){GL_SRC_ALPHA, GL_ONE};
```

Alternatively, you can simply set the blendAdditive property to YES, which is the same as setting blendFunc to GL_SRC_ALPHA and GL_ONE:

```
self.blendAdditive = YES;
```

The normal blend mode is set using GL_SRC_ALPHA and GL_ONE_MINUS_SRC_ALPHA, which creates transparent particles:

```
self.blendFunc = (ccBlendFunc){GL_SRC_ALPHA, GL_ONE_MINUS_SRC_ALPHA};
```

Particle Texture

Without a texture, all particles would be flat, colored squares, as in Figure 9-3. To use a texture for a particle effect, provide one using the CCTextureCache method addImage, which returns the CCTexture2D for the given image file:

```
self.texture = [[CCTextureCache sharedTextureCache] addImage:@"fire.png"];
```

Particle textures look best if they're cloudlike and roughly spherical. It's often detrimental to the particle effect if the texture has high-contrast areas, resembling a particular shape or form, like the redcross.png from the shoot-'em-up game. This makes it easier to see individual particles because they don't blend too well with each other. Some effects can use this to their advantage, like the aforementioned stars circling the player's head. In addition, cartoonlike images or gradients work best, whereas photorealistic images tend to create an undefinable pixel mess. To demonstrate this, Figure 9-6 shows three different textures applied to the same particle effect.

Figure 9-6. The same particle effect using different textures. Photorealistic images are not ideal

The most important aspect of particle textures is that the image must be at most 64x64 pixels in size. The smaller the texture size, the better it is for the performance of the particle effect.

Particle Designer

Particle Designer is an interactive tool for creating particle effects for cocos2d and iOS OpenGL applications. You can download the trial version at `http://particledesigner.71squared.com`.

This is an invaluable tool that will save you a lot of time creating particle effects. Its power is that you can immediately see what happens onscreen when you change a particle effect's properties, and you can share your creations with others and get inspiration from other developers' particle effects.

Introducing Particle Designer

By default, Particle Designer's user interface shows a visual list of particle effects. To edit a particular effect, select it and switch to the Emitter Config view (Figure 9-7) by either double-clicking it or clicking the Emitter Config button in the upper right-hand corner.

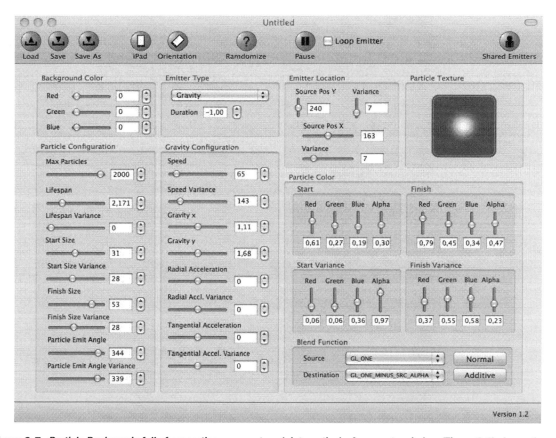

Figure 9-7. Particle Designer is full of properties you can tweak interactively. A separate window (Figure 9-8) shows the effect as you edit it

You should recognize these parameters from the description of the self-made particle effect properties. Only a few properties aren't available and can't be edited in Particle Designer. One is the positionType, and another is the endRadiusVar property for the radius emitter mode. The latter means you can't create particle effects that rotate outward in radius mode. But you can always load a Particle Designer effect and then tweak it in code by overriding certain properties, like setting the positionType to kCCPositionTypeFree, as you'll do later in Listing 9-4. This is just a minor nuisance compared to actually seeing onscreen how your effect changes as you move the sliders.

The only unusual control is the Particle Texture. There's no button to load an image, and double-clicking the field doesn't do anything either. The trick here is that the Particle Texture box only accepts images that are dragged and dropped onto it. Just drag any image from Finder over to this box, and the box will turn green, signaling that it will accept that image. Once you drop the image, it will be used by the particle effect.

Caution   Particle Designer will warn you if you drop an image that's larger than 512x512 pixels. It will use the image anyway but will scale the image down to 512x512 pixels, regardless of its original aspect ratio. Do keep in mind that texture sizes of over 64x64 pixels are probably overkill unless you have special requirements. A particle effect's performance is mainly influenced by the size of the texture and the number of particles.

The Particle Designer preview window in Figure 9-8 looks just like the iPhone Simulator. It can also be set to the iPad screen size, and you can change the orientation by clicking the iPad/iPhone and Orientation buttons in Particle Designer's menu bar, to the right of the Load, Save, and Save As buttons. By clicking and dragging inside the preview window, you can move the particle effect around, which helps you see how the effect might look on moving objects.

Figure 9-8. *By clicking and dragging inside Particle Designer's preview window, you can even move the particle effect around to see what it might look like on moving objects*

Notice that the Background Color settings aren't part of the actual effect. They will change the background color of the preview window. This is useful if your game has bright colors and you want to design a dark or dim effect and still be able to see what you're doing.

If you lack inspiration, you can always make use of the Ramdomize button. You can also ponder about the meaning of the word *ramdomize*, which is how it's spelled in Particle Designer. The Urban Dictionary tells me that *ramdom* is a cooler form of random. So, I'm guessing the developers just thought their randomizer to be extra cool. Well, it's definitely inspiring even though it doesn't randomize all the available properties. For example, Ramdomize will never change the emitter type, the emitter location, and many emitter type–specific parameters.

Once you find your inspiration, you'll want to slide the sliders and watch what happens in the preview window. Take your time and tweak an effect until you like it. Careful, though, because it's a very captivating, even mesmerizing, activity, and you'll easily find yourself making new particle effects just for the fun of it.

Caution   Be careful when designing particle effects! First, keep in mind that your game has to calculate and render a lot of other things, too. If the effect you're currently designing runs at 60 FPS in Particle Designer's preview window, that doesn't mean it won't kill your framerate when you use it in your game. Always test new particle effects in your game and keep an eye on the framerate. Also, make sure to run these tests on a device—in particular on older devices! Your game's performance in the iPhone/iPad Simulator is often misleading and thus must be regarded as completely irrelevant. The same goes for the Particle Designer preview window.

Using Particle Designer Effects

I'm assuming that, hours later, you've made the perfect particle effect and now you'd like to use that in cocos2d. I made mine, and the first step is to save the particle effect. When you click the Save or Save As button in Particle Designer, you get the dialog shown in Figure 9-9.

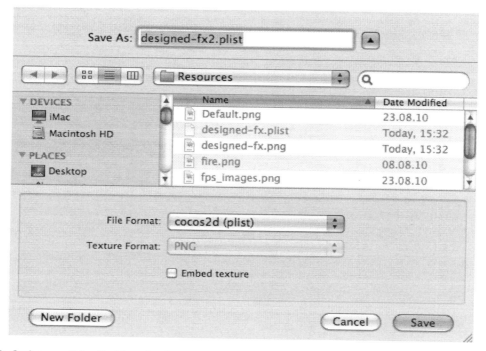

Figure 9-9. *Saving a particle effect from Particle Designer requires you set the file format to cocos2d. Embedding the texture into the plist file is optional*

For the saved particle effect to be usable by cocos2d, you must set the File Format setting to cocos2d (plist). You can also check the Embed texture box, which will save the texture into the plist file. The benefit is that you only have to add the plist file to your Xcode project; the downside is that you then can't change the effect's texture without loading the particle effect back into Particle Designer.

After saving the effect, you have to add the effect plist and, if you didn't embed the texture, the effect's PNG file to your Xcode project's Resources group. In the ParticleEffects01 project, I've added both variants, one effect with a separate PNG texture and another effect that has the texture embedded in the plist file.

Listing 9-4 shows how I modified the runEffect method to load the Particle Designer effects.

Listing 9-4. Using a Particle Effect Created with Particle Designer

```
-(void) runEffect
{
    ...

    switch (particleType)
    {
        ...

        case ParticleTypeDesignedFX:
            system = [CCParticleSystemQuad particleWithFile:@"fx1.plist"];
            break;
        case ParticleTypeDesignedFX2:
            system = [CCParticleSystemQuad particleWithFile:@"fx2.plist"];
            system.positionType = kCCPositionTypeFree;
            break;
        case ParticleTypeSelfMade:
            system = [ParticleEffectSelfMade node];
            break;

        default:
            // do nothing
            break;
    }
    ...
}
```

You initialize a CCParticleSystem with a Particle Designer effect by using the particleWithFile method and providing the particle effect's plist file as parameter. In this case, I chose the CCParticleSystemQuad since it is faster than CCParticleSystem and can be batched with CCParticleBatchNode. Most importantly, Particle Designer effects require the quad particle system because CCParticleSystem isn't compatible with effects created with Particle Designer.

Sharing Particle Effects

What's very cool about Particle Designer is that you can share your creations with other Particle Designer users. From the Particle Designer menu, simply choose Share and then Share Emitter to open a dialog that lets you enter a title and description for your particle effect, as shown in Figure 9-10.

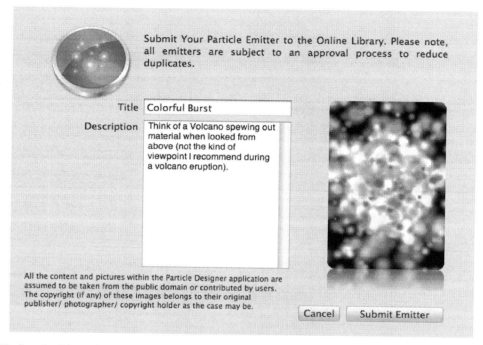

Figure 9-10. *By submitting a Particle Effect to the Online Library, you can share your creations with other users*

Caution   As the message in Figure 9-8 indicates, you should be careful to only upload artwork for which you have the rights to share and distribute or for which you are the copyright holder. Otherwise, you risk violating someone's copyright or may be violating a nondisclosure or other agreement if you work under contract.

In Figure 9-11, you can see the effect I just submitted in the lower right-hand corner.

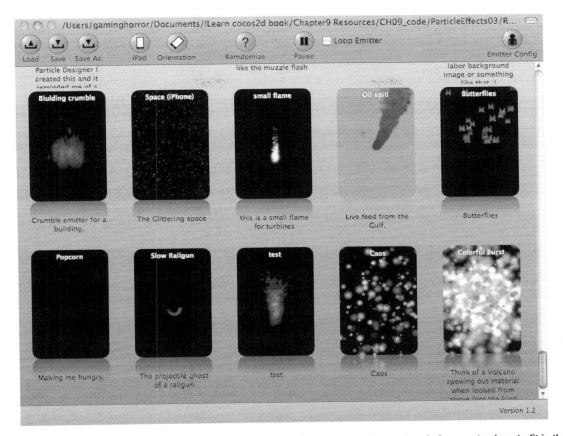

Figure 9-11. The submitted effect quickly appears in the Online Library. Apparently my description was too long to fit in the display area

Shared particle effects may not always be perfect for your requirements, but they often provide good starting points for your own effects. They help you achieve the desired effect much faster and, at the very least, they can be an inspiration. I encourage you to scroll through the list of effects and try as many as you can to gain a good sense of what's possible, what looks good, and what just doesn't work.

Shoot 'em Up with Particle Effects

I'd love to see some of these effects in the game! Let's take the shoot-'em-up game to a new level. You'll find the results in this chapter's ShootEmUp04 project, along with added sound effects, as well as in Figure 9-12.

Figure 9-12. I killed the boss, and I can't see a darn thing. But those particles are so beautiful!

In the Enemy class, the gotHit method is the perfect place to add destructive particle explosions, as Listing 9-5 shows. I decided the boss monster should have its own particle effect, mostly because it's so big. And purple.

Listing 9-5. Adding an Explosion Effect to the Shoot 'em Up Game

```
-(void) gotHit
{
    hitPoints--;
    if (hitPoints <= 0)
    {
        self.visible = NO;

        // Play a particle effect when the enemy was destroyed
        CCParticleSystem* system;

        if (type == EnemyTypeBoss)
        {
            system = [CCParticleSystemQuad particleWithFile:@"fx-explosion2.plist"];
            [[SimpleAudioEngine sharedEngine] playEffect:@"explo1.wav"
                                              pitch:1.0f
                                                pan:0.0f
                                               gain:1.0f];
        }
        else
        {
            system = [CCParticleSystemQuad particleWithFile:@"fx-explosion.plist"];
            [[SimpleAudioEngine sharedEngine] playEffect:@"explo2.wav"
                                              pitch:1.0f
                                                pan:0.0f
                                               gain:1.0f];
        }
```

```
        // Set some parameters that can't be set in Particle Designer
        system.positionType = kCCPositionTypeFree;
        system.autoRemoveOnFinish = YES;
        system.position = self.position;

        [[GameLayer sharedGameLayer] addChild:system];
    }
    else
    {
        [[SimpleAudioEngine sharedEngine] playEffect:@"hit1.wav"
                                  pitch:1.0f
                                    pan:0.0f
                                   gain:1.0f];

    }
}
```

You have to add the particle effects `fx-explosion.plist` and `fx-explosion2.plist` as resources to the Xcode project. The particle system is initialized as before. Since the particle effect should and must be independent from the enemy that creates it, a few preparations are necessary. First, set the `autoRemoveOnFinish` flag to YES so that the effect automatically removes itself. This works because both explosions run only for a short time. The effect also needs the current position of the enemy so that it's displayed at the correct position.

I add the particle effect to the `GameLayer` because the enemy itself can't display the particle effect. To start, it's invisible and so will be any child nodes added to it. It also might be respawned very soon, which would interfere with the particle effect's position. But most importantly, all `Enemy` objects are added to a `CCSpriteBatchNode`, which does not allow you to add anything but `CCSprite` objects. If the particle effect were added to the `Enemy` object, a runtime exception would be inevitable.

For playing sound effects, the `SimpleAudioEngine` class usually suffices. To use it, you must import the `SimpleAudioEngine.h` header file in every file you're using the `SimpleAudioEngine` class because cocos2d doesn't treat the CocosDenshion audio engine as an integral part of the engine.

As you play the game with the new particle effects, you may notice that the first time one of these effects displays, the game play stops for a short moment. That's because cocos2d is loading the particle effect's texture—a rather slow process, whether the texture is embedded into the plist, as in this case, or provided as a separate texture. To avoid that, I'm preloading the particle effects and sound files in the `GameLayer`:

```
-(id) init
{
    if ((self = [super init]))
    {
        ...
        // To preload the textures, play each effect once off-screen
        [CCParticleSystemQuad particleWithFile:@"fx-explosion.plist"];
        [CCParticleSystemQuad particleWithFile:@"fx-explosion2.plist"];
```

```
    // Preload sound effects
    [[SimpleAudioEngine sharedEngine] preloadEffect:@"explo1.wav"];
    [[SimpleAudioEngine sharedEngine] preloadEffect:@"explo2.wav"];
    [[SimpleAudioEngine sharedEngine] preloadEffect:@"shoot1.wav"];
    [[SimpleAudioEngine sharedEngine] preloadEffect:@"shoot2.wav"];
    [[SimpleAudioEngine sharedEngine] preloadEffect:@"hit1.wav"];
  }
  return self;
}
```

The init method now creates each particle system for each particle effect once, but it doesn't add it as child anywhere. This causes the texture to be cached by cocos2d. If you chose not to embed the texture inside the particle effect plist file, you can preload the particle effect textures simply by calling the CCTextureCache addImage method:

```
[[CCTextureCache sharedTextureCache] addImage:particleFile];
```

Summary

This chapter was truly a visual joy ride! The stock effects provided by cocos2d give a good indication of what the particle effect is able to deliver. They're quick and easy to use.

But it was also excruciating to create a particle effect in source code. There are so many properties to tweak; some are exclusive to specific emitter modes; some have misleading names, and they aren't exactly straightforward to figure out. With the explanation for each property, however, you should now have a good understanding how a particle effect is put together and what the most important parameters are.

We then saw how particle effects can shine with Particle Designer. This tool is extremely helpful—and lots of fun—to work with. Suddenly, when you can move sliders and see the results immediately onscreen, it changes your whole view on particle effects, and even more so since you can share your creations with others and experiment with other designers' effects.

Finally, the shoot-'em-up game got a makeover and now plays particle explosions and sounds when bullets are fired and enemies are destroyed. This makes for a much more lively game.

In the next chapter I set the shoot-'em-up game aside for a bit to tell you all you need to know about tilemaps.

Chapter 10

Working with Tilemaps

In the next two chapters, I introduce you to the world of tile-based games. Whether you've been playing games since the age of classic role-playing games like Ultima or you've just recently joined your Facebook friends in Farmville, I'm sure you've already played a game that uses the tilemap concept for displaying its graphics.

In tilemap games, the graphics consist of a small number of images, called *tiles*, which align with each other; placing them on a grid allows you to build rather convincing game worlds. The concept is very attractive because it conserves memory, compared to drawing the whole world as individual textures, while still allowing a lot of variety.

This chapter introduces general tilemap concepts by using the simplest tilemaps of all: *orthogonal tilemaps*. They're most often built from square tiles, rarely from non-square rectangular tiles, and typically display the world in a top-down fashion. This chapter discusses the various display styles of tilemaps, and the next chapter focuses on isometric tilemaps, building on the tilemap programming basics that you'll learn in this chapter.

What Is a Tilemap?

Tilemaps are 2D game worlds made of individual tiles. You can create large world maps with just a handful of images that all have the same dimensions. This means tilemaps are very efficient at conserving memory for large maps (game worlds). It's no wonder that they first appeared in the early days of computer games. Many classic role-playing games used square tiles to create fantastic fantasy worlds. These games looked a bit like the tilemap in Figure 10-1, which is also a perfect example of an orthogonal tilemap. It looks like an aerial view, looking straight down. For this reason, orthogonal tilemaps usually look flat.

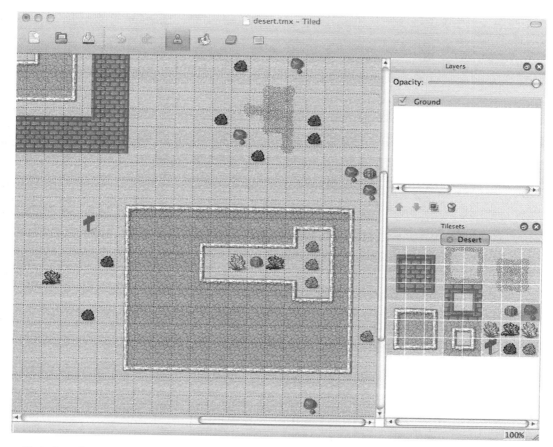

Figure 10-1. An orthogonal tilemap in Tiled (Qt) Map Editor

Tiles in an orthogonal tilemap actually don't need to be square; you can create orthogonal tilemaps from rectangular images as well. Those were most often used by Asian role-playing games, such as Dragon Quest. While still using an orthogonal perspective, it allowed the designers to create objects that are seemingly taller than wide. This enabled the designers to create the illusion of volumes, like houses, by painting them as several tiles and allowing game characters to be partially obstructed by tiles.

That method really came to shine with Ultima 6 and in particular Ultima 7. By skewing the perspective with which tiles were drawn, the effect came close to isometric tilemaps while still being orthogonal tilemaps. Using this method, the designers were able to create the illusion of depth, as you can see in Figure 10-2.

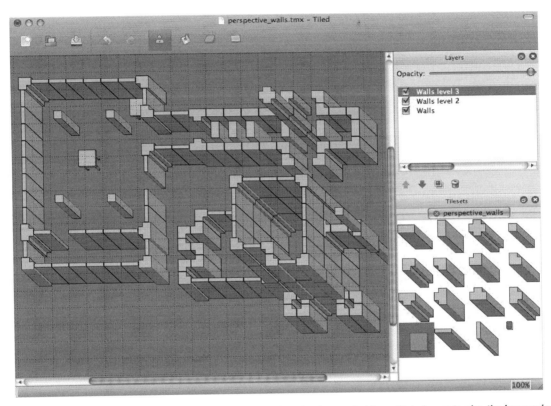

Figure 10-2. An orthogonal tilemap with perspective tiles designed to be created in multiple layers to give the impression of depth. This tilemap style came to fame with Ultima 7

Isometric tilemaps take this one step further by not just drawing the tiles in a certain perspective but also by rotating them by 45 degrees. Isometric tilemaps are very effective in tricking our minds into believing that there really is a third dimension in this world, even though all the images are still essentially flat. Isometric tilemaps achieve this impression of depth by using tile images that are drawn as diamond shapes (rhombuses) and allowing tiles closer to the viewer to draw over the tiles further away from the viewer. See Figure 10-3 for an example of an isometric tilemap. I discuss isometric tilemaps in the next chapter in greater detail.

Figure 10-3. An isometric tilemap in Tiled (Qt) Map Editor

The tilemaps in Figures 10-2 and 10-3 prove that tilemaps don't need to be flat-looking. You can use the layering or stacking of tiles with some games that allow players to interact with the game world, as many of the Farmville fan videos show to great effect. Several Farmville users have used nothing but crop fields to build houses and even tall skyscrapers just by stacking tiles. They make use of the optical illusion that's possible with isometric tilemaps.

You usually edit tilemaps with an editor, and the one directly supported by cocos2d is called Tiled (Qt) Map Editor. Tiled is free, is open source, and allows you to edit both orthogonal and isometric tilemaps with multiple layers. Tiled also enables you to add trigger areas (object layer), which you can use in a game to trigger certain actions when a character enters the area. They also serve as a way to add arbitrary positions to the map so that you can, for example, define spawn locations. By editing tile properties, you can determine what type of tile it is. You can also use this to block characters from entering certain tiles or, for example, to take damage when moving over a lava tile.

> **Note**   Qt refers to Nokia's Qt framework, on which Tiled is built. Because there's also a defunct Java version of Tiled, it's important to make this differentiation by writing Tiled (Qt). The Java version is no longer updated but contains a few extra features that may be worth checking out. In this and the following chapter, I use and discuss Tiled (Qt).

Preparing Images with TexturePacker

Before you start working with the Tiled (Qt) Map Editor, you need to prepare the tilemap graphics. The set of tile images for a tilemap is commonly called a *tileset*. Technically it's just a texture atlas containing tile images, but Tiled (Qt) can only load tilesets in PNG (recommended) or JPG format.

In the Tilemap01 project for this chapter, you'll find a number of square tile images in the Assets/tiles folder. Add all these tile images to TexturePacker and then uncheck Allow Rotation, set Algorithm to Basic, and set Sort by to Name. These settings ensure that the tiles are ordered and aligned correctly for Tiled. The resulting tileset in TexturePacker should look similar to Figure 10-4.

Figure 10-4.   Creating a texture atlas of a few square tiles using TexturePacker

For Tiled it's crucial that the tiles stay at the same position—this is why sorting by name and disallowing rotation is so important—because Tiled refers to individual tiles in the tileset by position (tile index) and offset only. That means that if tiles in the texture change places, the tilemap in Tiled will look completely different. The tilemap still refers to the same tile positions in the tileset, but instead of a grass tile there might now be a water tile at that position, for example.

Tiled (Qt) Map Editor

The most popular tool to create tilemaps for use with cocos2d is the Tiled (Qt) Map Editor that I've already mentioned in the preceding sections. The TMX files it creates are natively supported by the cocos2d game engine. TMX files are simply XML files that, if need be, you could edit with a text editor.

Tiled is available as a free download, and at the time of this writing the latest version is 0.8.1. You can download Tiled from its home page, at `www.mapeditor.org`.

If you'd like to support the development of Tiled, consider making a donation to the project's developer, Thorbjørn Lindeijer. You can find the donate button on the web site.

Creating a New Tilemap

The first thing after you've downloaded and started Tiled is to go to the View menu and check both the Tilesets and Layers items. This will show the list of layers and the current tileset on the right-hand side of the Tiled window which you'll need to refer to frequently. Then choose File ➤ New to create a new tilemap, bringing up the New Map dialog pictured in Figure 10-5.

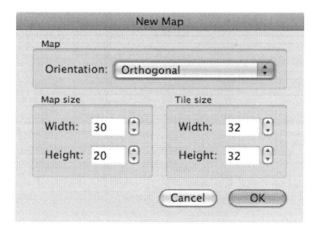

Figure 10-5. *Creating a new tilemap in Tiled*

Currently, Tiled supports orthogonal (rectangular) tilemaps as well as isometric tilemaps. Hexagonal maps are not supported. The map size is given in tiles, but Tiled will show you the size of the map in pixels as well. In this case, the new map will be 30×20 tiles, with the tile images having 32 × 32-pixel dimensions. It's crucial that the tile size matches the size of your tile images, or they will not align.

The new map will be completely empty, and there's no tileset loaded that you can draw from. You can add a tileset by selecting Map ➤ New Tileset from Tiled's menu. This opens the New Tileset dialog (shown in Figure 10-6), where you can browse for the proper tileset image. A tileset is just a name for an image containing multiple tiles with equal spacing, so you could also call it a texture atlas containing only images of the same size.

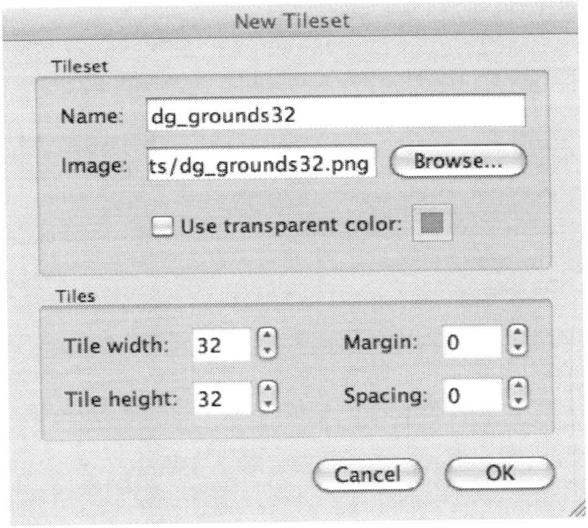

Figure 10-6. Creating a new tileset from an image file

> **Note** The function Map ➤ Add External Tileset is used only to import a previously exported tileset to share the same tileset with multiple TMX maps. You can export a tileset by right-clicking the tileset view in the lower right-hand corner of the Tiled window and then choosing Export Tileset As.

You'll use the dg_grounds32.png tileset. These tiles were drawn by David E. Gervais and published under the Creative Commons License, meaning you are free to share and remix his work as long as you give credit to him. You can download more of his tilesets from this web site: http://pousse.rapiere.free.fr/tome/index.htm.

In Figure 10-6, I have already added the dg_grounds32.png tileset image by locating it through the Browse button in the Resources folder of the Tilemap01 project. If you check the "Use transparent color" check box, transparent areas will simply be drawn in pink (the default color). You can leave this box unchecked for now because the tiles in use have no transparent areas.

The tile width and height are the dimensions of individual tiles in the tileset. They should match the tile size of 32 × 32 pixels, which you set when creating the new map. The Margin and Spacing settings determine how many pixels away from the image border the tiles are and how many pixels of space are between them. In the case of the dg_grounds32.png, there's no spacing at all, so I set both values to 0.

If you had your tiles aligned by TexturePacker to create a tileset texture, you must enter the pixel-padding value used by TexturePacker in the Margin and Spacing fields. By default, TexturePacker uses a padding of 0 pixels.

When loading a new tileset image, make sure the tileset image is already located in your project's Resource folder. You should then also make sure to save the tilemap TMX file to the same folder where the tileset image used by the tilemap is located. Otherwise, cocos2d might fail to load the tileset image; trying to load the TMX file will then cause a runtime exception. The culprit is that TMX files reference the tileset image relative to the location the TMX file is saved to. If they're not both in the same folder, cocos2d may be unable to find the image because the folder structure isn't preserved when the app is installed in the simulator or on the device.

TIP   TMX files are plain XML files, so you might want to peek inside if you're curious. If you see the image file referenced with parts of a path, then cocos2d is unlikely to load the referenced image file. The image reference should list just the image filename without any path components, like so: `<image source="tiles.png"/>`.

How to create Tilemaps for Retina and iPad Resolutions

Tiled has no concept of varying resolutions for tilemaps. But cocos2d supports all the usual extensions like -hd, -ipad and -ipadhd for tilemap files. Problem is, how to convert an existing tilemap to an HD tilemap or vice versa?

The answer lies in manually editing the TMX files created by Tiled in Xcode or with a text editor. Following is the entire contents of the tilemap.tmx file used in this chapter:

```
<?xml version="1.0" encoding="UTF-8"?>
<map version="1.0" orientation="orthogonal" width="24" height="16" tilewidth="40"
tileheight="40">
 <tileset firstgid="1" name="tiles" tilewidth="40" tileheight="40" spacing="0" margin="0">
  <image source="tiles.png" width="128" height="128"/>
 </tileset>
 <layer name="Tile Layer 1" width="24" height="16">
  <data encoding="base64" compression="zlib">
eJztlNOKgCAMRr9Km+//xBEssLU/Qe8SDuqEM2VMAGgLAc8OmRH/Nojl3ycR+Q9G7mU8kOP6HOdhpDubR/
OTcHt4OUnxazXI5Cn4vsXz31TmZPq1RcW7rpq/P4t8GqS45P2tPoz6Kev3erEZscz/sPL/+Yc9LqVyBq0=
  </data>
 </layer>
</map>
```

I've highlighted in bold the entries you need to modify. Because this is a standard-resolution tilemap, you need to multiply all the numeric values by two to convert the tilemap to a Retina resolution tilemap. Be careful not to change the map's parameters by accident, especially because both map and tileset have `tilewidth` and `tileheight` parameters. And if you convert a Retina tilemap to standard resolution, you'd divide the numeric values by two. In that case all the values should be even numbers so they're divisible by two with no remainder.

You also need to change the source image name so that it uses the `tiles-hd.png` image that you can create with TexturePacker as described in Chapter 6. Then save the modified tilemap as `tilemap-hd.tmx`.

Unfortunately this process is tedious and error-prone because you have to do this after every modification to the tilemap, or you can choose to edit both standard and Retina resolution tilemaps at the same time—but that's still twice the work, or four times the work if you want to support standard, Retina, iPad, and Retina iPad resolutions. In that case, you'd have to keep these files up to date:

- Standard resolution: `tilemap.tmx` and `tilemap.png`
- Retina resolution: `tilemap-hd.tmx` and `tilemap-hd.png`
- iPad resolution: `tilemap-ipad.tmx` and `tilemap-ipad.png`
- iPad Retina resolution: `tilemap-ipadhd.tmx` and `tilemap-ipadhd.png`

You can always design and test your tilemap in one resolution and only convert it on occasion to other resolutions. You might also consider writing a script or a small app that automates that process for you. A good starting point is the Tilemap HD/SD conversion tool available here: `http://wasabibit.com/WasabiBit/Dev_Notes.html`.

The alternative is to create your tilemaps with iTileMaps on an iOS device. It lets you automatically create SD/HD versions of the tilemaps you're creating. You can try out the free version to see if iTileMaps is an option for you. You can find more information on the iTileMaps homepage: `www.klemix.com/page/iTileMaps.aspx`.

Designing a Tilemap

With the tileset loaded, you're faced with a blank map, an invitation for your creativity to come up with great ideas for a tilemap. What's even better is to get rid of the blank tilemap as the very first step. It's very helpful to start the tilemap with a default floor tile. I selected the Bucket Fill tool and picked a bright grass tile so that my tilemap is now a lush meadow—sort of. You can see it in Figure 10-7.

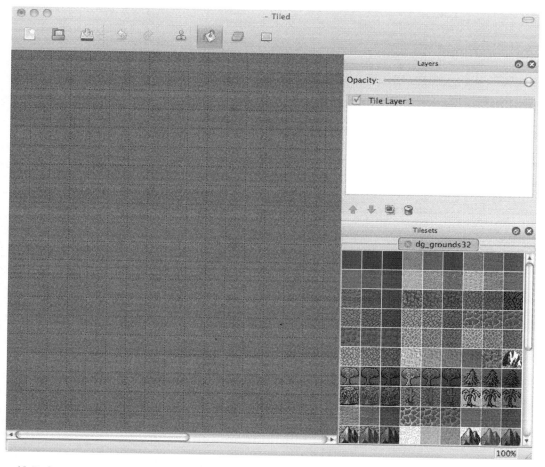

Figure 10-7. An empty map with the dg_grounds32 tileset loaded, waiting for your inspiration

Tip If you ever notice something missing from Tiled's window, check the View menu. You can hide and unhide the Tilesets, Layers, and History views. This is important because it's the only way to bring back these views in case you clicked the X button on one of these views.

Tiled uses four modes for editing the tilemap, indicated by the four rightmost icons on the toolbar. They are Stamp Brush (hotkey B), which allows you to draw the current selection in the tileset; Bucket Fill (hotkey F), which fills areas of connected, identical tiles; Eraser (hotkey E), which erases tiles; and Rectangular Select (hotkey R), with which you can select a range of tiles and then copy and paste the selection.

You can also zoom the tilemap. If you have a mouse with a scroll wheel, hold down the Command key and roll the scroll wheel to zoom in and out. Alternatively, you can also zoom in and out by pressing the Command key with either the plus and minus sign, respectively.

You'll spend most of your time picking a tile from the tileset and drawing it onto the tilemap with the Stamp Brush selected. Placing tile by tile, you'll create your tile-based game world.

You can also edit tiles in multiple layers by adding more layers in the Layers view. From the menu, choose Layer ➤ Add Tile Layer to create a new layer for tiles. Using multiple tile layers allows you to switch out areas of the tilemap in cocos2d. In the TileMap01 example project, I use it to switch parts of the map between winter and summer.

You can also choose Layer ➤ Add Object Layer to add a layer for adding objects. There are two types of objects: the regular objects are simply rectangles that you can place, and the other type of objects are tile objects that let you freely place a tile anywhere on the map, without snapping to the tile grid. You can use the rectangle objects to annotate the map with custom information, such as spawn points, teleport locations, or trigger areas. The tile objects are most commonly used to place smaller things like swords, flowers, candles, and other items directly onto the tile world.

To work with objects, additional buttons are available in the Tiled toolbar: Select Objects (hotkey S), Insert Objects (hotkey O), and Insert Tile Objects (hotkey T). To insert a rectangle object, click the Insert Objects icon and click in the tilemap world to create point objects (rectangles with zero width and height), or click and drag down and to the right to create a rectangle. To insert a tile object, click the Insert Tile Objects icon, select a tile from the tileset, and then click the tilemap world to add a new tile object.

Some functionality in Tiled is hidden in context menus. For example, you can delete the rectangle objects I just mentioned by right-clicking them in the Tilemap view and selecting Remove Object. Note that you also need to have the object layer highlighted in the Layers list view for the context menu to appear.

You can also edit properties of objects, layers, and tiles by right-clicking them and clicking the corresponding Properties menu item. One use for that is to create an additional tile layer by using Layer ➤ Add Tile Layer. This will be a layer used to tell the game about certain properties of tiles. I called it GameEventLayer because it will be used to define trigger areas for certain game events.

With GameEventLayer selected, choose Map ➤ New Tileset and load game-events.png from the same folder as dg_grounds32.png. It contains only three tiles. Right-click one, select Tile Properties, and add the isWater property, as shown in Figure 10-8.

Figure 10-8. *Adding a tile property*

> **Caution**   Keep in mind that each tile layer creates some overhead, especially if you set tiles in multiple layers at the same location. This will cause both layers to be drawn and can adversely affect the game's performance. I recommend keeping the number of tile layers to a minimum. Two to four tile layers should be sufficient for most games. Be sure to take a look at your game's framerate on the device after you've added a new tile layer and drawn on it.
>
> Also be aware that Tiled allows you to add more than one tileset for a layer. However, cocos2d supports only one tileset per layer.

You can then draw over the tilemap using the tile whose properties you just added the isWater property to. Ideally, draw it over the river. To see the tiles underneath what you're drawing, you can use the Opacity slider for the GameEventLayer in the Layers view. Or click the layer's check box to hide or unhide everything drawn on this particular layer.

Just be sure to enable all layer check boxes before saving the TMX tilemap. Cocos2d doesn't load layers that are unchecked in Tiled.

When you're done with this, you should have a tilemap similar to the one in Figure 10-9. Save it in the same `TileMap01 Resources` folder where the tileset images are.

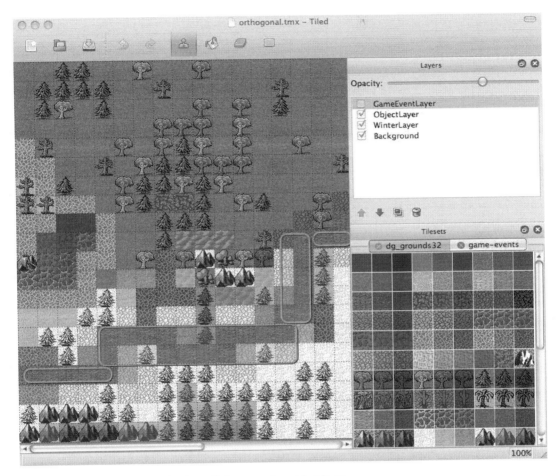

Figure 10-9. A completed tilemap with three tile layers and an object layer

Using Orthogonal Tilemaps with Cocos2d

To use TMX tilemaps with cocos2d, you first have to add the TMX file and the accompanying tileset image files as resources to your Xcode project. In the TileMap01 project, I added `orthogonal.tmx` along with the `tilesets dg_grounds32.png` and game-events.png. Loading and displaying the tilemap is very straightforward; the following code is the interface of the `TileMapLayer` class:

```
#import "cocos2d.h"

enum
{
    TileMapNode = 0,
};

@interface TileMapLayer : CCLayer
{
}

+(id) scene;
@end
```

And this is the `TileMapLayer` implementation which loads a tilemap and hides the `GameEventLayer`:

```
#import "TileMapLayer.h"
#import "SimpleAudioEngine.h"

@implementation TileMapLayer
+(id) scene
{
    CCScene *scene = [CCScene node];
    TileMapLayer *layer = [TileMapLayer node];
    [scene addChild: layer];
    return scene;
}

-(id) init
{
    if ((self = [super init]))
    {
        CCTMXTiledMap* tileMap = [CCTMXTiledMap tiledMapWithTMXFile:@"orthogonal.tmx"];
        [self addChild:tileMap z:-1 tag:TileMapNode];

        CCTMXLayer* eventLayer = [tileMap layerNamed:@"GameEventLayer"];
        eventLayer.visible = NO;

        self.isTouchEnabled = YES;
    }
    return self;
}
@end
```

The `CCTMXTiledMap` class is initialized with the name of the TMX file and then added as a child with a tag so that it can be retrieved later. An instance variable would of course work just as well. The next step is to retrieve the `CCTMXTiledMap` used for game events by using the `layerNamed` method and providing the name of the layer as it was named in Tiled. Because the game events layer will be used only as hints for code to determine properties of certain tiles, this layer shouldn't be rendered at all. Note that if you uncheck the layer in Tiled, it won't be displayed, but you won't have access to its tiles and tile properties either.

If you run the project now, you'll see a tilemap just like in Figure 10-10.

Figure 10-10. The orthogonal tilemap in the iPhone Simulator

Right now you can't do anything with the tilemap, but I'd like to change that. For example, I'd like to be able to find the isWater tiles. I've added the ccTouchesBegan method, as shown in Listing 10-1, to determine the tile that the player is touching.

Listing 10-1. Determining a Tile's Properties

```
-(void) ccTouchesBegan:(NSSet *)touches withEvent:(UIEvent *)event
{
    CCNode* node=[self getChildByTag:TileMapNode];
    NSAssert([node isKindOfClass:[CCTMXTiledMap class]], @"not a CCTMXTiledMap");
    CCTMXTiledMap* tileMap=(CCTMXTiledMap*)node;

    // Get the position in tile coordinates from the touch location
    CGPoint touchLocation=[self locationFromTouch:touches.anyObject];
    CGPoint tilePos=[self tilePosFromLocation:touchLocation tileMap:tileMap];

    // Check if the touch was on water (e.g., tiles with isWater property)
    BOOL isTouchOnWater=NO;
    CCTMXLayer* eventLayer=[tileMap layerNamed:@"GameEventLayer"];
    int tileGID=[eventLayer tileGIDAt:tilePos];

    if (tileGID !=0)
    {
        NSDictionary* properties=[tileMap propertiesForGID:tileGID];
        if (properties)
        {
            NSString* isWaterProperty=[properties valueForKey:@"isWater"];
```

```
            isTouchOnWater = isWaterProperty.boolValue;
        }
    }

    // Decide what to do depending on where the touch was
    if (isTouchOnWater)
    {
        [[SimpleAudioEngine sharedEngine] playEffect:@"alien-sfx.caf"];
    }
    else
    {
        // Get the winter layer and toggle its visibility
        CCTMXLayer* winterLayer = [tileMap layerNamed:@"WinterLayer"];
        winterLayer.visible = !winterLayer.visible;
    }
}
```

The CCTMXTiledMap is retrieved as usual. The location of the touch is first converted into screen coordinates and then used to retrieve the tilePos containing the indices into the tilemap at that specific screen location. I'll get to the tilePosFromLocation method in a minute. For now, just know that it returns the index of the touched tile.

At this point, I have to introduce the concept of global identifiers (GIDs) for tiles, which are unique integer numbers assigned to each tile used in a tilemap. The tiles in a map are consecutively numbered, starting with 1. A GID of 0 represents an empty tile. With the tileGIDAt method of the CCTMXLayer, you can determine the GID number of the tile at the given tile coordinates.

Next, the CCTMXLayer named GameEventLayer is obtained from the tilemap. This is the layer where I defined the isWater tile and drew it over the river tiles. The tileGIDAt method returns the unique identifier for this tile. If the identifier happens to be 0, it means there is no tile at this position on this layer—in that case, it's already clear that the touched tile can't be an isWater tile.

The CCTMXTiledMap has a propertiesForGID method, which returns an NSDictionary if there are properties available for the tile with the given identifier (GID). This NSDictionary contains the properties edited in Tiled (see Figure 10-8). The dictionary stores any key/value pairs as NSString objects. To see what's in a particular NSDictionary for debugging purposes, you can use a CCLOG statement like this:

```
CCLOG(@"NSDictionary 'properties' contains:\n%@", properties);
```

This will print out a line similar to the following in the Debugger Console window:

```
2010-08-30 19:50:52.344 Tilemap[978:207] NSDictionary 'properties' contains:
{
    isWater = 1;
}
```

You'll be dealing with a variety of NSDictionary objects while working with tilemaps. Logging its contents allows you to peek inside any NSDictionary, or any iPhone SDK collection class, for that matter. This will frequently come in handy.

You can retrieve each property in an NSDictionary by its name through the NSDictionary method valueForKey, which returns an NSString. To get a Bool value from the NSString, you can simply use the NSString's boolValue property. In much the same way, you can retrieve integer and floating-point values using NSString's intValue and floatValue properties, respectively.

At the end of ccTouchesBegan, I check whether the touch was on water, and if so, a sound is played. Otherwise, I retrieve the WinterLayer and toggle its visible property by negating it. Changing seasons has never been this simple! The effect should illustrate how you can use multiple layers in Tiled to achieve changes on a global scale without having to load a completely separate tilemap.

For more local changes to individual tiles, you can use the removeTileAt and setTileGID methods to remove or replace tiles of a specific layer during game play:

```
[winterLayer removeTileAt:tilePos];
[winterLayer setTileGID:tileGID at:tilePos];
```

Locating Touched Tiles

I mentioned the tilePosFromLocation method earlier, and I'll repeat the two relevant lines from the ccTouchesBegan code here before getting to the implementation of locationFromTouch and tilePosFromLocation:

```
// Get the position in tile coordinates from the touch location
CGPoint touchLocation = [self locationFromTouch:touches.anyObject];
CGPoint tilePos = [self tilePosFromLocation:touchLocation tileMap:tileMap];
```

First, the position of the touch is mapped to screen coordinates. I've done this before, but because you'll be needing this code a lot, I've provided it in Listing 10-2 for your reference.

Listing 10-2. Determining the Position of a Touch

```
-(CGPoint) locationFromTouch:(UITouch*)touch
{
    CGPoint touchLocation = [touch locationInView:touch.view];
    return [[CCDirector sharedDirector] convertToGL:touchLocation];
}
```

With the touch location converted to screen coordinates, the tilePosFromLocation method is called. It gets both the touch location and a pointer to the tileMap as parameters. The method in Listing 10-3 contains a bit of math, which I'll explain in a second—hold your breath:

Listing 10-3. Converting Location to Tile Coordinates

```
-(CGPoint) tilePosFromLocation:(CGPoint)location tileMap:(CCTMXTiledMap*)tileMap
{
    // Tilemap position must be offset, in case the tilemap is scrolling.
    CGPoint pos = ccpSub(location, tileMap.position);

    // scaling tileSize to Retina display size
    float pointWidth = tileMap.tileSize.width / CC_CONTENT_SCALE_FACTOR();
    float pointHeight = tileMap.tileSize.height / CC_CONTENT_SCALE_FACTOR();
```

```
    // Cast to int makes sure that result is in whole numbers
    pos.x = (int)(pos.x / pointWidth);
    pos.y = (int)((tileMap.mapSize.height * pointHeight - pos.y) / pointHeight);

    // Ensure coordinates are always within tilemap bounds.
    pos.x = fmaxf(0, fminf(tileMap.mapSize.width - 1, pos.x));
    pos.y = fmaxf(0, fminf(tileMap.mapSize.height - 1, pos.y));
    return pos;
}
```

Still with me? If you've worked with tilemaps before, this bit of code should be familiar, but if not, you may be at a loss. I'll explain. The first thing this method does is subtract the current tileMap.position from the touch location. The upcoming changes to the Tilemap project will add tilemap scrolling, so the tilemap's position will most likely not be at 0,0, and that needs to be factored in by subtracting the tilemap's position from the location.

To make the viewpoint scroll farther up (north) and to the right (east), you actually have to change its position by negative amounts. That's because the tilemap starts at position 0,0, which positions the map's bottom left-hand corner at the very bottom left of the screen. The tilemap's 0,0 point coincides with the screen's 0,0 point initially. If you were to move the tilemap to position 100,100, it would seem as if the viewpoint were moving toward the left and down. The common mistake is to assume that you're moving the viewpoint, which you are not. The tilemap layer is what's moving, and to scroll farther toward the center of the tilemap, you have to offset the tilemap by negative values.

The rest is simple math: to get the proper offset from the tilemap (whose position you know is always negative), you have to subtract the touch location and tileMap.position. The concrete numbers reveal that subtracting a negative number is actually an addition:

location(240, 160) – tileMap.position(-100, -100) = pos(340, 260)

With the tilemap layer moved –100,–100 pixels away from the screen's 0,0 point, and the touch being at 240,160 pixels on the screen, the total offset of the touch location from the tilemap's position is 340,260 pixels away from the current tileMap.position.

With the scrolling offset taken into account, you can get the tile coordinates for the tile at this location into the tilemap. At this point, you have to consider that the tile coordinates' 0,0 tile is at the top left-hand corner of the tilemap. Contrary to screen coordinates, where the 0,0 point (point of origin) is at the lower left-hand corner, the tilemap coordinates start at the upper left-hand corner. Figure 10-11 shows the x,y coordinates of a series of tiles. The screenshot was made with the Tiled Java version by enabling View ➤ Show Coordinates, which is a feature that isn't available yet in the Tiled Qt version.

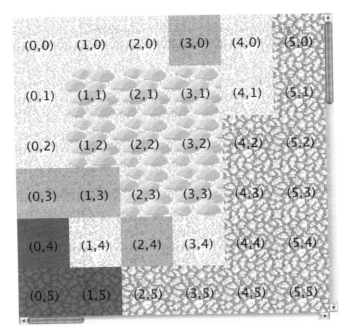

Figure 10-11. The coordinate system of an orthogonal tilemap

So you're not confused, here's the code that calculates the tile coordinate's x position:

```
float pointWidth = tileMap.tileSize.width / CC_CONTENT_SCALE_FACTOR();
pos.x = (int)(pos.x /  pointWidth);
```

The `tileMap.tileSize` property is the size of the tiles in the tileset, which in this case is 32×32 (see also Figure 10-6). By dividing the tilemap's `tilesize` with the `CC_CONTENT_SCALE_FACTOR()`, the width (and height) are converted to point coordinates. Internally, cocos2d handles tilemap sizes as pixel coordinates—this is one of the few exceptions where you'll have to deal with conversion between pixel and point coordinates to ensure correct behavior on both standard- and Retina-resolution devices.

If the touch were at the 340 x position, the calculation would reveal the following:

```
340 / 32 = 10.625
```

That can't be right, though. You're looking for a tile's x coordinate, which is never a fractional number! The reason is, of course, that the touch was somewhere inside the tile we're looking for (that is, inside a 32×32 square area). The simple trick of casting the result to an `int` value will get rid of the fractional part and assign this to `pos.x`:

```
pos.x = (int)10.625        // pos.x == 10
```

Casting to an `int` will remove the fractional part. You can safely get rid of the fractional part because it's simply not relevant—actually it's harmful. If you didn't cast away the fractional part but used the noninteger coordinate—in this example, 10.625—to try to retrieve the tile at a tile coordinate 10.625, you'd receive a runtime error because there is only a tile at x coordinates 10 and 11, not at 10.625.

You use a slightly more complicated calculation to get the tile's y coordinate:

```
float pointHeight=tileMap.tileSize.height / CC_CONTENT_SCALE_FACTOR();
pos.y=(int)((tileMap.mapSize.height * pointHeight - pos.y) / pointHeight);
```

Note that the parentheses are important to make sure the division is done last. In actual numbers, this calculation may be easier to understand. As shown in Figure 10-5, the `tileMap.mapSize` is 30 × 20 tiles, and as I mentioned earlier, `tileMap.tileSize` is 32 × 32 pixels. The calculation then looks like this:

```
pos.y = (int)((20 * 32 - 260) / 32)
```

Multiplying `tileMap.mapSize.height` with `pointHeight` returns the full height of the tilemap in points. This is necessary because the tilemap starts counting y coordinates from top to bottom, whereas screen y coordinates count from bottom to top. By calculating the bottommost y coordinate of the tilemap and subtracting the current y position 260 from that, you get the correct y position of the touch into the tilemap, in points. And because it's a point coordinate, which can have a fractional part, you need to divide by the `pointHeight` and then cast down to an int value to get the tile's y coordinate.

Before the coordinates are returned, they're clipped to valid coordinates within the tilemap width and size. The `fminf` and `fmaxf` functions return whichever of the two values is smaller or larger respectively; used in combination they clip the coordinates to within 0 and tilemap size or width minus 1. This is far shorter than using a series of `if` statements.

Working with the Object Layer

The `orthogonal.tmx` tilemap I've created as an example tilemap for this chapter also contains an object layer, fittingly named `ObjectLayer`. You can create object layers in Tiled by choosing Layer ➤ Add Object Layer. Then you can click inside the tilemap and draw rectangles. I think the name *object layer* is a bit unfortunate and misleading, because most games will use these rectangles as points of interest and trigger areas, and not as actual objects.

In the Tilemap01 project, I've added a bit more code to the `ccTouchesBegan` method to interact with the object layer. Listing 10-4 shows the relevant part of the code, which follows directly after the `isWater` check:

Listing 10-4. Detecting If a Touch Was Inside an ObjectLayer Rectangle

```
// Check if the touch was within one of the rectangle objects
CCTMXObjectGroup* objectLayer=[tileMap objectGroupNamed:@"ObjectLayer"];

BOOL isTouchInRectangle=NO;
int numObjects=objectLayer.objects.count;
for (int i=0; i<numObjects; i++)
{
    NSDictionary* properties=[objectLayer.objects objectAtIndex:i];
    CGRect rect=[self getRectFromObjectProperties:properties tileMap:tileMap];

    if (CGRectContainsPoint(rect, touchLocation))
```

```
    {
        isTouchInRectangle = YES;
        break;
    }
}
```

Because object layers are a different kind of layer, you can't get them via the `layerNamed` method of the tilemap. The object layer in cocos2d is the class `CCTMXObjectGroup`— another unfortunate naming mishap, because Tiled calls it an *object layer*, not an *object group*. In any case, you can get the `CCTMXObjectGroup` for the object layer named simply `ObjectLayer` by using the tilemap's `objectGroupNamed` method and specifying the object layer's name as defined in Tiled.

Next, I iterate over the `objectLayer.objects` `NSMutableArray`, which contains a list of `NSDictionary` items. Sound familiar? Yes, these are the same `NSDictionary` properties returned by the tilemap's `propertiesForGID` method, as shown earlier—except that the contents of these `NSDictionary` items are given by Tiled and aren't user-editable. They simply contain the coordinates for each rectangle. The method `getRectFromObjectProperties` returns the rectangle:

```
-(CGRect) getRectFromObjectProperties:(NSDictionary*)dict tileMap:(CCTMXTiledMap*)tileMap
{
    float x, y, width, height;

    x = [[dict valueForKey:@"x"] floatValue] + tileMap.position.x;
    y = [[dict valueForKey:@"y"] floatValue] + tileMap.position.y;
    width = [[dict valueForKey:@"width"] floatValue];
    height = [[dict valueForKey:@"height"] floatValue];

    return CGRectMake(x, y, width, height);
}
```

The keys x, y, width, and height are set by Tiled. I simply retrieve them from the `NSDictionary` via `valueForKey` and use the `floatValue` method to convert the values from `NSString` to actual floating-point numbers. The x and y values need to be offset with the `tileMap`'s position, because the rectangles need to be moving along with the tilemap. At the end, a `CGRect` is returned by calling the `CGRectMake` convenience method.

The code in ccTouchesBegan then simply checks whether the touch location is contained in the rect via `CGRectContainsPoint`. If it is, the isTouchInRectangle flag is set to `true`, and the for loop is aborted by using the `break` statement. There's no need to check another rectangle for containing the touch location. At the end of ccTouchesBegan, the isTouchInRectangle flag is then used to decide whether to play a particle effect at the touch location. So, this code is creating an explosion particle effect whenever you touch inside a rectangle:

```
if (isTouchOnWater)
{
    [[SimpleAudioEngine sharedEngine] playEffect:@"alien-sfx.caf"];
}
else if (isTouchInRectangle)
{
    CCParticleSystem* system = [CCParticleSystemQuad particleWithFile:↵
        @"fx-explosion.plist"];
    system.autoRemoveOnFinish = YES;
    system.position = touchLocation;
    [self addChild:system z:1];
}
```

Drawing the Object Layer Rectangles

When you run the book's Tilemap01 project, you'll notice that the object layer rectangles are drawn over the tilemap, as shown in Figure 10-12. This isn't a standard feature of tilemaps or object layers. Instead, the rectangles are drawn using OpenGL ES code. Every CCNode has a -(void) draw method that you can override to add custom OpenGL ES code. I tend to use this a lot to debug my code visually by drawing lines, circles, and rectangles that may be used for collision and distance tests, among other things. In this case, actually seeing where the object layer areas are is very useful. Visualizing such information beats looking up and comparing coordinates in the debugger. Our minds are much better at assessing visual information than they are at comparing and calculating numbers. Use this fact to your advantage!

Figure 10-12. The tilemap with object layer rectangles displayed using OpenGL ES code

The -(void) draw method just needs to be in the class, and it will be called automatically every frame. However, you should refrain from using the draw method to modify properties of nodes because that can interfere with drawing the nodes. Listing 10-5 shows the draw method of the TileMapLayer class.

Listing 10-5. *Drawing ObjectLayer Rectangles*

```
#ifdef DEBUG
-(void) draw
{
    [super draw];

    CCNode* node=[self getChildByTag:TileMapNode];
    NSAssert([node isKindOfClass:[CCTMXTiledMap class]], @"not a CCTMXTiledMap");
    CCTMXTiledMap* tileMap=(CCTMXTiledMap*)node;

    // Get the object layer
    CCTMXObjectGroup* objectLayer=[tileMap objectGroupNamed:@"ObjectLayer"];

    // make the lines thicker
    glLineWidth(2.0f * CC_CONTENT_SCALE_FACTOR());
    ccDrawColor4F(1, 0, 1, 1);
```

```
    int numObjects = objectLayer.objects.count;
    for (int i=0; i<numObjects; i++)
    {
        NSDictionary* properties = [objectLayer.objects objectAtIndex:i];
        CGRect rect = [self getRectFromObjectProperties:properties tileMap:tileMap];

        CGPoint dest = CGPointMake(rect.origin.x+rect.size.width, ↵
            rect.origin.y+rect.size.height);
        ccDrawRect(rect.origin, dest);
        ccDrawSolidRect(rect.origin, dest, ccc4f(1, 0, 1, 0.3f));
    }

    // reset line width
    glLineWidth(1.0f);
}
#endif
```

First, I get the tilemap by its tag and then the CCTMXObjectGroup by using the objectGroupNamed method. I then set the line width to 2 pixels with the OpenGL ES method glLineWidth. Multiplying with CC_CONTENT_SCALE_FACTOR() ensures that the line width scales to 4 pixels on Retina devices, because CC_CONTENT_SCALE_FACTOR() returns 2.0f on Retina devices, otherwise 1.0 f. This affects line thickness and color of all subsequent lines drawn with OpenGL ES—not just in the current method but possibly other nodes that use OpenGL ES code for drawing (for example, any of the convenience methods for drawing lines, circles, and polygons defined in cocos2d's CCDrawingPrimitives.h header file). That's why I reset glLineWidth after I'm done drawing. It's good style in OpenGL code to leave its state like you found it; otherwise, it might alter the way other draw code produces its output. OpenGL is a state machine, so every setting you change is remembered and may affect subsequent drawing methods. To avoid this, any OpenGL settings you change should be set back to a safe default after you're done drawing.

> **Note**   Code inside the -(void) draw method is always drawn at a z-order of 0. It's also drawn before all other nodes at z-order 0, which means that any OpenGL ES code will be overdrawn by other nodes if they're also at z-order 0. In the case of the object layer draw code, I had to add the tileMap at a z-order of −1 for the rectangles to be drawn over the tilemap.

Just as before, I iterate over all object layer objects and get their properties from NSDictionary to get the CGRect of that object, which is then used in the ccDrawRect and ccDrawSolidRect methods. Unfortunately, these methods don't take a CGRect as input but an origin and destination CGPoint. Therefore, you have to create the destination point manually by adding the corresponding sizes to the origin coordinates.

Note that the draw method is enclosed in #ifdef DEBUG and #endif statements. This means that the object layer rectangles won't be drawn in release builds, because they're only needed for debugging and illustration purposes—the end user should never see them.

Scrolling the Tilemap

The best part comes last: scrolling. It's actually straightforward because you only need to move the CCTMXTiledMap. In the Tilemap01 project, I've added the call to the centerTileMapOnTileCoord method in ccTouchesBegan right after obtaining the tile coordinates of the touch:

```
-(void) ccTouchesBegan:(NSSet *)touches withEvent:(UIEvent *)event
{
    ...
    // Get the position in tile coordinates from the touch location
    CGPoint touchLocation = [self locationFromTouches:touches];
    CGPoint tilePos = [self tilePosFromLocation:touchLocation tileMap:tileMap];

    // Move tilemap so that the touched tile is at the center of the screen
    [self centerTileMapOnTileCoord:tilePos tileMap:tileMap];
    ...
}
```

Listing 10-6 shows the centerTileMapOnTileCoord method, which moves the tilemap so that the touched tile is at the center of the screen. It also stops the tilemap from scrolling farther if any tilemap border already aligns with the screen edge.

Listing 10-6. Centering the Tilemap on a Tile Coordinate

```
-(void) centerTileMapOnTileCoord:(CGPoint)tilePos tileMap:(CCTMXTiledMap*)tileMap
{
    // center tilemap on the given tile pos
    CGSize screenSize = [CCDirector sharedDirector].winSize;
    CGPoint screenCenter = CGPointMake(screenSize.width * 0.5f, ↵
        screenSize.height * 0.5f);

    // tile coordinates are counted from upper left corner, this maps coordinates to lower left
corner
    tilePos.y = (tileMap.mapSize.height - 1) - tilePos.y;

    // scaling tileSize to Retina display size
    float pointWidth = tileMap.tileSize.width / CC_CONTENT_SCALE_FACTOR();
    float pointHeight = tileMap.tileSize.height / CC_CONTENT_SCALE_FACTOR();

    // point is now at lower left corner of the screen
    CGPoint scrollPosition = CGPointMake(-(tilePos.x * pointWidth), ↵
        -(tilePos.y * pointHeight));

    // offset point to center of screen and center of tile
    scrollPosition.x + = screenCenter.x - pointWidth * 0.5f;
    scrollPosition.y + = screenCenter.y - pointHeight * 0.5f;

    // make sure tilemap scrolling stops at the tilemap borders
    scrollPosition.x = MIN(scrollPosition.x, 0);
    scrollPosition.x = MAX(scrollPosition.x, -screenSize.width);
    scrollPosition.y = MIN(scrollPosition.y, 0);
    scrollPosition.y = MAX(scrollPosition.y, -screenSize.height);
    CCLOG(@"tilePos: (%i, %i) moveTo: (%.0f, %.0f)",
```

```
        (int)tilePos.x, (int)tilePos.y, scrollPosition.x, scrollPosition.y);

    CCAction* move=[CCMoveTo actionWithDuration:0.2f position:scrollPosition];
    [tileMap stopAllActions];
    [tileMap runAction:move];
}
```

After obtaining the center position of the screen, I modify the `tilePos` y coordinate, because tilemap coordinates are counted from top to bottom (see Figure 10-11), and screen coordinates increase from bottom up. In effect, I convert the `tilePos` y coordinate as if it were counted from bottom up. In addition, I subtract 1 from the map's height to account for the fact that tile coordinates are counted from 0. In other words, if the map's height were 10, only the tile coordinates 0 to 9 would be valid.

The tilemap sizes (which are in pixel coordinates) are converted to points just as shown earlier in Listing 10-3. This ensures that scrolling works on both standard-resolution and Retina-resolution devices.

Next, create the `scrollPosition` CGPoint, which will become the position the tilemap will be moved to. The first step is to multiply the tile coordinates with `pointWidth` and `pointHeight`, respectively. You may be wondering why I negate the `tilePosInPixels` coordinates. It's simply because if I want the tiles to move from top right to bottom left, I have to move the tilemap down and to the left by decreasing the coordinates.

The next big block modifies the coordinates of the `scrollPosition` to center the tile on the screen's center point. You also need to take into account the center of the tile itself, which is why half the `tileSize` is deducted from the `screenCenter` offset.

Using the Objective-C language's `MIN` and `MAX` macros ensures that the `scrollPosition` is kept within the bounds of the tilemap so as to not reveal anything past the borders of the tilemap. `MIN` and `MAX` return the minimum and maximum values of their two parameters and are a more compact and readable solution than conditional assignments using `if` and `else` statements.

Finally, use a `CCMoveTo` action to scroll the tilemap node so that the touched tile is centered on the screen. The result is a tilemap that scrolls to the tile that you tap. You can use the same method to scroll to a tile of interest—for example, the player's position.

Tip   As for the player character itself, the next chapter has an implementation of isometric tilemaps. You can apply the same principle to orthogonal tilemaps. And this cocos2D forum thread will get you started with pathfinding on orthogonal tilemaps, source code included: www.cocos2d-iphone.org/forum/topic/19463.

If you're interested in a complete, working, ready-made solution for a hack-and-slash game on orthogonal tilemaps, including a great tutorial, I recommend looking at Nate Weiss' Action-RPG Engine: www.iphonegamekit.com.

Summary

You should now have a fair understanding of what tilemaps are, and you should know how to work with the Tiled (Qt) Map Editor to create a tilemap with multiple layers and properties your game can use.

Loading and displaying a tilemap with cocos2d is a simple task that quickly grows in complexity when it comes to obtaining tile and object layers, modifying them, and reading their properties. You also learned how to determine the tile coordinate of a touch location and how to use tile coordinates to scroll the tilemap so that it centers the touched tile on the screen.

I even got you acquainted with custom drawing and a bit of OpenGL ES code to render the object layer rectangles on the tilemap for debugging purposes.

In the next chapter you'll learn how to work with isometric tilemaps and what it takes to implement a player character moving over the isometric world.

Isometric Tilemaps

With isometric tilemaps you can get the best of both worlds—using two-dimensional graphics to achieve a three-dimensional look. This is why isometric tilemap games are so widely popular. Isometric tilemap games started to get a strong foothold in the late 1990s but slowly disappeared with the increasing 3D rendering performance of desktop computers and consoles. They've reemerged with force in recent years in mobile games and web games, where 3D rendering is very costly or unavailable. Examples range from classic computer role-playing games like Ultima VII and Diablo to current Facebook-hype Farmville and many of its official and unofficial companion games.

Isometric games allow you to create believable game worlds that seem to have spatial depth with relatively simple graphics and tools. In addition, 2D graphics require far less powerful devices than real 3D computer graphics.

Figure 11-1 shows an example of the isometric tilemap game you'll build in this chapter. You'll control a ninja character who sneaks around in this world, avoiding collisions with walls and mountains. The ninja will also be able to hide behind certain objects, such as trees and cacti.

Figure 11-1. An isometric tilemap game

> **Note**   All tilesets used in this chapter were created by David E. Gervais and publishedunder the Creative Commons license. You can download more of his work at
> `http://pousse.rapiere.free.fr/tome/index.htm`.

Designing Isometric Tile Graphics

To help you understand how to design isometric graphics, I'll first introduce the concept of projection. In a 3D world, you can look at the objects from all sides, because 3D worlds can freely project the 3D world onto your two-dimensional screen from any angle and position. This conversion from a three-dimensional world onto a two-dimensional screen is called *perspective projection*. Taking a photograph is also a form of perspective projection of the real world onto a 2D image. Both projections retain the perspective of the viewer's point of view.

In an isometric tilemap world, each individual tilemap image is already a projection of a seemingly three-dimensional object onto a flat surface. This projection is usually performed with a special form of parallel projection called *isometric projection*. The image then becomes more or less skewed, but our minds still recognize it as a three-dimensional object.

> **Tip**   To learn more about the various projection techniques and technical details of each, I recommend browsing the section about parallel projection on Wikipedia at
> `http://en.wikipedia.org/wiki/Parallel_projection`.

In terms of tilemaps, Figure 11-2 shows the concrete steps for creating an isometric projection of an orthogonal image. The square is first rotated by 45 degrees and then scaled down along its y-axis to give it its typical isometric diamond shape.

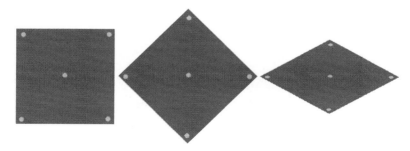

Figure 11-2. *An orthogonal turned isometric by rotating it by 45 degrees and then compressing it vertically*

However, Figure 11-2 is just the theoretical approach to illustrate the projection of the isometric shape. You can't turn an orthogonal image into an isometric image by simply rotating and compressing it, because the rotation would affect the image content. It would just look flat and very wrong, just like Figure 11-3.

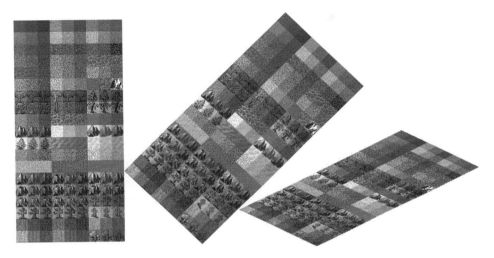

Figure 11-3. Turning an orthogonal tileset into an isometric tileset—it's not that simple!

Instead, consider the diamond shape from Figure 11-2 as your drawing canvas of the floor. The simplest isometric tiles you can design are flat ground tiles. Just fill the diamond shape with a certain pattern, and you get yourself usable isometric tiles. Figure 11-4 shows a number of flat-colored isometric tiles laid out next to each other, creating a ground floor pattern. Ground floor tiles are not impressive and look very flat. Yet they are essential as the game world's background layer.

Figure 11-4. Ground floor isometric tiles have no depth. They're used as solid surface areas

To add actual visual depth to an isometric tilemap, you need to have object tiles that extend beyond the diamond shape. The most commonly used approach is to draw three-dimensional objects as if they were viewed at a 45-degree angle and then draw them up and over the diamond shape, typically extending no more than one tile above. In the example in Figure 11-5, you can see this quite nicely by looking at the doorway. The door arch is drawn mostly over the isometric tile above the one that the door's frame is standing on. This gives the arch its visual depth.

Figure 11-5. Add depth by drawing objects up to twice as high as the diamond shape

Isometric tilemaps allow object tiles to overlap one another because the tiles are drawn from back to front, which means object tiles closer to the viewer are always drawn over tiles behind them, adding to the feeling of depth. But this approach requires careful design of individual tiles and the tilemap itself, because too much overlap or overlapping the wrong tiles can quickly destroy the illusion of depth.

As a good practice, try not to overlap object tiles that have wildly different shapes but use the same or similar color palette. In the case of Figure 11-5, for example, you would not want to place the crystal tile directly behind the doorway. The loss in contrast and merging outlines of these tiles could easily destroy the perception of depth.

Likewise, although you can create isometric object tiles that span much higher than twice the tile height, it's very hard to create a convincing 3D look if objects appear very high because the player will see only part of the tilemap. If you were building a huge castle whose walls span a dozen tiles high and the player approached them from below, the walls could easily be mistaken for a large section of ground floor. You can even end up creating optical illusions like the drawings of M. C. Escher because the isometric tiles do not get smaller the farther away from the screen they are. So, there's always a fine line between what works and what doesn't when designing isometric tiles and tilemaps.

Figure 11-6 shows a finely crafted isometric tileset named dg_iso32.png, which contains a good variation of ground floor tiles; object tiles such as walls, trees, and houses; and adornment objects or items that can be placed on any ground tile. The tiles in this set are each 54x49 pixels in size. The height can be chosen arbitrarily; it can be more or less than 49 pixels and depends on how much overlap between tiles you like in your tilemap. The actual height of the diamond shape is 27 pixels. This will become important when you create the tilemap in Tiled (Qt) Map Editor.

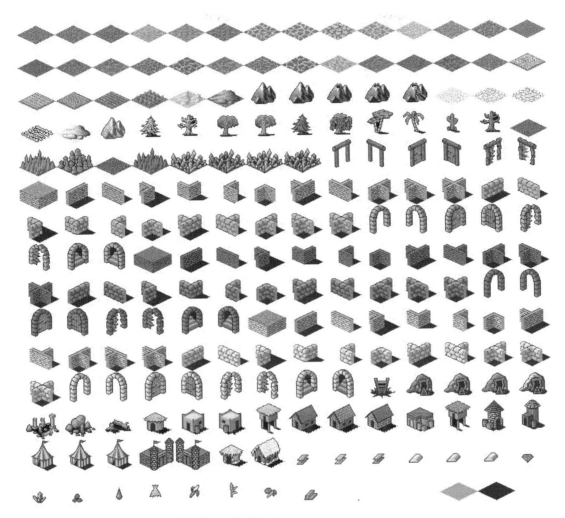

Figure 11-6. David Gervais's finely crafted isometric tileset

Isometric Tilemap Editing with Tiled

You'll use the Tiled Map Editor once again to create the isometric tilemap. Basic tilemap editing is the same as with orthogonal maps, but you have to follow certain crucial steps to correctly set up a new isometric tilemap and load an isometric tileset.

Creating a New Isometric Tilemap

Open Tiled and choose File ➤ New to open the New Map dialog in Figure 11-7. Set the orientation obviously to Isometric, and the map size to 30 tiles wide and high, just right for our example project. The odd thing here is the tile size width and height, which seem to be off a bit.

I already mentioned that the individual tiles in dg_iso32.png are 54x49 pixels. The size of the diamond shape, which you have to consider when laying down tiles, is 54x27 pixels. Yet the tile size in the New Map dialog is 52x26. This is because David Gervais designed his tiles to require overlapping of 2 pixels in the horizontal and 1 pixel in the vertical direction in order to close all gaps between the tiles.

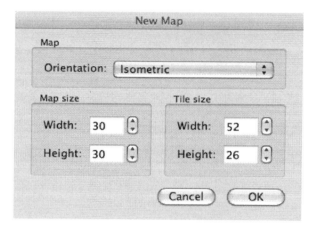

Figure 11-7. *Create a new isometric tilemap in Tiled*

This offset is on purpose, because isometric tiles are often designed to overlap each other a little. In this case, the size of the tiles in the Tiled isometric map must be 2 pixels less wide and 1 pixel less high than the actual size of the diamond shapes in the tileset. Other isometric tilesets may require different offsets, or even no offset at all.

If you see any artifacts like the ones in Figure 11-8, you've set the wrong tile size when creating a new isometric map with David Gervais' tileset. You can find this erroneous tilemap as isometric-no-offset.tmx in the project's Resources folder, for illustration purposes.

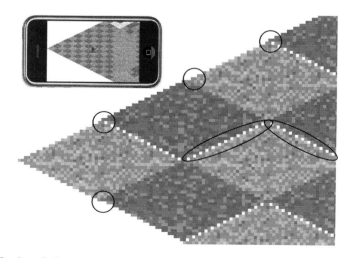

Figure 11-8. *Artifacts like these indicate a tile-size offset problem*

If you did make a mistake and picked incorrect offsets and you don't want to lose the tilemap you've just spent hours designing, or if you have other reasons to tweak the tilemap size or tileset size, there's a simple way to do this, but it requires manipulating the TMX file directly because there's no such option in Tiled itself.

The following trick makes it easy to experiment with various offsets until you get it just right. Close Tiled if it's currently running and then select the TMX file in your Xcode project; you'll see that it's displayed as a plain-text XML file. You can edit the file with any other text editor just as well. At the beginning of the file, you'll find the map section:

```
<map version="1.0" orientation="isometric" width="30" height="30" tilewidth="54"↵
    tileheight="27">
```

You can edit the `tilewidth` and `tileheight` parameters until you've found the correct offsets for the tilemap. Likewise, if you're having problems determining the tile size of the isometric tileset you're using, you can modify the `tilewidth` and `tileheight` parameters of the tileset(s):

```
<tileset firstgid="1" name="dg_iso32" tilewidth="54" tileheight="49">
    <image source="dg_iso32.png"/>
</tileset>
```

Just make sure to close and reload the TMX file in Tiled after you made any manual changes to it, because Tiled won't automatically reload the file.

Creating a New Isometric Tileset

Next you need to load a tileset containing isometric tiles. For this chapter you'll be using the `dg_iso32.png` tileset image found in the IsoTilemap01 project's `Resources` folder. In Tiled, choose Map ➤ New Tileset . . . and browse to the `dg_iso32.png` file.

Notice that Tiled will set default tile width and height according to the settings in the New Map dialog, shown in Figure 11-7. For isometric tilemaps, the defaults always need to be corrected because of the overlap of isometric tiles. As I mentioned earlier, the `dg_iso32.png` tileset uses a tile width of 54 pixels and a tile height of 49 pixels. Note that you have to use the full canvas height of the isometric tiles, not the diamond shape height of 27 pixels. Figure 11-9 shows the correct setup for this tileset.

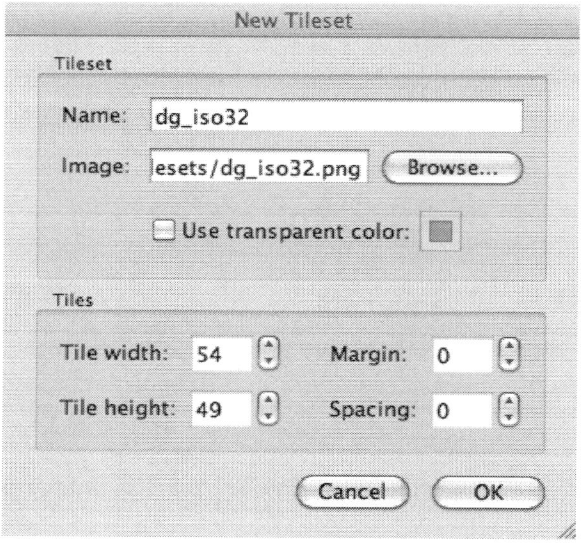

Figure 11-9. *Adding the tileset with width 54 pixels and height 49 pixels*

Laying Down Some Ground Rules

The most important rule for designing isometric maps is that you need at least two layers so that game characters can walk behind certain tiles. One layer is for flat ground objects and floor tiles, and the other is for all other objects that either overlap other tiles or are not fully opaque, such as items. In the tileset of Figure 11-6, the first two rows are ground tiles and need to be placed on the ground floor, whereas in row 3 the mountains as well as almost all tiles in row 4 and after need to be placed on the Objects layer.

In Tiled, add two new layers via Layer ➤ Add Tile Layer … and name them Ground and Objects. Make sure the Objects layer is drawn on top of the Ground layer. When designing your tilemap, you should take great care to lay down only fully opaque, flat floor tiles on the Ground layer. All other tiles have to be placed on the Objects layer.

Cocos2d has issues with properly displaying game characters and other sprites behind partially occluding tiles in tilemaps, unless you apply the following steps. As one part of the solution, you need to add a special property named cc_vertexz to tiled layers. I explain the solution in more detail shortly; for now, select the Ground layer and click Layer ➤ Layer Properties. … Add a new property named cc_vertexz and set its value to –1000. Do the same with the Objects layer but instead of entering –1000, enter the string *automatic*, as in Figure 11-10.

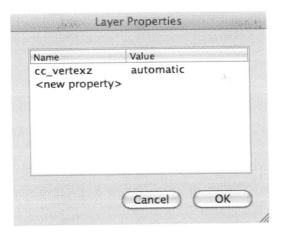

Figure 11-10. The Objects layer needs the cc_vertexz property set to automatic

Now you can spend some time designing a nice-looking tilemap, or you can simply load the one I designed in the IsoTilemap01 project. Be sure to put only floor tiles on the Ground layer and only overlapping and transparent tiles on the Objects layer. When you're done, you should have a nice-looking tilemap like the one in Figure 11-11.

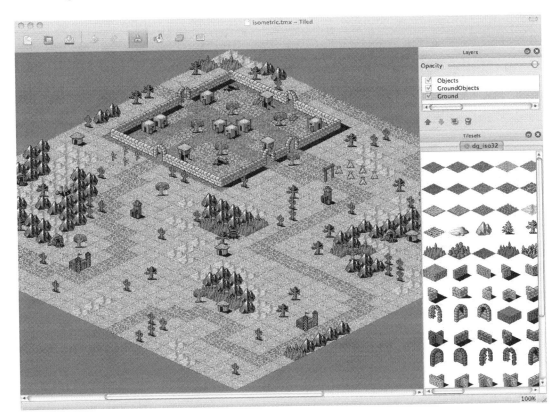

Figure 11-11. A completed isometric tilemap in Tiled using David Gervais's tileset

Isometric Game Programming

Let's use this isometric tilemap in a cocos2d game. As you might expect, some things will have to change compared to working with orthogonal tilemaps. In particular, you need to set up cocos2d properly to allow isometric tiles to partially occlude game characters. Determining a touched tile also requires different code than orthogonal tilemaps, and when scrolling, you can no longer stop scrolling at the borders of the tilemap because the tilemap itself has a diamond shape.

Loading the Isometric Tilemap in Cocos2d

This is easy. Compared to orthogonal tilemaps, you don't need to change anything except load the isometric.tmx file instead of orthogonal.tmx.

```
CCTMXTiledMap* tileMap=[CCTMXTiledMap tiledMapWithTMXFile:@"isometric.tmx"];
[self addChild:tileMap z:-1 tag:TileMapNode];
tileMap.position=CGPointMake(-500, -300);
```

I do set the isometric tilemap's position to –500, –300 right away, assuming the tilemap size is 30x30 tiles. This approximately centers the screen on the lower corner of the small village on the north of the tilemap in Figure 11-11. I do this to illustrate the following point about properly setting up Cocos2D for isometric tilemaps, and in Figure 11-12 you can see there's something obviously wrong with the tilemap.

Figure 11-12. Without 2D projection, the Ground layer will render incorrectly

Set up Cocos2d for Isometric Tilemaps

If you followed the creation of the tilemap thus far and you set the cc_vertexz properties on the ground and objects layers in Tiled as described earlier, the resulting tilemap may look like the one in Figure 11-12. Somehow, the Ground layer is zoomed far out, and tiles from the Objects layer seem to be floating in midair. It looks like a scary place to be.

The way to fix this and enable proper rendering of overlapping sprites is to initialize cocos2d in a different way from how the cocos2d Application template in Xcode sets things up. It initializes cocos2d in a standard way, which is fine for most games but fails to work properly with isometric tilemap games. In the IsoTilemap01 project, the cocos2d startup code is altered to the code in Listing 11-1 with the changes and additions highlighted in bold.

Listing 11-1. Manually Initializing cocos2d's `EAGLView`

```
- (BOOL)application:(UIApplication *)application
didFinishLaunchingWithOptions:(NSDictionary *)launchOptions
{
    // Create the main window
    window_ = [[UIWindow alloc] initWithFrame:[[UIScreen mainScreen] bounds]];

    // Create an CCGLView with a RGB565 color buffer, and a depth buffer of 24-bits
    CCGLView *glView = [CCGLView viewWithFrame:[window_ bounds]
                              pixelFormat:kEAGLColorFormatRGB565
                              depthFormat:GL_DEPTH_COMPONENT24_OES
                        preserveBackbuffer:NO
                                sharegroup:nil
                             multiSampling:NO
                           numberOfSamples:0];

    director_ = (CCDirectorIOS*)[CCDirector sharedDirector];
    [director_ setProjection:kCCDirectorProjection2D];
    ...
```

You have to change two things for isometric tilemaps. First, you need to enable the OpenGL depth buffer to allow a more fine-grained control over the z-ordering of objects. Second, `CCDirector` has to use a 2D projection to work with the depth buffer.

Tip If you're a Kobold2D user, you can make these changes in the `config.lua` file. Look for the GLViewDepthFormat and Enable2DProjection settings and change them to these values:
`GLViewDepthFormat = GLViewDepthFormat.Depth24Bit,`
`Enable2DProjection = YES,`

You first create a `UIWindow` and then decide on a `CCDirector` type to use and set the animation interval to 60 frames per second. This is the default behavior.

The `EAGLView` line is important because for overlapping tiles to render properly, you have to specify a depth buffer with the `depthFormat` parameter. In this case, it's `GL_DEPTH_COMPONENT24_OES`, which creates a depth buffer of 24 bits. To conserve memory, you can also use a 16-bit depth buffer, which may be sufficient.

Depth buffering allows OpenGL to determine whether a certain pixel is in front or behind another pixel so it can decide whether to actually draw the new pixel or discard it. This comes at a cost of additional memory usage—nearly 2 MB for a 24-bit depth buffer on Retina devices—but it allows sprites and tiles to correctly overlap one another.

The other really important line in the initialization is setProjection, which puts cocos2d in 2D projection mode. This changes a couple of OpenGL parameters that affect the way cocos2d renders nodes. In this case, it fixes the issue in Figure 11-12 where the ground floor is not rendered as expected, with the final result shown in Figure 11-13. But it also enables you to finely tune the z-order of sprites by using the vertexZ property rather than the zOrder property of sprites.

Figure 11-13. With 2D projection, the Ground layer is displayed as expected

By default, cocos2d's z-ordering of nodes is based on the z value when you're adding a node via the addChild method. Nodes with a lower z-order are drawn before nodes with a higher z-order. Nodes that have the same z-order are drawn in the order in which they've been added to the node hierarchy, meaning nodes added last will be drawn over nodes added before that node. This allows cocos2d to order nodes without using a depth buffer.

If you enable depth buffering, you can also use the vertexZ property to change each node's draw order freely. Cocos2d requires this freedom in order to let the cc_vertexz tilemap property work its magic. Later you'll manipulate the vertexZ property of the player character to correctly draw the player sprite in front of or behind other isometric tiles.

Locating an Isometric Tile

The next thing to do is determine from a touch location the coordinates of the touched tile. You can find this code in the IsoTilemap01 project. Before I get to that, let's see what the interface and implementation of the TileMapLayer class look like thus far. It's nothing you haven't seen before:

```
// TileMapLayer.h
#import "cocos2d.h"

enum
{
    TileMapNode = 0,
};
```

```
@interface TileMapLayer : CCLayer
{
}
+(CCScene *) scene;
@end

// TileMapLayer.m
#import "TileMapLayer.h"

@implementation TileMapLayer
+(CCScene *) scene
{
    CCScene *scene = [CCScene node];
    TileMapLayer *layer = [TileMapLayer node];
    [scene addChild: layer];
    return scene;
}

-(id) init
{
    self = [super init];
    if (self)
    {
        CCTMXTiledMap* tileMap = [CCTMXTiledMap tiledMapWithTMXFile:@"isometric.tmx"];
        [self addChild:tileMap z:-1 tag:TileMapNode];

        // offset the tilemap's start position to move it into view
        tileMap.position = CGPointMake(-500, -500);

        self.isTouchEnabled = YES;
    }
    return self;
}
@end
```

If you refer to Figure 10-11 in the previous chapter, you'll recall that the tilemap indices of orthogonal tilemaps have their origin point (0, 0) at the top-left corner. Now, with isometric tilemaps, there is no top-left corner anymore. The tilemap itself is rotated by 45 degrees, which makes the topmost tile the point of origin. Figure 11-14 illustrates this well. Tiles toward the bottom right have increasing X coordinates, while Tiles toward the bottom left have increasing Y coordinates. The bottommost tile then has the coordinates 29, 29 in a map consisting of 30x30 tiles.

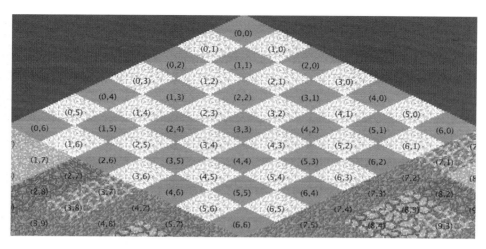

Figure 11-14. *The coordinate system of an isometric tilemap*

This may seem strange at first, but if you lean your head a bit to the right, you may notice that the tile coordinates follow the exact same order as in orthogonal tilemaps, except that the whole map is rotated by 45 degrees.

You can now straighten your head again, because I need you to focus on the modified tilePosFromLocation method, which calculates the touched tile coordinates from a touch location on the screen. As Listing 11-2 shows, it's a wee bit more complex than the orthogonal counterpart.

Listing 11-2. *Calculating the Tile Coordinates from a Touch Location*

```
-(CGPoint) tilePosFromLocation:(CGPoint)location tileMap:(CCTMXTiledMap*)tileMap
{
    // Tilemap position must be subtracted, in case the tilemap position is scrolling
    CGPoint pos = ccpSub(location, tileMap.position);

    float halfMapWidth = tileMap.mapSize.width * 0.5f;
    float mapHeight = tileMap.mapSize.height;
    float pointWidth = tileMap.tileSize.width / CC_CONTENT_SCALE_FACTOR();
    float pointHeight = tileMap.tileSize.height / CC_CONTENT_SCALE_FACTOR();

    CGPoint tilePosDiv = CGPointMake(pos.x / pointWidth, pos.y / pointHeight);
    float inverseTileY = mapHeight - tilePosDiv.y;

    // Cast to int makes sure that result is in whole numbers
    float posX = (int)(inverseTileY+tilePosDiv.x - halfMapWidth);
    float posY = (int)(inverseTileY - tilePosDiv.x+halfMapWidth);

    // make sure coordinates are within isomap bounds
    posX = MAX(0, posX);
    posX = MIN(tileMap.mapSize.width - 1, posX);
    posY = MAX(0, posY);
    posY = MIN(tileMap.mapSize.height - 1, posY);

    return CGPointMake(posX, posY);
}
```

Subtracting the tilemap position to take scrolling of the tilemap into account is the same as in the orthogonal version of this method. Next I create a number of variables, just to make the code a bit more readable and have less to type, and then divide the map size width by half. I then create a CGPoint tilePosDiv, which is the pixel location within the tilemap divided by the tilemap's width and height (in points, not pixels), and an inverseTileY variable, which is simply the inverse of the tilemap's y coordinates. This inversion is necessary because the tilemap y coordinates count from top down, whereas screen y coordinates count from bottom up.

Now you can get to actually calculating the x,y coordinates of the touched tile. The calculation starts with the inverse y coordinate, which will be in the range of 0 to 29 for a tilemap that has a height of 30 tiles. It defines the vertical position in the tilemap from which you'll be looking for the x and y tile coordinates horizontally.

This becomes clearer if you look at Figure 11-4 and locate tile coordinate (3,3). You'll notice that when you move on a horizontal line to the left of tile coordinate (3,3), the x coordinates decrease and the y coordinates increase: (2,4), (1,5), (0,6). Similarly, if you move to the right of tile coordinate (3,3), the x coordinates increase while the y coordinates decrease: (4,2), (5,1), (6,0).

That means you can get both x and y tile coordinates from the inverseTileY position. In the case of the x tile coordinate, you add the tilePosDiv.x coordinate and then subtract halfMapWidth. For the y tile coordinate, you subtract the sum of tilePosDiv.x and halfMapWidth from inverseTileY.

Tip   I'll spare you the details of the mathematical concepts behind this calculation, because you can apply the code as is and don't need to change anything. If you're interested in understanding the intricate details of isometric projection and the mathematics behind it, I recommend reading the excellently illustrated article by Herbert Glarner at www.gandraxa.com/isometric_projection.aspx.

By applying the Objective-C MIN and MAX macros, I ensure that the returned tile coordinate is within the bounds of the tilemap. In other words, it will return coordinates from (0,0) to (29,29) for the 30x30 tilemap used by the isometric tilemap projects.

Scrolling the Isometric Tilemap

With the tilePosFromLocation method updated to work with isometric tilemaps, the IsoTilemap01 project continues by implementing isometric tilemap scrolling, using the tile coordinates returned from the tilePosFromLocation method. Just as in the orthogonal tilemap project, you do this using the centerTileMapOnTileCoord method, shown in Listing 11-3.

Listing 11-3. Scrolling the Screen to Center on a Specific Tile Coordinate

```
-(void) centerTileMapOnTileCoord:(CGPoint)tilePos tileMap:(CCTMXTiledMap*)tileMap
{
    // center tilemap on the given tile pos
    CGSize screenSize=[CCDirector sharedDirector].winSize;
```

```
    CGPoint screenCenter=CGPointMake(screenSize.width * 0.5f,↵
        screenSize.height * 0.5f);

    // get the ground layer
    CCTMXLayer* layer=[tileMap layerNamed:@"Ground"];
    NSAssert(layer !=nil, @"Ground layer not found!");

    // internally tile Y coordinates are off by 1
    tilePos.y -=1;

    // get the pixel coordinates for a tile at these coordinates
    CGPoint scrollPosition=[layer positionAt:tilePos];

    // negate the position to account for scrolling
    scrollPosition=ccpMult(scrollPosition, -1);

    // add offset to screen center
    scrollPosition=ccpAdd(scrollPosition, screenCenter);

    // move the tilemap
    CCAction* move=[CCMoveTo actionWithDuration:0.2f position:scrollPosition];
    [tileMap stopAllActions];
    [tileMap runAction:move];
}
```

First, the screen center position is determined as before. Then you want to use the convenience method of the layer, positionAt, which returns a screen position for a tile coordinate. To do so, get the Ground layer and assert that it exists. It doesn't matter which layer you use, as long as all layers use the same size tiles.

Before calling the positionAt method, I have to subtract 1 from the tile y coordinate to fix a persistent offset problem. Seasoned programmers may be worried that using a tile y coordinate of 0 and subtracting 1 from it could lead to an invalid index and thus a disastrous crash. But in this case, the positionAt method doesn't use the tile coordinates as indices, and it works with any tile coordinate, even negative ones.

The positionAt method returns the pixel position of the given tile coordinate within the tilemap and stores it in the scrollPosition variable. This method isn't specific to isometric tilemaps; it works for all tilemap types: orthogonal, isometric, and hexagonal. Internally, cocos2d checks which type of tilemap is currently being used and then uses the appropriate calculation, because they differ in profound ways. If you're interested in the specific implementation of each of these calculations, take a look at the methods positionForOrthoAt, positionForIsoAt, and positionForHexAt in the cocos2d CCTMXLayer.m implementation file.

Because the tilemap may be scrolling, in which case it will have a negative position, the scrollPosition is multiplied by –1, negating it. After that I just add the screenCenter position to it, and I know where to scroll to. The move action is the same as before and moves the tilemap so that the touched tile is centered onscreen.

This World Deserves a Better End

Because of the diamond-shaped nature of isometric tilemaps, it's inevitable that the scrolling tilemap will reveal parts outside of the tilemap, as shown in Figure 11-15. Indeed, the tilePosFromLocation method ensures that the returned tile coordinate is always within bounds, so you can use that safely even if the player touches outside the tilemap. But if you don't want the player to see the end of your isometric tilemap world, you'll have to use a trick.

Figure 11-15. *It's the end of the world as we know it (and it feels wrong)*

Open Tiled and load the isometric.tmx file from the IsoTilemap01 project's Resources folder. What you want to do is to add a border around the existing map and fill it with tiles that give the impression of an impassable area. In Tiled, use Map ➤ Resize Map … to bring up the Resize dialog shown in Figure 11-16. You need to add 10 tiles to each side of this tilemap to completely fill the border. Depending on the tile size, you'll have to experiment to find the minimum number of tiles that needs to be appended. In this case, enter **50** as the new width and height and also enter **10** in the offset boxes. This makes the tilemap 20x20 tiles larger and also moves everything you've edited previously to the center so that you end up with a border of 10 tiles on each side.

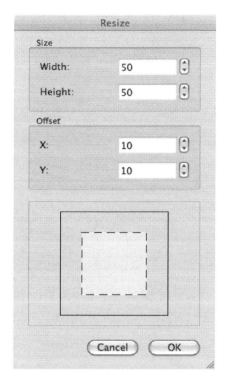

Figure 11-16. *Resizing the map in Tiled to add a border*

You can now fill this border area to give the impression of an area of the map that's simply impassable. It helps to choose a darker ground tile to hint to the player that this area can't be entered, and of course you should add impenetrable objects onto the Objects layer and around the border of the playable area. Your result should look something like Figure 11-17. I saved my version into the Resources folder of the project and named it isometric-with-border.tmx. So if you don't want to do the editing, you only need to load isometric-with-border.tmx instead of the isometric.tmx file.

Figure 11-17. *A convincing impassable map border area*

Note   The impassable area in Figure 11-17 does look quite repetitive and boring. You may be tempted to add more detail to that area, but that's a double-edged sword. On one side, more details and variations within the impassable area will make it look better. On the other, it can also fool the player into thinking about and, even worse, spending time trying to reach that one spot in the impassable area that looks like it could be visited. For example, houses or cave entrances are places the player would want to explore, so avoid using those in the border area. The player might assume it's a secret area and he simply has to figure out how to get there. If you have a player thinking like this, it's bad for your game. You don't want to tempt the player into trying things that are absolutely impossible to achieve. It just wastes his time and it ends in frustration.

The IsoTilemap02 project implements the code that prevents you from scrolling outside the playable area by defining the inner tile coordinates of the playable area. I added two CGPoint variables, playableAreaMin and playableAreaMax, to the TileMapLayer class:

```
@interface TileMapLayer : CCLayer
{
    CGPoint playableAreaMin, playableAreaMax;
}
```

The playable area variables are initialized with a border size of 10 tiles in the init method of the class:

```
-(id) init
{
    self = [super init];
    if (self)
    {
        ...

        const int borderSize = 10;
        playableAreaMin = CGPointMake(borderSize, borderSize);
        playableAreaMax = CGPointMake(tileMap.mapSize.width - 1 - borderSize, ↵
                                      tileMap.mapSize.height - 1 - borderSize);
    }
    return self;
}
```

The playable area is defined as anything within the bounds of the tile coordinates (10, 10) to (39, 39). All tiles outside this area should be considered not part of the playfield. All that remains is to update the tilePosFromLocation method by replacing the MIN/MAX lines to implement this rule of the playable area. Instead of keeping the tile coordinates within the bounds of the whole tilemap, you now want to keep it within the bounds of the playable area, as such:

```
posX = MAX(playableAreaMin.x, posX);
posX = MIN(playableAreaMax.x, posX);
posY = MAX(playableAreaMin.y, posY);
posY = MIN(playableAreaMax.y, posY);
```

If you try this, you'll see that only the tiles within the playable area can be centered onscreen. What's more, clicks outside the playable area aren't just ignored; the tilemap scrolls as close as possible to the tile you clicked. This way, you don't destroy the player's impression of a world that seemingly extends far beyond what the player can see.

Adding a Movable Player Character

By adding a player character moving about the tilemap world, you get closer to an actual isometric game. In this case, I chose `ninja.png` as the player character and added it to the IsoTilemap02 project. The player is a class derived from `CCSprite`, aptly named `Player`. Listing 11-4 shows the header file.

Listing 11-4. The Player Class Interface

```
#import <Foundation/Foundation.h>
#import "cocos2d.h"

@interface Player : CCSprite
{
}

+(id) player;
@end
```

The `+(id) player` method in Listing 11-5 allocates and initializes the sprite with the `ninja.png` file.

Listing 11-5. The Player Class Implementation

```
#import "Player.h"

@implementation Player
+(id) player
{
    return [[self alloc] initWithFile:@"ninja.png"];
}
@end
```

You then create the player in the `TileMapLayer` class's `init` method:

```
#import "Player.h"

...

-(id) init
{
    self = [super init];
    if (self)
    {
        ...

        CGSize screenSize = [CCDirector sharedDirector].winSize;
```

```
        // Create the player and add it
        player=[Player player];
        player.position=CGPointMake(screenSize.width / 2, screenSize.height / 2);
        // offset player's texture to best match the tile center position
        player.anchorPoint=CGPointMake(0.3f, 0.1f);
        [self addChild:player];
    }
    return self;
}
```

You will also have to update the TileMapLayer interface to add the player instance variable and forward-declare the Player class:

```
@class Player;

@interface TileMapLayer : CCLayer
{
    CGPoint playableAreaMin, playableAreaMax;
    Player* player;
}
```

The player's position is set to the center of the screen on purpose. Because you already have a method that allows you to center a specific tile on the screen, centering the player sprite on the screen as well makes it behave as if it were moving across the tilemap, when in fact it always remains at the same position. You don't have to move the player sprite at all!

The player's anchorPoint is offset a little from its default of (0.5f, 0.5f) to (0.3f, 0.1f) to approximately center the sprite's feet on the center position of the tile. Otherwise, it might look wrong because all other game objects like trees and cacti have their roots, literally speaking, at the center of the tile. So, it's only natural to try to place the player's feet at that position as well.

If you try this now, even though the player sprite never moves, it looks as if the player is walking about the tilemap world. Perfect!

Well, not quite. If you move over mountains and walls and trees and buildings, the player sprite is always drawn in front of them.

Enabling the Player to Move Behind Tiles

To allow the player to be partially hidden by object tiles in front of him, such as buildings, walls, trees, and whatnot, you have to change his vertexZ value as he moves around on the map. At the start of this chapter, when you created the Objects layer in Tiled, you gave it a property named cc_vertexz and set it to automatic. This instructed cocos2d to assign consecutive vertexZ values to the tiles in that layer. Figure 11-18 shows you which vertexZ values the tiles are assigned in a tilemap that's 50x50 tiles in size. This is different from the tile indices shown in Figure 11-14 because the vertexZ values increase in both X and Y directions. You could say that vertexZ values decrease with each horizontal row of the tilemap.

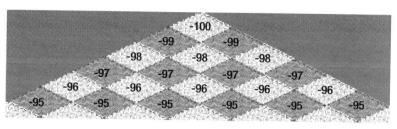

Figure 11-18. The vertexZ values of tiles in the 50x50 tilemap

This is reflected in code by the updateVertexZ method added to the Player class:

```
-(void) updateVertexZ:(CGPoint)tilePos tileMap:(CCTMXTiledMap*)tileMap
{
    float lowestZ=-(tileMap.mapSize.width+tileMap.mapSize.height);
    float currentZ=tilePos.x+tilePos.y;
    self.vertexZ=lowestZ+currentZ - 1.5f;
}
```

The lowest vertexZ value is simply the sum of the map size width and height in the negative. Likewise, you can get the difference of any tile coordinate in the tilemap to the lowest vertexZ value, which is the tile at position 0, 0. It's the sum of the X and Z coordinates of that position. For example, the tile at position 2, 2 is 2+2=4 less than the lowest vertexZ value. If you add the two, you get −100+4=−96. Since the player sprite is added to the TileMapLayer after the tilemap, it will render on top of tiles with the same vertexZ value. Because of this, I also subtract 1.5 so that the end result is a vertexZ value of −96.5 if the player is standing on the tile coordinate 2, 2. That also places the player behind any object on the same tile. If you want your player to be in front of any object on the same tile, you should subtract 1.0f or less.

To make this code work, you also have to define the updateVertexZ method in the Player class's interface:

```
@interface Player : CCSprite
{
}

+(id) player;
-(void) updateVertexZ:(CGPoint)tilePos tileMap:(CCTMXTiledMap*)tileMap;
@end
```

And then you should call the updateVertexZ method every time the tilemap is moved, which is done in the ccTouchesBegan method of the TileMapLayer class:

```
-(void) ccTouchesBegan:(NSSet *)touches withEvent:(UIEvent *)event
{
    CCNode* node=[self getChildByTag:TileMapNode];
    NSAssert([node isKindOfClass:[CCTMXTiledMap class]], @"not a CCTMXTiledMap");
    CCTMXTiledMap* tileMap=(CCTMXTiledMap*)node;

    CGPoint touchLocation=[self locationFromTouches:touches];
    CGPoint tilePos=[self tilePosFromLocation:touchLocation tileMap:tileMap];

    [self centerTileMapOnTileCoord:tilePos tileMap:tileMap];
```

```
// update the player's vertexZ
[player updateVertexZ:tilePos tileMap:tileMap];
}
```

If you try this now, you'll see that the ninja player will hide behind walls, trees, and other large objects, like a good ninja does.

Moving the Player, Tile by Tile

So far, the player (actually, the screen) moves faster the further away from the center the screen is touched. The player also moves across the tiles freely, but he really should be moving from tile to tile in only four directions. The IsoTilemap03 project changes the control mechanism to one that allows you to move the player in one of the four allowed directions as long as you keep a finger on the screen. The move direction depends on where you touch the screen relative to the player.

This requires some additions to the TileMapLayer interface, shown in Listing 11-6.

Listing 11-6. The TileMapLayer Class Interface

```
typedef enum
{
    MoveDirectionNone=0,
    MoveDirectionUpperLeft,
    MoveDirectionLowerLeft,
    MoveDirectionUpperRight,
    MoveDirectionLowerRight,

    MAX_MoveDirections,
} EMoveDirection;

@class Player;

@interface TileMapLayer : CCLayer
{
    CGPoint playableAreaMin, playableAreaMax;
    Player* player;

    CGPoint screenCenter;
    CGRect upperLeft, lowerLeft, upperRight, lowerRight;
    CGPoint moveOffsets[MAX_MoveDirections];
    EMoveDirection currentMoveDirection;
}
```

The EMoveDirection enum is later used to determine in which direction the player intends to walk, with MoveDirectionNone signaling no movement. Let's look at changes in the implementation of the TileMapLayer class's init method in Listing 11-7.

Listing 11-7. Initializing the Player's Movement Directions

```
// divide the screen into 4 areas
screenCenter=CGPointMake(screenSize.width / 2, screenSize.height / 2);
upperLeft=CGRectMake(0, screenCenter.y, screenCenter.x, screenCenter.y);
```

```
lowerLeft=CGRectMake(0, 0, screenCenter.x, screenCenter.y);
upperRight=CGRectMake(screenCenter.x, screenCenter.y, screenCenter.x,↵
    screenCenter.y);
lowerRight=CGRectMake(screenCenter.x, 0, screenCenter.x, screenCenter.y);

moveOffsets[MoveDirectionNone]=CGPointZero;
moveOffsets[MoveDirectionUpperLeft]=CGPointMake(-1, 0);
moveOffsets[MoveDirectionLowerLeft]=CGPointMake(0, 1);
moveOffsets[MoveDirectionUpperRight]=CGPointMake(0, -1);
moveOffsets[MoveDirectionLowerRight]=CGPointMake(1, 0);

currentMoveDirection=MoveDirectionNone;

// continuously check for walking
[self scheduleUpdate];
```

The four CGRect variables, upperLeft, lowerLeft, upperRight, and lowerRight, divide the screen into four quadrants, each of which is the touch area to move the player in the desired direction. Thus, a touch in the lower-right area of the screen will move the player to the right and down along the tilemap.

The moveOffsets array contains a CGPoint for each move direction that, when added to the current tile coordinate, will return the next tile coordinate in that direction. The currentMoveDirection variable simply holds which direction the player is moving toward, and you need a scheduleUpdate to continuously check whether the player still wants to move.

The ccTouchesBegan method (Listing 11-8) has changed to simply check which quadrant of the screen received the touch and then sets the currentMoveDirection. The newly added ccTouchesEnded method sets the currentMoveDirection back to MoveDirectionNone.

Listing 11-8. Moving the Player Based on Touch Location

```
-(void) ccTouchesBegan:(NSSet *)touches withEvent:(UIEvent *)event
{
    // get the position in tile coordinates from the touch location
    CGPoint touchLocation=[self locationFromTouches:touches];

    // check where the touch was and set the move direction accordingly
    if (CGRectContainsPoint(upperLeft, touchLocation))
    {
        currentMoveDirection=MoveDirectionUpperLeft;
    }
    else if (CGRectContainsPoint(lowerLeft, touchLocation))
    {
        currentMoveDirection=MoveDirectionLowerLeft;
    }
    else if (CGRectContainsPoint(upperRight, touchLocation))
    {
        currentMoveDirection=MoveDirectionUpperRight;
    }
    else if (CGRectContainsPoint(lowerRight, touchLocation))
    {
        currentMoveDirection=MoveDirectionLowerRight;
    }
}
```

```
-(void) ccTouchesEnded:(NSSet *)touches withEvent:(UIEvent *)event
{
    currentMoveDirection = MoveDirectionNone;
}
```

The gist of the work has now been moved to the update method, which is scheduled to be called every frame:

```
-(void) update:(ccTime)delta
{
    CCNode* node = [self getChildByTag:TileMapNode];
    NSAssert([node isKindOfClass:[CCTMXTiledMap class]], @"not a CCTMXTiledMap");
    CCTMXTiledMap* tileMap = (CCTMXTiledMap*)node;

    // if the tilemap is currently being moved, wait until it's done moving
    if (tileMap.numberOfRunningActions == 0)
    {
        if (currentMoveDirection != MoveDirectionNone)
        {
            CGPoint tilePos = [self tilePosFromLocation:screenCenter tileMap:tileMap];

            CGPoint offset = moveOffsets[currentMoveDirection];
            tilePos = CGPointMake(tilePos.x+offset.x, tilePos.y+offset.y);
            tilePos = [self ensureTilePosIsWithinBounds:tilePos];

            [self centerTileMapOnTileCoord:tilePos tileMap:tileMap];
        }
    }

    // continuously fix the player's Z position
    CGPoint tilePos = [self floatTilePosFromLocation:screenCenter tileMap:tileMap];
    [player updateVertexZ:tilePos tileMap:tileMap];
}
```

The tilemap has a running action only when it is moving, so I give it a new move action only if it has no move action currently running and the currentMoveDirection isn't MoveDirectionNone. The tilePosFromLocation is no longer retrieved from the screen touch location, but instead the screenCenter position is used. Since the player is always centered on the screen, this is a convenient shortcut to the tile coordinate at the center of the screen.

The moveOffsets array returns a CGPoint that is added to tilePos to get the new tile coordinate we intend to move to. Because this can be outside the playable area, the new tile coordinate is run through the ensureTilePosIsWithinBounds method. It's the same code we used before to keep the tile coordinate within the playable area but refactored into a separate method to avoid duplicating this code. Lastly, the centerTileMapOnTileCoord method is called to move and center the screen on the desired tile coordinate, which also adds the move action.

The methods ensureTilePosIsWithinBounds and floatTilePosFromLocation have been refactored to be reusable. Previously they were merged into the tilePosFromLocation method. The refactored methods still perform the same functions but individual aspects such as adjusting the tile position to be in the playable area can now be used by other code too. Following are the refactored methods:

```
-(CGPoint) ensureTilePosIsWithinBounds:(CGPoint)tilePos
{
    tilePos.x=MAX(playableAreaMin.x, tilePos.x);
    tilePos.x=MIN(playableAreaMax.x, tilePos.x);
    tilePos.y=MAX(playableAreaMin.y, tilePos.y);
    tilePos.y=MIN(playableAreaMax.y, tilePos.y);
    return tilePos;
}

-(CGPoint) floatTilePosFromLocation:(CGPoint)location tileMap:(CCTMXTiledMap*)tileMap
{
    CGPoint pos=ccpSub(location, tileMap.position);
    float halfMapWidth=tileMap.mapSize.width * 0.5f;
    float mapHeight=tileMap.mapSize.height;
    float tileWidth=tileMap.tileSize.width / CC_CONTENT_SCALE_FACTOR();
    float tileHeight=tileMap.tileSize.height / CC_CONTENT_SCALE_FACTOR();

    CGPoint tilePosDiv=CGPointMake(pos.x / tileWidth, pos.y / tileHeight);
    float mapHeightDiff=mapHeight - tilePosDiv.y;

    // Cast to int makes sure that result is in whole numbers
    float posX=(mapHeightDiff+tilePosDiv.x - halfMapWidth);
    float posY=(mapHeightDiff - tilePosDiv.x+halfMapWidth);
    return CGPointMake(posX, posY);
}

-(CGPoint) tilePosFromLocation:(CGPoint)location tileMap:(CCTMXTiledMap*)tileMap
{
    CGPoint pos=[self floatTilePosFromLocation:location tileMap:tileMap];
    pos=[self ensureTilePosIsWithinBounds:CGPointMake((int)pos.x, (int)pos.y)];
    return pos;
}
```

With the player now moving across the tilemap tile by tile, we can keep updating the player's vertexZ value. Previously, the vertexZ value was set to the target tile coordinate immediately, which caused the player to be drawn below all object tiles he was moving over. By continuously updating the vertexZ value as the player moves across the tilemap, his z position is now more accurate and removes any overlap glitches from the previous IsoTilemap02 project.

Note   When you're moving the player through an arc, you'll notice that as he moves through the arc he'll suddenly appear in front of the arc or disappear behind it, depending on the direction he's moving. This is an unavoidable side effect of 2D isometric tilemaps. You can reduce this effect only by drawing your archways higher than any character in your game. You could also split the arc into three tiles so that only the middle section is passable, whereas the two sides of the archway are regarded as blocking tiles.

Stop Player on Collisions

Lastly, you don't want the player to walk over walls and mountains. He may be a ninja, but he's not *that* good. To solve that problem, add a new layer in Tiled via Layer ➤ Add Tile Layer … and name it Collisions; then move the Opacity slider just above the Layers list to about the middle. Now pick a tile from the tileset whose color is a strong contrast to the tilemap, because you'll use it to draw collision areas over the tilemap, and they should be easily recognizable despite having a low opacity.

I chose one of the purple tiles. Right-click the tile of your choice and select Tile Properties … from the context menu. Note that this command has no equivalent in the Tiled menu; tile properties can be accessed only by right-clicking a tile. In the Tile Properties dialog shown in Figure 11-19, add a property named `blocks_movement` and set the value to 1. Actually, I'm going to ignore the value in code; it's only important that the `blocks_movement` value exists.

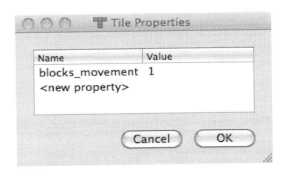

Figure 11-19. Add a blocks_movement tile property

With the Collisions layer selected, draw on the tilemap with the tile that has the `blocks_movement` property set. Place a tile everywhere you don't want the player to move onto—for example, walls, mountains, houses, and so on.

The tilemap `isometric-with-border.tmx` in the IsoTilemap03 project is already prepared with a Collisions layer. The Collisions layer is only for checking whether a tile can be moved on and should not be displayed in the game, so the first thing you do in the `init` method of the `TileMapLayer` class is to set this layer invisible (see Listing 11-9).

Listing 11-9. Hiding the Collisions Layer

```
CCTMXTiledMap* tileMap=[CCTMXTiledMap tiledMapWithTMXFile:↵
    @"isometric-with-border.tmx"];
[self addChild:tileMap z:-1 tag:TileMapNode];

CCTMXLayer* collisionsLayer=[tileMap layerNamed:@"Collisions"];
collisionsLayer.visible=NO;
```

To check whether a certain tile coordinate is blocked, I've added the `isTilePosBlocked` method to the IsoTilemap03 project, as shown in Listing 11-10.

Listing 11-10. Determine Whether a Tile Is Blocked

```
-(BOOL) isTilePosBlocked:(CGPoint)tilePos tileMap:(CCTMXTiledMap*)tileMap
{
    CCTMXLayer* layer=[tileMap layerNamed:@"Collisions"];
    NSAssert(layer !=nil, @"Collisions layer not found!");

    BOOL isBlocked=NO;
    unsigned int tileGID=[layer tileGIDAt:tilePos];
    if (tileGID>0)
    {
        NSDictionary* tileProperties=[tileMap propertiesForGID:tileGID];
        id blocks_movement=[tileProperties objectForKey:@"blocks_movement"];
        isBlocked=(blocks_movement !=nil);
    }

    return isBlocked;
}
```

The code first tries to get a tile at the given tile coordinate from the Collisions layer. If there is no tile there, the tileGID will be 0, and you can safely assume that this tile is not blocked. But if there is a valid tileGID at the tilePos coordinate, the tileMap is queried for the properties of the tile, which returns an NSDictionary object. If the dictionary's objectForKey method returns a valid object for the key named blocks_movement, the tile is blocked.

The place to check for collision is in the update method, as shown in Listing 11-11.

Listing 11-11. Checking for Collision in the update Method

```
-(void) update:(ccTime)delta
{
    ...

    // if the tilemap is currently being moved, wait until it's done moving
    if ([tileMap numberOfRunningActions] == 0)
    {
        if (currentMoveDirection !=MoveDirectionNone)
        {
            CGPoint tilePos=[self tilePosFromLocation:screenCenter tileMap:tileMap];

            CGPoint offset=moveOffsets[currentMoveDirection];
            tilePos=CGPointMake(tilePos.x+offset.x, tilePos.y+offset.y);
            tilePos=[self ensureTilePosIsWithinBounds:tilePos];

            if ([self isTilePosBlocked:tilePos tileMap:tileMap] == NO)
            {
                [self centerTileMapOnTileCoord:tilePos tileMap:tileMap];
            }
        }
    }

    ...
}
```

Before moving the tilemap, the `isTilePosBlocked` method is called to see whether the player can actually move there. If the destination tile coordinate is not blocked, he will move; otherwise, he won't.

Adding More Content to the Game

So far, we have a game where you guide a character through an isometric tilemap world. Hiding behind trees and avoiding collisions are just the foundation for a game set in this world. What if you want to add more actors to the world, whether enemies or nonplayer characters (NPCs)?

In principle, you animate them just as you'd move the player, except that the player is centered onscreen whereas NPCs can be anywhere on the tilemap. Still, you only need to determine which direction the NPC should walk toward and then move him like the layer is moved in the `centerTileMapOnTileCoord` method. The only difference is that the actions are run on the NPC, and the directions need to be reversed, because you aren't moving the layer; the NPC is moving on the layer.

As soon as you have NPCs wandering around, the next step is to ask how you can get them to move from A to B while avoiding obstacles and finding the shortest route. The answer to that is the A* pathfinding algorithm, which is an industry standard and has been adapted and tweaked for many situations. Tile-based games are ideal candidates for this particular pathfinding algorithm, because actor positions are usually restricted to the tile coordinates. For an in-depth introduction to the A* pathfinding algorithm and, honestly, to a lot of game programming topics in general, you must visit Amit's A* pages at `http://theory.stanford.edu/~amitp/GameProgramming/`.

And you'll want to visit Amit's Game Programming Information pages in general. He links to articles concerning artificial intelligence and tile-based games, including procedural world generation. A lot of the articles may seem dated, but, in fact, most of them are timeless and are still valuable sources of information. Check them out at `www-cs-students.stanford.edu/~amitp/gameprog.html`.

Summary

In this chapter, you learned what's special about isometric tilemaps, how isometric tiles are designed, and how to create a tilemap with a perceived depth. You learned how to create and improve such an isometric tilemap with Tiled by adding an impassable border and preventing collisions.

You also learned the techniques necessary to set up a tilemap for use with cocos2d and how to set up cocos2d itself with 2D projection and a depth buffer for correct rendering of overlapping tiles and sprites.

Finally, you added a player whose sprite is correctly clipped depending on whether it's in front or behind tiles. You can also move the player around tile by tile by tapping and holding the screen relative to the player sprite to make him go in that direction. That he will do unless the direction is blocked by a mountain, wall, or any other movement-blocking tile that you set in Tiled.

So far, you've worked with games that need to be controlled and animated in discrete steps. You were responsible for implementing all the actor's movement and rotation as well as checking for collisions. In the next two chapters, I introduce you to physics engines, which allow you to lean back as you watch your game's objects bounce around and collide with each other all by themselves. If this is the first time you've worked with a physics engine, it will be a magical experience. Hold on to your hat!

Chapter 12

Physics Engines

Physics engines are what drive popular iOS games like Angry Birds, Stick Golf, Jelly Car, and Stair Dismount. They allow you to create a world that feels dynamic and lifelike.

Cocos2d is distributed with two physics engines: Box2D and Chipmunk. Both are designed to work only in two dimensions, so they're a perfect fit for cocos2d.

In this chapter, you'll learn the basics of both of these physics engines, and along the way you'll probably come to appreciate one more than the other. I'll briefly explain the differences between them, but for the most part it's a choice based on personal preference.

If you've never worked with a physics engine before, don't worry—I'll also give you a quick introduction to their basic concepts and key elements.

Basic Concepts of Physics Engines

You can think of a physics engine as an animation system for game objects. Of course, it's up to the game developer to connect and synchronize game objects like sprites with the physics objects, called *rigid bodies*. They're called that because physics engines animate them as if they were stiff, nondeformable objects. This simplification allows physics engines to calculate a large number of bodies.

There are generally two types of bodies: *dynamic* (moving) and *static* (immovable) objects. The differentiation is important because static bodies never move—and should never be moved—and the physics engine can rely on certain optimizations based on the fact that static bodies never collide with each other.

Dynamic bodies, on the other hand, collide with each other and with static bodies. They also have at least three defining parameters in addition to their position and rotation. One is *density*, or *mass*—in other words, a measure of how heavy an object is. Then there is *friction*—how resistant or slippery the dynamic body is with respect to moving over surfaces. Finally, there is *restitution*, which determines the bounciness of the object. Although impossible in the real world, physics engines can create dynamic bodies that never lose momentum as they bounce, or even gain speed every time they bounce off of some other body.

Both dynamic and static bodies have one or more shapes that determine the area the body encompasses. Most often the shape is a circle or a rectangle, but it can also be a polygon, a number of vertices forming any complex shape, or merely a straight line. The shapes of a body determine where other bodies and their shapes collide. And in turn, each collision generates *contact points*—the points where the two bodies' shapes intersect. You can use these contact points to play particle effects or add scratch marks at exactly the places where the bodies have collided.

Dynamic bodies are animated by the physics engine through applying forces, impulses, and torque instead of setting their position and rotation directly. Modifying position and rotation directly is not advised, because physics engines make certain predictions that no longer hold true if you manually reposition bodies.

Finally, you can connect bodies together using a selection of *joints*, which limit the movement of connected bodies in various ways. Some joints may have motors, which can act as the drive wheel of a car, for example, or as friction for the joint so that the joint tries to snap back to its original position.

Limitations of Physics Engines

Physics engines have their limits. They have to take shortcuts because the real world is prohibitively complex to simulate. The use of rigid bodies is an example. In some extreme cases, physics engines may not be able to catch every collision—for example, when bodies are moving very fast they may tunnel through each other. Although this has been proven to happen in quantum physics, real-world objects that we can actually see with our own eyes have yet to show that effect.

Rigid bodies can sometimes penetrate each other and get stuck, especially if they're constrained by joints that hold two or more bodies together and limit their range of motion. This can lead to undesirable trembling motions of the bodies as they struggle to move apart while keeping their joint constraints satisfied. You may have seen this even in modern games; for example, the ragdolls of dead actors in a first-person shooter game can sometimes be seen in very unnatural body positions, their limbs not coming to rest at all, causing the entire ragdoll to tremble or worse. Such events continue to amaze and amuse players. Do a search for "physics glitch" on your favorite video site and you'll see what I mean.

And of course there can be game-play issues. With rigid bodies, you never know what will happen given enough players interacting with them. Eventually some players may manage to block themselves and trap themselves in a dead-end situation, or they may figure out how to exploit the physics simulation to be able to move to areas they shouldn't be able to reach.

The Showdown: Box2D vs. Chipmunk

As I mentioned, cocos2d is distributed with two physics engines: Box2D and Chipmunk. How should you choose between them?

In a lot of cases, it boils down to a matter of taste. Most developers argue along the lines of the programming language in which the physics engines are implemented: Box2D is written entirely in C++, whereas Chipmunk is written in C.

You may favor Box2D over Chipmunk simply because of its C++ interface. Being written in C++ has the added advantage that it integrates better with the likewise object-oriented Objective-C language. You may also appreciate that Box2D uses a verbose language throughout, as opposed to the many one-letter variable names common in Chipmunk. In addition, Box2D makes use of operator overloading so that you can, for example, add two vectors simply by writing the following:

```
b2Vec2 newVec = vec1+vec2;
```

But if you're not very familiar with C++, you may find its steep learning curve daunting. To that end, the Chipmunk physics engine may be more welcoming to you if you're more familiar with C language syntax or prefer a lightweight implementation of a physics engine that may be easier to pick up and learn. It's been part of the cocos2d distribution for many months longer than Box2D has, which has also spawned more tutorials and forum posts about Chipmunk, although Box2D tutorials are catching on. Chipmunk also offers several commercial versions from Indie to Enterprise Editions; the higher-end editions include additional performance optimizations and an Objective-C API. Learn more about the commercial version features here: http://chipmunk-physics.net/chipmunkPro.php.

One warning ahead of time: Chipmunk uses *C structures*, which expose internal fields. If you're experimenting and don't know what certain fields are used for, and they're not documented, that means you shouldn't change them—because they're used only internally.

There is also the popular Chipmunk SpaceManager, which adds an easy-to-use Objective-C interface to Chipmunk. SpaceManager also makes it easy to attach cocos2d sprites to bodies and adds debug drawing, among other things. You can download Chipmunk SpaceManager here: http://code.google.com/p/chipmunk-spacemanager. Unfortunately, at the time of writing the latest version 0.1.3 of SpaceManager isn't compatible with cocos2d 2.0. I'm sure a compatibility update will be made eventually.

In terms of functionality, you can safely choose either engine. Unless your game relies on one particular feature that one physics engine has and the other doesn't, you can use either to great effect. Especially if you have no familiarity with either one, feel free to choose the one that appeals to you more, based on the language and coding style.

The rest of this chapter introduces you to the basics of both physics engines so you can decide for yourself which one appeals to you more. In Chapter 13, you'll learn how to build a playable pinball game with bumpers, flippers, and lanes built with Box2D and the VertexHelper tool.

Box2D

The Box2D physics engine, written in C++, was developed by Erin Catto, who has given presentations about physics simulations at every Game Developers Conference (GDC) since 2005. It was his GDC 2006 presentation that eventually led to the public release of Box2D in September 2007. It's been in active development ever since.

Because of its popularity, the Box2D physics engine is distributed with cocos2d. You can create a new project using Box2D by choosing the cocos2d Box2D application template from Xcode's File ➤ New Project dialog. This project template adds the necessary Box2D source files to the project and provides a test project in which you can add boxes that bounce off each other, as shown in Figure 12-1. The boxes also fall according to gravity, depending on how you're holding your device.

Figure 12-1. The PhysicsBox2D example project

Caution   Because the Box2D physics engine is written in C++, you have to use the file extension `.mm` instead of `.m` for all your project's implementation files. This tells Xcode to treat the implementation file's source code as either Objective-C++ or C++ code. With the `.m` file extension, Xcode will compile the code as Objective-C and C code and won't understand Box2D's C++ code, which will result in numerous compile errors for every line of code that uses or makes a reference to Box2D. So if you're getting a lot of errors related to Box2D, check that your implementation files all end in `.mm`, and if not, rename them.

Documentation for Box2D is available in several places. First, you can read the Box2D manual online at www.box2d.org/manual.html, which introduces you to common concepts and shows example code. The Box2D API reference is distributed with Box2D itself, which you can download at http://code.google.com/p/box2d. You can also find the Box2D API reference in the Box2D version distributed with the book's source code. The API reference is in the folder `/Physics Engine Libraries/Box2D_v2.1.2/Box2D/Documentation/API`—to view it, locate and open the file `index.html` in that folder. You can also browse the Box2D API reference (and other libraries) for the version included in Kobold2D by visiting this URL: www.learn-cocos2d.com/api-ref.

If you like Box2D, you should also consider donating to the project; you can do so via the Donate button on its home page: www.box2d.org.

The World According to Box2D

Because the Box2D example project provided by cocos2d is quite complex, I decided to break it down into smaller pieces and re-create the example project step by step, but not without adding some extras and variations.

Listing 12-1 shows the HelloWorldLayer header file from the PhysicsBox2D01 project.

Listing 12-1. The Box2D HelloWorldLayer Interface

```
#import "cocos2d.h"
#import "Box2D.h"
#import "GLES-Render.h"

#define PTM_RATIO 32
#define TILESIZE 32
#define TILESET_COLUMNS 9
#define TILESET_ROWS 19

enum
{
    kTagBatchNode,
};
@interface HelloWorldLayer : CCLayer
{
    CCTexture2D* spriteTexture;
    b2World* world;
    GLESDebugDraw* debugDraw;
}
+(CCScene*) scene;
@end
```

It's fairly standard, except that it includes the Box2D.h header file and adds a member variable of type b2World. This is the physics world—think of it as the container class that will store and update all physics bodies.

The init method in Listing 12-2 calls initPhysics to set up the physics world. I'll get to that next. The rest of the init code creates a CCSpriteBatchNode, keeps a reference to the sprite batch texture, and adds a label to the screen. Notice that the dealloc method calls delete on the world and debugDraw instance variables. Because these are C++ class instances, you have to release (delete) them manually. ARC does not manage memory of C or C++ objects.

Listing 12-2. The HelloWorldLayer initialization

```
#import "HelloWorldLayer.h"
#import "PhysicsSprite.h"

@implementation HelloWorldLayer

+(CCScene*) scene
{
    CCScene* scene = [CCScene node];
    HelloWorldLayer* layer = [HelloWorldLayer node];
```

```
        [scene addChild: layer];
        return scene;
    }
-(id) init
{
    self = [super init];
    if (self)
    {
        self.isTouchEnabled = YES;

        CCSpriteBatchNode* batchNode=[CCSpriteBatchNode ↵
                                batchNodeWithFile:@"dg_grounds32.png"];
        spriteTexture=batchNode.texture;
        [self addChild:batchNode z:0 tag:kTagBatchNode];

        [self initPhysics];

        CGSize screenSize=[CCDirector sharedDirector].winSize;
        [self addNewSpriteAtPosition:ccp(screenSize.width / 2, screenSize.height / 2)];

        CCLabelTTF* label=[CCLabelTTF labelWithString:@"Tap screen"
                                    fontName:@"Marker Felt"
                                    fontSize:32];
        [self addChild:label z:0];
        label.color = ccc3(0, 0, 255);
        label.position = ccp(screenSize.width / 2, screenSize.height - 50);

        [self scheduleUpdate];
    }
    return self;
}
-(void) dealloc
{
    delete world;
    world=NULL;
    delete debugDraw;
    debugDraw=NULL;
}
```

The Box2D world is initialized in the initPhysics method by creating a new b2World object with a gravity vector, as shown in Listing 12-3. This also adds collisions at the screen borders and enables debug drawing.

Listing 12-3. Initializing the Box2D World

```
-(void) initPhysics
{
    b2Vec2 gravity;
    gravity.Set(0.0f, -10.0f);
    world = new b2World(gravity);

    world->SetAllowSleeping(true);
    world->SetContinuousPhysics(false);
```

```
debugDraw = new GLESDebugDraw(PTM_RATIO);
world->SetDebugDraw(debugDraw);

uint32 flags = 0;
flags += b2Draw::e_shapeBit;
//          flags += b2Draw::e_jointBit;
//          flags += b2Draw::e_aabbBit;
//          flags += b2Draw::e_pairBit;
//          flags += b2Draw::e_centerOfMassBit;
debugDraw->SetFlags(flags);

// Define the ground body.
b2BodyDef groundBodyDef;
b2Body* groundBody=world->CreateBody(&groundBodyDef);

// Define the ground box shape.
CGSize screenSize=[CCDirector sharedDirector].winSize;
float boxWidth=screenSize.width / PTM_RATIO;
float boxHeight=screenSize.height / PTM_RATIO;
b2EdgeShape groundBox;
int density=0;

// bottom
groundBox.Set(b2Vec2(0, 0), b2Vec2(boxWidth, 0));
groundBody->CreateFixture(&groundBox, density);
// top
groundBox.Set(b2Vec2(0, boxHeight), b2Vec2(boxWidth, boxHeight));
groundBody->CreateFixture(&groundBox, density);
// left
groundBox.Set(b2Vec2(0, boxHeight), b2Vec2(0, 0));
groundBody->CreateFixture(&groundBox, density);
// right
groundBox.Set(b2Vec2(boxWidth, boxHeight), b2Vec2(boxWidth, 0));
groundBody->CreateFixture(&groundBox, density);
}
```

Remember that Box2D is written in C++. To instantiate one of Box2D's classes, you have to add the new keyword in front of the class's name. If Box2D were written in Objective-C, the equivalent line might look like this:

```
world=[[b2World alloc] initWithGravity:gravity allowSleep:allowBodiesToSleep];
```

In other words, the new keyword in C++ is equivalent to sending the alloc message to an Objective-C class followed by an init message. That of course means you also have to deallocate the Box2D world, as seen in Listing 12-2. In C++ you do this using the delete keyword:

```
-(void) dealloc
{
    delete world;
    world=NULL;
    delete debugDraw;
    debugDraw=NULL;
}
```

The Box2D world in Listing 12-3 is initialized with an initial gravity vector and allows bodies to fall asleep.

Sleeping bodies? It's a trick that allows the physics simulation to quickly skip over objects that don't need processing. A dynamic body goes to sleep when the forces applied to it have been below a threshold for a certain amount of time. In other words, if the dynamic body is moving and rotating very slowly or not at all, the physics engine will flag it as sleeping and won't apply forces to it anymore—that is, unless an impulse or force applied to the body is strong enough to make the body move or rotate again. This trick allows the physics engine to save time by not processing the bodies that are at rest. Unless all your game's dynamic bodies are in constant motion, you should enable this feature as in Listing 12-3.

The continuous physics setting causes Box2D to track collisions of fast-moving objects more accurately. It effectively prevents fast-moving objects to penetrate or pass through other objects at the expense of speed. In fact, you should probably leave this setting disabled until you actually experience bugs due to fast-moving objects not colliding with each other.

The gravity passed to Box2D is a b2Vec2 struct type. It's essentially the same as a CGPoint, because it stores x and y float values. In this case, and fortunately for us in the real world too, gravity is a constant force. The 0, −10 vector is constantly applied to all dynamic bodies, making them fall down, which in this case means toward the bottom of the screen.

Debug drawing may be helpful during development but also has a negative impact on performance. Unless you need it, it may be better to leave it disabled. The HelloWorldLayer class performs the debug drawing in the draw method but encloses it in #if DEBUG statement to make sure debug drawing is disabled in release builds:

```
#if DEBUG
-(void) draw
{
    [super draw];

    ccGLEnableVertexAttribs(kCCVertexAttribFlag_Position);
    kmGLPushMatrix();
    world->DrawDebugData();
    kmGLPopMatrix();
}
#endif
```

Restricting Movement to the Screen

World setup, check. What next? Well, you should limit the movement of the Box2D bodies to within the visible screen area. For that, you'll need a static body. The simplest way to create a static body is by using the world's CreateBody method and then adding fixtures (collision information) to it. I'll repeat the relevant code from Listing 12-3 here:

```
// Define the ground body.
b2BodyDef groundBodyDef;
b2Body* groundBody = world->CreateBody(&groundBodyDef);
```

Bodies are always created through the world's CreateBody method. This ensures that the body's memory is correctly allocated and freed. The b2BodyDef is a struct that holds all the data needed to create a body, such as position and the body type. By default, an empty body definition creates a static body at position 0, 0.

Note   The &groundBodyDef variable is passed with a leading & (ampersand) character to the CreateBody method. That's C++ for "Give me the memory address of groundBodyDef." If you look at the definition of the CreateBody method, it requires a pointer passed to it: b2World::CreateBody(const b2BodyDef *def);. Because pointers store a memory address, you can get that address of a nonpointer variable by prefixing it with the ampersand character.

The body itself doesn't do anything. To make it enclose the screen area, you have to create a shape with four sides:

```
// Define the ground box shape.
CGSize screenSize=[CCDirector sharedDirector].winSize;
float boxWidth=screenSize.width / PTM_RATIO;
float boxHeight=screenSize.height / PTM_RATIO;
b2EdgeShape groundBox;
int density=0;

// bottom
groundBox.Set(b2Vec2(0, 0), b2Vec2(boxWidth, 0));
groundBody->CreateFixture(&groundBox, density);
// top
groundBox.Set(b2Vec2(0, boxHeight), b2Vec2(boxWidth, boxHeight));
groundBody->CreateFixture(&groundBox, density);
// left
groundBox.Set(b2Vec2(0, boxHeight), b2Vec2(0, 0));
groundBody->CreateFixture(&groundBox, density);
// right
groundBox.Set(b2Vec2(boxWidth, boxHeight), b2Vec2(boxWidth, 0));
groundBody->CreateFixture(&groundBox, density);
```

Look at how the b2EdgeShape groundBox variable is reused. Each Set method call is followed by a call to groundBody->CreateFixture(), which uses the -> operator to denote that groundBody is a C-style pointer and passes &groundBox. Because Box2D makes a copy of groundBox, you can safely reuse the same shape to create all four sides enclosing the screen area without modifying or overriding the previous lines. Because the body is a static body (the default setting for Box2D bodies), density has no effect and is set to 0.

Notice that the screen width and height is divided by a PTM_RATIO constant to convert them from pixels to meters. Why meters, and what's PTM_RATIO? Box2D is optimized to work best with dimensions in the range of 0.1 to 10 meters (1 meter is approximately 3.28 feet). It's tuned for the metric system, so all distances are considered to be meters, all masses are in kilograms, and time is measured in—quite oddly—seconds. If you're not familiar with the meters, kilograms, and seconds (MKS) system, don't worry—you don't have to meticulously convert feet into meters and pounds into kilograms. The conversion to meters is just a way to keep the distance values for Box2D in the desirable range of 0.1 to 10, and the masses used by bodies don't resemble real-world masses anyway. The masses of bodies often need to be tweaked by feel rather than by using realistic weights.

You should try to keep the dimensions of objects in your world as close to 1 meter as much as possible. That's not to say that you can't have objects that are smaller than 0.1 meters or larger than 10 meters, but you may run into glitches and strange behavior if you create relatively small or large bodies.

The PTM_RATIO is defined like this:

```
#define PTM_RATIO 32
```

It's used to define that 32 pixels on the screen equal 1 meter in Box2D. A box-shaped body that's 32 pixels wide and high will be 1 meter wide and high. A body that's 4×4 pixels in size will be 0.125×0.125 meters in Box2D, whereas a relatively huge object of 256×256 pixels will be 8×8 meters in Box2D and still well within acceptable Box2D dimensions. The PTM_RATIO lets you scale the size of Box2D objects down to the dimensions within which Box2D works best, and a PTM_RATIO of 32 is a good compromise for a screen area that may be as large as 1024×768 points on the iPad.

Converting Points

Note that the b2Vec2 struct is different from CGPoint, which means you can't use a CGPoint where a b2Vec2 is required, and vice versa. In addition, Box2D points need to be converted to meters and back to pixels. To avoid making any mistakes, such as forgetting to convert from or to meters or simply making a typo and using the x coordinate twice, wrapping this repetitive code into convenience methods like these is highly recommended:

```
-(b2Vec2) toMeters:(CGPoint)point
{
    return b2Vec2(point.x / PTM_RATIO, point.y / PTM_RATIO);
}

-(CGPoint) toPixels:(b2Vec2)vec
{
    return ccpMult(CGPointMake(vec.x, vec.y), PTM_RATIO);
}
```

This allows you to write the following code to easily convert between CGPoint and pixels to b2Vec2 and meters:

```
// Box2D coordinates to Cocos2D point coordinates
b2Vec2 vec=b2Vec2(200, 200);
CGPoint pointFromVec=[self toPixels:vec];

// Cocos2D point coordinates to Box2D coordinates
CGPoint point=CGPointMake(100, 100);
b2Vec2 vecFromPoint=[self toMeters:point];
```

Adding Boxes to the Box2D World

With a static body containing the objects within screen boundaries, all that's missing is something to be kept within the screen boundaries. How about little boxes, then?

I've added David Gervais' orthogonal tileset image dg_grounds32.png to the Resources folder of the PhysicsBox2D01 project. The tiles are 32×32 pixels, so they make perfect 1×1-meter boxes.

The addNewSpriteAt method shown in Listing 12-4 is part of the cocos2d Box2D application template project but slightly modified to make use of all the tiles in the tileset.

Listing 12-4. Adding a New Dynamic Body with a Sprite

```
-(void) addNewSpriteAtPosition:(CGPoint)pos
{
    int idx=CCRANDOM_0_1() * TILESET_COLUMNS;
    int idy=CCRANDOM_0_1() * TILESET_ROWS;
    CGRect tileRect=CGRectMake(TILESIZE * idx, TILESIZE * idy, TILESIZE, TILESIZE);

    PhysicsSprite* sprite=[PhysicsSprite spriteWithTexture:spriteTexture
                                                      rect:tileRect];

    CCNode* batchNode=[self getChildByTag:kTagBatchNode];
    [batchNode addChild:sprite];

    sprite.position=pos;

    // Define the dynamic body.
    b2BodyDef bodyDef;
    bodyDef.type=b2_dynamicBody;
    bodyDef.position=[self toMeters:pos];
    b2Body* body=world->CreateBody(&bodyDef);
    body->SetUserData((__bridge void*)sprite);

    // Define a box shape for our dynamic body.
    b2PolygonShape dynamicBox;
    dynamicBox.SetAsBox(0.5f, 0.5f);

    // Define the dynamic body fixture.
    b2FixtureDef fixtureDef;
    fixtureDef.shape=&dynamicBox;
    fixtureDef.density=1.0f;
    fixtureDef.friction=0.3f;
    body->CreateFixture(&fixtureDef);

    [sprite setPhysicsBody:body];
}
```

First, a sprite is created from the CCSpriteBatchNode by using PhysicSprite's spriteWithTexture initializer and supplying a CGRect that's 32×32 pixels in size, to randomly pick one of the tileset's tiles as the sprite's image.

Cocos2d provides the PhysicsSprite class. It's essentially a regular CCSprite that has an additional physics body instance variable. It uses the physics body to set the sprite's position and rotation every time the sprite is rendered. This has the added advantage that you don't need to manually update the sprite's position and rotation properties, and it works well with ARC because you don't need to store the sprite with the body's SetUserData(void* data) function.

But I do store the sprite in the body's userdata anyway, because I need the sprite later on during collision detection in order to tint its color to visualize the collision. Because the userdata is a void* pointer, assigning an Objective-C object to void* with ARC enabled requires a special bridge cast, like this:

```
body->SetUserData((__bridge void*)sprite);
```

You also need a bridge cast to obtain the physics sprite from the body's userdata:

```
PhysicsSprite* sprite=(__bridge PhysicsSprite*)body->GetUserData();
```

After the sprite, a body is created, but this time the b2BodyDef type property is set to b2_dynamicBody, which makes it a dynamic body that can move around and collide with other dynamic bodies. Later, when you're iterating over the bodies in the world, this allows you to quickly access the body's sprite.

The body's shape is a b2PolygonShape set to a box shape that's half a meter in size. The SetAsBox method creates a box shape that's twice the given width and height, so the coordinates need to be divided by 2—or, as in this case, set to 0.5f to create a box shape whose sides are 1 meter wide and high.

The dynamic body also needs a fixture that contains the body's essential parameters—first and foremost, the shape, but also the density, friction, and restitution—which influence how the body moves and bounces around in the world. Consider the fixture to be a set of physics parameters used by bodies.

Updating the Box2D World

The physics bodies won't do anything unless you regularly call the Step method of the Box2D world. You do this in the update method, shown in Listing 12-5.

Listing 12-5. Updating Each Body's Sprite Position and Rotation

```
-(void) update:(ccTime)delta
{
    int32 velocityIterations=8;
    int32 positionIterations=1;
    world->Step(delta, velocityIterations, positionIterations);
}
```

You animate the Box2D world by regularly calling the Step method. It takes three parameters. The first is timeStep, which tells Box2D how much time has passed since the last step. It directly affects the distance that objects will move in this step. Although you're using the time delta here, passing the delta time as timeStep isn't recommended, because the delta time fluctuates, and so the speed of the physics bodies won't be constant. This effect rears its ugly head when the device may be taking a tenth of a second to do background processing, such as sending or receiving an e-mail in the background. This can make all physics objects move large distances in the next frame. In a game, you'd rather have the game slow down or even stop for a tenth of a second and then carry on where you left off. Without a fixed time step, the physics engine would try to cope with a short interruption by moving all objects based on the time difference. If the time difference is large, the objects will move a lot more in a single frame, and that can lead to them suddenly moving a large distance.

The second and third parameters to the Step method are the number of iterations. They determine the accuracy of the physics simulation and also the time it takes to calculate the movement of the bodies. It's a trade-off between speed and accuracy. In the case of position iterations, you can safely err on the side of speed and require only a single iteration—you don't normally need more position accuracy in games unless you experience objects not coming to rest, colliding in unnatural ways, or missing collision entirely. Velocity is more important, however; a good starting point for velocity iterations is eight. More than ten velocity iterations have no discernible effect in games, but just one to four iterations won't be enough to get a stable simulation. The fewer the velocity iterations, the more bumpily and restlessly the objects will behave. I encourage you to experiment with these values.

Collision Detection

Box2D has a b2ContactListener class, which you're supposed to subclass if you want to receive collision callbacks. The following collision detection code is in the PhysicsBox2D01 project but not the regular cocos2d Box2D project template.

Create a new class in Xcode and name it ContactListener. Then rename the implementation file to ContactListener.mm so it has the file extension .mm. Then you can use both C++ and Objective-C code in the same file. Listing 12-6 shows the ContactListener header file.

Listing 12-6. The ContactListener Class's Interface

```
#import "Box2D.h"

class ContactListener : public b2ContactListener
{
private:
    void BeginContact(b2Contact* contact);
    void EndContact(b2Contact* contact);
};
```

It's a C++ class, so the class definition is a little different. Note the trailing semicolon after the last bracket. Forgetting that semicolon is a common error. The BeginContact and EndContact methods are defined by Box2D and get called whenever there's a collision between two bodies.

In the implementation, I merely change the sprite's colors to magenta while the two bodies are in contact and set it back to white when they're no longer in contact, as shown in Listing 12-7.

Listing 12-7. Checking for the Beginning and Ending of Collisions

```
#import "ContactListener.h"
#import "cocos2d.h"
#import "PhysicsSprite.h"

void ContactListener::BeginContact(b2Contact* contact)
{
    b2Body* bodyA=contact->GetFixtureA()->GetBody();
    b2Body* bodyB=contact->GetFixtureB()->GetBody();
    PhysicsSprite* spriteA=(__bridge PhysicsSprite*)bodyA->GetUserData();
    PhysicsSprite* spriteB=(__bridge PhysicsSprite*)bodyB->GetUserData();
```

```
    if (spriteA != NULL && spriteB != NULL)
    {
        spriteA.color=ccMAGENTA;
        spriteB.color=ccMAGENTA;
    }
}

void ContactListener::EndContact(b2Contact* contact)
{
    b2Body* bodyA=contact->GetFixtureA()->GetBody();
    b2Body* bodyB=contact->GetFixtureB()->GetBody();
    PhysicsSprite* spriteA=(__bridge PhysicsSprite*)bodyA->GetUserData();
    PhysicsSprite* spriteB=(__bridge PhysicsSprite*)bodyB->GetUserData();

    if (spriteA != NULL && spriteB != NULL)
    {
        spriteA.color=ccWHITE;
        spriteB.color=ccWHITE;
    }
}
```

b2Contact contains all the contact information, including two sets of everything suffixed with A and B. These are the two contacting bodies; no differentiation is made as to which is colliding with the other—they're both simply colliding with each other. If, for example, you have an enemy colliding with a player's bullet, you'd want to damage the enemy, not the bullet. It's up to you to determine which is which. Also keep in mind that the contact methods may be called multiple times per frame, once for each contact pair.

It's a bit convoluted to get to the sprite from the contact through the fixture to the body and then get the user data from that. The Box2D API reference certainly helps you find your way through the hierarchy, and with a little experience it'll become second nature.

To actually get the ContactListener connected with Box2D, you have to add it to the world. In HelloWorldLayer, import the ContactListener.h header file and add a ContactListener* contactListener to the class as a member variable:

```
#import "cocos2d.h"
#import "Box2D.h"
#import "GLES-Render.h"
#import "ContactListener.h"

...

@interface HelloWorldLayer : CCLayer
{
    CCTexture2D* spriteTexture;
    b2World* world;
    ContactListener* contactListener;
    GLESDebugDraw* debugDraw;
}

...

@end
```

In the initPhysics method of HelloWorldLayer, you can then create a new ContactListener instance and set it as the contact listener for the world:

```
-(void) initPhysics
{
    b2Vec2 gravity;
    gravity.Set(0.0f, -10.0f);
    world=new b2World(gravity);
    world->SetAllowSleeping(true);
    world->SetContinuousPhysics(false);

    contactListener=new ContactListener();
    world->SetContactListener(contactListener);

    ...
```

What remains is to delete the contactListener in the dealloc method to free its memory, because it's a C++ class object:

```
-(void) dealloc
{
    delete world;
    world=NULL;
    delete debugDraw;
    debugDraw=NULL;
    delete contactListener;
    contactListener=NULL;
}
```

Now the boxes in the PhysicsBox2D01 project will be tinted purple whenever they touch other boxes. The implementation isn't perfect, as you'll notice. Some boxes clearly collide but may not be colored. The problem is that EndContact may be called for a body which still has other contacts. But for demonstration purposes it suffices.

Joint Venture

With joints, you can connect bodies together. The type of joint determines which way the connected bodies are connected. In this example method, you create four bodies total. Three are dynamic bodies connected to each other using a *revolute joint*, which keeps the bodies at the same distance but allows them to rotate 360 degrees around each other. If you find it hard to imagine how these objects might behave, you should try them in the PhysicsBox2D01 project. In this case, working code can explain it better than words or a static image could. The fourth body is a static body to which one of the dynamic bodies is also attached using a revolute joint.

For clarity and brevity I've extracted the code that creates the PhysicsSprite into the createPhysicsSpriteAt method, and the createBodyFixture method takes care of creating the body's shape and fixture.

```
-(void) addSomeJointedBodies:(CGPoint)pos
{
    // Create a body definition and set it to be a dynamic body
    b2BodyDef bodyDef;
    bodyDef.type=b2_dynamicBody;
```

```
        bodyDef.position=[self toMeters:pos];
        bodyDef.position=bodyDef.position+b2Vec2(-1, -1);
        b2Body* bodyA=world->CreateBody(&bodyDef);
        [self createBodyFixture:bodyA];

        PhysicsSprite* spriteA=[self createPhysicsSpriteAt:pos];
        [spriteA setPhysicsBody:bodyA];
        bodyA->SetUserData((__bridge void*)spriteA);

        bodyDef.position=[self toMeters:pos];
        b2Body* bodyB=world->CreateBody(&bodyDef);
        [self createBodyFixture:bodyB];

        PhysicsSprite* spriteB=[self createPhysicsSpriteAt:pos];
        [spriteB setPhysicsBody:bodyB];
        bodyB->SetUserData((__bridge void*)spriteB);

        bodyDef.position=[self toMeters:pos];
        bodyDef.position=bodyDef.position+b2Vec2(1, 1);
        b2Body* bodyC=world->CreateBody(&bodyDef);
        [self createBodyFixture:bodyC];

        PhysicsSprite* spriteC=[self createPhysicsSpriteAt:pos];
        [spriteC setPhysicsBody:bodyC];
        bodyC->SetUserData((__bridge void*)spriteC);

        b2RevoluteJointDef jointDef;
        jointDef.Initialize(bodyA, bodyB, bodyB->GetWorldCenter());
        bodyA->GetWorld()->CreateJoint(&jointDef);

        jointDef.Initialize(bodyB, bodyC, bodyC->GetWorldCenter());
        bodyA->GetWorld()->CreateJoint(&jointDef);

        // create an invisible static body to attach to
        bodyDef.type=b2_staticBody;
        bodyDef.position=[self toMeters:pos];
        b2Body* staticBody=world->CreateBody(&bodyDef);
        jointDef.Initialize(staticBody, bodyA, bodyA->GetWorldCenter());
        bodyA->GetWorld()->CreateJoint(&jointDef);
}
```

b2BodyDef is reused for all bodies; only the position is modified for each body, and a PhysicsSprite is created and assigned as user data to the body.

b2RevoluteJointDef is filled with data by using the Initialize method, providing two bodies to connect to each other and a coordinate where the joint is located. By using one body's GetWorldCenter coordinate, that body will be centered on the joint and allowed only to rotate around itself.

The joint is created by the CreateJoint method of the b2World class. Even though the HelloWorldLayer class in the PhysicsBox2D01 project has a b2World member variable, I wanted to illustrate that you can also get the world through any body—it doesn't matter which one—with the body's GetWorld method. This is good to know, because in the ContactListener discussed earlier, you don't have a b2World member variable, so you'll have to get the b2World pointer through one of the contact bodies.

Chipmunk

The Chipmunk physics engine was developed by Scott Lembcke of Howling Moon Software. Chipmunk was actually inspired by an early version of Box2D, before it became a full-fledged physics engine. More information about Chipmunk and its documentation are found on Scott's home page at `http://chipmunk-physics.net`. And if you need help, you can find that in the Chipmunk forums: `http://chipmunk-physics.net/forum`.

Chipmunks in Space

For the Chipmunk tutorial, you'll build the same project as before. You can find the resulting code in the PhysicsChipmunk01 project. Listing 12-8 shows the Chipmunk version of the `HelloWorldLayer` header file.

Listing 12-8. The Chipmunk HelloWorld Interface

```
#import "cocos2d.h"
#import "chipmunk.h"

#define TILESIZE 32
#define TILESET_COLUMNS 9
#define TILESET_ROWS 19

enum
{
    kTagBatchNode,
};

@interface HelloWorldLayer : CCLayer
{
    CCTexture2D* spriteTexture;
    cpSpace* space;
    cpShape* walls[4];
}

+(CCScene*) scene;
@end
```

There's nothing unusual here, except for the `cpSpace` and `cpShape` instance variables. Instead of *world*, Chipmunk calls its world a *space*. It's just a different term for the same thing. The Chipmunk space contains all the rigid bodies. And the wall shapes define the screen boundary collisions. The `walls` array is only needed so the walls can be removed from the Chipmunk space when the scene is deallocated. Chipmunk doesn't automatically manage the memory of its physics objects the way Box2D does. Because Chipmunk is a C library, ARC can't manage Chipmunk's memory either.

The initialization and dealloc part of `HelloWorldLayer` isn't much different from the Box2D version, as you can see here:

```
#import "HelloWorldLayer.h"
#import "PhysicsSprite.h"

@implementation HelloWorldLayer
```

```
+(CCScene*) scene
{
    CCScene* scene=[CCScene node];
    HelloWorldLayer* layer=[HelloWorldLayer node];
    [scene addChild:layer];
    return scene;
}
-(id) init
{
    self=[super init];
    if (self)
    {
        self.isTouchEnabled=YES;

        CGSize screenSize=[CCDirector sharedDirector].winSize;

        CCLabelTTF* label=[CCLabelTTF labelWithString:@"Tap screen"
                                             fontName:@"Marker Felt"
                                             fontSize:36];
        label.position=ccp(screenSize.width / 2, screenSize.height - 30);
        [self addChild:label z:-1];

        CCSpriteBatchNode* batchNode=[CCSpriteBatchNode ↵
            batchNodeWithFile:@"dg_grounds32.png"];
        spriteTexture=batchNode.texture;
        [self addChild:batchNode z:0 tag:kTagBatchNode];

        [self initPhysics];
        [self addNewSpriteAtPosition:ccp(200,200)];

        [self scheduleUpdate];
    }
    return self;
}

-(void) dealloc
{
    for (int i=0; i<4; i++)
    {
        cpShapeFree(walls[i]);
    }
    cpSpaceFree(space);
}
...
```

You can see in the dealloc method how the four wall segments are freed using cpShapeFree, and
following that the space is freed with cpSpaceFree. So let's see how things are created in the first
place. Same as before, you do the Chipmunk initialization in the initPhysics method:

```
-(void) initPhysics
{
    cpInitChipmunk();
    space=cpSpaceNew();
    space->gravity=CGPointMake(0, -100);
    ...
}
```

The very first thing you must do before using any Chipmunk methods is call `cpInitChipmunk`. After that, you can create the space with `cpSpaceNew`.

Notice how Chipmunk can use the same `CGPoint` structure used in the iPhone SDK. Chipmunk internally uses a structure called `cpVect`, but in cocos2d you can use both interchangeably. I use a `CGPoint` to set the gravity to –100, which means downward acceleration that's roughly the same as that used in the Box2D project. You'll also commonly see the method `ccp`, which is identical to `CGPointMake`.

Boxing-In the Boxes

To keep all the boxes within the boundaries of the screen, you need to create a static body whose shape defines the screen area. You do this in the second part of the `initPhysics` method, shown in Listing 12-9.

Listing 12-9. Creating the Screen Border Collisions

```
-(void) initPhysics
{
    ...
    CGSize screenSize=[CCDirector sharedDirector].winSize;
    float boxWidth=screenSize.width;
    float boxHeight=screenSize.height;
    // bottom
    walls[0]=cpSegmentShapeNew(space->staticBody, ccp(0, 0), ↵
                            ccp(boxWidth, 0), 0.0f);

    // top
    walls[1]=cpSegmentShapeNew(space->staticBody, ccp(0, boxHeight), ↵
                            ccp(boxWidth, boxHeight), 0.0f);

    // left
    walls[2]=cpSegmentShapeNew(space->staticBody, ccp(0, 0), ↵
                            ccp(0, boxHeight), 0.0f);

    // right
    walls[3]=cpSegmentShapeNew(space->staticBody, ccp(boxWidth, 0), ↵
                            ccp(boxWidth, boxHeight), 0.0f);

    for (int i=0; i<4; i++)
    {
        walls[i]->e=1.0f;
        walls[i]->u=1.0f;
        cpSpaceAddStaticShape(space, walls[i]);
    }
}
```

Unlike Box2D, with Chipmunk you don't have to take any pixel-to-meter ratio into account. You can use the screen size in pixels as it is to define the corner points and to work with Chipmunk bodies in general.

Four wall segments are added to the `walls` array. Each is a segment shape, which in essence is just a line from A to B that blocks physics objects. You create the walls as static shapes with the cpSpaceAddStaticShape method, but not before setting some parameters on the wall. This is where Chipmunk gets a little too lazy for my taste. It takes some getting used to to remember that e stands for elasticity (bounciness) and u of all things means friction. Both values are coefficients, meaning if you set them to 1 they will not be elastic and will cause no friction.

Adding Ticky-Tacky Little Boxes

To add boxes to the world, you use the same code in the init method of HelloWorldLayer as in the Box2D example. Refer to Listing 12-4 to refresh your memory.

I'll go straight to creating the dynamic body for new boxes, which is what the addNewSpriteAtPosition method does (Listing 12-10).

Listing 12-10. Adding a Body with a Sprite, Chipmunk Style

```
-(void) addNewSpriteAtPosition:(CGPoint)pos
{
    int idx=CCRANDOM_0_1() * TILESET_COLUMNS;
    int idy=CCRANDOM_0_1() * TILESET_ROWS;
    CGRect tileRect=CGRectMake(TILESIZE * idx, TILESIZE * idy, TILESIZE, TILESIZE);
    PhysicsSprite* sprite=[PhysicsSprite spriteWithTexture:spriteTexture
                                                      rect:tileRect];
    sprite.position=pos;

    CCNode* batchNode=[self getChildByTag:kTagBatchNode];
    [batchNode addChild:sprite];

    const int numVertices=4;
    float halfTileSize=TILESIZE * 0.5f;
    CGPoint verts[] =
    {
        ccp(-halfTileSize, -halfTileSize),
        ccp(-halfTileSize, halfTileSize),
        ccp(halfTileSize, halfTileSize),
        ccp(halfTileSize, -halfTileSize),
    };
    float mass=1.0f;
    cpBody* body=cpBodyNew(mass, ↵
        cpMomentForPoly(mass, numVertices, verts, CGPointZero));

    body->p=pos;
    cpSpaceAddBody(space, body);

    cpShape* shape=cpPolyShapeNew(body, numVertices, verts, CGPointZero);
    shape->e=0.4f;
    shape->u=0.4f;
    cpSpaceAddShape(space, shape);

    [sprite setPhysicsBody:body];
    body->data=(__bridge void*)sprite;
}
```

You create the dynamic body for the box with the cpBodyNew method with the given mass and a *moment of inertia*. The moment of inertia determines the resistance of a body to move, and it's calculated by the helper method cpMomentForPoly, which takes the body's mass and the vertices of its 32×32-pixel box shape.

The body's position, p, is then updated, and the body is added to the space via the cpSpaceAddBody method. Note that contrary to Box2D, you don't have to convert pixels to meters; you can work with pixel coordinates directly.

The array of vertices are the corners of the box shape. Because the corner positions are positioned relative to the center of the box you're creating, they're all half a tile's size away from the center. Otherwise, the box shape would be twice as big as the tile.

The cpPolyShapeNew method then takes the body as input, the verts array, and the number of vertices in the array, as well as an optional offset, which is set to CGPointZero in this case. Out comes a new cpShape pointer for the box shape. The shape's elasticity and friction are set to values that give a similar behavior to the Box2D boxes, and after the sprite is set as user data to the data field, the shape is added to the space via cpSpaceAddShape. And finally, there's also a Chipmunk version of the PhysicsSprite class which gets the body assigned so it can update its position and rotation based on the Chipmunk body.

The Chipmunk body also gets the sprite assigned to its data field. Again this requires a bridge cast so ARC won't complain.

Updating the Chipmunk Space

You have to update the Chipmunk space every frame to advance the physics simulation. You do this in the update method in Listing 12-11.

Listing 12-11. Updating the Chipmunk Space

```
-(void) update:(ccTime)delta
{
    const int iterations=10;
    for (int i=0; i<iterations; i++)
    {
        cpSpaceStep(space, 0.005f);
    }
}
```

Just as with Box2D, you have to advance the physics simulation using a step method. In this case, it's cpSpaceStep, which takes the space and a time step as input. A fixed time step works best, and just like in Box2D, using a fixed time step as opposed to passing the delta time is highly recommended. This is probably even truer for Chipmunk, as I noticed very odd effects when using the delta time. As long as the framerate doesn't fluctuate heavily (it really shouldn't anyway), using a fixed-time-step approach works very well.

The PhysicsSprite class does all the position and rotation updates for you.

A Chipmunk Collision Course

C callback methods handle collisions in Chipmunk. In the PhysicsChipmunk01 project, I've added the contactBegin and contactEnd static methods (in Listing 12-12), which do exactly the same as their Box2D counterparts—change the color of boxes that are in contact to magenta.

Listing 12-12. Collision Callbacks a la Chipmunk

```
static int contactBegin(cpArbiter* arbiter, struct cpSpace* space, void* data)
{
    BOOL processCollision=YES;

    cpBody* bodyA;
    cpBody* bodyB;
    cpArbiterGetBodies(arbiter, &bodyA, &bodyB);

    PhysicsSprite* spriteA=(__bridge PhysicsSprite*)bodyA->data;
    PhysicsSprite* spriteB=(__bridge PhysicsSprite*)bodyB->data;
    if (spriteA !=nil && spriteB !=nil)
    {
        spriteA.color=ccMAGENTA;
        spriteB.color=ccMAGENTA;
    }

    return processCollision;
}
static void contactEnd(cpArbiter* arbiter, cpSpace* space, void* data)
{
    cpBody* bodyA;
    cpBody* bodyB;
    cpArbiterGetBodies(arbiter, &bodyA, &bodyB);

    PhysicsSprite* spriteA=(__bridge PhysicsSprite*)bodyA->data;
    PhysicsSprite* spriteB=(__bridge PhysicsSprite*)bodyB->data;
    if (spriteA !=nil && spriteB !=nil)
    {
        spriteA.color=ccWHITE;
        spriteB.color=ccWHITE;
    }
}
```

The contactBegin method should return YES if the collision should be processed normally. By returning NO or 0 from this method, you can also ignore collisions. To get to the sprites, you first have to get the shapes from the cpArbiter, which just like b2Contact holds the contact information. Via the cpArbiterGetShapes method and passing two shapes as out parameters, you get the colliding shapes from which you can then retrieve the individual PhysicsSprite pointers. If they're both valid, you can change their color.

As with Box2D, these callbacks don't get called by themselves. In the HelloWorldLayer initPhysics method, right after the space is created, you must add the collision handlers using the cpSpaceAddCollisionHandler method:

```
-(void) initPhysics
{
    cpInitChipmunk();
    space=cpSpaceNew();
    space->gravity=CGPointMake(0, -100);

    unsigned int defaultCollisionType=0;
    cpSpaceAddCollisionHandler(space, defaultCollisionType, defaultCollisionType,
                               &contactBegin, NULL, NULL, &contactEnd, NULL);
```

The default collision type for shapes is 0, and because I don't care about filtering collisions, both collision type parameters are set to 0. You can assign each body's shape an integer value to its collision_type property and then add collision handlers that are called only if bodies of matching collision types collide. This is called *filtering collisions* and is described in the Chipmunk manual, at http://files.slembcke.net/chipmunk/release/ ChipmunkLatest-Docs/#cpShape.

The next four parameters are pointers to C callback methods for the four collision stages: *begin*, *pre-solve*, *post-solve*, and *separation* (the same as the EndContact event in Box2D). These serve the same purpose as the corresponding callbacks in Box2D. Most of the time you'll be interested only in the begin and separation events.

I pass NULL for pre-solve and post-solve, because I'm not interested in handling these. You can use these methods to influence the collision or to retrieve the collision force in the post-solve step. The final parameter is an arbitrary data pointer you can pass on to the callback methods if you need it. I don't, so I set it to NULL as well.

With that, you have a working collision callback mechanism.

Joints for Chipmunks

The Chipmunk example project also needs its own implementation of addSomeJointedBodies. The setup is more verbose than for Box2D, as shown in Listing 12-13. You'll recognize most of the code as setting up static and dynamic bodies—if you find that code familiar, feel free to skip to the end where the joints are created.

Listing 12-13. Creating Three Bodies Connected with Joints

```
-(void) addSomeJointedBodies:(CGPoint)pos
{
    float mass=1.0f;
    float moment=cpMomentForBox(mass, TILESIZE, TILESIZE);

    float halfTileSize=TILESIZE * 0.5f;
    int numVertices=4;
    CGPoint vertices[] =
    {
        ccp(-halfTileSize, -halfTileSize),
        ccp(-halfTileSize, halfTileSize),
```

```
        ccp(halfTileSize, halfTileSize),
        ccp(halfTileSize, -halfTileSize),
    };

    // Create a static body
    cpBody* staticBody=cpBodyNew(INFINITY, INFINITY);
    staticBody->p=pos;

    CGPoint offset=CGPointZero;
    cpShape* shape=cpPolyShapeNew(staticBody, numVertices, vertices, offset);
    cpSpaceAddStaticShape(space, shape);

    // Create three new dynamic bodies
    float posOffset=1.4f;
    pos.x+= TILESIZE * posOffset;
    cpBody* bodyA=cpBodyNew(mass, moment);
    bodyA->p=pos;
    cpSpaceAddBody(space, bodyA);

    shape=cpPolyShapeNew(bodyA, numVertices, vertices, offset);
    cpSpaceAddShape(space, shape);

    PhysicsSprite* spriteA=[self createPhysicsSpriteAt:pos];
    [spriteA setPhysicsBody:bodyA];
    bodyA->data=(__bridge void*)spriteA;

    pos.x+= TILESIZE * posOffset;
    cpBody* bodyB=cpBodyNew(mass, moment);
    bodyB->p=pos;
    cpSpaceAddBody(space, bodyB);

    shape=cpPolyShapeNew(bodyB, numVertices, vertices, offset);
    cpSpaceAddShape(space, shape);

    PhysicsSprite* spriteB=[self createPhysicsSpriteAt:pos];
    [spriteB setPhysicsBody:bodyB];
    bodyB->data=(__bridge void*)spriteB;

    pos.x+= TILESIZE * posOffset;
    cpBody* bodyC=cpBodyNew(mass, moment);
    bodyC->p=pos;
    cpSpaceAddBody(space, bodyC);

    shape=cpPolyShapeNew(bodyC, numVertices, vertices, offset);
    cpSpaceAddShape(space, shape);

    PhysicsSprite* spriteC=[self createPhysicsSpriteAt:pos];
    [spriteC setPhysicsBody:bodyC];
    bodyC->data=(__bridge void*)spriteC;

    // Create the joints and add the constraints to the space
    cpConstraint* constraint1=cpPivotJointNew(staticBody, bodyA, staticBody->p);
    cpConstraint* constraint2=cpPivotJointNew(bodyA, bodyB, bodyA->p);
    cpConstraint* constraint3=cpPivotJointNew(bodyB, bodyC, bodyB->p);

    cpSpaceAddConstraint(space, constraint1);
    cpSpaceAddConstraint(space, constraint2);
    cpSpaceAddConstraint(space, constraint3);
}
```

In this example, you're creating a pivot joint with `cpPivotJointNew`, which is the same as the `b2RevoluteJoint` used in the Box2D example. Each joint is created with the two bodies that should be connected to each other and one of the bodies' center position as the anchor point. The `cpPivotJointNew` method returns a `cpConstraint` pointer, which you'll have to add to the space using the `cpSpaceAddConstraint` method.

Summary

In this chapter, you learned the basics of the two physics engines distributed with cocos2d: Box2D and Chipmunk. You now have two working examples of these physics engines at your disposal, which should help you decide which one you'd like to use.

You learned how to set up a screen area that contains all the little boxes created from a tilemap as dynamic bodies. You now also know the basics of detecting collisions and how to create joints to connect bodies together in both physics engines.

In the next chapter, you'll be making a game that uses the Box2D physics engine.

Chapter 13

Pinball Game

I'd like to put the Box2D physics engine to good use, so in this chapter you'll be making an actual pinball game. Pinball tables are all about using our physical world and turning that into a fun experience. With a physics engine, however, you're not just limited to real-world physics.

You can create some elements of the pinball table, such as bumpers and balls, by simply choosing the right balance of friction, restitution, and density. Other elements need joints to work—a revolute joint for the flippers and a prismatic joint for the plunger. And of course, you need lots of static shapes that define the collision polygons of the table.

Because it would be impractical to define collision polygons in source code, at least for the level of detail necessary to build a believable pinball table, I'll introduce another useful tool: PhysicsEditor. With that, you can create collision polygons by simply drawing the vertice—or, even faster, let PhysicsEditor trace the shape's outlines with a single mouse click.

At the end of this chapter, you'll have a fully playable pinball game, as depicted in Figure 13-1.

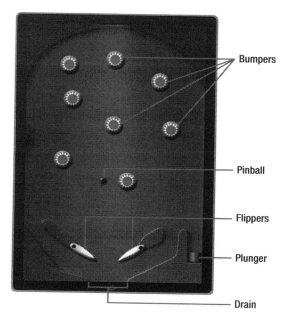

Figure 13-1. The pinball table built in this chapter

Shapes: Convex and Counterclockwise

Let's start with the requirements of collision polygons. The first thing you need to be aware of when defining collision polygons for Box2D and Chipmunk is that these engines expect the collision polygons to have the following properties:

- Vertices defined in a counterclockwise fashion
- Polygons as convex shapes

A *convex* shape is a shape where you can draw a straight line between any two points without the line ever leaving the shape. In *concave* shapes, you can draw a straight line between two points such that the line is not entirely contained within the shape. Figure 13-2 illustrates the difference between convex and concave shapes.

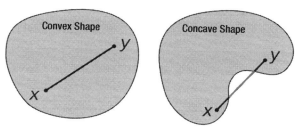

Figure 13-2. Convex and concave shapes

Defining the vertices of a convex shape in a counterclockwise fashion can be illustrated by drawing a convex shape in your mind. You place one vertex anywhere and then go left to place another. Then go down and to the right, and you will have drawn a rectangle in a counterclockwise fashion. Or place another vertex and then go right, up, and then left, and you will have drawn a counterclockwise shape. It doesn't matter where you start with the first vertex, but it's very important to follow the counterclockwise orientation of vertices.

Fortunately, if you're working with PhysicsEditor, you don't have to care about polygon vertex order (orientation) or whether the polygon is convex or concave. PhysicsEditor automatically takes care of that for you transparently. PhysicsEditor splits concave shapes into one or more convex shapes. The physics objects loader shipped with PhysicsEditor then assigns all the shapes to a single Box2D body. It's still good practice to try to avoid shapes being split in order to have as few collision shapes per body as possible to get the best performance.

> **Tip**   How do you know if you made a mistake and accidentally created a clockwise-oriented or concave collision shape? Well, every physics engine reacts differently. Some will tell you up front by throwing an error. But in the case of Box2D, if a moving body hits a collision shape that is not well formed, the moving body will simply stop moving when it gets close to that shape. If you ever see that effect happening in your Box2D game, check the nearby collision polygons.

Working with PhysicsEditor

Armed with the knowledge about properly defining collision polygons, it's time for you to check out the PhysicsEditor tool, which you can download from `www.physicseditor.de`. After opening the downloaded PhysicsEditor disk image and dragging `PhysicsEditor.app` to your application's folder, you're ready to run PhysicsEditor (see Figure 13-3). In the PhysicsEditor disk image, you'll also find a folder named `Loaders` that contains the loader code (shape cache) for Box2D and Chipmunk plist files created by PhysicsEditor. You'll be using the `GB2ShapeCache` class found in the `Loaders/generic-box2d-plist` folder in the example projects of this chapter to load the shapes created by PhysicsEditor.

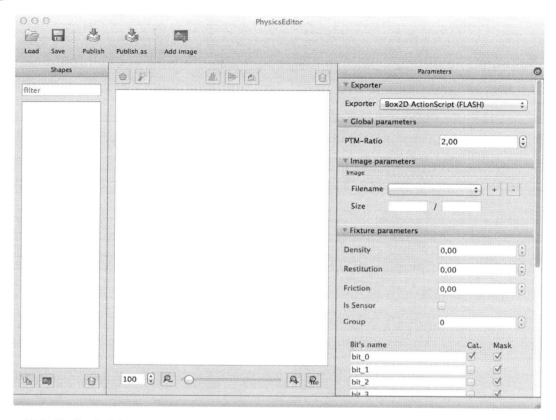

Figure 13-3. The PhysicsEditor application

If you've previously downloaded the PhysicsEditor disk image, you should download the latest version again because the GB2ShapeCache class may have been updated—for example, to be compatible with Box2D v2.2.

After adding the GB2ShapeCache files to your project, you'll notice that the project won't compile without errors anymore. The problem is that GB2ShapeCache wasn't written with ARC in mind. But that's easy to fix: simply go through the Edit ➤ Refactor ➤ Convert to Objective-C ARC ... process again and allow Xcode to make the necessary changes to the GB2ShapeCache files.

You should now drag and drop the PNG files located in the PhysicsBox2DPinball01 project's Assets/pinball folder onto the leftmost pane in PhysicsEditor, labeled Shapes.

Note   You'll be using only the HD resolution images to create physics shapes with PhysicsEditor. You don't have to create separate HD and SD resolution physics shapes. The physics simulation world is independent from the graphical representation of the objects and thus independent of the screen resolution.

The first thing you should modify in PhysicsEditor is the settings for the exporter. PhysicsEditor can export to several game engines, supports both Box2D and Chipmunk physics engines, and even allows you to create your own custom export format. To write files compatible with cocos2d, you must set the Exporter setting on the rightmost pane to Box2D generic (PLIST). Setting the exporter first is important because it enables or disables some features of the PhysicsEditor GUI, depending on the targeted physics engine's capabilities.

Next you should set the PTM-Ratio setting to 240. This value's unit is in pixels per meter, meaning 240 pixels will equal 1 meter in the Box2D physics simulation world. The dimensions of the Box2D physics world matter because Box2D is optimized to work best with objects of 1 to 10 meters in size. You can easily run a simulation with larger or smaller objects, but Box2D loses precision and can show odd behavior when you have very large (tens or even hundreds of meters) or very small objects (small or tiny fractions of a meter).

Because you're using high-resolution images in PhysicsEditor, the PTM-Ratio of 240 will create a pinball table that is 4 meters high (960 Retina-resolution pixels divided by 240) and 2.6 meters wide (640 Retina-resolution pixels divided by 240). The actual pixels to meter ratio in cocos2d will be half the PTM-Ratio setting of PhysicsEditor—in this case, 120 pixels per meter. This is because the cocos2d coordinate system is in points, which means both the standard-resolution display and Retina displays have the same dimension: 320x480 points. A point equals 1 pixel on standard displays and 2 pixels on Retina displays. The size of the table in the Box2D physics world is unaffected by the actual screen resolution. If you work only with standard-resolution images and have Retina support disabled in your app, the PTM-Ratio setting in PhysicsEditor will equal that in Cocos2D.

Defining the Plunger Shape

Let's start with the plunger, the spring that kicks the ball into play. Select the plunger image on the leftmost pane and click the Add polygon button on the center view's toolbar. This creates a new triangle shape on the center working area and highlights it. Because you need a rectangular shape, double-click one of the sides to add a fourth vertex. If you add too many vertices, you can right-click or Option-click a vertex and choose Delete point to remove it.

Move the four vertices to the four corners of the plunger by clicking and dragging them. Create a rectangular shape that encompasses the entire plunger, including the spring. Doing so will avoid problems when the ball by accident falls below the plunger's head.

You may have noticed the little bluish circle with the + inside. This is the anchor point of the shape, which coincides with the anchor point of the shape's sprite. Later, when you position the shape in cocos2d, the shape's anchor point will be centered on the coordinates you provide.

Move the anchor point to the bottom center of the plunger image to make it easier to position the plunger. You can drag the blue circle, but in many cases you'll want to place it very accurately. In those cases, you can modify the anchor point's absolute pixel position or the relative position in the Parameters pane under Image Parameters.

Figure 13-4 shows the plunger shape being edited.

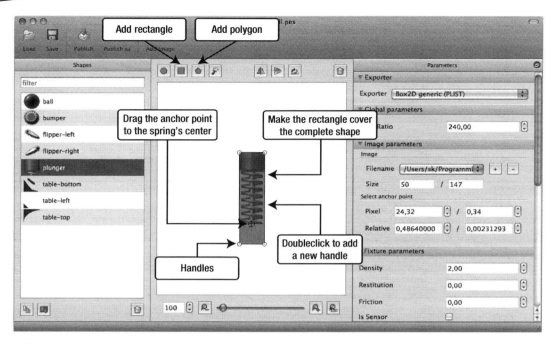

Figure 13-4. Manually defining a shape in PhysicsEditor

Instead of creating the shape from a polygon, you could have also used the Add Rectangle button. (But then I wouldn't have been able to tell you how to add or delete vertices and how to drag them.)

You can and should also set the collision bits for the plunger under the Fixture parameters section in the Parameters pane. The collision bits allow you to define which shapes collide and which don't. You'll use the collision bit settings to prevent the plunger from colliding with any shapes but the ball.

To make working with collision bits easier, you can change the names of collision bits. The collision bit names aren't exported; they serve only to remind you what each bit's used for. By default, the bits are called `bit_0` to `bit_15`. You'll want to change the names of the first five bits to `Ball`, `Bumper`, `Flipper`, `Plunger`, and `Wall`, respectively.

Box2D shapes collide with each other only when the category bit (the check box column labeled Cat.) and the mask bit (the check box column labeled Mask) of both shapes are set. Typically you'll want to assign each shape to just one particular category. In the case of the plunger, make sure that only the category bit for the `Plunger` category is set. In other words, you're assigning the plunger's shape to be in the `Plunger` collision bit category. With the Mask check box, you then set which other categories this shape is allowed to collide with with. In the case of the plunger, you should set only the Mask check box for the `Ball` category, allowing the plunger to collide with the ball. Figure 13-5 shows the correct settings for the Plunger collision category and mask flags.

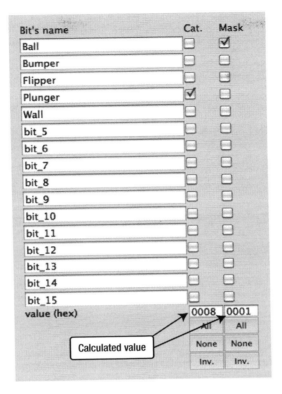

Figure 13-5. *Collision parameters for the plunger*

Note   So far, the plunger would collide with the ball, but the ball wouldn't collide with the plunger. Keep in mind that defining collisions is a two-way process, and in this case you still have to put the ball in the Ball category and check the ball's Mask bit that corresponds with the Plunger category to have both ball and plunger collide with each other.

You can also set the mask bit for the same category, allowing multiple objects of the same category to collide with each other. In the case of the ball shape, it would make sense to set the Mask bit of the Ball category to allow ball-to-ball collisions. This will be useful if you want to extend the pinball game to support a multiple balls on the table at the same time.

Below the Cat. and Mask columns are the buttons All, None, and Inv., which allow you to check all, uncheck all, or invert the check boxes' checked status. They're helpful to avoid clicking possibly dozens of check boxes one after another.

Defining the Table Shapes

The pinball table consists of three separate shapes named table-bottom, table-left, and table-top. The table background image is split up to make it easier to edit its shapes and to make it easier to create different pinball layouts without having to replace the entire image.

Select the `table-top` image in the Shapes pane to start editing the shape for the topmost part of the pinball table. As you can see in Figure 13-6, it's a concave shape. With the manual method used to define the plunger, it would be difficult and error-prone to create all the vertices of this round shape manually, let alone ensure that the resulting shape is convex. PhysicsEditor makes that a lot easier for you: it traces the shape's outline and creates a suitable shape with a single mouse click!

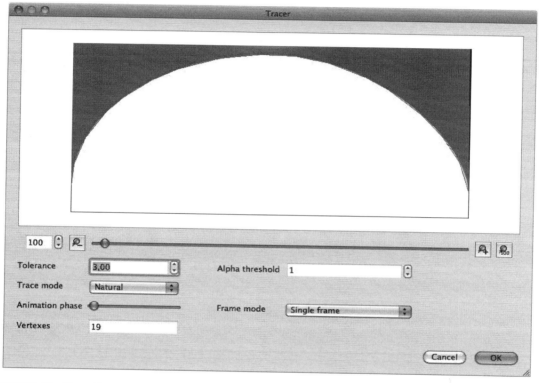

Figure 13-6. *The Shape Tracer creates shapes automatically*

Click the magic wand icon in the toolbar called the Shape Tracer to open the Shape Tracer dialog shown in Figure 13-6.

The Shape Tracer shows the shape's image and an overlay of the shape it's going to create when you click the OK button. Below the image are a slider and buttons to its left and right that control the zoom level of the image. The image zoom settings don't affect how the shape is created.

The most important setting you'll want to adjust in the Shape Tracer is the Tolerance setting. Tolerance changes how accurately the image is traced to create a shape, which directly influences the number of vertices used for the shape, and the number of vertices of a shape in turn influence the performance of the physics simulation. Generally, you should always strive to achieve adequate collision responses with the least amount of vertices. The more important accurate collisions are for your game, the more vertices you should allow for some objects. At the same time, if you add many objects using the same shape, using a shape with fewer vertices will result in better performance.

By experimenting with the Tolerance setting, I found that a good compromise in this case is a Tolerance value of 4,0. This creates a shape with 18 vertices, and it's the highest Tolerance value that still traces the image's shape quite accurately. The default Tolerance setting of 1,0 would have created a shape with 31 vertices, so I was able to save 13 vertices. But you'll notice if you cycle through the Tolerance values that even a Tolerance value of only 1,5 will already cut down the number of vertices to 20.

Tip You can use the Frame Mode setting in the Shape Tracer to create a shape for an animation (sequence of images). To create an animation in PhysicsEditor, you'll have to add more image files to a shape under Image Parameters in the Parameters pane, in the default PhysicsEditor window. By clicking the + button next to the Filename setting, you can add additional images to a single shape; then you can have the shape trace create a shape that's either the intersection or the union of each animation frame's shape.

When you're satisfied with the traced shape, click the OK button to close the Shape Tracer dialog. This creates the new shape. You still have to perform a quick manual tweak for the pinball table's collisions to work smoothly. Because the screen area defines the collision on the sides of the pinball table, you should drag the lower left-hand and lower right-hand corner vertices as well as the upper left-hand and upper right-hand corner vertices slightly outside the screen area and downward and upward, respectively, so that they're clearly outside the black frame border drawn around the table-top image. See Figure 13-7 for a visual hint.

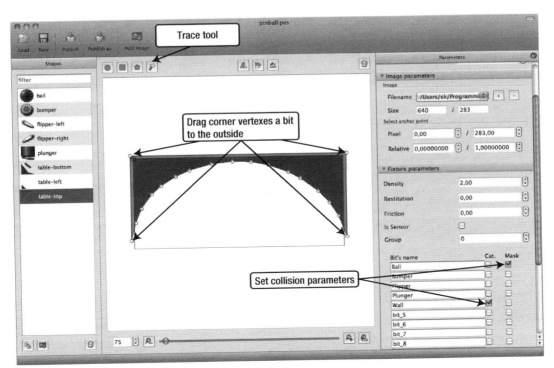

Figure 13-7. Finalizing the table's top shape

By extruding these two vertices, the shape will form a soft transition to the sides of the screen borders. Without extruding them, the ball might get reflected from the tips of these vertices because of the slight inaccuracies always present in physics simulations.

Now move the anchor point (the blue circle with the +) to the top left-hand corner, preferably by using the anchor point settings in the Parameters pane under Image Parameters. Set the Relative values to 0,0 and 1,0, respectively, to move the anchor point to the top left-hand corner. This anchor point position will later let you align the image exactly with the screen border by simply positioning it to 0,480 in point coordinates.

Note   If you don't see the anchor point circle, and there are no anchor point settings under Image Parameters, you don't have the Exporter setting in the Parameters pane set to the Box2D generic (PLIST) format.

The last step is to adjust the collision bits of the table-top shape. Check the category (Cat.) check box of the Wall row and then set the Mask check box in the Ball row. This will enable collisions of the pinball table with the ball. Accordingly, you'll have to set the same collision bits for the table-left and table-bottom shapes because they're all part of the Wall category and should collide with the Ball category.

Use the Shape Tracer to create the shape for the table-left image in the same way. Under Image Parameters, move the anchor point to Pixel coordinates 0,0 and 50,0. Don't forget to set the collision bits just like earlier for table-top.

Now you'll trace the shape for the table-bottom image. This requires a few additional steps because the table-bottom image actually consists of four individual, disjointed elements that need to have individual shapes. Version 1.0.4 of PhysicsEditor traces only contiguous shapes, so you need to open the Shape Tracer a total of four times. Each time you open the Shape Tracer, click the part of the image you want to trace and click OK to create the shape. A Tolerance setting of 4,0 works well for all four shapes. You should end up with four shapes covering all the four elements of the table-bottom image. Don't forget to set the collision bits exactly like you did for table-top, as shown in Figure 13-7.

Defining the Flippers

Select the flipper-left image and open the Shape Tracer. Notice that the resulting shape initially suggested by the Shape Tracer doesn't make much sense—the shape is a lot larger than the image would suggest.

That's because the image has glow and shadow effects that create an aura around the shape itself and that's nearly invisible on a light background. To enable the Shape Tracer to create a better shape, adjust the Alpha threshold setting. The default value is 0, which means that all pixels that are not entirely transparent will be considered when the shape is traced. In this case, you want to consider only the fully opaque pixels for the shape. If you set the Alpha threshold to 254, as in Figure 13-8, you get a much better result.

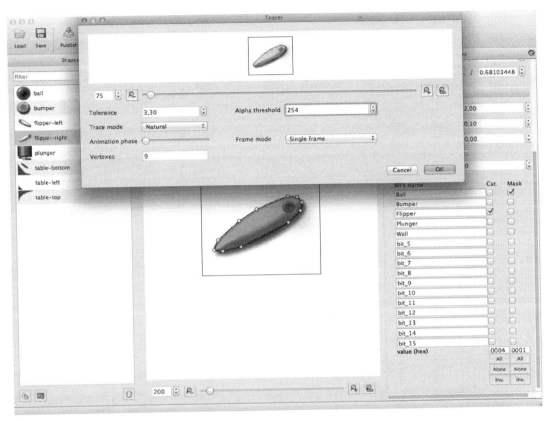

Figure 13-8. *Tracing the shape of a flipper with an alpha threshold to ignore the image shadow*

> **Tip**   If for any reason the Shape Tracer result isn't what you want, and neither the Tolerance nor the Alpha threshold setting lets you fix the shape, you can still manually edit the shape after closing the Shape Tracer. Just click any vertex and drag it. You can also double-click a vertex to remove it or double-click a line segment between two vertices to add a new vertex.

Repeat the same process for the flipper-right image. And don't forget to set the collision bits for both flippers. You'll want to check the Flipper category and the Mask check box in the Ball row. Figure 13-8 shows the correct collision bit settings.

You should set the anchor point of the left flipper to Pixel coordinates 27,78—and 97,79 for the right flipper.

Defining the Bumper and Ball

The ball and bumper images are both circles, so you can use the Add Circle command from the toolbar to create a circle shape. The circle shape has only one "vertex" that acts as a handle to resize the circle shape.

Starting with the bumper, change the circle shape's size and position so that it overlaps the solid part of the bumper while ignoring the bumper's shadow. Set the bumper's anchor point to Pixel coordinates 33, 42 so that the anchor point is centered on the bumper. Set the collision bits category check box next to Bumper, and set the Mask check box of the Ball row.

To simulate the bumper's bounce effect, modify the Fixture parameter in the Parameters pane labeled Restitution. *Restitution* is the amount of elasticity with which an object repels other colliding objects. A restitution of 0 means that the collision is not elastic at all and will stop the incoming object. A restitution of 1 simulates a perfect elastic collision, allowing the colliding object to continue at the same speed after colliding.

Because in this case you want to simulate an additional repelling force coming from the bumper, you can use a value of 1,5 or higher to have the colliding object move away from the collision at a higher speed than it had when it impacted.

Lastly, create the circle shape for the ball image. Size and position the circle shape so that it overlays the entire ball image. Set the anchor point Relative values to 0,5 and 0,5.

As for the ball's collision bits, set the category check box next to Ball and check all the Mask check boxes for the other categories: Ball, Bumper, Flipper, Plunger, and Wall. You can also simply click the All button at the bottom of the Mask column. Because you don't use the other bits, it doesn't matter if they are checked, too.

Some of the ball's Fixture Parameters affect how the ball behaves on the table. I set the Density to 8,0, Restitution to 0,3 and Friction to 0,7. These settings give the ball just a little bit of bounce. Feel free to tweak these settings and observe how the ball's behavior changes.

Save and Publish

Lastly you should save the current PhysicsEditor .pes file. You can later open the .pes file to continue editing shapes. You shouldn't add the .pes file to your Xcode project; it's used only by PhysicsEditor.

To use the shapes in cocos2d, you use the Publish button. This creates a .plist file that the GB2ShapeCache class distributed with PhysicsEditor can read. For the PhysicsBox2DPinball01 project, I published the shapes as pinball-shapes.plist in the Resources folder of the project. Add this file to the Resources group in Xcode.

Programming the Pinball Game

Now you can move on to the implementation phase and actually program the pinball game. You'll learn how to lay out the table before moving on to the interactive elements like the ball, plunger, bumpers, and flippers. But before we get to that, I'd like to introduce you to the essential BodySprite class, which synchronizes a cocos2d sprite with a Box2D body not unlike the `PhysicsSprite` class provided by cocos2d's Box2D project template. The main difference is that `BodySprite` uses the `GB2ShapeCache` class to create its `b2Body` object and will also destroy its body when a `BodySprite` object is released from memory.

Caution   Keep in mind that the pinball project uses Box2D, which is written in C++. This requires you to use the `.mm` file extension instead of `.m` for all class implementation files so that the compiler correctly switches to compiling C++ code instead of C code. Whenever you create a new Objective-C class, you have to rename the implementation file so that it uses the `.mm` file extension. Otherwise, you'll see a lot of compile errors seemingly caused by the Box2D source code.

Forcing Portrait Orientation

The pinball table is designed to be played in portrait orientation, but cocos2d sets up its project templates to use only landscape orientation. You can easily fix that by opening `AppDelegate.m` and locating the method `shouldAutorotateToInterfaceOrientation`. This method should return YES for all supported orientations, otherwise it should return NO. You can use the `UIInterfaceOrientationIsPortrait` macro to test whether a given interface orientation is a portrait mode. If so, it will return YES.

```
-(BOOL) shouldAutorotateToInterfaceOrientation: ↵
    (UIInterfaceOrientation)interfaceOrientation
{
    return UIInterfaceOrientationIsPortrait(interfaceOrientation);
}
```

Kobold2D users can also use the Supported Device Orientation buttons on the Summary tab of the application target's properties to change which orientations are supported and which aren't.

The BodySprite Class

The idea behind the `BodySprite` class is that you want to use a self-contained object for all your dynamic classes. So far, you simply added the body to the `PhysicSprite`'s `physicsBody` property, and it's easy to forget to add the sprite itself as `userdata` to the body. The `BodySprite` class is designed to make the `PhysicsSprite` class more self-contained.

`BodySprite` is derived from `PhysicsSprite` and therefore contains a Box2D `physicsBody` property and instance variable. With all classes for the pinball game elements being derived from the `BodySprite` class, you have a common class to work with, which you can then further probe for its type. For example, you can use the `isKindOfClass` method to determine at runtime from any `BodySprite*` pointer which class you're working with. The `isKindOfClass` method is supported by all classes that derive from `NSObject`.

In addition, the `BodySprite` class header file includes commonly used headers such as `Box2d.h` and `Helper.h` (see Listing 13-1). The Helper class contains helpful functions you've used before, such as `toPixels` and `toMeters`, as well as `locationFromTouch` and `screenCenter`. The `Constants.h` file contains the `PTM_RATIO` because it will be needed by multiple classes.

Listing 13-1. The BodySprite Header File

```objc
#import "cocos2d.h"
#import "Constants.h"
#import "Helper.h"
#import "PhysicsSprite.h"
#import "GB2ShapeCache.h"

@interface BodySprite : CCSprite
{
}
/**
 * Creates a new shape
 * @param shapeName: Name of the shape and sprite
 * @param inWorld: Pointer to the world object to add the sprite to
 * @return BodySprite object
 */
-(id) initWithShape:(NSString*)shapeName inWorld:(b2World*)world;

/**
 * Changes the body's shape
 * Removes the fixtures of the body replacing them
 * with the new ones
 * @param shapeName name of the shape to set
 */
-(void) setBodyShape:(NSString*)shapeName;

@end
```

You use the initializer method `initWithShape` to initialize both the body and the sprite by using the supplied shape name as defined in PhysicsEditor. It assumes that both the name of the image and the name of the shape are identical.

Caution   By default TexturePacker retains the file extension of images so that your shape might be named "plunger," but the sprite frame name might be "plunger.png." To fix that, you have to check the Trim sprite names check box in the TexturePacker Output pane. The `pinball.tps` file used in this chapter has this check box already set; it removes the `.png` extension from the sprite frame names. That way, both the TexturePacker sprite frames and PhysicsEditor shape names will be identical.

For the texture atlas, you use TexturePacker and add the `pinball` folder as a smart folder reference, meaning that TexturePacker will keep the texture atlas contents up to date with all changes to the images in the `pinball` folder. Refer to Chapter 6 for instructions on how to set up a smart folder reference.

You also need to set an additional option you haven't used yet: trim sprite names. This feature removes the `.png` suffix from the sprite names. The advantage is that you can use the same names for the physics shapes and the sprites. The only caveat is that you'll have to refer to sprite frame names without the `.png` extension, which admittedly out of habit is sometimes easy to forget.

Listing 13-2 shows the BodySprite class implementation file.

Listing 13-2. The BodySprite Class Implementation

```
#import "BodySprite.h"

@implementation BodySprite

@synthesize body;

-(id) initWithShape:(NSString*)shapeName inWorld:(b2World*)world
{
    // init the sprite itself with the given shape name
    self=[super initWithSpriteFrameName:shapeName];
    if (self)
    {
        // create the body
        b2BodyDef bodyDef;
        physicsBody=world->CreateBody(&bodyDef);
        physicsBody->SetUserData((__bridge void*)self);

        // set the shape
        [self setBodyShape:shapeName];
    }
    return self;
}

-(void) setBodyShape:(NSString*)shapeName
{
    // remove any existing fixtures from the body
    b2Fixture* fixture;
    while ((fixture=physicsBody->GetFixtureList()))
    {
        physicsBody->DestroyFixture(fixture);
    }

    // attach a new shape from the shape cache
    if (shapeName)
    {
        GB2ShapeCache* shapeCache=[GB2ShapeCache sharedShapeCache];
        [shapeCache addFixturesToBody:physicsBody forShapeName:shapeName];

        // Assign the shape's anchorPoint (the blue+in a circle in PhysicsEditor)
        // as the BodySprite's anchorPoint. Otherwise image and shape would be offset.
        self.anchorPoint=[shapeCache anchorPointForShape:shapeName];
    }
}
```

```
-(void) dealloc
{
    // remove the body from the world
    physicsBody->GetWorld()->DestroyBody(physicsBody);
}
```

@end

The BodySprite implementation initializes the sprite with the initWithSpriteFrameName method. Then it calls the world's CreateBody method and sets self as the user data pointer of the body, allowing you to later access the BodySprite class in the Box2D collision callback methods. Because you're using ARC, you need to __bridge cast self to void* to tell the compiler that self is passed into the C++ method SetUserData as a weak reference. In other words, you're telling ARC that Box2D won't release the memory of the self object, and that you accept that if self is released from memory by ARC, the body's userdata will be an invalid pointer. Because BodySprite releases the Box2D body when it's released, this won't cause any issues because the body is released from memory before the self object.

Tip   The CCNode class also has a userData property, which you can use in the same way as b2Body's userData field, including the requirement to use (__bridge void*) casts. But CCNode also has a userObject property, which is of type id and has the same purpose as userData. If you need to store an arbitrary Objective-C class object in a CCNode object, use the userObject property to avoid having to perform a __bridge cast.

The PhysicsEditor GB2ShapeCache class is used to add the fixtures to the body using the provided shapeName. The PhysicsBox2DPinball01 project already includes the necessary files. To make use of the GB2ShapeCache class in a new projects, just remember to add the GB2ShapeCache.h and GB2ShapeCache.mm files from the PhysicEditor.dmg disk image folder /Loaders/generic-box2d-plist to your Xcode project and then re-run the Convert to Objective-C ARC process described earlier.

The key point to take away here is that the BodySprite is a CCSprite that manages the allocation, deallocation, and configuration of the Box2D body for you. It also ensures that you can access the BodySprite class and thus the cocos2d sprite wherever you normally have access only to the Box2D body object. Thus, the BodySprite class becomes the glue that brings the physics body together with the cocos2d sprite.

If a sprite derived from BodySprite goes out of scope—for example, if you remove it as a child from its cocos2d parent node—then BodySprite will take care of destroying the Box2D body for you. This is the most important distinction from cocos2d's PhysicSprite class, which only gets you halfway there.

In addition, you can change the sprite's body shape by calling setBodyShape. This removes any existing fixtures from the body and then adds the fixtures associated with the given shapeName from the GB2ShapeCache. This will change only the collision shape of the body and preserve the body's current state of motion, like its velocity, position, and rotation. Keep in mind that calling this method is time-consuming and should be done only as needed. It's certainly not a good idea to change a body's shape every frame.

All classes inheriting from BodySprite now have to concern themselves only with setting the correct shape name and any code that's unique to the class.

Creating the Pinball Table

The pinball's table is made up of three individual images and associated shapes, named table-top, table-left, and table-bottom. You'll create the table using the TablePart class, which inherits from BodySprite. The TablePart header only adds the static initializer method tablePartInWorld, as seen in Listing 13-3.

Listing 13-3. TablePart Class Interface

```
#import "BodySprite.h"

@interface TablePart : BodySprite
{
}
+(id) tablePartInWorld:(b2World*)world position:(CGPoint)pos name:(NSString*)name;
@end
```

The TablePart implementation in Listing 13-4 is also rather unimpressive because its only purpose is to initialize the BodySprite and then set body's position to the desired location. This will also update the sprite's position automatically the next time the update method of the PinballTableLayer class is executed (refer to Listing 13-3).

The TablePart class also sets the body type to b2_staticBody, which makes each TablePart a nonmoving object. This has two advantages, one being that Box2D doesn't need to perform certain calculations on static objects, and the other simply that objects colliding with a static body willn't affect a static body's position or rotation at all.

Listing 13-4. TablePart Class Implementation

```
#import "TablePart.h"
#import "Helper.h"

@implementation TablePart
-(id) initWithWorld:(b2World*)world position:(CGPoint)pos name:(NSString*)name
{
    if ((self=[super initWithShape:name inWorld:world]))
    {
        // set the body position
        physicsBody->SetTransform([Helper toMeters:pos], 0.0f);

        // make the body static
        physicsBody->SetType(b2_staticBody);
    }
    return self;
}
```

```
+(id) tablePartInWorld:(b2World*)world position:(CGPoint)pos name:(NSString*)name
{
    return [[self alloc] initWithWorld:world position:pos name:name];
}
@end
```

To create the three required TablePart instances (and later other pinball elements), I've created the TableSetup class, which creates the various BodySprite instances that will make up the bodies of the pinball table. TableSetup inherits from CCSpriteBatchNode to improve the rendering performance of the pinball table's elements.

This is the header file of the TableSetup class:

```
#import "cocos2d.h"
#import "Box2D.h"

@interface TableSetup : CCSpriteBatchNode
{
}

+(id) setupTableWithWorld:(b2World*)world;
@end
```

And because that's so unspectacular, let's turn our attention to the implementation of the TableSetup class of the project, shown in Listing 13-5.

Listing 13-5. TableSetup Class Implementation

```
#import "TableSetup.h"
#import "Constants.h"
#import "TablePart.h"

@implementation TableSetup
-(id) initTableWithWorld:(b2World*)world
{
    if ((self=[super initWithFile:@"pinball.pvr.ccz" capacity:5]))
    {
        // add the table blocks
        [self addChild:[TablePart tablePartInWorld:world
                                        position:ccp(0, 480)
                                            name:@"table-top"]];
        [self addChild:[TablePart tablePartInWorld:world
                                        position:ccp(0, 0)
                                            name:@"table-bottom"]];
        [self addChild:[TablePart tablePartInWorld:world
                                        position:ccp(0, 263)
                                            name:@"table-left"]];
    }

    return self;
}
```

```
+(id) setupTableWithWorld:(b2World*)world
{
    return [[self alloc] initTableWithWorld:world];
}
@end
```

As of now, the job of the `TableSetup` class is to create the three `TablePart` classes that make up the static background elements of the pinball table. It also sets the correct position of each `TablePart` instance, which is influenced by their shape's `anchorPoint`. For example, the table-top image has its shape `anchorPoint` set to the upper left-hand corner of the image so that positioning it at (0, 480) aligns the image and shape correctly at the top border of the screen. Because `TablePart` inherits from `BodySprite`, which inherits from `CCSprite`, it's legal and quite convenient to add these classes directly to the `TableSetup` class, which inherits from `CCSpriteBatchNode`.

You'll later extend the `TableSetup` class to add the other pinball table elements—plunger, ball, bumpers, and flippers.

> **Tip**   Did you notice the use of the `ccp` method? It's exactly the same as the `CGPointMake` method, but some cocos2d developers prefer to use `ccp` over `CGPointMake` simply because it's shorter to type. You'll find the entire `ccp` line of helpful math functions defined in `CGPointExtension.h`. They tend to come in handy particularly when you're developing physics games. Box2D also brings its own math functions that are defined in `b2Math.h`. The reason is that Box2D's vector classes like `b2Vec2` are C++ classes, and not C structs like `CGPoint`, meaning the Box2D data structures generally can't be used with the `ccp` methods.

The `TableSetup` class itself is initialized by the `PinballTableLayer` class, which is based on the `HelloWorldLayer` class of the Box2D project from Chapter 12. Listing 13-6 shows the interface of the `PinballTableLayer` class.

Listing 13-6. PinballTableLayer Class Header File

```
#import "cocos2d.h"
#import "Box2D.h"
#import "GLES-Render.h"
#import "ContactListener.h"

@interface PinballTableLayer : CCLayer
{
    b2World* world;
    ContactListener* contactListener;
    GLESDebugDraw* debugDraw;
}

+(id) scene;
@end
```

It contains references to the `ContactListener` and `GLESDebugDraw` classes. The latter I'll get to shortly; the `ContactListener` class will play a role when you're adding the pinball game's plunger. For now, look at the initialization of the `PinballTableLayer` class in Listing 13-7.

Listing 13-7. Initialization of the PinballTableLayer Class

```
#import "PinballTableLayer.h"
#import "BodySprite.h"
#import "Constants.h"
#import "Helper.h"
#import "GB2ShapeCache.h"
#import "TableSetup.h"

@implementation PinballTableLayer
-(id) init
{
    if ((self=[super init]))
    {
        // pre load the sprite frames from the texture atlas
        [[CCSpriteFrameCache sharedSpriteFrameCache]↵
            addSpriteFramesWithFile:@"pinball.plist"];

        // load physics definitions
        [[GB2ShapeCache sharedShapeCache] addShapesWithFile:@"pinball-shapes.plist"];

        // init the box2d world
        [self initPhysics];

        // load the background from the texture atlas
        CCSprite* background=[CCSprite spriteWithSpriteFrameName:@"background"];
        background.anchorPoint=ccp(0,0);
        background.position=ccp(0,0);
        [self addChild:background z:-3];

        // Set up table elements
        TableSetup* tableSetup=[TableSetup setupTableWithWorld:world];
        [self addChild:tableSetup z:-1];

        [self scheduleUpdate];
    }
    return self;
}

...

@end
```

The `CCSpriteFrameCache` loads the sprite frames from the texture atlas created with TexturePacker by loading the `pinball.plist` file.

More importantly, this is followed by loading the `pinball-shapes.plist` file into the `GB2ShapeCache` class. It is important to do this first before calling any other Box2D method so that the shape cache's `ptmRatio` is correctly set to the value from the PhysicsEditor setting

PTM-Ratio. If you'll recall, PTM-Ratio was one of the first PhysicsEditor settings you modified at the beginning of this chapter.

The pixel-to-meters macro PTM_RATIO used in Chapter 12 has been changed from a simple constant value to the following definition, which you'll find in the Constants.h header file:

```
#import "GB2ShapeCache.h"
#define PTM_RATIO ([GB2ShapeCache sharedShapeCache].ptmRatio * 0.5f)
```

This improved PTM_RATIO macro now retrieves the points-to-meter ratio from the GB2ShapeCache class. And that's why you have to make sure the shape cache is initialized before using the PTM_RATIO macro.

The shape cache's ptmRatio is divided by two (multiplied by 0.5f) because the shapes created in PhysicsEditor were based on the Retina-resolution images, whereas cocos2d's resolution-independent point coordinates used for positioning nodes always assume the iPhone's screen resolution to be 480x320 points.

The initPhysics method still performs the initialization of the Box2D physics engine. The Box2D init code is essentially the same as in the previous chapter, with two exceptions: the static screen boundary shape that keeps dynamic objects inside the screen area defines no top or bottom shapes, allowing dynamic bodies to fall outside the screen through the bottom. We'll need that for the ball to be able to roll into the table's drain. You don't need the top shape because there will be a pinball table shape blocking the entire upper area of the screen.

In addition to that, the collision parameters for the left and right boundary are set in the init code, because these shapes aren't defined with the help of PhysicsEditor. The categoryBits must be set to the Wall bit (collision bit 4 in PhysicsEditor), and the maskBits must be set to the Ball bit (collision bit 0 in PhysicsEditor). The bit values are specified in hexadecimal format, indicated by the leading 0x. You'll find that PhysicsEditor displays those hexadecimal values below the Cat. and Mask columns under Fixture Parameters.

The following is the initBox2dWorld method, with the changes and additions, compared to the Box2D initialization code from Chapter 12 highlighted:

```
-(void) initPhysics
{
    b2Vec2 gravity;
    gravity.Set(0.0f, -10.0f);
    world=new b2World(gravity);
    world->SetAllowSleeping(true);
    world->SetContinuousPhysics(true);

    contactListener=new ContactListener();
    world->SetContactListener(contactListener);

    debugDraw=new GLESDebugDraw(PTM_RATIO);
    world->SetDebugDraw(debugDraw);

    uint32 flags=0;
    flags += b2Draw::e_shapeBit;
    flags += b2Draw::e_jointBit;
    //      flags += b2Draw::e_aabbBit;
    //      flags += b2Draw::e_pairBit;
```

```
//        flags += b2Draw::e_centerOfMassBit;
debugDraw->SetFlags(flags);

// Define the ground body.
b2BodyDef groundBodyDef;

// Call the body factory which allocates memory for the ground body
// from a pool and creates the ground box shape (also from a pool).
// The body is also added to the world.
b2Body* groundBody = world->CreateBody(&groundBodyDef);

// Define the ground box shape.
CGSize screenSize = [CCDirector sharedDirector].winSize;
float boxWidth = screenSize.width / PTM_RATIO;
float boxHeight = screenSize.height / PTM_RATIO;
b2EdgeShape groundBox;
int density = 0;

// left
groundBox.Set(b2Vec2(0, boxHeight), b2Vec2(0, 0));
b2Fixture* left = groundBody->CreateFixture(&groundBox, density);
// right
groundBox.Set(b2Vec2(boxWidth, boxHeight), b2Vec2(boxWidth, 0));
b2Fixture* right = groundBody->CreateFixture(&groundBox, density);

// set the collision flags: category and mask
b2Filter collisonFilter;
collisonFilter.groupIndex = 0;
collisonFilter.categoryBits = 0x0010; // category = Wall
collisonFilter.maskBits = 0x0001;     // mask = Ball

left->SetFilterData(collisonFilter);
right->SetFilterData(collisonFilter);
}
```

You've enabled continuous physics for this project because the ball can move at high speeds. Without continuous physics it's possible that the ball may penetrate or pass through other objects, or leave the table entirely.

If you run the project now, you'll see . . . a pinball table. Great. But how do you know that the collision shapes are properly placed and active?

Box2D Debug Drawing

This is where the GLESDebugDraw class defined in the GLES-Render files comes in handy. It's also the reason why in Listing 13-7 you added all child objects using a negative z-order. Remember that any drawing done by OpenGL ES code in a node's draw method is drawn at a z-order of 0. If you want the OpenGL ES drawings to actually be drawn over other nodes, you need to give those nodes a negative z-order.

Have another look at the part of the initPhysics method of the PinballTableLayer class that initializes the Box2D debug drawing:

```
debugDraw=new GLESDebugDraw(PTM_RATIO);
world->SetDebugDraw(debugDraw);

uint32 flags=0;
flags+= b2Draw::e_shapeBit;
flags+= b2Draw::e_jointBit;
//      flags+= b2Draw::e_aabbBit;
//      flags+= b2Draw::e_pairBit;
//      flags+= b2Draw::e_centerOfMassBit;
debugDraw->SetFlags(flags);
```

An instance of the GLESDebugDraw class is created, using the pixel-to-meter ratio given by the PTM_RATIO macro, and then stored in the PinballTableLayer instance variable debugDraw. The debugDraw instance is then passed to the Box2D world via the SetDebugDraw method. You can define what to draw by setting the bits defined in b2DebugDraw, with the e_shapeBit being the most important because it draws the collision shapes of all bodies. Feel free to try out the other bits too, but too much information is a real concern with debug drawing. It makes it harder to see what you actually want to be seeing, and the more that's drawn, the lower the performance will be.

You also have to override the draw method of the PinballTableLayer class and call the debugDraw->DrawDebugData() method to actually draw the debug info. Because you don't want the end user to see the debug info, the draw method is enclosed in an #ifdef DEBUG ... #endif statement so that it's visible only in debug builds:

```
#if DEBUG
-(void) draw
{
    [super draw];

    ccGLEnableVertexAttribs(kCCVertexAttribFlag_Position);
    kmGLPushMatrix();
    world->DrawDebugData();
    kmGLPopMatrix();
}
#endif
```

Adding the Ball

Can you imagine a pinball game without a pinball? I can't, so let's add one to the PhysicsBox2DPinball01 project and have a look at its implementation. The aptly named Ball class is derived from BodySprite and also implements the CCTargetedTouchDelegate protocol for experimentation purposes (see Listing 13-8).

Listing 13-8. The Ball Class's Interface

```
#import "BodySprite.h"
#import "Box2D.h"

@interface Ball : BodySprite<CCTargetedTouchDelegate>
{
    BOOL moveToFinger;
    CGPoint fingerLocation;
}

+(id) ballWithWorld:(b2World*)world;
@end
```

There's the usual static initializer ballWithWorld, which takes a b2World pointer as input. Then you have the member variable moveToFinger, which determines whether the ball should move toward the touch location, and the fingerLocation CGPoint variable, which specifies the actual location of the finger. We can use those to have a little fun with the ball as long as the pinball game doesn't yet have any other interactive elements to move the ball. Take a look at the Ball initialization and cleanup methods in Listing 13-9.

Listing 13-9. The init and cleanup Methods of the Ball Class

```
#import "Ball.h"

@implementation Ball
-(id) initWithWorld:(b2World*)world
{
    if ((self=[super initWithShape:@"ball" inWorld:world]))
    {
        // set the parameters
        physicsBody->SetType(b2_dynamicBody);
        physicsBody->SetAngularDamping(0.9f);

        // set random starting point
        [self setBallStartPosition];

        // enable handling touches
        [[CCDirector sharedDirector].touchDispatcher addTargetedDelegate:self
                                            priority:0
                                    swallowsTouches:NO];

        // schedule updates
        [self scheduleUpdate];
    }
    return self;
}

+(id) ballWithWorld:(b2World*)world
{
    return [[self alloc] initWithWorld:world];}

-(void) cleanup
```

```
{
    [super cleanup];
    [[CCDirector sharedDirector].touchDispatcher removeDelegate:self];
}
```

Just as with the `TablePart` class, the initialization begins by calling the `BodySprite` init method `initWithShape`, which takes care of setting up the body and sprite. Well, it almost does—because you do have to set the body type to be a `b2_dynamicBody` to let Box2D know that this body should be treated as a movable object.

In addition, the angular damping value of the body is set to `0.9f`, which makes the ball's angular motion more resistant to change. This allows the ball to slide over a surface without rolling too much, which is standard behavior for heavy pinballs made of metal.

Tip   Tweaking physics values is usually very labor-intensive and requires careful consideration of each change. It's also frequently underestimated by both designers and programmers alike. That's because all physics attributes are interrelated or interdependent. For example, if you change the density (mass), friction, or restitution of one object, you'll inevitably alter the behavior of any colliding object. Notice that this example pinball game, although it does a fairly good job of simulating a pinball game, would still require a lot of tweaking and fine-tuning of the ball's behavior and collision responses for everything to feel just right and to be a fair and fun pinball table. PhysicsEditor can help you with the tweaking of values by providing you a single, convenient interface for editing any shape's physics parameters.

The `setBallStartPosition` method repositions the ball somewhere in the area where you'll later add the plunger. By slightly randomizing the ball's position, the plunger will later shoot the ball into play more realistically, meaning unpredictably to some extent. Whenever the ball falls into the drain, the `setBallStartPosition` method is called again to place the ball back to its start position.

```
-(void) setBallStartPosition
{
    // set the ball's position
    float randomOffset = CCRANDOM_0_1() * 10.0f - 5.0f;
    CGPoint startPos = CGPointMake(305 + randomOffset, 80);

    physicsBody->SetTransform([Helper toMeters:startPos], 0.0f);
    physicsBody->SetLinearVelocity(b2Vec2_zero);
    physicsBody->SetAngularVelocity(0.0f);
}
```

The `physicsBody->SetTransform` method positions the ball's body, and as with all bodies in this example game, the `PhysicsSprite` class takes care of synchronizing the body's sprite with the body's position. The position in pixels must of course be converted to Box2D's meter units, which is done by using the `Helper` class's `toMeters` method. The second parameter of the `SetTransform` method is the rotation of the body.

Just changing the body's position isn't enough. The body would still keep its current velocity (angular and linear) and would simply keep on moving. The last two lines of the `setBallStartPosition` method thus reset the linear and angular velocity of the body to 0. Linear velocity determines a body's speed and direction, whereas angular velocity determines how fast and in which direction the body rotates.

To actually make the ball appear on the pinball table, you also have to add it to the scene. Do that in the `init` method of the `TableSetup` class by adding these lines below the initialization of the `TablePart` objects:

```
#import "TableSetup.h"
#import "Constants.h"
#import "TablePart.h"
#import "Ball.h"

@implementation TableSetup
-(id) initTableWithWorld:(b2World*)world
{
    if ((self=[super initWithFile:@"pinball.pvr.ccz" capacity:5]))
    {

        . . .

        Ball* ball=[Ball ballWithWorld:world];
        [self addChild:ball z:-1];
    }
    return self;
}
```

If you ran the game now, you'd see the ball in the lower left-hand corner drop to the ground, and that's it. You don't have any way to move it yet, so you need to add some simple ball movement code for testing the bumpers before you get to add the plunger.

Forcing the Ball to Move

So far, the ball is just dropping down, and that's it. You need a way, at least temporary, to control the ball. The `Ball` class implements the `CCTargetedTouchDelegate` and has registered itself to receive touches. Let's check what the touch delegate methods do:

```
-(BOOL) ccTouchBegan:(UITouch *)touch withEvent:(UIEvent *)event
{
    moveToFinger=YES;
    fingerLocation=[Helper locationFromTouch:touch];
    return YES;
}

-(void) ccTouchMoved:(UITouch *)touch withEvent:(UIEvent *)event
{
    fingerLocation=[Helper locationFromTouch:touch];
}
```

```
-(void) ccTouchEnded:(UITouch *)touch withEvent:(UIEvent *)event
{
    moveToFinger = NO;
}
```

These methods specify that while a finger is touching the screen, the ball moves toward the finger; and while the finger is moving, the fingerLocation is constantly updated.

Next, take a quick look at the update method of the Ball class:

```
-(void) update:(ccTime)delta
{
    if (moveToFinger == YES)
    {
        [self applyForceTowardsFinger];
    }

    if (sprite.position.y < -(sprite.contentSize.height * 10))
    {
        [self setBallStartPosition];
    }

    // limit speed of the ball
    const float32 maxSpeed = 6.0f;
    b2Vec2 velocity = physicsBody->GetLinearVelocity();
    float32 speed = velocity.Length();
    if (speed > maxSpeed)
    {
        velocity.Normalize();
        physicsBody->SetLinearVelocity(maxSpeed * velocity);
    }

    // reset rotation of the ball
    physicsBody->SetTransform(physicsBody->GetWorldCenter(), 0.0f);
}
```

I'll get to the applyForceTowardsFinger method next. But while we're here, notice how you check to see whether the ball has gone down the drain. The sprite's y position is compared with the sprite image's height multiplied by 10. Why the multiplication? That's just to give the impression that it takes a short moment for the ball to roll back before it reappears. If the ball has fallen down far enough outside the screen area, the setBallStartPosition resets the ball's position, and the fun begins anew.

Problem is, that doesn't seem to work initially. Unfortunately, the PhysicsSprite class doesn't update the sprite's position property at all. But that's an easy fix. You only need to add one line near the end of the nodeToParentTransform method in the PhysicsSprite class:

```
-(CGAffineTransform) nodeToParentTransform
{
    b2Vec2 pos = physicsBody->GetPosition();
    float x = pos.x * PTM_RATIO;
    float y = pos.y * PTM_RATIO;

    ...
```

```
    self.position = CGPointMake(x, y);

    // Rot, Translate Matrix
    transform_ = CGAffineTransformMake(c, s, -s, c, x, y);
    return transform_;
}
```

The Ball's update method also ensures that the ball has a maximum speed that it will never exceed. I've chosen the maxSpeed value to be 6.0 merely by trial and error. The length of the linear velocity vector of the ball's body is the ball's current speed. If the body's speed exceeds maxSpeed, the body should be slowed down to maxSpeed without changing its direction. You achieve that by first normalizing the velocity vector, which results in a vector that still points in the same direction but has a length of exactly one unit; this is called a *unit vector*. With a length of one unit, all you need to do is to multiply this unit vector by maxSpeed to cap the body's velocity to maxSpeed.

The last line simply causes the body's rotation to be reset; in other words, the body never rotates. This is to prevent the ball's sprite from rotating. Because the ball's image has a highlight and a shadow, you can only create the illusion of a light source shining on the ball if the highlight and shadow of the ball stay in place.

Because the body's world center is set as the position, the position of the body remains the same, and only its rotation is updated. Doing so doesn't stop the physical effect of a spinning ball colliding with or sliding along hard surfaces because that effect is calculated from the body's angular velocity, which remains unaffected. You can safely reset the ball's rotation, because from the perspective of the physics engine, the ball's shape being a circle means that the ball's surface features are the same from any direction. A circle is completely symmetrical.

Now have a look at the applyForceTowardsFinger method, which makes the ball accelerate toward the finger, as in Listing 13-10.

Listing 13-10. Accelerating the Ball Toward the Touch Location

```
-(void) applyForceTowardsFinger
{
    b2Vec2 bodyPos = physicsBody->GetWorldCenter();
    b2Vec2 fingerPos = [Helper toMeters:fingerLocation];

    b2Vec2 bodyToFingerDirection = fingerPos - bodyPos;
    bodyToFingerDirection.Normalize();

    b2Vec2 force = 2.0f * bodyToFingerDirection;
    physicsBody->ApplyForce(force, physicsBody->GetWorldCenter());
}
```

You have the two positions of the body and the finger, and then you subtract the finger position from the body position. For example, if the body's position were at the screen center (160, 240), and the finger is touching near the upper right-hand corner of the screen at (300, 450), then subtracting the body position from the finger position, being the subtraction of the individual x and y coordinates, results in (300 - 160, 450 - 240) = (140, 210). The vector bodyToFingerDirection is now (140, 210). It's called the direction from bodyPos to fingerPos because if you added bodyToFingerDirection to bodyPos, you'd get to the coordinates of fingerPos.

> **Note** The b2Vec2 struct makes use of a technique called operator overloading, which makes it possible to subtract, add, or multiply two or more b2Vec2 structs with each other. Operator overloading is a feature of the C++ language; it's not available in Objective-C—so you can't subtract, add, or multiply CGPoint variables this way.

So, the bodyToFingerDirection vector is now pointing from the body to the finger. When Normalize is called on the bodyToFingerDirection vector, it's turned into a *unit vector*, as mentioned earlier. A unit vector is a vector of length 1—or one unit. This allows you to multiply it with a fixed factor, in this case doubling its length, to create a constant force vector pointing in the direction of the finger. You can then use the ApplyForce method of the body to apply this as an external force to the body's center. You could also use a position other than the center, but in that case, the body would start spinning.

The end result is that the ball accelerates toward the point on the screen that your finger is touching. The ball will usually overshoot, slow down, and return. A little bit like the gravitational pull the sun exerts on our planet, albeit a lot more dramatically.

However, as someone interested in astronomy, I do have to correct myself. Gravity is a force that falls off by the square of the distance between two objects pulling on each other. If you want a more realistic simulation of gravity in your game, simply replace the applyForceTowardsFinger code with that in Listing 13-11.

Listing 13-11. Simulating Gravitational Pull

```
-(void) applyForceTowardsFinger
{
    b2Vec2 bodyPos = physicsBody->GetWorldCenter();
    b2Vec2 fingerPos = [Helper toMeters:fingerLocation];
    float distance = bodyToFingerDirection.Length();
    bodyToFingerDirection.Normalize();

    // "real" gravity falls off by the square over distance
    float distanceSquared = distance * distance;
    b2Vec2 force = ((1.0f / distanceSquared) * 20.0f) * bodyToFingerDirection;
    physicsBody->ApplyForce(force, physicsBody->GetWorldCenter());
}
```

The multiplication by 20.0f in this case is a magic number. It's just there to make the gravitational pull noticeable enough. Now the ball will speed up more the closer it gets to your finger and will barely move if you touch the screen relatively far away from the ball.

Although the applyForceTowardsFinger code serves only as a temporary control mechanism, you could use the gravity code in Listing 13-11 to create magnetic objects on your pinball table.

Adding the Bumpers

Now that you have a ball you can move with your finger, let's make things a bit more interesting by introducing bumpers to the game. What are bumpers? They're the round, mushroom-shaped objects that force the ball away when it touches them.

> **Note**   Sometimes people confuse bumpers with the flippers that the player controls or the usually triangular slingshots just above the flippers. If you want to refresh your memory about pinball terminology, the Wikipedia article on pinball can help clarify it: en.wikipedia.org/wiki/Pinball.

Listing 13-12 shows the, once again, rather simple header file of the Bumper class.

Listing 13-12. The Bumper Class's Interface

```
#import "BodySprite.h"

@interface Bumper : BodySprite
{
}

+(id) bumperWithWorld:(b2World*)world position:(CGPoint)pos;
@end
```

Once more, the Bumper class is derived from BodySprite. The initialization looks very much like Listing 13-9, in which the ball was initialized, so I'll just focus on the important part in Listing 13-13.

Listing 13-13. Initializing the Bumper

```
#import "Bumper.h"

@implementation Bumper
-(id) initWithWorld:(b2World*)world position:(CGPoint)pos
{
    if ((self=[super initWithShape:@"bumper" inWorld:world]))
    {
        // set the body position
        physicsBody->SetTransform([Helper toMeters:pos], 0.0f);
    }
    return self;
}

+(id) bumperWithWorld:(b2World*)world position:(CGPoint)pos
{
    return [[self alloc] initWithWorld:world position:pos];
}
@end
```

The only key ingredient for the Bumper class is to set its restitution parameter to above 1.0f—in this case you've already set it to 1.5f in PhysicsEditor. This gives any rigid body touching the surface of the bumper an impulse that is 50 percent higher than the force with which the bumper was hit. The result is something that's not possible in the real world (except in real pinball): the impacting object increases its velocity after hitting the bumper's surface. It's physics engine magic, and in this case it's very desirable because you save yourself a lot of headaches in implementing the bumper's logic. Box2D does it for you.

What's left is to add some bumpers by adding the following lines in the `init` method of the `TableSetup` class, and don't forget to import the `Bumper.h` file. Feel free to reposition the bumpers as you desire:

```
// add some bumpers
[self addBumperAt:ccp( 76, 405) inWorld:world];
[self addBumperAt:ccp(158, 415) inWorld:world];
[self addBumperAt:ccp(239, 375) inWorld:world];
[self addBumperAt:ccp( 83, 341) inWorld:world];
[self addBumperAt:ccp(157, 294) inWorld:world];
[self addBumperAt:ccp(260, 286) inWorld:world];
[self addBumperAt:ccp( 67, 228) inWorld:world];
[self addBumperAt:ccp(183, 189) inWorld:world];
```

To make adding bumpers more convenient, I added the method `addBumperAt` to the `TableSetup` class:

```
-(void) addBumperAt:(CGPoint)pos inWorld:(b2World*)world
{
    Bumper* bumper = [Bumper bumperWithWorld:world position:pos];
    [self addChild:bumper];
}
```

Have a look now and try how the bumpers feel in the `PhysicsBox2DPinball01` project—pretty close to actual pinball bumpers, I think.

The Plunger

I hate to take control away from you, but for now I must. You're adding the plunger now, and being able to control the ball with your fingers might get in the way. So, go into the `Ball` class's `update` method and comment out the call to `applyForceTowardsFinger`:

```
if (moveToFinger == YES)
{
    // disabled: no longer needed
    // [self applyForceTowardsFinger];
}
```

Now you can add the `Plunger` class, which I've already done in the `PhysicsBox2DPinball01` project. Listing 13-14 shows the `Plunger` class's interface, which is also derived from `BodySprite`.

Listing 13-14. The Plunger's Header File

```
#import "BodySprite.h"

@interface Plunger : BodySprite
{
    b2PrismaticJoint* joint;
}

+(id) plungerWithWorld:(b2World*)world;
@end
```

The Plunger class has a member variable for b2PrismaticJoint, which it's going to use to propel itself upward. A prismatic joint allows only one axis of movement—a telescope bar would be a good example of a prismatic joint in the real world. You can only move the smaller pipe inside the larger pipe, which allows the telescope bar to be extended and retracted, but only in one direction.

Initializing the plunger is also straightforward, as Listing 13-15 shows. I edited the plunger's physics settings in PhysicsEditor. In particular, I set the friction to a very high value and set restitution to 0. This ensures that the ball is launched smoothly by remaining in close contact with the plunger during the time the plunger is propelled upward.

Listing 13-15. Initializing the Plunger

```
#import "Plunger.h"

@implementation Plunger
-(id) initWithWorld:(b2World*)world
{
    if ((self=[super initWithShape:@"plunger" inWorld:world]))
    {
        CGSize screenSize=[CCDirector sharedDirector].winSize;
        CGPoint plungerPos=CGPointMake(screenSize.width - 13, -32);

        physicsBody->SetTransform([Helper toMeters:plungerPos], 0);
        physicsBody->SetType(b2_dynamicBody);

        [self attachPlunger];
    }
    return self;

}
+(id) plungerWithWorld:(b2World*)world
{
    return [[self alloc] initWithWorld:world];
}
```

Most interesting is the call to attachPlunger and the actual creation of the prismatic joint in this method, shown in Listing 13-16.

Listing 13-16. Creating the Plunger's Prismatic Joint

```
-(void) attachPlunger
{
    // create an invisible static body to attach joint to
    b2BodyDef bodyDef;
    bodyDef.position=physicsBody->GetWorldCenter();
    b2Body* staticBody=physicsBody->GetWorld()->CreateBody(&bodyDef);

    // Create a prismatic joint to make plunger go up/down
    b2PrismaticJointDef jointDef;
    b2Vec2 worldAxis(0.0f, 1.0f);
    jointDef.Initialize(staticBody, physicsBody, physicsBody->GetWorldCenter(),↵
        worldAxis);
    jointDef.lowerTranslation=0.0f;
    jointDef.upperTranslation=0.35f;
    jointDef.enableLimit=true;
    jointDef.maxMotorForce=80.0f;
    jointDef.motorSpeed=40.0f;
    jointDef.enableMotor=false;

    joint=(b2PrismaticJoint*)physicsBody->GetWorld()->CreateJoint(&jointDef);
}
```

First, a static body is created at the same location as the plunger's dynamic body. It acts as the larger pipe of a telescope bar held in place so that only the inner pipe may spring upward when released. Remember physics (or *Mythbusters*, for that matter): every action has an equal and opposite reaction. To avoid the opposite reaction—a downwards-oriented movement of the other body of the prismatic joint—it's turned into a static, unmovable body holding the plunger in place.

The worldAxis restricts the prismatic joint's movement to the y-axis (in other words, up and down). The worldAxis is expressed as a normal vector with values from 0.0f to 1.0f; when the y-axis is set to 1.0f, the worldAxis becomes parallel to the y-axis. If you were to set both x- and y-axes to 0.5f, the worldAxis would be a 45-degree angle. b2PrismaticJointDef is initialized with the staticBody and the world center position of the plunger's dynamic body. As the anchor point for the joint the worldAxis is used, which restricts motion of the prismatic joint along the y-axis.

Now follows a set of parameters. The lower and upper translations define how far along the axis the plunger is allowed to move. In this case, it's allowed to move 0.35f meters upward, which is exactly 42 points or 84 pixels on Retina display devices and 42 pixels on non-Retina devices. The enableLimit field is set to true so that this movement limit is actually adhered to by the connected bodies. Because the static body doesn't move, the plunger moves the full extent. If both were dynamic bodies, both bodies would be able to move, which would be undesirable in this case, as mentioned earlier.

Next, set maxMotorForce to 80.0f (the unit in this case is Newton-meters, which is a unit of torque). In Chipmunk this is called the body's *moment*. The maxMotorForce value limits the torque, or energy, of the joint's movement. The motorSpeed then determines how quickly, if at all, this maxMotorForce is reached. I determined both values merely by trial and error until it felt about right. The ball is now catapulted up and around with just about the right speed. The motor is initially disabled because I only want the plunger to go off when there's a ball touching it.

The joint is then created using the world's CreateJoint method and stored in the joint member variable. Because CreateJoint returns a b2Joint pointer, it has to be cast to a b2PrismaticJoint pointer before assignment.

Notice that it's unnecessary to destroy the joint that the Plunger class is keeping as a member variable. The joint is automatically destroyed when either body it's attached to is destroyed, and in this case the BodySprite's dealloc method destroys the body.

The plunger must also be added to the table. As usual, you do this in the initTableWithWorld method of the TableSetup class after importing the Plunger.h header file. Simply append the following code:

```
// Add plunger
Plunger *plunger = [Plunger plungerWithWorld:world];
[self addChild:plunger z:-1];
```

Creating a Universal Contact Listener

To launch the ball automatically on contact, you need some way to react to collisions. The Box2D physics engine includes the b2ContactListener class. To process collisions, you have to create a custom class that inherits from b2ContactListener and overrides at least one of the collision callback methods BeginContact, EndContact, PreSolve, and PostSolve. You've already created a ContactListener C++ class in Chapter 12. Now it's time to apply some Objective-C to collision callbacks.

On the C++ side you commonly end up with code that looks similar to Listing 13-17. In principle, you retrieve the two colliding bodies from the b2Contact class. In this particular case, each body's user data pointer holds a pointer to a BodySprite object, which lets you compare the classes to decide how to further process the collision. The verbosity of the code is further increased because a contact's two bodies may be in any order, even if the same objects collide frequently. That means during any contact, the plunger might be either bodyA or bodyB, and the ball would be the corresponding other body. So, you always have to test for both cases.

Listing 13-17. A Very Common but Tedious Way to Process Box2D Collisions

```
void ContactListener::BeginContact(b2Contact* contact)
{
    b2Body* bodyA = contact->GetFixtureA()->GetBody();
    b2Body* bodyB = contact->GetFixtureB()->GetBody();
    BodySprite* bodySpriteA = (BodySprite*)bodyA->GetUserData();
    BodySprite* bodySpriteB = (BodySprite*)bodyB->GetUserData();

    if ([bodySpriteA isKindOfClass:[Plunger class]] &&↵
        [bodySpriteB isKindOfClass:[Ball class]])
    {
        Plunger* plunger = (Plunger*)bodySpriteA;
        // ... perform custom code for collision handling
    }
}
```

```
    else if ([bodySpriteB isKindOfClass:[Plunger class]] &&↵
            [bodySpriteA isKindOfClass:[Ball class]])
    {
        Plunger* plunger = (Plunger*)bodySpriteB;
        // ... perform custom code for collision handling
    }
}
```

The previous approach also requires you to import the header files for each colliding BodySprite class. Over time, the collision-handling class knows about most game objects and can become quite complex and hard to read. Instead, you want to have each BodySprite class handle the collision events that it's involved in. This keeps the code cleanly separated and easier to maintain and turns the job of the collision handling class to one of delegating the collision events to the colliding objects.

The ContactListener class (Listing 13-18) in the PhysicsBox2DPinball01 project defines two additional methods next to the regular Box2D collision callback methods to perform the delegation of collision events.

Listing 13-18. The ContactListener Class Definition

```
class ContactListener : public b2ContactListener
{
private:
    void BeginContact(b2Contact* contact);
    void PreSolve(b2Contact* contact, const b2Manifold* oldManifold);
    void PostSolve(b2Contact* contact, const b2ContactImpulse* impulse);
    void EndContact(b2Contact* contact);

    void notifyObjects(b2Contact* contact, NSString* contactType);
    void notifyAB(b2Contact* contact,
                    NSString* contactType,
                    b2Fixture* fixtureA,
                    NSObject* objA,
                    b2Fixture* fixtureB,
                    NSObject* objB);
};
```

The regular Box2D contact methods are implemented in Listing 13-19. The BeginContact and EndContact methods simply delegate the contact information to the notifyObjects methods but also provide the information about whether it was a begin or end contact event by passing an appropriate NSString object. The reason it's a string and not a flag or enumeration will become clear shortly. Because you don't care about the PreSolve and PostSolve events, they remain empty stubs, but could be extended by also calling notifyObjects with the contact and an appropriate string.

Listing 13-19. Implementation of the Box2D Contact Methods

```
/// Called when two fixtures begin to touch.
void ContactListener::BeginContact(b2Contact* contact)
{
    notifyObjects(contact, @"begin");
}

/// Called when two fixtures cease to touch.
void ContactListener::EndContact(b2Contact* contact)
{
    notifyObjects(contact, @"end");
}

void ContactListener::PreSolve(b2Contact* contact, const b2Manifold* oldManifold)
{
    // do nothing
}

void ContactListener::PostSolve(b2Contact* contact, const b2ContactImpulse* impulse)
{
    // do nothing
}
```

What does the notifyObjects method do? Extracting the two colliding bodies and obtaining their user data pointer is similar to Listing 13-17. But take note of the differences:

```
void ContactListener::notifyObjects(b2Contact* contact, NSString* contactType)
{
    b2Fixture* fixtureA = contact->GetFixtureA();
    b2Fixture* fixtureB = contact->GetFixtureB();

    b2Body* bodyA = fixtureA->GetBody();
    b2Body* bodyB = fixtureB->GetBody();

    NSObject* objA = (NSObject*)bodyA->GetUserData();
    NSObject* objB = (NSObject*)bodyB->GetUserData();

    if ((objA != nil) && (objB != nil))
    {
        notifyAB(contact, contactType, fixtureA, objA, fixtureB, objB);
        notifyAB(contact, contactType, fixtureB, objB, fixtureA, objA);
    }
}
```

In this case, you simply assume the user data pointer to be a pointer to an Objective-C class derived from NSObject. This provides the flexibility that any object can respond to collision events, not just BodySprite objects. If both user data pointers are not nil, then the notifyAB method is called twice, the second time with the A and B variables switched. This ensures that both objA and objB receive the collision notification, and the notifyAB method only needs to handle one case.

The job of the notifyAB method is to construct the selector that should be called and, if possible, call the selector with any contact information that the receiving object might need in order to handle the collision. Listing 13-20 shows the implementation of the notifyAB method.

Listing 13-20. Implementation of the Box2D Contact Methods

```
void ContactListener::notifyAB(b2Contact* contact,
                               NSString* contactType,
                               b2Fixture* fixture,
                               NSObject* obj,
                               b2Fixture* otherFixture,
                               NSObject* otherObj)
{
    NSString* format = @"%@ContactWith%@:";
    NSString* otherClassName = NSStringFromClass([otherObj class]);
    NSString* selectorString = [NSString stringWithFormat:format, contactType, ↵
        otherClassName];
    SEL contactSelector = NSSelectorFromString(selectorString);

    if ([obj respondsToSelector:contactSelector])
    {
        Contact* contactInfo = [[Contact alloc] initWithObject:otherObj
                                         otherFixture:otherFixture
                                         ownFixture:fixture
                                         b2Contact:contact];
        [obj performSelector:contactSelector withObject:contactInfo];
        contactInfo = nil;
    }

}
```

The format string defines the general naming format of the selectors that will be called. The syntax of the selectors that notifyAB calls is as follows:

```
<contactType>ContactWith<otherClassName>:(Contact*)contactInfo
```

The contactType is the string you pass to the notifyObjects method, which will be either "begin" or "end" in the current implementation. The otherClassName string is obtained from the NSStringFromClass method, which takes the class of the otherObj. For the collision events of the ball and the plunger, the selectorString will be one of the following, depending on the contactType and the otherObj class name:

```
beginContactWithBall
endContactWithBall
beginContactWithPlunger
endContactWithPlunger
// and so on ...
```

Before performing the selector, notifyAB first checks whether obj actually responds to that selector. In the current implementation, only the Plunger class implements one of the selectors: beginContactWithBall. All other selectors will never be performed because they don't exist (yet).

The Contact class is also defined in ContactListener.h and merely acts as a container object holding any collision information that you might want to pass to receiving classes. By using a container class, the selector format doesn't need to change when you decide to pass more or less information, simply because the only parameter is a pointer to a Contact object, and the information is encapsulated within the Contact class.

> **Tip**   There's also a technical reason for using a container class. The performSelector method of the NSObject class knows only three variants: with zero, one, or two parameters. Because you definitely like to pass on more than two parameters to the receiving object, there's simply no other choice than to use a container class. Whenever you find the performSelector method limiting, remember that you can always create a container class holding any information that you'd like to pass on to the class implementing the selector.

Because Contact is such a simple class, Listing 13-21 shows both interface and implementation in one listing.

Listing 13-21. Interface and Implementation of the Contact Class

```
@interface Contact : NSObject
{
@private
    NSObject* otherObject;
    b2Fixture* ownFixture;
    b2Fixture* otherFixture;
    b2Contact* b2contact;
}
-(id) initWithObject:(NSObject*)otherObject_
        otherFixture:(b2Fixture*)otherFixture_
         ownFixture:(b2Fixture*)ownFixture_
          b2Contact:(b2Contact*)b2contact_;
@end

@implementation Contact
-(id) initWithObject:(NSObject*)otherObject_
        otherFixture:(b2Fixture*)otherFixture_
         ownFixture:(b2Fixture*)ownFixture_
          b2Contact:(b2Contact*)b2contact_
{
    self=[super init];
    if (self)
    {
        otherObject=otherObject_;
        otherFixture=otherFixture_;
        ownFixture=ownFixture_;
```

```
        b2contact = b2contact_;
    }
    return self;
}
@end
```

The only notable aspect of the Contact class is that you can't keep the contact for later use. The notifyAB method sets the object to nil immediately after the contactSelector message was sent to indicate that it's only a temporary object. Directly after the call to the Box2D contact methods, the b2Contact object is released by Box2D, and so the otherFixture, ownFicture, and b2contact pointers will be invalid, and accessing them would cause a crash.

Responding to Contact Events

Now whenever the ball and the plunger get in contact, the beginContactWithBall method in the Plunger class is called:

```
-(void) endPlunge:(ccTime)delta
{
    // stop the motor
    joint->EnableMotor(NO);
}

-(void) beginContactWithBall:(Contact*)contact
{
    // start the motor
    joint->EnableMotor(YES);

    // schedule motor to come back, unschedule in case the plunger is hit repeatedly
    [self scheduleOnce:@selector(endPlunge:) delay:0.5f];
}
```

As soon as the ball touches the plunger, the plunger's motor is enabled, which propels the plunger and thus the ball upward. The endPlunge method is scheduled to stop the motor after a short time. I took extra care to correctly unschedule the selectors. For example, it's very likely that the beginContactWithBall method is called repeatedly within a short time period, because there may be more than one contact point (Box2D reports each contact point individually); or simply, the ball might bounce a little and lose contact, but the plunger's motor ensures that the plunger will touch the ball again after a short time.

Similarly, you'll find the two methods beginContactWithPlunger and beginContactWithBumper implemented in the Ball class. Both types of contact will simply play a sound effect:

```
-(void) playSound
{
    float pitch = 0.9f + CCRANDOM_0_1() * 0.2f;
    float gain = 1.0f + CCRANDOM_0_1() * 0.3f;
    [[SimpleAudioEngine sharedEngine] playEffect:@"bumper.wav"
                                    pitch:pitch
                                      pan:0.0f
                                     gain:gain];
}
```

```
-(void) endContactWithBumper:(Contact*)contact
{
    [self playSound];
}
-(void) endContactWithPlunger:(Contact*)contact
{
    [self playSound];
}
```

> **Tip**   Keep in mind that Box2D reports each individual contact of two colliding objects, causing the contact methods to be called more than once for the same two objects. In some cases, you may want to set a Bool variable to YES in order to note that a contact has already happened. The corresponding contact method should first check whether the variable is set, and if it is, skip the code. You should later set the variable back to NO in a scheduled update method to reenable contact events. By doing so, you can avoid contact code being run multiple times and avoid undesirable side effects like too many sounds played at once.

The Flippers

The final ingredients are the flippers, with which you control the action. The two flippers will be controlled by touching the screen on either the left or right side, as Listing 13-22 shows.

Listing 13-22.   The Flipper Interface

```
#import "BodySprite.h"

typedef enum
{
    kFlipperLeft,
    kFlipperRight,
} EFlipperType;

@interface Flipper : BodySprite<CCTargetedTouchDelegate>
{
    EFlipperType type;
    b2RevoluteJoint* joint;
    float totalTime;
}

+(id) flipperWithWorld:(b2World*)world flipperType:(EFlipperType)flipperType;
@end
```

Each flipper is anchored using a b2RevoluteJoint. Take a look at the flipper initWithWorld method in Listing 13-23 to see how the flippers are created.

Listing 13-23. Creating a Flipper

```
-(id) initWithWorld:(b2World*)world flipperType:(EFlipperType)flipperType
{
    NSString* name = (flipperType == kFlipperLeft) ? @"flipper-left" : @"flipper-right";
    self = [super initWithShape:name inWorld:world];

    if (self)
    {
        type = flipperType;

        // set the position depending on the left or right side
        CGPoint flipperPos = (type == kFlipperRight) ? ccp(210, 65) : ccp(90, 65);

        // attach the flipper to a static body with a revolute joint
        [self attachFlipperAt:[Helper toMeters:flipperPos]];

        // receive touch events
        [[CCDirector sharedDirector].touchDispatcher addTargetedDelegate:self
                                                                priority:0
                                                          swallowsTouches:NO];

    }
    return self;
}

+(id) flipperWithWorld:(b2World*)world flipperType:(EFlipperType)flipperType
{
    return [[self alloc] initWithWorld:world flipperType:flipperType];
}

-(void) cleanup
{
    [super cleanup];

    // stop listening to touches
    [[CCDirector sharedDirector].touchDispatcher removeDelegate:self];
}
```

The Flipper class also registers itself with the CCTouchDispatcher to receive touch input events. The common misconception is that only the CCLayer class can receive input, but in fact CCLayer is merely conveniently preconfigured to receive touches. Any class can register itself with the CCTouchDispatcher class as a delegate, provided that the class also removes itself as a touch delegate, usually in the cleanup method.

As with the other pinball elements, the flippers are added to the TableSetup class after importing the Flipper.h file and initialized as left and right flipper by using the EFlipperType enum from Listing 13-22.

```
// Add flippers
Flipper *left = [Flipper flipperWithWorld:world flipperType:kFlipperLeft];
[self addChild:left];

Flipper *right = [Flipper flipperWithWorld:world flipperType:kFlipperRight];
[self addChild:right];
```

> **Note**   I could have used the flipper's shape names instead, but I wanted to hide this
> implementation detail. No one but the `Flipper` class should be concerned with what the flipper's
> frame and shape names are.

The `attachFlipperAt` method creates the revolute joints (see Listing 13-24), with a few
modifications for the right flipper in order to change the direction and upper limit of the right
flipper's rotation. The point the flippers rotate around will be the anchor point of their shapes,
which is editable in PhysicsEditor.

Listing 13-24. Creating the Flipper Revolute Joint

```
-(void) attachFlipperAt:(b2Vec2)pos
{
    physicsBody->SetTransform(pos, 0);
    physicsBody->SetType(b2_dynamicBody);

    // turn on continuous collision detection to prevent tunneling
    physicsBody->SetBullet(true);

    // create an invisible static body to attach to'
    b2BodyDef bodyDef;
    bodyDef.position=pos;
    b2Body* staticBody=physicsBody->GetWorld()->CreateBody(&bodyDef);

    // setup joint parameters
    b2RevoluteJointDef jointDef;
    jointDef.Initialize(staticBody, physicsBody, staticBody->GetWorldCenter());
    jointDef.lowerAngle=0.0f;
    jointDef.upperAngle=CC_DEGREES_TO_RADIANS(70);
    jointDef.enableLimit=true;
    jointDef.maxMotorTorque=100.0f;
    jointDef.motorSpeed=-40.0f;
    jointDef.enableMotor=true;

    if (type == kFlipperRight)
    {
        // mirror speed and angle for the right flipper
        jointDef.motorSpeed *=-1;
        jointDef.lowerAngle=-jointDef.upperAngle;
        jointDef.upperAngle=0.0f;
    }

    // create the joint
    joint=(b2RevoluteJoint*)physicsBody->GetWorld()->CreateJoint(&jointDef);
}
```

You may be wondering why the flipper's body is set as a bullet. Trust me, I'm not going to shoot
flippers at you! Physics engines traditionally have a problem with detecting collisions of objects

moving at high speeds because such an object can travel great distances between two collision tests, seemingly "tunneling" through other collidable objects. That may be fine for subatomic particles, but not for our flippers and the ball.

The SetBullet method enables a special, continuous collision detection method for fast-moving objects that takes into account the path the object must have taken between two collision tests. Thus, the bullet mode is able to detect collisions that would have otherwise been missed, at the expense of performance. The bullet mode should be used judiciously and only when absolutely needed. In the pinball game, I noticed that both the flippers and the ball would sometimes "miss" each other, so I have them both treated as fast-moving objects to get more accurate collision detection.

The static body is created to attach the flipper to an unmovable body, to keep the flipper anchored in place. b2RevoluteJointDef uses lowerAngle and upperAngle as the rotation limits, which are in radians. I'll set the upperAngle to 70 degrees and convert it to radians with the CC_DEGREES_TO_RADIANS macro provided by cocos2d.

The revolute joint also has maxMotorTorque and motorSpeed fields, which are used to define the speed and immediacy of the movement of the flippers. However, unlike the plunger, the motor is enabled all the time, and changes direction every time the sign of the motorSpeed variable is changed. While the flippers are down, the motor will force them down so that they don't bounce when the ball hits them.

In the ccTouchBegan method, the location of the touch is obtained, which is validated with the isTouchForMe method before actually reversing the motor.

```
-(BOOL) ccTouchBegan:(UITouch*)touch withEvent:(UIEvent*)event
{
    BOOL touchHandled = NO;

    CGPoint location = [Helper locationFromTouch:touch];
    if ([self isTouchForMe:location])
    {
        touchHandled = YES;
        [self reverseMotor];
    }

    return touchHandled;
}

-(void) ccTouchEnded:(UITouch*)touch withEvent:(UIEvent*)event
{
    CGPoint location = [Helper locationFromTouch:touch];
    if ([self isTouchForMe:location])
    {
        [self reverseMotor];
    }
}
```

The isTouchForMe method implements the check to figure out on which side of the screen the touch was and whether the current instance of the class is the correct flipper to respond to this touch.

```
-(bool) isTouchForMe:(CGPoint)location
{
    if (type == kFlipperLeft && location.x<[Helper screenCenter].x)
    {
        return YES;
    }
    else if (type == kFlipperRight && location.x>[Helper screenCenter].x)
    {
        return YES;
    }

    return NO;
}
```

Reversing the motor speed then simply allows the flipper to spring up and to spring back down again when the touch ends and the motor speed is reversed again.

```
-(void) reverseMotor
{
    joint->SetMotorSpeed(joint->GetMotorSpeed() * -1);
}
```

The rest is just physics. If the ball is on the flipper, and you touch the screen on the correct side, the flipper will be accelerated upward, pushing the ball with it. Depending on where on the flipper the ball lands, it will be propelled more or less straight upward.

Summary

In this chapter, you learned how to use the PhysicsEditor tool to define the collision shapes for the bodies used in the pinball game. With just the ball in place, I illustrated how you can simulate acceleration toward a point, including how to model the effects of gravity or magnetism more or less realistically.

I hope this chapter gave you an impression of how much fun physics can be, regardless of what you may have experienced in physics class. But then again, you didn't build pinball machines in physics class—or did you?

If you'd like to go beyond this example—for example, using more joints or taking more control of the collision process—I refer you to the Box2D manual, at www.box2d.org/manual.html.

On the other hand, if you need more information about individual classes and structs, you should look at the Box2D API reference. It's provided in the Documentation folder of the Box2D download, which you can obtain from http://code.google.com/p/box2d. Because the Box2D API reference isn't available online, I'm hosting it on my site at www.learn-cocos2d.com/api-ref/latest/docs.html.

To get help with Box2D, you can check out the official Box2D forums at www.box2d.org/ forum/ index.php and look at the Physics subsection of the cocos2d forums at www.cocos2d-iphone. org/forum/forum/7.

If you're interested in learning more about PhysicsEditor, I can recommend the PhysicsEditor blog (www.physicseditor.de/blog) in which Andreas Löw shows off some cool PhysicsEditor tips and tricks. If you have a support request for Andreas, you can simply write an e-mail to support@code-and-web.de.

Chapter

14

Chapter

Game Center

Game Center is Apple's social network solution. It enables you to authenticate players, store their scores and display leaderboards, and track and display their achievement progress. Players can invite friends to play, or choose to quickly find a match and play a game with anyone.

This chapter introduces you not only to Game Center and the Game Kit API but also to the basics of online multiplayer programming and, of course, how to use Game Center together with cocos2d.

Because a lot of Apple's examples are intentionally incomplete, you'll be developing a GameKitHelper class in this chapter. This class will remove some of the complexities of Game Center programming for you. It will make it easier for you to use Game Kit and Game Center features and let you easily reuse the same code for other games.

To configure your application for use with Game Center, you're going to use iTunes Connect. The information on the iTunes Connect web site is considered confidential Apple information, so I can't discuss it in this book. However, I will point you to Apple's excellent documentation for each step—and quite frankly, setting up leaderboards and achievements on iTunes Connect is possibly the easiest aspect of Game Center.

Enabling Game Center

Game Center is the service that manages and stores player accounts and each player's friend lists, leaderboards, and achievements. This information is stored online on Apple's servers and accessed either by your game or by the Game Center app that's installed on all devices running iOS 4.1 or newer.

> **Note**   The easiest way for a user to check whether a device supports Game Center is to locate the Game Center app on the device. If it exists, the device is ready for Game Center; otherwise, it's not. If the Game Center app isn't available, but the device is eligible for upgrading to iOS 4.1, Game Center support will become available after upgrading the device's operating system via iTunes.
>
> If you don't have access to a Game Center–enabled device, you can still program and test Game Center features using the iPhone/iPad Simulator. With the exception of matchmaking, all Game Center features can be tested in the Simulator.

On the other side, the Game Kit API is what you use to program Game Center features. Game Kit provides programmatic access to the data stored on the Game Center servers and is able to show built-in leaderboards, achievements, and matchmaking screens. But Game Kit also provides features besides Game Center—for example, peer-to-peer networking via Bluetooth and voice chat. These are the only two Game Kit features already available on devices running iOS 3.0 or newer.

The final ingredient in this mix is iTunes Connect. You set up your game's leaderboards and achievements through the iTunes Connect web site. But most importantly, iTunes Connect lets you enable Game Center for your game in the first place. You'll start with that step first, so you should do this before you've even created an Xcode project for your game.

Your starting point for learning more about Game Center and the steps involved in creating a game that uses Game Center is at Apple's Getting Started with Game Center web site: `http://developer.apple.com/devcenter/ios/gamecenter`.

Creating Your App in iTunes Connect

The very first step is to log in with your Apple ID on the iTunes Connect web site: `http://itunesconnect.apple.com`.

Then you want to add a new application, even if it doesn't exist yet. For most fields that iTunes Connect asks you to fill out, you can enter bogus information. There are only two settings that you have to get right. The first is, obviously, to enable Game Center when iTunes Connect asks you whether the new application should support Game Center.

The other is to enter a Bundle ID (also referred to as Bundle Identifier) that matches the one used in the Xcode project. Because you don't have an Xcode project yet, you're free to choose any Bundle ID you want. Apple recommends using reverse domain names for Bundle IDs with the app's name appended at the end. The catch is that the Bundle ID needs to be unique across all App Store apps, and there are tens of thousands of them.

For the book's example, I chose `com.learn-cocos2d` to be the app's Bundle ID. Because this Bundle ID is now taken by me, you'll have to use your own Bundle ID. If you want, you can simply suffix it with a string of your choosing or choose an entirely new string.

> **Note** Remember to use your own Bundle ID whenever I refer to the `com.learn-cocos2d` Bundle ID.

For a detailed description of how to create a new app and how to set up Game Center for an app on iTunes Connect, refer to Apple's iTunes Connect Developer Guide: `http://itunesconnect.apple.com/docs/iTunesConnect_DeveloperGuide.pdf`.

Specifically, the "Game Center" section explains in great detail how to manage the Game Center features on iTunes Connect.

Setting Up Leaderboards and Achievements

For the most part, after enabling Game Center for an app, what you'll be doing on iTunes Connect is setting up one or more leaderboards to hold your players' scores or times, and setting up a number of achievements that players can unlock while playing your game.

To access the Game Center leaderboards and achievements, you refer to them by ID. To be able to query and update the correct leaderboards and achievements, you should note the leaderboard category ID strings and the achievement ID strings.

I've set up one leaderboard with a score format of Elapsed Time and a leaderboard category ID of `Playtime`. For achievements I've entered one achievement, with an achievement ID of `PlayedForTenSeconds`, that grants the player five achievement points.

Feel free to set up additional leaderboards and achievements, but keep in mind that the example code in this chapter relies on at least one leaderboard with a category ID of `Playtime` and one achievement with an achievement ID of `PlayedForTenSeconds` to exist.

AppController and NavigationController

Now it's time to create the actual Xcode project. You can start the project from any cocos2d project template. The cocos2d 2.0 templates actually include rudimentary Game Center functionality. You can also use an already existing project with no Game Center support.

Beginning with version 2.0, cocos2d removed the `RootViewController` class in favor of a `UINavigationController` class. This class is created in the `AppDelegate` files, which declare the `AppController` class. Note that `AppController` is simply the name for the app delegate class in cocos2d projects. You can obtain a reference to the `AppController` from anywhere via the `UIApplication` class' `delegate` property:

```
AppController* app = (AppController*)[UIApplication sharedApplication].delegate;
```

You can then access the navigation controller via the `navController` property:

```
[app.navController presentModalViewController:viewController animated:YES];
```

You may be wondering what you need the navigation controller for. Game Center needs a view controller like the UINavigationController class to be able to show its built-in UIKit user interface. The navController provided by cocos2d makes Game Center integration a lot easier.

Configuring the Xcode Project

Enter the Bundle ID you've entered for your app in iTunes Connect. Remember that I'm using com.learn-cocos2d as the Bundle ID for the example projects, but you can't use it because it's already taken now, and Bundle IDs must be unique.

Locate the Info.plist file in your project's Resources folder and select it. You can then edit it in the Property List editor, as shown in Figure 14-1. Set the Bundle identifier key to have the same value as your app's Bundle ID. In my case, that's com.learn-cocos2d, and in your case it will be whatever string you chose as the app's Bundle ID.

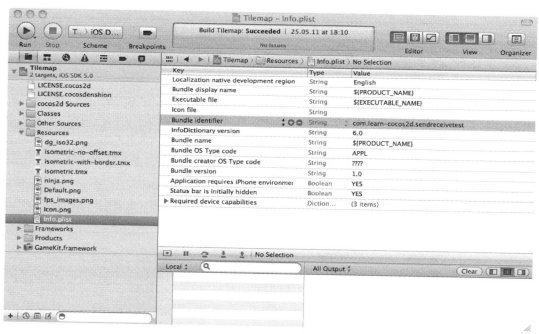

Figure 14-1. The Bundle identifier key must match your app's Bundle ID

You can actually use Game Kit—and Game Center, for that matter—in two ways. One is to require Game Center, as the cocos2d project templates do, which means your app will run only on devices that support Game Center and are running iOS 4.1 or newer. However, for the examples I've written, I didn't make Game Center a requirement because it's relatively easy to check whether Game Center is available and then not use it if it isn't. This allows your game to be run on devices running iOS 4.0, just without all the Game Center features. Kobold2D projects link with Game Center but don't require it.

If you do want to require Game Kit and Game Center to be present, you can set this in your app's Info.plist UIRequiredDeviceCapabilities list. By adding another key named gamekit with a Boolean value and checking the check box, as shown in Figure 14-2, you can tell iTunes and potential users that your app requires Game Kit and thus requires iOS 4.1 or newer.

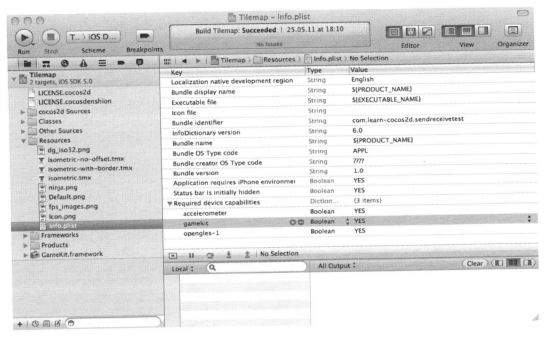

Figure 14-2. Making Game Kit a strict requirement

You can learn more about iTunes requirements and the UIRequiredDeviceCapabilities key in Apple's Information Property List Key Reference: http://developer.apple.com/library/ios/#documentation/General/Reference/InfoPlistKeyReference/Introduction/Introduction.html.

> **Caution** If you add the gamekit key but later decide you don't want to make Game Kit a requirement, make sure you remove the gamekit entry. If you simply uncheck the gamekit check box, it actually tells iTunes that your app isn't available on devices that support Game Center—the exact opposite of what you might expect. To actually make Game Kit an optional requirement, you have to remove the gamekit entry altogether.

To verify that your project links with the Game Kit framework, select the application target in your project. Select the root entry in the Project Navigator, which is the project itself and labeled Tilemap in Figure 14-2. Then choose the appropriate target (not the one named cocos2d-library) and switch to the Build Phases tab. Unfold the Link Binary With Libraries section to see the list of libraries this target is currently linked with. There should be a GameKit.framework in the list.

If not, below that list are two + and – buttons with which you can add or remove libraries. To add another library, click the + button. You'll see another list pop up like the one in Figure 14-3. Locate the `GameKit.framework` entry and click the Add button. Because you have a lot of libraries to choose from, and they're not always sorted alphabetically, it helps to filter the list by entering *GameKit* in the text field above the list.

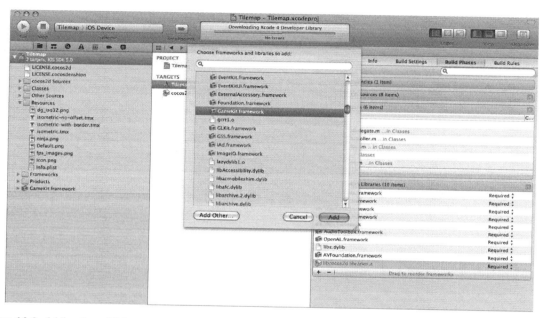

Figure 14-3. *Adding GameKit.framework*

`GameKit.framework` will be added to the Linked Libraries list when you click the Add button. By default, new libraries are added as Required, which is displayed to the right of each library. The setting Required means your app will work only on devices where the `GameKit.framework` library is available. If that's what you want, and you've added the gamekit key to `Info.plist`, you can leave it at that. Otherwise, change the setting to Optional in order to be able to run the app even on devices that don't have Game Center available. You can account for that with a relatively simple check in code (discussed shortly in Listing 14-3) and then disable any Game Kit features in case a device doesn't support Game Kit. Cocos2d projects require Game Kit by default, whereas Kobold2D projects have it set as optional.

Finally, you'll want the `GameKit.h` header file to be available in all your project's source files. Instead of adding it to each and every source file, you should add it to your project's `Prefix.pch` file. This is the precompiled header that contains header files from external frameworks to allow the project to compile faster. But it also has the added benefit that every header file added to the prefix header will make its definitions available to every source code file in the current project.

You can find the `Prefix.pch` file in the Supporting Files group. Open the one in your project and add the GameKit header to it, as shown in Listing 14-1.

Listing 14-1. Adding the GameKit Header to Your Project's Prefix Header

```
#ifdef __OBJC__
    #import <Foundation/Foundation.h>
    #import <UIKit/UIKit.h>
    #import <GameKit/GameKit.h>
#endif
```

That's it—your app is set up for use with Game Center.

Game Center Setup Summary

To summarize, enabling Game Center for your app requires the following steps:

1. Create a new app in iTunes Connect:
   a. Specify a Bundle ID for the new app.
   b. Enable Game Center for this app.

2. Set up your initial leaderboards and achievements in iTunes Connect:
   a. Note the leaderboard category IDs and achievement IDs. (Also note that you'll likely continue to edit and add leaderboards and achievements throughout the development of your game.)

3. Edit Info.plist:
   a. Enter the app's Bundle ID in the Bundle identifier field.
   b. Optionally require Game Kit by adding a Boolean value labeled gamekit to the UIRequiredDeviceCapabilities list.

4. Add the necessary Game Kit references:
   a. If needed, add the GameKit.framework to your application target's Linked Binary with Libraries build phase. Change its Type setting from Required to Optional if Game Kit isn't strictly required by your app.
   b. Add #import <GameKit/GameKit.h> to your project's prefix header file.

Before you proceed, make sure you've followed each step. You can always go back and make the necessary changes later. But if you don't do all of these steps at the beginning, chances are you'll get errors or something won't work, but the associated error message won't necessarily point you to a mistake or oversight concerning one of these steps.

Common causes for Game Center to not work properly are a mismatch between the Bundle ID in the project's Info.plist file and the Bundle ID set up for your app in iTunes Connect.

Game Kit Programming

Before you get into programming Game Center with the Game Kit API, I'd like to mention the two important resources on Apple's developer web site.

There is the Game Kit Programming Guide, which provides a high-level, task-based overview of Game Kit and Game Center concepts: `http://developer.apple.com/library/ios/#documentation/NetworkingInternet/Conceptual/GameKit_Guide/Introduction/Introduction.html` .

For in-depth detailed information about the Game Center classes and protocols, you can refer to the Game Kit Framework Reference: `http://developer.apple.com/library/ios/#documentation/GameKit/Reference/GameKit_Collection/_index.html` .

The GameKitHelper Delegate

I mentioned earlier in this chapter that you'll use a GameKitHelper class to provide easier access to Game Kit and Game Center features. Because connecting to an online server causes responses to be delayed by several milliseconds, if not seconds, having a central class manage all Game Center–related features is a good idea. All the Game Center examples are based on the isometric game developed in Chapter 11. You'll find the following example code in the IsoTilemap04 project.

One of your game's classes can then use this functionality and register itself as a GameKitHelper delegate to get notified of events as they occur. To do that, the delegate must implement the GameKitHelper @protocol that's defined in the GameKitHelper.h header file (Listing 14-2). Only classes implementing this protocol can be assigned to the GameKitHelper delegate property to receive the protocol messages. The protocol is simply a list of method definitions that a class using the protocol must implement. If any of the methods in the protocol aren't implemented, the compiler will let you know about that.

Listing 14-2. The GameKitHelper Header File

```
#import "cocos2d.h"
#import <GameKit/GameKit.h>

@protocol GameKitHelperProtocol<NSObject>
@optional
-(void) onLocalPlayerAuthenticationChanged;
-(void) onFriendListReceived:(NSArray*)friends;
-(void) onPlayerInfoReceived:(NSArray*)players;
@end

@interface GameKitHelper : NSObject<GKLeaderboardViewControllerDelegate, ↵
    GKAchievementViewControllerDelegate>
{
    id<GameKitHelperProtocol>delegate;
    BOOL isGameCenterAvailable;
    NSError* lastError;
}

@property (nonatomic, retain) id<GameKitHelperProtocol>delegate;
@property (nonatomic, readonly) BOOL isGameCenterAvailable;
@property (nonatomic, readonly) NSError* lastError;

+(GameKitHelper*) sharedGameKitHelper;
```

```
// Player authentication, info
-(void) authenticateLocalPlayer;
-(void) getLocalPlayerFriends;
-(void) getPlayerInfo:(NSArray*)players;
@end
```

For your convenience, the GameKitHelper class also stores the last error in its lastError property. This lets you check whether any error occurred and, if so, what kind of error, without actually receiving the Game Center messages directly. The GameKitHelper class is a singleton, which was described in Chapter 3, so I'll leave the singleton-specific code out of the discussion.

I discuss the remaining properties and methods shortly. For now, take a look at how the TileMapLayer class is extended so that it can function as the delegate for GameKitHelper. The essential changes to the header file are importing GameKitHelper.h and specifying that TileMapLayer implements GameKitHelperProtocol:

```
#import "GameKitHelper.h"

...

@interface TileMapLayer : CCLayer<GameKitHelperProtocol>
{
    ...
}
```

Then you can set the TileMapLayer class to be the delegate of the GameKitHelper class, in the init method:

```
-(id) init
{
    self = [super init];
    if (self)
    {
        GameKitHelper* gkHelper = [GameKitHelper sharedGameKitHelper];
        gkHelper.delegate = self;
        [gkHelper authenticateLocalPlayer];
        ...
```

Note that you're responsible for setting the GameKitHelper delegate back to nil when appropriate—for example, shortly before changing scenes. Because GameKitHelper keeps a reference to the delegate, ARC won't release the delegate object from memory. That would not only keep the delegate itself in memory but all of its member variables as well, including all its children if it's a CCNode class.

Checking for Game Center Availability

The GameKitHelper class starts by checking for Game Center availability right in its init method (Listing 14-3). It needs to do that only once because the conditions never change while the app is running.

Listing 14-3. Testing for Game Center Availability

```
-(id) init
{
    if ((self = [super init]))
    {
        // Test for Game Center availability
        Class gameKitLocalPlayerClass = NSClassFromString(@"GKLocalPlayer");
        BOOL isLocalPlayerAvailable = (gameKitLocalPlayerClass != nil);

        // Test if device is running iOS 4.1 or higher
        NSString* reqSysVer = @"4.1";
        NSString* currSysVer = [UIDevice currentDevice].systemVersion;
        BOOL isOSVer41 = ([currSysVer compare:reqSysVer
                                        options:NSNumericSearch] != NSOrderedAscending);

        isGameCenterAvailable = (isLocalPlayerAvailable && isOSVer41);
        NSLog(@"GameCenter available = %@", isGameCenterAvailable ? @"YES" : @"NO");

        [self registerForLocalPlayerAuthChange];
    }
    return self;
}
```

The first test is simply to check whether a specific Game Center class is available. In this case, the Objective-C runtime method NSClassFromString is used to get one of the Game Center classes by name. If this call returns nil, you can be certain that Game Center is unavailable.

But it's not quite that simple. Because Game Center was already partially available in beta versions prior to iOS 4.1, you also need to check whether the device is running at least iOS 4.1. You do that by comparing the reqSysVer string with the systemVersion string.

Once both checks are made, you combine the results using the && (and) operator, so that both must be true for isGameCenterAvailable to become true. The isGameCenterAvailable variable is used to safeguard all calls to Game Center functionality within the GameKitHelper class. This avoids accidentally calling Game Center functionality when it's not available, which would crash the application.

Note that this is how Apple recommends you check for Game Center availability. You shouldn't use any other methods—for example, determining the type of device your game is running on. Although certain devices are excluded from using Game Center, the preceding check already accounts for this.

Authenticating the Local Player

The local player is a fundamental concept to Game Center programming. It refers to the player account that's signed into the device. This is important to know because only the local player can send scores to leaderboards and report achievement progress to the Game Center service. The very first thing a Game Center application needs to do is authenticate the local player. If that fails, you can't use most of the Game Center services, and in fact Apple recommends not using any Game Center functionality unless there is an authenticated local player.

In the GameKitHelper init method, the registerForLocalPlayerAuthChange method is called so that GameKitHelper receives events concerning authentication changes for the local player. This is the only Game Center notification that's sent through NSNotificationCenter. You register a selector to receive the message, as shown in Listing 14-4.

Listing 14-4. Registering for Local Player Authentication Changes

```
-(void) registerForLocalPlayerAuthChange
{
    if (isGameCenterAvailable == NO)
        return;

    NSNotificationCenter* nc = NSNotificationCenter.defaultCenter;
    [nc addObserver:self
            selector:@selector(onLocalPlayerAuthenticationChanged)
                name:GKPlayerAuthenticationDidChangeNotificationName
              object:nil];
}
```

As you can see, isGameCenterAvailable is used here to skip the rest of the method in case Game Center isn't available. You'll notice other methods doing the same thing, and I'll refrain from repeating this in the book's code.

The actual method being called by NSNotificationCenter simply forwards the message to the delegate, but only if the delegate implements the onLocalPlayerAuthenticationChanged message. Because the GameKitHelper delegate methods are marked as @optional, this precaution is necessary to avoid crashes.

```
-(void) onLocalPlayerAuthenticationChanged
{
    if ([delegate respondsToSelector:@selector(onLocalPlayerAuthenticationChanged)])
    {
        [delegate onLocalPlayerAuthenticationChanged];
    }
}
```

Note The local player's signed-in status may actually change while the game is in the background and the user runs the Game Center app and signs out. That's because of the multitasking nature introduced with iOS 4.0. Essentially, your game must be prepared to handle the local player logging out and some other player signing in at any time during game play. Typically, you should end the current game session and return to a safe place—for example, the main menu. But you should consider saving the current state of the game for each local player as they sign out so that when they sign back in, the game continues exactly where that player left the game.

The actual authentication is performed by the authenticateLocalPlayer method, in Listing 14-5.

Listing 14-5. Authenticating the Local Player

```
-(void) authenticateLocalPlayer
{
    if (isGameCenterAvailable == NO)
        return;

    GKLocalPlayer* localPlayer = GKLocalPlayer.localPlayer;
    if (localPlayer.authenticated == NO)
    {
        [localPlayer authenticateWithCompletionHandler: ↵
        ^(NSError* error)
        {
            [self setLastError:error];
        }];
    }
}
```

At first glance, that's relatively straightforward. The localPlayer object is obtained, and if it's not authenticated, the authenticateWithCompletionHandler method is called. And the NSError object returned by the method is set to the lastError and . . . hey, wait a second. That's all part of the method's parameter?

Yes. These inline methods are called *block objects*, which I introduced at the end of Chapter 3. Blocks are also used by CCMenuItem classes. I'll explain blocks again in the next section as a refresher. For now, just know that the block object is a C-style method that's passed as a parameter to the authenticateWithCompletionHandler method. It's run only after the authentication request has returned from the server.

If you call the authenticateLocalPlayer method, your game will display the Game Center sign-in dialog, shown in Figure 14-4. If you have an Apple ID, you can sign in with your Apple ID and password. Or you can choose to create a new account.

Figure 14-4. Game Center sign-in dialog

But there's a third possibility—if Game Center detects that there's already a signed-in player on this device, it simply greets you with a "Welcome back" message. How do you sign out in that case? Through the Game Center app, which also exists on the iPhone/iPad Simulator for that very reason.

If you run the Game Center app, select the first tab that reads either Me or Sandbox and then click the label at the bottom that starts with Account:. You'll get a pop-up dialog that allows you to view your account or sign out. After signing out through the Game Center app, the next time you run your app, and it's going through the player authentication process, the sign-in dialog in Figure 14-4 will be shown again.

> **Note**   If the [GKLocalPlayer localPlayer].underage property is set after the local player was authenticated, some Game Center features are disabled. You can also refer to the underage property if your game should disable optional features that aren't suitable for underage players.

Now, about error handling, you'll notice that GameKitHelper uses the setLastError method wherever there's an error object returned. This lets the delegate class check whether any error occurred through the lastError property. If it's nil, then there was no error.

However, only the last error object is kept around, and the next method returning an NSError object will replace the previous error, so it's crucial to check for the lastError property right away if error handling is important in that particular case. In some cases, you can safely ignore errors. They might lead only to temporary problems, like an empty friends list. Regardless, the setLastError message copies the new error and then prints out diagnostic information so you can always keep an eye on the kinds of errors that occur during development:

```
-(void) setLastError:(NSError*)error
{
    lastError = error.copy;

    if (lastError != nil)
        NSLog(@"GameKitHelper ERROR: %@", [lastError userInfo].description);
}
```

If you receive an error and want to know more about it, refer to Apple's Game Kit Constants Reference, which describes the error constants defined in the GameKit/GKError.h header file: http://developer.apple.com/library/ios/#documentation/GameKit/Reference/GameKit_ConstantsRef/Reference/reference.html.

After the local player has successfully signed in, you can access his friend list, leaderboards, and achievements. But before I get to that, let's sidestep for a moment and review the important aspects of block objects.

Block Objects

The inline method shown in Listing 14-5 is called a *block object*, commonly referred to simply as a *block*. You might have heard of *closures*, *anonymous functions*, or *lambda* in other languages, which are essentially the same concept. Block objects are a C-language extension introduced by

Apple to make multithreaded and asynchronous programming tasks easier. In layman's terms, block objects are C callback functions that can be created within other functions, assigned to variables for later use, passed on to other functions, and run asynchronously at a later time. Because a block object has read access to the local variables of the function or scope it was defined in, it typically requires fewer arguments than a regular callback method. Optionally, with the __block storage specifier, you can also allow the block object to modify variables in its enclosing scope.

> **Tip**   Refer to Apple's Blocks Programming Topics documentation if you're interested in more details about block objects: `http://developer.apple.com/library/mac/#documentation/Cocoa/Conceptual/Blocks/Articles/00_Introduction.html`. You'll also find more examples near the end of Chapter 3 where I explain how to use blocks with menus, specifically the CCMenuItem classes.

I'll cut out the actual block object from Listing 14-5 to discuss it separately:

```
^(NSError* error)
{
    [self setLastError:error];
}
```

It looks like a method, except it has no name and it begins with a caret symbol (^). The NSError pointer is the only variable passed to it, but commas can delimit multiple variables, as in this example:

```
^(NSArray* scores, NSError* error)
{
    [self setLastError:error];
    [delegate onScoresReceived:scores];
}
```

If that reminds you of a C method's parameters, you're correct. If you want, you can consider a block to be a C method whose name is ^ and that can be passed to one of the many Game Kit methods taking block objects as parameters.

I'd like to point out two technicalities. First, local variables can be accessed in a block. But they can't normally be modified, unless they're prefixed with the __block keyword. Consider this code snippet:

```
__block bool success = NO;
[localPlayer authenticateWithCompletionHandler:↵
^(NSError* error)
{
    success = (error == nil);
    lastError = error;
}];
```

With blocks, it's only legal to modify a local variable declared outside the block's scope if the variable is declared with the __block keyword. In this case, the success variable is declared locally outside the block but is modified within the block, so it must be prefixed with the __block keyword. On the other hand, the `lastError` variable is a member variable of the class. You can modify member variables within blocks without using the __block keyword.

Also, in the case of Game Kit, you'll be frequently passing block objects to Game Kit methods, but the block objects won't be run until a later time. You're probably used to code being executed in sequence, but in Game Kit programming it's not! The block passed to a Game Kit method is called only when the call completes a round-trip to and from the Game Center server. That takes time because data needs to be transmitted to the Game Center servers and processed, and then a result needs to be returned to the device. Only then does the block object get executed.

Let's take an example. You may find yourself tempted to write something like this:

```
__block bool success = NO;

[localPlayer authenticateWithCompletionHandler: ↵
^(NSError* error)
{
    success = (error == nil);
}];

if (success)
    NSLog(@"Local player logged in!");
else
    NSLog(@"Local player NOT logged in!");
```

However, this example will always report that the player isn't logged in. Why? Well, the execution path is such that the `authenticateWithCompletionHandler` will take your block as a parameter and store it while it sends a request to the server and waits for the response to come back. However, the execution continues right away after the `authenticateWithCompletionHandler` method, and that's where the `success` variable decides which log statement to print. The problem is, the `success` variable is still set to NO because the block hasn't been executed yet.

Several milliseconds later, the server responds to the authentication, and that triggers the completion handler—the block object—to be run. If it returns without error, the `success` variable is set to YES. But alas, your logging code has already been run, so the assignment has no effect.

Note that this isn't a problem of block objects in general; some methods immediately, or even repeatedly, run a block right away before returning back to you. But in the case of almost all Game Kit methods, the block objects are used exclusively as pieces of code that will be run whenever the Game Center server has responded to a particular request. In other words, the block objects used by Game Kit are run asynchronously after an unspecified delay (and possibly not at all if the connection is interrupted).

Receiving the Local Player's Friend List

When the local player signs in or out, the `onLocalPlayerAuthenticationChanged` method is received and forwarded to the delegate. The delegate in these examples is the `TileMapLayer` class, which implements this method to ask for the local player's friend list in Listing 14-6.

Listing 14-6. Asking for the List of Friends

```
-(void) onLocalPlayerAuthenticationChanged
{
    GKLocalPlayer* localPlayer = GKLocalPlayer.localPlayer;
    if (localPlayer.authenticated)
    {
        GameKitHelper* gkHelper = [GameKitHelper sharedGameKitHelper];
        [gkHelper getLocalPlayerFriends];
    }
}
```

It checks whether the local player is authenticated, and if so, it calls the getLocalPlayerFriends method of the GameKitHelper class right away. Take a look at that in Listing 14-7.

Listing 14-7. GameKitHelper Requesting the Friends List

```
-(void) getLocalPlayerFriends
{
    if (isGameCenterAvailable == NO)
        return;

    GKLocalPlayer* localPlayer = GKLocalPlayer.localPlayer;
    if (localPlayer.authenticated)
    {
        [localPlayer loadFriendsWithCompletionHandler:↵
        ^(NSArray* friends, NSError* error)
        {
            [self setLastError:error];
            if ([delegate respondsToSelector:@selector(onFriendListReceived:)])
            {
                [delegate onFriendListReceived:friends];
            }
        }];
    }
}
```

Because the getLocalPlayerFriends method doesn't know when it's called or by whom, it plays things safe by checking again that the local player is actually authenticated. Then it calls the GKLocalPlayer class's loadFriendsWithCompletionHandler method, for which you'll supply another block object that's run when the server returns a list of player identifiers as strings. Unsurprisingly, this list of identifiers is stored in the friends array.

Once the call to loadFriendsWithCompletionHandler has succeeded, you can access the current player identifiers of the local player's friends through the GKLocalPlayer class:

```
NSArray* friends = GKLocalPlayer.localPlayer.friends;
```

Note that the friends array can be nil or not contain all friends. In the delegate that receives the onFriendsListReceived message, and in all other GameKitHelper delegate methods for that matter, you should check whether the received parameter is nil before working with it. If it's nil, you can refer to the lastError property of the GameKitHelper class to get more information about the error for debugging, logging, or possibly presenting it to the user when it makes sense to do so.

The delegate method onFriendsListReceived simply passes the player identifiers back to GameKitHelper, requesting more info about the player identifiers in the friends list:

```
-(void) onFriendListReceived:(NSArray*)friends
{
    GameKitHelper* gkHelper = [GameKitHelper sharedGameKitHelper];
    [gkHelper getPlayerInfo:friends];
}
```

That's straightforward, so let's turn our attention back to the GameKitHelper class's getPlayerInfo method. If the playerList array contains at least one entry, it will call the loadPlayersForIdentifiers static method of the GKPlayer class, as shown in Listing 14-8.

Listing 14-8. Requesting Players from a List of Player Identifiers

```
-(void) getPlayerInfo:(NSArray*)playerList
{
    if (playerList.count > 0)
    {
        // Get detailed information about a list of players
        [GKPlayer loadPlayersForIdentifiers:playerList withCompletionHandler:↵
        ^(NSArray* players, NSError* error)
        {
            [self setLastError:error];
            if ([delegate respondsToSelector:@selector(onPlayerInfoReceived:)])
            {
                [delegate onPlayerInfoReceived:players];
            }
        }];
    }
}
```

Again, a block object is used to handle the returned results from the server. And as always, the lastError property is updated before calling the delegate's onPlayerInfoReceived method. The players array should now contain a list of GKPlayer class instances, which the delegate then simply prints to the Debugger Console window in the absence of a proper friend list user interface:

```
-(void) onPlayerInfoReceived:(NSArray*)players
{
    for (GKPlayer* gkPlayer in players)
    {
        CCLOG(@"PlayerID: %@, Alias: %@", gkPlayer.playerID, gkPlayer.alias);    }
}
```

The GKPlayer class has only three properties: the player identifier, an alias, and the isFriend flag, which is true for all the players in this particular case. The alias is simply the player's nickname.

If you created a new sandbox account, you won't have any friends, so it's normal for the list to be empty. You can fix that by signing out of Game Center with the Game Center app, creating another account by running your app again, and finally sending a friend request to your previous sandbox account.

Leaderboards

In the IsoTilemap04 project, I added functionality for posting and retrieving leaderboard scores. I hooked into the onPlayerInfoReceived method in the TileMapLayer class to submit a dummy score to Game Center, under the Playtime category:

```
-(void) onPlayerInfoReceived:(NSArray*)players
{
    GameKitHelper* gkHelper = [GameKitHelper sharedGameKitHelper];
    [gkHelper submitScore:1234 category:@"Playtime"];
}
```

The submitScore method shown in Listing 14-9 is implemented in GameKitHelper and calls the onScoresSubmitted message back to the delegate. Because there's no return parameter to pass on, it simply reports through the success value if the score was transmitted without an error.

Listing 14-9. Submitting a Score to a Leaderboard

```
-(void) submitScore:(int64_t)score category:(NSString*)category
{
    if (isGameCenterAvailable == NO)
        return;

    GKScore* gkScore = [[GKScore alloc] initWithCategory:category];
    gkScore.value = score;

    [gkScore reportScoreWithCompletionHandler:↵
    ^(NSError* error)
    {
        [self setLastError:error];

        BOOL success = (error == nil);
        if ([delegate respondsToSelector:@selector(onScoresSubmitted:)])
        {
            [delegate onScoresSubmitted:success];
        }
    }];
}
```

The score value is of type int64_t, which is the same as long long. That's right, long long. The long data type is a 32-bit integer value whereas long long means it's a 64-bit integer value, so it can store an incredibly large number—one with 19 digits. That allows for more than 4 billion times greater values than a regular 32-bit integer can represent!

A temporary GKScore object is created and initialized with a leaderboard category identifier, which you define in iTunes Connect. In this case, the category ID is Playtime. The GKScore object also gets the score assigned, and then its reportScoreWithCompletionHandler method is called, which will transmit the score to the Game Center server and to the correct leaderboard.

The delegate receives the onScoresSubmitted message and subsequently calls the retrieveTopTenAllTimeGlobalScores method to get the top ten scores:

```
-(void) onScoresSubmitted:(bool)success
{
    if (success)
    {
        GameKitHelper* gkHelper = [GameKitHelper sharedGameKitHelper];
        [gkHelper retrieveTopTenAllTimeGlobalScores];
    }
}
```

The GameKitHelper class's retrieveTopTenAllTimeGlobalScores simply wraps the call to retrieveScoresForPlayers and feeds it with preconfigured parameters:

```
-(void) retrieveTopTenAllTimeGlobalScores
{
    [self retrieveScoresForPlayers:nil
                          category:nil
                             range:NSMakeRange(1, 10)
                       playerScope:GKLeaderboardPlayerScopeGlobal
                         timeScope:GKLeaderboardTimeScopeAllTime];
}
```

Feel free to add more wrapper methods for retrieving scores as you see fit, depending on your game's needs. Because there are a variety of ways to retrieve leaderboard scores and several filters to reduce the number of scores retrieved, it makes sense to use wrapper methods to reduce the potential for human error. Listing 14-10 shows the retrieveScoresForPlayers method in full.

Listing 14-10. Retrieving a List of Scores from a Leaderboard

```
-(void) retrieveScoresForPlayers:(NSArray*)players
                        category:(NSString*)category
                           range:(NSRange)range
                     playerScope:(GKLeaderboardPlayerScope)playerScope
                       timeScope:(GKLeaderboardTimeScope)timeScope
{
    if (isGameCenterAvailable == NO)
        return;

    GKLeaderboard* leaderboard = nil;
    if (players.count > 0)
    {
        leaderboard = [[GKLeaderboard alloc] initWithPlayerIDs:players];
    }
    else
    {
        leaderboard = [[GKLeaderboard alloc] init];
        leaderboard.playerScope = playerScope;
    }
```

```
    if (leaderboard != nil)
    {
        leaderboard.timeScope = timeScope;
        leaderboard.category = category;
        leaderboard.range = range;

        [leaderboard loadScoresWithCompletionHandler:↵
        ^(NSArray* scores, NSError* error)
        {
            [self setLastError:error];
            if ([delegate respondsToSelector:@selector(onScoresReceived:)])
            {
                [delegate onScoresReceived:scores];
            }
        }];
    }
}
```

First, a GKLeaderboard object is initialized. Depending on whether the players array contains any players, the leaderboard may be initialized with a list of player identifiers to retrieve scores only for those players. Otherwise, the playerScope variable is used, which can be set to either GKLeaderboardPlayerScopeGlobal or GKLeaderboardPlayerScoreFriendsOnly to retrieve only friends' scores.

Then the leaderboard scope is further reduced by the timeScope parameter, which allows you to obtain the all-time high scores (GKLeaderboardTimeScopeAllTime), only those from the past week (GKLeaderboardTimeScopeWeek), or only today's scores (GKLeaderboardTimeScopeToday).

Of course, you also have to specify the category ID for the leaderboard—otherwise, GKLeaderboard wouldn't know which leaderboard to retrieve the scores from. Finally, an NSRange parameter lets you refine the score positions you'd like to retrieve. In this example, a range of 1 to 10 indicates that the top ten scores should be retrieved.

Make sure you limit the score retrieval using all these parameters (especially the NSRange parameter) to reasonably small chunks of data. Although you could, it's not recommended to retrieve all the scores of a leaderboard. If your game is played online a lot, and many scores are submitted, you might be loading hundreds of thousands—if not millions or billions—of scores from the Game Center servers. That would cause a significant delay when retrieving scores.

With the leaderboard object set up properly, the loadScoresWithCompletionHandler method takes over and asks the server for the scores. When the scores are received, it calls the delegate method with onScoresReceived, passing on the array of scores. The array contains objects of class GKScore sorted by leaderboard rank. The GKScore objects provide you with all the information you need, including the playerID, the date the score was posted, and its rank, value, and formattedValue, which you should use to display the score to the user.

Fortunately for you, Apple provides a default leaderboard user interface. Instead of using the scores I just retrieved, I'll ignore them and use the onScoresReceived delegate method to bring up the built-in leaderboard view:

```
-(void) onScoresReceived:(NSArray*)scores
{
    GameKitHelper* gkHelper = [GameKitHelper sharedGameKitHelper];
    [gkHelper showLeaderboard];
}
```

Game Kit has a GKLeaderboardViewController class, used to display the Game Center leaderboard user interface, as shown in Listing 14-11.

Listing 14-11. Showing the Leaderboard User Interface

```
-(void) showLeaderboard
{
    if (isGameCenterAvailable == NO)
        return;

    GKLeaderboardViewController* leaderboardVC = ↵
        [[GKLeaderboardViewController alloc] init];
    if (leaderboardVC != nil)
    {
        leaderboardVC.leaderboardDelegate = self;
        [self presentViewController:leaderboardVC];
    }
}
```

The leaderboardDelegate is set to self, which means the GameKitHelper class must implement the GKLeaderboardViewControllerDelegate protocol. The GameKitHelper class already implements this protocol:

```
@interface GameKitHelper : NSObject<GKLeaderboardViewControllerDelegate, ↵
    GKAchievementViewControllerDelegate>
{
    ...
}
```

Then you must implement the leaderboardViewControllerDidFinish method, used to simply dismiss the view and to forward the event to the delegate:

```
-(void) leaderboardViewControllerDidFinish:(GKLeaderboardViewController*)viewController
{
    [self dismissModalViewController];
    if ([delegate respondsToSelector:@selector(onLeaderboardViewDismissed)])
    {
        [delegate onLeaderboardViewDismissed];
    }
}
```

Now there's a bit of behind-the-scenes magic going on. I've added a few helper methods to GameKitHelper that deal specifically with presenting and dismissing the various Game Kit view controllers making use of the UINavigationController instance cocos2d sets up in the AppController class. This navigation controller will be used to display the Game Center views, as shown in Listing 14-12.

Listing 14-12. Using Cocos2d's Root View Controller to Present and Dismiss Game Kit Views

```
#import "AppDelegate.h"

...

-(UINavigationController*) appNavigationController
```

```
{
    AppController* app = (AppController*)[UIApplication sharedApplication].delegate;
    return app.navController;
}

-(void) presentViewController:(UIViewController*)vc
{
    UINavigationController* navController = [self appNavigationController];
    [navController presentModalViewController:vc animated:YES];
}

-(void) dismissModalViewController
{
    UINavigationController* navController = [self appNavigationController];
    [navController dismissModalViewControllerAnimated:YES];
}
```

The GKLeaderboardViewController will load the scores it needs automatically and present you with a view like the one in Figure 14-5.

Figure 14-5. The Game Kit leaderboard view

The leaderboard view—and all other Game Kit views, for that matter—is presented in Portrait mode by default, even if your app uses only landscape orientations. This is rather annoying for landscape apps, but there seems to be no obvious way to change this behavior via methods or properties of the view itself.

To allow the Game Kit views to be presented in landscape orientation, you have to extend each Game Kit view with a category and implement (override) the shouldAutorotateToInterfaceOrientation method. You then have it return YES for all the interface orientations the view is allowed to autorotate to. You can use the method UIInterfaceOrientationIsLandscape to force the Game Kit views to be presented in landscape orientation. The following code is an implementation that forces the GKLeaderboardViewController view to display itself in landscape orientation:

```
@interface GKLeaderboardViewController (OrientationFix)
-(BOOL) shouldAutorotateToInterfaceOrientation:↵
    (UIInterfaceOrientation)interfaceOrientation;
@end

@implementation GKLeaderboardViewController (OrientationFix)
-(BOOL) shouldAutorotateToInterfaceOrientation:↵
    (UIInterfaceOrientation)interfaceOrientation
{
    return UIInterfaceOrientationIsLandscape(interfaceOrientation);
}
@end
```

You can apply the same principle to the GKAchievementViewController, the GKMatchmakerViewController and in general to any self-contained, ready-made view controller. This procedure is the only way to force a specific orientation on Game Kit views, and it's not a hack but the recommended (and only) solution.

Achievements

In the IsoTilemap04 project you're also calling the GameKitHelper showAchievements method when the leaderboard view is dismissed. This brings up the Achievements view (Listing 14-13).

Listing 14-13. *Showing the Achievements View*

```
-(void) showAchievements
{
    if (isGameCenterAvailable == NO)
        return;

    GKAchievementViewController* achievementsVC = ↵
        [[GKAchievementViewController alloc] init];
    if (achievementsVC != nil)
    {
        achievementsVC.achievementDelegate = self;
        [self presentViewController:achievementsVC];
    }
}
```

This is very similar to showing the leaderboard view in Listing 14-11. Once more, the GameKitHelper class also has to implement the proper protocol, named GKAchievementViewControllerDelegate:

```
@interface GameKitHelper : NSObject<GKLeaderboardViewControllerDelegate,↵
    GKAchievementViewControllerDelegate>
```

The protocol requires the GameKitHelper class to implement the achievementViewControllerDidFinish method, which is also strikingly similar to the one used by the leaderboard view controller:

```
-(void) achievementViewControllerDidFinish:(GKAchievementViewController*)viewControl
{
    [self dismissModalViewController];
    if ([delegate respondsToSelector:@selector(onAchievementsViewDismissed)])
    {
        [delegate onAchievementsViewDismissed];
    }
}
```

You can see an example of the achievements view in Figure 14-6, in which one achievement is already unlocked. To show the achievements view in landscape mode, refer to the example I presented in the previous heading about leaderboards.

Figure 14-6. The Game Kit achievements view

So, what else can you do with achievements?

Obviously, you want to determine whether an achievement has been unlocked, and actually you want to report all the progress a player makes toward completing an achievement. For example, if the achievement's goal is to eat 476 bananas, then you'd report the progress to Game Center every time the player eats a banana. In this example project, you're simply checking for time elapsed, and then you report progress on the PlayedForTenSecs achievement. You do that in the TileMapLayer's update method, shown in Listing 14-14.

Listing 14-14. Determining Achievement Progress

```
-(void) update:(ccTime)delta
{
    totalTime += delta;
    if (totalTime > 1.0f)
    {
        totalTime = 0.0f;

        NSString* playedTenSeconds = @"PlayedForTenSecs";
        GameKitHelper* gkHelper = [GameKitHelper sharedGameKitHelper];
        GKAchievement* achievement = ↵
            [gkHelper getAchievementByID:playedTenSeconds];
        if (achievement.completed == NO)
        {
            float percent = achievement.percentComplete + 10;
            [gkHelper reportAchievementWithID:playedTenSeconds
                            percentComplete:percent];
        }
    }
    ...
}
```

Every time a second has passed, the achievement with the identifier PlayedForTenSecs is obtained through GameKitHelper. If the achievement isn't completed yet, then its percentComplete property is increased by 10 percent, and the progress is reported through GameKitHelper's reportAchievementWithID method (Listing 14-15).

Listing 14-15. Reporting Achievement Progress

```
-(void) reportAchievementWithID:(NSString*)identifier percentComplete:(float)percent
{
    if (isGameCenterAvailable == NO)
        return;

    GKAchievement* achievement = [self getAchievementByID:identifier];
    if (achievement != nil && achievement.percentComplete < percent)
    {
        achievement.percentComplete = percent;
        [achievement reportAchievementWithCompletionHandler:↵
        ^(NSError* error)
```

```
        {
            [self setLastError:error];
            if ([delegate respondsToSelector:@selector(onAchievementReported:)])
            {
                [delegate onAchievementReported:achievement];
            }
        }];
    }
}
```

To avoid unnecessary calls to the Game Center server, the achievement's `percentComplete` property is verified to actually be smaller than the `percent` parameter. Game Center doesn't allow achievement progress to be reduced and thus will ignore such a report. But if you can avoid actually reporting this to the Game Center server in the first place, you avoid an unnecessary data transfer. With the limited bandwidth available on mobile devices, every bit of data not transmitted is a good thing.

> **Tip**   Reporting an achievement's progress may fail for a number of reasons—for example,
> the device might have lost its Internet connection. Be prepared to save any achievements that
> couldn't be transmitted. Then retry submitting them periodically or when the player logs in the next
> time. The `KKGameKitHelper` class provided with Kobold2D contains additional code to cache
> achievements that failed transmission to the Game Center server..

This still leaves the question open: where do the achievements come from in the first place? They're loaded as soon as the local player signs in. To make this possible, extend the block object used in `authenticateWithCompletionHandler` to call the `loadAchievements` method if there wasn't an error:

```
[localPlayer authenticateWithCompletionHandler:↵
^(NSError* error)
{
    [self setLastError:error];

    if (error == nil)
    {
        [self loadAchievements];
    }
}];
```

The `loadAchievements` method uses the `GKAchievement` class's `loadAchievementsWithCompletionHandler` method to retrieve the local player's achievements from Game Center (Listing 14-16).

Listing 14-16. Loading the Local Player's Achievements

```
-(void) loadAchievements
{
    [GKAchievement loadAchievementsWithCompletionHandler:↵
    ^(NSArray* loadedAchievements, NSError* error)
```

```
    {
        [self setLastError:error];
        if (achievements == nil)
        {
            achievements = [[NSMutableDictionary alloc] init];
        }
        else
        {
            [achievements removeAllObjects];
        }
        for (GKAchievement* achievement in loadedAchievements)
        {
            [achievements setObject:achievement
                            forKey:achievement.identifier];
        }
        if ([delegate respondsToSelector:@selector(onAchievementsLoaded:)])
        {
            [delegate onAchievementsLoaded:achievements];
        }
    }];
}
```

Inside the block object, the achievements member variable is either allocated or has all objects removed from it. This allows you to call the loadAchievements method at a later time to refresh the list of achievements. The returned array loadedAchievements contains a number of GKAchievement instances, which are then transferred to the achievements NSMutableDictionary simply for ease of access. The NSDictionary class lets you retrieve an achievement by its string identifier directly instead of having to iterate over the array and comparing each achievement's identifier along the way. You can see this in the getAchievementByID method in Listing 14-17.

Listing 14-17. *Getting and Optionally Creating an Achievement*

```
-(GKAchievement*) getAchievementByID:(NSString*)identifier
{
    if (isGameCenterAvailable == NO)
        return;

    GKAchievement* achievement = [achievements objectForKey:identifier];

    if (achievement == nil)
    {
        // Create a new achievement object
        achievement = [[GKAchievement alloc] initWithIdentifier:identifier];
        [achievements setObject:achievement forKey:achievement.identifier];
    }

    return achievement;
}
```

This is where you need to be careful. The getAchievementByID method creates a new achievement if it can't find one with the given identifier, assuming that this achievement's progress has never been reported to Game Center before. The loadAchievements method in Listing 14-16 only obtains achievements that have been reported to Game Center at least once. For any other achievement, you have to create it first. So, getAchievementsByID will always return a valid achievement object, but you'll only notice whether that achievement is really set up for your game when you try to report its progress to Game Center.

You can also clear the local player's achievement progress. Do this with great care and not without asking the player's permission. On the other hand, during development, the resetAchievements method in Listing 14-18 comes in handy.

Listing 14-18. Resetting Achievement Progress

```
-(void) resetAchievements
{
    if (isGameCenterAvailable == NO)
        return;

    [achievements removeAllObjects];

    [GKAchievement resetAchievementsWithCompletionHandler:↵
    ^(NSError* error)
    {
        [self setLastError:error];
        BOOL success = (error == nil);
        if ([delegate respondsToSelector:@selector(onResetAchievements:)])
        {
            [delegate onResetAchievements:success];
        }
    }];
}
```

Matchmaking

Now we enter the realm of matchmaking—connecting players and inviting friends to play a game match together. To start hosting a game and to bring up the corresponding matchmaking view, I've added a call to GameKitHelper's showMatchmakerWithRequest method after the achievements view has been dismissed, as shown in Listing 14-19.

Listing 14-19. Preparing to Show the Host Game Screen

```
-(void) onAchievementsViewDismissed
{
    GKLocalPlayer* localPlayer = [GKLocalPlayer localPlayer];
    if (localPlayer.authenticated)
    {
        GKMatchRequest* request = [[GKMatchRequest alloc] init];
        request.minPlayers = 2;
        request.maxPlayers = 4;
```

```
        GameKitHelper* gkHelper = [GameKitHelper sharedGameKitHelper];
        [gkHelper showMatchmakerWithRequest:request];
    }
}
```

A GKMatchRequest instance is created, and its minPlayers and maxPlayers properties are initialized, indicating that the match should have at least two and at most four players. Every match must allow for two players, obviously, and you can create a peer-to-peer match with up to four players. *Peer-to-peer networking* means that all devices are connected with each other and can send and receive data to and from all other devices. This stands in contrast to a server/client architecture, where all players connect to a single server and send and receive only to and from this server. In peer-to-peer networks, the amount of traffic generated grows exponentially, so most peer-to-peer multiplayer games are strictly limited to a very low number of allowed players.

Note   Game Center can connect up to 16 players, but only if you have a hosted server application to manage all matches using client/server architecture. That requires a huge amount of work and know-how to set up and use properly, so I'll leave it out of this discussion and focus only on peer-to-peer networking.

The showMatchmakerWithRequest method is implemented in a strikingly similar way to the code that brings up the leaderboard and achievement views, as Listing 14-20 shows.

Listing 14-20. Showing the Host Game Screen

```
-(void) showMatchmakerWithRequest:(GKMatchRequest*)request
{
    GKMatchmakerViewController* hostVC = [[GKMatchmakerViewController alloc]↵
        initWithMatchRequest:request];
    if (hostVC != nil)
    {
        hostVC.matchmakerDelegate = self;
        [self presentViewController:hostVC];
    }
}
```

Figure 14-7 shows an example matchmaking view, waiting for you to invite a friend to your match. You can also wait until Game Center finds an automatically matched player for your game, but because you're currently developing the game, it's rather unlikely that anyone but you is currently playing it.

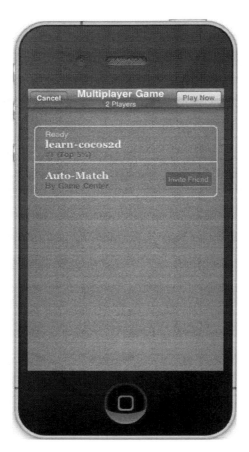

Figure 14-7. The host game matchmaking view

If you followed the leaderboard and achievement view examples, you know that each required the GameKitHelper class to implement a protocol, and with matchmaking it's no different. I also added GKMatchDelegate because you're going to need it soon.

```
@interface GameKitHelper : NSObject< GKLeaderboardViewControllerDelegate,↵
    GKAchievementViewControllerDelegate, GKMatchmakerViewControllerDelegate,↵
    GKMatchDelegate>
```

The GKMatchmakerViewControllerDelegate protocol requires three methods to be implemented: one for the player pressing the Cancel button, one for failing with an error, and one for finding a suitable match. The latter deserves a mention:

```
-(void) matchmakerViewController:(GKMatchmakerViewController*)viewController
            didFindMatch:(GKMatch*)match
```

```
{
    [self dismissModalViewController];
    [self setCurrentMatch:match];
    if ([delegate respondsToSelector:@selector(onMatchFound:)])
    {
        [delegate onMatchFound:match];
    }
}
```

If a match was found, this match is set as the current match, and the delegate's onMatchFound method is called to inform it about the newly found match.

Instead of hosting a match, you can also instruct Game Center to try to automatically find a match for you, as shown in Listing 14-21. If successful, the delegate receives the same onMatchFound message.

Listing 14-21. Searching for an Existing Match

```
-(void) findMatchForRequest:(GKMatchRequest*)request
{
    if (isGameCenterAvailable == NO)
        return;

    GKMatchMaker* matchmaker = [GKMatchMaker sharedMatchmaker];
    [matchmaker findMatchForRequest:request withCompletionHandler:↵
    ^(GKMatch* match, NSError* error)
    {
        [self setLastError:error];

        if (match != nil)
        {
            [self setCurrentMatch:match];
            if ([delegate respondsToSelector:@selector(onMatchFound:)])
            {
                [delegate onMatchFound:match];
            }
        }
    }];
}
```

While Game Center is searching for a match, you should give the user visual feedback, like an animated progress indicator, because finding a match can take several seconds or even minutes. That's where the CCProgressTimer class comes in handy (discussed in Chapter 5). You should also give your user a means to cancel the matchmaking process, and if she does so, you should call the cancelMatchmakingRequest method:

```
-(void) cancelMatchmakingRequest
{
    [[GKMatchmaker sharedMatchmaker] cancel];
}
```

At this point, the match has been created, but all the players might not yet be connected to the match. As players join the game, the match:didChangeState method of the GKMatchDelegate protocol is called for each player connecting or disconnecting. Only when the expectedPlayerCount of the match has been counted down to 0 by the Game Kit framework should you start the match. The GKMatch object updates the expectedPlayerCount property automatically, as Listing 14-22 shows.

Listing 14-22. Waiting for All Players Before Starting the Match

```
-(void) match:(GKMatch*)match player:(NSString*)playerID↩
    didChangeState:(GKPlayerConnectionState)state
{
    switch (state)
    {
        case GKPlayerStateConnected:
            if ([delegate respondsToSelector:@selector(onPlayerConnected:)])
            {
                [delegate onPlayerConnected:playerID];
            }
            break;
        case GKPlayerStateDisconnected:
            if ([delegate respondsToSelector:@selector(onPlayerDisconnected:)])
            {
                [delegate onPlayerDisconnected:playerID];
            }
            break;
    }

    if (matchStarted == NO && match.expectedPlayerCount == 0)
    {
        matchStarted = YES;
        if ([delegate respondsToSelector:@selector(onStartMatch)])
        {
            [delegate onStartMatch];
        }
    }
}
```

If at any time during your game a player drops out and the expectedPlayerCount property becomes greater than 0, you can call addPlayersToMatch to fill up the now empty space with a new player, as in Listing 14-23 (assuming that your game supports players joining a match in progress). Because there's no guarantee that a player will actually be found, you shouldn't interrupt the game while GKMatchmaker is looking for a new player.

Listing 14-23. Adding Players to an Existing Match

```
-(void) addPlayersToMatch:(GKMatchRequest*)request
{
    if (isGameCenterAvailable == NO)
        return;
    if (currentMatch == nil)
        return;

    [[GKMatchmaker sharedMatchmaker] addPlayersToMatch:currentMatch
                                matchRequest:request
                              completionHandler: ↩
```

```
    ^(NSError* error)
    {
        [self setLastError:error];
        BOOL success = (error == nil);
        if ([delegate respondsToSelector:@selector(onPlayersAddedToMatch:)])
        {
            [delegate onPlayersAddedToMatch:success];
        }
    }];
}
```

Sending and Receiving Data

Once all players are connected, and the match has officially started, you can start sending and subsequently receiving data. The easiest way to do that is to send data to all players, as shown in Listing 14-24.

Listing 14-24. Sending and Receiving Data

```
-(void) sendDataToAllPlayers:(void*)data sizeInBytes:(NSUInteger)length
{
    if (isGameCenterAvailable == NO)
        return;

    NSError* error = nil;
    NSData* packet = [NSData dataWithBytes:data length:length];
    [currentMatch sendDataToAllPlayers:packet
                         withDataMode:GKMatchSendDataUnreliable
                                error:&error];
    [self setLastError:error];
}
-(void) match:(GKMatch*)match didReceiveData:(NSData*)data ↵
    fromPlayer:(NSString*)playerID
{
    if ([delegate respondsToSelector:@selector(onReceivedData:fromPlayer:)])
    {
        [delegate onReceivedData:data fromPlayer:playerID];
    }
}
```

The sendDataToAllPlayers method takes a void pointer as input and wraps it into an NSData object. You can send any data as long as you provide the correct length of that data packet. Typically, networked programs send structs like CGPoint (or any custom struct) to make this process easier, because you can then use sizeof(myPoint) to get the length (size in bytes) of such a data structure.

Also, to speed up transmission, most data is sent unreliably. Data that's sent frequently can especially be sent unreliably because if a packet ever gets lost, the clients simply have to wait for the next packet to arrive. If you do need every packet to arrive—for example, because it contains crucial information that's sent only once—then you should set the data mode to GKMatchSendDataReliable. This instructs GameKit to simply transmit the packet again if it couldn't be delivered. Because GameKit has to receive a return packet from clients to acknowledge that they received the packet, this adds additional traffic.

What data you should send and how often you should send it depend entirely on the game itself. The ground rule is to send as little as you can, as rarely as possible. For example, instead of transmitting each player's position every frame, you should send a packet for each movement action, because the movement in the tilemap game is always 32 pixels in one direction and done by a CCMoveAction. So, it's sufficient to send when the move should start and in which direction it should be—that saves a lot of traffic compared to sending each player's position every frame.

In the IsoTilemap04 project you'll get an introduction to sending and receiving packets over a network. The most important aspect to creating network packets is that the receiver must be able to identify the type of packet received by looking at a common header data. Typically, and this is also what the Apple documentation recommends, you define C structs with a common struct field as the first entry for each packet. The NetworkPackets.h file defines the structs, as shown in Listing 14-25.

Listing 14-25. Defining Network Packets as C Structs in NetworkPackets.h

```
typedef enum
{
    kPacketTypeScore = 1,
    kPacketTypePosition,
} EPacketTypes;

typedef struct
{
    EPacketTypes type;
} SBasePacket;

// the packet for transmitting a score variable
typedef struct
{
    EPacketTypes type;

    int score;
} SScorePacket;

// packet to transmit a position
typedef struct
{
    EPacketTypes type;

    CGPoint position;
} SPositionPacket;
```

You'll see that all packet structs have the EPacketTypes type field, and it's the first field in each struct. This allows you to cast any packet to one of type SBasePacket to allow the receiver to inspect the packet type, and based on that, the receiver can then safely cast the struct to the actual packet.

Listing 14-26 shows an example of this. It's the onReceivedData method from the TileMapLayer class.

Listing 14-26. Receiving Packets and Determining Packet Type

```
-(void) onReceivedData:(NSData*)data fromPlayer:(NSString*)playerID
{
    SBasePacket* basePacket = (SBasePacket*)data.bytes;

    switch (basePacket->type)
    {
        case kPacketTypeScore:
        {
            SScorePacket* scorePacket = (SScorePacket*)basePacket;
            CCLOG(@"\tscore = %i", scorePacket->score);
            break;
        }
        case kPacketTypePosition:
        {
            SPositionPacket* positionPacket = (SPositionPacket*)basePacket;

            if (playerID ! = [GKLocalPlayer localPlayer].playerID)
            {
                CCTMXTiledMap* tileMap = ↩
                    (CCTMXTiledMap*)[self getChildByTag:TileMapNode];
                [self centerTileMapOnTileCoord:positionPacket->position
                                    tileMap:tileMap];
            }
            break;
        }
        default:
            CCLOG(@"unknown packet type %i", basePacket->type);
            break;
    }
}
```

This code first casts the received data bytes to a pointer to an SBasePacket struct. Notice in Listing 14-25 that that's the struct that contains only the type field. Because you've declared that all packets must have this field at its first entry, any packet can be safely cast to SBasePacket. The switch statement inspects the type, and depending on the network packet, further processing is done—but not without casting the packet to the actual packet type. For example, if the basePacket->type is kPacketTypeScore, the basePacket is cast to an SScorePacket to allow the code to access the score field.

> **Tip**   When checking packets, it's a good idea to add the default option. You'll frequently add new packets, and from time to time you'll forget to handle this particular packet type on the receiving end. So, logging this as an error or even throwing an exception is recommended. Otherwise, you may see bugs in your app that could be hard to track down.

Actually sending the packets is relatively easy and follows the same principle. You first create a new variable with one of the packet structs as its data type. Then you fill in each field of the struct and pass it to the GameKitHelper method sendDataToAllPlayers.

In Listing 14-27, the packets are created on the stack. You don't need to allocate memory because Game Kit makes a copy of the struct and thus takes over the memory management of the packet. Because sendDataToAllPlayers required a pointer, the packet is prefixed with the reference operator (ampersand character) &packet to denote that the packet variable's address is passed instead of the packet itself.

Listing 14-27. Sending Packets via GameKitHelper

```
// send a bogus score (simply an integer increased every time it is sent)
-(void) sendScore
{
    if ([GameKitHelper sharedGameKitHelper].currentMatch != nil)
    {
        bogusScore++;

        SScorePacket packet;
        packet.type = kPacketTypeScore;
        packet.score = bogusScore;

        [[GameKitHelper sharedGameKitHelper] sendDataToAllPlayers:&packet
                                            sizeInBytes:sizeof(packet)];
    }
}
// send a tile coordinate
-(void) sendPosition:(CGPoint)tilePos
{
    if ([GameKitHelper sharedGameKitHelper].currentMatch != nil)
    {
        SPositionPacket packet;
        packet.type = kPacketTypePosition;
        packet.position = tilePos;

        [[GameKitHelper sharedGameKitHelper] sendDataToAllPlayers:&packet
                                            sizeInBytes:sizeof(packet)];
    }
}
```

The most important part of sending packets is to make sure you set the right packet type. If you assign the wrong packet type, the receiver won't know what to do with the packet. It might mistake it for a different type of packet, causing a crash because the receiver might try to access a nonexisting field. Or the receiver might simply work with unrelated data, causing all kinds of bugs. Imagine the score becoming the player's position, or vice versa. To avoid these kinds of issues, particularly if you have many different packet types, creating methods like createPositionPacket and createScorePacket may be helpful, which you call with all the required parameters for the packet while the method itself fills in the correct packet type.

In Figure 14-8 you can see the Tilemap16 project in action. Every time the player is moved on the iPhone, a position packet is sent over the network. The iPad is connected to the current match, receives the position packet, and moves the player character accordingly.

Figure 14-8. If the player moves on the iPhone, the iPad will update its view from the position packet it received

Summary

I hope this chapter and the provided GameKitHelper class help you get comfortable with Game Center programming. Sure, network programming is no easy task, but I've laid a lot of the groundwork for you, and even block objects are no longer foreign territory for you. In particular, the checklist of tasks to enable Game Center support for your game should help you avoid a lot of the initial pitfalls faced by developers.

Over the course of this chapter, you've become comfortable using the leaderboard and achievement features of Game Center. Those things alone bring your game to a new level. And with the user interface provided by Game Center, you don't even have to write your own user interface to display leaderboards and achievements.

I then introduced you to the matchmaking features of Game Center, which allow you to invite friends to join your game, find random players on the Internet, and allow them to send and receive data.

With this chapter, I departed a little from pure cocos2d programming; in fact, you can apply what you just learned about Game Center to any iOS app. In the next chapter, I tackle another subject that's not pure cocos2d game programming either but is frequently asked for: mixing UIKit views with cocos2d.

Chapter **15**

Cocos2d and UIKit Views

For most iOS developers there's a clear dividing line: if you want to program "regular" apps with no or little multimedia content, you'll be using Cocoa Touch and its UIKit framework to create the iPhone's and iPad's native user interfaces.

But if you want to develop iOS games and multimedia applications, you want to use cocos2d and have little incentive to use anything but CCSprite and CCMenu to create your game's scenes and user interfaces.

A great number of developers are experienced only in either environment, and they often find it confusing to cross the border from Cocoa Touch to cocos2d and vice versa. In almost all these cases, the programmers want to combine the best of both worlds, leveraging their existing knowledge of either Cocoa Touch or cocos2d to create hybrid applications.

Because Cocoa Touch and cocos2d work fundamentally in different ways and require a different mind-set, it's usually not straightforward to create such hybrids. This chapter will help you transition in both directions. You'll learn how to add Cocoa Touch views and features to a cocos2d application; at the same time, you'll also learn how you can plug in cocos2d to an existing Cocoa Touch application.

What Is Cocoa Touch?

Cocoa Touch is the name of the application programming interface (API) used to create iOS applications. It's of course inspired by Cocoa, the API for programming Mac OS X applications.

Cocoa Touch is comprised of several frameworks, including Core Animation, Core Data, Map Kit, Store Kit, and Web Kit, just to name a few. But strictly speaking, even cocos2d is a Cocoa Touch library because the OpenGL ES framework, as well as Core Audio, OpenAL, and AV Foundation (AV stands for Audio/Video) frameworks that cocos2d is built on, are part of Cocoa Touch.

It's no wonder then that most programmers refer specifically to UIKit when they're asking about how to integrate Cocoa Touch views into cocos2d. UIKit is the framework that provides programmers with the native iOS controls and views used to build the graphical user interfaces (GUIs) of iOS applications. At the same time, other frameworks such as iAd, Web Kit, Game Kit, and Map Kit typically include specialized views, and they're mostly built with the GUI elements provided by UIKit.

So, technically, even if programmers discuss integration issues of Game Center with cocos2d, they often refer to the views as being part of UIKit, even though the actual view is provided by Game Kit or Web Kit, for example. For reference, here are the cocos2d forum topics tagged with UIKit and Cocoa Touch:

```
http://www.cocos2d-iphone.org/forum/tags/uikit
http://www.cocos2d-iphone.org/forum/tags/cocoa-touch
```

Using Cocoa Touch and cocos2d Together

Before you get to work with the code in this chapter, I want to step back for a moment and discuss why one would want to mix cocos2d with Cocoa Touch (UIKit views), what the limitations are, and what the differences between Cocoa Touch and cocos2d are.

Why Mix Cocoa Touch with cocos2d?

There are many good reasons to mix Cocoa Touch and cocos2d. Essentially, they all boil down to a better user experience or faster development.

For one, if you're a cocos2d programmer, you'll be adding some Cocoa Touch views to your application sooner or later, most commonly to generate some revenue with iAd or if you're writing a Game Center–enabled game. But you also might want to provide users with a native-looking user interface, which you can design efficiently with Interface Builder and later skin with textures that maintain the game's look and feel so that your user interface doesn't look like the Settings app. A great example of such a skinned app is Carcassone—you have to look twice to see that its user interface is actually entirely made with UIKit views.

Although you can make reasonably good user interfaces with cocos2d, there's simply a much greater variety of already existing controls available from UIKit that cocos2d doesn't provide. Cocos2d provides CCMenu and that's about it in terms of user interface controls. And the occasional reimplementation of popular UIKit views in cocos2d always lacks in feel and features. Sliders, on/off toggle buttons, navigation views, and tab bars can all be highly useful in designing your game's user interface, especially in those games or parts of the game where performance is not of the utmost importance.

If you're a Cocoa Touch programmer and you need some multimedia content in your game, it's much easier to rely on cocos2d to do that job and do it with high performance rather than programming it directly with OpenGL ES. After all, cocos2d shields you from OpenGL ES and provides an interface that's much easier to use.

Cocoa Touch does provide powerful graphical frameworks like Core Graphics and Core Animation. But they suffer from a major disadvantage: they're often not fast enough for real-time games. They were designed to display and animate user interface elements, not games.

Limitations of Mixing Cocoa Touch with cocos2d

When designing your app or game that mixes Cocoa Touch views with the cocos2d view, you should be aware of some limitations. Most obviously, UIKit views aren't designed for high performance, so you may notice a drop in performance, especially if you use UIKit views in fast-paced games and during game play.

For example, it's more favorable for performance to rely on `CCLabelBMFont` to display the score during game play than using a UITextField for the same purpose. And likewise, you should prefer to use `CCMenu` for the in-game pause menu button rather than using a UIButton. In menu screens, though, those performance considerations are usually not a problem, and you can see improved productivity from being able to use Interface Builder to create your menu screens.

You should also be aware that any UIKit view can only be either in front of the entire cocos2d view or entirely behind it. You can't have a UIKit view that's in front of some of the cocos2d scene's sprites, labels, effects, and so on, while at the same time being behind other cocos2d sprites, labels, effects, or other nodes. In other words, you can't "sandwich" a UIKit view between two or more cocos2d nodes.

You can do the opposite, however, although with some limitations and manual labor. You can "sandwich" the cocos2d view: UIKit views in the background, then a transparent cocos2d view with some nodes, and then some more UIKit views in the foreground. This approach requires a little more work setting up the view hierarchy and making the cocos2d view transparent. Imagine playing a full-motion video in the background, over which you draw cocos2d sprites, and the rest of the user interface is made up of UIKit views.

But touch input remains a problem: either the UIKit views and not the cocos2d view will receive input, or those UIKit views added to the cocos2d view and the cocos2d view itself will receive input but not the views in the background. This has to do with the fact that the cocos2d view receives all touches on the screen simply because it occupies the entire screen. So, you need to write additional code to process the touches on the cocos2d view and then decide whether the cocos2d view should forward the touches—for example, if the user didn't touch any of the cocos2d sprites currently displayed on screen.

Allowing all views to receive input is possible, and I'll provide you with a basic solution later in this chapter. But it's up to you to improve and adapt it for your own needs. Depending on your needs, the necessary code changes may actually be substantial and challenging in order to fully support UIKit views both in front of the cocos2d view and behind it and have all views reacting properly to touch input.

How Is Cocoa Touch Different from cocos2d?

Let's take a look at the major differences of Cocoa Touch programming compared to working with cocos2d. One difference is the Model-View-Controller pattern common to Cocoa Touch applications but essentially missing from cocos2d. And then you also have to consider the differences caused by cocos2d's OpenGL ES view because it behaves differently in some aspects than a regular `UIView`.

The Model-View-Controller Pattern

Probably the first and biggest difference for programmers coming from a Cocoa Touch background is that cocos2d doesn't strictly adhere to the Model-View-Controller (MVC) pattern, which is commonplace in Cocoa and Cocoa Touch.

The MVC pattern divides the programming tasks into the three subsets: model, view, and controller. The model contains any algorithms that run behind the scenes and maintains the state of the world; in essence, the model represents knowledge. The view is the visual representation of the model and renders the current state of the world based on the model data. And the controller essentially provides a means for the user to interact with the world through user input, but it's also used to react to other external events such as receiving data over the network. The model, view, and controller are each separate classes to decouple the user interface from business (or game) logic.

In games, you can apply the MVC pattern, and many have attempted to do so with cocos2d. You'll find a good number of articles on the subject if you search for *cocos2d mvc*, and my personal favorite treatment of the subject is this two-part article by Bartek Wilczyński:

```
http://xperienced.com.pl/blog/how-to-implement-mvc-pattern-in-cocos2d-game
http://xperienced.com.pl/blog/how-to-implement-mvc-pattern-in-cocos2d-gamepart-2
```

For Cocoa Touch programmers, the fact that cocos2d doesn't follow the MVC pattern may come as a culture shock. But it's one you can work around. On the other hand, as a cocos2d programmer, you likely won't even notice that you're using MVC because the entire Cocoa Touch framework is designed for the MVC pattern. You'll happily use the controllers and views provided to you, and you'll find no problem adding the logic and algorithms (the model) into either controller or view, or both. That's also a valid pattern, albeit more tightly coupled and less maintainable in large projects.

Cocos2d's View Uses OpenGL ES

Instead of relying on UIKit for displaying its graphics, cocos2d creates an OpenGL ES view. This means cocos2d has more direct access to graphics resources and can render its view much faster.

Of course, behind the scenes, all UIKit views are also rendered by OpenGL ES; there's just a lot more stuff going behind the scenes that's needed for graphical user interfaces but is essentially a waste of performance if you want to make games. You may remember the very early games that were written entirely with UIKit, Core Graphics, and Core Animation? If not, good for you. They were often slow and unresponsive.

One immediately noticeable difference between Cocoa Touch and cocos2d is the coordinate system. Cocos2d has the origin point (0,0) at the lower left-hand corner of the screen, whereas UIKit views have their origin point at the upper left-hand corner. You need to consider the differences in coordinate systems used by UIKit and OpenGL ES when positioning but also when manually rotating UIKit views.

And because cocos2d is programmed to interact directly with the graphics hardware, it uses its own hierarchy of displaying graphical elements. In cocos2d that's the CCNode hierarchy where you can add any CCNode-based class to any other CCNode, with a CCScene as the very first element in that hierarchy. The UIKit framework, on the other hand, operates with a view hierarchy where you add UIView-based classes to another, often with a UIWindow as the topmost element. Both view hierarchies are incompatible, so you can't add a UIView to a CCNode, and vice versa. This is noticeable when you change from one CCScene to another using a CCTransitionScene. While the cocos2d nodes all move aside, the UIKit views remains fixed in place unless you also move them separately and in sync with the cocos2d animation. It's actually a good idea to avoid this kind of situation in the first place.

Alert: Your First UIKit View in cocos2d

The simplest and most straightforward example for using a UIKit view with cocos2d is found in the example project CocosWithCocoa01. It displays a UIAlertView on top of the cocos2d scene created from the default cocos2d project template. To re-create the project from scratch, open Xcode and go to File ➤ New ➤ New Project to bring up the New Project dialog. In that dialog, select cocos2d under the iOS list and create the cocos2d project.

Let's modify the HelloWorldLayer class to display a UIAlertView. The interface in HelloWorldLayer.h needs only one small addition; namely, the HelloWorldLayer class needs to support the UIAlertViewDelegate protocol:

```
@interface HelloWorldLayer : CCLayer <UIAlertViewDelegate>
{
}
```

All other changes are made to the HelloWorldLayer.m implementation file. The init method of the "Hello World" sample is modified to use a color gradient background, just so you see the visual effect of the UIAlertView darkening the screen, and to call the showAlertView method.

```
-(id) init
{
    if ((self = [super init]))
    {
        CCLayerGradient* layer = [CCLayerGradient layerWithColor:ccc4(100,150,255,255)
                                                        fadingTo:ccc4(255,200,50,100)
                                                     alongVector:ccp(0.75f, 0.25f)];
        [self addChild:layer];

        CCLabelTTF *label = [CCLabelTTF labelWithString:@"Hello World"
                                               fontName:@"Marker Felt"
                                               fontSize:64];
        CGSize size = [CCDirector sharedDirector].winSize;
        label.position = ccp(size.width / 2, size.height / 2);
        [self addChild:label];

        self.isTouchEnabled = YES;
        [self showAlertView];
    }
    return self;
}
```

The showAlertView method allocates a UIAlertView with a title, two buttons, and the message text "Hello Cocoa Touch!" For a delegate, you'll be using self now that you've added the UIAlertViewDelegate protocol to the HelloWorldLayer class.

Finally, you can show the alert view. Listing 15-1 shows the resulting code.

Listing 15-1. A UIAlertView Is Created and Shown over cocos2d's View (CCGLView Class)

```
-(void) showAlertView
{
    UIAlertView* alertView = [[UIAlertView alloc] initWithTitle:@"UIAlertView Example"
                                                  message:@"Hello Cocoa Touch!"
                                                  delegate:self
                                          cancelButtonTitle:@"Well"
                                          otherButtonTitles:@"Done", nil];
    [alertView show];
}
```

> **Tip**   It's not necessary to add a UIAlertView to another view. This makes it very straightforward
> to create UIAlertView messages. The only drawback is that UIAlertView will always be drawn
> above everything else and will swallow all touches as long as it's displayed. No amount of sending
> views to back or reordering the view hierarchy will change that. If you need a simple solution for
> a pause menu, UIAlertView is your cheap and dirty friend, especially during development. But
> keep in mind that while touches are disabled, you'll still be receiving acceleration events, which
> you'll have to turn off or ignore while the UIAlertView is shown.

The HelloWorldLayer class will receive all events from the UIAlertView and can respond to them
by simply implementing one or more of the UIAlertViewDelegate methods. For this example,
I decided to respond to the didDismissWithButtonIndex message (see Listing 15-2), which
is sent whenever the user taps a button, which always dismisses the UIAlertView regardless
of which button was tapped. Another CCLabelTTF, with a string and color that depend on the
buttonIndex, is added to the cocos2d scene at a random position every time the alert view is
dismissed.

Listing 15-2. Responding to the UIAlertView didDismissWithButtonIndex Message

```
-(void) alertView:(UIAlertView*)alertView↵
    didDismissWithButtonIndex:(NSInteger)buttonIndex
{
    NSString* message = @"Well";
    ccColor3B labelColor = ccYELLOW;
    if (buttonIndex == 1)
    {
        message = @"Done";
        labelColor = ccGREEN;
    }
    CCLabelTTF* label = [CCLabelTTF labelWithString:message
                                     fontName:@"Arial"
                                     fontSize:32];
    CGSize size = [CCDirector sharedDirector].winSize;
```

```
label.position = CGPointMake(CCRANDOM_0_1() * size.width,↵
    CCRANDOM_0_1() * size.height);
label.color = labelColor;
[self addChild:label];

// keep the alert view alive by bringing it up again
[self showAlertView];
}
```

The showAlertView method is called again whenever the alert view has been dismissed, so the alert view will keep showing up again, allowing you to add another label to the cocos2d view. You can see the result in Figure 15-1.

Figure 15-1. A UIAlertView is displayed over the cocos2d view

Embedding UIKit Views in a cocos2d App

Next you'll be embedding more commonly used UIKit views in cocos2d. One of the simplest and most common is the UITextField, which you'll add on top of cocos2d, as you've done before. It gets more complicated when you move it to the background of cocos2d, which requires making the cocos2d view transparent.

Finally, I'll show you how you can add your Interface Builder views into a cocos2d app, instead of creating the views programmatically.

Adding Views in Front of the cocos2d View

In the CocosWithCocoa01 project, I've added UITextField views on top of the cocos2d view. The UITextField is a simple text entry box that automatically brings up the iPhone keyboard when you tap it.

```
-(void) addSomeTextFields
{
    // regular text field with rounded corners
    UITextField* textField = [[UITextField alloc] initWithFrame:↵
        CGRectMake(40, 20, 200, 24)];
    textField.text = @"Regular UITextField";
    textField.borderStyle = UITextBorderStyleRoundedRect;

    // get the cocos2d view (it's the CCGLView class which inherits from UIView)
    UIView* glView = [CCDirector sharedDirector].view;

    // add the text field view to the cocos2d CCGLView
    [glView addSubview:textField];
}
```

It's important to note that the process of programmatically creating any UIView class is very similar to how you create the UITextField. You pick the desired class derived from UIView and then call alloc and initWithFrame. You can create most UIView controls by just providing a frame rectangle. However, you usually have to set some properties afterward to configure the control; in this example, I've set the textField to use the rounded style as well as setting the initial text.

Caution The frame rectangle is where many programmers first notice the different coordinate systems of cocos2d nodes and UIView classes. Whereas in cocos2d the origin (0, 0) is at the lower left-hand corner of the screen, the origin for UIView classes is at the upper left-hand corner of the screen. This means that the UITextField is actually 20 pixels below the top border of the screen and not 20 pixels above the bottom border. You'll have to keep this in mind when working with UIView classes.

Because the UITextField, like most other UIView classes, doesn't have a show method, you need some other way to attach it to the view hierarchy. Because the cocos2d view is the CCGLView class, which in turn inherits from UIView, you can simply add the UITextField to the cocos2d view as a subview. The CCDirector has a view property that lets you access the cocos2d view and then call the addSubview method on it to add the textField. By default this adds the view on top of the cocos2d view.

If you try this now, you'll see a text field on your scene, and when you tap the text field, the iPhone keyboard will come up, and you can start editing text. No extra code needed. Except the keyboard won't go away anymore.

That's by design because the Return key might be a valid key to start a new line rather than to stop editing. So, you need some way to dismiss the keyboard. To do so, open the HelloWorldLayer header file and add the UITextFieldDelegate protocol like so:

```
@interface HelloWorldLayer : CCLayer <UIAlertViewDelegate, UITextFieldDelegate>
{
}
```

Doing so allows the `HelloWorldLayer` class to respond to `UITextFieldDelegate` methods like `textFieldShouldReturn`. For this to work, you must assign the `HelloWorldLayer` class instance to the `UITextField` by assigning `self` to the delegate property. Add the bold line at the end of the initialization block of the `UITextField`:

```
// regular text field with rounded corners
UITextField* textField = [[UITextField alloc] initWithFrame:↵
    CGRectMake(40, 20, 200, 24)];
textField.text = @"  Regular UITextField";
textField.borderStyle = UITextBorderStyleRoundedRect;
textField.delegate = self;
```

Most UIKit views have this delegate method and an accompanying delegate protocol. So, if you ever wonder how you can respond to events of a certain `UIView`, it's usually done by implementing the class's accompanying delegate protocol and responding to the appropriate message. Of course, one very common and repeated mistake you'll make (I know I do) is to forget to actually assign the delegate to the class interface. So, whenever a delegate method isn't being called, or you get a compiler warning on the line where you assign the delegate object, you should check whether that object's class uses and implements the view's delegate protocol.

In our case, the `textFieldShouldReturn` message of the `UITextFieldDelegate` protocol is sent whenever the user taps the Return key on the iPhone keyboard:

```
-(BOOL) textFieldShouldReturn:(UITextField *)textField
{
    // dismiss the keyboard
    [textField resignFirstResponder];

    // if the text is empty, remove the text field
    if (textField.text.length == 0)
    {
        [textField removeFromSuperview];
    }
    return YES;
}
```

By sending the `resignFirstResponder` message to the `textField`, the keyboard will be dismissed. Simply as an exercise on how to remove a UIView from the cocos2d view, I've added a condition that sends the `removeFromSuperview` message to the `textField` if the `textField` is empty when the user presses Return. Notice how this entire method doesn't care which `UITextField` is sending the message, nor does it care where in the view hierarchy the `textField` was added. You'll take advantage of that next by adding another `UITextField`.

If you try what you have so far, you'll notice that the keyboard is dismissed when you press Return, and if you've deleted all characters from the text field, the entire text field will vanish.

> **Tip**   Keep in mind that if it's possible that your scene changes while the user is editing text in a
> UITextField, you would have to manually send the resignFirstResponder message to all
> text fields in order to dismiss the keyboard. Otherwise, the keyboard may remain visible during and
> after the scene change, and the user won't be able to dismiss it anymore. To avoid this situation,
> it's preferable to also respond to the textFieldDidBeginEditing message and use that to
> temporarily disable any buttons or events that could change the current scene. Then reenable the
> buttons or events when you receive the textFieldShouldReturn message.

Skinning the UITextField with a UIImage

No, I'm not going to peel off the text field's skin! If you haven't heard the term *skinning* before, it
basically means adding (or changing) a texture to a user interface control or view. Essentially you
change the native look of the control or view and replace it with your own.

In Listing 15-3 you're adding some more code at the bottom of the addSomeTextFields method
in order to create a second UITextField that uses a texture as background.

Listing 15-3. Skinning a UITextField View

```
-(void) addSomeTextFields
{
    ...

    // text field that uses an image as background (aka "skinning")
    UITextField* textFieldSkinned = [[UITextField alloc] initWithFrame:↵
        CGRectMake(40, 60, 200, 24)];
    textFieldSkinned.text = @"With background image";
    textFieldSkinned.delegate = self;

    // load and assign the UIImage as background of the text field
    CCFileUtils* fileUtils = [CCFileUtils sharedFileUtils];
    NSString* file = [fileUtils fullPathFromRelativePath:@"background-frame.png"];
    UIImage* image = [[UIImage alloc] initWithContentsOfFile:file];
    textFieldSkinned.background = image;

    // get the cocos2d view (it's the CCGLView class which inherits from UIView)
    UIView* glView = [CCDirector sharedDirector].view;

    // add the text field view to the cocos2d CCGLView
    [glView addSubview:textField];
    [glView addSubview:textFieldSkinned];
}
```

Creating the UITextField should be familiar, and you also add self as a delegate of the text
field. The code that dismisses the keyboard and removes the text field when it's empty (see
Listing 15-2) now works for this new UITextField as well.

The next part is what cocos2d users with little or no Cocoa Touch programming experience
may find odd. You can't just add a CCSprite or the sprite's texture to a UIView. You need a

UIImage class for skinning Cocoa Touch views, which you can then comfortably create via initWithContentsOfFile. Or not? Well, the returned UIImage might be nil.

It turns out that cocos2d allows you to use filenames without specifying a path because internally it adds the path to the application's bundle file for you. This full path to a bundle file looks something like this on an iOS device, and the path will be different when running the app in the Simulator or on another device:

```
/var/mobile/Applications/...lots of letters.../CocosWithCocoa.app/background-frame.png
```

Because UIImage and most other Cocoa Touch classes dealing with files expect the full path to the file, you have to use the CCFileUtils method fullPathFromRelativePath to create an NSString, which contains the full path to the file in the app bundle. Then you get a valid UIImage, and you can assign it to the background property. You can see what this looks like in Figure 15-2.

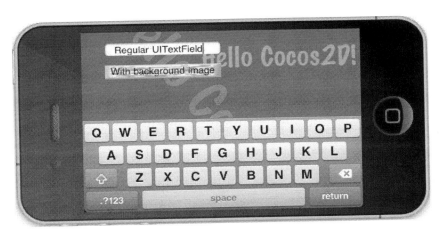

Figure 15-2. Two UITextField views with the iPhone keyboard raised

Tip   The background image of a UIView will always be scaled and stretched to fit the UIView's frame. This will often blur or otherwise distort the texture. To avoid that, you should design background images of UIViews to the exact dimensions of the UIView. Alternatively, design the texture for the largest possible size of the UIView so that even if it's scaled, it's scaled down and doesn't lose as much image quality compared to upscaling the texture.

Adding Views Behind the cocos2d View

What if you want to add a UIView behind the cocos2d view? For example, to play a video in the background? You need to change a few things to allow UIKit views in the background. You'll find these code changes in the CocosWithCocoa02 project.

Moving the UITextFields to the Background

Adding the UITextField views to the app's window is straightforward. For this example, you get to skip over the UITextField initialization code in the addSomeTextFields method because it doesn't change. The only change is in adding the UITextField views as subviews of the cocos2d view's superview, which happens to be the app's UIWindow object:

```
-(void) addSomeTextFields
{
    // get the cocos2d view (it's the CCGLView class which inherits from UIView)
    UIView* glView = [CCDirector sharedDirector].view;
    // The window is the superview of the cocos2d view
    UIView* window = glView.superview;

    // UITextField initialization code omitted
    ...

    // add the text fields to the window
    [window addSubview:textField];
    [window addSubview:textFieldSkinned];
}
```

You can simply access the window because it happens to be the superview of the cocos2d glView . The *superview* is the Cocoa term for what you would call the parent node in the cocos2d node hierarchy. You can then add the text fields to the window instead of the glView.

However, you won't notice a difference if you run the project now. Because you've added the text fields after the cocos2d view, they're automatically rendered after the cocos2d view by default. This is the same behavior as in the cocos2d node hierarchy. To actually move the text fields to the back, you can either send the sendSubviewToBack message to all of them or, more easily, send the bringSubviewToFront message to the glView, like so:

```
    // add the text fields to the window
    [window addSubview:textField];
    [window addSubview:textFieldSkinned];

    // send the cocos2d view to the front so it is in front of the other views
    [window bringSubviewToFront:glView];
```

Note that the sendSubviewToBack and bringSubviewToFront messages are sent to the view that contains the view that should be sent to the back or front. In this case, that's the window. If you run the project now, you'll see a difference. But you won't be seeing the text fields anymore. What's the problem now?

Making the cocos2d View Transparent

By default, the cocos2d view is completely opaque. Anything behind the glView will be obstructed because the cocos2d CCGLView is filled each frame with an opaque clear color. It also has its opaque property set to YES. You can easily remedy this by adding the following lines to the addSomeTextFields method:

```
// make the cocos2d view transparent
glClearColor(0, 0, 0, 0);
glView.opaque = NO;
```

The opaque flag is set to NO, and the glClearColor is all zero. It's not strictly necessary to use a black color however; it's sufficient to reduce the alpha channel (fourth parameter) of glClearColor so that the clear color is at least somewhat transparent. But for this example and in most cases, you don't want the background to be tinted or just partially opaque. You may also wonder why setting the view's opaque property to NO isn't enough to make the view transparent. The answer is simple: OpenGL ES doesn't respect that property and draws its clear color anyway.

This is only half of the story. What's easy to forget and something you just have to know is that cocos2d's CCGLView has to be set up with a pixelFormat that actually uses an alpha channel. Without the alpha channel, you can't make the cocos2d view transparent.

By default, cocos2d initialized the CCGLView with the kEAGLColorFormatRGB565 pixel format. This pixel format uses 16 bits per pixel and has no alpha channel. The only other pixelFormat currently supported is kEAGLColorFormatRGBA8, which has 8 bits per color channel plus an 8-bit alpha channel, which results in 32 bits per pixel. Obviously, this has an impact on performance and memory usage because the framebuffer memory size doubles. That's the reason why the kEAGLColorFormatRGB565 pixel format is the default, but there's really no other choice than to use kEAGLColorFormatRGBA8 if you want to make the cocos2d view transparent.

Open the AppDelegate.m file, and in the applicationDidFinishLaunching method look for the line that initialized the CCGLView. Then change that to use the kEAGLColorFormatRGBA8 pixel format:

```
CCGLView *glView = [CCGLView viewWithFrame:[window bounds]
                          pixelFormat:kEAGLColorFormatRGBA8
                          depthFormat:0];
```

Kobold2D users can make that change in the config.lua file by changing the GLViewColorFormat setting accordingly:

```
GLViewColorFormat = GLViewColorFormat.RGBA8888,
```

Now you can run the app again, and you'll see the "Hello Cocos2D!" labels being drawn over the text fields. There's only one issue remaining: the text fields underneath the cocos2d view won't respond to your touches!

Properly Propagating Touch Events via Hit Testing

The easiest way to have the views behind the cocos2d view respond to touch events is to completely disable touch input on the cocos2d view. You won't be receiving any messages from the CCTouchDispatcher anymore if you add this line:

```
// This will disable all touch events on the cocos2d view
glView.userInteractionEnabled = NO;
```

Now the text fields behind the cocos2d view will act normally, but touch input for the cocos2d view is disabled. UIKit views, which are in front of the cocos2d view, should also work normally and respond to touches, unless you've added them to the cocos2d glView directly instead of the window.

You may be wondering why disabling touch input on the cocos2d view is the best, or at least the easiest, option. For that, you have to understand that the cocos2d view is a UIView that spans the entire screen area. Although you can see through it now that you've set it up to be transparent, it still responds positively to the UIView hitTest event. After all, any touch is somewhere on the screen, and because the cocos2d view is as big as the screen and doesn't take into account what's actually displayed inside its view, it responds positively to the hit test. So, any touch that reaches the cocos2d view will be processed by it or the CCTouchDispatcher class. Anything underneath the cocos2d view is cut off from receiving touch events.

Unfortunately, cocos2d doesn't have a built-in system to forward the hitTest event to its nodes for them to decide whether they actually need to respond to the touch. I present you with a solution that uses the node's bounding boxes and requires extending the CCGLView class with a category.

> **Caution**   Only add the following hit test code to the CCGLView class if you absolutely need it in your project. It will have a negative effect on performance whenever a touch event is fired, which is basically the whole time the user has at least one finger on the touchscreen. The more nodes there are in your scene, the larger the performance penalty will be.

Open the HelloWorldLayer.h file and add this category interface, preferably before the HelloWorldLayer interface:

```
@interface CCGLView (hittest)
-(UIView*) hitTest:(CGPoint)point withEvent:(UIEvent*)event;
@end
```

Now at the beginning of the HelloWorldLayer.m file add the CCGLView hit test category implementation shown in Listing 15-4. The hitTest method is part of the UIView class and gets called when the UIKit framework is trying to determine which view wants to respond to a touch event. The method either returns a UIView instance, which should receive the touch input, or returns nil to signal that the hit test was unsuccessful, in which case the UIKit framework keeps looking for other views that might want to process the touch event.

Listing 15-4. Preparing to Hit Test All cocos2d Scene Children

```
@implementation CCGLView (hittest)

...

-(UIView*) hitTest:(CGPoint)point withEvent:(UIEvent*)event
{
    UIView* hitView = [super hitTest:point withEvent:event];

    if (hitView == self)
    {
        CCScene* runningScene = [CCDirector sharedDirector].runningScene;
        CCArray* sceneChildren = runningScene.children;
        CGPoint glPoint = [[CCDirector sharedDirector] convertToGL:point];
```

```
        BOOL hit = [self hitTestNodeChildren:sceneChildren point:glPoint];
        return (hit ? self : nil);
    }
    return hitView;
}
@end
```

In this case, you first call the super implementation to receive the view the `hitTest` would normally return. In almost all cases, this will be the `CCGLView` itself, but because you can add subviews to the `CCGLView`, it might return a subview, and in this case you want to allow the subview to handle the touch.

Otherwise, the `runningScene` is obtained from the `CCDirector`, which gives you access to the cocos2d node hierarchy via the `children` array. Because the `hitTest` point is in Cocoa Touch coordinates, you also have to convert it to GL coordinates before passing both the `sceneChildren` and the `glPoint` to the `hitTestNodeChildren` method shown in Listing 15-5. If that method returns a hit, the `hitTest` responds by returning `self`. Otherwise, it lets the `hitTest` fail by returning `nil`, allowing all views behind the cocos2d view to take their turn and proceed with the hit testing.

The `hitTestNodeChildren` method in Listing 15-5 is more complicated and harder to understand because it uses recursion to traverse the cocos2d node hierarchy. In other words, the function can call itself to go even deeper into the cocos2d node hierarchy. Add the `hitTestNodeChildren` method just above the `hitTest` method.

Listing 15-5. Recursively Testing All Nodes to Test If Their boundingBox Contains a Given Point

```
@implementation CCGLView (hittest)
-(BOOL) hitTestNodeChildren:(CCArray*)children point:(CGPoint)point
{
    BOOL hit = NO;

    if (children.count > 0)
    {
        Class sceneClass = [CCScene class];
        Class layerClass = [CCLayer class];

        for (CCNode* node in children)
        {
            // check the node's children first
            hit = [self hitTestNodeChildren:node.children point:point];

            // abort search on first hit
            if (hit)
            {
                break;
            }

            // scenes/layers are typically full screen, so do not hitTest them
            if ([node isKindOfClass:sceneClass] || [node isKindOfClass:layerClass])
            {
                continue;
            }
```

```
                // check the node itself
                hit = CGRectContainsPoint(node.boundingBox, point);

                // abort search on first hit
                if (hit)
                {
                    break;
                }
            }
        }

        return hit;

}
...

@end
```

The first half of the `for` loop simply traverses deeper into the cocos2d node hierarchy by calling the function recursively with the current node's children. If any of the recursive calls have found a hit, the loop is aborted right there.

In the second half, the actual node being iterated is checked. This performs the actual hit test by first making sure you're not testing a `CCScene` or `CCLayer` class node. The reason is that they both typically have their `boundingBox` set to the entire screen area. If you'd test any of these classes, you'd always "hit" them, and that's exactly what you're trying to avoid.

Now that you're sure the test is on a node with a reasonable bounding box, the actual check is as simple as testing for whether the point is inside the `boundingBox`:

```
hit = CGRectContainsPoint(node.boundingBox, point);
```

Again, if there was a hit, the loop aborts, and the method returns. This is an optimization because you only ever need to find any node that responds positively to the hit test.

Obviously, this solution has some drawbacks. For one, it assumes that a node should get a touch event if the touch is inside its `boundingBox`. What it doesn't know is whether there's some kind of game state that would prevent the node from processing the touch—for example, if the node is a `CCMenuItem` that's currently disabled. Or if the touch is on a sprite that actually performs a pixel-perfect collision check; in that case, the bounding box check is too broad. Moreover, the `boundingBox` is excessively large when the node is rotated because it's an axis-aligned bounding box that changes in size as the node rotates.

What you can do to alleviate this situation is add a `hitTest` method to a `CCNode` class category, which performs just the bounding box check by default but can be overridden by subclasses to perform more accurate or conditional checks.

Sandwiching the cocos2d View

Just to complete this test, I'd like to add another text field—but in front of the cocos2d view so that you truly have a sandwiched cocos2d view with UIKit views in the back and in the front, and all of them can respond to touches.

The change is rather simple; just add this code at the end of the `addSomeTextFields` method and make sure you add the `textFieldFront` as subview of the `window` and not the `glView`:

```
UITextField* textFieldFront = [[UITextField alloc] initWithFrame:↵
    CGRectMake(280, 40, 200, 24)];
textFieldFront.text = @"  On top of Cocos2D";
textFieldFront.borderStyle = UITextBorderStyleRoundedRect;
textFieldFront.delegate = self;

[window addSubview:textFieldFront];
```

Actually, you could also add the textFieldFront to the glView as a subview without any immediately noticeable change. But adding the text field to the window allows you to reorder it in the view hierarchy at any time; for example, you could move it behind the cocos2d view using the sendSubviewToBack method of the window. You wouldn't be able to do that if you add the view directly to cocos2d's glView.

Check out Figure 15-3 for the result. You'll have UIKit views on top of the cocos2d view and behind it. The text view at the back can still be edited and manipulated as the Cut, Copy, Paste, Replace button shows. More importantly, despite the accompanying text field being behind the cocos2d view, the Cut, Copy, Paste, Replace pop-over button is automatically on top of the cocos2d view. Just how it ought to be!

Figure 15-3. UIKit views on top and behind the cocos2d view, with input enabled for all of them

Adding Views Designed with Interface Builder

At this point, you may be wondering how you could add a view that was designed with Apple's Interface Builder. Let's tackle this now. Code-wise, it's surprisingly simple, and you can look it up in the CocosWithCocoa02 project if you want.

The first order of business is to create an Interface Builder resource file. In Xcode 4, you create it comfortably from within the project using the File ➤ New ➤ New File command from the menu or right-click a group and select New File.

You'll be prompted to choose a template from the file template dialog. As you can see in Figure 15-4, you should create the Interface Builder file using the UIViewController subclass template. This will also create the Interface Builder nib file for you and connect it with your view controller, which is essential for the view to work.

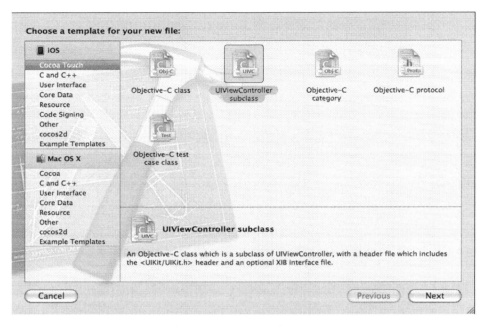

Figure 15-4. Create an Interface Builder view by creating a UIViewController subclass

Make sure the check box With XIB for user interface in Figure 15-5 is checked, and make sure the Subclass of text is the UIViewController. I decided to save this template using the filename MyView.m. You should end up with three new files in your project: MyView.h, MyView.m, and MyView.xib.

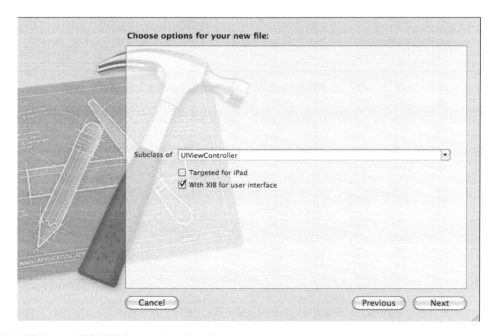

Figure 15-5. Make sure "With XIB for user interface" is checked

> **Note**   The developer documentation and even the Cocoa Touch API refer to Interface Builder files as nib files, even though they use the extension `.xib`. They used to have the `.nib` extension, and it simply stuck as a tradition even though the file extension was changed years ago. So, nib and xib are used interchangeably and refer to the same thing.

If you click the `MyView.xib` file, you'll be presented with the Interface Builder, which is no longer a separate application but integrated into Xcode 4. You'll see an iPhone screen's view, onto which you can drag and drop views from the Object Library, accessible via View ➤ Utilities ➤ Object Library in case it's not currently visible.

With Interface Builder, you can easily create your UIKit user interface visually. Because it's beyond the scope of the book to explain the Interface Builder workflow, I'll refer you to Apple's Xcode 4 User Guide and specifically the section on Designing User Interfaces:

```
http://developer.apple.com/library/mac/#documentation/ToolsLanguages/Conceptual/Xcode4UserGuide/
InterfaceBuilder/InterfaceBuilder.html
```

While I'm at it, if you need a refresher or introduction to views and windows, take a look at Apple's View Programming Guide for iOS:

```
http://developer.apple.com/library/ios/#documentation/WindowsViews/Conceptual/ViewPG_iPhoneOS/
Introduction/Introduction.html
```

> **Note**   Unfortunately, you can't use Interface Builder to design your cocos2d view. For that you have to use a separate editor like CocoShop, CocoaBuilder, LevelHelper, or any other editing tool with cocos2d support that fits your need. See Chapter 17 for a list of cocos2d editing tools.

For now, it's sufficient to just add any views to the Interface Builder view, like sliders, buttons, labels, and whatnot. But ideally you should at least do the following: select the main view and bring up the Attributes Inspector via View ➤ Utilities ➤ Attributes Inspector. The first attribute under Simulated Metrics is called Orientation, and you should change that to Landscape because the application is currently only capable of running in Landscape mode. If you don't do that, your views will be rotated by 90 degrees when you run the application.

The `MyView` class doesn't need to be modified; the default implementation works just fine. You can directly load the `MyView.xib` file by adding the following code at the end of the `addSomeTextFields` method:

```
// add an Interface Builder view
MyView* myViewController = [[MyView alloc] initWithNibName:@"MyView" bundle:nil];
[window addSubview:myViewController.view];
[window sendSubviewToBack: myViewController.view]; // optional
```

Notice that the `initWithNibName` takes the name of the xib file as a parameter but without the `.xib` extension. If you add the extension, you'll receive an error message that the xib could not be loaded. The bundle parameter is nil, which means the app should look for the file in the main bundle.

Because the MyView class inherits from UIViewController, you can access the actual view with the myViewController.view property. You'll add that to the window, and if you want, you can also issue an sendSubviewToBack message to put the view in the background.

You can now create and add views designed with Interface Builder to a cocos2d app. Your result might look something like the one in Figure 15-6.

Figure 15-6. The resulting project shows the MyView.xib file designed with Interface Builder in the bottom half

Embedding the cocos2d View in Cocoa Touch Apps

Many developers don't realize it's actually possible to embed a cocos2d view in a regular application using UIKit views as its main user interface. The cocos2d view doesn't even have to be full-screen!

The difficulty merely lies in setting up the project. I'll show you how it's done.

Creating a View-Based Application Project with cocos2d

Fire up your Xcode 4 and create a copy of the ARC-enabled cocos2d template, or simply follow the steps in Chapter 2 again. The important bit is that you need the cocos2d-library target.

Then add a new target to the project via File ➤ New ➤ Target. Select the Single View Application template, as shown in Figure 15-7, and name the new target ViewBasedAppWithCocos2D. Make sure to enable Automatic Reference Counting for this new target, and for this example I decided not to use Storyboards. You'll end up with a target that has a view controller class, the corresponding .xib files for iPhone and iPad, and an app delegate class. If you run it right now, you'll see a blank iPhone view with just the status bar on top.

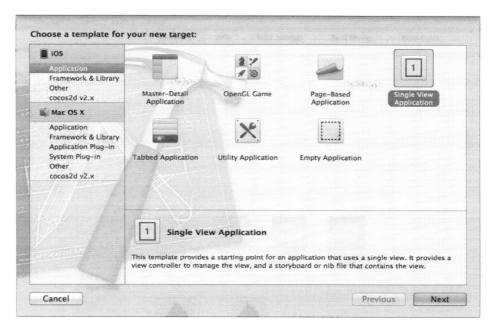

Figure 15-7. The starting point for embedding a cocos2d view is the Single View Application template

The next step is to link the cocos2d-library with the ViewBasedAppWithCocos2D target. You can do this as described in Chapter 2 by selecting the target and switching to the Build Phases tab. Under the Link Binary with Libraries section, click the + button to bring up the add dialog. In this case you'll want to add not only the libcocos2d-library.a file but also the frameworks required by cocos2d. They are:

- AudioToolbox.framework
- AVFoundation.framework
- GameKit.framework
- libz.dylib
- OpenAL.framework
- OpenGLES.framework
- QuartzCore.framework

Note that you can select all libraries in one go by holding down the Command key while selecting the items in the list. The added frameworks and libraries may be added to the root of the project in the Project Navigator. You can safely drag them into the Frameworks group where they belong, just to get them out of sight because you don't need to work with them.

On the target's Build Settings tab, locate the Header Search Paths setting. You need to add the path to the Kazmath library here, which is:

`"cocos2d-2.x-ARC-iOS/libs/kazmath/include"`

Alternatively you can simply add the entire project folder to the search path. You can do that by setting Header Search Paths to this:

`./**`

You may also remove the original application target and scheme because you won't need them anymore.

You can now build and run the `ViewBasedAppWithCocos2D` target. It should build the cocos2d source code now. But of course without a user interface, it's the same dull and empty app as it was before. Let's change that!

Designing the User Interface of the Hybrid App

Select the `ViewController_iPhone.xib` file in the Project Navigator to see the Interface Builder view. Using the Object Library (View ➤ Utilities ➤ Object Library), drag and drop the following objects onto the view. You can arrange these objects in the design area in any way you like:

- View (basic rectangular drawing region)
- Switch (on/off control)
- Segmented Control (multiple buttons in a single control)

Now select the newly added view object and switch to the Identity Inspector (View ➤ Utilities ➤ Identity Inspector). You'll notice that the first item shows that the view is derived from the `UIView` class. Because this should become the cocos2d `CCGLView`, use the drop-down button to select a custom class from the list. One of the first items should be the `CCGLView` class. If not, scroll the list until you find the `CCGLView` or simply type in the name of the class. The resulting user interface mockup should look something like Figure 15-8.

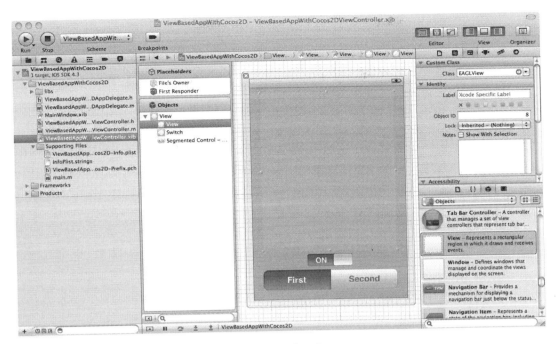

Figure 15-8. *The Interface Builder view of the hybrid app's user interface*

Interface Builder will automatically instantiate the CCGLView for you. You only need to attach the CCDirector with this particular view. The On/Off Switch should serve as the toggle button that turns the cocos2d view on and off.

First, some preparations. Select the CCGLView view and switch to the Attributes Inspector (View ➤ Utilities ➤ Attributes Inspector). Check the Hidden check box so that the view is initially hidden. With the Attributes Inspector still open, select the On/Off Switch and change its initial State to Off. You'll hide and unhide the CCGLView programmatically.

Note   The cocos2d CCDirector class can manage only one CCGLView at a time, mainly because the CCDirector class is a singleton. An app using multiple cocos2d views at the same time is not currently possible without significant changes to cocos2d. Support for multiple cocos2d views is on the development roadmap.

Now you need to make the connection from the buttons on the view to the ViewController class. The easiest way to do so is to open an Assistant Editor in Xcode 4 via View ➤ Editor ➤ Assistant. You can customize the layout of the Assistant Editor with one of the selections available under View ➤ Assistant Editor. The Assistant Editor will automatically display the ViewController.h file.

In the Interface Builder view, select the On/Off Switch and right-click it. It doesn't matter if you select it from the list or click its view. The context menu that opens shows a list of events that the control sends. Click the circle next to the Value Changed event and drag it over to the Assistant Editor. You'll notice that it will highlight a line with the label Insert Action if you drag it somewhere below the class @interface brackets and above the @end statement. That's where you should drop the arrow to make the connection. A pop-up view will show up and ask you for the name of the event. I decided to call mine switchChanged. You can leave all the other settings at their default values and then make the connection by clicking the Connect button in the pop-up view.

Interface Builder has automatically created the necessary code for you in order to receive the particular event that you just connected. There's new code both in the interface and implementation sections of the ViewController class. Before you review the code changes, you should also connect the same Value Changed event of the Segmented Control and name it sceneChanged.

This concludes the user interface design part of this project. Now let's move on to hooking up cocos2d.

Start Your cocos2d Engine

If you followed the user interface design part, you'll find two empty methods called switchChanged and sceneChanged in the ViewController.m class implementation file, next to some other boilerplate code that was added by the View-based Application template.

The first step is to get cocos2d up and running. One thing that's comfortable when working with cocos2d projects created from one of the cocos2d templates is that you rarely need to add a header file to any of your classes. That's because the cocos2d.h file is imported in the project's prefix header. Because this is not the case in the View-based Application template, open the ViewBasedAppWithCocos2D-Prefix.pch file in the Supporting Files group and add the cocos2d header:

```
#import <Availability.h>

#ifndef __IPHONE_4_0
#warning "This project uses features only available in iPhone SDK 4.0 and later."
#endif

#ifdef __OBJC__
    #import <UIKit/UIKit.h>
    #import <Foundation/Foundation.h>
    #import "cocos2d.h"
#endif
```

Now open the AppDelegate.m file. Because this app delegate class was created by Apple's Single View project template, cocos2d isn't being initialized. You have to add the necessary cocos2d startup code manually. You need to add the highlighted code in Listing 15-7 to the didFinishLaunchingWithOptions method.

Listing 15-7. Setting Up the Director in AppDelegate.m

```
- (BOOL)application:(UIApplication *)application ↵
    didFinishLaunchingWithOptions:(NSDictionary *)launchOptions
```

```
{
    self.window = [[UIWindow alloc] initWithFrame:[[UIScreen mainScreen] bounds]];
    // Override point for customization after application launch.
    if ([[UIDevice currentDevice] userInterfaceIdiom] == UIUserInterfaceIdiomPhone) {
        self.viewController = [[ViewController alloc] ↵
            initWithNibName:@"ViewController_iPhone" bundle:nil];
    } else {
        self.viewController = [[ViewController alloc] ↵
            initWithNibName:@"ViewController_iPad" bundle:nil];
    }

    // initialize cocos2d director
    CCDirectorIOS* director = (CCDirectorIOS*)[CCDirector sharedDirector];
    director.wantsFullScreenLayout = NO;
    director.projection = kCCDirectorProjection2D;
    director.animationInterval = 1.0 / 60.0;
    director.displayStats = YES;
    [director enableRetinaDisplay:YES];

    // find the CCGLView in the xib view
    NSArray* subviews = self.viewController.view.subviews;
    for (int i = 0; i < subviews.count; i++)
    {
        UIView* subview = [subviews objectAtIndex:i];
        if ([subview isKindOfClass:[CCGLView class]])
        {
            director.view = (CCGLView*)subview;
            break;
        }
    }

    self.window.rootViewController = self.viewController;
    [self.window makeKeyAndVisible];
    return YES;
}
```

That's surprisingly little code to get cocos2d running. As usual, you set the animation interval, projection, enable Retina mode, and the rest is just connecting the director with the CCGLView. The latter part simply goes over the list of subviews in the view controller's view to find one that's subclassed from CCGLView. Once the right view is found, it's assigned to the director as the director's view.

To enable the fps display via displayStats you'll also have to add all of the fps_images png files from any cocos2d project to your project via the File ➤ Add Files To … command. Otherwise, the framerate counter won't be displayed.

Next you need to add a cocos2d scene class to the project. Using the File ➤ Add Files to "ViewBasedAppWithCocos2D"… menu item, browse into the cocos2d project you created earlier and then locate and select both the header and implementation files of the HelloWorldLayer class. Make sure the Copy items into destination group's folder (if needed) check box is checked. Alternatively, you can also create a new cocos2d scene class from a cocos2d file template or manually. You'll be using the HelloWorldLayer class throughout this example.

Import the `HelloWorldLayer` class in the `ViewController.m` file so that you can run it as your main cocos2d scene:

```
#import "HelloWorldLayer.h"
```

All that's left now is to actually start up cocos2d and show and hide its `CCGLView`. The `switchChanged` method in Listing 15-8 contains all the code that's needed to run and show or stop and hide cocos2d.

Listing 15-8. Starting and Stopping the cocos2d Scene

```
- (IBAction)switchChanged:(id)sender
{
    UISwitch* switchButton = (UISwitch*)sender;
    CCDirectorIOS* director = (CCDirectorIOS*)[CCDirector sharedDirector];

    if (switchButton.on)
    {
        // if there's no running scene yet, add one
        if (director.runningScene == nil)
        {
            [director runWithScene:[HelloWorldLayer scene]];
        }

        [director startAnimation];
        director.view.hidden = NO;
    }
    else
    {
        [director stopAnimation];
        director.view.hidden = YES;
    }
}
```

There's only one special case in this code that checks whether there's a currently running scene. If there's none, you know that this is the first time the user tapped the On/Off switch and so you must run the first scene. You can easily start and stop the cocos2d engine at any time.

It gets a lot more complicated if you want to shut down cocos2d entirely and boot it up again. Most of the time you want to avoid that. You can reduce the memory usage of cocos2d temporarily by cleaning all caches. All cocos2d cache classes have methods to uncache unused or all cached assets. Before stopping cocos2d you may also want to switch to an empty scene to make sure cocos2d isn't referencing any assets for the time being. If you do that, the memory footprint of cocos2d is pretty minimal, and you can avoid the hassle of completely shutting down and rebooting cocos2d. Not only would this add additional loading time, it's also prone to cause a variety of issues. Although cocos2d supports it, this shutdown and restart behavior is barely tested and gets very little to no support.

Notice that the director methods `startAnimation` and `stopAnimation` are used to run and stop cocos2d. Just for the very first time when there is no running scene, you need to call `runWithScene`. But if you want to run a different scene each time cocos2d is restarted, you should call `replaceScene` directly after the call to `startAnimation`. The `runWithScene` method can be called only once during the lifetime of the application and must not be used again.

Technically, the stopAnimation method only stops cocos2d from refreshing its view. Unless the view is hidden or obstructed by another view, the last frame cocos2d has rendered will remain as a static image in the CCGLView. That's why hiding the CCGLView is a good idea. Calling stopAnimation is necessary to ensure that certain UIKit views are responsive and animate smoothly, in particular all views derived from UIScrollView. It's good practice to call stopAnimation whenever you hide the cocos2d view, to conserve performance for the foreground views as well as conserve battery power. Once the foreground view is dismissed, you call startAnimation again and you can unhide the CCGLView, and the cocos2d view and director continue where they were.

> **Tip**   If you want to see how this app behaves with autorotation, you have to make a small change to the ViewBasedAppWithCocos2DViewController class. Simply return YES from the shouldAutorotateToInterfaceOrientation method to enable rotation to all orientations. Although your app doesn't support it well (it's not designed for landscape orientation), it serves to show that the cocos2d view will be correctly autorotated.

Changing Scenes

The last step to complete this project is to use the Segmented Control's buttons to change scenes in the cocos2d view. Listing 15-9, taken from the ViewController class, shows the code that was added to the sceneChanged method.

Listing 15-9. Changing Scenes Whenever You Press a UIKit Button

```
- (IBAction)sceneChanged:(id)sender
{
    CCDirector* director = [CCDirector sharedDirector];
    if (director.view.hidden == NO)
    {
        UISegmentedControl* sceneChanger = (UISegmentedControl*)sender;
        int selection = sceneChanger.selectedSegmentIndex;

        CCScene* newScene = [HelloWorldLayer scene];
        CCScene* trans = nil;
        if (selection == 0)
        {
            trans = [CCTransitionSlideInL transitionWithDuration:1 scene:newScene];
        }
        else if (selection == 1)
        {
            trans = [CCTransitionShrinkGrow transitionWithDuration:1 scene:newScene];
        }
        else
        {
            trans = [CCTransitionSlideInR transitionWithDuration:1 scene:newScene];
        }
        [director replaceScene:trans];
    }
}
```

Because the user can press the Segmented Control buttons at any time, even before the cocos2d view is initialized, the first thing this method does is to check that the `director.view` exists and is not hidden. Otherwise, the remaining code could crash the app.

The `sender` parameter is always the control that triggered the event. Here I rightfully assume that it's a `UISegmentedControl`. If you ever change the control, you have to change the control's class here as well. Via the `selectedSegmentIndex`, you get the index of the currently selected button, which is then used to decide which transition to use for the new scene. I'm simply creating a new instance of the same `HelloWorldLayer` class; of course, you can also use different scene classes for each button if you want. At last, `trans` is used with the `director` method `replaceScene` to actually change the scene to the new one using a transition.

> **Note** The cocos2d transitions will act only on the cocos2d view and its nodes. UIKit views will be unaffected by the cocos2d transitions. But you can use `UIView` animations and transitions on the cocos2d view. You can learn more about `UIView` animations here:
> `http://developer.apple.com/library/ios/#documentation/WindowsViews/`
> `Conceptual/ViewPG_iPhoneOS/AnimatingViews/AnimatingViews.html`.

I spiced up my `HelloWorldLayer` scene with some additional cocos2d labels in the background and labels for the buttons. You'll find these code changes to the `HelloWorldLayer` class in the ViewBasedAppWithCocos2D project. The result looks something like Figure 15-9.

Figure 15-9. A cocos2d view in a view-based application

Summary

This chapter provided you with everything you need to know to successfully and painlessly mix cocos2d with regular UIKit views. You now have the option to choose how much UIKit you want in your cocos2d app and when, where, and how you'd like your cocos2d view in your UIKit app.

The trickiest aspects were making the cocos2d view transparent in order to allow UIKit views in the background as well as performing hit tests on cocos2d nodes in an attempt to allow all views to receive input, whether UIKit or cocos2d and regardless of where they are in the view hierarchy.

Adding cocos2d to a UIKit app also proved to be fairly simple, even if you need to turn the cocos2d view on and off only at specific times. You may have also taken away that the cocos2d view doesn't need to be full-screen at all but can be any size, or even resized while the app is running.

But you also learned that mixing cocos2d and UIKit views is not without drawbacks, specifically performance-wise. Keep a watchful eye on your app's performance by testing it regularly on a device, particularly on first- and second-generation devices. You only get the best performance if you avoid using UIKit views for your game scene, but for menu scenes they can be a great help and timesaver.

Kobold2D Introduction

In more than two years of working with cocos2d, I found plenty of opportunity and need to improve the cocos2d development workflow by adding helpful code snippets, extending cocos2d classes, enabling easier cross-platform development, automating often-repeated tasks, simplifying the cocos2d upgrade process, and providing complete and accurate documentation. Eventually, this culminated in the inception of Kobold2D, a game engine that's still very much based on cocos2d-iphone but improves the workflow for cocos2d developers.

The goal of Kobold2D is to make it easier for new developers to work with cocos2d while at the same time satisfying my own needs for a professional work environment (and I hope yours too!).

Kobold2D merges the cocos2d engine with popular libraries many developers have been using with cocos2d in the past. Some of these libraries have almost become essential add-ons, including Lua, the new cocos2d-iphone-extensions project, SneakyInput, Chipmunk SpaceManager, ObjectAL, and iSimulate. Kobold2D makes these libraries readily accessible and usable by all developers—you just have to import a library's header files and call library methods.

And by the time you're reading this I will have a version of KoboldScript available for you at www.koboldscript.com. KoboldScript is a Lua scripting interface for cocos2d with statemachines and game components.

In this chapter, I introduce you to the key concepts of working with Kobold2D and how it changes the way you develop cocos2d-based apps. I guide you through the Kobold2D version of the DoodleDrop project to illustrate how easy it is to write a game that also runs on Mac OS computers—and to give you an introduction on Kobold2D user input processing.

You can learn more about Kobold2D and download it at www.kobold2d.com.

Benefits of Using Kobold2D

I view Kobold2D as a game-development kit rather than a game engine. It's more like a Linux distribution with the cocos2d-iphone project as its "kernel" and multiple other modules tacked onto it, all ready to use after installation.

To stick with the analogy, if cocos2d-iphone were a Linux kernel with just its command-line interface, Kobold2D would be providing the graphical user interface and the essential applications that make the operating system more powerful, enjoyable to work with, and accessible to a broader user base.

At the same time, the command line is still there; it has simply become part of a bigger whole.

Kobold2D Is Ready to Use

Kobold2D installs like a regular application. There's no need to run a script in the Terminal app or perform any other such error-prone tasks. Download and run the package installer, follow the onscreen instructions, and you're done. It's quick and painless.

After installing Kobold2D, you can build one of the 15 template projects right away; most of them are based on projects you've worked on throughout the book. With the exception of the app start-up process, which is now simply a configuration file, everything you've learned about cocos2d in this book and elsewhere still applies.

The Kobold2D installer also adds the various API references to the Documentation tab of the Xcode Organizer window.

Kobold2D Is Free

Kobold2D is free and distributed under the MIT License. All the included libraries use either the MIT License or a compatible license.

The only exception is iSimulate, which requires the paid iSimulate app from the App Store to unlock all features. The free iSimulate Lite, for example, doesn't support the forwarding of multitouch events to the iOS Simulator.

Kobold2D Is Easy to Upgrade

A big incentive for Kobold2D was to simplify and streamline upgrading cocos2d in existing projects. The downside of using the cocos2d Xcode project templates is that a copy of the entire cocos2d source code resides in each and every project, making the upgrade process unnecessarily tedious and error-prone.

Kobold2D fixes that by keeping your code separate from any library's code. If a new version of Kobold2D is released, and you want your project to use the updated code, simply run the Kobold2D Project Upgrader tool of the newly installed Kobold2D version. It will scan previous Kobold2D versions and offer to upgrade each individual project with a click of the mouse. The only task that remains for you to upgrade your code is the unavoidable code maintenance because of API changes—for example, classes that may have been renamed in cocos2d or other libraries, or library methods whose parameters have changed.

Kobold2D Includes Popular Libraries

A central aspect of Kobold2D is to spare developers the pain of adding third-party libraries to cocos2d projects. Correctly setting up third-party libraries often requires intricate knowledge of the build system, an intuition about how to read compiler and linker errors, and possibly even small but crucial source code changes in the right places. It can take hours, if not days, for someone else's code to compile and link successfully on all platforms: iOS (ARMv6 and ARMv7), iOS Simulator, and Mac OS X both in 32-bit and 64-bit variants, and all of those either with or without ARC.

That's what Kobold2D provides: lib service. Kobold2D 2.0 includes the following libraries.

Libraries for both iOS and Mac OS X projects:

- Kobold2D (game engine code, Objective-C)
- cocos2d-iphone (2D graphics, Objective-C)
- cocos2d-iphone-extensions (utility code, Objective-C)
- Box2D (physics, C++)
- GBox2D (Box2D physics, Objective-C)
- Chipmunk (physics, C)
- Chipmunk SpaceManager (Chipmunk physics, Objective-C)
- CocosDenshion (audio, Objective-C)
- Lua (scripting)

Libraries available only for iOS projects:

- ObjectAL (audio, Objective-C)
- SneakyInput (joystick, Objective-C)
- iSimulate (library for iSimulate app)

Whenever an essential library such as cocos2d is updated, a new release of Kobold2D will follow within days, if not hours. There's no need for you to get active on the library front.

> **Note** You may be wondering why I didn't include cocos3d in Kobold2D 2.0 even though it's part of Kobold2D 1.x. The reason is that cocos3d is targeting OpenGL ES 1.1 and is therefore incompatible with cocos2d 2.0 or any other source code that uses OpenGL ES 2.0. The cocos3d roadmap lists OpenGL ES 2.0 support as TBD, meaning when it'll be available is unknown. Once it is, I'll add it back in.

Some readers may wonder whether this means that Kobold2D apps are bloated, with all those libraries being included. You may be surprised to hear that early tests showed that Kobold2D apps are actually slightly smaller compared to cocos2d-iphone apps, even though Lua is built into Kobold2D. The reason is that the Kobold2D projects are set up to allow the linker to throw away any code that isn't used in your app. That means if, for example, you don't include any of the Box2D headers, none of the Box2D library code will be linked with your app. But if you do want to start using Box2D, it's as simple as adding the Box2D.h header file to your project, and you're ready to start writing Box2D-enabled physics apps.

Kobold2D Takes Dual-Platform to Heart

By having one target for each platform (iOS and Mac OS X) by default in its project templates, Kobold2D allows you to build and run your code on both platforms from within the same Xcode project.

Developing for both iOS and Mac OS platforms is also encouraged by the Kobold2D API, which goes a long way toward ensuring that game engine code compiles for both platforms. For example, if you try to read the mouse button states on iOS, the code still compiles, and the result is a safe default, which in this case would simply report that no mouse button is pressed.

The Kobold2D Workspace

After downloading and installing Kobold2D, you'll find the most recent version of Kobold2D in a versioned subfolder of ~/Kobold2D—for example, ~/Kobold2D/Kobold2D-2.0. The installer will also open the Kobold2D Project Starter.app for you, which allows you to start a new Kobold2D project from one of the supplied project templates (see Figure 16-1).

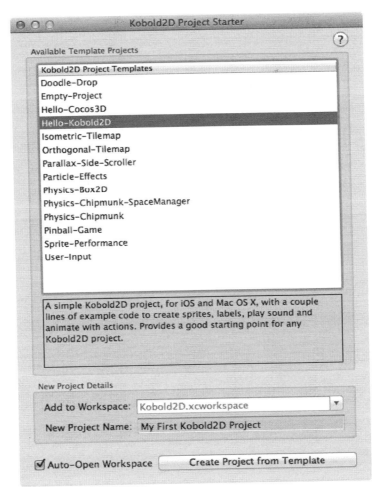

Figure 16-1. *The Kobold2D Project Starter tool lets you start new projects easily*

Select the Hello-Kobold2D template, enter any text in the New Project Name text field, and click Create Project from Template. You can also change the Add to Workspace text if you want to add the new project to a custom workspace (it will be created if necessary). By default, Kobold2D projects are added to the Kobold2D.xcworkspace.

Xcode should now open the Kobold2D workspace that contains your new project, as shown in Figure 16-2.

Figure 16-2. The Kobold2D Xcode 4 workspace view with the Hello Kobold2D Mac OS X project running

Caution Kobold2D uses the new workspace concept of Xcode 4, which allows you to combine multiple projects in a single workspace window. If you open the `.xcodeproj` file of a Kobold2D project either from the most recently used list or by double-clicking it in Finder, the project won't build successfully. You can easily spot this problem because the Kobold2D-Libraries project will be absent from the Project Navigator pane. Make sure to always open the corresponding `.xcodeworkspace` file that contains the `.xcodeproj` that you want to work with.

The Hello Kobold2D Template Project

Let's take a closer look at the Hello Kobold2D project (Figure 16-2) to demonstrate several key concepts of Kobold2D.

The Hello World Project Files

In Figure 16-3 you'll see the groups and files in the My First Kobold2D Project, which was created from the Hello-Kobold2D template project.

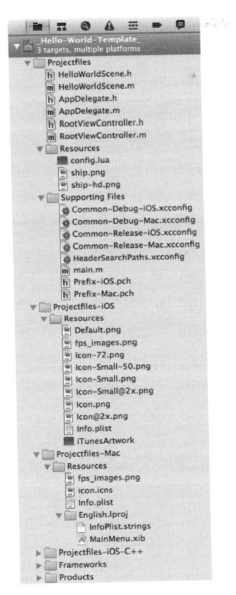

Figure 16-3. The default group structure of a Kobold2D project

The immediately noticeable difference compared to a regular cocos2d project is that three groups begin with Projectfiles, and there is the additional BuildSettings group. The idea behind that is to have a Projectfiles group and folder that contain the source code and resource files common to all platforms. The majority of your source code and resources will be in this folder. The additional Projectfiles-iOS and Projectfiles-Mac groups should contain only files used by that particular platform. These groups are meant as suggestions; you're of course free to structure your project's group as you see fit.

The `BuildSettings` group contains several `.xcconfig` files, which are the textual format for Xcode build settings. Normally you don't need to modify these files, but in some cases you may want to,—or example, to enable iSimulate. One huge benefit of the `.xcconfig` files is that you can document them, and accordingly you'll find several notes for each build setting, what it does, what it affects, and when you might want to enable or disable it. The other big benefit of `.xcconfig` files is that Kobold2D controls each project's default settings. Should an Xcode or cocos2d update require different build settings, then that change will be shipped with Kobold2D instead of leaving it up to you. In the past, this has caused a lot of grief whenever certain build settings became incompatible with cocos2d.

Almost all Kobold2D project templates provide targets for both iOS and Mac OS X, which are suffixed with `-iOS` and `-Mac`, respectively. I hope that the readily available Mac target will encourage you and other developers to consider cross-platform development from the start and to publish more apps to both the iOS and Mac App Store. It's certainly a lot easier to take cross-platform development into account from the start rather than porting the app once it's finished.

How Kobold2D Launches an App

Kobold2D simplifies the start-up process, in particular how much custom code is needed in your project (by default: none). Kobold2D does all the initialization performed by the main function, the app delegate, and the root view controller behind the scenes.

Furthermore, Kobold2D lets you easily modify the start-up settings, such as the first scene or layer to display, the device orientation, the render settings, the Mac window size, Retina support, and many more. All these settings are centralized in the `config.lua` script file.

Main and AppDelegate

The `main.m` file is the entry point for each application; it contains the `main` method. The Kobold2D implementation simply calls its internal method `KKMain`:

```
#import "kobold2d.h"

int main(int argc, char *argv[])
{
    return KKMain(argc, argv, NULL);
}
```

`KKMain` takes both `argc` and `argv` arguments and a third, optional parameter that can be used to pass additional parameters to the start-up process if needed. Because that's rarely, if ever, needed, you can just pass NULL. `KKMain` hides the complexity of launching the app for either the iOS or Mac OS platform. It also initializes Lua and parses the `config.lua` file, which provides app configuration settings. I discuss the `config.lua` file in the next section.

At this point, it makes sense to show you the `AppDelegate` class of a Kobold2D project, or, rather, what's left of it. Here's the interface:

```
#import "KKAppDelegate.h"

@interface AppDelegate : KKAppDelegate
{
}
@end
```

Nothing there. Maybe there's more in the implementation part of the app delegate?

```
#import "AppDelegate.h"

@implementation AppDelegate
// Called when Cocos2D is fully setup and you are able to run the first scene
-(void) initializationComplete
{
}
@end
```

Nope. I can already hear you: dude, where's my app delegate?

Kobold2D takes care of the entire app start-up process for you and hides it within the KKAppDelegate class from which the AppDelegate class inherits. In particular, KKAppDelegate correctly sets up cocos2d based on the config.lua settings and encapsulates platform-specific app delegate code. This allows Kobold2D to integrate changes to the app delegate class introduced by newer cocos2d versions and makes them available to your projects.

The KKAppDelegate class is a regular UIApplicationDelegate on iOS and an NSApplicationDelegate class on Mac OS; you can implement (override) any of the app delegate protocol methods yourself whenever you need to do so. However, you should make sure to call the super implementation of overridden methods to ensure that KKAppDelegate still performs its duties.

The only custom method that you may find useful is initializationComplete, which is called after the app and cocos2d have been fully initialized but before the first scene is about to be run. You can call the CCDirector runWithScene method inside initializationComplete to run a specific scene. However, that's not required, because the config.lua file has a setting FirstSceneClassName that lets you specify just the name of the class that cocos2d should run as its first scene without writing any code.

In essence, the Kobold2D classes KKMain and KKAppDelegate provide the common functionality developers expect from these classes. Furthermore, they provide the foundation code for any Kobold2D project, enabling you to use Lua for configuration files, among other things. You also have less code to maintain. In particular, if there's an essential change to these classes in iOS, Mac OS, or cocos2d, Kobold2D will take care of these changes or additions for you.

The Start-up Configuration File

Kobold2D always loads the Lua script file config.lua, which is in the Resources group of each Kobold2D project.

The config.lua script file returns a Lua table containing all the game's settings. A Lua table is a flexible data structure that combines the features of dictionaries (indexed by string) and arrays (indexed by value). You can create deeply nested Lua tables—which in terms of possibilities equal XML files or property lists, but with a relatively simple, readable syntax with built-in error-reporting.

Lua scripts are text files, so naturally they're easier to edit than property lists, regardless of whether you're using a property list editor or editing the property list XML file directly. And Lua scripts allow you to comment on each line to explain your rationale, the range of valid values, and so on. You can't do that with property list files because property list editors don't allow you to comment on entries.

> **Note**   Lua support for Kobold2D was originally provided by the Wax library created by Corey
> Johnson. Wax allows all Lua scripts to call any Objective-C method and to instantiate Objective-C
> classes, including cocos2d classes. However, Kobold2D avoids Wax scripting, and eventually most
> of the Wax project was removed. Instead, Kobold2D uses Lua only to load settings files like
> config.lua, executing Lua scripts and calling Lua functions. This is fast. For actual game scripting
> with Lua, the add-on product KoboldScript is currently in development. You can get more info about
> KoboldScript on www.koboldscript.com.

The config.lua file contains settings for just about everything you might want to tweak during the
start-up process. Listing 16-1 shows an example config.lua file.

Listing 16-1. The config.lua Script Contains All Start-up Settings for Kobold2D

```lua
local config =
{
    KKStartupConfig =
    {
        -- load first scene from a CCScene or CCLayer derived class with this name
        FirstSceneClassName = "HelloWorldLayer",

        MaxFrameRate = 60,
        DisplayFPS = YES,

        EnableUserInteraction = YES,
        EnableMultiTouch = NO,

        -- Render settings
        DefaultTexturePixelFormat = TexturePixelFormat.RGBA8888,
        GLViewColorFormat = GLViewColorFormat.RGB565,
        GLViewDepthFormat = GLViewDepthFormat.DepthNone,
        GLViewMultiSampling = NO,
        GLViewNumberOfSamples = 0,

        Enable2DProjection = NO,
        EnableRetinaDisplaySupport = YES,
        EnableGLViewNodeHitTesting = NO,
        EnableStatusBar = NO,

        -- Orientation & Autorotation
        -- Kobold2D uses the supported orientations from the Target's Summary pane
        -- (same as Info.plist "Supported interface orientations")

        -- iAd setup
        EnableAdBanner = YES,
        LoadOnlyPortraitBanners = YES,
        LoadOnlyLandscapeBanners = NO,
        PlaceBannerOnBottom = NO,
        AdProviders = "iAd, AdMob",     -- comma seperated list
        AdMobRefreshRate = 15,
        AdMobFirstAdDelay = 5,
```

```
        AdMobPublisherID = "YOUR_ADMOB_PUBLISHER_ID",
        AdMobTestMode = YES,

        -- Mac OS specific settings
        AutoScale = NO,
        AcceptsMouseMovedEvents = NO,
        WindowFrame = RectMake(1024-640, 768-480, 640, 480),
    },
}

return config
```

Most of these settings should be self-explanatory and may seem familiar to you. The settings are documented in the KKStart-upConfig class in the Kobold2D API Reference and here: www.kobold2d.com/display/KKDOC/Config.lua+Settings+Reference.

For example, the FirstSceneClassName setting lets you specify the name of a class inheriting from CCScene or CCLayer (automatically wrapped inside a CCScene), which will be the first scene run by the CCDirector. You can enable iAd or AdMob ad banners, or provide the default window position and size for Mac builds.

The big advantage of using a Lua-based configuration file is that the entire start-up code is part of the Kobold2D code and can be updated in new versions if it needs to be. As Kobold2D matures, more settings will be added to the start-up config, depending on what developers need to change or include most in their apps. In addition, you can create and use custom config.lua settings. The Hello World project provides an example of loading custom settings. I'll get to that in the next section.

Tip   You can learn more about Lua from the free *Programming in Lua* book, available online on the official Lua home page at www.lua.org/pil. The book is for an older version of Lua but is still largely relevant. You may also want to browse the Lua reference manual at www.lua.org/manual to get a quick overview of the language. Lua has grown to be the number-one scripting language for game developers over the past ten years. It has a very small memory footprint and speed-wise often comes close to 80 to 90 percent of the performance achievable with C programming.

The Hello Kobold2D Scene and Layer

Let's move on to the actual scene class HelloWorldLayer, which is set as the first scene via the config.lua setting FirstSceneClassName = "HelloWorldLayer". You'll notice that this first scene is actually derived from CCLayer. Kobold2D realizes that and automatically wraps the HelloWorldLayer class into a CCScene instance behind the scenes.

Tip   To avoid writing the repetitive + (id) scene method in each CCLayer class, you can simply call the + (id) nodeWithScene method in Kobold2D:

[[CCDirector sharedDirector] replaceScene:[MyGameLayer nodeWithScene]];

The HelloWorldLayer interface declaration is pretty unspectacular and provides only three instance variables that will later be loaded from the config.lua file:

```
#import "cocos2d.h"

@interface HelloWorldLayer : CCLayer
{
    NSString* helloWorldString;
    NSString* helloWorldFontName;
    int helloWorldFontSize;
}

@property (nonatomic, copy) NSString* helloWorldString;
@property (nonatomic, copy) NSString* helloWorldFontName;
@property (nonatomic) int helloWorldFontSize;

@end
```

At this point, you should take note of a particular addition to the config.lua file. There's an additional Lua table labeled HelloWorldSettings in Listing 16-2, which provides three familiar-looking settings: HelloWorldString, HelloWorldFontName, and HelloWorldFontSize.

Listing 16-2. Custom config.lua Settings

```
local config =
{
    KKStartupConfig =
    {
        -- start-up settings removed for brevity
    },

    HelloWorldSettings =
    {
        HelloWorldString = "Hello Kobold2D!",
        HelloWorldFontName = "Marker Felt",
        HelloWorldFontSize = 50,
    },
}
```

With the exception of the uppercase first letter, these settings match the properties of the HelloWorldLayer class in name and data type. I'm sure you can see the connection here. Indeed, the KKConfig class method injectPropertiesFromKeyPath, shown in Listing 16-3, loads the values from the HelloWorldSettings subtable and injects them into the correspondingly named properties of the target class, in this case self.

Listing 16-3. Injecting (Assigning) the Custom Settings to Class Properties

```
[KKConfig injectPropertiesFromKeyPath:@"HelloWorldSettings" target:self];
```

By *inject* I mean if there is a Lua table named HelloWorldSettings, then each setting it contains will be assigned to a correspondingly named property of the target class, in this case self. For example, the setting HelloWorldString will be assigned to the class property helloWorldString if it has the correct data type (NSString*) and isn't set to be a readonly property.

> **Tip** By using KKConfig, you can easily make your app data-driven, which for example allows designers and artists to tweak your app's behavior without having to modify source code. Data-driven development also comes to shine when you have a variety of game objects with the same or similar settings. You don't want these settings spread throughout your code—you want to centralize them in a single file that provides the necessary overview.

After injection, the three properties will contain the same values as the HelloWorldSettings Lua table. They're ready to be used by the label:

```
CCLabelTTF* label = [CCLabelTTF labelWithString:helloWorldString
                                fontName:helloWorldFontName
                                fontSize:helloWorldFontSize];
```

Listing 16-4 shows the HelloWorldLayer implementation in its entirety. Apart from the previous call to KKConfig and the use of the CCDirector extensions and platform macros discussed earlier, it's still 100-percent cocos2d code.

Listing 16-4. Hello Kobold2D Implementation File

```
#import "HelloWorldLayer.h"

@implementation HelloWorldLayer
@synthesize helloWorldString, helloWorldFontName;
@synthesize helloWorldFontSize;

-(id) init
{
    if ((self = [super init]))
    {
        CCDirector* director = [CCDirector sharedDirector];

        CCSprite* sprite = [CCSprite spriteWithFile:@"ship.png"];
        sprite.position = director.screenCenter;
        [self addChild:sprite];

        // get the hello world string from the config.lua file
        [KKConfig injectPropertiesFromKeyPath:@"HelloWorldSettings" target:self];

        CCLabelTTF* label = [CCLabelTTF labelWithString:helloWorldString
                                        fontName:helloWorldFontName
                                        fontSize:helloWorldFontSize];

        label.position = director.screenCenter;
        label.color = ccGREEN;
        [self addChild:label];

        // print out which platform we're on
        NSString* platform = @"(unknown platform)";

        if (director.currentPlatformIsIOS)
        {
            // add code
```

```
                platform = @"iPhone/iPod Touch";

            if (director.currentDeviceIsIPad)
                platform = @"iPad";
            if (director.currentDeviceIsSimulator)
                platform = [NSString stringWithFormat:@"%@ Simulator", platform];
        }
        else if (director.currentPlatformIsMac)
        {
            platform = @"Mac OS X";
        }

        CCLabelTTF* platformLabel = [CCLabelTTF labelWithString:platform
                                                       fontName:@"Arial"
                                                       fontSize:24];
        platformLabel.position = director.screenCenter;
        platformLabel.color = ccYELLOW;
        [self addChild:platformLabel];

        glClearColor(0.2f, 0.2f, 0.4f, 1.0f);
    }
    return self;
}

@end
```

Notice the way I determine the platform (iOS, Mac OS) and device type (iPad, iOS Simulator) using director properties such as currentPlatformIsIOS and currentDeviceIsSimulator. These are some of the extensions to CCDirector I mentioned earlier.

You may be wondering why I haven't used preprocessor macros like __IPHONE_OS_VERSION_ MAX_ALLOWED to determine platform and device type. First, in Kobold2D I wouldn't have used the hard-to-remember and verbose SDK macros. Instead, Kobold2D provides the simpler macros KK_PLATFORM_IOS and KK_PLATFORM_MAC to differentiate between the two supported platforms. If needed, you can also differentiate between iOS device and iOS Simulator by using the macros KK_PLATFORM_IOS_DEVICE and KK_PLATFORM_IOS_SIMULATOR.

The real reason for not using preprocessor macros and why conditional compilation with #ifdef should be used only as a last-resort measure is this: the compiler is your friend! Every time your code is compiled, the compiler lets you know that everything is in order or tells you whatever is technically or syntactically wrong with your code. It may be annoying at times, but the compiler is only letting you know that you made a mistake or forgot something. Allowing as much code as possible to be compiled by the compiler every time you build the code is so important for cross-platform development that the added overhead of platform and device runtime tests are entirely negligible.

Once you do cross-platform development, you'll likely spend a lot of time working on and compiling code for only one platform. Any code that's within an #ifdef for the other platform is invisible to the compiler, and it won't complain about errors. Now as soon as you switch targets and compile for the other platform, you'll likely run into errors that were thus far ignored due to the use of #ifdef. These errors may be related to code changes that you made an hour ago, a day ago, or maybe even a week ago.

Not only does it cause a lot of mental load to figure out which code change caused the error and what the correct fix will be, it's also frustrating because you'll frequently find that switching target platforms results in build failures. Either you'll spend more time than necessary building code regularly for both target platforms or you'll simply give up, maybe with the good intention of porting the project when it's finished. However, porting a completed project is much more work than developing it for both platforms from the beginning.

Code that compiles works. At least it's technically correct. Immediate build errors are more likely to be corrected right away and easier to fix because you still have the most recent code changes in your short-term memory.

Running Hello World with iSimulate

To enable iSimulate you have to open the `BuildSettings-iOS.xcconfig` file, which is located in the `BuildSettings` group of your Kobold2D project. The only thing you have to do is to remove the comment from this line:

```
OTHER_LDFLAGS[sdk = iphonesimulator*][arch = *] = $(OTHER_LDFLAGS) $(FORCE_LOAD_ISIMULATE)
```

Now if you run the Hello World project on the iPhone or iPad Simulator, you'll notice a network connection dialog as in Figure 16-4, which is the reason iSimulate is disabled by default. Several

Figure 16-4. Network connection warning caused by iSimulate

users have complained about it; some were confused why Kobold2D projects would want to accept incoming network connections. You'll also notice the iAd banner that shows up because it was enabled in `config.lua`.

Note If you see an `bannerView:didFailToReceiveAdWithError` error in your log with the message "The operation couldn't be completed. (ADErrorDomain error 1.)," then this is most likely caused by the app not being set up for iAd. The iAd service needs to be enabled for each app and each developer in iTunes Connect. You'll find more information about enabling iAd for your app at `https://itunesconnect.apple.com/docs/iTunesConnect_DeveloperGuide.pdf`.

As I said, the incoming network connections warning dialog is caused by iSimulate. The iSimulate library needs to accept incoming connections from the iSimulate app, which you can run on your WiFi-enabled iOS device in order to remote control the simulator. In other words, iSimulate enables you to test your game using your device but running in the Simulator. All the features the Simulator doesn't have—such as GPS, accelerometer, or multitouch—can be simulated with the iSimulate app. It can be a real time-saver.

For example, if you have iSimulate running on your device and connected to your Mac, you will receive messages like `accelerometer:didAccelerate:` in your app, even though the Simulator doesn't have an accelerometer. This makes iSimulate an invaluable tool if you consider that running your app is usually a lot faster than deploying it to a device. I recommend giving it a try with Kobold2D's User-Input template project.

iSimulate is available on the App Store and normally costs $15.99: `http://itunes.apple.com/app/isimulate/id306908756`.

DoodleDrop for Mac with KKInput

So far, all the projects throughout the book were written for iOS. If you install Kobold2D, you'll notice that not only are most of the book's projects included in Kobold2D, almost all of them also have a Mac OS version.

So, what would it take to make a project like DoodleDrop from Chapter 4 work both on Mac and on iOS? Not that much actually. It turns out that by far the biggest change is related to handling user input. Thankfully, Kobold2D provides a platform-agnostic user input handler that simplifies user input dramatically by allowing you to test the state of input devices at any time in any class and method.

First, the `accelerometer:didAccelerate` event method has been removed because it's no longer needed. Instead, `KKInput` will be responsible for providing the app with acceleration values. You tell it to activate accelerometer input and to set the filtering factor in the `init` method of the DoodleDrop `GameLayer` class:

```
// Yes, we want to receive accelerometer input events.
[KKInput sharedInput].accelerometerActive = YES;
[KKInput sharedInput].acceleration.filteringFactor = 0.2f;
```

Enabling the accelerometer will first test whether the device supports the Core Motion framework. If so, acceleration values will be provided by Core Motion, which gives us a tiny performance benefit. In all other cases, the standard UIAccelerometer interface is used to obtain acceleration values. The filtering factor is a percentage that determines how responsive the game character will react to sudden changes in acceleration.

Listing 16-5 shows the modified DoodleDrop update method that includes user input handling for both platforms.

Listing 16-5. Handling User Input for Both Platforms with KKInput

```
-(void) update:(ccTime)delta
{
    KKInput* input = [KKInput sharedInput];
    if (isGameOver)
    {
        if (input.anyTouchEnded ||↵
            [input isKeyDown:kKKKeyCode_Space] ||↵
            [input isKeyDown:kKKKeyCode_Return])
        {
            [self resetGame];
        }
    }
    else
    {
        [self acceleratePlayerWithX:input.acceleration.smoothedX];

        if ([input isKeyDown:kKKKeyCode_LeftArrow])
        {
            [self acceleratePlayerWithX:-keyAcceleration];
        }
        else if ([input isKeyDown:kKKKeyCode_RightArrow])
        {
            [self acceleratePlayerWithX:keyAcceleration];
        }

        // The rest of the update code remained unchanged.
        ...
    }
}
```

The update method processing is split into handling the gameover and the rest of the code that runs while the game is commencing. If the game is over, you simply check whether any touch ended, or the spacebar or Return key is being held down, before resetting the game and starting over.

While the game is running, the player's velocity is updated either based on the input.acceleration.smoothedX value or based on a constant keyAcceleration value when either the left or right arrow key is held down. The acceleratePlayerWithX method is shown in Listing 16-6 (coming up soon), which contains the code previously in the accelerometer:didAccelerate method.

KKInput provides you with built-in high-pass and low-pass filters via properties of the KKAcceleration class exposed by the input.acceleration property. You can access the raw acceleration, the smoothed (low-pass filtered), and the instantaneous (high-pass filtered) values. In most games, you want to use the smoothed values, which provide steady acceleration and cancel out sudden, short-lived movements. Instantaneous acceleration values are useful whenever you want to react to sudden acceleration movements, such as shaking or quickly flipping the device.

You'll notice that the input code doesn't use conditional compiling via #ifdef. If you run this code on Mac, the anyTouchEnded method is guaranteed to return NO all the time. Likewise, when running on iOS, the isKeyDown method always return NO, because there's no keyboard available. And the input.acceleration values are all 0 on Mac OS.

If it seems wasteful to you to test for keyboard events on iOS and touch events on Mac OS, please keep in mind that the additional overhead is minimal while the benefit of always compiling all your code guarantees that it continues to work for both platforms. If the platform-specific code is extensive, you can always branch it using the Kobold2D CCDirector extensions like currentPlatformIsIOS and currentPlatformIsMac.

Listing 16-6. Updating the Player's Velocity

```
-(void) acceleratePlayerWithX:(double)xAcceleration
{
    // adjust velocity based on current accelerometer acceleration
    playerVelocity.x = (playerVelocity.x * deceleration) + ↩
        (xAcceleration * sensitivity);

    // we must limit the maximum velocity of the player sprite, in both directions
    if (playerVelocity.x > maxVelocity)
    {
        playerVelocity.x = maxVelocity;
    }
    else if (playerVelocity.x < -maxVelocity)
    {
        playerVelocity.x = -maxVelocity;
    }
}
```

Everything else requires no changes to create the Mac OS port, thanks to the fact that no hard-coded positions and offsets were used. Nevertheless, it makes sense for game play reasons to restrict the Mac window size to that of an iPhone in config.lua:

```
WindowFrame = RectMake(300, 300, 320, 480),
```

The Lua function RectMake creates a rectangle with the given origin (300, 300) and size (320, 480). RectMake creates rectangles that are compatible with CGRect or NSRect, depending on the platform. Additional Lua utility functions are PointMake and SizeMake.

Summary

I hope that this chapter has given you a good impression of how working with Kobold2D will help you make games and apps easier and have more possibilities. On the `www.kobold2d.com` web site, you'll have access to the API documentation of all libraries, a programming guide, the support forum, the feedback section, and a road map that allows you to see how Kobold2D development is progressing. And you definitely should check up on the progress I'm making regarding KoboldScript at `www.koboldscript.com`. KoboldScript is the Lua game-scripting interface for Kobold2D and cocos2d.

One of the most important features of Kobold2D is its ability to use Lua tables to define settings. You'll then be able to feed these settings directly into properties of class instances with just a single call to the `KKConfig` class. This is even more important if you work with others who need to make changes to the app but don't want or shouldn't have to change the source code.

Kobold2D also makes dual-platform development for iOS and Mac OS easier and provides a convenient, one-stop class for handling user input, as you saw in this section. You'll also find plenty of template projects in Kobold2D based on projects created throughout the book and subsequently ported to work on Mac OS.

What's left is for you to go to `www.kobold2d.com` now to download the latest version, install it, and start experimenting with the provided template projects.

Out of the Ordinary

This final chapter contains no source code. I'm not even going to talk much about the cocos2d engine. Instead, I'd like to focus on where you can look after finishing this book, if you want to ask questions and learn more. Without a doubt, the number one place to go after reading this book is www.learn-cocos2d.com. Every other week I publish an in-depth article about example code, guidance, references, the state of affairs, and the occasional opinion piece. You'll also find links to the Cocos2D Podcast and my LearnCocosTV channel.

You should also investigate which technologies may be useful to implement in your game, such as advertising, analytics, one of the many social networking libraries, and even server technology used in persistent world games.

Everything you ever wanted to know is probably somewhere on the Internet. It may simply be hiding. If you want to know where to find art, audio, and freelancers, you're in luck—I provide good starting points in this chapter.

I also give you a glimpse into marketing and public relations in this final chapter. Those are topics I'm often asked about, and they're full of mystery and misunderstandings. I discuss working with a publisher and how you can benefit from such a relationship and also how to market your game and yourself.

For an independent developer, it's very important to be recognized by the community as a creative, enthusiastic game developer and to connect with the community. All your social networking efforts will then help you promote your game simply by being able to reach out to more like-minded people. If you can build a network of followers, the success of your game will follow. A lot of people get that mixed up and think it's the other way around. It's not.

You'll also learn about the reference games and apps made available with cocos2d. They'll give you a good impression of what's possible with the cocos2d game engine and also what you can achieve as an independent developer. One of the most exciting learning tools is other people's source code, so I've included a list of commercial cocos2d source code projects that are on sale for exactly this reason.

Most of all, "out of the ordinary" should be the guiding principle for whatever you do. Create something that's different, and don't be afraid to *be* different.

Additional Resources for Learning and Working

The purpose of this section is to help you find answers to your questions, get support for a particular problem, obtain more source code to learn from and base your own games on, and of course introduce you to all the cocos2d tools and some of the best cocos2d reference games.

It is also the purpose of my blog at `www.learn-cocos2d.com/blog`. You'll find the latest updates and cocos2d game development tips and tricks on my blog, where I post a new in-depth article every other Thursday.

Where to Find Help

Whether you're facing a technical problem that you can't solve on your own or need more people to work on your game, you can get help. In addition, if you're looking for art, audio, or tools, I know just where you can find what you're looking for, or at least where you can begin your search.

> **Tip**   If you get stuck and don't know what else to try, just writing down what the problem is, what you're trying to achieve, and what you've done so far can help. Most of the time it frees your mind to think of things you haven't tried yet, and more often than not it leads to a solution. If not, at least you now have a summary you can post to a forum or Q&A site, which will help you get a good answer more quickly. The art of asking questions is all about making it easy for others to answer them.

Cocos2d Home Page

This may seem obvious, but if you have a question related to cocos2d, you should stop by and join the cocos2d community in the forum: `http://cocos2d-iphone.org/forum`.

In the cocos2d forum, you can ask about anything related to cocos2d. It has subforums for hot topics like audio programming, physics engines, social networks, cocos3d, and ads, as well as a general forum for Objective-C and iPhone SDK–related questions. For the most part, the cocos2d community is friendly and very helpful, and a lot of great example code and development stories have been shared on the forum.

Before asking questions, be sure to search both the forum and the official cocos2d documentation wiki: `http://cocos2d-iphone.org/wiki/doku.php`.

In addition, you can announce your newly released game in the cocos2d games forum. Don't forget to also add it to the list of games made with cocos2d. You can do this on the cocos2d Games page: `www.cocos2d-iphone.org/games`.

Cocos2D Central

I launched a community hub called Cocos2D Central for everything related to cocos2d. Most importantly, there are forum sections for cocos2d, the book, Kobold2D, and my game kits. Cocos2D Central also hosts the official forum of cocos2d-javascript, the web browser port of cocos2d.

In the Resources section, there are several small tutorials available, and the Downloads section hosts all files I currently offer for download, including the cocos2d installer and the source code for this book.

Stack Exchange Network

Forums are a great way for communities to interact with each other. But as such, they tend to get a little chatty, and searching for a specific answer can be cumbersome because the forum's content isn't strictly limited to solving problems.

That's exactly where Q&A web sites like Stack Exchange shine. You go in, ask a particular question, and get answers. Because the focus is on Q&A, it's easier to find existing answers. And if you really like a question or answer, you can vote it up so it will be listed higher on search results.

I'm regularly amazed by the show of expertise from contributors on the Stack Exchange network. This is in part thanks to the built-in badge and points system, making it very rewarding to both ask interesting questions and write thoughtful, in-depth answers. The Stack Exchange network is comprised of several free Q&A web sites, the most popular and my personal favorite being `http://stackoverflow.com`, which is about programming questions in general.

You won't find as many questions about cocos2d on Stack Overflow as you will on the official cocos2d forum, but the questions on Stack Overflow are good ones, and almost all of them get good answers. There's a bit of confusion about the use of search tags on the site, with both *cocos2d* and *cocos2d-iphone* used to tag questions regarding the iPhone version of cocos2d. This can be attributed to the success of cocos2d for iPhone, in that it has become synonymous with the name cocos2d itself. Use these two links to find all the cocos2d for iPhone–related questions on Stack Overflow:

- `http://stackoverflow.com/questions/tagged/cocos2d`
- `http://stackoverflow.com/questions/tagged/cocos2d-iphone`

Stack Exchange is expanding as a Q&A web sites network. One of the latest additions is the Game Development Q&A web site. On this site you can ask general game programming questions and about anything game development–related in general, including design, marketing, and sales. Check out the Game Development Stack Exchange site at `http://gamedev.stackexchange.com`.

Tutorials and FAQs

Plenty of tutorials for cocos2d are on the Web, but one tutorial writer clearly stands out from the crowd: Ray Wenderlich. He's written more than a dozen cocos2d tutorials and published them on his web site: `www.raywenderlich.com/tag/cocos2d`. Besides cocos2d tutorials, on this site you'll also find other highly interesting iPhone SDK–related tips and tricks. In at least one particular case, this is also helpful for cocos2d developers, where Ray explains how to save and load your app's data. This can be applied to saving and loading games as well (see `www.raywenderlich.com/1914/how-to-save-your-app-data-with-nscoding-and-nsfilemanager`).

The iDevBlogADay articles on my Learn & Master cocos2d web site (`www.learn-cocos2d.com/category/idevblogaday`) are mainly tutorials and guides. You learn how to enable ARC in cocos2d projects, gain insights in the iOS Sales Statistics, how to write a Webcam Viewer with cocos2d, and how to upgrade an existing cocos2d project to a newer version—and a lot more.

You should definitely join the Twitterverse and create a list or saved search for cocos2d and kobold2d. There are so many really good tutorials, but they're spread far and wide. Another great way to keep track of great articles about iOS development in general is to visit the Cocoa Literature web site (`http://cocoalit.com`) every now and then. Cocoa Literature aggregates only the best and most helpful articles.

Source Code Projects to Benefit From

Personally, I learn best by browsing through other people's code. One of the first things I did when I got cocos2d and found the documentation lacking was to invest in the Sapus Tongue source code project to see how cocos2d is actually being used in a game. It was very helpful for getting started quickly.

> **Note**   Since Zynga acquired certain assets of Sapus Media, the Sapus Tongue Source Code and Level SVG products are no longer available. However, the source code products I'm introducing in the following sections are excellent replacements.

The advantage of commercially sold source code compared to the open source projects is that you rarely get support for the latter, and they're almost never updated, to the point that most of the open source projects you'll find are using versions of cocos2d prior to v1.0—with one exception, the official cocos2d-iphone-extensions project: `www.cocos2d-iphone.org/forum/topic/17546`.

The following source code projects are all commercial offerings. I refrain from listing prices because they're subject to change. You can also browse these products on my Affiliate Products page, where you can also find newer products not listed in the book: `www.learn-cocos2d.com/store/affiliate-products`.

Quexlor Action-RPG Engine Code and Tutorial

The Action-RPG Engine was formerly known as the iPhone Game Kit. It's one of the first source code game kits for cocos2d and was created by Nathanael M. Weiss. The game Quexlor: Lands of Fate (see Figure 17-1) is a role-playing hack-and-slash game following in the footsteps of Diablo, featuring a large tilemap world with multiple levels, various monsters, and plenty of items. The game kit comes with a huge amount of royalty-free graphics created by Reiner Prokein, a comprehensive *Make Your Own iPhone Game* e-book, and a publishing guide that explains in detail how to submit your game to the App Store. Obviously, you also get the game's excellently crafted source code, but that almost seems secondary.

Figure 17-1. *Quexlor: Lands of Fate (iPad) is a game made with the iPhone Game Kit*

You can find the link to the Quexlor game on the App Store, an iPhone Game Creation for Beginner's Kit, and a whole lot more information about the RPG Engine on its web site, so I suggest taking a look: `www.iphonegamekit.com`.

Line-Drawing Game Starterkit

My Line-Drawing Game Starterkit is modeled after successful games like Flight Control and Harbor Master. If you like to create line-drawing games, this starter kit gets you going with drawing lines, moving objects along the paths, collision detection, and a clearly structured code base, including both iPhone and iPad versions.

Each purchase grants you a site license, which means your whole team is allowed to use the game's source code and assets. Because it's a starter kit, you're naturally allowed to make clones of the game. I also offer a 60-day money-back guarantee, and I'll be happy to help you learn the starter kit's source code and give directions on how to extend it.

Tip   If you start to follow @gaminghorror (me) on Twitter, you'll receive a direct message from me within a day. I will include a secret coupon code with which you can buy the Line-Drawing Game Starterkit at 30% off! Should you already be following me, tell a friend to follow me to get the coupon code.

The Line-Drawing Game Starterkit's product page contains the starter kit's feature list, links to the demo apps (see Figure 17-2), a code sample, and the complete documentation: www.learn-cocos2d.com/store/line-drawing-game-starterkit.

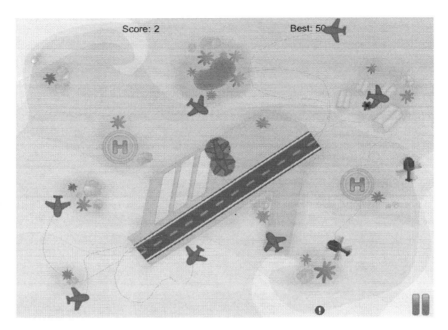

Figure 17-2. *The Line-Drawing Game Starterkit example game (iPad)*

The Space Game Starterkit

The Space Game Starterkit evolved from Ray Wenderlich's Space Game Tutorial (www.raywenderlich.com/3611/how-to-make-a-space-shooter-iphone-game) into a commercial starter kit for making a side-scrolling shoot-'em-up game.

As with the iPhone RPG Game Kit, there's added value in the form of four epic tutorials included in the purchase. The tutorials explain a lot of the details that go into making this particular game and games in general. Coming from Ray Wenderlich, you can expect high-quality code and tutorials.

Ray's wife, Vicki, provided the artwork for the Starterkit. You can reuse and modify the artwork as you like as long as you credit Vicki Wenderlich. She runs an iPhone art blog at www.vickiwenderlich.com.

Learn more about the Space Game Starterkit, pictured in Figure 17-3, in Ray Wenderlich's store: www.raywenderlich.com/store/space-game-starter-kit.

Figure 17-3. Ray and Vicki Wenderlich's Space Game Starterkit

iUridium Source Code

If you had a Commodore 64 home computer in the 1980s or early 1990s, chances are that you've played or at least heard of Uridium. Uridium was a fast-paced space game shooter with a unique feature: you could change the flight direction of your spaceship with a smoothly animated Immelmann turn, to fly over the enemy spacecraft from end to end to complete various objectives. If you will, it was one of the early free-roaming world type of games.

Nenad Alajbegovic has paid homage to Uridium by porting it to the iPhone; the iOS version is appropriately named iUridium. You get the entire source code for the game, which uses just about everything the cocos2d game engine has to offer, and then some. For example, Nenad implemented caching (pooling) of bullets and enemies to create a smooth game play. He also has UIKit views, Game Center leaderboards, and Facebook and Twitter integrated. The levels are created entirely as tilemaps and dynamically loaded from XML into the game's scene and layer nodes.

The license is fair, only asking you not to make a clone of iUridium but expressly allowing you to make your own side-scrolling shooter game. But you do have to replace all the artwork, music, and sound effects with your own.

You can find all the information about iUridium, pictured in Figure 17-4, on this web site: www.iuridium.com/?page_id=2.

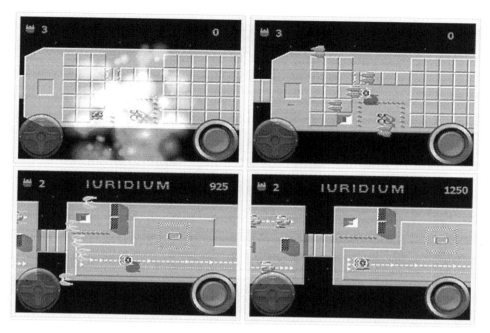

Figure 17-4. The iUridium's game source code is available for sale

BATAK Duel Source Code

Dan Nelson is the developer of BATAK Duel for iPhone. He created this game in five months with no prior iPhone game-development knowledge. He managed to integrate OpenFeint into the game, a menu system, and of course savegames. The app is rich in visuals, both by utilizing cocos2d's particle system as well as additional effects such as lighting, smoothly scrolling credits, and a transparent pop-up keyboard.

The license is fair, only asking you not to use any of the BATAK Duel artwork, music, and sound effects. You can find more information about the BATAK Duel source code, pictured in Figure 17-5, on this web site: `www.batakduel.com/blog/78`.

Figure 17-5. The source code of BATAK Duel for iPhone is for sale

Cocos2D Podcast

Mohammad Azam and I are recording the Cocos2D Podcast to report on recent events; to talk about hot topics; to interview game developers, tool authors, and bloggers; and to give listeners insider information and insights into game development with cocos2d.

The Cocos2D Podcast is available on cocos2dpodcast.wordpress.com, and new episodes are announced on www.learn-cocos2d.com/blog. Each episode runs between 30 to 60 minutes. Here's a selection of episode topics we've covered so far:

- Earning additional revenue using iAds, IAP, selling source code, and so on
- Michael Daley explains Particle Designer and Glyph Designer
- Ray Wenderlich talks about Cocos2d, his book, workshops, and more
- Andreas Löw explains TexturePacker and PhysicsEditor
- Vladu Bogdan expounds on LevelHelper and SpriteHelper
- Zynga acquires Cocos2d contributors

- Tools in Cocos2d iPhone game development
- Game engines and frameworks as alternatives to Cocos2d

Tools, Tools, Tools

In this book I've introduced you to what I think are the best tools for each purpose. However, there are usually alternatives. If you also read the first edition of this book, you know that I used different tools in that first edition than here in the second. In less than a year, some tools put on wings, and others essentially stopped progressing and fell behind.

Because that almost natural process is not going to change in the future, and it's hard to predict which tools are here to stay and which aren't over the coming years, I wanted to share an alphabetically sorted list of currently existing tools that you can use for cocos2d without going into describing them and regardless of their current state, except of course that they need to be usable and functional at the very least.

You can use the following tools for development with cocos2d. I highlighted my personal favorites in bold:

- Bitmap font tools
    - BMFont (Windows): www.angelcode.com/products/bmfont
    - Fonteditor: http://code.google.com/p/fonteditor
    - **Glyph Designer**: http://glyphdesigner.71squared.com
    - Hiero: http://slick.cokeandcode.com/demos/hiero.jnlp
    - LabelAtlasCreator: www.cocos2d-iphone.org/forum/topic/4357
- Particle editing tools
    - ParticleCreator: www.cocos2d-iphone.org/forum/topic/16363
    - **Particle Designer**: http://particledesigner.71squared.com
- Physics editing tools
    - Mekanimo: www.mekanimo.net
    - PhysicsBench: www.cocos2d-iphone.org/forum/topic/9064
    - **PhysicsEditor**: www.physicseditor.de
    - VertexHelper: www.cocos2d-iphone.org/archives/779
- Scene editing tools
    - CocosBuilder: http://cocosbuilder.com
    - Cocoshop: www.cocos2d-iphone.org/forum/topic/15668
    - LevelHelper: www.levelhelper.org
- Texture atlas tools
    - DarkFunction Editor: http://darkfunction.com

- SpriteHelper: www.spritehelper.org

- **TexturePacker**: www.texturepacker.com

- Zwoptex: zwoptexapp.com

- Tilemap editing tools

  - iTileMaps (iPad): www.klemix.com/page/iTileMaps.aspx

  - **Tiled Map Editor**: www.mapeditor.org

Cocos2d Reference Apps

The following is a list of games and apps made with cocos2d. They should serve as shining examples of what you can do with cocos2d as well as the creativity of cocos2d developers.

Instead of providing an iTunes link to each app in the book, I decided to create a post on my blog where I host all the links to the games mentioned here, and I'll update this list to include noteworthy games released after the book has been published. You can find the list of links to these apps, including other links of interest, on the Great Apps Made With cocos2d page: www.learn-cocos2d.com/2010/10/great-apps-made-with-cocos2d.

- **The Elements** (iPad) is a graphical representation of the periodic table of elements. The outstanding features are the plentiful photographs and smooth 360 animations that invite you to explore the elements that make up you, me, and the rest of the universe (excluding empty space, of which there's a lot I've been told). It's priced high but worth every cent, and if you need an app that will let you brag about your new iPad, this is it!

- **Bloomies** is a colorful gardening game, full of bees (see Figure 17-6). If that doesn't sway you, maybe the idea of fostering and nurturing your own

Figure 17-6. Bloomies from Phantoom Entertainment

garden does. The flowers need your constant attention, and the game play is addictive, just like any Tamagotchi-style game. Oh, and it happens to be made by two former colleagues of mine. It's just a beautiful game, and so is their follow-up game, Super Blast.

■ **StickWars** is a game where you defend your castle from incoming stick figures by flicking them in the air or literally shaking them to the ground. The developer, John Hartzog, had never before worked with Objective-C or on mobile devices, but he pulled it off. StickWars remains to this date within the top 100 games and continues to be updated even a year after the initial release.

■ **ZombieSmash** is also a castle defense game, except that this time hordes of zombies are attacking, and you get explosives, 16-ton weights, shotguns, and other cool items that make a bloody mess to fend them off (see Figure 17-7). Your castle is your barn, and if you can defend it, you'll be rewarded with a slow-motion animation of the final zombie losing its, err, unlife. The outstanding feature of this game is certainly the rag-doll animation system that allows zombies to walk, crawl, or otherwise try to move even if they've lost some of their limbs.

Figure 17-7. Zombie Smash by GameDoctors

■ **Super Turbo Action Pig** revives the simple game play concept of a scrolling level where your character always falls down, except when you touch the screen to boost his jetpack. The extraordinary part here is that the game's graphics are extremely well made and the overall presentation of the game, the trailer, the web site, and the humor set a great example.

- Then there's **Farmville**—do I even have to explain what it's about? It's an incredibly successful Facebook game that has millions of players worldwide building their farms in an isometric landscape. It just goes to show how powerful cocos2d is if a company like Zynga uses it to port its most successful game to the iPhone. It's notable that Zombie Farm came out on the iPhone before Farmville, and it was also created with cocos2d.

- **Melvin Says There's Monsters** (iPad) is a beautifully animated cartoon kid story with professional-quality voiceovers. The story is cleverly constructed and has an insightful turning point. It's a pleasure to watch even for an adult, and it also uses cocos2d's page-flip animations very effectively. If you have an iPad and kids, it's a must have!

- **Trainyard** is an innovative puzzle game that was clearly engineered with the user in mind. It features a mode for the color-blind, is optimized to use little battery power, saves and loads the game just as the user left it, and even allows users to share puzzle solutions on the Web, using a duplicate of the game engine written in Flash. All this, besides being a really innovative puzzle game where you lay tracks and combine trains to match them with colored train yards.

- **Abstract War 2.0** is a dual-stick shooter featuring colorful and vibrant geometric visuals (see Figure 17-8). It's obviously inspired by Geometry Wars on Xbox Live Arcade. It's an intense space-shooter with plenty of game modes. You can even play it in multiplayer mode via a Bluetooth connection, and it allows you to use your own iPod music.

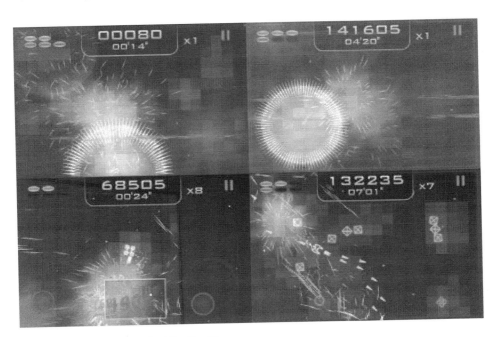

Figure 17-8. Abstract War 2.0 by Forzefield Studios SL

■ **Fuji Leaves** is an interesting music game, where dropping balls hit leaves, and depending on the speed and location of impact, a sound is played. With several balls on the screen bouncing around, you can dynamically create musical scores. It's intensely fascinating to play this game, trying to come up with interesting scores and just the right placement of leaves. Before you know it, an hour has passed.

The Business of Making Games

This section covers social gaming, ads, and In-App Purchase—basically, the business of making games. In this section, the focus isn't on technology; I talk about my experience as a professional and independent game developer and what it takes to make successful games.

At least the tips provided in this section will improve your odds to make a more successful game with the right people, and you'll learn how to market the game to your target audience.

Working with Publishers

In the early days of computer programming, developers single-handedly copied their game code onto floppy disks and shrink-wrapped it to sell it in local software and hardware stores. Those days are long gone, and with the increasing complexity of games, publishers have taken on the task of distributing and marketing games. This model has been the default for the past 20 years or so, but with the advent of the indie game scene in recent years, mostly driven by new technologies such as downloadable games, the Xbox Live Indie Games channel, and Apple's App Store, more and more game developers are turning to self-publishing again. So, why would you want to work with a publisher these days?

The first reason is technical support and testing. Publishers want to make sure that every game they release does not reflect badly on their reputations, so one of their goals is to release games with as few bugs as possible and with polished game play. If you're not used to this process, which includes the scrutiny of a quality assurance team, you'll be in for a surprise, and it may not always be a pleasant one—such as the game's release being held back due to yet another obscure and hard to-find bug. So, that's a bad thing? To the contrary, it forces you to work with an attention to detail that's all too often neglected and dismissed by hobbyist developers. And in the end, you'll be rewarded with a better game. In most cases, this also translates to more favorable reviews by press and players alike and thus more sales.

Working with an established publisher also reflects positively on you, simply because of the respected games already released by said publisher. I don't mean that in an ego-trip kind of way. You're not special because you're working with big-name publisher X—but you sure will learn a lot, and that's going to make you stand out from the crowd. It also improves your street cred and the chances of landing a better job or contract sometime down the road.

The experiences working with a publisher don't just involve game programming and the things you'll pick up from technical support and the quality assurance process. You'll also sign a contract and get a glimpse at all the legalese and paperwork involved (it's really not that bad).

Signing a standard contract with a publisher is more like opening a bank account. Everything is ready-made, and you just have to fill in a few blanks. Expect the publisher to take anywhere between 30 to 70 percent of the revenue. It depends a lot on what they do, in which phase of development they come on board, and whether they support you financially.

If you allow yourself to learn from working with a publisher, it can be very insightful to get an impression of the details that need to be specified to get everything in order from a financial and legal point of view. If the publisher has a good track record with other developers, you can feel assured that they're not going to screw you over. But you definitely need to understand the terms you're signing, because if you're used to posting your sales numbers, for example, those may now be covered by a nondisclosure agreement you signed with the publisher.

You do give up a certain amount of freedom, and you need to be able to live with it and trust the publisher to do the best job they can for those parts you're giving up. For example, if a publisher is asking you for a change in direction for certain aspects of your game, you should seriously consider it. At least most of them know what they're talking about, and they also know what's working and what isn't (this certainly isn't the case for all of them, though). However, because games is a very subjective field, publishers do have the tendency to favor proven sets of features over other risky but innovative ones—but less so on iOS, where publishers are more willing and able to give their developers creative freedom, if not total control over the design of the game.

In return for giving up some freedoms, they'll reward you with marketing your game. They know the channels, and they have a direct feed to the review web sites and the press. And that's possibly another area of expertise you'll learn a lot from. The press has a certain way they like to receive and consume the information they need to write a review about your game. Your publisher knows all about it will request a few things from you that you wouldn't have considered on your own, such as high-resolution artwork or a one-line catchphrase that really gets players interested in your game.

If you get the chance to cooperate with a publisher, my advice is to go for it at least once, no matter how much you value your creative freedom. Afterward, you'll understand much better what you're giving up and what you're receiving in return, at least in that particular case. Whatever your experience may be, the experience alone and what you'll learn should make it worthwhile (and maybe it will be rewarding enough to do it again—but if not, you'll know why).

There are several game publishers you may want to consider contacting. Your best shot would be those who market specifically for iOS or mobile devices, and in that area two names stand out from the crowd. One is ngmoco, which published Goldfinger, We Rule, We Farm, Epic Pet Wars, and Rolando. Visit ngmoco's web site at www.ngmoco.com. The other is Chillingo, who has released games like Minigore, the Quest, Knight's Rush, and of course Angry Birds. Chillingo's web site is www.chillingo.com.

Finding Freelancers

If you believe in your game and you're ready to invest money into it, you may want to get help from professional freelancers worldwide. Besides asking for jobs in the cocos2d forum itself, you can also post a job offer on one of the more popular outsourcing web sites. Likewise, you can also offer your expertise as a freelancer to employers on these sites. Plenty of web sites offer such services; you'll even find some that can hook you up with someone close to where you live.

I'll refer you to the ones that I know work best and have a good reputation: they're eLance (www.elance.com) and Guru (www.guru.com).

They both work on the same principle. You post a job offer, which could be a small task or an entire project. Then you receive proposals from candidates, from which you can pick one or more to do the job. Once you've received, reviewed, and approved the work, you pay the freelancer. Abuse can be reported and basically locks the offender out of the platform, so although you need to be able to trust people you've never worked with, the risks are minimal for both parties. I recommend choosing smaller tasks to start with. Just as if you were to get into the stock market, by starting small you can get a good feel for how this works and what can happen.

Finding Free Art and Audio

The alternative to hiring someone to do the work for you is to find the work available on the Internet (preferably for free). However, be careful about anything that's "free." I'm not saying that it might have a catch; I'm warning about the common misconception that free means "can be used freely." It may not cost you anything to get an image or audio file that's free, but that doesn't tell you anything about what you're legally allowed to do with it. That's typically where a license should come into play but often doesn't. A lot of people publish their own source code, artwork, audio, and writings for free on the Internet but forget to add a proper license file to it if the work is intended to be used by others. The problem is that by default, the author has the copyright and retains all rights to how the work can be used. If there's no explicit waiver, preferably in the form of a license, then you should not use this work (especially not in commercial products, and that includes $0.99 apps sold via the iTunes App Store).

For reference, I'd like to point you to Funplosion Labs, which has an article listing web sites where you can get free game graphics and audio. Funplosion also disclaims this with a warning about the copyright and a link to the license agreement for each web site (see `http://funplosion.com/free-assets.html`).

And don't forget the wonderful OpenGameArt website (`http://opengameart.org`) where you'll find not just art but also sound and music for free.

Caution   Be wary of the General Public License (GPL), especially if used by a source code library that you want to use or integrate into a commercial app. Using GPL-licensed code in your own project requires you to open source your own project's source code. Not just that, but anyone else is subsequently given the right to use your source code and to copy, modify, and redistribute it. Note that the Lesser General Public License (LGPL) license is not as stringent. Similarly there are two Creative Commons licenses. The CC-BY 3.0 is non-restrictive, whereas the Share-Alike version CC-BY-SA 3.0 requires you to share your project with that same license. Refer to this link for a comparison of common source code licenses:

`http://developer.kde.org/documentation/licensing/licenses_summary.html`.

Finding the Tools of the Trade

Sometimes you may wish you had a tool that just does *that*, whatever *that* might be. There are times as a game developer where you need to process data, modify images, or build whole worlds—things that are tedious and error-prone to do in code or simply too time-consuming to do on your own because you'd rather focus on writing your game.

My tip is to use the Indie Game Tools web site, which collects, categorizes, and allows others to rate game design tools for independent game developers. The focus here isn't on expensive software used by professional studios but on low-cost and free solutions for about anything, from game engines to converters, from scripting languages to server technologies, and from asset packages to game editors. Maintained by Robert "Robc" Charney, it's the place I go to see if there's a tool available that fits my bill. Visit the site here: `http://indiegametools.com`.

Just a minor caveat: don't put too much weight on the ratings of individual tools. The number of ratings is very small, so there can be huge differences between similar tools, and the ratings may be biased by both unhappy users and proactive communities. You should leave your mark and add some of your own ratings so that over time the ratings become more accurate. In addition, some tools simply can't be compared by rating; they may have totally different uses, making it unfair to compare them based on their rankings on the Indie Game Tools web site.

Marketing

So, you made a game and submitted it to the App Store. Now what? How do people find your game in the first place?

The story starts at the beginning. The moment you begin working on your game should also be the starting point for your marketing efforts. Get a web site up and running and post your development experiences and maybe some work-in-progress screenshots. That should be your first step to connect with other game developers.

In terms of the marketing and business aspects, I'd like to save you some time. The following link is to the Big List of Indie Marketing and Business Tips, and I have to say that's an understatement. You'll find most of the meaningful and intelligent articles ever written on the subject on just this one page, so be sure to look at it even if you're only mildly interested in the marketing and business aspects of indie game development. Check it out at `www.pixelprospector.com/indev/2010/08/the-big-list-of-indie-marketingand-business-tips`.

Still interested in marketing? Good, check out the free e-book *Videogame Marketing and PR*, written by Scott Steinberg. You can get it on the book's web site: `www.sellmorevideogames.com`.

Marketing Your Game and Yourself

If you're really not sure whether your game is going to be a success based on how much fun it's going to be, one rather effective way to increase your chances is to make a game that's very presentable and colorful and just looks like great fun in screenshots. With the low barrier to entry on mobile devices because of the low price points, a great-looking game with little in terms of play depth more often than not will outperform and outsell a complex game with multiple game modes and many hours of potential game play. It may pain some developers because it goes against everything they believe in, but it's an unavoidable fact of life. Of course, if you can combine the two and create an innovative, fun game that just looks great, the opportunities are endless.

If you browse reviews, there's one thing you should give a lot of attention to. The most prominently featured screenshots are always action scenes from the game, usually with a lot of things going on at the same time. This has almost become an art form; professional developers will even develop specialized tools to stage scenes where they can take the best possible action screenshots, without having to play the game and rely on luck to get it just right. Maybe you should consider that, too. So, the best artwork you can create or pay for should definitely be a priority for you, and so should making a convincing trailer for your game. Outstanding presentation is a very important buy-in to get to talk with a publisher as well.

This advice goes for your blog as well. You do have a blog, don't you? If not, start one right now! You can get a free blog on `http://wordpress.com`, and you'll learn how to work with the most popular blogging software along the way. As your blog matures, you may want to consider hosting your blog on your own server; you can do that with WordPress as well, but with a lot more options for customization through plug-ins and themes.

Your blog is an important way of marketing yourself. The most important aspect here is that self-marketing will indirectly benefit anything you do from now on. Blogging gets you in touch with other like-minded people, who sooner or later will be willing to help you, sometimes for free. If you're really making a name for yourself in your development community, that's good news because it can get you attention from publishers who follow the same channels you're working in. Note that this is in contrast to most of the players of your game, to whom you'll have to reach out on a different level.

And because your blog should be your public face, it should be you who's talking. Don't put on a mask and try to sound like a big corporation—for example, by saying things like what you're doing is going to revolutionize the way we play games. I call that … a term I won't put in this book, but I'm sure you know what I mean.

Make sure you don't come across as cocky on your blog, but likewise don't belittle yourself. You may be a beginner, but you're learning, so focus on what you've learned. The things you do learn will seem like things that millions of other developers already know, so you might wonder whether you should really blog about them. I'm familiar with these thoughts, and frankly speaking, you'll always have doubts about whether what you write is going to be of interest to others. It is, trust me. And if it isn't, no big deal. The truth is, even though there are millions of developers who may already know about what you post, there are millions more who don't and who will be able to learn from you.

And remember to put your best skills up front and avoid blogging about your weaknesses. You may not know it all, but you can learn it. If you really want to know how multiplayer game programming can be enhanced by predicting client movements, learn about it. The Web is a great resource—collect what you find and blog about what you found and learned. Others will respect you for it. Blogging takes years of practice, so it's best to start now because it will pay off in the end—possibly in ways you can't even imagine right now.

Another important way of marketing yourself is Twitter. Once you have something to tell the world, you'll be happy to be able to reach out to dozens, hundreds, if not thousands of your followers at once. Twitter is a very effective marketing tool. How to use it effectively is a matter of following simple steps. First, don't protect your tweets—it seriously limits the number of people who are going to follow you. (I certainly won't.) Then provide an interesting bio, which should include your interests, what you do, and anything else that makes you seem like an interesting person to follow. Simply using a joke, poem, or quote as your bio is a no-no. And don't forget to link to your blog! The most important things are to tweet regularly and tweet about things others might find interesting. Tweeting only about yourself and your products (or just retweeting other's posts) isn't going to convince many people to follow you.

Public Relations and Press Releases

If you work alone and you don't want to cooperate with a publisher, hiring a public relations (PR) firm or agent to give yourself and your game a better chance in the market may be a wise decision. But it could also be downright stupid and pointless. In the latter case, it's usually not the fault of whoever is doing the PR; it's a matter of understanding the benefits of PR—what it takes to make it work effectively—and assessing whether it's worth spending thousands of dollars on.

As an independent developer, you're likely to have a very limited budget. Even entry-level prices for PR agents are going to make your jaw drop to the floor. If that's the case, walk away and get back to working on your game. Your gut reaction is correct.

Now, if you already have a game out there and it's presentable, and you've earned not just money but also some influence with the people around you, things may be a little different. Perhaps you have some money to spare, you've learned a lot from your first game, your second one is even better, and you already have players waiting for it to come out. Can you give it a boost with the help of professional PR? In this case it's more likely.

If you take on the help of a PR agent, you should definitely try to find one who has a track record of working for the game industry—preferably with independent game developers and the mobile games niche. They're not easy to find, so ask around. Using a PR agent who isn't into game development is a waste of time and money—you need to have PR with the ability to reach out to your game's target audience. But most of all, the deciding factor should really be your game.

If you know you have something special, testers tell you so, and the game just looks gorgeous, then investing a few thousand dollars in PR might be a good choice. The PR agent will want game reviewers to write about your game and game development sites to take notice of your special abilities. If these aren't clearly visible, professional PR won't be able to make a big difference. PR works best if you can provide gorgeous screenshots and an intriguing, funny, and captivating trailer movie.

How do you know if your game is something special? By asking the people who wouldn't hesitate to tell you what they don't like. Family and friends are typically too kind to provide the sometimes harsh criticism needed to improve a game. You should ask on forums for private beta testers and provide them with an appetizer, which could be a screenshot or a description of your game's special features, so that they'll be more interested to try your game. How you deal with criticism and feature requests, and generally how you interact with your testers, is also a matter of PR. Dealing with user feedback, and specifically criticism, is a vital skill you should hone as early as possible.

But who's to say you can't try for yourself first? There are press release services specifically for independent developers that cost a fraction of what a professional PR agent would charge you. And writing a press release isn't that hard if you follow the rules. The following press release services tap into exactly the right channels for game players and developers. The hottest candidates are the Indie Press Release Service, at `www.gamerelease.net`, and the Game Press Release Submission Service at Mitorah Games, at `www.mitorahgames.com/Submit-Game-Press-Release.html`.

Unsurprisingly, both services are run by independent developers themselves. Specifically, Juuso Hietalahti created the Indie Press Release Service and also runs the very insightful www.gameproducer.net blog. This blog is especially interesting if you want to learn more about production and marketing aspects.

You should also consider the Games Press web site, which is frequented by game journalists worldwide (see www.gamespress.com/about_howtosubmit.asp).

Engaging Players for More Revenue

Every platform has a number of peripheral technologies that are helpful if not essential, at least in some cases and for some developers. On the iOS platform, this includes the ever-growing list of social networking platforms to choose from, besides Apple's Game Center. Then there's server development kits that you might need for developing persistent games that ought to connect to your own server, be it to find and run matches of more than four players or simply to save characters, progress, settings, and worlds online.

And, although sometimes seen as dubious, providing ads in games can create an additional revenue stream, especially for free games and lite versions. Often in conjunction with ads, you can also investigate whether it would help your game to add analytics and metrics in order to find out where players fail most often, what buttons they click the most, and how frequently they play individual game modes. This can help you tweak your game to be more fun for more players.

Engaging Your Players

The big buzzword in the game industry is clearly *social*. Whether buzz or bubble, whether it has investors, reviewers, and players pay attention or yawn, the social gaming component is growing stronger and has become expected. Social gaming entails anything from passively pushing updates to networks like Twitter and Facebook to directing player interaction in multiplayer games.

In addition, push notifications are a powerful tool for you to remind your users about important events happening in your app. Be it an update, new content, or just the next game you released, it gives you an additional channel to keep your users engaged with your apps and your brand.

Social Networks

Besides Apple's Game Center technology, there are a number of different social networking platforms. All are more or less similar in that they allow players to connect, post high scores, earn achievements, and do many other things, including posting game events to Twitter and Facebook—and all of them are free for both players and developers!

Because their feature sets are constantly evolving, and the market for social networks is booming, the final decision is up to you. I list the big players here and mention some of their outstanding features.

> **Note**   Most of the social networking SDKs as well as ShareKit (http://getsharekit.com) already include support for connecting your users with Twitter and Facebook, so you don't need to learn and implement the separately available Facebook and Twitter APIs. If all you need is access to Twitter, you should have a look at the excellent MGTwitterEngine API from Matt Gemmell, at http://mattgemmell.com/2008/ 02/22/mgtwitterengine-twitter-from-cocoa. And if you need to integrate Facebook into your app, the official Facebook iOS SDK is located on GitHub: http://github.com/facebook/facebook-ios-sdk.

- **OpenFeint** is the perceived leader of iOS social networking SDKs. It boasts Game Center compatibility and turn-based multiplayer features to stand out from the crowd. But first and foremost it's very popular, with an audience of players numbering in the millions. Have a look at OpenFeint's developer portal: www.openfeint.com/developers.

- **Scoreloop** sets itself apart from the competition by offering additional revenue streams via downloadable content, sharing virtual goods and in-game currencies. It also includes analytics to determine what your players are doing. Take a feature tour on the Scoreloop home page: www.scoreloop.com.

- **Plus+** is the social networking platform created by ngmoco, a big publisher of iOS games. It's currently available only to ngmoco's development partners. Ngmoco is looking for select developers to partner with; if you think you have what it takes, then you might want to apply on its developer web site: http://plusplus.com/developers.

- Chillingo's **Crystal** is the other big iOS publisher's social networking platform. And as with Plus+, access is limited to developers working with Chillingo and Electronic Arts, the new owners of Chillingo. You can get information on the Crystal SDK on http://devsupport.crystalsdk.com.

If you're missing Agon-Online in this list, you probably haven't heard the news that it shut down on June 30, 2011. As for Geocade, it is still available at www.geocade.com but simply does not play a role among its competitors.

Socket Server Technology for Multiplayer Games

If you're looking to build a multiplayer game that requires more sophisticated server-side game logic and storage than the social networking platforms are able to offer, you'll have to write your own socket server. Luckily, the hard part of writing a server/client architecture with socket connection and other networking voodoo has already been done for you.

Hosting your online games on a socket server has several advantages. For some games, it's very important that players can't cheat, so running the most critical game logic isolated on the server while being able to verify the data coming from clients can prevent a lot of common cheating mechanisms. A server-based approach is also the only way to write a game that supports a lot of players at once. With peer-to-peer technology, you quickly run into scalability issues, because each device's bandwidth is rather limited, and every player in a peer-to-peer match adds computational overhead to every device connected to that match. Apple's Game Kit restricts peer-to-peer connections between devices to a maximum of four players for that reason. The server hardware is ultimately more powerful and has a higher bandwidth than any device connected to it, which lets you host more players in the same match. In addition, the server hosts the database and usually runs verifications that ensure that players haven't tampered with their app or the stream of data coming in to defeat cheats and exploits.

- **Electrotanks's Electroserver** is a feature-rich server technology used by professionals worldwide. It's priced accordingly, but it does have a free version that allows for up to 25 concurrent users to be connected with the game server. If that's sufficient for you, give it a try: `www.electrotank.com`.

- **SmartFoxServer** by gotoAndPlay() follows in the tracks of Electroserver. It's not as feature rich, but it's very popular among independent game developers, mostly because it has a completely free Lite version, while the Basic and Pro versions still allow up to 20 users for free. In general, the prices are more affordable for independent developers. Compare the SmartFoxServer editions on the products page: `www.smartfoxserver.com/products`.

- **Exit Games** follows a two-pronged approach by offering a networking component called Photon and a managed service for developing persistent online games called Neutron. Neutron natively supports the development of turn-based multiplayer games, and it can suspend and resume game sessions. Photon has a free version that supports up to 50 concurrent users per app or server, and Neutron has a free trial version. Compare features and prices on the Exit Games web site: `www.exitgames.com`.

Push Notification Providers

Push notifications are those little alert messages popping up on your iPhone's screen, whether you're using it or not. Some apps use them to inform users about the stock market, about a live sporting event, or simply to let you know that there's a new comic strip available. The uses are endless. The greatest power of push notifications is that it gives your users an incentive to keep using your app; they won't forget it as easily if they let the app remind them about news and events.

You may have heard of Apple's push notification service, but if not, you can learn more about it in Apple's Push Notification Programming Guide: `http://developer.apple.com/library/ios/#documentation/NetworkingInternet/Conceptual/RemoteNotificationsPG/Introduction/Introduction.html`.

Push notifications allow apps to broadcast messages to individual devices. If you implement one of the social networking platforms, you'll get this feature for free, and you don't need to care about the complexities of push notification programming. However, in some cases you may need to implement your own solution, and for that you need a push notification provider. That's a server that can communicate with Apple's servers and the iOS devices. You can write your own server with the free and open source apns-sharp library (see `http://code.google.com/p/apns-sharp`) or you can sign up for the Mono Push service (`www.monopush.com`) or Urban Airship (`http://urbanairship.com`).

iCloud

With iOS 5 Apple introduced iCloud, its cloud-based storage solution for storing documents and simple key-value data on the cloud. What cloud? Well, obviously not that white, fluffy stuff floating way above your head. Cloud storage simply means storing data on a remote server, and the *cloud* part refers to the fact that you don't know exactly which server your data is stored on, or how. You just send data to the cloud, and the cloud server stores it. The next time you want your data back, the cloud server finds it for you and delivers it back to you.

Cloud storage allows game developers to store savegames in the cloud so that the game's progress isn't locked into a particular device and app. If your app is available for both iOS and Mac OS, you could store savegames in the cloud, and the user can continue where he left off on both versions and on any of his devices and computers.

Or you could save the persistent world of your Mac OS massively multiplayer game to the cloud, and the iPhone app could allow the user to change the player's inventory, sell items on the auction house, and do all the other chores while he's on the road.

You can learn more about iCloud here: `http://developer.apple.com/icloud`.

Earning More Revenue

Don't we all want to make more money? With apps, you can do so by displaying ads or by selling in-game content via In-App Purchase. Both are powerful tools—in particular for free apps, because apps that cost nothing get on average about ten times more downloads than apps that cost $.99.

Ads and Analytics

Advertisements provide a way to generate additional revenue from apps and games. It can be very lucrative if the app is very popular, but frankly speaking, it's also easy to put off users by displaying ads, and it's much more likely to make little to no money. It's still worth experimenting with advertisements—for example, if you use them as a motivator in free versions of your app by letting your users know that the full version removes the ads—besides offering all the other cool features the players want, of course.

Regardless of whether you dislike ads, there's another reason to evaluate the ad space. That's because most advertising SDKs can also provide you with insightful metrics and analytics. This not only includes statistical data such as which iOS version your users have installed and which device they're using but also includes custom metrics, such as which game mode is played most often and where players tend to fail more frequently. This allows you to tweak the difficulty and the user interface layout according to how the users are actually using your app. It also helps you plan upgrades and marketing strategy.

- **iAd** by Apple is the first contender when it comes to advertising on iOS devices. You can get an overview of the iAd Network on Apple's advertising web site: `http://advertising.apple.com`.

- **AdMob for App Developers** is also a very popular ad platform among game developers. You can learn more about the iOS version of AdMob at `www.admob.com/appdevs`, whereas the Mobile Analytics product is hosted here: `http://analytics.admob.com`. AdMob also offers AdWhirl (`www.adwhirl.com`), which allows you to display ads from a variety of ad providers.

- **Flurry Analytics** is the only product that focuses solely on metrics and analytics. Note that Flurry bought Pinch Media, and its products have merged into Flurry Analytics, in case you're wondering why I'm not mentioning the very popular Pinch Analytics. Begin your research into Flurry Analytics here: `www.flurry.com/product/analytics/index.html`.

In-App Purchase

Even if you sell your app, you could publish a free (lite) version of it that uses In-App Purchase to unlock the full version while the user is running the app. For you it can be as little as setting a BOOL variable to YES after the purchase is made, but for the user it's so much more convenient not having to go back to the App Store to make the purchase. I have no data on this, but you can expect that a significant percentage of users won't make the purchase simply because it means quitting your app, waiting for the App Store to load, entering their password, and then waiting for the download to finish.

To get acquainted with In-App Purchase, you can (and should) read Apple's extensive and detailed In-App Purchase Programming Guide: `http://developer.apple.com/library/ios/#documentation/NetworkingInternet/Conceptual/StoreKitGuide/Introduction/Introduction.html`.

But then again, you may want to get started as quickly as possible and learn as you go. With a technology as complex and involving as In-App Purchase, getting started can be quite frustrating, but Ray Wenderlich's tutorial will help you get up on your feet: `www.raywenderlich.com/2797/introduction-to-in-app-purchases`.

Because Apple is constantly improving its technologies, some of the information in the tutorial may no longer apply. In such a case, it's very helpful to study the Technical Note TN2259: Adding In-App Purchase to your iOS and Mac Applications: `http://developer.apple.com/library/ios/#technotes/tn2259/_index.html`. This is a relatively short guide that helps you overcome the typical hurdles of implementing

In-App Purchase, including links to set up your contracts, tax and banking information, and a FAQ.

Summary

I hope you enjoyed learning about some of the surrounding technologies and resources that may be useful for creating your game and becoming a successful game developer, including where to get help and where to find royalty-free game art and audio.

As mentioned in this chapter, marketing and public relations will definitely need to be on your table if you want to actually earn a living from making games. I've only scratched the surface of those here, but it should be enough to help you get started.

Finally, remember to buy and use other cocos2d games in order to learn from them. As a game developer, you need to be constantly playing new games to feed your creativity with new ideas, and you also need to learn what players are saying about other developers' games. Improving your knowledge of how games are made is just as important—purchasing one or several commercial cocos2d source code projects is certainly going to be a wise investment.

This book ends here, but your journey has just begun. I'm sure you'll still have lots of questions, and for that reason I've launched the community web site Cocos2D Central on `http://cocos2d-central.com`. Feel free to stop by and ask me anything about cocos2d, the book, my game kits, marketing, publishers, Xcode, Objective-C, or anything else related to game development. I will continue to blog about cocos2d on the book's `www.learn-cocos2d.com` web site. I'm looking forward to hearing from you.

I hope you have enjoyed reading this book as much as I did writing it. Thank you for reading it!

Index

E

◼G

Made in the USA
Lexington, KY
22 September 2012